The Political Economy of Development and Underdevelopment in Africa

While Africa is too often regarded as lying on the periphery of the global political arena, this is not the case. African nations have played an important historical role in world affairs. It is with this understanding that the authors in this volume set out upon researching and writing their chapters, making an important collective contribution to our understanding of modern Africa. Taken as a whole, the chapters represent the range of research in African development, and fully tie this development to the global political economy. African nations play significant roles in world politics, both as nations influenced by the ebbs and flows of the global economy and by the international political system, but also as actors, directly influencing politics and economics. It is only through an understanding of both the history and present place of Africa in global affairs that we can begin to assess the way forward for future development.

Toyin Falola is the Frances Higginbotham Nalle Centennial Professor in History at the University of Texas at Austin. A Fellow of the Nigerian Academy of Letters, he is the author or editor of more than 100 books.

Jessica Achberger received her PhD in History from the University of Texas at Austin. Her dissertation focused on the foreign policy and economic development of Zambia, particularly in terms of its relationship with China. An historian of both Africa and Asia, she is interested particularly in linkages between the two continents. She is currently a Fellow at the Southern African Institute of Policy and Research in Lusaka, Zambia.

Routledge African Studies

1 **Facts, Fiction, and African Creative Imaginations**
   Edited by Toyin Falola and Fallou Ngom

2 **The Darfur Conflict**
   Geography or Institutions?
   Osman Suliman

3 **Music, Performance and African Identities**
   Edited by Toyin Falola and Tyler Fleming

4 **Environment and Economics in Nigeria**
   Edited by Toyin Falola and Adam Paddock

5 **Close to the Sources**
   Essays on Contemporary African Culture, Politics and Academy
   Abebe Zegeye and Maurice Vambe

6 **Landscape and Environment in Colonial and Postcolonial Africa**
   Edited by Toyin Falola and Emily Brownell

7 **Development, Modernism and Modernity in Africa**
   Edited by Augustine Agwuele

8 **Natural Resources, Conflict, and Sustainable Development**
   Lessons from the Niger Delta
   Edited by Okechukwu Ukaga, Ukoha O. Ukiwo and Ibaba Samuel Ibaba

9 **Regime Change and Succession Politics in Africa**
   Five Decades of Misrule
   Edited by Maurice Nyamanga Amutabi and Shadrack Wanjala Nasong'o

10 **The Political Economy of Development and Underdevelopment in Africa**
   Edited by Toyin Falola and Jessica Achberger

The Political Economy of Development and Underdevelopment in Africa

Edited by Toyin Falola
and Jessica Achberger

Routledge
Taylor & Francis Group
NEW YORK   LONDON

First published 2013
by Routledge
711 Third Avenue, New York, NY 10017

Simultaneously published in the UK
by Routledge
2 Park Square, Milton Park, Abingdon, Oxon OX14 4RN

Routledge is an imprint of the Taylor & Francis Group, an informa business

© 2013 Taylor & Francis

The right of Toyin Falola and Jessica Achberger to be identified as the authors of the editorial material, and of the authors for their individual chapters, has been asserted in accordance with sections 77 and 78 of the Copyright, Designs and Patents Act 1988.

All rights reserved. No part of this book may be reprinted or reproduced or utilised in any form or by any electronic, mechanical, or other means, now known or hereafter invented, including photocopying and recording, or in any information storage or retrieval system, without permission in writing from the publishers.

Trademark Notice: Product or corporate names may be trademarks or registered trademarks, and are used only for identification and explanation without intent to infringe.

Library of Congress Cataloging-in-Publication Data
Africa Conference (Tex.) (2011 : University of Texas at Austin)
  The political economy of development and underdevelopment in Africa / edited by Toyin Falola and Jessica Achberger.
    p. cm. — (Routledge African studies ; 10)
  Includes bibliographical references and index.
Originated from the 2011 Africa Conference, Africa in World Politics, held at the University of Texas-Austin from March 25 to 27, 2011
  1. Economic development—Political aspects—
Africa. 2. Africa—Economic conditions. 3. Africa—Foreign economic relations. 4. Economic development—International cooperation. I. Falola, Toyin. II. Achberger, Jessica. III. Series: Routledge African studies ; 10.
  HC800.A553325 2011
  338.96—dc23
  2013002632

ISBN13: 978-0-415-81888-9 (hbk)
ISBN13: 978-0-203-38774-0 (ebk)

Typeset in Sabon
by IBT Global.

To the people of Africa, and to the people who work endlessly to promote development.

Contents

List of Figures and Tables   xi
Acknowledgments   xiii

Introduction   1
TOYIN FALOLA AND JESSICA ACHBERGER

PART I
Historical Roots of African Underdevelopment

1   Africa and the Making of the Global Environmental Narrative: Challenges and Opportunities for the Continent's Development Initiatives   19
MARTIN S. SHANGUHYIA

2   Indigenization versus Domiciliation: A Historical Approach to National Content in Nigeria's Oil and Gas Industry   47
JESSE SALAH OVADIA

3   Globalization and Rural Land Conflict in North-West Cameroon: A Historical Perspective   74
EMMANUEL M. MBAH

4   Evolving Political Accountability in Kenya   93
JACOB BUTLER

PART II
Africa in the New Global Economy

5   Towards a Contextualized Appraisal of Securities Regulation in East Africa   111
JUNE MCLAUGHLIN

6   The Impact of Changing Global Power Relations on African
    Governance of Foreign Direct Investment   128
    ROSHEN HENDRICKSON

7   Globalization and Regional Impulses from the Global South: A
    Comparative Study of ECOWAS and ASEAN   147
    OKPEH OCHAYI OKPEH, JR.

8   The Political Implication of Past and Present Nigerian Financial Crises 176
    MUHAMMED TANKO

9   Transcending an Elitist Approach and Making a Paradigm Shift
    from Growth without Development to a "Populist" Development 192
    HAUWA'U EVELYN YUSUF AND ADEFARAKAN ADEDAYO YUSUF

PART III
Forging New International Connections

10 The Political Economy of Rising Asian Interests in Africa:
    Problems, Prospects, and Challenges   213
    OLUSEGUN M. OSINIBI

11 The Impact of the BRICS Countries on Africa's Socioeconomic
    Development in the Post-Cold War Era   228
    ALEXIUS AMTAIKA

12 How Ready is Nigeria for Chinese Investments?   267
    JOHN E. ANEGBODE AND CLETUS E. ONAKALU

13 The New Scramble for Africa? Indo-Kenyan Economic
    Relations, 1980–2010   279
    FELIX KIRUTHU, MARY KINYANJUI AND FRANCIS MUCHOKI

PART IV
The Way Forward for Twenty-First-Century Development

14 French Foreign Policy in Rwanda: Language, Personal
    Networks, and Changing Contexts   307
    CÉLINE A. JACQUEMIN

15 The Question of Development in Africa   331
EBUNOLUWA O. ODUWOLE

16 A Critique of the Notion of Africa as the "Third World":
Towards a New Perspective   342
MIKE O. ODEY

17 American Pharmaceutical Influence on Uganda's HIV/AIDS
Relief System   363
BEN WEISS AND JESSICA ACHBERGER

18 An African's View of the Aftermath of Copenhagen's Climate
Change Conference   379
OLIVIER J. TCHOUAFFE

19 Globalization and Developing Economies: Eco-Tourism and
Sustainable Development in Cross River State, Nigeria   396
DONALD OMAGU

Contributors   423
Index   429

Figures and Tables

FIGURES

11.1	The BRICS countries' share of the global economy, 2010.	230

TABLES

2.1	Selected Statistics on Employment and GDP in Nigeria	49
2.2	Projected Nigerian Content Value Contributions	58
2.3	NNPC-NCD Gap Analysis	59
2.4	Nigerian Content Measurement of Contractor Inputs	67
2.5	Contractor's Nigerian Content Categorization	67
8.1	Sectoral Contribution to GDP Growth in Nigeria, 2003–2007 (percent)	178
8.2	Regression Results	187
12.1	Electrical Energy Production in Some African Countries	273
14.1	Conference of Heads of States from France and African Countries	319
16.1	Growth Rate of the Fastest Growing Economies in 2010	357
17.1	PEPFAR Mother-to-Child Transmission Prevention Program Coverage	365
17.2	Number of Individuals put on Antiretroviral Drugs by PEPFAR Globally	365
17.3	Provision of Antiretroviral Treatment from 2000 to 2007 in Uganda	367
17.4	HIV/AIDS Expenditures in 2006	367
17.5	PEPFAR's HIV/AIDS treatment in Nigeria, 2007	372
17.6	PEPFAR Provided Treatment in its Fifteen Focus Nations	373

Acknowledgments

The preparation of a manuscript such as this requires the hard work and dedication of many individuals. First, we would like to thank the organizers and support staff of the 2011 Africa Conference at the University of Texas at Austin. The conference co-coordinators, Jessica Achberger and Charles Thomas, could not have put together such a well-organized and successful event if not for the support of Tosin Abiodun, Lady Jane Aquiah, Emily Brownell, Roy Doron, Ryan Groves, Jason Morgan, Segun Obasa, Adam Paddock, and Danielle Sanchez.

We would also like to thank all the participants of the 2011 Conference, Africa in World Politics, which made it such a success. The fruitful dialogue from the Conference made a significant contribution to the chapters of this volume. This volume is a reflection of the power of collaboration, and each chapter was aided by the valuable comments received from panel chairs, co-participants, and conference attendees.

Finally, we would like to thank our families for their continuing support of us in our endeavors as academics. It is through their support that we are able to dedicate ourselves to this work.

Toyin Falola and Jessica Achberger
Austin, Texas and Lusaka, Zambia
June 2012

Introduction

Toyin Falola and Jessica Achberger

Of all the topics within the realm of political economy, questions surrounding development have been the overwhelming focus of scholars of Africa. Important work is being done to understand why, fifty years after independence, many African nations are still plagued by chronic underdevelopment. There are a number of answers to this question, including a colonial legacy, neocolonial influence, and bad governance and corruption, as well as less widely accepted views such as environmental determination. However, most scholars appreciate that it is not just one singular factor that is plaguing the Africa continent but rather a combination of many, which differ on a country-to-country basis. The question asked by this volume, then, is how does internal African development relate to Africa's place in global affairs?

The Political Economy of Development and Underdevelopment in Africa originated from the 2011 Africa Conference, Africa in World Politics, held at the University of Texas-Austin from March 25 to 27, 2011. The intention of this international, interdisciplinary conference was to facilitate the exchange of ideas among scholars and professionals interested in Africa's historical and contemporary place in global politics. The nineteen chapters in this volume represent and reflect the numerous papers presented at the conference that were concerned with African political economy and the role of Africa in the global narrative.

Africa's role in the global political economy is not a recent phenomenon. Since the precolonial period, the African continent has played a vital role in world affairs. Undoubtedly the most notorious example of this is the transatlantic slave trade, in which, from the sixteenth to the nineteenth centuries, upwards of 10 million Africans were sent to the New World as slaves.[1] However, the people of Africa also played a significant role in trade via the Indian Ocean. While this is a much less researched field than the transatlantic slave trade, the trade between Asia, Africa, and the Middle East was a hugely significant process from antiquity onward and, some argue, through to the present day. Africans played key roles as traders along the East African coast, and Indian, Chinese, and Arab influences and artifacts are found as far inland as Botswana.[2]

Africa's role in global political and economic affairs only increased with colonialism. Although the colonies, divided by Europe at the Berlin Conference of 1884–1885, did not act autonomously during the period of colonial rule, they were crucial to the economies of the colonizers.[3] Africans participated in the global economy through trade with Europeans, fought in the global political struggles of World Wars I and II, and effectively disrupted the entire status quo of the global system in their calls for nationalism, which began during the interwar years and continued up to the "decade of independence" in the 1960s.[4] Among the newly independent nations this influence only grew, especially in light of the Cold War. The struggle between the global superpowers—the United States and the Soviet Union as well as China—significantly increased the influence of any single African nation's political and economic ideology and actions in terms of its Cold War alignment.[5] This process was only accentuated by African nations' participation in international organizations such as the United Nations, where each has one vote and a voice on the global political platform.[6]

The twenty-first century has brought a number of changes to the global economy. The rise of Brazil, Russia, India, and China threatens to upset the established international order; the recession of 2008 has wreaked havoc not only on the U.S. domestic economy but also the international economy; and the bailouts of a number of European nations have affected all global politics and economics. While Africa is too often regarded as lying on the periphery of the global political arena, this is not the case. African nations have played an increasingly important historical role in world affairs, and they are likely to continue to do so. It is with this understanding that the authors of this volume began researching and writing their chapters, making an important collective contribution to our understanding of modern Africa.

CONCEPTUALIZATION

The study of development, and subsequently underdevelopment, is not particularly new to African studies. After the optimism of nationalism in the 1960s gave way to falling commodity prices, coups, and secession movements across the African continent, scholars looked for a new way to understand African history, politics, and economics. The seminal work on development of the 1970s, Walter Rodney's *How Europe Underdeveloped Africa*, paved the way for birth of the "underdevelopment school," taking a more realistic and less optimistic view of Africa. Rodney and the scholars of underdevelopment placed the blame solely on the former European colonial powers as regards both colonialism and, after independence, neocolonialism, for Africa's struggle to develop both politically and economically.

While scholars today are less often given to singular theories such as blame on the West, they still too often focus on one single aspect of development, which is understandable considering the amount of expertise that would be required to be comprehensive. There are several examples of the new arguments being made regarding African development. For instance, many scholars of late have begun pointing to the hurt, rather than the help, that western aid to Africa was causing. Although there have been numerous volumes on this topic, perhaps the most widely discussed has been Dambisa Moyo's book *Dead Aid*, a manifesto proclaiming that trade, not aid, is what Africa truly needs. Another example has been the surge of literature on the growing Chinese presence in Africa. Many of these new books leave much wanting for serious academics, but several scholars, namely political scientists such as Chris Alden and Ian Taylor, have been forging the way for a better understanding of this important topic in African studies.

Edited volumes have been the most common venue for the most recent conversation on development. With the United Nations Millennium Development Goals (MDGs) just a few years away from expiry, scholars are taking the opportunity to reflect on the past while looking ahead to the future. While there is no room here to discuss all the new literature and themes within the greater purview of understanding and promoting African development, several recent edited volumes that address pressing issues and themes within the broader field of development deserve special mention. Most volumes specialize, including *China and Africa Development Relations,* edited by Christopher Dent; *Climate Change and Sustainable Urban Development in Africa and Asia*, edited by Belinda Yuen and Asfaw Kumssa; and the IDRC's edited volume *Managing Natural Resources for Development in Africa: a Resource Book,* edited by Washington Ochola, Pascal Sanginga, and Issac Bekalo. However, other volumes cover a wider range of development topics, bringing them together in conversation with one another. These include the very recently published *Globalization and Sustainable Development in Africa,* edited by Bessie House-Soremekun and Toyin Falola, and *Africa towards 2030: Challenges for Development Policy,* edited by Erik Lundsgaarde. We must also note that beyond these volumes there is important work being done in both single-authored and edited publications aiming to relate HIV/AIDS, the environment, and domestic and international political economy to our understanding of development.

The volume of material that already exists and is still being produced is unquestionably overwhelming. Yet it is clear that there is a need to continue the discussion on African development, particularly in relation to political economy. In the twenty-first century, Africa faces numerous development challenges, most of which must viewed in light of the global political and economic narrative and not as isolated issues. Therefore the intention of this volume is to bring together the diverse new research taking place on African political economy, specifically in relation to development. More succinctly, the objectives of this volume are as follows.

First, these chapters define development itself, particularly in the context of Africa, as well as how the concept has changed and is further changing over time. It links African political economy, both domestic and in terms of foreign policy, with the greater question of development, creating a nuanced view of a complicated topic. The book argues that without first understanding the history of postcolonial African nations, any suggestions to encourage future development will be without contextualization.

The following chapters explore Africa's changing role in the global economy, proving that while Africa may often be left out of international politics, its markets are intricately tied to the rest of the world. Several chapters interrogate the new Asian presence in Africa, in particular the rising power of China, examining both the positive and negative aspects of these new and/or changing relationships. Others examine a subset of the myriad arguments being put forth to promote African development, including changes in foreign policy, political accountability, health care, and environmental sustainability.

The volume stresses that there is not just one answer to why Africa is plagued with chronic underdevelopment, just as there is not one answer to how to encourage development in the twenty-first century. Finally and most importantly, it asserts African agency in the development narrative, as well as African influence on the global historical narrative.

The contributors to this volume represent a wide range of backgrounds and experience. The fields of history, political science, economics, and development studies are represented, as well as scholars from Africa, Europe, and America. This diverse pool of authors allows the volume to cover such a wide range of topics with the utmost expertise, bringing together scholarship that would otherwise be divided along disciplinary and continental lines. It is this interdisciplinary focus that makes this volume so valuable in the study of development in Africa.

OUTLINE OF CHAPTERS

The Political Economy of Development and Underdevelopment in Africa is designed to serve as both a scholarly volume and a reader, providing undergraduate and graduate students with a guide to the many issues and interrelated questions surrounding African development. As displayed in this volume's table of contents, the book is made up of four thematic parts. The authors of Part I, the "Historical Roots of African Underdevelopment," delve into the initial roots of modern issues, providing a long-term understanding of the oil industry and land conflicts and proving that current challenges must be viewed through a historical lens.

In the first chapter, "Africa and the Making of the Global Environmental Narrative: Challenges and Opportunities for the Continent's Development Initiatives," Martin Shanguhyia examines both historical and contemporary conceptions of the African environment, particularly as concerns the debate on environmental crises and the politics pertaining to these crises. Shanguhyia argues that Africa is central to the global environmental narrative, "especially as concerns the politics of causes, consequences, and solutions to environmental problems that are perceived to bear global implications."

His review ranges from the early twentieth century to the present day, a period of great globalization, in which events such as colonization and war created and manifested themselves in environmental concerns. Africa's resources have long been at the center of European and American engagement with the continent, creating environmental issues out of political and economic motivations. More recently, concerns over the environment have found their own way into political debate, as people have begun to realize the human impact and are now promoting "sustainable development."

Shanguhyia's chapter examines studies that speak to the environmental interdependence of nations as well as Africa's place in conceptualizing and contesting the proposed initiatives on environmental practices. Specifically he argues that the view of Africa as a "victim" in the global environmental narrative has predicated the need for "tools" to be given by the international community. This has "expanded existing avenues for local and particularly international intervention into the continent in ways that exhibit both obvious and latent forms of external presence and domination." Yet Africa is constantly negotiating its own place and terms, and this includes land-related environmental problems, particularly issues surrounding climate change.

Chapter 2, "Indigenization versus Domiciliation: A Historical Approach to National Content in Nigeria's Oil and Gas Industry," by Jesse Salah Ovadia, examines a specific aspect of the African environment—its natural resources. Ovadia looks at those of Nigeria, namely oil and gas, and their relation to income disparity. He takes contemporary policies and places them in the historical context of the indigenization of Nigeria's oil to assess "key differences in theory and practice and draw conclusions relevant to the region as a whole."

Specifically, Ovadia examines the theories of domiciliation and indigenization and argues that ultimately both "fall short on the promise of delivering social and human development." Ovadia takes a long view of indigenization, looking at the oil industry in Nigeria from 1960 to 2000 and examining legislation as theory and practice as reality. He also points to issues of income disparity in the current policy of Nigerian content, claiming that although "it cannot be denied that Nigerian content promotes a shift from foreign ownership to indigenization . . . there is much skepticism about the extent to which Nigerian content involves Nigerian participation in ownership and the encouragement of investment by the Nigerian elite." It is too soon to know how successful the current theory will be in practice, but Ovadia makes a strong claim that an examination of the history ensures that "the primary beneficiaries will not be the Nigerian people."

In Chapter 3, "Globalization and Rural Land Conflict in North-West Cameroon: A Historical Perspective," Emmanuel Mbah argues that the influence of global forces has been increasing in Cameroon; he interrogates how globalization specifically has affected rural land and boundaries in North-West Cameroon. Mbah first examines globalization and conflict in terms of land conflict in African generally and North-West Cameroon in particular. He identifies the "globalization-induced economic factors that contribute directly or indirectly to rural land disputes in North-West Cameroon," including primary resources, accessibility, land scarcity, population growth, development, and soil fertility.

The combination of these factors results in "precolonial communal land exploitation patterns [that] are no longer tenable in the region." Previously land was viewed as unlimited, but in postcolonial Cameroon land has become scarce, as well as "an important social security resource." Mbah recommends that in addition to normal conflict-resolution strategies, economic strategies should be deployed to deal with the scarcity of land induced by globalization. Specifically he argues that economic diversification as well as improved farming techniques would go far in reducing conflicts over land.

The final chapter in Part I, "Evolving Political Accountability in Kenya," by Jacob Butler, explores how Kenyan politics have changed since the first multiparty elections in 1992. Whereas previously opposition was dealt with through violence and detention, leaders in a functioning democracy were held to be accountable. Using a historical perspective, Butler examines the evolution of political accountability in Kenya, arguing "the push for accountability by the voting public, the media, civil society groups, and the international community has been a highly contested and evolved into battle as entrenched politicians have abused power in order to avoid being held accountable, thus allowing them to engage in politics as usual."

After first defining political accountability, Butler discusses accountability and the "lack thereof" in Kenya's political system since 1992. The discussion looks at three main actors in the "game" of accountability: the media, the judiciary system, and the international actors involved in Kenyan domestic politics. Ultimately Butler concludes that "the push for political accountability in Kenya is an ongoing process," as long as its citizens continue to push for transparency and proper governance from their leaders.

Part II of this volume explores "Africa in the New Global Economy," connecting current global economic issues to questions surrounding development. Authors in this section interrogate the roles of foreign direct investment, regional and global markets, and financial crises in African development and Africa's full integration in the global economy. The current crisis in the global economy is often discussed in terms of the United States and Europe and, increasingly, China. The influence of these large economies has significant effects on the entire global system, including the nations of Africa. What is less recognized but also important is the need for economic stability in developing nations, including many in Africa. The interconnectedness of the global system and the crucial role a stable economy plays in creating a stable political and social system necessitates a closer look into Africa's role in the global economy.

In the first chapter of Part II, Chapter 5, "Toward a Contextualized Appraisal of Securities Regulation in East Africa," June McLaughlin examines the ideological underpinnings of stock exchanges and the macroissues involved in securities regulation in East Africa—specifically the historical role of development institutions in the creation of security exchanges and the dominant economic policies. McLaughlin argues that stock exchanges are inherently proponents of neoclassical economic theory, "which makes unrealistic assumptions about decision making devoid of any cultural context." Therefore it is critical to understand how stock exchanges influence a uniquely African economic context.

In particular, the Nairobi Stock Exchange, the Uganda Securities Exchange, the Dar es Salaam exchange, and the Rwanda over-the-counter exchange are used as case studies, examining the creation, implementation, and regulation of each exchange in turn. McLaughlin then moves on to describe the interdisciplinary dialogue that exists around these exchanges, using various perspectives to provide a better understanding of the regulation of stock exchanges in general. She argues that "How exchanges develop historically informs how we think about them. Once they exist we need to examine them within their context." This chapter serves to begin to place these exchanges within this context and to examine them within their own unique historical perspectives.

Throughout postcolonial African history, governments have sought foreign direct investment (FDI). In Chapter 6, "The Impact of Changing Global Power Relations on African Governance of Foreign Direct Investment," Roshen Hendrickson examines changing global power relations and their effect on FDI in Africa. Previously, the main sources of FDI for African nations came from the West; however, other nations, specifically Asian nations like China and India, have recently increased their investments. Hendrickson explains in her chapter that while FDI is popular among African nations, it is not regulated, and research indicates that it does not guarantee economic growth.

She argues that " The potential for FDI to contribute to economic development in Africa depends on the way rules, agreements, and norms impact the likelihood that FDI will create jobs, transfer knowledge and technology, and protect the environment, workers' rights, and human rights." In her chapter, Hendrickson first examines the history of the governance of FDI and the implications for African economies. She then explores changing global power relations, looking at the decline of the United States and the increasing initiatives and influence of newly developing global economic powers like China and Brazil. These changing power dynamics are having a profound effect on African nations, which depend so heavily on FDI, providing decreased neoliberal economic regulation for African economies and increased competition for African resources—both of which have the potential to contribute to sustainable economic growth in Africa.

Okpeh O. Okpeh Jr., the author of Chapter 7, "Globalization and Regional Impulses from the Global South: A Comparative Study of ECOWAS and ASEAN," argues that the end of the Cold War has brought about immense transformations in the political and economic order of the world—that is, "globalization." The chapter looks at how countries of the global south are responding to globalization and how regionalism, specifically the Economic Community of West African States (ECOWAS) and the Association of Southeast Asian Nations (ASEAN), helps members states meet the challenges of globalization.

Okpeh examines the global context of what he terms the "new regionalism." He then takes a closer look at regionalism in the African and Asian contexts historically and then in the contemporary period with a comparison of ECOWAS and ASEAN. He argues that such a comparison is useful because it allows us to assess the performance of these two organizations, to relate individual nations' experiences to global development, and to draw conclusions on the interplay between globalization and regionalism as related to economic development.

Okpeh postulates that in the future "the stability of the international system envisaged in the increasing integration of the world as a consequence of globalization appears elusive." In fact, it seems more likely that regional organization will proliferate in this environment and remain a "major force," ultimately affecting not just economic policy but also foreign policy, which helps nations to weather crises like the global economic crisis.

The global financial crisis of 2008 had a profound effect on the world's economy. Although it began in the United States and slowly unfolded in the Eurozone, economic globalization ensured that no nation would not somehow feel its effects. In Chapter 8, "The Political Implication of Past and Present Nigerian Financial Crises," Muhammed Tanko examines how financial crises, both throughout history and the current crisis, have affected the Nigerian economy in comparison with the rest of the world. In order to gather a full picture of the effects of the Nigerian financial crises, Tanko uses a two-step analysis of data, first looking at development generally and then employment in particular.

In turn, he identifies the areas having a major impact on the capital market: federal government medium- and long-term bonds; external trade and financial flows; the non-oil sector; the banking sector; and, finally, the labor force and unemployment. Tanko concludes that the impact of the current Nigerian financial crisis has had "different ramifications" for different sectors. He argues that the banking sector in particular mirrored global trends, but that it was "largely contained because of its limited integration with the global financial system." However, the crisis combined with internal management issues in the banks, in turn affecting several sectors of the Nigerian economy. In light of his conclusions, Tanko recommends that the Nigerian economy take a few key steps to move forward and away from the present crisis. The first step is to diversify the economy away from oil and to stem the mismanagement of resources and other forms of corruption. He also suggests the encouragement of a "safe and sound" banking system, so as to fund domestic development projects. Most importantly, however, he suggests that an understanding of the past and present financial crises in Nigeria is key to ensuring that the economy will be able to manage any future difficulties.

In Chapter 9, "Transcending an Elitist Approach and Making a Paradigm Shift from Growth without Development to 'Populist' Development," Hauwa'u Evelyn Yusuf and Adefarakan Adedayo Yusuf examine the problem of depending on an elite group to promote development. In the authors' view, dependence on elites has been a particular problem for Africa because "the historical epoch that gave birth to them, particularly the ravaging capitalist system and the prevailing international economic order, affected not only their conceptualization of issues but also their ability to promote progress in the region." For the last fifty years then, the continent has been "drifting."

Using a historical model of tracing development, the authors take several African case studies in a comparative perspective, also comparing them to the Asian countries of Malaysia and Singapore, which have had a much different story of development. In the first section, they examine Africa's potential for development and the reasons why it has been lagging behind countries like those in Asia. Next they look specifically at how elites have conceptualized African development. Finally, they argue that "emotional intelligence" is the key to making the necessary paradigm shift to populist development. Overall, they argue, that the elite of Africa "must rethink and relearn development" and that it must be "conceptualized from an inclusive and not exclusive perspective."

In a subset of the changing global economy, Part III, "Forging New International Connections," explores the rise of the BRIC countries and its effects on the African continent. Chapters in this section explore the rising Asian influence in Africa in terms of both its benefits and its challenges. The authors explore how investment and aid have changed in the post-Cold War era, examining case studies such as Nigeria's recent and future relations with China and the longer history of India's presence in Kenya.

In the first chapter of this section, "The Political Economy of Rising Asian Interests in Africa: Problems, Prospects, and Challenges," Olusegun Osinibi examines both the positive and negative aspects of increasing Asian interest and influence in Africa. As a continent of great natural resources, Africa has become increasingly appealing to the governments of Asia, which require raw materials for both large populations and a growing manufacturing industry. Osinibi looks first at the historical roots of the relationship between Africa and Asia and its effects on present cooperation. This present cooperation is then explicated in both political and economic initiatives and an analysis of the political economy of increasing initiatives. Finally, Osinibi examines how Africa has continued to be underdeveloped in comparison with other regions and how Asian interests can benefit and provide solutions for ensuring African development.

Osinibi believes that "The prospects of strong sociopolitical and economic cooperation between Africa and Asia raise much optimism in view of the boundless human and natural resources available on both continents." However, the joint goals of political, economic, and sociocultural cooperation are not being realized owing to corruption, poverty, and poor governance in Africa and an unfavorable balance of trade between Africa and Asia. Once these issues have been properly dealt with, "it is then that the immense benefits of Asia's rising interest in Africa will be evident for all to see."

In Chapter 11, "The Impact of the BRICS countries on Africa's Socioeeconomic Development in the Post-Cold War Era," Alexius Amtaika discusses the BRICS countries of Brazil, Russia, India, China, and South Africa and their role in African development. In Asia, South America, and Africa, the BRICS countries have recently had a surge of influence "evident in political economy, trade, investment and decision-making spheres, in international bodies and in the affairs of other countries beyond their continents." Rivaling the western hegemonic power of the G8 countries, the BRICS countries, since the end of the Cold War, have become increasingly organized and powerful, creating both a "glimmer of hope" for other developing nations and concerns over a new form of imperialism.

Amtaika's chapter, therefore, examines the impact that the BRICS countries have had on African nations, specifically in the area of socioeconomic development. He examines both aid and investment, highlighting the positive and negative aspects of the "new world order" with which Africa is forced to contend. He argues that the BRICS countries can have a positive influence on Africa, but that "realizing the continent's potential requires a radical reform of the nature of African politics and politicians." In the end, it is up to individual African nations to realize their goals for socioeconomic development.

Chapter 12, "How Ready Is Nigeria for Chinese Investments?" is an examination by John Anegbode and Cletus Onakalu of the historical and contemporary relationship between Nigeria and China. Anegbode and Onakalu argue that although Nigeria has a long-standing diplomatic relationship with China, dating back to 1971, the trade between Nigeria and China has increased significantly in the last decade. Therefore the chapter, in addition to interrogating the relationship between China and Africa generally, examines a specific Nigerian case: that of the Niger Delta crisis and its implications for corruption and leadership challenges to Chinese investments in Nigeria.

Chinese investments have increased in several important sectors of the Nigerian economy, specifically in energy resources. Consequently, the Niger Delta crisis can be seen as a major threat to Chinese investment in Nigeria. Other threats also abound, including corruption, poor leadership, and the problem of inferior Chinese goods. Owing to the internal issues in Nigeria, the authors argue that before it can enter into agreements with other nations, Nigeria must address its own "multifaceted problems." They argue for stricter punishments for Nigerians who are found to be corrupt, following the example of China, as well as for Chinese investors to comply with the rules and regulations of their host country. As it stands, however, "Nigeria is not yet ready to accommodate China's investment."

In Chapter 13, "The New Scramble for Africa? Indo-Kenyan Economic Relations, 1980–2010," Felix Kiruthu, Mary Kinyanjui, and Francis Muchoki, further investigating the role of the new "developing" powerhouses, explore the specific example of Kenya's relations with India. They argue that while much attention has been paid to the relationship between China and Africa, little attention has been given to that between India and Africa. Yet although the historical relations between India and the African nations differ quite markedly from the Chinese example, India has also shown great "enthusiasm" in "reaching out to Africa."

The period of "new economic relations" is defined in this chapter as the era since 1980, and the authors examine the reasons, nature, and dynamics of these relations from a political economy approach. Specifically they argue that "Indo-African relations after independence have been characterized by issues that are deemed to be of mutual interest between African countries like Kenya and India, regardless of whether they are political, social or economic in nature." On viewing these issues through a historical lens, it becomes clear that the foundation for relations between India and Kenya was laid long before 1980, allowing for the current large- and small-scale operations. Yet these operations have done little to promote Kenyan infrastructure, reminiscent of western investments. There is potential for improvement, however, with increased skills and technology transfers as well as ethical business operations.

The final section of this volume, Part IV, "The Way Forward for Twenty-First-Century Development," covers a range of ideas on the promotion of African development. Some of these are new ideas, like environmental regulation and sustainable tourism, while others look at familiar topics in new ways, such as U.S. HIV/AIDS aid programs in Uganda and evolving political accountability in Kenya. It is in this section that we can begin to take lessons from previous chapters and apply them in direct and nuanced ways to specific African challenges, moving forward for development in the new century.

In 2010, French President Sarkozy hosted the French Africa summit, outlining French policy toward Africa, which has undergone much change since the end of the Cold War. These former and current policies are examined by Céline Jacquemin in Chapter 14, "French Foreign Policy in Rwanda: Language, Personal Networks, and Changing Contexts." Specifically, Sarkozy redefined French policy away from a previous basis of Francophone loyalty to one "founded on mutual interests and shared goals." Jacquemin asks how these new policies can benefit France and Rwanda in particular and the African continent in general.

She explains that although the Francophone policy of favoring French-speaking African nations has remained at the center of French foreign policy, new policies allow for relations with English-speaking nations and an attempt to gain new allies. France finds the need for allies critical, as the French have competition not only from the United States and United Kingdom but now also from China and India, evidenced in their support of the efforts of either Nigeria or South Africa to gain a permanent seat on the United Nations Security Council. Overall, despite major changes in French foreign policy toward Africa, Jacquemine argues, "Francophonie continues to remain the main foundation of the relationship between France and its former colonies," but this is certain to change more in the post-Cold War political era.

Chapter 15, "The Question of Development in Africa," more broadly interrogates the contemporary issues surrounding this topic. In this chapter, Ebunoluwa Oduwole argues that, in addressing all the various indices of development, it becomes clear that Africa is "far behind developing, let alone developed." Specifically the chapter examines the indices of human development, the environment, and safety in the context of determining the level of development of a nation. Oduwole is clear that rapid development is possible but that any such development is hindered by the social, political, and, most importantly, moral climate within African nations. While Oduwole's arguments apply to many African nations, she focuses on Nigeria, and in particular on how corruption has affected development.

After defining development and looking briefly at the example of Nigerian corruption, Oduwole discusses what she believes is one of the most important factors affecting a nation's development: the moral factor. Although not denying the importance of political, economic, and social stability, she argues that "the mind-set factor, which can be described as a set of ideas that shapes one's behavior and outlook and places the interest of the society far above that of the self, is crucial." Oduwole concludes African development should be achieved by internal development "through a commitment to political will" by both the leadership and citizenry of a country.

Since decolonization, there have been a number of terms used to define previously colonized nations, including the "Third World." In Chapter 16, "A Critique of the Notion of Africa as the 'Third World': Toward a New Perspective," Mike O. Odey argues against this labeling and instead argues for the term "developing" to be used in referring to African nations. These concepts are used by Odey as analytical tools in defining Africa at different stages of world history. Specifically, he argues that the old terminology implies that Africa has not changed for the better since decolonization and could even be defined as "racially prejudiced."

The main question Odey uses to guide his argument is: How has Africa developed since the end of the Cold War? After giving a brief background on world classifications, he looks at how African nations are developing, albeit gradually and despite all odds. For Odey, this view represents the arguments of the "realists" and "optimists" of African development. Yet as a self-proclaimed pragmatist, he acknowledges that development, including African development, does not happen in a vacuum. Therefore, he argues for the importance of considering the interdependence of all nations in an increasingly globalizing world. Once the world realizes that African development will encourage the development of the entire global economy, "the stigma of the old Third World formation will be jettisoned when all these are achieved and Africa will wear a new look of development."

Looking at a crucial aspect of twenty-first-century development for Africa, Ben Weiss and Jessica Achberger, in "United States' Pharmaceutical Influence on Uganda's HIV/AIDS Relief System," examine the influence of the United States on the distribution of antiretroviral drugs in Uganda. Specifically the authors examine the role of the President's Emergency Plan for AIDS Relief (PEPFAR), which since its creation in 2003 has contributed to one of the most dramatic drops in AIDS rates worldwide. Yet because of the economic recession and increasing budget cuts, programs like PEPFAR are in danger of ceasing to exist. This, the authors argue, could have detrimental effects on Uganda's health care system.

The chapter looks at the current methods of distributing antiretroviral drugs and draws conclusions about the potential effects of a major budget cut. The authors argue that Uganda is entirely too dependent on American aid for these programs and that the fundamentals of the Ugandan health care system (including things such as improved transportation and clinic access) need to be overhauled before the situation reaches the point of crisis. While PEPFAR has no doubt significantly contributed to the decrease in AIDS rates in Uganda and other countries including Nigeria, "pharmaceutical and logistical dependence on the United States will always threaten Uganda's ability to have a sustainable HIV/AIDS treatment program."

Climate change is a hot topic that has been on everyone's lips for the last several years. International conferences, such as the one in Copenhagen in 2009, have provided well-publicized forums for discussion of the global environment. In Chapter 18, "Copenhagen: An African's Reading on the Aftermath of the Copenhagen's Climate Change Conference (2009)," Olivier Tchouaffe points out that Africa is at the center of the global environmental crisis, despite its peripheral status in relation to the United States, the European Union, China, and India at conferences such as the one at Copenhagen.

Africa has been discouraged from playing an active role in the conversation about climate change, yet it is inevitable that all will be affected, as "climate change does not recognize borders." Tchouaffe argues that "climate change is a global challenge that requires substantial questions, definite answers, and incentives." Therefore the chapter "aims to deconstruct the globalization discourses around climate change and the African continent" and determine Africa's rightful place in the dialogue, as well as the strategies that should be employed.

In the final chapter, "Globalization and Developing Economies: Eco-Tourism and Sustainable Development in Cross River State, Nigeria," Donald Omagu explains that eco-tourism, although relatively new, is the fastest-growing sector of tourism, especially in developing countries. International tourists are lured to developing countries with the promise of an exotic vacation, but also with the idea that their trip will be both environmentally and socially responsible. As Omagu explains, "Eco-tourism presents an environmentally friendly and potentially complementary intervention option" for people in developing countries to generate income. It encourages residents of environmentally sensitive areas to respect the land and provides an opportunity for a cross-cultural educational experience for tourists from abroad.

Eco-tourism, however, does not come without its challenges, and Omagu discusses both the prospects and key issues facing eco-tourism in Cross River State, Nigeria. Specifically, Omagu argues, "without appropriate planning and management, the cost of Cross River State eco-tourism may accrue to the extent that its benefits are lost." The chapter concludes by emphasizing the key factors to be addressed so as to avoid such a loss in Cross River State.

Taken as a whole, the chapters in this volume represent the broad range of research in African development and fully tie this development to the global political economy. African nations play significant roles in world politics, both as nations influenced by the ebbs and flows of the global economy and by the international political system and also as actors directly influencing politics and economics. It is only through an understanding of both the history and present place of Africa in global affairs that we can begin to assess the way forward for future development.

NOTES

1. On the trans-Atlantic slave trade see, A. E. Afigbo, Carolyn A. Brown, and Paul E. Lovejoy, eds., *Repercussions of the Atlantic Slave Trade: the Interior of the Bight of Biafra and the African Diaspora* (Trenton, NJ: Africa World Press, 2011); and Toyin Falola and Matt Childs, eds., *The Yoruba Diaspora in the Atlantic World* (Bloomington, IN: Indiana University Press, 2004).
2. See, for instance, Jeremy Prestholdt, *Domesticating the World: African Consumerism and the Genealogies of Globalization* (Berkeley and Los Angeles, CA: University of California Press, 2008).
3. On the colonial economy, see P. J. Cain and A. G. Hopkins, *British Imperialism, 1688–2000* (New York: Longman, 2002); Allister Hinds, *Britain's Sterling Colonial Policy and Decolonization, 1939–1958* (Westport, CT: Greenwood Press, 2001); and Marcello De Cecco, *The International Gold Standard: Money and Empire* (New York: St. Martin's Press, 1984.)
4. See Claude Ake, *A Political Economy of Africa* (Harlow; Essex, UK: Longman, 1981); A. Adu Boahen, *Africa under Colonial Domination 1880–1935* (London: Heinemann, 1985); and Toyin Falola, *The Dark Webs: Perspectives on Colonialism in Africa* (Durham, NC: Carolina Academic Press, 2005).

5. For an excellent look at the role of the Third World generally, see Odd Arne Westad, *The Global Cold War: Third World Interventions and the Making of Our Times* (Cambridge, UK: Cambridge University Press, 2005). For a look at southern Africa specifically, see Sue Onslow, ed., *Cold War in Southern Africa: White Power, Black Liberation* (New York: Routledge, 2009).
6. See, for instance, Adekeye Adebajo, *From Global Apartheid to Global Village: Africa and the United Nations* (Scottsville, South Africa: University of Kwa-Zulu-Natal Press, 2009).

REFERENCES

Adebajo, Adekeye. *From Global Apartheid to Global Village: Africa and the United Nations*. Scottsville, South Africa: University of Kwa-Zulu-Natal Press, 2009.
Afigbo, A. E., Carolyn A. Brown, and Paul E. Lovejoy, eds. *Repercussions of the Atlantic Slave Trade: the Interior of the Bight of Biafra and the African Diaspora*. Trenton, NJ: Africa World Press, 2011.
Ake, Claude. *A Political Economy of Africa*. Harlow; Essex, UK: Longman, 1981.
Alden, Chris. *China in Africa*. London: Zed Books, 2007.
Alden, Chris, Daniel Large, and Ricardo Soares de Oliveira. *China Returns to Africa: A Rising Power and a Continent Embrace*. New York: Columbia University Press, 2008.
Boahen, A. Adu. *Africa under Colonial Domination, 1880–1935*. London: Heinemann, 1985.
Cain, P. J., and A. G. Hopkins. *British Imperialism, 1688–2000*. New York: Longman, 2002.
De Cecco, Marcello. *The International Gold Standard: Money and Empire*. New York: St. Martin's Press, 1984.
Dent, Christopher M. *China and Africa Development Relations*. Oxford, UK: Routledge, 2011.
Falola, Toyin. *The Dark Webs: Perspectives on Colonialism in Africa*. Durham, NC: Carolina Academic Press, 2005.
Falola, Toyin, and Matt Childs, eds. *The Yoruba Diaspora in the Atlantic World* Bloomington, IN: Indiana University Press, 2004.
Hinds, Allister. *Britain's Sterling Colonial Policy and Decolonization, 1939–1958*. Westport, CT: Greenwood Press, 2001.
House-Soremekun, Bessie, and Toyin Falola. *Globalization and Sustainable Development in Africa*. Rochester, NY: University of Rochester Press, 2011.
Lundsgaarde, Erik. *Africa toward 2030: Challenges for Development Policy*. Basingstoke; Hampshire, UK: Palgrave Macmillan, 2012.
Moyo, Dambisa. *Dead Aid: Why Aid Is Not Working and How There Is a Better Way for Africa*. New York: Farrar, Straus and Giroux, 2009.
Ochola, Washington Odongo, P. C. Sanginga, and Isaac Bekalo. *Managing Natural Resources for Development in Africa: A Resource Book*. Nairobi: copublished by The University of Nairobi Press in association with International Development Research Centre, International Institute of Rural Reconstruction, Regional Universities Forum for Capacity Building in Agriculture, 2010.
Onslow, Sue, ed. *Cold War in Southern Africa: White Power, Black Liberation*. New York: Routledge, 2009.
Prestholdt, Jeremy. *Domesticating the World: African Consumerism and the Genealogies of Globalization*. Berkeley and Los Angeles, CA: University of California Press, 2008.

Rodney, Walter. *How Europe Underdeveloped Africa*. Washington, DC: Howard University Press, 1981.
Taylor, Ian. *China's New Role in Africa*. Boulder, CO: Lynne Rienner, 2009.
Westad, Odd Arne. *The Global Cold War: Third World Interventions and the Making of Our Times*. Cambridge, UK: Cambridge University Press, 2005.
Yuen, Belinda, and Asfaw Kumssa. *Climate Change and Sustainable Urban Development in Africa and Asia*. Dordrecht: Springer, 2011.

Part I
Historical Roots of African Underdevelopment

1 Africa and the Making of the Global Environmental Narrative
Challenges and Opportunities for the Continent's Development Initiatives

Martin S. Shanguhyia

This study analyzes the historical and contemporary perceptions and constructions of Africa within the global environmental narrative, particularly as concerns the debate on environmental crises. It further explores the extent to which the continent and its peoples have engaged the politics that pertain to these crises. The principal contention is that Africa has been central in the framing of global environmental issues, especially as concerns the politics of causes, consequences, and solutions to environmental problems that are perceived to bear global implications. The period of focus is the twentieth century into the present, a time of unprecedented globalization of modern environmental issues. During this period, environmental concerns have largely been a manifestation of broader political, military, economic, and social trajectories that shaped European and American societies during momentous times, including imperial expansion, colonization, the Great Depression, the two World Wars, the Cold War, and decolonization as well as increased use of technology and science after 1945.[1]

By extension, these developments have been imperative in promoting Africa's engagement with the global community. Africa's natural environment, ranging from its physical geography to tangible resources such as land/soil, forests, water, and minerals have been at the core of determining economic and political initiatives at the state and international levels. Indeed, the assertion by James C. McCann in this regard—that Africa has never been ecologically isolated but that its physical environment has enabled a porous relationship allowing for centuries of the exchange of goods, ideas, and people with the international community—is instructive in this exposition.[2] Consequently a closer analysis will also reveal that local economic initiatives in Africa since the precolonial through colonial times have been linked to the continent's environmental resources in an integrated global economy.[3] Most recently, Africa has found itself positioned in the midst of a world where debates about globalization occupy the center stage, so much so that the quest for development on the continent has also been conceptualized with a "world systems" analysis.[4] This attests to continued trends toward interdependence between the communities and nations of the world. More critical, however, is the way in which politics about the environment within and outside of Africa have played a fundamental role in reinforcing local/national development inside the globalization process and the positioning of Africa within that process.

An important trend in this period, especially after the 1980s, has been the growing worldwide realization of the massive impact occasioned by a pervasive human interaction with the natural environment. This, in turn, has elicited the need for global environmental governance so as to promote what has been termed "sustainable development" based on the world's natural resources.[5] Since colonial times, Africa and its people have not escaped contact with these developments, and the outcome of that contact within the environmental domain is largely the theme of this discussion. It is these seemingly western-initiated global currents that have helped shape Africa's place in world environmental politics both as a subject and an object of discussion. This is particularly the case given that the above developments of the twentieth and early twenty-first century have served to increase the engagement with Africa by the international community, particularly western nations' institutions and nongovernmental organizations, which have been instrumental in globalizing environmental issues.

In order to appreciate these international linkages between Africa and the global engagement of the environmental narrative, this study revisits interpretations that view modern environmental politics at the global level as being the outcome of the realization that natural resources are of a global nature. That is, this study resonates with analyses that create links between local/regional environmental concerns and the international environmental system in the bid to create an understanding of cause and effect in environmental dilemmas as well as solutions to such dilemmas.[6] Such views have been boosted by notions that perceive the existence of a high degree of interdependence between nations of the world, thereby requiring international cooperation in resource use and management.[7] It is this movement, mainly born in the West and embraced by the colonial and postcolonial states, that has sought to incorporate Africa and its peoples in environmental issues at the global level.

This discussion goes further to identify with studies that critique the presumed primacy of the global perspective in the configuration and prioritization of specific environmental problems as well as the management approaches to environmental resources and social and economic development sectors.[8] Thus, while it is evident that the globalization of environmental issues has aided modern transnational networks—which continue to produce and sustain unequal power relations in the global arena—this process has also been seen to provide "junctures," spaces, or opportunities for regions like Africa and its peoples to reconceptualize and contest seemingly universal global ideas or externally imposed initiatives about environmental practices.[9] Processes of contestation have also not been without opportunities for accommodation and assertion of African interests and aspirations.

The basic argument in this discussion is threefold: first, Africa and its peoples have been portrayed in global environmental debates partly as culprits in fomenting some ecological crises but mostly as victims needing the "tools"—knowledge, financing, and technology—to deal with environmental problems. This narrative, created by state officialdom and aided by local and international stakeholders in African resources, has been sustained through space and time, from colonial through modern times, although with varying degrees of intensity. Second, the need to provide these tools so that Africa and its people can confront the perceived environmental problems has introduced new and expanded avenues for local and particularly international intervention into the continent in ways that exhibit both obvious and latent forms of external presence and domination. For Africa, this has come by way of an increasing presence of international (and national) interventions into the colonial and the postcolonial states. Third, having been reluctantly drawn into the global engagement with the environment, Africa has not remained passive but has staked out opportunities and navigated through the debate in ways deemed beneficial to its peoples. Therefore one of the critical questions raised here is this: How has Africa and its people contested or engaged the global ideas about the environment?

Multiple environmental regimes exist that can be used to identify the various ways in which Africa has engaged or been involved in the environmental issues at the global level. However, this analysis focuses mainly on land-related environmental problems, especially desertification and land degradation as well as climate change. These have featured prominently in global debates and have been persistently linked directly to the livelihoods and, therefore, the current and future survival of the majority of Africa's population.

AFRICA'S ENGAGEMENT WITH COLONIAL ENVIRONMENTAL CONCERNS: DESERTIFICATION/LAND DEGRADATION

Concerns about desertification and increasing cases of drought in Africa stretch back to ancient times but have been increasingly raised since colonial times. The Sahara, Sahel, and the sprawling plateau and grasslands of northeastern, eastern, central, and southern Africa have particularly raised concerns as far as desiccation and drought are concerned. This was especially the case in the French and British colonies in West Africa, where colonial officials from the 1930s onward raised the specter of the expansion of the Sahara southward. This expansion, experts and colonial officials feared, threatened to push the Sahelian conditions into the northern margins of the Ivory Coast, Gold Coast, and Nigeria, thereby threatening water and land resources in those areas.[10] In the ensuing research and debate into the problem, European ecological experts focused on local African farming practices to identify the causes of desertification in the region. Overcultivation, overgrazing, deforestation, and grass fires set by African herders and farmers in West Africa's Savanna were cited as facilitating the perceived desertification problem. In 1935, E. P. Stebbing, an influential ecologist who engaged with environmental issues in British colonies in India and Africa, was certain that the Kano region of northern Nigeria would be swallowed up by the Sahara in a "space of the next fifty years or less" and blamed the impending desolation as being caused "principally by man." Stebbing attributed this degeneration to locally induced deforestation, intensive cultivation, and a "wasteful" industrial activity of iron-smelting that increased extraction of fuel wood from the standing vegetation.[11]

It should be noted that western scientific knowledge was at the core of framing the causes and nature of these environmental threats at the time. The limit of that knowledge was illustrated in the conflict in opinion over the extent and actual causes of desertification in West Africa or if indeed desiccation was affecting the region. There was no consensus as to whether these parts of West Africa were actually arid. This was emphasized by Brynmor Jones, the British geologist attached to Nigeria who commented on the problem: "It is doubtful if the term 'arid' is applicable to any of the British colonies in West Africa, since even the driest part of them [around Lake Chad] receives a mean annual rainfall of 15 inches."[12] While Stebbing attributed human causes to desertification, Brynmor inferred from the scanty historical evidence of climatic changes for that region that a series of droughts due to scarce rainfall led to any dry conditions.[13]

With both British and French ecological experts involved in identifying the causes, nature, and impact of desertification in colonial West Africa, the problem was viewed as one that transcended colonial borders, and its perception as an international problem was evident in the search for solutions. Consequently collaborative rather than "isolated" efforts were sought with a proposal to establish an international vegetation belt stretching from the Ivory Coast through northern Nigeria to the Lake Chad area. An Anglo-French commission was subsequently constituted in 1936 to investigate the state of desiccation in West Africa.[14] The commission's findings contradicted Stebbing's gloomy depictions and predictions of the nature, causes, and effects of desertification in the area. Generally, in spite of such differences in opinion, views involving destructive African farmers and herders as causes of ecological decline were pervasive in the emergent official environmental narrative in colonial West Africa. Focus on local land practices was aided by the failure to establish a natural/climatic link to desertlike conditions in the savanna parts of West Africa, so much so that state intervention was urged in order to regulate the agricultural activities of the local African communities, such as shifting cultivation and grazing.[15] Overall, French and British colonial administrations in West Africa were persuaded to denigrate African farming practices and then intervened in ways that esteemed western technical knowledge in the management of African ecologies. Such was the case even when practical experimentation with western technical planning for some projects failed to materialize in that region.[16]

While desertification dominated the environmental debate in West Africa in the 1930s, claims of land degradation defined colonial agricultural debates in British colonies in eastern and southern Africa. Before that period, Africa's encounter with the western world at the close of the nineteenth century and especially at the onset of the twentieth had opened the way for the unprecedented extraction of the continent's natural resources by the colonial powers following colonial conquest. This is not to overlook the human, economic, and environmental debacles occasioned by earlier centuries of contact between Africa and the international community that were well manifested in the transactions of the international slave trade.[17] Yet with the onset of colonialism—particularly in times of economic uncertainty, such as those generated by the Depression years of the early 1930s as well as political conflicts as occasioned by the two World Wars—questions about access to and use of resources became priorities at the national and international agendas of the colonial powers. Africa's role in sustaining these countries in times of economic uncertainty meant that the continent and its people became central to any debate that involved the extraction and use of land-based natural resources.

Colonial eastern Africa suffered a series of droughts and locust invasions in the Depression years, which were also a time when soil erosion was associated with official visions of social and economic decline in African reserves.[18] Drought spells reduced agricultural production, thereby occasioning food shortages. Yet colonial officials in Kenya, Tanganyika, and Uganda, unable to effectively address the famine that resulted from natural forces, focused instead on drought to heighten images of desolation in African rural areas; thus they catapulted land degradation and soil erosion to the top of the agricultural agenda of those areas.[19] In South Africa, official concerns about environmental degradation of natural resources and on the dangers of soil erosion were voiced as far back as the mid-nineteenth century, but they gained momentum after the beginning of the twentieth. Then, both settler and African farming and herding practices on the veldts, particularly grass fires and deforestation activities, came under scrutiny.[20] Soil erosion and desiccation led to forecasts of gloom as fears were expressed that the *dongas* that dotted the veldts were turning South Africa into a desert country.[21] Thus, as was the case with the desertification problem in West Africa, the natural causes of land degradation in eastern and southern Africa, whose most visible symptom was soil erosion, were often overlooked in favor of local human causes.

It was mainly in the search for solutions to the perceived environmental crises (especially land degradation) in eastern and southern Africa in the 1930s that international links to the issues became evident and globalization of soil erosion became fashionable for institutions and western experts who engaged the problem at first hand and for colonial states in Africa seeking solutions from the West. Local ecological problems pertaining to land degradation and soil erosion warranted technical solutions born in the West, especially in the southwestern plains of the United States, where the Dust Bowl had threatened the agricultural landscape and with it the region's livelihoods and economy.[22] The Dust Bowl aided in the internationalization of land degradation as a global problem needing the global sharing of agrotechnical information to resolve it. Such international solutions found their way into the colonial technical and administrative departments in eastern and southern Africa in the 1930s through the postwar period.[23] The western conservation ideology found expression in official intervention policies in African peasant agriculture, justified by the colonial state's concerns about the welfare of the soil.

William Beinart has exposed the colonial development ideology behind the intrusive interventionist conservation programs that were aimed at confronting land degradation in southern Africa.[24] The vision of the state and its capitalist agents was guided by capitalist aspirations focused on rational planning of the agrarian sector so as to secure certain economic gains. Metropolitan commercial firms seized the moment to supplement state efforts to enforce the conservation ethic among African rural communities so as to shore up these companies' capitalist interests. In colonial Uganda, the Empire Cotton Growers Association, faced with fears of soil erosion and its potential impact on cotton-producing areas in eastern Africa, put its weight behind imperial and international efforts to enforce conservation measures in areas such as the Teso District.[25]

The global conflict of 1939–1945 enhanced the role of Africa's environmental resources, especially in global politics, as the belligerent powers depended on those resources for victory against their enemies. As the soil conservation programs started in the 1930s and were carried into the 1940s, European colonial powers in Africa encountered the contradiction of conserving resources that they also needed to exploit as part of Africa's war effort. Priority was accorded to surplus extraction over conservation to the extent that the quality of land deteriorated rapidly in eastern and southern Africa during and after the war. Subsequently, Britain in particular revisited the conservation ethic with vengeance with its postwar reconstruction program in its African colonies. The intrusive nature of the colonial state had never been so evident in Africa's rural areas since colonial conquest earlier in the century, as earlier efforts were mooted to ensure a balance between increased production and soil conservation initiatives in African reserves.

The proliferation into African rural landscapes of western ecological and agricultural experts, aided by the technical and administrative departments of the colonial state in the postwar period to deal with land degradation and soil conservation, is synonymous with what some historians of Africa have dubbed the "second colonial occupation."[26] The 1930s images of desolation and a grim future for African rural populations in the colonial script in eastern and southern Africa were resurrected in the postwar period and linked to reports of increased soil erosion and land degradation. There was a sense of urgency to help save African communities that, apart from being depicted as the victims of the perceived environmental decline, were also blamed for having caused the problem through inefficient farming activities. Thus, by the mid-1940s, the colonial environmental narrative had hardly changed except that it was trumpeted with increased intensity. Western environmental experts were tapped to disseminate western scientific and technical knowledge to African farmers and thus help save the rural ecologies from turning to waste.

The postwar conservation program in the African colonies was implemented as part of the international economic need to help European powers to recover from the war's destruction. While depending on the United States for an economic bailout, France and Britain still looked to their colonies to supply resources so as to aid in their post-war reconstruction programs. In 1947, for example, Sir Stafford Cripps, the chancellor of the exchequer, made clear to a conference of colonial governors that the ultimate solution at the economic difficulties of the sterling area was to be found in the British colonies. Therefore, for Britain, the shortages of essential commodities as well as the dollar crisis after the war were instrumental in London's policies; these were directed at massive intervention in the rural agriculture of colonies such as Kenya, Tanganyika, and Nyasaland.[27] For Africa, and especially the British colonies, this implied the official execution of economic and social engineering programs with the objective of promoting "overall development" in rural areas.[28] Existing studies on the second colonial occupation in Africa after 1945 into the 1950s are replete with images of expanded and intensive colonial agrarian programs of a dual nature: increased production as well as soil conservation initiatives by governments, all of which tied local economic and environmental initiatives to the international system.

Enforced land management initiatives by colonial states in Africa often elicited resistance from rural populations for their inadequacies in accommodating land tenure patterns, traditional land practices, and forces in the agricultural markets for rural household production as well as the agricultural labor resources of those households. More importantly, such responses were automatic reactions against the limitations of employing internationally acquired land management knowledge to Africa's rural landscapes. As a result of such limits, some colonial officials were reluctantly persuaded to rethink their indifference toward African modes and tools of production. For example, some colonial agricultural projects were driven by notions that privileged imported ecological practices in rural areas; when they failed, their failure served to open avenues for a colonial dialogue on the potential long-term value of using local African knowledge in the management of agrarian ecologies. Such alternatives were often voiced by only a few but sometimes also by influential colonial agricultural officials who experienced growing frustration on seeing that these African tropical ecologies were too dynamic and complex to warrant a linear or one-sided external management approach. That is, the importance of recourse to local/indigenous agricultural practices came to be realized.

Recent studies have revealed how some officials in Kenya's Department of Agriculture, for example, acknowledged that while African agricultural practices were always criticized, such local practices were more suited to the local environments than those suggested by colonial experts. In Northern Rhodesia (Zambia), for example, the Agricultural Department gradually modified its negative view of shifting cultivation, a traditional farming system whose ecological values had been assumed to be wasteful.[29] In Uganda, a section of the colonial administration realized the need to reclaim the production of indigenous food crops in the bid to boost food reserves, since these were being undermined by the enforcement of new export crops.[30] From comprehensive research done by Paul Richards on British territories on West Africa, particularly in colonial Nigeria, we have a sense of colonial shift in the perceptions of the value of African "peasant agricultural practices" toward the cultivation of indigenous food crops suitable to those rural ecologies that were previously dedicated to the production of new but unsuccessful crops. The failure of these crops was due in part to the indifference of African farmers to the new agricultural ideas, since these were being enforced without consulting the local community.[31]

Such colonial trends in the post-Depression and post-World War II periods highlight the imposing nature of international knowledge regarding the management of Africa's rural ecologies as well as the dilemmas involving the efficacy of that knowledge system. However, the fact that such assumptions never worked in some rural ecologies attests to how far colonial experts had "misread" the African landscape.[32] Those trends also attest to those "recovering" African ecological practices that were deemed rational in confronting the ecological crises of the 1930s and 1940s.

The extent to which such recovery efforts succeeded depended on other intervening, more powerful, forces such as the economic needs of the colonial states and metropolitan countries—needs such as those occasioned by the postwar reconstruction programs. Such rural development initiatives imposed a burden of surplus production alongside enforced soil conservation initiatives aimed at "normalizing" African agriculture so as to ensure a sustained supply of raw materials for Britain's postwar recovery. This often required a more concerted recourse to more specialized western methods of land management that had been applied in the previous decade, which in turn elicited active and overt resistance from the local population.

Such resistance in Tanganyika ranged from chants of "We don't want terraces, give us back our old ways," by a large crowd of demonstrators in the Uluguru Highlands of the Morogoro District in Tanganyika in 1955, to the refusal by women in Shambaa to construct *matuta* (ridges) on their farms.[33] This could be attributed to the labor costs and surplus opportunities that

African households counted as lost if they were to go along with these enforced conservation measures. These postwar development programs based on externally imposed ecological management also opened new avenues for marginalized African groups, especially women, to assert their traditional rights over property and labor. Fiona Mackenzie has demonstrated how gender cut across the changing socioeconomic landscape of the Kikuyu in Central Kenya as accessibility to land faded with time, so that the traditional rights to land by Kikuyu women were contested by men. At the same time, the colonial government's emphasis on western knowledge of soil conservation was interpreted by Kikuyu women as an assault on their status as custodians of indigenous knowledge in land management, resulting in the Murang'a women's riot of 1948.[34] Generally the need of the Kikuyu in central Kenya to reassert alternative normal land relations and rational land management counter to those initiated by the colonial states, in collaboration with local and international capital, can be seen in the outbreak of the Mau Mau War in Kenya. One of the major catalysts to this conflict must be identified not only in the land alienation schemes of the colonial state but also in the enforcement of land management practices that were not viable in the overcrowded reserves of Kikuyuland.[35]

Such local African resistance notwithstanding, the immediate postwar exigencies in Europe and Africa served to engage the African environmental sector by seeking to exploit the continent's agricultural resources. The momentous drift toward independence in the 1950s and the early years of the new African states continued to be enmeshed in development initiatives that reflected a continued focus on rural agricultural landscapes as environments whose efficient management was believed to hold the key for the future of Africa. This engagement was also influenced by growing global concerns about the state of the planet amid the increased exploitation of natural resources to furnish human needs. Some have subsequently viewed the post-World War II period as laying the foundation for the current global concerns with environmental problems and the search for their solutions. Such thinking, which clearly echoed trends already heralded in the environmental narrative already associated with colonial Africa, depicts this period as critical in facilitating humanity's pervasive impact on the natural environment and calls for a global responsibility in confronting environmental problems.[36]

Consequently, and particularly after 1950 into the early years of independence, the drive to modernize African agricultural practices was factored into the overall development project as promoted by influential western nonstate actors such as the World Bank. Episodic or sustained environmental crises and the inability of the new African states to contain them or prevent the perceived human causes of ecological degradation were seen as impediments to sustainable long-term development efforts on the continent warranting external interventions. As a result, the need for external interventions in Africa were driven by what Arturo Escobar describes as western-conceived "objects," such as poverty, lack of technology and capital, high population growth, and outdated agricultural practices, which western discourses used to depict the "abnormalities" of the African peasant farmer.[37] Perhaps such thinking was given impetus by natural environmental crises that engulfed some parts of Africa a decade after independence, particularly the Sahelian droughts of the 1970s and 1980s and the related economic and social problems. Local attempts to confront the challenges occasioned by the Sahelian droughts and the economic and environmental conservation efforts that accompanied developmental efforts in some African states in the 1970s and 1980s attests to the default mode of the global system that demonstrated the limits of Africa's engagement with environmentally induced challenges.

THE SAHELIAN DROUGHTS AND THE ENVIRONMENTAL AND ECONOMIC CHALLENGES OF THE POSTCOLONIAL AFRICAN STATE

While the intermittent droughts and claims of desiccation in the 1930s did not lead to gloom as predicted by ecologists in those early decades, new fears were brought to bear following prolonged occurrences of drought and arid conditions in the Sahelian parts of Africa in the late 1960s and particularly the early 1970s. The resulting drought conditions were perceived to produce social and economic problems for communities inhabiting this ecological belt to the extent that the desertification debate was revisited in earnest and the problem elevated to an international crisis. There was continuity in the causation narrative as the Sahelian populations were criticized for their mismanagement of the land, overgrazing, and deforestation activities, reminiscent of similar views in the 1930s in West Africa.[38] In the most recent analysis, Michael Mortimore has underscored the importance of prolonged irregular precipitation over claims of resource abuse as causes of the Sahelian desertification and the resultant famines of the 1970s.[39]

Newly independent West African countries were urged to adopt a regional collaborative effort since the problem and the effects of desertification were seen to transcend national borders even as the causes were known to be local, embedded in the activities of the African herder and the sedentary farmer in fixed geographical locations of the Sahel. Beyond the call for regional efforts, the global dimensions of desertification also invited suggestions for a global strategy to confront it. Part of this strategy was driven by the globalization of the problem beyond Africa to include Asia and Latin America, as the United Nations took the initiative to host a conference on desertification in 1977 in Nairobi.[40] In doing so, and particularly in identifying solutions to the problem, desertification was cast along class/economic lines, projecting it as a real threat to the less developed countries of the world. The state of poverty in these regions, it was argued, amplified the incapacity of the local peoples and governments to deal with environmental crises, thereby requiring financial and technical resources from the richer western nations to combat the problem.[41] In this way, concerns over desertification in postcolonial Africa highlighted the persistent historical practices within the environmental domain that created social and cultural differences between the western (external) and African worlds, with the former seeking to privilege its power and knowledge over the latter. Such a trajectory is synonymous with what Escobar further describes as a "production of the Third World through articulation of knowledge and power" that has been the basis of the global discourse on development.[42]

Just like the 1970s, the 1980s were critical for Africa as far as its economic agenda was concerned, particularly with regard to the role of the environment in shaping the outcomes of that agenda from an international perspective. The economic crises of the 1970s and the budgetary deficits it created, itself aided by corrupt patron-client political regimes, led to an accumulation of debt that filtered into the 1980s.[43] African governments needing massive bailouts turned to the same international financial institutions whose funding of the stalled "green revolution" projects in the earlier decades had not only failed but had also contributed to the national debt of most African states. The prescription and the adoption of the World Bank's structural adjustment policies in the 1980s—which were aimed at eliminating financial, technical, and inefficient social policies of African governments—only expanded the international engagement with Africa's economic aspirations and, with it, the environmental sector. This was often achieved by perpetuating existing global relations in solving problems related to the "modernization" of development.

Thus, as far as Africa's environmental sector was concerned, the mainly market-driven structural adjustment policies of the 1980s failed to accrue sustainable benefits to the populations that dominated the marginal, less productive environments. In such ecological regions across the drier parts of western, eastern, and southern Africa, environmental degradation and especially soil erosion were evident, thereby compromising the productivity of those areas. For example, structural adjustment policies aimed at boosting export crops in Senegal and Ghana largely proved to be "extractive," hence contributing to degradation and the loss of soil fertility, inasmuch as they served to revitalize some aspects of economic planning, particularly in Ghana.[44] Such trends were symptomatic of the fact that the adjustment policies widened income gaps between populations within any given country, forcing poor segments of those populations to maximize their survival strategies by extracting land resources in ways that were seen to increase ecological degradation.[45]

The extreme end of the criticism of such "green" development as driven by structural policies has pointed to its failure to achieve balance between elimination of fiscal debts and eradication of poverty and attendant environmental problems.[46] More importantly, the imposing presence of the World

Bank and the International Monetary Fund through structural adjustment policies facilitated the integration of Africa into the global economy in a neocolonial fashion, since these international financial institutions as well as western governments determined Africa's economic policy.[47] Such policy has tended to emphasize concentration on the production of primary, often agricultural export commodities, which, as already noted, have been expected to thrive in depressed ecologies. Such scenarios have partly reinforced Africa's dependence on the international flow of capital, which has been directed at programs that should "normalize" environmental practices.

Apart from the economic and social dilemmas occasioned by the structural adjustment policies in the 1980s, the decade was also marked by a prolonged drought, whose debilitating effects were manifested in a famine that plagued parts of northeastern Africa, especially Ethiopia. Drought spells and food shortages were also experienced as far south as Mozambique and parts of the South African veldts. Mainstream western media fed the world with appeals, including images of human misery and environmental desolation wrought by months of failed rainfall. The Ethiopian famine provided an opportunity for some western scholars and international development stakeholders to reassess the "African problem," which was felt to amount to a "crisis."[48] The problem was cast within "western modernity," whereby progress in the western sense had stalled in Africa while the rest of the world proceeded along "most of the normally accepted indicators of progress." Benchmarks of "modern society" were perceived to be at a state of decay in Africa: breakdown of the transport infrastructure, with trucks unable to operate for lack of spare parts, as well as lack of electricity, chronic food shortages, and declining living standards, were indices used to describe problems that were exposed by the drought of the 1980s. It was further urged that the long-term solution lay in a reappraisal of development in Africa as promoted by western countries and other agencies.[49]

Such representations of Africa in the global environmental discussions further confirm that notions of nature/environment and poverty have been at the core of "modernity" as a western cultural project exported to other parts of the world.[50] It further resonates with the argument that the so-called Third World has been "produced" through an articulation of power and knowledge that defines the modern development discourse.[51] Generally, however, the perceived environmental crises of the 1980s and their impact on sub-Saharan countries revived the narrative of an expanding Sahara and gave credence to both national and international efforts to adopt specific intrusive measures. At the national level, countries like Mali reinforced former colonial environmental policing acts aimed at protecting existing forest and other vegetation cover, so much so that the already marginalized populations bore the economic costs of the ensuing conservation program through heavy fines for "destroying" forests for their fuel energy needs.[52]

Mali's experience is evidence of the ability of some postcolonial states to perpetuate interventionist environmental policies reminiscent of colonial times. Furthermore, it exposes the postcolonial states' response to local environmental crises with the urgency created by the international arena, so that Mali's preoccupation with its environmental conservation agenda in the 1980s was also motivated by the internationalization of the Sahelian crisis. By extension, the environmental programs of Moussa Traore's government had the intended objective of attracting international funding for Mali's "green projects."[53] Thus, some postindependent African states have, owing to challenges posed by environmental concerns, been facilitators of the movement across international borders of capitalist investments, thus reinforcing international intervention in local livelihoods via environmental programs. Jeremy Swift has emphasized this point as regards the desertification narrative, which was used by African governments to ask for antidesertification measures and was used to justify increased flows of international aid to Africa. Consequently the emergence of the environmental crisis narrative with regard to Africa has been the result of intersecting interests of local and international actors, mainly the colonial and postcolonial states, scientists/technical experts, and aid donors.[54] Yet it is still worth emphasizing that local actors, such as African states and the local populations, have often responded positively to powerful international currents in global environmental debates. This may continue to be the trend with the more imposing global politics on climate change and global warming.

AFRICA IN THE ERA OF POLITICS ON CLIMATE CHANGE

Probably more than any other environmental issues, the phenomenon of climate change (and the related aspect of global warming) has amplified the view that the natural environment is a shared heritage that calls for collaborative initiatives to address the causes and effects of environmental problems. The debate on climate change has served to expose continuities and changes in the way that the international community has engaged these issues while focusing on Africa. This is also true insofar as Africa has responded to those issues. Furthermore, as far as the continent is concerned, climate-related concerns are not new, as it has already been demonstrated in the preceding discussion that climatic patterns had an immense influence on colonial and postcolonial debates on desertification and drought in West Africa.[55] The persistence of the Sahelian drought, particularly in West Africa, has not only been termed "the most striking multidecadal regional climate shift documented in the 20th century" but has also been perceived to induce international climatic and ecological changes across the Atlantic into the Caribbean in the form of masses of dust that have loaded aerosols into the atmosphere on a scale that contributes to climatic vagaries associated with the latter region.[56] This attests to the importance of climate in shaping discourses that continue to govern Africa's engagement with the global community and how local/regional climatic shifts in Africa can also be conceptualized along global scales. But it is the vengeance with which the global community has visited climate change in modern times, and the increased positioning of Africa in this debate, that warrants attention. This is because of the immense political and economic implications of atmospheric change for Africa and for the relations it continues to generate between the continent and the international community.

The debate on climate change and its global impact has its origin in the West and has recently been at the core of the environmental movement, which has sought to globalize the atmospheric issues of the depletion of the ozone layer and the resultant global warming. The debate has been conceived and made to thrive on scientific and technical information produced by western institutions and that—according to Gareth Porter, Janet Welsh Brown, and Pamela S. Chasek—has provided a "new political force" for the environmental movement to hoist climate change on the agenda seeking to promote transnational cooperation to confront environmental problems. This globalization has involved linking the impact of climate change to the global extraction and use of natural resources and to related economic issues such as trends in world trade, all embedded in western interests.[57]

The fact that technical construction of the evidence on climate change is built on western foundations and institutions parallels similar trends in the making of the environmental narrative in colonial Africa. Furthermore, it is the view that African communities are among the most imperiled by an unchecked global warming due to the perception of exiting social and economic problems that also brings to memory predictions of doom to the continent that were voiced in the 1930s. That is, the current global environmental narrative on climate change, while founded in the West, has often looked to Africa for reasons to give it momentum and legitimacy. Such reasons, well grounded in popular media, national, and international reports, have presented Africa and its peoples as likely to be hit the hardest in the event that causes of global warming remain unchecked and solutions to this phenomenon neglected.

Consequently the term *vulnerability* has been pushed by international agencies to explain that Africa's existing social, economic, and political institutional frameworks are hardly prepared for extreme vagaries of climate change and are therefore incapable of dealing with them. Mainstream debates on the subject have focused on threats posed by climate change to resources that provide for African livelihoods, imply the urgency of the need to confront global warming. Aside from revisiting the Sahelian droughts of the 1980s, pointers have been directed to recent droughts as well as floods in eastern and southern and parts of West Africa to emphasize the potential dangers of climate change on the continent. As a direct case in point, there were the El Niño rains of 1997–1998 in eastern Africa, which raised concerns about the impact of changing climatic patterns on agricultural systems and food security in this particular region.[58]

Furthermore, the increased incidence of water insecurity for about 3 million Africans annually has been touted as a problem warranting attention at the top of the climate change agenda. The need to focus on Africa's water resources in the wake of claims of global warming is even more imperative given that agriculture, Africa's most pervasive economic undertaking for millions of rural households, depends on rainwater.[59] Thus the need to prioritize water in the global environmental debate has also brought to the fore issues such as food and shelter, which together form what has been referred to in external interventionist programs as the "Brown Agenda."[60] Consequently, more than the related sectors such as fisheries and forestry, it is the agricultural sector in Africa that has received the most attention owing to its vital economic role on the continent both for rural and urban African populations. This sector forms the core of the rural economy and accounts for 50 percent of the continent's exports, yet it is perceived to face the highest risk from changes induced by climate change. The 2010 projections have it that if effective interventions against the negative impact of global warming are not implemented, about 240 million Africans will be undernourished by the 2080s.[61]

Some empirical studies have revealed a likely decrease in dry-land farm income with increased global warming, thereby strengthening the need for irrigation as a meaningful strategy for coping with climate change across Africa.[62] Further concerns have been directed at the shrinking land resources that hold potential for agricultural production and other sustainable livelihoods in Africa, such as the drying of the Chadian Basin wetlands and of Lake Faguibine in northern Mali, as reasons to engage climate change-related developments on the continent.[63] A closer connection has also been drawn between global warming and massive displacement of African populations across international borders, thereby increasing the prospect of environmental refugees as well as the political marginalization of certain ethnic communities especially in the Sahel states.[64]

More critically, the focus on Africa's vulnerability to global warming has in turn invigorated the debate about the means for confronting climate change at the global level.[65] Mitigation, a process calling for a commitment to cut down on carbon dioxide emissions into the atmosphere, has multiplied terrains of contest within the international community on the one hand and between the industrial powers and African states on the other. The most industrialized nations, which account for the largest budgetary emission of gases, have continuously procrastinated over endorsing their commitment to reduce such emissions owing to the potential financial and other economic implications for their divestment in alternative technologies. Consequently, from Kyoto to Copenhagen and through the Cancún climate talks, evidence has emerged of the leading industrial powers' reluctance to bear the costs of managing the global environment for the "rest of the world."[66] African countries contribute less to industrial emissions and other consumption patterns considered to deplete the ozone layer and increase global warming; they consider it a moral obligation for the West and other industrialized nations to bear that burden. The continued vacillation of the West on this issue validates the argument that global environmental politics have been founded on the economic development of the West and are aimed at protecting those interests.[67] In the mid-1970s, Volkov asserted that when governments of industrial capitalist countries adopt the concept of interdependence at international conferences, they do so in only a bid so to protect their own political and economic interests at the expense of developing countries. This observation could as well apply to the current dilemmas facing climate change negotiations.[68]

As long as the debate about the management of "global resources" and especially climate change and global warming continues to be conceptualized within economic and technological terms by the industrialized and emerging rich nations, many countries in Africa—and their counterparts in Asia and Latin America—will struggle to level the terms of reaching an international consensus on the way forward. A history of global negotiations on climate change and global warming illustrates the prevalence of western and industrial capitalism in the management of the environment. In a way, what this means for Africa is that the much-needed financial and related aid to promote environment-based economies is bound to be pegged on meeting the capitalist interests of western nations and corporations seeking to invest in Africa's environmental and economic sectors. Climate-based environmental challenges in Africa therefore have the potential to redefine or reinforce conditions for channeling the flow of international aid and capital on to the continent. A closer analysis of the outcome of most of the international talks on climate—given the imposing role of what has been referred to as "climate capitalism"—continues to reveal a trend toward such a global imbalance.[69]

Although also fraught with politics, mainstream thinking within the international arena has often advocated for strengthening Africa's capacity to withstand the effects of climate change, hence the drive for adaptation—another of the approaches floated by international stakeholders in the environmental/development nexus.[70] Adaptation has served to increase the presence of foreign aid and donors engaging in social, economic, and environmental projects aimed at increasing Africa's capacity to deal with the effects of climate change; more importantly, however, it has exposed the power and economic imbalances that exist between Africa and the industrial West. This imbalance is reflected in the fact that the financial, policy formulation, and some technical aspects required for building adaptation strategies are themselves driven from outside of the continent. However, such a scenario has not been without opportunities for the continent to assert its position in the current global environmental politics and the solutions being sought to confront global warming.

Such opportunities have been manifested in several ways but mainly through efforts by international actors to integrate indigenous African practices and values in confronting potential problems linked to climate change, projecting emerging trends of global collective concerns for the dangers of climate change and possible solutions to these problems. Therefore, in the effort to balance, if not neutralize, the seemingly universal western technological and scientific solutions aimed at achieving adaptation to climate change, there is a shift to recognizing and integrating African traditional practices and values in those solutions. There is a growing realization that there exists the potential for such practices and values that have been used by specific African communities across the continent to adapt to vagaries in climate for thousands of years, offering a "natural laboratory" in current efforts to help such communities cope with climate change. These have ranged from fast-maturing crops, commercial group investments in crops and livestock, and social networks to the diversification in off-farm income-generating activities. Such activities have been identified by international researchers to possess the potential to check climate change-related challenges in rural areas of Sudan, South Africa, and Mozambique.[71] In the semidry ecology of Kitui in eastern Kenya, research has shown how households adapt to drought in the short term by harnessing indigenous plants for food and raw materials for informal entrepreneurial economic ventures such as handicrafts and finding fuel wood for the burning of construction bricks. There is a need, therefore, to strengthen the capacity for adaptation in this frequently drought-stricken area by targeting strategies to make them useful in the long term.[72]

In a more pragmatic way, international scientists and the Intergovernmental Authority on Development (IGAD), a six-nation organization in eastern and northeastern Africa, are collaborating in tapping into the indigenous African understanding of rainfall regimes by the Ngaanyi rainmaking clan of the Banyore community of western Kenya.[73] On the other hand, the Consultative Group on International Agricultural Research (CGIAR), in collaboration with rural farmers, has launched a program to revamp "orphaned" and also indigenous crops, such as millet, sorghum, cassava, and pigeon pea. Most of these are known both for their nutritional value and their resilience against drought-related agricultural regimes.[74] The latter case illustrates the continued presence and role of multilateral institutions in the production of environmental knowledge in developing regions such as Africa, even in instances where such efforts emphasize recourse to indigenous or "peoples" solutions to environmental challenges. The reason for this is the premium attached to the financial capacity required to rehabilitate such solutions into a "modern" environmental problem—that of global warming—which is still understood in a western sense. Such financial investments have remained a preserve of international financial institutions and the western economies that fund them. The funding of the CGIAR, for example, has networks with the industrial West and the

World Bank, making it possible for these agencies to retain an interest in the activities initiated by this organization anywhere on the African continent. In this way, some scholars have considered multilateral institutions as "handmaidens" of international capital in developing countries insofar as their involvement in environmental activities is concerned.[75] Whether this is a valid assessment or not, their presence and role in Africa attests to the extent to which Africa has been "captured" and is embedded in the globalization of environmental dilemmas and the search for their solutions.

While the pervasiveness of external, mainly scientific knowledge has been railed against for its shortcomings in solving environmentally related problems in Africa, there has been recognition of the shortcomings of local communities as well in providing solutions for all such problems. This interpretation calls for the need to have science to play a complementary role to local solutions in matters of environmental regulation.[76] The efforts to understand dynamics of global change through the application to traditional knowledge of rainfall patterns to modern scientific methods, as is the case with IGAD's initiatives in western Kenya, is illustrative of the emerging trends in this direction. Then there is the question of the collective bargaining of African states in the global politics on climate change and other "globally conceptualized" environmental issues. This is a critical issue given that issues of global significance are themselves driven by imposing currents of political power by either individual or single states. The inability by African and other developing states in Asia, Latin America, and the Caribbean to assert their will at international conferences on climate change has been attributed to problems ranging from handicapped negotiating power given their lack of political clout in global power relations, to the already mentioned structural imbalance in the generation and flow of environmental knowledge that is skewed in favor of the industrialized nations.[77]

However, the need to assert the African voices in modern global environmental politics, especially in international forums on climate change, is gradually becoming clearer, particularly among the continent's ruling elite. There is a nearly unanimous consensus in Africa's political leadership that the West should not expect Africa to contribute to bearing the costs of emission of the industrial gases causing global warming given the continent's negligible contributions to the global budgetary emissions of such gases into the atmosphere. Jean Ping, the president of the commission of the African Union (AU), represented a common African position at the Copenhagen climate change talks in a communication that requested "polluting countries" to finance the transfer and implementation of climate adaptation technology in Africa.[78] A rare but significant alternative to the existing international order in environmental power relations was emphasized by President Yoweri Museveni of Uganda, who termed the emission of gases by the West an act of "aggression" against Africa.[79] Yet Africa's collective bargaining at international climate talks has proved elusive, given the differential economic and developmental gaps between African countries.

South Africa, the most industrialized of them all, has tended to identify with the industrialized or emerging rich nations' stand as far as cutting back on emissions is concerned.[80]

Generally, Africa has consciously identified climate change and the attendant problem of global warming as real, given its current and future potential or tangible impact on the continent's economic and political well-being. Thus, the AU, through its Commission on Climate Change and Development in Africa, expressed "grave concern" about the vulnerability of Africa's socioeconomic and productive systems to climate change and called attention to the continent's low mitigation and response capacities. The AU subsequently gave support to a study titled "Climate Information for Development Needs: An Action Plan for Africa—Report and Implementation Strategy" and urged member states, the private sector, the public, and development stakeholders to mobilize for action in climate change initiatives at the national and regional levels.[81] More critical is the way in which Africa's leadership has acknowledged and endorsed the various international frameworks designed to address climate change, such as the 1992 United Nations Framework Convention on Climate and the Kyoto Protocol, upon which successive international talks continue to be based.[82] Subsequently, the AU as well as the respective member states have adapted to the global trends of building continental and regional institutional frameworks to address the twin issues of climate change and global warming. The global connections of these initiatives have been reiterated by a commitment by the African leadership to "improve climate risk management" by engaging the help of international multilateral and bilateral development organizations.[83] This attests to the unintended acquiescence of Africa to the globalization of development occasioned by the current environmental challenges and attendant world politics.

Most critical for the continent are the economic opportunities offered by the challenges of climate change. There is increasing recognition by Africa's leaders, at least at the continental level, for opportunities to pursue sustainable development programs that embrace green/low-carbon growth. Thus the greening of the African economy is an opportunity to start new businesses, develop new markets, and lower energy costs while also contributing to job growth.[84] Yet if low economic growth rates are not arrested, the lack of a financial base to invest in these opportunities makes it imperative for African states to depend on flows of international financial aid that could perpetuate external terms in local environmental initiatives that continue to operate in a global framework, as has been the case over the years.

CONCLUSION

At the onset of the twenty-first century, Africa found itself faced with long-drawn-out challenges of attaining sustainable forms of economic and political development. Yet with positive gains already being made in the political liberalization that started in early 1990s, such gains have not been matched by any durable economic and environmental programs. These developments have occurred against a deep historical background that has largely been defined by the continent's relationship with the international community, aided by local African states, based on the politics of access, use, and management of Africa's natural environment. While it remains the foundation on which positive economic and social gains can be made, Africa's environmental resource base has, on the other hand, attracted international stakeholders in the form of international powers and multinational organizations that have largely determined the way forward in the continent's quest for meaningful development. The internationalization of the global economy and the integration of Africa into that economy have meant that Africa's environmental resources, which are perceived to be crucial in sustaining the international system, have also been internationalized. The emergence of climate change and global warming as major issues have reinforced the central place of Africa in global debates. These issues have involved not only the question of how to overcome this atmospheric challenge but also the potential impact of these atmospheric processes on economic development and the management of related environmental issues relating to African livelihoods. Generally, however, the globalization of environmental crises and the solutions mooted to overcome them has presented not only challenges but also opportunities for African states and the local populations to assert themselves. Consequently efforts to recover and use local environmental knowledge systems, strengthening African environmental institutional capacity, as well as trends toward adopting collective environmental agendas by African states at international environmental meetings are manifestations of counteractions against the highly challenging aspects of globalization of resource management

NOTES

1. For a concise exposition on these developments as related to environmental changes in the twentieth century, see J. R. McNeill, "Social, Economic, and Political Forces in Environmental Change: Decadal Scale (1900 to 2000)," in Robert Costanza, Lisa J. Graumlich, and Will Stephen, eds., *Sustainability or Collapse?An Integrated History and Future of People on Earth* (Cambridge, MA: Massachusetts Institute of Technology, 2007), 301–328. For a more detailed version, see J. R. McNeill, *Something New Under the Sun: An Environmental History of the Twentieth Century World* (New York: Norton, 2000).
2. James McCann, *Greenland, Brownland, Blackland: An Environmental History of Africa, 1800–1900* (Oxford: James Currey, 1999), 11.
3. This is the emphasis in such classic works as Walter Rodney, *How Europe Underdeveloped Africa* (Washington, DC: Howard University Press, 1982); Andre Gunder Frank, *Dependent Accumulation* (New York: Monthly

Review Press, 1979); Immanuel Wallerstein, *World-Systems Analysis: An Introduction* (Durham, NC: Duke University Press, 2004).
4. For an exposition on a "world systems" theory, see Wallerstein, *World-Systems Analysis: An Introduction* (Durham, NC: Duke University Press, 2004).
5. James Gustave Speth, "Globalization and the Environment," in James Gustave Speth, ed., *Worlds Apart: Globalization and the Environment* (London: Island Press, 2003), 1–18. "Sustainable Development" as implied in such global views of the environment, refers to a development that fulfils present needs without impinging on the ability of the future generations to meet their own needs and follow a definition bequeathed by the World Commission and Environment in *Our Common Future* (Oxford, UK: Oxford University Press, 1987), 8.
6. See, for example, Maurice Strong, "Global Sustainable Development," in Steven Vertovec and Darrel Posey, eds,. *Globalization, Globalism, Environments, and Environmentalism* (Oxford, UK: Oxford University Press, 2002), 103; William G. Moseley and B. Ikubolajeh Logan, eds., *African Environment and Development: Rhetoric, Programs, Realities* (Burlington, VT: Ashgate, 2004).
7. For example, Lester Brown, *Interdependence of Nations*, Foreign Policy Association Headline Series No. 212 (New York: Foreign Policy Association, October 1972).
8. Such an approach is illustrated by works in Vigdis Broch-Due and Richard A. Schroeder, eds., *Producing Nature and Poverty in Africa* (Stockholm: Elanders Gotab, 2000).
9. Ibid., 13.
10. E. P. Stebbing, "The Encroaching Sahara: The Threat to the West African Colonies," *The Geographical Journal*, Vol. 85, No. 6 (June, 1935):507. See also Jeremy Swift, "Desertification: Narratives, Winners, and Losers," in Melissa Leach and Robbin Mearns, eds., *The Lie of the Land: Challenging Received Wisdom on the African Environment* (London: James Currey, 1996), 73–77.
11. Stebbing, "The Encroaching Sahara," 409, 509.
12. Brynmor Jones, "Desiccation and the West African Colonies," *The Geographical Journal*, Vol. 91, No. 5 (May, 1938):401.
13. Ibid., 406–416. Brynmor further acknowledged the inadequate archaeological evidence of climatic changes in the area, as well as lack of reliable meteorological data.
14. Ibid., 518; Stebbing, "The Encroaching Sahara," 401.
15. Brynmor, "Desiccation," 412.
16. On brief comments concerning this intervention in colonial West Africa, see James L. A. Webb Jr., "Ecology and Culture in West Africa," in Emmanuel Kwaku Akyeampong, ed., *Themes in West Africa's History* (Oxford, UK: James Currey, 2006), 46–49. For an example of the failure of wetland agricultural enterprise by the French colonial government in the Niger flood plain, see Monica van Beusekom, *Negotiating Development: African Farmers and Colonial Experts at the Office du Niger, 1920–1960* (Portsmouth, NH: Heinemann, 2002).
17. Frederick Cooper, "Africa in the World Economy," in Frederick Cooper, Allen Isaacman, Florencia E. Mallon, William Roseberry, and Steve J. Stern, eds., *Confronting Historical Paradigms: Peasants, Labor, and the Capitalist World System in Africa and Latin America* (Madison, WI: The University of Wisconsin Press, 1993), 109–115; For other details, see also John K. Thornton, *Africa and Africans in the Making of the Atlantic World, 1400–1680*

(Cambridge, UK: Cambridge University Press, 1998); and Robin Law, *The Slave Coast of West Africa, 1550–1750: The Impact of the Atlantic Slave Trade on African Society* (Oxford, UK: Clarendon Press, 1991).
18. Studies on the engagement by colonial states of soil erosion and conservation initiatives in eastern Africa at the onset of the 1930s are numerous. However, for a groundbreaking work that ties the problem to international solutions, see David Anderson, "Depression, Dust Bowl, Demography, and Drought: The Colonial State and Soil Conservation in East Africa during the 1930s," *African Affairs*, Vol. 83, No. 332 (July, 1984):321–343. See also Grace Carswell, *Cultivating Success in Uganda: Kigezi Farmers and Colonial Policies* (Nairobi: The British Institute of Eastern Africa, 2007).
19. Ibid., 332.
20. William Beinart, "Soil Erosion, Conservationism and Ideas about Development: A Southern African Exploration, 1900–1960," *Journal of Southern African Studies*, Vol. 11, No. 1 (Oct., 1984):54–56.
21. Ibid., 55.
22. A classic account on the Dust Bowl phenomenon in the United States remains that by Donald Worster, *Dust Bowl: The Southern Plains in the 1930s* (Oxford, UK: Oxford University Press, 1979).
23. On the imposition of western modes of conservation in addressing ecological problems in eastern and southern Africa between 1930 and 1950, see Anderson, "Depression:" David Anderson, *Eroding the Commons: The Politics of Ecology in Baringo 1890–1963* (London/Nairobi/Athens, OH: James Currey, 2002); William Beinart, "Soil Erosion"; and Kate Showers, *Imperial Gullies: Soil Erosion and Conservation in Lesotho* (Athens: Ohio University Press, 2005).
24. Beinart, "Soil Erosion," 59–60.
25. Anderson, "Depression," 332.
26. D. A. Low and John Lonsdale, "Introduction: Towards the New Order 1945–1963," in D. A. Low and A. Smith, eds., *History of East Africa*, Vol. 3 (Oxford, UK: Oxford University Press, 1976), 12–16.
27. For a direct relationship between metropolitan interests and intrusive presence of the colonial state in eastern Africa, see Michael Cowen, "The British State and Agrarian Accumulation in Kenya," in Martin Fransman, ed., *Industry and Accumulation in Africa* (London: Heinemann, 1982).
28. Frederick Cooper, *Africa since 1940: The Past of the Present* (New York: Cambridge University Press, 2002), 31.
29. Hellen Tilley, "African Environments and Environmental Sciences: The African Research Survey, Ecological Paradigms & British Colonial Development 1920–1940," in William Beinart and Joann McGregor, eds., *Social History and African Environments* (London: James Currey, 2003), 115–117.
30. Ibid., 116–117.
31. Paul Richards, *Indigenous Agricultural Revolution: Ecology and Food Reproduction in West Africa* (London: Hutchison, 1985); and Tilley, "African Environments," 117–118.
32. This wholesome argument is aptly made by James Fairhead and Melissa Leach, *Misreading the African Landscape* (Cambridge, UK: Cambridge University Press, 1996).
33. For the resistance in Uluguru, see Pamela A. Maack, "'We Don't Want Terraces!' Protest and Identity under the Uluguru Land Usage Scheme," in Gregory Maddox, James G. Giblin, and Isaria N. Kimambo, eds., *Custodians of the Land: Ecology and Culture in the History of Tanzania* (Athens: Ohio University Press, 1996), 152–174. For details on the women's resistance in Shambaa, see Steven Feierman, *Peasant Intellectuals: Anthropology and*

History in Tanzania (Madison, WI: University of Wisconsin Press, 1990), 181–203.
34. Fiona D. Mackenzie, *Land, Ecology, and Resistance in Kenya, 1880–1962* (Portsmouth, NH: Heinemann, 1998), 202. As for the other dynamics of the Murang'a peasant uprising, particularly as regards colonial authority and environment-related problems, see David Throup, *Economic and Social Origins of Mau Mau* (Ohio University Press: Athens, 1988), 139–170.
35. Tabitha Kanogo, *Squatters and the Roots of Mau Mau* (London: James Currey, 1987), 96–120; and Throup, *Economic and Social Origins*, 120–138.
36. James Gustave Speth, ed., *Worlds Apart: Globalization and the Environment* (London: Island Press, 2003), 3.
37. Arturo Escobar, *Encountering Development: The Making and Unmaking of the Third World* (Princeton, NJ: Princeton University Press, 1995), 41.
38. Michael H. Glantz, "The UN and Desertification: Dealing with a Global Problem," in Michael H. Glantz, ed., *Environmental Degradation in and Around Arid Lands* (Boulder, CO: West View Press, 1977), 4, 5.
39. Michael Mortimore, *Adapting to Drought: Farmers, Famines, and Desertification in West Africa* (Cambridge, UK: Cambridge University Press, 1989), 186.
40. Lloyd Timberlake, *Africa in Crisis: The Causes, the Cures of Environmental Bankruptcy* (Washington, DC: Earthscan, 1986), 59.
41. Ibid., 5–6.
42. Escobar, *Encountering Development*, 12.
43. Cooper, *Africa Since 1940*, 115.
44. Raymond L. Bryant and Sinead Bailey, *Third World Political Ecology* (London: Routledge, 1997), 92.
45. Calistous Juma and Richard Ford in consultation with Wanjiku Mwagiru, "Facing Africa's Ecological Crisis," in Ann Seidman and Frederick Anang, eds., *Towards a New Vision of Self Sustainable Development* (Trenton, NJ: Africa World Press, 1992), 188.
46. Bryant and Bailey, *Third World*, 92; and Bruce Rich, *Mortgaging the Earth: The World Bank, Environmental Impoverishment, and the Crisis of Development* (London: Earthscan, 1994), 186.
47. Thomas M. Callaghy, "Africa and the World Political Economy: Still Caught between a Rock and a Hard Place," in John W. Harbeson and Donald Rothchild, eds., *Africa in World Politics: Reforming Political Order* (Boulder, CO: West View Press, 2009), 42–43.
48. A detailed analysis of the 1980s Sahelian drought in northeastern Africa remains that by Timberlake, *Africa in Crisis*.
49. Ibid., 7.
50. Vigdis Broch-Due, "Producing Nature and Poverty in Africa: An Introduction," in Broch-Due and Schroeder, *Producing Nature*, 31.
51. Escobar, *Encountering Development*, 12.
52. Tor A. Benjaminsen, "Conservation in the Sahel: Policies and People in Mali, 1900–1998," in Broch-Due and Shroeder, *Producing Nature*, 94–108.
53. Ibid., 97.
54. The point is aptly analyzed by J. Swift in "Desertification," 88–90.
55. For more a more recent study on the technical and scientific data on Africa's climate change since 1900 within the context of current concerns about global warming, see Mike Hume, Ruth Doherty, Todd Ngara, Mark New, and David Lister, "Africa Climate Change: 1900–2100," *Climate Research*, Vol. 17 (2001):145–168; and Mike Hulme, Ruth Doherty, Todd Ngara, and Mark New, "Global Warming and Africa Climate Change: A Reassessment," in Pak Sum Low, ed., *Climate Change and Africa* (Cambridge, UK: Cambridge University Press, 2005): 29–49.

56. N. J. Mantua, "Decadal Chronology of the 20th-Century Changes," in Graumlich and Stephen, eds., *Sustainability or Collapse?*, 290.
57. Gareth Porter, Janet Welsh Brown, and Pamela S. Chasek, *Global Environmental Politics*, 3rd ed. (Boulder, CO: West View Press, 2000), 1.
58. Howard D. Leathers and Phillips Forster, *The World Food Problem: Tackling the Causes of Undernourishment in the Third World* (Boulder, CO: Lynne Rienner, 2004), 204.
59. Servaas van den Bosch, "Bring Water into Climate Change Negotiations," http://ipsnews.net/news.asp?idnews=52421/
60. See a detailed treatment of the "Brown Agenda" in Rodney R. White, "Environmental Priorities for Africa: Linkages between Climate Change and Basic Human Needs," *Canadian Journal of African Studies*, Vol. 31, No. 2 (1997): 301–314.
61. Economic Commission for Africa, *Economic Report on Africa* (2010), 104.
62. *The World Bank Economic Review*, Vol. 20, No. 3 (2006):367–388.
63. *The Los Angeles Times*, June 11, 2008; Diana Gregor, "Africa: Mass Migration as a Result of Environmental Changes," *Media Global*, New York, August 6, 2010.
64. Gregor, "Africa." As concerns the global connection between climate change and human displacement, see Frank Biermann and Ingrid Boas, "Preparing for a Warmer World: Towards a Global Governance System to Protect Climate Refugees," in *Global Environmental Politics*, Vol. 10, No. 1 (Feb. 2010):60–88; a study linking climate change to political marginalization is that by Clionadh Raleigh, "Political Marginalization, Climate Change, and Conflict in African Sahel States," in *International Studies Review*, Vol. 12. (2010):69–86. Raleigh maintains that small, politically insignificant ethnic groups in African Sahelian states would encounter the most conflicts occasioned by environmental pressures.
65. For more on Africa's vulnerability to climate change, see M. Boko et al., "Africa Climate Change 2007: Impacts, Adaptation, and Vulnerability" in M. L. Parry et al., eds., *Contribution of Working Group II to the Fourth Assessment Report of the Intergovernmental Panel on Climate Change* (Cambridge, UK: Cambridge University Press, 2007), 433–467, and *Economic Report on Africa* (The Economic Commission for Africa, 2010), 103–111.
66. Subsequently, there has been fallout in the media in Africa as far as this western stand is concerned and what it portends for Africa. See, for example, Saliem Fakir, "South Africa: Was Copenhagen the Death of Multilateral Environmental Agreements," *The South African Civil Society Information*, http://allafrica.com/stories/201001130800.html; Laurie Pichegru and Tema Gyuse, "Africa: Cooking Up a Climate Deal," *Inter Press Service*, http://allafrica.com/stories/201008080001.html; and Michelle Pressend, "Africa: From Cancun to Durban—Climate Change Negotiations Cop 'Out'," *The South African Civil Society Information*, http://allafrica.com/stories/201012140636.html
67. Porter, Brown, and Chasek, *Global Environmental Politics*, 2–3.
68. As emphasized in Glantz, "The UN and Desertification," 11.
69. See, for example, Patrick Bond, "Africa: 'Climate Capitalism' Won At Cancun—Everyone Else Loses," http://allafrica.com/stories/201012170825.html
70. Adaptation involves broader interventionist prescriptions aimed at helping human societies to adjust so as to survive or thrive in the midst of destabilizations occasioned by climate change. It is hoped that adaptation can reduce vulnerability and increase resilience. Oli Brown, Anne Hammill, and Robert Macleman, "Climate Change as the 'New' Security Threat: Implications for Africa," *International Affairs*, Vol. 83, No. 6 (2007):1149.

71. Jim Giles,"How to Survive a Warming World," *Nature*, Vol. 446 (April 12, 2007):716–717.
72. Siri Eriksen, "The Role of Indigenous Plans in Household Adaptation to Climate Change: The Kenya Experience," in Low, *Climate Change in Africa*, 248–259.
73. "IGAD Leaders to Tackle Food Crisis," *Daily Nation*, July 1, 2008, http://www.nation.co.ke/News/-/1056/237198/-/sfbkme/-/index.html.
74. http://www.cgiar.org/monthlystory/july_15_2010.html
75. Bryant and Bailey, *Third World*, 83, 100–102.
76. William Beinart, "African History and Environmental History," *African Affairs*, Vol. 99 (2000):294–295.
77. Joyeeta Gupta, *The Climate Change Convention and Developing Countries: From Conflict to Consensus?* (London: Kluwer Academic Publishers, 1997), viii, ix.
78. http://climate-l.iisd.org/news/african-union-announces-position-on-climate-change See also The African Union, Division of Communication and Information, *Communication no. 175/2009*, September 18, 2009.
79. Alexis Akeowo, "Is Global Warming Drowning Africa?" *Time*, September 21, 2007.
80. See "Africa: Cooking Up a Climate Deal," *The Inter Press News Service Agency*, http://ipsnews.net/africa/nota.asp?idnews=52423
81. Economic Commission for Africa, *Africa Climate Advisory Bulletin*, Addis Ababa, January 29–30, 2007.
82. Ibid.
83. Ibid.
84. United Nations Economic Commission for Africa. *The Economic Report on Africa* (2010), 109.

REFERENCES

African Union, Division of Communication and Information. Communication no. 175/2009. September 18, 2009: http://climate-l.iisd.org/news/african-union-announces-position-on-climate-change

Akeowo, Alexis. "Is Global Warming Drowning Africa?" *Time*, September 21, 2007, http://www.time.com/time/world/article/0,8599,1664429,00.html.

Anderson, David. *Eroding the Commons: The Politics of Ecology in Baringo 1890–1963*. Athens, OH: James Currey, 2002.

———. "Depression, Dust Bowl, Demography, and Drought: The Colonial State and Soil Conservation in East Africa during the 1930s." *African Affairs*, Vol. 83, No. 332 (July 1984): 321–343.

Beinart, William. "African History and Environmental History." *African Affairs*, Vol. 99 (2000): 269–302.

———. "Soil Erosion, Conservationism and Ideas about Development: A Southern African Exploration, 1900–1960." *Journal of Southern African Studies*, Vol. 11, No. 1 (October 1984): 52–83.

Benjaminsen, Tor A. "Conservation in the Sahel: Policies and People in Mali, 1900–1998." In Vigdis Broch-Due and Richard A. Schroeder, eds. *Producing Nature and Poverty in Africa*. Stockholm: Elanders Gotab, 2000.

Biermann, Frank, and Ingrid Boas. "Preparing for a Warmer World: Towards a Global Governance System to Protect Climate Refugees." *Global Environmental Politics*, Vol. 10, No. 1 (February 2010): 60–88.

Boko, M., et al. "Africa Climate Change 2007: Impacts, Adaptation, and Vulnerability" in M. L. Parry et al., eds. *Contribution of Working Group II to the*

Fourth Assessment Report of the Intergovernmental Panel on Climate Change. Cambridge, UK: Cambridge University Press, 2007.

Bond, Patrick. "Africa: 'Climate Capitalism' Won At Cancun—Everyone Else Loses": http://allafrica.com/stories/201012170825.html

Broch-Due, Vigdis, and Richard A. Schroeder. *Producing Nature and Poverty in Africa.* Stockholm: Elanders Gotab, 2000.

Brown, Lester. *Interdependence of Nations.* New York: Foreign Policy Association Headline Series no. 212, October 1972.

Brown, Oli, Anne Hammill, and Robert Macleman. "Climate Change as the 'New' Security Threat: Implications for Africa." *International Affairs,* Vol. 83, No. 6 (2007): 1141–1154.

Bryant, Raymond L., and Sinead Bailey. *Third World Political Ecology.* London: Routledge, 1997.

Callaghy, Thomas M. "Africa and the World Political Economy: Still Caught between a Rock and a Hard Place." In John W. Harbeson and Donald Rothchild, eds. *Africa in World Politics: Reforming Political Order.* Boulder, CO: West View Press, 2009.

Carswell, Grace. *Cultivating Success in Uganda: Kigezi Farmers and Colonial Policies.* Nairobi: The British Institute of Eastern Africa, 2007.

CGIAR Monthly Report. July 15, 2010: http://www.cgiar.org/monthlystory/july_15_2010.html

Cooper, Frederick. *Africa since 1940: The Past of the Present.* New York: Cambridge University Press, 2002.

———. "Africa in the World Economy." In Frederick Cooper, Allen Isaacman, Florencia E. Mallon, William Roseberry, and Steve J. Stern, eds. *Confronting Historical Paradigms: Peasants, Labor, and the Capitalist World System in Africa and Latin America.* Madison, WI: University of Wisconsin Press, 1993.

Cowen, Michael."The British State and Agrarian Accumulation in Kenya." In Martin Fransman, ed. *Industry and Accumulation in Africa.* London: Heinemann, 1982.

Economic Commission for Africa, *Economic Report on Africa,* 2010.

Economic Commission for Africa. *Africa Climate Advisory Bulletin.* Addis Ababa, January 29–30, 2007.

Escobar, Arturo. *Encountering Development: The Making and Unmaking of the Third World.* Princeton, NJ: Princeton University Press, 1995.

Fairhead, James, and Leach, Melissa. *Misreading the African Landscape.* Cambridge, UK: Cambridge University Press, 1996.

Fakir, Saliem."South Africa: Was Copenhagen the Death of Multilateral Environmental Agreements." *The South African Civil Society Information,* January 12, 2010: http://www.sacsis.org.za/site/article/408.1

Feierman, Stephen. *Peasant Intellectuals: Anthropology and History in Tanzania.* Madison: University of Wisconsin Press, 1990.

Giles, Jim. "How to Survive a Warming World," *Nature,* Vol. 446 (April 12, 2007): http://www.nature.com/nature/journal/v446/n7137/pdf/446716a.pdf

Glantz, Michael H. "The U.N. and Desertification: Dealing with a Global Problem." In Michael H. Glantz, ed. *Environmental Degradation in and around Arid Lands.* Boulder, CO: West View Press, 1977.

Gregor, Diana. "Africa: Mass Migration as a Result of Environmental Changes." *Media Global,* August 6, 2010, http://allafrica.com/stories/201008090190.html.

Gunder, Andre Frank. *Dependent Accumulation.* New York: Monthly Review Press, 1979.

Gupta, Joyeeta. *The Climate Change Convention and Developing Countries: From Conflict to Consensus?* London: Kluwer Academic Publishers, 1997.

Gustave, James Speth. "Globalization and the Environment." In James Gustave Speth, ed. *Worlds Apart: Globalization and the Environment*. London: Island Press, 2003.
Hulme, Mike, Ruth Doherty, Todd Ngara, and Mark New. "Global Warming and African Climate Change: A Reassessment." In Pak Sum Low, ed. *Climate Change and Africa*. Cambridge, UK: Cambridge University Press, 2005.
Hulme, Mike, Ruth Doherty, Todd Ngara, Mark New, and David Lister. "Africa Climate Change: 1900–2100." *Climate Research*, Vol. 17 (2001): 145–168.
"IGAD Leaders to Tackle Food Crisis." *Daily Nation*. July 1, 2008. http://www.nation.co.ke/News/-/1056/237198/-/sfbkme/-/index.html
Jones, Brynmor. "Desiccation and the West African Colonies." *The Geographical Journal*, Vol. 91, No. 5 (May 1938): 401–423.
Juma, Calistous, and Richard Ford in consultation with Manjiku Mwagiru. "Facing Africa's Ecological Crisis." In Ann Seidman and Frederick Anang, eds. *Towards a New Vision of Self Sustainable Development*. Trenton NJ: Africa World Press, 1992.
Kanogo, Tabitha, *Squatters and the Roots of Mau Mau*, London: James Currey, 1987.
Law, Robin. *The Slave Coast of West Africa, 1550–1750: The Impact of the Atlantic Slave Trade on African Society*. Oxford, UK: Clarendon Press, 1991.
Leathers, Howard D., and Phillip Forster. *The World Food Problem: Tackling the Causes of Undernourishment in the Third World*. Boulder, CO: Lynne Rienner, 2004.
Low, D. A., and John M. Lonsdale. "Introduction: Towards the New Order 1945–1963." In D. A. Low and A. Smith, eds. *History of East Africa*, Vol. 3. . Oxford, UK: Oxford University Press, 1976.
Maack, Pamela A. "'We Don't Want Terraces!': Protest and Identity Under the Uluguru Land Usage Scheme." In Gregory Maddox, James G. Giblin, and Isaria N. Kimambo, eds. *Custodians of the Land: Ecology and Culture in the History of Tanzania*. Athens, OH: Ohio University Press 1996.
Mackenzie, Fiona D. *Land, Ecology, and Resistance in Kenya, 1880–1962*. Portsmouth, NH: Heinemann, 1998.
McCann, James Greenland. *Brownland, Blackland: An Environmental History of Africa, 1800–1900*. Oxford, UK: James Currey, 1999.
McNeill, J. R. "Social, Economic, and Political Forces in Environmental Change: Decadal Scale (1900 to 2000)." In Robert Costanza, Lisa J. Graumlich, and Will Stephen, eds. *Sustainability or Collapse? An Integrated History and Future of People on Earth*. Cambridge, MA: Massachusetts Institute of Technology, 2007.
McNeill, J. R. *Something New Under the Sun: An Environmental History of the Twentieth Century World*. New York: Norton, 2000.
Moseley, William G., and Ikubolajeh B. Logan, eds. *African Environment and Development: Rhetoric, Programs, Realities*. Burlington, VT: Ashgate, 2004.
Pichegru, Laurie, and Tema Gyuse. "Africa: Cooking Up a Climate Deal." *Inter Press Service*, August 8, 2010: http://allafrica.com/stories/201008080001.html
Porter, Gareth, Janet Welsh Brown, and Pamela S. Chasek. *Global Environmental Politics*, 3rd ed. Boulder, CO: West View Press, 2000.
Pressend, Michelle. "Africa: From Cancun to Durban—Climate Change Negotiations Cop 'Out'." *The South African Civil Society Information*, December 13, 2010: http://allafrica.com/stories/201012140636.html
Raleigh, Clionadh. "Political Marginalization, Climate Change, and Conflict in African Sahel States." *International Studies Review*, Vol. 12 (2010): 69–86.
Rich, Bruce. *Mortgaging the Earth: The World Bank, Environmental Impoverishment, and the Crisis of Development*. London: Earthscan, 1994.

Richards, Paul. *Indigenous Agricultural Revolution—Ecology and Food Reproduction in West Africa*. London: Hutchison, 1985.

Rodney, Walter. *How Europe Underdeveloped Africa*. Washington, DC: Howard University Press, 1982.

Showers, Kate. *Imperial Gullies: Soil Erosion and Conservation in Lesotho*. Athens: Ohio University Press, 2005.

Siri Eriksen, "The Role of Indigenous Plans in Household Adaptation to Climate Change: The Kenya Experience." In Pak Sum Low, ed. *Climate Change and Africa*. Cambridge, UK: Cambridge University Press, 2005.

Stebbing, E. P. "The Encroaching Sahara: The Threat to the West African Colonies." *The Geographical Journal*, Vol. 85, No. 6 (June, 1935): 506–519.

Strong, Maurice. "Global Sustainable Development." In Steven Vertovec and Darrel Posey, eds. *Globalization, Globalism, Environments, and Environmentalism*. Oxford, UK: Oxford University Press, 2002.

Swift, J. "Desertification: Narratives, Winners, and Losers." In Melissa Leach and Robbin Mearns, eds. *The Lie of the Land: Challenging Received Wisdom on the African Environment*. London: James Currey, 1996.

Thornton, John K. *Africa and Africans in the Making of the Atlantic World, 1400–1680*. Cambridge, UK: Cambridge University Press, 1998.

Throup, David. *Economic and Social Origins of Mau Mau*. Athens: Ohio University Press, 1988.

Tilley, Helen. "African Environments and Environmental Sciences: The African Research Survey, Ecological Paradigms & British Colonial Development 1920–1940." In William Beinart and Joann McGregor, eds. *Social History and African Environments*. London: James Currey, 2003.

Timberlake, Lloyd. *Africa in Crisis: The Causes, the Cures of Environmental Bankruptcy*. Washington, DC: Earthscan, 1986.

van Beusekom, Monica. *Negotiating Development: African Farmers and Colonial Experts at the Office du Niger, 1920–1960*. Portsmouth, NH: Heinemann, 2002.

van den Bosch, Servaas. "Bring Water into Climate Change Negotiations." August 8, 2010: http://ipsnews.net/news.asp?idnews=52421/

Wallerstein, Immanuel. *World-Systems Analysis: An Introduction*. Durham, NC: Duke University Press, 2004.

Webb, James L. A. Jr. "Ecology and Culture in West Africa." In Emmanuel Kwaku Akyeampong, ed. *Themes in West Africa's History*. Oxford, UK: James Currey, 2006.

White, Rodney R. "Environmental Priorities for Africa: Linkages between Climate Change and Basic Human Needs." *Canadian Journal of African Studies*, Vol. 31, No. 2 (1997): 301–314.

World Bank Economic Review Vol. 20, No. 3 (2006): 367–388.

The World Commission on Environment and Development. *Our Common Future*. Oxford, UK: Oxford University Press, 1987.

Worster, Donald. *Dust Bowl: The Southern Plains in the 1930s*. Oxford, UK: Oxford University Press, 1979.

2 Indigenization versus Domiciliation
A Historical Approach to National Content in Nigeria's Oil and Gas Industry

Jesse Salah Ovadia*

Nigeria is often cited as the prime example of the phenomenon many academics and social commentators have labeled "the resource curse."[1] With its vast crude oil resources, Nigeria has generated hundreds of billions of dollars of revenue yet has very little to show beyond a legacy of underdevelopment and conflict. In Nigeria, the political elites have engaged in massive appropriation of the country's oil revenues and amassed untold wealth. The "achievements" of Nigerian oil development include 85 percent of oil revenues accruing to 1 percent of the population. In fact, Michael Watts has estimated that of US$400 billion in revenues, as much as US$100 billion has "simply gone 'missing' since 1970" (2006: 11–12).

By contrast, oil is often associated in the popular mindset with the notion of striking it rich; hence the moniker *black gold*. Crude oil has been the world's most important commodity for most of the last century, and Nigeria's proven reserves dwarf those of the rest of the continent. In the last two decades, Nigeria's reserves have soared with the discovery of large reservoirs of oil off Nigeria's coast in water beyond 1,000 meters of depth. Similarly, around the Gulf of Guinea, Nigeria's neighbors from Sierra Leone to Angola are "striking it rich" with their own deepwater oil finds. These finds are being driven by updated geological knowledge of deepwater hydrocarbon basins, the development of new extraction technologies, and political and economic realities that make deepwater drilling economically feasible.

Cyril Obi (2010) calls the resource curse "smoke and mirrors," arguing that as "an ideological notion of oil resource-determinism," the concept obscures more accurate understandings of the role of oil in political-economic issues. Nigerian academic Pat Utomi, who was a presidential candidate in 2007 and 2011, points out that

> The whole curse of [the] oil phenomenon is not a factor driven by "if there is oil there is going to be a resource curse problem." It is driven by lack of elite commitment to a long-term strategy. . . . If there was a leadership elite clever enough to move in that direction, I don't see why oil would have to be a curse. It would be a driver for development.[2]

In other words, different economic policy decisions would result in different outcomes within the structural limits of the (admittedly rapidly changing) socioeconomic reality.

Nigeria's latest effort to cultivate social and economic development through its fossil fuel wealth is now moving at an accelerated pace owing to the recent passage of the Nigerian Oil and Gas Industry Content Development Act of 2010 (henceforth referred to as the Nigerian Content Act, or NCA). In order to understand this groundbreaking law and its potential in a moment of changed geopolitical realities for oil producers in Africa's Gulf of Guinea, it is necessary to review the history of Nigeria's efforts to exert national control over the industry and increase the benefit derived from its oil wealth. Such a project allows new entrants into the business of crude oil production to learn from Nigeria's history of failed policies and failed development and serves as a poignant reminder of how easily seemingly well-intentioned policies can go astray.

Shell BP (formerly Shell D'Arcy) made its first strike in 1956 in Oloibiri, 65 miles west of Port Harcourt. In 1958, the first year of production, the total average daily production was 5,100 barrels per day (Ariweriokuma 2009: 25). From those modest beginnings, crude oil has become the defining commodity of the Nigerian economy. The importance of oil to Nigeria is reflected in the Economist Intelligence Unit's review of the country:

> According to official Nigerian government estimates, the oil sector accounts for 70–80% of federal government revenue (depending on the oil price), around 90% of export earnings and around 25% of GDP, measured at constant basic prices. . . . Manufacturing is tiny in comparison, contributing under 5% of GDP, while the services sector and the retail and wholesale sectors have continued to grow and accounted for over a third of GDP in 2007. (EIU 2009, citing NBS 2009)

As Pat Utomi argues, the notion of an enclave sector applies strongly to Nigeria: "In the main, the oil sector has remained an enclave sector, significantly disconnected from the rest of the Nigerian economy with very little multipliers beyond the rent that accrues to government."[3] Utomi underlines that an additional concern in connecting the industry to national economies is the low levels of employment generated by the upstream oil and gas sector.[4] Connecting the industry to the national economy and addressing this concern is fundamental to promoting economic if not social development.

Both the miniscule levels of national employment generated by the oil and gas industry (a subset in the dataset of the Mining and Quarrying Sector) and the significantly larger levels of employment generated by manufacturing, despite the vast difference in GDP contribution, can be seen in Table 2.1. As one expatriate working in Nigeria commented, "In Nigeria, extractive industry involves a lot of extraction, but not a lot of industry."[5] The contrast is particularly significant for analyzing the impact of the

NCA, which focuses on domiciling manufacturing and services related to the oil sector in-country.

Nigeria's focus on local content is now a decade in the making.[6] The theory behind local content is that by encouraging Nigerian participation in the oil and oil services sectors, more of the money invested annually in extracting the country's resource wealth (estimated to be roughly US$12 billion per year) can be captured domestically and used to spur growth in other sectors of the economy. It is still too early to come to meaningful conclusions on the impact of recent changes, which only solidified into the NCA in 2010. However, at this juncture, a detailed look at the current policies within the historical context of policies to promote national control of the Nigerian oil sector helps bring focus the theoretical principles behind the current drive for "Nigerian content" and suggests the outcomes that might emerge.

Today Nigeria is at a crossroads in that its current local content policies have the potential to succeed where previous policies failed to promote economic growth and development. The developmental effects of local content can be thought of as falling into two broad categories: policies designed to increase national ownership premised on the assumption that profits will trickle down to the general populace (premised on a notion of "trickle-down effects") and policies designed to increase economic activity and job creation through "knock-on effects" from the oil industry. It is important to note that the former, though still very much a part of the current local content drive, were the explicit focus of "indigenization" or "Nigerianization" policies in decades past, while the latter newly emphasized "domiciliation" within Nigerian content.

Table 2.1 Selected Statistics on Employment and GDP in Nigeria

	Total Working Population	Total Employed in Mining and Quarrying	Total Employed in Manufacturing	Oil and Gas Contribution to GDP (%)	Manufacturing Contribution to GDP (%)
2004	47,993,400	67,142 (0.14%)	836,234 (1.74%)	25.72%	3.50%
2005	49,486,362	69,001 (0.14%)	907,877 (1.83%)	24.86%	3.60%
2006	52,326,923	72,962 (0.14%)	959,990 (1.83%)	21.85%	3.71%
2007	54,030,000	81,045 (0.15%)	821,256 (1.52%)	19.60%	3.82%
2008	61,958,542	93,302 (0.15%)	944,324 (1.52%)	17.35%	3.82%

Source: NBS 2009.

This chapter places today's Nigerian content policies in the historical context of indigenization in Nigeria's oil and oil services in order to assess the key differences in theory and practice and draw conclusions relevant to the region as a whole. Nigeria's content policies will undoubtedly generate some employment, as well as significant new wealth, by creating knock-on effects in other sectors of the economy (domiciliation). However, Nigerian content is also premised on the familiar fallacious notion that Nigerian ownership and participation in benefits the oil sector will trickle down to the ordinary citizen (indigenization). It will be argued that both indigenization and domiciliation fall short on the promise of delivering social and human development. For this reason, local content policies, which have largely been ignored by many of the key actors in Nigerian and international civil society, must be given new attention in order to ensure that they deliver the best possible outcome.

NATIONAL CONTENT AND CONTROL AND INDIGENIZATION IN NIGERIA, 1960–2000

When Shell BP first began pumping oil in the Niger Delta, Nigeria was a British colony with a largely agrarian economy. The rapid expansion of oil exploration and production, however, took place after 1960 in a newly independent nation. Oil revenues flowed rapidly into the new state. Despite the massive amount of money expended in the Nigerian Civil War (1967–1970), the 1960s and '70s were a time of considerable expansion of roads, hospitals, and schools across the rest of the country. Oil revenues also formed the basis for the construction of the country's first oil refinery at Port Harcourt in 1965 and for the creation of numerous public sector enterprises, which unfortunately were often highly inefficient owing to poor management and their utilization for purposes of political patronage (Ariweriokuma 2009: 34). Polices promoting national content and control ("Nigerianization") have a long history in Nigeria's oil and gas industry—dating at least as far back as the passage of the Petroleum Act in 1969. For the following three decades, national content in Nigeria was defined by policies of indigenization. Underlying these policies were three sets of rationales or justifications. The policies would, in theory, provide revenue to the government of Nigeria, empower Nigerians by providing them with new opportunities, and give Nigeria control over key industries of strategic significance. In practice, in each of these respects, national content was a complete failure.

As Atsegbua has argued, de facto control of the industry by Nigeria requires that management and the day-to-day running of the industry be in the hands of Nigerians (2004: 99–108, citing Asante and Stockmeyer 1982). Therefore indigenization in the Nigerian oil and gas industry focused both on ownership and on the training and participation of Nigerians. In the Petroleum Act of 1969, there are some very basic protections for Nigerian companies as well as a number of regulations regarding training and the development of human capacity. The basic protections for Nigerian oil companies are found in the First Schedule of Section 23, which allows for the revocation of an oil prospecting licence or oil mining lease where the licensee or lessee is controlled by a country that does not permit citizens of Nigeria or Nigerian companies to acquire, hold, and operate petroleum concessions.[7]

More ambitiously, the Petroleum Act called for the large-scale Nigerianization of top-level positions over a defined period of time. Part IV of the act requires the holders of all oil prospecting licenses (OPLs) and oil mining leases (OMLs) to submit to the government "a detailed programme for the recruitment and training of Nigerians . . . in all phases of petroleum operations" and to submit twice-yearly reports on the execution of the program. This requirement works together with the First Schedule of Section 37, which requires the holder of an oil-mining lease (OML) to employ Nigerians for 75 percent of managerial and supervisory positions within 10 years of the grant[8]:

> The holder of an oil mining lease shall ensure that—
> (a) within ten years from the grant of his lease—
>   (i) the number of citizens of Nigeria employed by him in connection with the lease in managerial, professional and supervisory grades (or any corresponding grades designated by him in a manner approved by the Minister) shall reach at least 75% of the total number of persons employed by him in those grades; and
>   (ii) the number of citizens of Nigeria in any one such grade shall be not less than 60% of the total; and
> (b) all skilled, semi-skilled and unskilled workers are citizens of Nigeria.

According to Nwaokoro, the government, through the NNPC (National Nigerian Petroleum Company), already has all the power it needs to exert control over both procurement of Nigerian goods and services and employment of Nigerians: "The obligations of the Petroleum Act befall the 'holder' of a mining lease—which is the national oil company, NNPC" (2010: 60). Despite the existence of these powers and although the law is still in effect, the goals of the government and the NNPC related to national content were never achieved.

In 1972, the government of Nigeria instituted the Nigerian Enterprises Promotion Decree, often called the Indigenization Decree. This marked the beginning of the policy of indigenization in Nigeria, pursued most explicitly from roughly 1972 to 1979. The aim of the decree was to encourage the participation of Nigerians in the economy by requiring the transfer of foreign capital to indigenous hands. In two schedules, the decree listed 22 industrial and service activities exclusively reserved for Nigerian citizens or associations (Schedule 1) and 33 commercial and industrial activities also reserved for Nigerians, but which could be carried out by expatriates under certain conditions (Schedule 2). Although few of these activities related directly to the oil and gas industry, some notable areas affecting the industry included:

   i. Haulage of goods by road (Schedule 1)
  ii. Manufacture of blocks, bricks and ordinary tiles for building and construction (Schedule 1)
 iii. Boat building (Schedule 2)
  iv. Coastal and inland waterways shipping (Schedule 2)
   v. Construction industries (Schedule 2)
  vi. Distribution agencies for machines and technical equipment (Schedule 2)
 vii. Manufacture of cement (Schedule 2)
viii. Manufacture of wire, nails, washers, bolts, nuts, rivets and other similar articles (Schedule 2)
  ix. Manufacture of paints, varnishes or other similar articles (Schedule 2)
   x. Shipping (Schedule 2)

One of the main methods of skirting indigenization was the practice of "fronting," whereby the former expatriate owner sold the targeted business to Nigerians but retained effective control. Several methods of fronting employed with respect to the Indigenization Decree are discussed by Nicholas Balabkins. One of the major consequences of the Indigenization Decree, described by Balabkins as "unintended," was "the concentration of economic power in the hands of a few Nigerians" (1982: 179). Both fronting and the concentration of power, among the most cited reasons for continued underdevelopment in Nigeria, have also been a concern amongst the planners formulating Nigeria's local content strategy.

Around the same time as the Indigenization Decree, the government of Nigeria began taking equity participation in the international oil companies (IOCs) operating in Nigeria, starting in April 1973 with a 35 percent stake in Shell BP's Nigerian operations. By April 1974, the government held a 55 percent stake in all the subsidiaries of the IOCs in Nigeria. A new Indigenization Decree was instituted in January 1977. In the words of Balabkins, the aim of the new decree was to "transfer the ownership and effective management of the modern sector of industry and commerce ultimately into the hands of Nigerian citizens" (1982: 195). The new decree of 1977 included all activities carried on in Nigeria, and there were no exemptions for any expatriate firms. Three categories of activities were created—one in which activity was reserved exclusively for Nigerians, one in which Nigerians were to have at least 60 percent equity participation in the enterprise, and one in which Nigerians were to have no less than 40 percent equity participation. All industrial fields not listed were automatically in the third category, requiring 40 percent indigenous equity participation.

By 1979, the government of Nigeria had increased its equity participation in the IOCs to 60 percent. At the end of that year, with the nationalization of BP's 20 percent stake in Shell BP, the government's equity in Shell Nigeria became 80 percent. Although they had the largest share in all the IOCs, they did not, Atsegbua contends, have de facto control. For the oil sector, one of the key lessons of the indigenization experience was the need for Nigerian management in the oil and gas industry. The lack of such indigenous managerial capacity was one of the key reasons that the Indigenization Decree was not successful. In Atsegbua's words, "The inability of Nigeria to exercise de facto control over its oil industry is the result of the absence of domestic personnel for management positions in the subsidiaries of the IOCs" (2004: 106–107). Of course this did not ensure control, as Nigerians appointed to such positions might feel more loyalty and affinity to the viewpoints of their overseas headquarters.

A similar process was happening during this period in the oil services sector. Beginning in 1977, the NNPC began holding equity interest in several multinational oil service companies (OSCs). Over the years, while their operations in Nigeria have grown significantly, the asset base of these OSCs has remained stagnant. Despite efforts to exert national control, the industry made few contributions to national development. Profits reported in Nigeria were very low compared to the turnover, while the multinational OSCs did not have standard fabrication yards in Nigeria. This ensured that fabrication contracts would be handled by their home offices and most materials would be sourced from sister companies, which quoted high noncompetitive prices. They also made little effort to procure widely available chemicals in Nigeria and failed to make any plans to change these practices (Ariweriokuma 2009: 102–103).

A proper study of why indigenization failed, analyzing the political-economic and sociocultural factors that undermined these policies, is beyond the scope of this work. However, the lessons of this era's failures have been internalized by the architects of Nigerian content. In summing up the experience of indigenization at an industry conference on local content in August 2010, Austin Avuru, CEO of Seplat Petroleum, noted: "The policy generated handsome profits for Nigerian Dealers without building capacity. . . . The result was economic stagnation and collapse of entire program" (Avuru 2010). One positive outcome of national control in multinational OSCs was more active participation by Nigerians at the management level. This led to some of the first set of Nigerian engineers employed in such positions to start their own OSC companies. The NNPC continued equity participation in multinational OSCs until 2006. In the nearly three decades during which the NNPC attempted to exert control over the sector, little change occurred and little was done to increase the sector's benefit to the Nigerian economy (Ariweriokuma 2009: 103).

NATIONAL CONTENT IN OTHER LEGAL REGIMES

There are several other legal regimes that are of significance in understanding national content in Nigeria's oil and gas industry. Among these are the petroleum arrangements between the NNPC (on behalf of the Nigerian government) and the petroleum operators. The four main types of agreements are joint operating agreements (JOAs), production sharing contracts (PSCs), service contracts (SCs), and the memoranda of understanding (MOUs) that Nigeria signed with each of the IOCs in 1986. Although they are not public documents, it is well known that there are provisions regarding national content several of these arrangements.

After entering into partnership with the IOCs in the 1970s, JOAs were signed, setting out the terms of the joint venture. The sections of the JOA related to national content are listed by Etrikerentse (2004: 227–229):

- Article 2.2.8(vi) states "Operator shall give preference to a contractor that is organized under the laws of Nigeria to the maximum extent possible, provided there is no significant difference in price or quality between such contractor and others"
- In the schedule to the JOA on contract procedure, Section 4.3.2 states that all work done in Nigeria shall use, as far as practicable, indigenous human and material resources
- Section 4.5 states that the local part of the work done by foreign contractors shall where practicable, be performed by contractor's local subsidiary
- Section 5.5 requires the operator to "maintain policies and practices which create a competitive environment/climate amongst local and/or overseas suppliers"
- Section 5.5.1 states that "Fabrication whenever practicable shall be done locally provided standards are not jeopardized. To this effect, joint operators recognize and shall accommodate local offers at a premium of 3%."

Atsegbua (2004) adds that Section 5.5.2 of the JOA calls for the involvement of indigenous companies in the supply of goods and services.

Beginning in the 1990s, owing to funding problems with the joint venture arrangement, the government of Nigeria began signing PSCs with the IOCs instead of new exploration and production being conducted under the JOAs. Most of the PSCs are for exploration and production in Nigeria's deep water, where the initial investment required is substantially larger. Less is publicly known about the local content clauses in PSCs. Additionally, there may be slight differences depending on when the PSC was signed. However, what is well known is that in all the PSCs there are clauses requiring the preparation and implementation of plans and programs for the training and education of Nigerians for all job classifications in accordance with the Petroleum Act 1969 as well as a premium on commercial offers of locally sourced goods and services (Atsegbua 2004). Many of these provisions have been completely ignored by both the IOCs and NNPC. As one Nigerian content manager noted during an internal presentation to the Nigerian AGIP Oil Company, in terms of the national content provisions of the JOAs and PSCs, "the effect was not felt."[9]

Nevertheless, Nwaokoro insists that "Nigeria's 1993 model PSC remains an excellent vehicle for enhancing local content" (2010: 60). Explaining, he refers to numerous clauses in the 1993 PSC for offshore deep water that make clear the NNPC's authority to assert control, approve work plans and budgets, and approve all foreign contracts and purchase orders above US$250,000 and all local contacts and purchase orders above ₦1 million. Nwaokoro concludes that: "Read together, the above provisions clearly show that the Nigerian government, through NNPC, retains significant control over procurement of goods and services" (2010: 62). Nwaokoro's analysis does suggest more of a problem with capacity and willingness to enforce regulations then a need for a new legal structure. However, deeper analysis of the historical context in which these regimes were created and enforced shows the value of a fresh approach.

THE MOVEMENT TOWARD A STRATEGY OF DOMICILIATION AND PROMOTION OF LOCAL CONTENT

With greater awareness of the limitations of early efforts at national content, a slow rumble began to build among industry insiders that a new approach was needed to increase the benefit to the nation from the petroleum industry. However, backward steps preceded the current push toward Nigerian content. For example, in 1988 many of the guidelines on staff release were suspended, leading to abuse of the expatriate quota system that promoted Nigerianization. This trend continued until 1997, when new regulations regarding utilization of the expatriate quota and new reporting requirements for expatriate labor were announced. It was only after the return to civilian rule in 1999 that the local content push began anew.

The 1990s also saw the implementation of a Discretionary Allocation Policy (DAP) to award oil prospecting licenses to indigenous entrepreneurs, as well as the Marginal Fields Program (which is discussed below). By 1992, under the DAP, twenty indigenous companies had been awarded licenses. By 1996, the figures had climbed to thirty-eight. Unfortunately the policy was used primarily for political patronage and elite accumulation and had little impact on national control or national content. Reflecting on the DAP in a 2004 presentation on local content development, then-director of the Department of Petroleum Resources (DPR) Macaulay A. Ofurhie conceded, "Indeed the policy on discretionary award has attracted some justifiable criticisms since it was first implemented, more so, as most of the favoured companies had been unable to muster the required know-how to deliver on the implicit trusts vested on them by the state" (Ofurhie 2004). By the year 2000, the slow rumble in the Nigerian oil and gas industry had transformed into a real and concrete movement to institute local content policies. As Ernest Nwapa, currently executive secretary of the Nigerian Content Development and Monitoring Board (NCDMB), describes, "For the past 50 years, since oil exploration started at a commercial level in Nigeria, the strategy was just to import goods and services. So, any economy that is based on importing all its goods and services without balancing trade ends up being an impoverished economy."[10]

Tracing exactly where this movement originated and where momentum came from is very difficult for an outsider to do since there are numerous people claiming credit through conflicting accounts of what actually happened. The push for local content began with a workshop in Abuja in 2001; it was called the National Workshop on Improvement of Local Content and Indigenous Participation in the Upstream Sector of the Petroleum Industry. The workshop was organized by National Petroleum Investment and Management Services (NAPIMS), a subsidiary of the NNPC. Therefore the group general manager of NAPIMS, M. A. Fiddi, is essentially correct to claim that, in terms of Nigerian content, "the whole thing started off from NAPIMS."[11] The workshop in Abuja also had strong support from the new Obasanjo administration, as evidenced by the participation of Dr. Rilwanu Lukman, presidential advisor on petroleum and energy. The workshop produced a communiqué with a recommendation for the establishment of a National Committee on Local Content Development (NCLCD). Following approval from the board of the NNPC, the committee was inaugurated in October 2001 under the leadership of NAPIMS. It produced a report in April 2002 highlighting the committee's finding that the Nigerian content of goods and services in the upstream sector of the oil and gas industry in Nigeria was less than 5 percent, meaning that: "95% of the yearly expenditure of about US$8 billion flows out of the country" (NCLCD 2002: 5).

The committee's report included a definition of local content, strategies for measurement, and recommendations. Among the recommendations were targets for aggregate local content value in the oil and gas industry from all the categories of 40 percent by 2005 and 60 percent by 2010. The committee also recommended a new local content initiative to restructure the industry and to allow DPR and NAPIMS to effectively monitor and enforce a new Nigerian content development policy. The most important of the NCLCD's recommendations was the drafting of legislation for a Nigerian content development bill. The draft bill, included in Volume I of the NCLCD report, placed responsibility on the DPR to ensure compliance and monitor performance.

The DPR was one of many industry stakeholders actively involved in the committee. After the release of the NCLCD report, the DPR, for a time, became the principal actor moving forward the local content initiative. Under DPR Director Ofurhie, a Nigerian content unit was created in 2002 as a special unit under the director's office. One of its key actions was to produce a study on local content in Nigeria. The study was commissioned by the Norwegian Agency for Development Cooperation (NORAD) and executed through Norwegian Oil and Gas Partners (INTSOK) within the context of a memorandum of understanding between Norway and Nigeria. It was conducted under the authority of the Office of the Advisor to the President on Petroleum and Energy, DPR, NNPC, and NAPIMS between August 2002 and April 2003 and included a review of six oil-producing countries—Brazil, Indonesia, Malaysia, Mexico, Nigeria, and Norway. It then proceeded to analyze Nigeria in further detail to identify opportunities for local content development and make recommendations. Chief among the recommendations was putting in place a legal framework for local content policy (Heum et al. 2003).

At the same time, local content was being advanced by a group at the Lagos Business School (LBS) led by Pat Utomi and Fabian Ajogwu, SAN. The two faculty members spearheaded a series of workshops and conferences put on by LBS on how Nigerians can participate more in the oil and gas industry. This effort involved several well-known professors from the school and major players from the industry. Ajogwu was also a member of the Local Content Development Steering Committee set up to guide local content development and coordinate between the IOCs, NNPC, Netco (another subsidiary of NNPC), DPR, and NAPIMS. Discussions at this committee were important in shaping not only the content but also the intent of the Nigerian content initiative.

The Nigerian content bill drafted by the NCLCD was submitted to the special advisor to the president and thereafter submitted to the National Assembly.[12] However, in 2003, prior to the release of the INTSOK study, there was a change in the Obasanjo administration. Edmund Daukoru became the presidential advisor on petroleum and energy and F. M. Kupolokun, who was special assistant and advisor to the president, became the group managing director of the NNPC. At this point Nigerian content entered a new phase. It would take until April 2010 for a very different Nigerian content bill to be passed into law.

According to F. M. Kupolokun, when he moved from special advisor to the president to the NNPC in November 2003, local content was a major priority for him: "I had clear ideas on what I wanted to do."[13] Kupolokun commissioned two international consulting firms to study local content issues and other successful cases such as Brazil, Norway, and Malaysia, which had been previously considered in the INTSOK study. He then created the Nigerian Content Division (NCD) within the NNPC and appointed a group general manager to head the division; originally Joseph Akande, who was later replaced by Ernest Nwapa. At some point the targets for Nigerian content were also changed to 45 percent by 2005 and 70 percent by 2010. The estimates on how the 70 percent target could be achieved are shown in Table 2.2; however neither target was met and Nigerian content now stands at around 35 percent according to most NCDMB estimates.

Table 2.2 Projected Nigerian Content Value Contributions

Sector	Average Annual Amount Spent ($m)	Value Contribution ($m)				
		2006	2007	2008	2009	2010
Engineering	900	270	340	495	605	720
Installation	1,100	220	233	263	295	330
Construction	1,100	330	465	528	625	770
Fabrication	1,500	500	610	705	850	1,000
Procurement	5,400	475	600	1,000	1,700	2,500
Others (including Gulf of Guinea hub)		105	320	650	1,150	1,480
TOTAL	10,000	1,900	2,568	3,631	5,225	6,800

Source: Ariweriokuma 2009: 114, citing NNPC-NCD, 2006.

Through the NCD, the NNPC released a series of Nigerian content directives. The first set of directives focused on three areas: manufacturing, materials, and engineering. The original 10 directives were later increased to 15 and further revised to 23 directives by 2006. Kupolokun and the NCD then ordered more consulting work to be done, including a gap analysis, which resulted in further policies to address the gap in Nigerian content targets on human capacity and fabrication and actually existing capacity (see Table 2.3).[14] As Kupolokun explains, "It's one thing to say this is what I want; its another thing whether you have in place the capacity to deliver."[15]

The Local Content Development Steering Committee, in which Fabian Ajogwu participated, quickly identified front-end engineering and design (FEED) as one of the key areas to address. As Ajogwu explains, "FEED was like the Kingdom of Heaven. If you got that, everything else would follow." This was because FEED had a large out-of-country spend, was a key to capacity building and technology transfer, and was a necessary step for larger milestones. The committee was also keen on a database of Nigeria's human capacity, though this never materialized.[16] As described by Dauda Anako Maliki, who produced a study on Nigerian content for NNPC under the NNPC Chief Officers' Management Development Programme, there was a "fresh approach" to Nigerian content after 2005 (Maliki 2009). A new bill was drafted by the Nigerian Content Division under Joseph Akande. Fabian Ajogwu, a regular consultant to the NCD, was hired to vet the draft and offer comments and suggestions. Although the bill passed the Nigerian Senate, it died with the end of the Obasanjo administration. It was revived in 2008 in a new form that called for the creation of the NCDMB instead of entrusting implementation and monitoring to DPR.

A final piece of the puzzle was put in place with the creation Nigerian Content Consultative Forum at a series of inaugural meetings in June 2005.

Table 2.3 NNPC-NCD Gap Analysis

Subsectors	Capacity Element	Current Available Capacity	Post-Gap Analysis Requirement
Engineering	In-country engineering, person-hours	1.5 million	5 million
	Skill discipline engineers [sic]	1,000	3,600
	Engineering companies (500,000 person-hour minimum capacity)	none	5 or 6
Fabrication	Annual tonnage of fabrication including FPSO modules and LNG	25,000MT	150,000MT
	Certified welders/fitters	2,000	10,000
	Integrated fabrication yards (25,000MT–30,000MT min. capacity)	none	6
	Deep sea port & facilities for FPSO integration	none	2
Manufacturing	Annual tonnage of steel pipes	none	1 million MT
	Annual tonnage of Portland cement	2.23 million MT	11.8 million MT
Shipping and logistics	50% of annual equity crude for export	no indigenous company	180 million bbls (worth $900 million)
	Lighters and medium-sized vessels for coastal services	25	Over 250
	Qualified Nigerian ship captains, crewman and divers	220	over 4,000

Source: NNPC-NCD 2008.

The forum contains working subcommittees for the various industry groupings (including fabrication and engineering). By 2007–2008, the NNPC-NCD had ordered all the IOCs to form NCDs in their organizations with a manager at the level of general manager. Despite progress, legislation was stalled in the National Assembly and compliance with NNPC's directives among the IOCs was half-hearted at best. Disagreeing with the notion that the directives were ignored, F. M. Kupolokun admits, "in a number of cases there was some tension where they just didn't want to do it." However, the chief executive of a major indigenous oil service company, who did not give permission to be quoted on the record, disagrees: "They've talked the talk, but they haven't walked the walk. There's been no implementation of Nigerian content. The directives issued by the NNPC were not followed by any of the MNCs. . . . The attitude is still 'how can we do as little as possible?'"[17]

Officials within NNPC have made similar statements. Writing in 2008, Ado Sule Ibrahim, an employee in the NNPC Chief Officers' Management Development Program, argued that until passage of a Nigeria content bill, the NNPC lacks the power to enforce its Nigeria content directives (Ibrahim 2008). Writing a study for the same program in 2010, prior to the passage of the NCA, Joseph Atibi Brown, Chief Geologist in the Planning Department of the NCD, contended that the law in needed due to lack of specific legal framework to support the set objectives:

> The impact of the absence of a legal framework and strategies for NCD, has adversely affected the entire oil and gas industry such as youth restiveness in oil and gas producing areas, capital flight, a completely non-existent linkage industries and underdevelopment of oil producing areas and the nation at large. (Brown 2010: ii)

OTHER RECENT LOCAL CONTENT POLICIES: MARGINAL FIELDS AND LOCAL CONTENT VEHICLES

Two other sets of policies have been used in recent times to promote national content in Nigeria's oil and gas sector. They are the Marginal Fields and Local Content Vehicles (LCV) programs. Both programs target Nigerian participation in the exploration and production of oil and gas. While the Marginal Fields Program is ongoing, the LCV program was used only in the 2005 bid round. These two programs are the most recent examples of ongoing indigenization efforts that seek to mask elite accumulation and rent-seeking under the guise of promoting national content and control.

The Marginal Fields Program targets small discoveries within the area of a concession, specifically those that have not been exploited by the operator of that concession despite the fact that they have proven reserves, because such exploitation would only be of marginal commercial value. The program was implemented in 1996 through an amendment to the Petroleum Act that allows the head of state order the farming out of a marginal field within a larger leased concession if it has been left undeveloped for a period not less than 10 years from the date of first discovery. The amendment was designed to take such fields, release them from the control of the IOCs, and allow Nigerian exploration and production companies to acquire these fields and exploit their resources.

Of course only a very small number of Nigerians have the necessary capital or connections to take advantage of the opportunities presented by the Marginal Fields Program. Additionally, the peculiar wording of the amendment (which was passed as a decree under military rule in the final years of the Abacha regime), granting the power to release marginal fields not to the government, DPR, or NNPC but solely to the head of state, seems to reinforce the idea that this program was intended more as patronage than as a method of promoting national content. Although the Marginal Fields Program was conceived of in the 1990s, it was stalled by opposition from several quarters until 2002, with much of the opposition coming from the IOCs. In early 2003, awards of twenty-four fields were finally made to thirty-one indigenous companies. The awards were granted for a period of 5 years and were automatically renewable for companies that had begun producing oil in that time frame. However, by the end of the first 5 years of the program, only five fields had entered into production (AOGR 2010: 4). Additionally, most of the Nigerian companies that won awards were heavily reliant on foreign "technical partners," which limited the transfer of knowledge, skills, and technology.

The LCV program was a concept developed for the 2005 bid round by Edmund Daukoru then the minister of state for energy. The program mandated that the government supply a list of Nigerian companies approved to participate in the round as LCVs. Each bid for a license was required to include a minimum 10 percent stake for LCVs, which would be involved as full-paying partners. The program was envisioned as a way to build the capacity of indigenous oil companies, with the IOC taking on particular responsibilities in each bid to train and develop the partnering LCVs' capacity. In theory, training was to involve the operator's assignment of particular tasks in its work program to the LCV to undertake under its supervision. Promoting the local content aspect of the bid round during a "roadshow" speech before the 2005 round, Daukoru argued that one of the major thrusts of the round was "To implement a viable and comprehensive Local Content policy that emphasizes quantifiable and measurable indigene participation, utilization of local goods and services utilization, technology transfer and capacity building, all of which are necessary to transform Nigeria into the hub of oil and gas development in the Gulf of Guinea" (Daukoru 2005).

In the same speech, Daukoru specifically argued that the LCV process "discourages the hawking of Nigerian acreage abroad." Unfortunately the LCV program ended up creating several complications in the round. According to a report by Chatham House, the LCV program "produced a rash of shell or paper companies, causing bidders serious difficulty with due diligence." The authors of the report conclude that the evidence suggests that the LCV scheme was "a mechanism to reward cronies with a slice of the action," and that bidders were steered to choose particular LCVs. Also of particular significance, the report notes, "Of the 100-plus LCVs which pre-qualified, only 10% had previous experience in oil exploration and development" (Vines et al. 2010: 13–14). In the end, according to Austin Avuru, most of the companies involved in the 2005 bid round as LCVs were unable to pay their share.[18]

No doubt it is important for Nigerian companies to have knowledge, capacity, and experience in oil exploration and production. Acknowledging this necessity, the Chatham House Report points to the Marginal Fields Program as a more useful mechanism for promoting national control. Egbert Immomoh, chairman of Afren PLC and a former deputy managing director of the Shell Petroleum Development Company (Nigeria), argues that the marginal fields exercise was useful for encouraging indigenous players to get into the upstream sector; however, he does note that although there are many indigenous players in the sector now, there are not many with producing fields. Immomoh says he never understood the idea of local content vehicles, commenting that they were likely "good for a few individuals who made a quick buck and then went to bed."[19]

However, Edmund Daukoru argues the LCV program is still superior to the Marginal Fields, which came into existence before he took office: "I was always against marginal fields.... It does not provide much revenue to the government and involves a lot of inefficiencies."[20] Daukoru believes that LCVs are a much better way to promote and develop indigenous upstream capacity since the companies involved will be part of the decision making:

> Because they are partners, they are entitled to all the documentation, paperwork, and can attend meetings and be involved in staffing. That is the surest way in my mind to grow the future E&P integrated companies. Nigerians can be providing welding services for a million years, can be providing diving services for a thousand years, they can do fabricating of wellhead platforms for as long as you like. The combination of a welder and these other professions will never come together to form an integrated E&P company ... that is why we came up with the concept of local content partners.[21]

Daukoru does admit that a major problem was that many of the LCVs sold their stakes shortly after the round. His view is that if these transactions were disallowed in future rounds, the program would be much more successful. "If they continue, they could be fixed as time went. These are new policy initiatives ... you plug the loopholes as you go."[22] In the end, both programs were guided by logic of indigenization that created policies of limited success, seemingly designed more to benefit a few well-connected elites than Nigeria as a whole.

THE NIGERIAN CONTENT LAW

On April 22, 2010, Goodluck Jonathan, in his capacity as acting president of Nigeria, signed the Nigerian Oil and Gas Industry Content Development Act (NCA). The NCA gives first consideration for awards of oil blocks, oil-fields, and oil lifting to "Nigerian independent operators," gives exclusive consideration to Nigerian indigenous service companies that meet certain conditions to bid on land and swamp operating areas, creates the Nigerian Content Monitoring and Development Board (NCDMB), requires a Nigerian content plan for all bidding on tenders in the industry, and lays out a series of regulations designed to domicile manufacturing and services relating to the oil and gas industry in-country.

Taking the definition of the 2002 NCLCD report, the NCA defines Nigerian content as "the quantum of composite value added to or created in the Nigerian economy by a systematic development of capacity and capabilities through the deliberate utilization of Nigerian human, material resources and services in the Nigerian oil and gas industry." Among the NCA's most controversial measures is a stipulation of a maximum of 5 percent of management positions for expatriate workers and a schedule containing minimum levels of Nigerian content in any project. This schedule sets minimum targets in engineering, fabrication, materials and procurement, services, research and development, shipping and logistics, and many other categories. Included in the Nigerian content regulations are also minimum levels of Nigerian content in finance, including 100 percent of general banking services, 70 percent of monetary intermediation, and 50 percent of the amount of loans for credit. It remains to be seen, however, whether, like in other areas, the Nigerian banking sector is capable of meeting the minimum levels of Nigerian content. Finally, the NCA also gives the NCDMB, which was essentially created out of the NNPC-NCD, authority to hand out hefty penalties—5 percent of the project sum for each project or cancellation of the project.

Although the IOCs have complained loudly about the onerous nature of the new reporting requirements, from 2005 to 2009 the IOCs had to submit monthly monitoring reports covering all major projects to the NCD using their templates (Maliki 2009: 7). Despite a lag of time from when the NCA was signed until the NCDMB was set up and in a position to collect data, by September 2010 the Department of Operations and Projects (formerly the Office of Planning in the NNPC-NCD) was, according to the head of the department, demanding plans for review and approval from all oil and gas companies for every project and contract.[23] However, in the first 6 months of the NCA, according to the manager of the Monitoring and Evaluation Department, the NCDMB did not issue any fines or penalties under the act.[24]

Officials have been very careful to distinguish the NCA from Nigerianization. According to a manager in the NCDMB, "We are not preaching Nigerianization. Nigerian content is not about Nigerianization. It's about domiciliation; doing it in Nigeria. So if you think that we cannot do this in Nigeria, tell us why and what you think needs to be done to do it in Nigeria."[25] This is a view often repeated by Nigerian content proponents. The visions articulated by Nigerian content advocates paint a rosy picture filled with more employment opportunities for Nigerians. Shortly after the passage of the NCA, Minister of Petroleum Diezani Alison Maduke was quoted in a statement released by NNPC as having said that "The Nigerian Content Law has the potential to generate over 30,000 jobs in the next 5 years" (Akogun 2010). In his vision of Nigerian content, Ernest Nwapa, who also talks frequently of 30,000 new jobs, describes the impact of positive GDP growth due to increased capture of the industry's annual spend:

> Essentially, our work is to increase the participation of Nigerians in the oil and gas industry, to grow capacity and local capabilities will enable more work to be domiciled in Nigeria and to improve the value of expenditure in the oil and gas industry that is retained in Nigeria and in that way increase employment, increase the well-being of Nigerians, and keep technological growth going.[26]

The NCDMB's vision is also shared by NNPC, which has set up a website devoted to Nigerian content:

> NNPC's "Nigerian Content" vision is to transform the oil and gas industry into the economic engine for job creation and national growth by developing in-country capacity and indigenous capabilities. In this way a greater proportion of the work will be done in Nigeria with active participation of all sectors of the economy and ultimately Nigeria will be positioned as the hub for service delivery within the West African sub-region and beyond. (Nigerian Content 2010)

It is hardly an exaggeration to say that a wide array of stakeholders share a similar view. Arguing that the NCA will be a great benefit to Nigerian workers, Louis Brown Ogbeifun, former national president of the Petroleum and Natural Gas Senior Staff Association of Nigeria (PENGASSAN), echoing most of Nigerian labor, suggests that "The recently passed [NCA] is a major breakthrough that the unions have been striving toward for a long time. We see it as something that will reduce unemployment in Nigeria."[27] In a rare occurrence, the Lagos Chamber of Commerce and Industry, which strongly opposed indigenization in the 1970s, agrees with labor. In the words of one of its senior economists,

> The benefits are clear. The private sector and the Lagos Chamber of Commerce and Industry support the Nigerian Content Act and encourage businesses to implement it. We believe it will create employment and benefit Nigeria, so we support it and call for it to be fully implemented by the federal government.[28]

A similar vision is also articulated by indigenous oil service companies through the influential Petroleum Technology Association of Nigeria (PETAN), a lobby group for indigenous oil service companies. Shawley

Coker, who is chairman of PETAN and represents the organization on the NCDMB's governing council, has said, "We hope that if these policies are well adhered to, they should have a multiplier effect and create employment."[29] Finally, as discussed above, albeit with reservations about some of the regulations, the oil industry also sees the potential benefits. According to the manager in charge of Nigerian content at Shell's joint venture company, the Shell Petroleum Development Company (SPDC), Nigerian content also has benefits for relations with Niger Delta communities: "It's all about empowering people; getting them gainfully employed in productive activities so they are able to send their children to school, improving their economic means of livelihood, making them productive, and improving their standard of living. This is what we do and how we contribute to nation-building."[30] This perspective reflects a strong commitment to Nigerian content, at least among Nigerian managers at international oil companies.

Local content policies did not form in a vacuum, absent of ideology and interest. It is therefore necessary to discuss the theory underpinning Nigerian content to better understand who benefits from it in theory and in practice. An examination of indigenization and other policies of national content and national control are important so that local content can be understood in its historical context. A Nigerian content manager at one of the major IOCs argues that indigenization was not "in the same vein as Nigerian content," since it was about transferring ownership of existing companies to Nigerians. Nigerian content, he contends, is about making things happen in Nigeria, domiciling work in Nigeria, encouraging project management and procurement in Nigeria, and promoting the growth of small and medium enterprises (SMEs).[31] As Ernest Nwapa puts it, "We're not saying that international companies cannot operate in the sector. All we're saying is 'come and do it here.'"[32]

This view is shared by Fabian Ajogwu, the LBS professor who was part of the team that prepared the NCA, as well as earlier workshops and committees:

> Local content should be about empowering the country and its people. It's not about seizing or nationalizing assets in the sector. I'm also of the school of thought that local content can only be achieved in an environment that is capitalistic in outlook but with guided regulation. . . . If you want a Nigerian to be involved, he should be able to find his equity. If the country so desires, it can set up a fund to assist him, but he should pay for his joint stock.[33]

This approach to national content and national control is significantly more acceptable to foreign governments and international oil companies. However, it represents a significant departure from indigenization and embracing of the tenets of orthodox neoliberalism.

THE PROMISE AND PITFALLS OF NIGERIAN CONTENT: AN INTRODUCTION

The promise of Nigerian content is very real. For this reason, Nigerians from all walks of life are filled with genuine optimism. The optimism, a hope that greater Nigerian participation in the oil and gas industry will bring greater social and economic development, is also optimism about a transformation to a more capitalistic mode of production and development. This optimism is captured by industry insider Austin Avuru: "There is clearly a very strong drive from Nigerian entrepreneurs not only to invest, but to add value to the industry. I think that in another 10 years you are going to see a thriving sector overall controlled by independent, indigenous, small-sized companies."[34]

The NCDMB is very firm in its resolve to ensure indigenous companies get the contracts. Jobs are given now to companies with higher Nigeria content. All contracts given now have more Nigerian companies involved. As an employee in the NCD of one of the major foreign joint venture companies, responsible for tracking procurement, explained, "You're seeing more companies that have never been given the opportunity getting jobs now for the first time. Sometimes we're forced to do that."[35] The industry as a whole remains skeptical of the ability of indigenous companies to offer goods and services of comparable quality. However, a Nigerian content manager at one of the larger Nigerian indigenous oil service companies explained why, in her view, Nigerian content policies will not affect the quality of products supplied: "If I can prove they aren't offering acceptable quality, I can go abroad. So that is their incentive to offer quality products and services."[36]

Although the industry may remain skeptical, the NCDMB believes it can monitor and enforce compliance with Nigerian content. While this is a large task, the head of the Monitoring and Evaluation Department at the NCDMB believes that ordinary Nigerians working in the industry will help the board enforce policy by anonymously reporting infractions.[37] This view would seem to be supported by one official in the Upstream Monitoring DPR who said that although Nigerian Content is no part of his job description, if he saw something he thought was a breach, he would report it.[38] Many Nigerians working for foreign and domestic companies have expressed similar views.

The key question in Nigerian content is how to evaluate the level of national content in any given project or activity. This question cuts to the heart of what kind of an impact Nigerian content can have and, more importantly, who benefits from it. Although as of 2010 no firm decisions have been made by the NCDMB about how to monitor Nigerian content, Tables 2.4 and 2.5, taken from NCDMB documents, shows the direction they are moving toward with one possible rubric. While Table 2.4 describes a rubric for measuring inputs in terms of materials and labor, Table 2.5 describes Nigerian content in terms of categorization of the contractors themselves. In this respect, Table 2.5 is notable in that it clearly promotes Nigerian ownership as a measurement of Nigerian content.

Table 2.4 Nigerian Content Measurement of Contractor Inputs

Description		Nigerian Content (%)
Procurement	Imported (sourced directly from foreign company)	0
	Imported (sourced through local company)	5
	Assembly done in Nigeria	20
	Manufacturing done in Nigeria with over 60% of input materials being imported or less than 40% local input materials	40
	Manufacturing done in Nigeria with over 60% local input materials	100
Labor cost	All gross payments to Nigerian citizens	100
	Non-Nigerian citizens employed in the direct performance and indirect support of the work and for the period of the work	20
	Training of Nigerian labor in-country	100
	Training carried out abroad	20

Source: NCDMB 2010b.

Table 2.5 Contractors' Nigerian Content Categorization

Category		Description	NC%
A	Wholly indigenous company	Equipment must be 100% owned or leased by the company	100
		At least 80% of directors must be Nigerian	
		At least 80% of top management must be Nigerian	
		At least 90% of senior field personnel must be Nigerian	
B	Major Nigerian shareholding company	Company registered in Nigeria with majority Nigerian shareholding	75
C	Alliance or joint venture	Company alliance between a Nigerian company and (category A) and a foreign company (category E)	50
D	Majority foreign shareholding company	Company registered in Nigeria with minority Nigerian shareholding	25
E	Foreign company	A foreign company registered in Nigeria with no Nigerian shareholding and whose assets belong to the offshore company	5

Source: NCDMB 2010b.

To enforce such a rubric, the NCDMB is moving toward a system in which the Nigerian Content Division of each IOC is responsible for completing a form for every contract (Form 1) and a form for every subcontractor on a given contract (Form 2) in order to win NCDMB approval. While Form 1 would include the details of the contract, including a breakdown of different activities (engineering, fabrication, procurement and services), the various subcontracts, their category of Nigerian content, and the value of the contract; Form 2 would be used to distinguish the total value of the activity, the foreign fees earned, and the Nigerian fees earned (for services) as well as the fees earned and man-hours worked by foreign and Nigerian labor at various levels from senior management to "junior/artisan" (local temporary staff) labor.[39]

Of the many pitfalls awaiting Nigerian content, most are well known to Nigerians. Speaking to a NAPE workshop, Shawley Coker warned of the need to "avoid the same pitfalls that derailed the Nigerianization ideals of the Indigenisation Decree of 1972." As he describes it, during the 1970s, "Government officials colluded with foreign owned companies to create Nigerian fronts. It was the era of entrenched paper companies, high business costs (given the chains of commission agents) and capital flight" (Coker 2010). In his 2004 presentation on local content, Macaulay Ofurhie warns about Nigerian fronts and explains how Nigerian content must be different:

> There have been reactions from some stake-holding units on the use of companies classifying companies on the basis of ownership. We have also been warned on the possible danger of manipulating the new policy to promote local fronts rather than local content which can stall the current aspirations. The Department is of the view the fear is unfounded. Whereas, the local content seeks to reward local investment and competence, [local fronting] seeks to glorify mediocrity and promote indigenous lackeys. Local content, unlike local fronting, aims at benefiting the larger society, while ensuring legitimate gains on labour and capital, local fronting concentrates on rewarding a tiny and often incompetent segment of the society to the detriment of the larger majority. (Ofurhie 2004)

Speaking about personal concerns with the new law, one senior official in DPR lamented that the problem with Nigerian content is that: "The whole game now is about contracts." Nigerian content, the official contended works to make sure Nigerians get the contracts, but once you have the contract, his concern was that a foreign company would still do the work:

> I'm a Nigerian, but I can have the backing of, let's say, Canada Inc. . . . I don't have anything, I've never drilled before, but I will bring that rig from Canada with Canadians on it. I will go because I have the

contacts, get all the necessary things, bid, have an office in Port Harcourt or Lagos or both, and the people can come and do the work.[40]

This concern has also been raised in connection with the role of "technical partners" in the Marginal Fields Program.

Responding to the suggestion that the oil operators are required to report in great detail on subcontractors, owners of equipment, sources of raw materials, etc., this official brought up some well-known concerns of all DPR officials: the problem of confirming what is in the reports, work plans, and submissions of the IOCs, not only in terms of Nigerian content but in general. For many public officials, there is a general sense that what the IOCs report is simply not a reflection of what is actually occurring on the ground: "But how do you confirm that? . . . I told you there is an issue of sincerity. It's not there. How do you validate?"[41] For these reasons, civil society has demanded, as one NGO representative suggested, that the names of everyone who get a contract award be published, along with dates of award and completion; and to ensure an "open, transparent process of bidding." Without this, he argued, under the guise of Nigerian content, contracts would be "dished out as political patronage."[42]

Concerns over Nigerian fronts and political patronage are connected to the pitfall of poor implementation. Shawley Coker has captured the hope that this moment represents for the Nigerian oil and gas industry, but also the recognition of the significant challenges that industry insiders knew awaited them: "Needless to say, there is a world of difference between the ideals of the law and the realization of the benefits it seeks to provide and protect. It would take the collective will and effort of the government, operators, service providers, stake-holding institutions, international investors and partners to make the [Nigerian Content Law] work." According to Coker, who, as mentioned above, is also a member of the governing council of the NCDMB, "the firmness with which the provisions of the law would be driven and defaulters sanctioned by the board (and relevant institutions) should set a sound regulatory tone for the industry" (Coker 2010). Still, the most stinging rebuke comes from the dissident DPR official, who questions the very connection between the government's decisiveness in setting targets and their strategy for meeting them: "There's no definitive plans, but there are targets. They've set targets, but there is no plan, no plan at all!"[43]

CONCLUSION

The NCA's adoption is a unique moment of opportunity for Nigeria and the Nigerian oil and gas industry. Nigerian content development is a movement to transform the structure of the Nigerian economy to promote greater national content and national control for the purposes of national development and security. The decisions being made now about Nigerian content will affect the direction and scope of how the Nigerian oil and gas industry shapes national development in years to come. It cannot be denied that Nigerian content promotes a shift from foreign ownership to indigenization. Yet there is much skepticism about the extent to which Nigerian content involves Nigerian participation in ownership and the encouragement of investment by the Nigerian elite. On the one hand, proponents of Nigerian content speak at great length about the potential benefits of domiciling economic activity in Nigeria, regardless of the national origins of the investors. On the other hand, the NCA as it was written and Nigerian content as conceived by those who developed its policies are understood to promote indigenization.

In explaining the thinking that went into the development of the NCA, Fabian Ajogwu, explains:

> Capital has no heart and it's not patriotic. It only sees returns on investments and minimum economic environments that guarantee the returns. . . . For local content to work, we need to present that Nigerian with returns on investments and a minimum economic environment which he would otherwise have rushed to Norway to find. There's no need to be emotional about it. It's just the truth. But with more opportunities for participation here locally with a regulatory framework supporting it, you have better chances of getting the elite involved, and they are already doing so.[44]

In the NCA, any clause that offers a benefit to an indigenous company has to be understood in the context of promoting Nigerian ownership. For example, Article 3 offers certain privileges to "Nigerian independent operators" (3.1) and "Nigerian indigenous service companies," though these terms are not defined anywhere in the law. While there are undoubtedly benefits to the country from promoting national companies, such benefits only accrue through these companies' engagement in productive economic activity. To ensure the promotion of productive activity, the NCDMB will have to evaluate the contribution of Nigerian companies and decide how much weight ownership should have in the measurement of Nigerian content. Although draft forms and procedures for the measurement of Nigerian content exist, it is still too early to know how Nigerian content will be evaluated by the NCDMB in practice.

Nigerian content is too new for anyone to express much more than an opinion about its effects. However, a look at the history of national content in Nigeria, the ideology behind the current Nigerian content push, and the shifts already observed by industry insiders suggests that unless more is done, the primary beneficiaries will not be the Nigerian people. Nigerians face two unattractive outcomes. While indigenization benefits the Nigerian elite and allows widespread rent-seeking and patronage, domiciliation exposes the country and the industry to the effects of neoliberal globalization (which also primarily benefits the elite of Nigeria, as well as foreign interests). To chart a course that allows Nigeria's resource wealth to reach the majority of its citizens is no easy task. However, it seems clear that Nigerian content policies are at the core of recent developments in the oil and gas industry that will help shape the country's future for generations to come

NOTES

*The field research for this work was carried out with the aid of a grant from the International Development Research Centre, Ottawa, Canada. Information on the centre is available on the web at www.idrc.ca. The author also gratefully acknowledges the support of York University, the York Centre for International and Security Studies, Stakeholder Democracy Network, and Social Action.
1. On the resource curse, see Sachs and Warner (1995, 2001) and Humphreys, Sachs, and Stiglitz (2007). For a critical response to this literature, see Zalik (2008) and Obi (2010).
2. Interview, November 2010.
3. Ibid.
4. In the context of the oil and gas industry, the "upstream" sector refers to exploration and production activities, as opposed to the "downstream," which refers to the refining and distribution of products derived from petroleum as well as the distribution of natural gas.
5. Comment made at a social event in Abuja, October 2010.
6. Since being articulated at the end of the 1990s, the term *local content* has been slowly replaced with *national content* and, more recently, *Nigerian content*. Although all three terms are used interchangeably in the oil industry today, it should be noted that the shift in terminology over time represents a conscious effort by the Nigerian government to define the nation as the primary stakeholder in the oil and gas industry—a key point of contention in ongoing struggles in the Niger Delta. These policies are distinct (in theory if not in practice) from policies of national content and control, or "Nigerianization." In this essay, *national content* refers to policies stretching back to the 1960s, while *local content* refers to the current national content push that began in 2001.
7. In the current amended Petroleum Act, this section is numbered Section 24.
8. In the current amended Petroleum Act, this section is numbered Section 38.
9. Meeting, November 2010.
10. Interview, October 2010.
11. Interview, November 2010.
12. "A Bill for an Act to make Provisions for Nigerian Content Development in the Upstream Sector of the Nigerian Petroleum Industry and for Matters Connected therewith" can be found in the *Official Gazette*, No. 72, September 2, 2003.
13. Interview, November 2010.
14. Results of the Gap analysis are reproduced in NNPC-NCD 2008.
15. Interview, November 2010.
16. Interview, December 2010. According to Ernest Nwapa, building an online database has again become a priority of the new NCDMB.
17. Interview, November 2010.
18. Interview, November 2010.

19. Interview, November 2010.
20. Interview, October 2010.
21. Ibid.
22. Ibid.
23. Interview, November 2010.
24. Interview, November 2010.
25. Interview, November 2010.
26. Interview, October 2010.
27. Interview, November 2010.
28. Meeting, November 2010.
29. Interview, December 2010.
30. Interview, October 2010.
31. Interview, November 2010.
32. Interview, October 2010.
33. Interview, December 2010.
34. Interview, November 2010.
35. Interview, November 2010.
36. Interview, December 2010.
37. Interview, 3 November 2010.
38. Interview, October 2010.
39. Draft versions of the NCDMB monitoring Forms 1 and 2.
40. Interview, November 2010.
41. Ibid.
42. Interview, October 2010.
43. Interview, November 2010.
44. Interview, December 2010

REFERENCES

Akogun, Kunle. "Nigerian Firms Now to Get Priority in Oil Sector." *This Day* [Lagos] April 23, 2010, http://www.oan-agency.com/site/newsdetail.php?recordID=Nigerian%20Firms%20Now%20to%20Get%20Priority%20in%20Oil%20Sector.

AOGR. "Marginal Fields: Status Update." *Africa Oil & Gas Report,* Vol. 11, No. 6 (2010): 4.

Ariweriokuma, Soala. *The Political Economy of Oil and Gas in Africa: The Case of Nigeria.* London: Routledge, 2009.

Asante, Samuel K.B. and Stockmeyer, Albrecht. "The Evolution of Development Contracts: The Issue of Effective Control," in *Legal and Institutional Arrangements in Minerals Development.* Mining Journal Books, 1982. Atsegbua, Lawrence. *Oil and Gas Law in Nigeria: Theory and Practice.* Lagos: New Era Publications, 2004.

Avuru, O. Austin. "Local Content Law: Pitfalls in Application." Presentation to the Nigerian Association of Petroleum Explorationists. Lagos, August 25, 2010.

Balabkins, Nicholas. *Indigenization and Economic Development: The Nigerian Experience.* London: JAI Press, 1982.

Brown, Joseph Atibi. *Nigerian Content and Oil and Gas Exploration in Nigeria: An Individual Project Report.* Abuja: NNPC Chief Officers' Management Development Program, April 2010.

Coker, Shawley. Local Capacity Building in an Enhanced Enabling Environment. Paper Presentation to the Nigerian Association of Petroleum Explorationists. Lagos. 25 August 2010. http://www.nape.org.ng/.

Daukoru, Edmund. "The Nigeria 2005 Oil and Gas Exploration and Production Acreage Bid Round." Port Harcourt: Keynote Address by the Presidential Advisor on Petroleum and Energy. March 24, 2005.

EIU. *Nigeria Country Profile*. London: Economist Intelligence Unit, 2009.

Etikerentse, G. *Nigerian Petroleum Law*. Lagos: Dredew Publishers, 2004.

Government of Nigeria. *Nigerian Oil and Gas Industry Content Development Act*. April 22, 2010.

Heum, Per, Christian Quale, Jan Erik Karlsen, Moses Kragha, and George Osahon. *Enhancement of Local Content in the Upstream Oil and Gas Industry in Nigeria: A Comprehensive and Viable Policy Approach*. Bergen: Institute for Research in Economics and Business Administration, Report No. 25/03, 2003.

Humphreys, Macartan, Jeffrey Sachs, and Joseph E. Stiglitz, eds. *Escaping the Resource Curse*. New York: Columbia University Press, 2007.

Ibrahim, Ado Sule. *Nigerian Content Development and Capacity Building in NNPC*. Abuja, Nigeria: NNPC Chief Officers' Management Development Program, August 2008.

Maliki, Dauda Anako. *Nigerian Content Implementation and Policy Targets in Oil and Gas Industry*. Abuja, Nigeria: NNPC Chief Officers' Management Development Program, August 2009.

NBS. *Nigeria Statistical Factsheets 2009*. Abuja, Nigeria: National Bureau of Statistics, 2009.

NCDMB. *Draft NCDMB Monitoring & Evaluation Directorate Procedure*. Nigerian Content Development and Monitoring Board, 2010. (Internal document.)

NCLCD. *Report of the National Committee on Local Content Development in the Upstream Sector of the Nigerian Petroleum Industry*, Vol. 1. National Local Content Committee, April 2002.

Nigerian Content. *Nigerian Content Website of the NNPC Group*. Nigerian National Petroleum Corporation, 2010: http://www.nigcontent.com/

NNPC-NCD. Nigerian Content Development in Oil & Gas Industry. Abuja, Nigeria: Nigerian Content Division, Nigerian National Petroleum Corporation, July 2008.

Nwaokoro, J. Emeka. "Signed, Sealed, but Will It Deliver? Nigeria's Local Content Bill and Cross-Sectoral Growth." *Journal of World Energy Law and Business*, Vol. 4, No. 1 (2010): 40–67.

Obi, Cyril I. "Oil as the 'Curse' of Conflict in Africa: Peering through the Smoke and Mirrors." *Review of African Political Economy*, Vol. 37, No. 126 (2010): 483–495.

Ofurhie, Macaulay A. "The Role of a Regulatory Agency in Local Content Development." Presentation to the National Association of Energy Correspondents. Lagos, October 7, 2004.

Sachs, Jeffrey, and Andrew M. Warner. *Natural Resource Abundance and Economic Growth*. NBER Working Paper No. 5398. Cambridge, MA: National Bureau of Economic Research, 1995.

———. "The Curse of Natural Resources." *European Economic Review*, Vol. 45, No. 4–6 (2001): 827–838.

Vines, Alex, Lillian Wong, Markus Weimer, and Indira Campos. *Thirst for African Oil: Asian National Oil Companies in Nigeria and Angola*. London: Royal Institute of International Affairs, 2010.

Wabote, Simbi. "Maintaining a Healthy Balance between Local and Foreign Involvement in Oil & Gas Service Delivery." Presentation to the Nigerian Association of Petroleum Explorationists. Lagos, August 25, 2010.

Watts, Michael. "Empire of Oil: Capitalist Dispossession and the Scramble for Africa." *Monthly Review*, Vol. 58, No. 4 (2006): 1–17.

Zalik, Anna. "Liquefied Natural Gas and Fossil Capitalism." *Monthly Review*, Vol. 60, No. 6 (2008): 41–53.

3 Globalization and Rural Land Conflict in North-West Cameroon
A Historical Perspective

Emmanuel M. Mbah

The rural land conflicts between villages in North-West Cameroon are rooted mainly in the recent economic transformations and developmental endeavors due to globalization within the last two decades. As defined by Jim Hite, globalization is "an ongoing process by which markets grow and expand into a network that reaches around the world."[1] Globalization is not a new phenomenon; the process goes as far back as the ancient period. The fifteenth century, however, marked the beginning of a rapid development in the process, brought about by innovations in the numerous technologies aimed at reducing distance. The expansion of the global market into North-West Cameroon was a gradual process that intensified only during the European colonization of the region in the late nineteenth and early twentieth centuries, first by the Germans in 1884 and later—with the defeat of Germany in the First World War—by the British from 1916 onward. In the last two decades, the pace of globalization has heightened, as capitalistic ventures now spread their tentacles over all of rural North-West Cameroon, facilitated in part by improved means of transport and communication.

Reducing or minimizing distance to and from markets is, therefore, an important component of globalization in rural African communities. In today's world, information on products spreads easily and markets move faster and more cheaply to and from any part of the globe than ever; it is no longer possible to isolate any community from market forces. These economic transformations, the shrinkage of distance, and changes in market conditions have particularly affected land-use patterns in rural communities, as has been the case in North-West Cameroon, where the value of land is up, prices have spiked, and the result has been conflict between villages and groups struggling to obtain permanent control over portions of rural land for profit. This essay aims at interrogating some of the global forces that have impacted rural land and boundaries in North-West Cameroon. It is divided into two major parts. The first part examines the issues of globalization, land scarcity, and conflict in rural Africa in general, while the remainder of the essay identifies and discusses those aspects of globalization that have introduced or heightened land conflict in rural Africa and North-West Cameroonin particular.

GLOBALIZATION, LAND SCARCITY, AND CONFLICT IN RURAL AFRICA

In precolonial/precapitalist African societies, land scarcity was not an issue because the importance of land was seen more in terms of its traditional and cultural values. In these societies, village land was communally owned and the chief was the custodian of such land. The notion of collective ownership ensured continuous harmony and unity within and between village groups exploiting the land. This also meant that such land would be collectively protected from aggressors.[2] The advent of European colonial rule coupled with the spread of capitalism to rural Africa destroyed the notion of communal land, replacing it with private or individual ownership.

Before the abolition of the transatlantic slave trade, African dependence on land was principally for the production of subsistence crops, hunting, and settlement needs. Since these uses did not require much land, disputes over land use were rare in precolonial African societies; serious land contestations occurred only over fertile stretches of land, truly rich hunting grounds, or areas that abounded with extractable resources. But when the transatlantic slave trade was abolished, Africans had to adjust to trade in commodities, especially primary landed commodities.[3] Although the change from trade in humans to trade in commodities led to a drastic reduction in the number of wars aimed at capturing slaves, it also led to an increase in conflict between individuals and communities for control over land and the resources therein. Land was becoming scarce and, hence more economically viable. This was a reversal of what previously occurred in sub-Saharan Africa, where there was plenty of land but very little labor and where "control over labor rather than land ownership was the ultimate determinant of wealth."[4]

The economic significance of land to rural African communities in this age of globalization (in raising incomes, providing employment, and exporting crops and other extractable resources as well as providing tax revenue for governments) has transformed land into a social security resource that has been responsible for rationalizing conflict. The problem was in part heightened by monetarist economic policies introduced in the continent by European colonizers, who promoted wide-scale capitalist commodity production and exchange in the continent. This questioned precolonial land ownership and tenure systems and introduced socioeconomic divisions accentuated by land ownership and productivity as well as the monetary value of land. In the 1920s in the Gold Coast (present-day Ghana), for example, the monetary value of cocoa production had increased from £4,764,067 in 1921 to £11,229,000 in 1928. Cocoa, coffee, tea, cotton, and many other crops encouraged by global capitalism of the European colonization of Africa needed extensive land for their cultivation and, as a result, many farmers in West Africa opened up plantations to cultivate these crops. These "rural capitalists" reinvested the gains from their initial harvests in more land purchases. Thus the unique dynamic of global capitalism of the colonial era "was the fact that Africans sold land which was supposed to have been communally owned."[5] The sale of land at a precipitous pace signaled the beginning of globalization/capitalism-induced land scarcity in Africa.

The intensification of cash cropping and animal husbandry in most areas of West Africa in the 1930s established a permanent commercial link between land, production, and overseas markets, as reflected in a reinvigorated local scramble for its possession and exploitation. It is from this scarcity-derived scramble induced by global capitalism that we identify the new political and economic sources of rural land disputes between individual farmers and groups and ethnic communities on the continent. Today, the traditional concepts of rural land in Africa are less the cause of conflict; the commercial notions of "investment [and] commodity production" are more responsible.[6]

The crystallization of the link between land use, scarcity, and conflict also occurred when European colonizers appropriated large areas for government programs, including land reservations for European traders, the development of trading posts, the construction of residential areas, land grants to missionaries, and for colonial schools, farms, and administrative offices. There is no doubt that land appropriations both during the colonial and postcolonial eras were a response to rapid globalization. But because much of the expropriated land spanned rural boundaries, disputes were introduced between communities sharing the border. Not unrelated to the issue of expropriation was competition between rival European companies, communities, and churches over land, especially where rural communities were split between different groups of European land seekers: "A grant of land to one meant a counter-grant to the other. Where disputed territory is involved, a spiral of conflict is immediately unleashed."[7] In the Aguleri-Unuleri conflict in eastern Nigeria, for example, the contested territory of Otuocha (which had been communally exploited by both groups in the past) became the subject of a grant/sale and countergrant/sale to Europeans, introducing misunderstandings between the parties.[8]

In rural areas, colonialism also created a new elitist class of petty bourgeoisie who were quite aware of the sociopolitical and economic global transformations taking place and hence had a taste for land and landed property on a scale never before witnessed on the continent. As elites in their various communities, they increasingly sought political support in order to promote their interests, including the protection of community land. They became actively involved in land disputes with other communities, recruiting lawyers and spending huge sums of money for its pursuit.[9] When independence came in the 1960s, the political importance of land as an asset that bestows power and authority to its owners was unmistakably clear. This explains the surge since then by elites to accumulate land for future profit and/or speculation in anticipation of future rising prices and higher values.

Whatever the case, scarcity makes it harder for nonindigenous people (deemed strangers in some parts of Africa) to have the same security of tenure as indigenous groups, especially during their initial period of settlement. As outsiders, the chief (the custodian of village land) can withdraw land allocated to a group "if they breach any conditions that may have been attached to the allocation," or "if they are deemed to behave contrary to local cultural norms," including any lukewarm attitude toward village ceremonies and projects.[10] In some cases, immigrants are pressured to offer tribute to village heads in order to remain in their good graces. Because of these constraints on nonindigenous people, many steer clear from considerable long-term investments on land that may not be theirs in the near future.[11] In Ivory Coast, the recent and heightened land squabbles resulting from scarcity have raised the difficult question of Ivorian belonging or Ivoirité, "a concocted distinction between 'pure' Ivoirians from the South and Muslim 'immigrants' in the North."[12] In Zimbabwe, Robert Mugabe has transformed the land question bequeathed by colonial rule into a serious political issue. In many African rural communities, land is at the core of political and social tensions because of its economic value.

Currently, land ownership and/or productivity constitute an important contributor in elevating the gross domestic product (GDP) of African states. Even the World Bank has emphasized the importance of land to rural African communities.[13] Thus, while privileged landowners can use land or landed resources to acquire the necessary credit to educate their children and even send them abroad for further education or as economic migrants, poor farmers find it difficult to secure access to the type of credit that could enable them purchase or rent land for those basic activities of the primary sector in order to keep themselves afloat. These poor farmers resort to arrangements of a nonpermanent nature to gain access to land. Such arrangements, also part of the process of globalization, may involve formal or informal contracts that can be renegotiated or revoked based on prevailing circumstances, including strain in relationships.

Meanwhile, increasing land scarcity has reduced the number of these nonpermanent arrangements on land in many rural African communities today, resulting in a high propensity for land conflict within and between village groups. Land that was thought of to be abundant in some African communities is now scarce. Scarcity is the result of too much pressure on land, raising its value/price and making access difficult. Camilla Toulmin has rightly observed that "the changing pressures, regulations and mechanisms for gaining access to land are generating increased conflict between user groups as option values rise" and that governments and foreign donors have renewed their interest in land issues in Africa both because of its increasing importance as well as its ability to generate conflict in this global age.[14] In North-West Cameroon, we see these conflicts playing out between villages, between farmers and grazers, and between indigenes and immigrants.

In many parts of Africa since independence, the increase in the cost or value of land has been accompanied by a corresponding increase in the human and cattle population. In Nigeria, acute land shortages with repercussions on the land holding system began to be felt as early as the 1970s. There, colonial authorities had failed to control the influx of cattle as well as to introduce regulatory policies on land exploitation. Overgrazing on the Mambilla Plateau in Nigeria, for example, has a direct effect on rural economies in the region; the consequences are frequently manifested through "occupational" boundary disputes. The August 1987 a violent confrontation between the Bachama and the Hausa of Tingno-Waduku in Northern Nigeria resulted from disputes over the struggle for land as an economic resource.[15]

In the Wukari region of Taraba state in Nigeria, the widespread migration of people of Tiv origin from the western sector of Cameroon into the Benue Valley that commenced in the eighteenth century had, by the early twentieth century, begun to exert considerable strain on land originally inhabited by the Jukuns and other neighboring communities in the region. Initially, relations between these groups were peaceful; but by the 1940s, the population dynamic in the Middle Belt region of Nigeria changed dramatically when people of Tiv descent became the most populous group. In Wukari Division, for example, the Tiv population had increased to three times that of the Jukun. Worried about the effects of the huge influx of Tiv farmers, the British took steps to arrest the situation by creating a Wukari Federation Local Council; it included all other groups in the region but excluded the Tiv, who were considered immigrants. Attempts by the Tiv in the 1940s for inclusion in this council have crystallized with related land/boundary issues to constitute the underlying sources of the Tiv-Jukun conflict.[16] What this means is that migrations, another important component of globalization, are an important contributor to rural land disputes in Africa.

In the Ivory Coast, the struggle over land rights has, since the 1960s, conditioned relations between the Baoule and their neighbors, including the Bete. While conflict between Baoule and these neighbors began during the period of European colonization, they have been intensified in postcolonial Ivory Coast for economic, ethnic, and political reasons.[17] In Mauritania, there are similar disputes between village groups and communities over control and ownership of fertile agricultural land and good pastures as well as the closest watering points. Here, available pastures and water constitute the underlying sources of conflict over rights of usage between neighboring nomadic pastoral groups, where "rainy season and dry season road tracks and watering points were the collective property of each faction or tribe."[18] Meanwhile, in Morocco, land possession is a major source of conflict between rural village communities where "the agricultural land tenure system, the local economy, and the commercial structure" of the region south of the Atlas Mountain have introduced cleavages between these groups.[19] Finally, in Kenya, the Rift Valley region has remained a highly contested zone between groups over farming and grazing lands.[20]

Similar examples of land disputes over usage and rights in this age of globalization abound throughout the African continent.

Environmental factors—including land deterioration through soil erosion, drought, deforestation, and cattle trampling—have also induced artificial scarcity, as land contestations heighten over more valuable plots. But while environmental factors may partly be responsible for scarcity, I agree with Derman and colleagues that "economic factors are far more important in predicting domestic armed conflict than are environmental factors."[21] Ethnicity is a lesser contributor to these recent conflicts; viewing ethnicity as the principal source of today's rural African conflict "seems . . . no more fruitful than seeing nation-states as the cause of international wars."[22] Ethnicity serves only as a crystallizing factor; it is not as important as those issues triggered by the demands of the new globalization.

The commoditization of land, "the penetration of capital and the attendant land grabbing and speculation [have diminished], with every passing day, the proportion of land available to the small-holding peasantry,"[23] who have to increase their share of subsistence or cash crop production in order to survive in a continent that has been economically stagnant for so long. The ongoing economic crisis has not made matters any easier:

> The crisis has destroyed the ability of Africans to build and maintain integrative projects, assuming that their leaders have the necessary will to do so. The crisis has also promoted civil and military forms of authoritarianism even as the propaganda of world opinion and the West, as well as the vast majority of the African people, demand multiparty democracy. Finally it has led to the growth of divisive competition for the ever decreasing national resources.[24]

The prevailing global economic crisis with its inequality and social differentiation has become fodder for contemporary rural land disputes on the continent. The reduction of state expenditures on social and economic amenities in rural communities, worsened by the implementation of structural adjustment programs, also part of the process of economic globalization, have not been successful, and have in part resulted to stagnation, poverty and misery, thereby permeating and expanding rural cleavages in Africa.

RURAL LAND CONFLICT IN NORTH-WEST CAMEROON

Globalization-induced economic factors that contribute directly or indirectly to rural land disputes in North-West Cameroon include the quest for sources of primary resources and other landed property, accessibility to urban areas and to means of communication, land scarcity and its growing economic value, population growth, developmental projects, soil fertility, and the impact of the current economic crisis. These factors have influenced the recurrence of past disputes, the outbreak of new ones, and the magnitude of hostilities that characterize conflict during this age of globalization.

Primary Resources

The struggle for control over primary agricultural resources as well as control over land where these resources flourish have on many occasions introduced disputes between individuals, villages, and ethnic groups in the region. These resources include, among others, raffia groves, palm and kola nut trees, and isolated fruit trees like plums, pears, and mangos as well as small patches of forest for the collection of firewood and building sticks. Land disputes are also frequent over land that is suitable for the cultivation of globally traded crops such as coffee, tea, and rice.

Raffia groves have for long been sources of rural land/boundary disputes in North-West Cameroon. The reasons for this are twofold. First, raffia groves are frequently found along natural boundary enclaves like valleys and along streams and rivers; these are favorable sites, in terms of relief and climate, for the flourishing of the raffia plant. But because the plant grows on both sides of a stream, making it a continuous grove, conflict is introduced between villages whose natural boundaries are along streams and rivers. A dispute usually commences when one village claims ownership over the entire raffia grove. Second, to inhabitants of the region, the raffia palm is an important economic item for the global market. From it is collected palm wine, an inexpensive but widely popular and locally consumed alcoholic drink. Palm wine has become increasingly important owing to formal or informal restrictions on the provision of beer during traditional death celebrations in some parts of the region, rendering it the next best alternative. The palm wine industry has been sufficiently developed and has flourished to serve not only the region but other areas of Cameroon, increasing its economic value. It is therefore not unrealistic for intervillage rural land/boundary disputes to ensue over rights to raffia groves.

Raffia groves also provide raw materials for construction and crafts. Bamboo collected from raffia plants is used in the construction of houses, in the making of beds and chairs, in decorations, and in the building of fences. Fiber, also collected from the raffia palm, is an important material for the weaving of colorful baskets and raffia bags. These bags are marketed globally, and it is not uncommon for western tourists to acquire them as souvenirs or gifts during their brief stays in the region. As a result, the economic importance of raffia groves and their role as sources of conflict between groups is unquestionable. During the construction of the Bali-Nyonga Station by the Germans, for example, the search for bamboo poles compelled Bali-Nyonga subjects to steal them from neighboring villages; such situations, which frequently resulted in hostilities, also questioned the actual boundaries between Bali-Nyonga and the respective villages.[25]

The dispute between Akum on the one hand and Nsongwa and Mbatu on the other, which started during colonial rule, resulted in part from claims and counterclaims made by the three villages over raffia groves and kola nut trees.[26] That between Bali-Nyonga and Guzang also resulted in part from claims made by the latter over raffia groves, plum and palm trees, and other primary resources. In its complaint to the British colonial administration, Guzang argued that part of its land, containing 501 raffia plants and 103 houses, had been left on the Bali-Nyonga side of a delineated boundary.[27] In the dispute between Mankon and Nsongwa, the chief of Nsongwa argued that the contested piece of land contained raffia groves and palm trees that he had brought from Bafut and planted himself.[28] Disputes over raffia groves and other agricultural resources, common all over the region today, are frequently heightened on contested land within easy reach to means of communication.

Accessibility

Access to means of communication, social amenities, and other infrastructures constitutes another economically induced source of rural land/boundary disputes nuanced by the effects of globalization in the region. The construction of a motor road from Bamenda through Bali to Mamfe by the Germans, in an age when the rest of the region lacked accessible road networks, was in part responsible for the numerous land/boundary disputes that cropped up on both sides of that road. Its construction was partly responsible for the dispute between Akum on the one hand and Nsongwa and Mbatu on the other, discussed earlier. The contested land, situated along this road, offered easy access to and from the Bamenda station, the Hausa settlement of Abakpwa below the station, right up to Mamfe through Batibo. The dispute intensified when markets to serve travelers and others in transit were opened along the road and in Bamenda town proper. The Kombe market, situated near the meeting point between Nsongwa and Mbatu, for example, developed for the sale of foodstuff and other necessities. The road reduced distance and facilitated movement of local traders and their produce to and from Bamenda town and station. This was particularly true of kola nut traders from the Abakpwa Hausa community in view of the bulk involved in transporting the produce. Accessibility to Bamenda town and station and the establishment of the Kombe market increased the value of the contested land.[29]

The construction of more roads in the region after independence has increased conflict over territories traversed by these roads. Because local markets and other business ventures are more connected to global markets by being situated along these highways, villages have either made new claims or renewed old ones, hitherto settled by authorities, over land on both sides of these new highways. The recent land/boundary dispute between Santa-Njong and Awing in Santa subdivision derives in great part to accessibility to roads and markets. The contested land is located near the tarred main highway linking Bamenda town in the North-West Province and Bafoussam in the West Province of Cameroon. While the village of Santa-Njong is located astride that highway, the village of Awing sits a considerable distance away from it and is connected only by a feeder road, which becomes muddy and difficult to traverse during the rainy season. Many in Santa-Njong are convinced that the claims of Awing over the land in question have more to do with accessibility than with customary rights of ownership.

Land Scarcity and the Growing Economic Value of Land

Any discussion of land scarcity in Africa in general and North-West Cameroon in particular is complicated by the fact that some villages have more land relative to their populations while others have very little. Within individual villages, some elites have more land than they can make use of while also preferring not to rent or sell it to the landless. Toulmin has argued that "land 'saturation' or scarcity is clearly a relative term, depending on local forms of land use, levels of productivity and market engagement, and patterns of income diversification."[30] For example, rural communities in Ivory Coast, with population densities of 80 to 100 persons per square kilometer, have a serious problem with scarcity because of a mode of production that relies heavily on the cultivation of tree crops on plantation scales. In Southern Benin, in contrast, scarcity becomes an issue at population densities of 250 to 300 persons per square kilometer.[31] A majority of villages in North-West Cameroon have densities significantly lower than what prevails in the two preceding examples. And as discussed below, relative scarcity, as witnessed by some villages in the region, is a result of many different factors.

In North-West Cameroon before the 1920s, land scarcity was not a serious issue. Before this period, plantation agriculture on the level of that of the Gold Coast and intensive cattle rearing were unpopular, and the cultivation of staple foods was at a subsistence level. From the 1920s, however, land that had hitherto been thought to be plentiful became scarce. A number of factors were responsible for this and all had to do with the rapid expansion of the global market in this region. These factors include the reintroduction of cattle in the region by British colonial authorities, the introduction of cash cropping on plantation scales, unfair land tenure systems and poor farming methods, the rapid increase in populations, and the precipitous rise in land speculation.

The reintroduction of cattle by British colonial authorities led to mass immigration of the Fulani with their cattle from the northern part of Nigeria as well as from the French portion of Cameroon from 1916 to take advantage of disease-free good pastures. The British aimed at promoting mixed agriculture in the region and the production of agricultural products alongside animal husbandry. They were convinced that because of the relatively low population density coupled with the vast mountainous grasslands, the region could support large herds of cattle. Through cattle taxes, otherwise known as *jangali*, Fulani cattle would constitute an important source of revenue for the colonial administration.[32] Jangali was "a capitation tax on cattle belonging to nomad herdsmen . . . a rough income tax."[33] Between 1930 and 1950, proceeds from this tax increased significantly and the British had good reasons to promote cattle herding by immigrant Fulani cattle owners.[34] By 1920, the first group of Fulani cattle owners under Ardo Sabga had already settled parts of the territory with a large herd of cattle.[35] This marked the beginning of Fulani migration into the region.

As the migrations continued, the prospect of increased revenues from cattle taxes loomed and by 1921 the British appointed a Fulani as headman, responsible for collecting taxes on an estimated cattle population of 7,057 head. By 1924, the cattle population had risen to approximately 12,000 head. The first documented collection of cattle taxes by the native authorities of Nso, Bali-Nyonga, and Kom took place in 1928, during which period the cattle population of Nso alone stood at 4,000 head. Jangali was increasingly becoming an important source of revenue for the British colonial administration:

> Revenues from jangali rose from £500 on 10,000 head in 1922, to £1793 in 1929. In 1936 the employment of an extra clerk to count cattle led to an increase of £2007 over the previous year's revenue. Jangali for 1937 amounted to £4,430 on 59,074 cattle head. By 1947 rates per head went up and revenues climbed to £19,616 on 156,883 cattle head. In 1956 there was an estimated 200,000 cattle head in this region, while jangali in 1957 amounted to £46,800.[36]

As the cattle population increased, so too did that of the Fulani. In the 1920s, only a small number of Fulani resided in the region. By 1953, their number had reached 10,000; by 1965, they numbered about 18,360.[37] The British gave many cattle-owning Fulani permits or certificates of occupancy to settle with their cattle on indigenous land. These certificates were granted over periods of between 7 to 25 years[38] at a rate of 500 acres per 50 cows, as was the case of the permit granted to Ardo Umam of Wum.[39] The shrinkage of distance to cattle markets that were now opened almost everywhere and the global exportation of cattle products (such as meat, hides, and skin) were added incentives for more Fulani to migrate to the region. But while the Fulani and cattle populations continued to increase, the available land, which had hitherto been considered vast and abundant, also began to shrink, rendering it more competitive.

Initially, the migrations posed no serious threats because the Fulani restricted their activities to mountaintops and slopes; these were perfect grazing sites but unfavorable for agriculture. The situation changed in the early 1930s, when the British introduced the planting of improved pasture species to supplement dry-season pastures. The Kikuyu grass, one of those improved species from Kenya, was widely distributed to the Fulani to plant against the dry season. Instead of planting it on the hills, the Fulani preferred to plant it in fertile valleys where yields were higher.[40] This meant that the fertile valleys that had been used by indigenous agricultural communities for subsistence food cultivation would have to be shared with the Fulani for their pasture requirements. In an era where rural populations were rapidly increasing as a result of high birth rates, low death rates, and rising life expectancies (due to the globalization of medicine, which came about as a result of the establishment of numerous mission dispensaries and hospitals during the colonial era), available land per person was definitely going to shrink.[41]

Meanwhile, by the 1930s, indigenous farmers were putting more land to agricultural use than before as a result of the introduction of plantation cropping for the global capitalist market. These global crops were not only competing with subsistence crops for land use but had become very important in view of their monetary value. The cultivation of coffee, tea, and rice started at about the same time as when locals began growing oil palms, raffia, and kola nuts on a plantation scale. These crops required considerable land.[42] The switch from subsistence to plantation-type agriculture heightened conflict over parcels of land in the region.

The introduction of Arabica coffee in the first half of the 1930s, in particular, reduced available land for the cultivation of food crops. When coffee was introduced, its cultivation was centered around individual compounds or in the immediate vicinity of village dwellings, where it had the advantage of shelter from kola nut, pear, mango, and other fruit trees. But because its cultivation took up much of the surrounding village land, farmers had to look for distant land to grow subsistence food crops. Fallow lands were used up for this purpose.[43] And because of population increases, and the high yields and revenues resulting from the cultivation of plantation crops for the global market, farmers in the region needed more land to increase their coffee, rice, oil palm, and raffia holdings.

The cultivation of rice and Arabica coffee was stimulated as far back as the 1950s, when the colonial agricultural department provided farmers with rice and coffee hullers and other processing machinery. While these new technologies stimulated cultivation and earnings, the proportion of land consecrated to their production also increased. Coffee in particular was very profitable. Harvest from a normal holding at the time, approximately 30 acres of land, amounted to about 6 tons. At two shillings per pound, the total value was £1,344. Costs were negligible because the family met labor requirements. Hence from 1949 to 1955 there was an annual increase of a thousand acres of newly planted coffee fields by peasant farmers in the region. In 1955, the agricultural department sold 55,000 coffee seedlings, scarcely enough to meet the demand for that year. Land became a scarce commodity as its global economic value increased. The reluctance of some rural farmers to adopt modern methods of agriculture promising higher yields complicated the land shortage problem. Many farmers have contumaciously stuck to the primitive method of shifting cultivation, with its wasteful fallow periods. As cultivable land became more and more limited, conflict ensued between groups in the region over boundaries and territorial space.[44] Thus, while the development of the primary sector of the African economy resulted in an increase in the commercial value of land, it also introduced land/boundary disputes between groups, precipitating numerous lawsuits over land ownership, a consequence of which was "widespread poverty, especially among the ruling houses and land-owning families."[45] Lawsuits over land, prevalent today in all areas of the region, are a testament to the increased global economic value attached to rural land.

The designation of large expanses of land as forest and game reserves and for educational and administrative uses, introduced by the respective colonial administrations (Germans and British), further reduced available rural land. Eucalyptus forests were opened in the Momo, Mezam (in Baforchu and Chomba), and Bui divisions while a game reserve, which took up a considerable stretch of land, was opened at Kimbi.[46] Individuals also planted large eucalyptus forests. In Ngyen-Mbo, for example, despite limited agricultural land, the Muna family owns large expanses of eucalyptus forest, located on cultivable land, while many locals have little or nothing. This, in part, explains the ferociousness with which the Ngyen-Mbo community has pursued its numerous disputes over land with neighboring Bali-Nyonga.

Traditional land tenure systems in the region have contributed in no small way in aggravating the land problem. In many rural communities in the region, land is the preserve of a few; the majority have little or nothing for food crop production. Indigenous land tenure systems function on the basis that "title to all land between . . . settlements, except economic crops actually planted by individuals such as raffia bushes, is vested in the Fon [chief]."[47] He uses his discretion to grant such land to his subjects when he pleases and is rewarded "in the form of tributes, services and even produce from the land."[48] Because of the apparent injustice in the system of land tenure, some individuals and rural elites, who in most cases are traditionally constrained against taking legal action to redress such unfairness, foment boundary disputes with neighboring villages to satisfy their land needs. The persistence of poor farming systems such as shifting cultivation, farming up and down mountain slopes (which frequently leads to soil erosion), and the absence of chemical fertilizers to improve productivity have crystallized with bad land tenure systems to heighten both the problem of land hunger and the resulting conflict.

Population Growth, Development, and Soil Fertility

Rapid population growth in North-West Cameroon has reduced the amount of farmland available to village communities and individual farmers. From

1953 to the present decade, the population of many villages has doubled or tripled. The population of the village of Balikumbat, for example, which stood at 6,350 in 1953, rose to 13,210 in 1976, then 15,658 in 1987, and 17,720 in 1995. While reducing the amount of farmland available to farmers, the growth rate has not been accompanied by available technology to maximize land use. In the meantime, retirees and those who have been made redundant by the global economic crisis and structural adjustment policies of the World Bank and the International Monetary Fund have returned to their respective villages to swell the rural population. These groups have been very active in the pursuit of conflict over land in recent times. The dispute between the previously mentioned Awing and Santa-Njong is also in part the result of rapidly exploding population numbers. Faced with farmland shrinkage, modern Awing now lays claim to land it lost about 75 years ago during colonial boundary delineations.

The need for additional land to provide for amenities that come with a globally changing landscape has reduced its availability for emergent populations in the region. Huge expanses of land in the region have been severed for the construction of schools, hospitals, roads, recreational centers, airports, and houses, which, through necessity, have the attendant effect of reducing available land for agriculture. This is especially so because these projects occupy land horizontally as opposed to vertically. The precipitous shrinkage of available rural land has frequently been translated into land/boundary disputes, especially in the south-central portions of the region, around the vicinity of Bamenda town, where land prices have skyrocketed. The conflict between the villages of Akum on the one hand and Nsongwa and Mbatu on the other can be attributed in part to land scarcity resulting from the growth and development of the town of Bamenda.[49] That between Bambili and Bambui, which started in the 1930s, has intensified today owing to land shortage; both villages have lost considerable portions of their ancestral land to government projects, including the construction of public institutions like the Cameroon College of Arts, Science and Technology; the Institute for Zoo Technical Research in Bambui; the Catholic Seminary; and many other schools and colleges. Additional portions are being used for cattle grazing and the remainder has become too small to accommodate the needs of indigenous farmers, who now attempt to grab land from their Babanki-Tungo, Banjah, Fungie, and Nkwen neighbors.[50] The expropriation of land by government for a tea estate at Ndu, the veterinary demonstration center in Jakiri, and many other such projects during and after the colonial period have further reduced the amount of cultivable land. The recent 2011 creation of the University of Bamenda is another endeavor that will further strip farmers of agricultural land and might lead to disputes in the affected communities.

Land/boundary disputes in the region occur frequently over fertile areas located along border enclaves between villages. Soil fertility constitutes an assurance of a fruitful harvest to these communities for subsistence as well as for the global market. But because all land does not have the same degree of fertility, the most fertile areas have become sources of conflict between villages. The 1984 land/boundary dispute between Bambili and Banjah, for example, resulted from the quest for fertile soils. The contested land is fertile and supports the cultivation of a variety of crops. This attracted subjects from Banjah, who started encroaching on portions of the territory claimed by Bambili on historical grounds. With encouraging harvests and in order to sustain their rapidly growing population, the villagers of Banjah claimed the land as theirs.[51] The disputes between the villages of Bambili and Babanki-Tungo, Balikumbat and Bafanji over Bangang, Bali-Nyonga and Chomba and many a rural land dispute in the Ndop plain area have all been influenced by soil fertility. The quests for fertile soils for the cultivation of food crops required by a rapidly growing population has influenced and will continue to stimulate land/boundary disputes in the region.

The Prevailing Economic Crisis

Finally, the ongoing economic crisis has crystallized the other factors, rendering rural land disputes in the region endemic. The crisis, which began in the late 1980s, reduced the amount of money in circulation and increased the prices of goods and services. Because of structural adjustment policies negotiated with the Bretton-Woods institutions by many African states, recruitment into the civil service ceased.[52] Unemployment rendered redundant many able-bodied persons who worked in the towns, forcing them to return to their respective villages, where their only alternative of coping in a rapidly globalizing world was to turn to the land. It is not surprising, then, to find many unemployed in the region taking an active role in land/boundary disputes. Meanwhile high unemployment rates, coupled with low wages and salaries, have stimulated farming activities and attracted many people to the land, increasing its value and rendering it very competitive. With the gradual application of technology and modern agricultural practices, even marginal lands, which hitherto had little or no economic value, have all been claimed by village communities in the province. The swampy land at Tuabi in the Mbengwi central subdivision, for example, which no one bothered about before the 1970s, has been progressively reclaimed and put to use. Thus it is without a doubt that global economic forces have played a very significant role in contributing to rural land conflict in the region. In many cases, issues related to ethnotribalism and the disruptive colonial boundary have only reinforced the quest to meet global challenges in the region.

The intensification and escalation of land/boundary disputes in the region usually occur during the farming season, from February to August. During this period, rival communities simultaneously strive to cultivate crops on contested land. In other situations, one village cultivates the contested land while the rival village waits to harvest. Both situations end in confrontations and destruction to crops and properties. Confrontation is also introduced when one party attempts to carry out construction work on contested territory. It is evident from the preceding pages that, with population increases and increases in the number of people who end up as quasiagriculturalists because of nothing else to do, the situation of land disputes induced by globalization will pose an even greater challenge in the future.

CONCLUSION

I have argued that the shrinkage of distance, population increase, rising unemployment, and rapidly expanding markets, among others things, have heightened conflict over land between rural communities in North-West Cameroon. As a result, precolonial communal land exploitation patterns are no longer tenable in the region. While land speculation, capital investment, and commodity production have risen arithmetically, populations (a large number of which are unemployed and landless) have risen geometrically, resulting in scarcity and hence conflict over land that was previously thought to be unlimited. Land has become an important social security resource for both individuals and communities, which explains the heightened state of conflict over its ownership and use.

In addition to normal conflict reduction and resolution strategies, there are economic measures that could be considered in addressing the problem of globalization-induced land scarcity. To begin with, the diversification of the economy, which at the moment is not keeping up with population increase, could help alleviate the problem of overreliance on land and landed resources. Industrialization aimed at creating jobs that lure the unemployed away from total dependence on the primary sector is one way of diversifying the economy. Second, improved methods of stock keeping that address the problem of land shrinkage would free up large expanses of land currently occupied by cattle, thereby reducing friction between pastoralists and agrarian communities, including the disputes over crop destruction and soil erosion that result from cattle trampling. Persuading and/or encouraging members of the community (through the use of subsidies) to adopt mixed farming techniques (intensive farming practices that maximize stock keeping and farming on smaller plots) can be very useful here. Finally, assuring soil fertility through the use of chemical fertilizers and/ or manure (subsidized by the government) would gradually eliminate the need for larger parcels; this would minimize the effects of land shrinkage, thereby reducing land disputes.

Globalization is here to stay. While I do acknowledge the fact that some land disputes in the region are so old and have been so politicized and ingrained in individual and group memories that they defy ordinary economic strategies for their resolution, addressing the problems associated with land ownership and use by examining their economic roots remains one of the surest ways of reducing present and future globalization-induced land conflict in North-West Cameroon.

NOTES

1. Jim Hite, "Land Use Conflicts on the Urban Fringe: Causes and Potential Resolution" (Clemson, SC: Strom Thurmond Institute, 1998), 2.
2. Verkijika G. Fanso, "Trans-Frontier Relations and Resistance to Cameroon-Nigeria Colonial Boundaries 1916–1945" (Doctoral dissertation, University of Yaoundé, 1982), 12–13.
3. A. Adu Boahen, *African Perspectives on Colonialism*, (Baltimore: Johns Hopkins University Press, 1987), 3–4.
4. Erik Gilbert and Jonathan T. Reynolds, *Africa in World History: From Prehistory to the Present* (Upper Saddle River, NJ: Pearson Education, 2004), 123.
5. Michael Crowder, *West Africa under Colonial Rule*, (Evanston, IL: Northwestern University Press, 1968), 349.
6. Bill Derman et al., eds., *Conflicts over Land and Water in Africa: Introduction* (Oxford: James Currey, 2007), 18.
7. Raphael Chima Ekeh, "Aguleri-Umuleri Conflict—The Theatre of Fratricidal War," in Monique Mekenkamp et al. (eds.), *Searching for Peace in Africa: An Overview of Conflict Prevention and Management Activities* (Utrecht, the Netherlands: European Platform for Conflict Prevention and Transformation, 1999), 360.
8. Ekeh, "Aguleri-Umuleri Conflict," 360.
9. Ekeh, "Aguleri-Umuleri Conflict," 360–61.
10. Paul Kishindo, "Customary Land Tenure and the New Land Policy in Malawi," (*Journal of Contemporary African Studies*, Vol. 22, No. 2 (May 2004):216–217.
11. Kishindo, "Customary Land Tenure and the New Land Policy in Malawi," 216.
12. Peter Schwab, *Africa: A Continent Self-Destructs* (New York: Palgrave Macmillan, 2001), 33–35. Also consult Camilla Toulmin, "Negotiating Access to Land in West Africa: Who Is Losing Out?" in Bill Derman, Rie Odgaard, and Espen Sjaastad, eds., *Conflicts Over Land and Water in Africa*, (Oxford, UK: James Currey, 2007), 96.
13. Derman et al., eds., *Conflicts Over Land and Water in Africa*, 23.
14. Camilla Toulmin, "Negotiating Access to Land in West Africa: Who Is Losing Out?" in Bill Derman et al., eds., *Conflicts over Land and Water in Africa*, (Oxford, UK: James Currey, 2007), 95.
15. Samuel G. Egwu, "Agrarian Question and Rural Ethnic Conflicts in Nigeria," in Okwudiba Nnoli (ed.), *Ethnic Conflicts in Africa* (Dakar, Senegal: CODESRIA Book Series, 1998), 62–63.
16. Judith Burdin Asuni, "The Tiv-Jukun Conflict in Wukari, Taraba State," in Mekenkamp et al,, eds., *Searching for Peace in Africa: An Overview of Conflict Prevention and Management Activities* (Utrecht, the Netherlands: European Platform for Conflict Prevention and Transformation, 1999), 353–354. It is believed by many in the region that the Jukuns who came from Yemen, together with the Kanuri, were the first to settle in Wukari. The Jukuns established the Kwararafa Kingdom, which attained its peak during the seventeenth century and cohabited peacefully with neighbors until the arrival of the Tivs.
17. Gilbert Gonnin, "Ethnicity, Politics and National Awareness in Côte d'Ivoire," in Okwudiba Nnoli, ed., *Ethnic Conflicts in Africa* (Dakar: CODESRIA Book Series, 1998), 161–174.

18. Oumar Moussa Ba, "The State, Elites and Ethnic Conflict in Mauritania," in Okwudiba Nnoli, ed., *Ethnic Conflicts in Africa* (Dakar: CODESRIA Book Series, 1998), 235–237.
19. Abdelghani Abouhani, "Tribal Conflict Management in Morocco," in Okwudiba Nnoli, ed., *Ethnic Conflicts in Africa* (Dakar: CODESRIA Book Series, 1998), 222.
20. Walter O. Oyugi, "Ethnic Politics in Kenya," in Okwudiba Nnoli, ed., *Ethnic Conflicts in Africa* (Dakar: CODESRIA Book Series, 1998), 289.
21. Derman et al., *Conflicts over Land and Water in Africa*, Introduction, 6.
22. Derman et al., *Conflicts over Land and Water in Africa*, 8.
23. Egwu, "Agrarian Question and Rural Ethnic Conflicts in Nigeria," 60.
24. Nnoli, "Ethnic Conflicts in Africa," 22.
25. E. M. Chilver and P. M. Kaberry, *Traditional Bamenda: The Precolonial History and Ethnography of the Bamenda Grassfields* (Buea, West Cameroon: Government Printer, 1968), 38.
26. No. 2124, Qf/b, 1939 (2), "Bangangu-Bambetu Land Dispute," 6, National Archives Buea, Hereafter Cited as NAB. Akum (Bangangu), Nsongwa, and Mbatu (Bambetu) all belong to the Ngemba clan of the Widikum ethnic group. Economic-induced inter-village rivalry, as opposed to ethnic/identity rivalry, was the underlying source of this conflict.
27. No. 9570, Qf/b, 1943 (1), "Bali–Guzang (Babujang) Boundary," 1–2, NAB; Fanso, "Trans-Frontier Relations," 49. While Bali Nyonga and Guzang belong to different ethnic groups, their ethnic differences had been buried by the marriage of a Bali Nyonga princess to the chief of Guzang. Because of this union, Guzang refrained from participating in the ethnic conflict between the Widikum ethnic group, of which it is a part, and the Bali Nyonga ethnic group. Therefore, the underlying source of the Bali Nyonga-Guzang conflict was economic.
28. No. 2341, Qf/b, 1938 (1), "Bande-Bangwa Boundary Dispute," 7 and 16, NAB. As mentioned in the introduction, the shrinkage of distance is a significant component of globalization.
29. No. 2124, "Bangangu–Bambetu Land Dispute," 6 and 14.
30. Toulmin, "Negotiating Access to Land in West Africa," 107.
31. Ibid.
32. Tambi Eyongetah and Robert Brain, *A History of the Cameroons* (London: Longman Group Ltd., 1979), 98.
33. *Cameroons under United Kingdom Administration: Report for the Year 1955* (published for the Colonial Office, London: Her Majesty's Stationery Office, 1956), 71.
34. Adamu Sale Suliy, "Farmer–Grazier Conflict in Bui Division, 1916–1989," (Master's thesis, University of Yaoundé, 1990), 9.
35. P. M. Kaberry, "Report on Farmer-Grazier [Grazer] Relations and the Changing Pattern of Agriculture in Nsaw (South Eastern Federation, Bamenda, Southern Cameroons)," in File No. Ab 17 (10), 1959, 125, NAB.
36. Kaberry, "Report on Farmer-Grazier [Grazer] Relations," 126.
37. Chilver and Kaberry, *Traditional Bamenda*, 1–2.
38. No. PM. 1230/S.1., Qf/a, 1963 (4), "FAO: Farmers-Graziers Relationship Problems," 2–6, NAB.
39. No. DWM. 676/261, April 19, 1969, "The Secretary to the Prime Ministers' Office, Buea, West Cameroon: Ardo Umam-Wum, Fencing Scheme," 1, NAB.
40. *Cameroons under United Kingdom Administration*, 106.
41. Ibid., 104–107.
42. Chilver and Kaberry, *Traditional Bamenda*, 37; Suliy, "Farmer–Grazier Conflict in Bui Division," 11–12.

43. Suliy, "Farmer–Grazier Conflict in Bui Division," 12.
44. *Cameroons under United Kingdom Administration*, 108.
45. Boahen, *African Perspectives on Colonialism*, 100–102.
46. Ibid., 108.
47. No. Qf/a, 1964 (1), "Land Tenure in West Cameroon," 3, NAB.
48. No. Qf/a, 1964 (1), "Land Tenure in West Cameroon," 3–4.
49. No. 2124, "Bangangu–Bambetu Land Dispute," 25.
50. Fidelis Makwondo Cheo, "Bambili and Her Neighbors: Inter-village Relations Since 1961" (Master's thesis, University of Yaoundé, 1996), 1, 49–50.
51. Cheo, "Bambili and Her Neighbors," 52.
52. Denis Amoussou-Yéyé, "Inter-Ethnic Relations and Socio-Political Dynamics in Benin," in Okwudiba Nnoli, ed., *Ethnic Conflicts in Africa* (Dakar, Senegal: CODESRIA Book Series, 1998), 398.

REFERENCES

Abouhani, Abdelghani. "Tribal Conflict Management in Morocco." In Okwudiba Nnoli, ed. *Ethnic Conflicts in Africa*. Dakar: CODESRIA Book Series, 1998.

Amoussou-Yéyé, Denis. "Inter-Ethnic Relations and Socio-Political Dynamics in Benin." In Okwudiba Nnoli, ed. *Ethnic Conflicts in Africa*. Dakar: CODESRIA Book Series, 1998.

Asuni, Judith Burdin. "The Tiv-Jukun Conflict in Wukari, Taraba State." In Monique Mekenkamp,

Paul van Tongeren, and Hans van de Veen, eds. *Searching for Peace in Africa: An Overview of Conflict Prevention and Management Activities*. Utrecht, the Netherlands: European Platform for Conflict Prevention and Transformation, 1999.

Ba, Oumar Moussa. "The State, Elites and Ethnic Conflict in Mauritania." In Nnoli, Okwudiba, ed. *Ethnic Conflicts in Africa*. Dakar: CODESRIA Book Series, 1998.

Boahen, A. Adu. *African Perspectives on Colonialism*. Baltimore: Johns Hopkins University Press, 1987.

Cameroons under United Kingdom Administration: Report for the Year 1955. London: Her Majesty's Stationery Office, 1956.

Cheo, Fidelis Makwondo. "Bambili and Her Neighbors: Inter-village Relations Since 1961." Master's thesis, University of Yaoundé, 1, 1996.

Chilver, E. M., and Kaberry, P. M. *Traditional Bamenda: The Precolonial History and Ethnography of the Bamenda Grassfields*. Buea, West Cameroon: Government Printer, 1968.

Crowder, Michael. *West Africa under Colonial Rule*. Evanston, IL: Northwestern University Press, 1968.

Derman, Bill, Rie Odgaard, and Espen Sjaastad, eds. *Conflicts Over Land and Water in Africa: Introduction*. Oxford, UK: James Currey, 2007.

Egwu, Samuel G. "Agrarian Question and Rural Ethnic Conflicts in Nigeria." In Okwudiba Nnoli, ed. *Ethnic Conflicts in Africa*. Dakar: CODESRIA Book Series, 1998.

Ekeh, Raphael Chima. "Aguleri-Umuleri Conflict—The Theatre of Fratricidal War." In Monique Mekenkamp, Paul van Tongeren, and Hans van de Veen, eds. *Searching for Peace in Africa: An Overview of Conflict Prevention and Management Activities*. Utrecht, the Netherlands: European Platform for Conflict Prevention and Transformation, 1999.

Eyongetah, Tambi, and Robert Brain. *A History of the Cameroons*. London: Longman Group, 1979.

Fanso, Verkijika G. "Trans-Frontier Relations and Resistance to Cameroon-Nigeria Colonial Boundaries 1916–1945." Doctoral dissertation, University of Yaoundé, 1982.

Gilbert, Erik, and Jonathan T. Reynolds, *Africa in World History: From Prehistory to the Present.* Cranbury, NJ: Pearson Education, 2004.

Gonnin, Gilbert. "Ethnicity, Politics and National Awareness in Côte d'Ivoire." In Okwudiba Nnoli, ed. *Ethnic Conflicts in Africa.* Dakar: CODESRIA Book Series, 1998.

Hite, Jim. "Land Use Conflicts on the Urban Fringe: Causes and Potential Resolution." Clemson, SC: Strom Thurmond Institute, 1998.

Kishindo, Paul. "Customary Land Tenure and the New Land Policy in Malawi." *Journal of Contemporary African Studies*, Vol. 22, No. 2 (May 2004):213–235.

Nnoli, Okwudiba. "Ethnic Conflicts in Africa: A Comparative Analysis." In Okwudiba Nnoli, ed. *Ethnic Conflicts in Africa.* Dakar: CODESRIA Book Series, 1998.

Oyugi, Walter O. "Ethnic Politics in Kenya." In Okwudiba Nnoli, ed. *Ethnic Conflicts in Africa.* Dakar: CODESRIA Book Series, 1998.

Schwab, Peter. *Africa: A Continent Self-Destructs.* New York: Palgrave Macmillan, 2001.

Suliy, Adamu Sale. "Farmer–Grazier Conflict in Bui Division, 1916–1989." Master's thesis, University of Yaoundé, 1990.

Toulmin, Camilla. "Negotiating Access to Land in West Africa: Who Is Losing Out?" Bill Derman, Rie Odgaard, and Espen Sjaastad, eds. *Conflicts Over Land and Water in Africa: Introduction.* Oxford, UK: James Currey, 2007.

4 Evolving Political Accountability in Kenya

Jacob Butler

The political structure of Kenya changed dramatically in 1992, when multiparty elections were held for the first time in the country's history. This development was a divergence from the past of Kenya as a one-party state in which public dissent and oppositional politics were dealt with by violence, detention, and loss of access to political patronage. In adopting the democratic principle of multiparty elections, Kenyan politicians entered into a new political world where accountability, a key characteristic of a functioning democracy, would be expected from leaders. Throughout this paper I analyze Kenya's evolving political accountability from a historical perspective. I argue that the push for accountability by the voting public, the media, civil society groups, and the international community has been a highly contested and has evolved into battle as entrenched politicians have abused power in order to avoid being held accountable, thus allowing them to engage in politics as usual. The chapter opens by indentifying a working definition of what political accountability is and its importance to democracy, followed by a discussion of accountability (or lack thereof) in Kenya. Next, I turn toward different arenas, where the game of political accountability manifests itself: the media, the judicial court system, and the involvement of international actors in domestic politics in Kenya.

DEFINING ACCOUNTABILITY

Before analyzing political accountability in the Kenyan context, it is important to identify just what accountability is and the role that it plays in a democratic political system. An encyclopedic definition of the term indicates that it is "the ability to ensure that officials in government are answerable for their actions."[1] This definition is beneficial in that there is definitely a correlation between "accountability" and "answers." However, it only tells half of the story, as there is also a lot more that goes into the word and processes surrounding it. In the book *The Self Restraining State: Power and Accountability in New Democracies,* Andreas Schedler and colleagues argue that there are two key concepts that are essential to political accountability: answerability (as mentioned above) and enforcement. Schendler et al. argue that answerability is defined by "the obligation of public officials to inform about and to explain what they are doing."[2] When "informing," leaders must provide reliable facts on a given topic, whereas when "explaining," they must provide reasons for their actions. Enforcement is "the capacity of accounting agencies to impose sanctions on power holders who have violated their public duties."[3] In other words, it is the ability to reward good and punish bad behaviors. In a democracy, this is most closely associated with citizens' ability to cast a ballot in the upcoming election.

However, these elections must be accepted by the population, oppositional parties, and international observers to be "free and fair" for enforcement to have any meaning. Schendler and colleagues state that accountability that exposes misdeeds, but does not (or lacks the ability to) impose consequences on guilty parties is comparable to acts of window dressing rather than real restrains on power. In addition to identifying the different connotations of accountability (answerability and enforcement), Schendler recognizes two major types of accountability: vertical and horizontal. Vertical accountability is a relationship between unequal parties as powerful actors (elite politicians) are held accountable by inferior groups such as citizens, civil society groups, and the mass media. Vertical accountability can also occur within the political system when higher-ranking officials hold subordinates accountable. On the other hand, horizontal accountability concerns actors on a level playing field. In democracies, this occurs via the separation of powers between different branches of government that are able to enforce a system of checks and balances on one another. In other words, the judiciary can hold the executive branch accountable, which has the same power over the legislative branch, and vice versa. These actors are all essentially equal and are thus able to police each other, possessing the ability for enforcement through use of impeachment, veto, etc.

ACCOUNTABILITY AND DEMOCRACY

Another key issue that needs to be addressed is the relationship between accountability and different political systems. In authoritarian regimes (arguably what Kenya was as a one-party state before 1992), rulers are not held publicly accountable for their actions by the populace. Ultimately, the authoritarian system prevents this from happening as there is a clear distinction between rulers and the ruled that does not allow citizens to question their leaders. This occurs because citizens living under authoritarian regimes often lack political rights, such as the freedom of speech and suffrage that allow for questions to be asked, thus promoting accountability. All that being said, accountability is not completely lacking under an authoritarian regime and is therefore not limited to democratic governments. In fact, authoritarian leaders are accountable to various actors as well. For example, they are accountable to whomever put them in power (possibly international actors), and to those who have the capacity and power to remove them from power (often the military).[4] The comparative lack of accountability in authoritarian regimes is in sharp contrast to the role and importance of accountability in a democratic political system. In fact, the level of accountability in a country is often used by researchers to assess democratic quality and its long-term viability in a particular context.[5] Further illustrating the importance of accountability is the recent tendency by international organizations like the World Bank and International Monetary Fund (IMF) to tie economic aid with adoption of democratic principles of "good governance" such as transparency, this practice a result of multimillion-dollar corruption scandals that have plagued the African continent.

Ultimately, if democracy is accepted as the "rule of the people," then the ability of those same people to exert influence (by maintaining accountability) onto their leaders is of upmost importance. "Without accountability 'the rule of the people' is emptied of all meaning for it is through this process that citizens ensure that all those who make decision for the whole community are able to justify those decisions as being in the interests of the community."[6] In other words, if elected leaders are inaccessible to citizens through two-way communication, then accountability is lacking. Furthermore, if the voting population is faced with a situation whereby all candidates have a history of abusing power, then the strength of the democracy has to be seriously questioned. In fact, many democratic theorists claim that the solitary use of elections to ensure accountability is not enough.[7] Baker claims that:

> It is not clear how effective the threat of punishment in a future election is on current government policy in situations where a degree of continuity among party alternatives does not exist, party policies are not well defined and voting is highly volatile. In addition, where incumbents have been dreamed to abuse the electoral system to their own advantage, it has proved relatively easy to manipulate results despite observers and commissions.[8]

Another example detailing the faults of relying solely on elections arises when politicians are able to campaign on what is politically popular but then diverge from these campaign promises with the only sanction being the failure to be reelected after their term is over. In this case, the will of the people has been put off until the next election, and there is no guarantee that the next candidate will uphold his or her promises either. Thus accountability has to be an ongoing, everyday process whereby politicians are subject to questions of "answerability" and possible "enforcement" on a continuing basis.

ACCOUNTABILITY AND IMPUNITY IN KENYA

Kenya is a glaring example of the need for improved accountability, as the political history of the country has been plagued by "bad governance, divisive ethnic based politics, tribal clashes, massacres, gross violations of human rights, gender violence, dehumanizing poverty, high-level corruption, economic stagnation, and impunity."[9] Following a failed coup in 1982, President Daniel arap Moi consolidated his power over the three branches of government through a series of laws that allowed him to dominate the political system. The Constitution was amended the same year establishing KANU, Moi's party, as the only legal party in the country. Furthermore, dissent was severely repressed through arrest, detention, torture, and killings, which resulted in a culture of silence and fear, plaguing society.[10] Repression was not limited to citizens, as media sources were censored and several publications that were critical of the regime were simply outlawed or their editors intimidated into compliance. Human rights abuses during this period are alleged to have been significant and were not helped by the fact that Moi possessed the ability to dismiss judges at will via a constitutional amendment. This situation persisted until international and domestic pressures forced Moi to repeal Section 2A of the constitution, which had declared Kenya to be a one-party state. As a result of this repeal, the first multiparty election in the country was held in 1992. That being said, Moi did not initially agree to this change himself, as he repeatedly argued that multiparty elections would result in chaos. That is, he went along with it only after international donors had suspended financial aid to the country.[11]

Following Moi's reluctant acceptance of multiparty elections, the transition from a one-party authoritarian regime to a democracy began, thus triggering an increased demand for accountability from political actors. Moi was able to win the 1992 and 1997 elections despite widespread irregularities, which undermined the idea of a free and fair process.[12] Specifically, he enjoyed the ability to choose the members of the Electoral Commission of Kenya (ECK), and political boundaries were gerrymandered to the benefit of KANU. Furthermore, nearly 4 million youth, an opposition support group who had recently become eligible to vote, were denied registration and marginalized.[13] Moi was also quick to intimidate and silence media members who were critical of his regime, and he was able to use the state-owned Kenya Broadcasting Company to highlight his party and disregard competitors. Finally, outright fraud was alleged, as voter turnouts exceeded 100 percent in some regions, and Moi even extended the voting period by one day, providing more time to ensure victory. Clearly these fraudulent elections do not speak well of the level of democracy or accountability in the country in the 1990s (without even mentioning the widespread corruption). Moi was essentially able to do whatever he had to do to win the election. Although Kenya was now no longer an authoritarian state, Moi still enjoyed a monopoly on power because he was able to silence critics and avoid questions of answerability. Furthermore, the lack of any consequences (enforceability) for his actions and his ability to manipulate the process gives credence to Baker's argument that elections on their own are not enough to ensure accountability. In many ways, "the government neither made nor allowed any steps in the pursuit of democratization, other than holding by-elections as required."[14]

Ultimately, fast-forwarding toward the present day (with different political actors) does not provide results that are very different. In 2002 Mwai Kibaki ran an anticorruption campaign and won; that election process went relatively well in comparison to previous examples. However, not long after Kibaki took office, allegations of widespread corruption involving high-ranking members of government began to leak out. John Githongo, a journalist appointed to an anticorruption position in the government, uncovered what came to be known as the Anglo-leasing scandal, in which hundreds of millions of dollars were embezzled through a contract given to a fake company. Citing a lack of commitment to fight corruption by the government and threats to his life, Githongo was forced to flee to the United Kingdom. This development is both encouraging and troubling from an accountability standpoint. On the one hand, the fact that Githongo's position in government even exists illustrates a commitment to at least appearing to adhere to principles of accountability and transparency. Furthermore, the fact that he refused to be bought off or silenced indicates there are individuals who are willing to take a stand against entrenched politicians. That being said, nothing has become of Githongo's allegations, as those implicated have not faced any consequences. Additionally, that Githongo received death threats points to the fact that politicians are committed to maintaining the status quo by any means necessary. Baker argues that "the greater the neglect of public political aims, incompetence, corruption, and weakness, the more reason there is to evade accountability. There is widespread reluctance to conduct their business in the open."[15] This statement sticks like glue to Kenyan political actors, as there is a long and rich history of corruption scandals across multiple regimes and a vested interest in remaining in the good graces of the international governments and organizations that provide the country with so much economic support. Politicians understand that every time a corruption scandal is disclosed, international investors become uneasy about exactly where their money is going and often threaten to suspend aid. Furthermore, these international investors demand that measures be taken to ensure economic transparency in order to pacify their own shareholders.

The country's most recent presidential election in 2007 was arguably a step backward on the accountability spectrum, as highly contested elections took a turn for the worse following relative peace on Election Day. After the ECK delayed the election results (amid widespread allegations of vote rigging), a sense of frustration and desire for victory in a winner-take-all system boiled over and widespread violence erupted across the country. Furthermore, there were allegations that much of the violence was politically orchestrated by members of the government. The chaos resulted in the deaths of over 1,000 people, and over 500,000 were internally displaced. The violence only ended when the two main candidates, Kibaki and Raila Odinga, agreed to form a power-sharing coalition in an agreement mediated by Kofi Annan of the United Nations. However, Jacqueline Klopp argues that creation of this power-sharing government ensured impunity, "since both parties include people guilty of corruption and violence, the grand coalition creates a common interest in perpetuating impunity and opposing the forces of accountability and transformation."[16] Ultimately the Commission of Inquiry into Post-Election Violence, also known as the Waki Commission, was formed and recommended the creation of a special tribunal in Kenya to prosecute those individuals who were responsible for orchestrating ethnic clashes. However, in actions that are all too familiar in Kenya, politicians repeatedly haggled over and delayed the process until the deadline to create such tribunal had passed.

As a result, Annan handed over a fateful envelope filled with the names of those responsible for inciting the violence to the International Criminal Court (ICC). Politicians have clearly demonstrated their desire to repress the push for accountability based on their refusal to enact legislation that would indict those responsible. In fact, some individuals who initially supported the idea of relying on the ICC for prosecution have flip-flopped, hoping to create a local tribunal that could be manipulated to achieve the desired results—in other words, continued impunity.[17] Some politicians have even argued that enforcement of accountability in the form of indictments and criminal trials would create a renewed threat of violence that could plunge the country into a civil war.[18] This argument sounds similar to the one used by Moi, that adoption of multiparty politics would lead to chaos, and it is evident that politicians are keen to use the fear card as a way of controlling the population when they dare to challenge the status quo. Furthermore, politicians argue that handing the case over to the ICC would create the illusion that Kenya was a failed state, which would have drastic consequences for the country's attempts to attract foreign investors and tourists.[19] This argument is interesting as Kenya is not even comparable to the neighboring failed state of Somalia in terms of lacking a functioning government that can enact legislation, mobilize a military, and provide border security. However, from the accountability perspective, there is some merit to the classification of Kenya as a failed state.

For example, this same scenario occurred in the 1990s, when Kenya had two other commissions of inquiry that named cabinet ministers as being responsible for inciting ethnic violence. However, the recommendations of the reports "were never fully implemented, and those responsible were not held accountable."[20] Time and time again politicians have proven that are not willing to adhere to the democratic principles of transparency, judicial independence, and acceptance of the rule of law. Politicians have continued to act as if they were above the law, and they ensure impunity by manipulating the system. Ultimately Kenyan politicians enjoy living in an environment that lacks accountability as corruption scandals, political violence, and a lack of meaningful constitutional reform do not lead to any significant consequences for anyone. Politicians have essentially been able to engage in politics as usual, relying on the use of political patronage and divisive ethnic tribalism to make sure that the voting population will be busy fighting each other over access to valuable resources rather than unifying to demand accountability from their leaders.

THE MEDIA AND ACCOUNTABILITY

Now that we have analyzed accountability as a concept and addressed its history in Kenya, it will helpful to examine an arena in which the struggle for increased accountability manifests itself. Undoubtedly the media are among the most important actors in the push for accountability. However, it is important to distinguish between the state-owned media and a free and independent press. State-owned media in an authoritarian regime often perform the function of cheerleaders and provide a forum for distribution of propaganda for the ruling regime. Furthermore, neutrality on the part of the state-owned media is not enough, as they are encouraged to attack and refute those who criticize the government. This practice is obviously a result of the fact that the government, as the owner of the organization, possesses the ability to hire and fire journalists and is the main means of the media's economic support. On the other hand, independent and free media sources perform the role of watchdog over governmental actors as they report on instances of abuse of power such as corruption. Some have even taken to comparing the press to a housefly, based on its habit of showing up when things start stinking.[21] Ultimately, an independent media is an ally of citizens in a democracy, as it asks critical questions of politicians on behalf of the entire community, demanding that politicians provide information on recent developments and accompanying justifications for their actions.

In discussing the role of the media in a democracy, Tettey argues as follows:

> Democracy is based on the notion of popular sovereignty. This requires that citizens be well informed if they are to participate in the political process and effectively play their role as the ultimate decision makers. A free and diverse press allows them to perceive a variegated view of issues on the basis of which they can make informed political decisions.[22]

Furthermore, the media provide a marketplace for ideas where different views and claims can be made that are then subjected to contestation, which increases the chance for the truth to emerge and to shape politics.[23] The media educate the population about ongoing political developments, provide a forum for civic engagement, and work to promote accountability by demanding answers from political actors. That being said, the media are engaged in a form of vertical accountability that lacks power of enforcement on those determined to abuse their power. The media can only voice public disapproval and are thus reliant on actors such as the judiciary (an equal to the executive) to sanction wrongdoing.

In the 1980s, all but nine of Africa's ninety daily newspapers were controlled by state governments, and the electronic media were fully in their control.[24] However, the independent media saw substantial growth, corresponding to the widespread transition toward democracy across Africa, and in turn helped to further accelerate the adoption of democratic principles by promoting accountability. Conversely, as mentioned earlier, independent media sources in Kenya were often the victim of widespread repression under the Moi regime, as journalists who were critical of government policies were arrested and often charged with sedition. Additionally, some publications were outright banned. Countless journalists were silenced through indictments that took them to court under the guise of protecting state security thus undermining existing laws that guaranteed freedom of expression.[25]

Journalists in Kenya who were lucky enough to have their cases heard in court (the alternative being violent intimidation) were faced with a judiciary that continually ruled in favor of the executive branch. The seemingly limitless authority enjoyed by African leaders allowed governments to influence press policy by withdrawing vital government advertising revenue from publications that dared to expose the misdeeds of politicians.[26] Moreover, private businesses were made to understand that advertising in a newspaper that was critical of government policy was sure to bring unwanted results when these same businesses applied for necessary licenses and contracts (which, of course, were controlled by the state). In one case, the government was even able to prevent a newspaper from ever being printed, as it had strong influence over the media organization's printing company.[27]

Despite their beneficial role as a watchdog for political accountability, there have been situations where the actions of members of the media have been counterproductive. Some of the new "alternative" media that appeared following the transition to democracy did not uphold high levels of professionalism, as journalists printed stories that lacked factual evidence or constituted essentially personal attacks that had nothing to do with important issues. Furthermore, there have been instances where journalists have attempted to extort payoffs from politicians by threatening to print damaging stories unless a bribe was paid. These actions diminish the integrity of all media organizations and give credence to the government's argument that the press is involved in personal vendettas against the state. Finally, some of the organizations further divide the populace by appealing to ethnic interests, which does not promote a unified population committed to demanding accountability. Another issue with the media is the fact that much of the population cannot afford a radio or television. Even the cost of a single magazine exceeds the daily wages of urban workers and is definitely out of reach for significant sections of the rural population.[28] Not surprisingly, the productions of most print and electronic media are consumed by the urban elite. Furthermore, those members of the population who are illiterate are marginalized, and unequal access to media sources hinders the idea of an informed electorate that can hold politicians accountable.

INDEPENDENCE OF THE JUDICIARY

As witnessed by the refusal and inability of the judicial branch to uphold freedom of expression involving the media, there are issues involving the enforcement aspect of accountability in Kenya. The media have done a commendable job of promoting answerability, but true accountability is not realized where horizontal institutions such as the judiciary cannot impose sanction on wrongdoing. "If a police officer kills someone in custody without due cause and still walks free, it does not satisfy the principle of accountability if a journalist documents this abuse of authority. . . . Unless there is some punishment for demonstrated abuses of authority, there is no rule of law and no accountability."[29] In a 1996 report, the International Bar Association determined that the there does not seem to be a proper degree of independence between the judiciary and the main executive arm in Kenya.[30] The ability of Moi to manipulate the judiciary in the past ensured that impunity would remain constant. As a result of the power enjoyed by the executive branch, cases were brought before "politically correct judges" who, because of their desire to protect their jobs and secure state favors, were willing to do everything possible to rule in favor of the presidency.[31]

Furthermore, those judges who placed judicial integrity above the interests of the state were punished, as evidenced in 1994 by the transfer of a chief magistrate to a post 130 kilometers away from Nairobi after he had demanded an investigation into a suspect's claims of police torture.[32] Baker argues that the courts should ensure that the executive, public officials, and powerful private institutions and individuals are subjected to the law and the constitution, and that these entities must have the pability to guarantee impartial justice.[33] This can be accomplished if the judiciary is elected or appointed independently so that it can act without executive interference. In the end, political actors must be forced to be accountable to both the people and the rule of law. In order for horizontal accountability to be realized, judges cannot defer to the state and leading politicians in matters that interest them.

INVOLVEMENT OF INTERNATIONAL ACTORS IN DOMESTIC POLITICS

International actors have played an increasingly important role in Kenyan domestic politics. For example, organizations like the Catholic Church, NGOs, and other civil society groups have increasingly demanded that the state fulfill its obligation to its citizens. Many of these organizations have fearlessly brought attention to human rights abuses and provide an important and powerful voice to the accountability concept of answerability. Furthermore, international organizations such as the World Bank and IMF, in cooperation with other national governments, provide a substantial amount of economic funding to the country. Therefore they have a vested interest in the politics of the country, and have often threatened to suspend aid upon discovery of corruption scandals or abuse of human rights. Owing to the government's dependency on this money, these international actors have a valuable bargaining chip on their side that they can use to influence policy.

However, some have argued that this relationship has made leaders in fact more accountable to external agencies than to their own electorate.[34] Stephen Brown argues that in Kenya, international donors actually discouraged measures that could have led to more comprehensive democratization during the 1992 and 1997 elections, which were plagued by instances of election fraud, as discussed earlier. Brown states:

> They did this by knowingly endorsing unfair elections and subverting domestic efforts to secure far-reaching reforms. In the face of anti-regime popular mobilization, donors' primary concern appeared to be the avoidance of any path that could lead to a breakdown of the political and economic order, even if this meant legitimizing and prolonging the regime's authoritarian rule.[35]

Brown argues that donors had spent $2.1 million on the 1992 elections and were determined to see them take place (even under unfair conditions), feeling that their procedural success outweighed the unfairness of the campaign.[36] He even goes so far to claim that donors deliberately suppressed evidence highlighting the irregularities of the election, as an internal donor report named eight constituencies where the poll could not be considered valid (and thus the results of the entire election); but in the public release of this document, this information was deleted.

In rationalizing these actions, Brown states "in Kenya donors advocated a more democratic government hoping it would lead to better economic governance. Yet they also feared instability that might accompany the transition to democracy, which would undermine economic reform."[37] As a result of the donors' overemphasis of the process of elections (as discussed earlier), their interest in maintaining economic prosperity, and their refusal to condemn the widespread electoral fraud, the Moi regime was able to remain in power and delay further democratic reform. Obviously this was an instance where these international actors had an opportunity to demand accountability from Kenyan politicians. However, their refusal to do so set the stage for continued abuses of power and a lack of improved accountability.

Another important role that international organizations have played in developing democracies is as election observers or monitors. Organizations such as the United Nations, Organization of African Unity, and the Council of Freely Elected Heads of Government (which is coordinated by former U.S. President Jimmy Carter) have increasingly become more involved with democratic elections around the world. Many times these groups are invited to oversee elections to provide a sense of legitimacy to the process. In addition, the groups can mobilize vast resources and provide cutting-edge technology that can be utilized during the election process. Furthermore, if conflict arises between opposition parties, these organizations can play the role of mediators.

Robert Pastor identifies this phenomenon as a "third dimension of accountability" and argues that "the presence of a prestigious group can deter electoral fraud and give local people a sense that their election has a larger importance (possibly increasing voter turnout)."[38] He goes on to say that:

> The most difficult question for monitors to answer is whether the election has been free and fair. To answer that effectively, monitors need to evaluate the entire electoral process. Irregularities of some kind occur, and the problem is to try to determine a patter to the irregularities that could have biased the election in favor of a particular party or candidate.[39]

However, Pastor argues that many of these international organizations are hesitant to criticize elections and rarely declare an election a fraud. This is often because the country they are working in is a member of the same organization. Thus a conflict of interest arises.

It is interesting to compare the ongoing involvement of the ICC in the fallout of deadly ethnic clashes following the 2007 election with the previous two examples. In December 2010, the ICC released the name of six Kenyans that they planned to prosecute for crimes committed during the postelection chaos of 2007. Those indicted include high-ranking political allies to both President Kibaki and Prime Minister Odinga. The ICC, as an international policing organization, is not concerned with economic prosperity or offending the Kenyan state; instead, its only interest is in bringing those politicians who incited the ethnic violence to justice. The ICC seems to be imposing horizontal accountability upon Kenyan politicians who seem to be unwilling to do so themselves. The argument can be made that the judiciary in Kenya is not a horizontal actor but rather a vertical one that works for the state to repress dissent.

However, Kenyan politicians are unable to manipulate the ICC and could be facing one of the first instances where horizontal accountability will be ensured and enforcement enacted. Luis Moreno-Ocampo, the chief prosecutor of the ICC, has even claimed to "use Kenya as a world example on how to fight impunity," and he is viewed as a savior by victims of the violence.[40] This has resulted in a sense of optimism among the population, who believe "the momentum against impunity is now unstoppable and will be far reaching. It will not be confined to the post election violence. It will involve many players and catch up with a wide range of crimes and misdeeds, past and present. Impunity of every kind will come under siege."[41] Shortly after the announcement of the six suspects by the ICC, Kenyan members of parliament overwhelmingly voted for the country to leave the ICC and have pushed for yet another delay to the court proceedings in order to set up a local tribunal.[42] In their arguments in favor of leaving the ICC, Kenyan politicians painted the organization as a "colonial, anti-African court" and said that Kenya was surrendering its sovereignty.[43]

CONCLUSION

Ultimately the push for political accountability in Kenya is an ongoing process. The media have enjoyed significant growth and play a vital role in ensuring that the "answerability" aspect of accountability is addressed. Furthermore, the culture of silence and fear has passed, and citizens and civil society groups today are empowered and are willing to speak out against governmental impunity. However, the inability and reluctance of domestic courts to invoke any sort of "enforceability" upon powerful politicians is a clear example of why accountability is failing. Additionally, the tragic events that followed the 2007 elections, and the subsequent refusal to address the issue domestically, do not speak well to the acceptance of accountability principles by the country's political actors. The involvement of the ICC in domestic issues is a new development, and its ability to impose negative sanctions on those who have abused power would send a strong message to Kenyan politicians that the old way of doing things has serious consequences. However, if Kenya does indeed decide to leave the ICC, the importance of the judicial branch is magnified. If the domestic court system continues to be a pawn used by powerful politicians to ensure impunity, then the future of accountability in Kenya does not look promising.

In the end, the desire of Kenyan politicians to leave the ICC will not have any impact upon the six currently accused. Barring any unforeseen concessions by the ICC, the Moreno-Ocampo Six, as they have been called, will have their day in court, and it is certain that Kenyan politicians and citizens will be following the results of the trial closely. Ultimately "the degree of accountability in a country is the outcome of the conflict between pressure from the populace and resistance from the power holders."[44] Therefore the level of accountability in Kenya will continue to evolve and be an ongoing and highly contested issue as long as the population continues to demand increased transparency and better governance from its leaders.

NOTES

1. Andreas Schedler, Larry Diamond, and Mark F. Plattner, *The Self-Restraining State: Power and Accountability in New Democracies* (Boulder, CO: Lynne Rienner, 1999), 14.
2. Ibid.
3. Ibid.
4. Bruce Baker, "Who Should Be Called to Account for Good Governance in Africa?" *Democratization*, Vol. 7, No. 2 (2000): 186.
5. Schedler et al., *The Self-Restraining State: Power and Accountability in New Democracies* (Boulder, CO: Lynne Rienner, 1999), 2.
6. Baker, "Who Should Be Called to Account," 186–187.
7. Schedler et al., *The Self-Restraining State*, 2.
8. Baker, "Who Should Be Called to Account," 203–204.
9. Wangari Maathai, "Scrap Constituencies and Empower Local Authorities," *Daily Nation*, November 16, 2009.
10. Angelique Haugerud, *The Culture of Politics in Modern Kenya* (Cambridge, UK: Cambridge University Press, 1995).
11. Ibid.
12. Korwa G. Adar, "Assessing Democratization Trends in Kenya: A Post-Mortem of the Moi Regime," *Commonwealth and Comparative Politics*, Vol. 28, No. 3 (2000): 107.
13. Ibid., 104.
14. Stephen Brown, "Authoritarian Leaders and Multiparty Elections in Africa: How Foreign Donors Help to Keep Kenya's Daniel Arap Moi in Power," *Third World Quarterly*, Vol. 22, No. 5 (2001): 732.
15. Baker, "Who Should Be Called to Account," 206.
16. Jacqueline M. Klopp, "Kenya's Unfinished Agenda," *Journal of International Affairs*, Vol. 62, No. 2 (2009): 144.
17. Macharia Gaitho, "Big Two Fail to Give Nod to ICC's Forays." *Daily Nation*, November 6, 2009.
18. Ken Wafula, "Special Tribunal Only Way Out," *Daily Nation*, November 16, 2009.
19. Rasna Warah, "After the Events of 2008, We Can't Claim Sovereignty," *Daily Nation*, November 16, 2009.
20. Klopp, "Kenya's Unfinished Agenda," 150.
21. Wisdom J. Tettey, "The Media and Democratization in Africa: Contributions, Constraints and Concerns of the Private Press," *Media, Culture, and Society*, Vol. 23, No. 1 (2001): 10.
22. Ibid., 8.
23. Ibid.
24. Ibid., 9.
25. Adar, "Assessing Democratization Trends in Kenya," 119.
26. Tettey, "The Politics of Media Accountability in Africa," 239.
27. Ibid., 241.
28. Ibid., 25.
29. Schedler et al., *The Self-Restraining State*, 17.
30. Adar, "Assessing Democratization Trends in Kenya," 122.

31. Ibid., 108.
32. Ibid., 122.
33. Baker, "Who Should be Called to Account," 195.
34. Ibid., 199.
35. Brown, "Authoritarian Leaders and Multiparty Elections in Africa," 726.
36. Ibid., 732.
37. Ibid., 735.
38. Pastor, *The Self-Restraining State*, 131.
39. Ibid.
40. Emeka-Mayaka Gekara, "Horse-Loving Prosecutor Who Strikes Fear into Lords of Impunity," *Daily Nation*, November 6, 2009.
41. Robert Shaw, "At Last, the Diabolical Forces of Impunity Are in Retreat," *Daily Nation*, November 18, 2009.
42. BBC News, "Kenya MPs Vote to Leave ICC Over Poll Violence Claims," December 23, 2010.
43. Ibid.
44. Baker, "Who Should Be Called to Account," 206.

REFERENCES

Adar, Korwa G. "Assessing Democratization Trends in Kenya: A Post-Mortem of the Moi Regime." *Commonwealth and Comparative Politics* Vol. 28, No. 3 (2000): 103–130.

Baker, Bruce. "Who Should Be Called to Account for Good Governance in Africa?" *Democratization* Vol. 7, No. 2 (2000): 186–210.

Brown, Stephen. "Authoritarian Leaders and Multiparty Elections in Africa: How Foreign Donors Help to Keep Kenya's Daniel Arap Moi in Power." *Third World Quarterly* Vol. 22, No. 5 (2001): 725–739.

Gaitho, Macharia. "Big Two Fail to Give Nod to ICC's Forays." *Daily Nation*, November 6, 2009, http://www.nation.co.ke/blogs/-/446672/683960/-/istl96z/-/index.html.

Gekara, Emeka-Mayaka. "Horse-Loving Prosecutor Who Strikes Fear into Lords of Impunity." *Daily Nation*, November 6, 2009, http://www.nation.co.ke/News/politics/-/1064/682642/-/xt4vp5z/-/index.html.

Haugerud, Angelique. *The Culture of Politics in Modern Kenya*. Cambridge, UK: Cambridge University Press, 1995.

"Kenya MPs Vote to Leave ICC Over Poll Violence Claims." *BBC News*, December 23, 2010, http://www.bbc.co.uk/news/world-africa-12066667.

"Kenya Police Ran 'Death Squads.'" *BBC News*, February 25, 2009, http://news.bbc.co.uk/2/hi/africa/7909523.stm.

Klopp, Jacqueline M. "Kenya's Unfinished Agenda." *Journal of International Affairs* Vol. 62, No. 2 (2009): 143–158.

Maathai, Wangari. "Scrap Constituencies and Empower Local Authorities" *Daily Nation*, November 15, 2009, http://www.nation.co.ke/oped/Opinion/-/440808/686662/-/4pnr5g/-/index.html.

Pastor, Robert. "The Third Dimension of Accountability: The International Community in National Elections." In Andreas Schedler, Larry Diamond and Mark F. Plattner, eds. *The Self-Restraining State: Power and Accountability in New Democracies*. Boulder, CO: Lynne Rienner, 1999.

Schedler, Andreas. "Conceptualizing Accountability." In Andreas Schedler, Larry Diamond, and Mark F. Plattner, eds. *The Self-Restraining State: Power and Accountability in New Democracies*. Boulder, CO: Lynne Rienner, 1999.

Schedler, Andreas, Larry Diamond, and Mark F. Plattner. "Introduction." In *The Self-Restraining State: Power and Accountability in New Democracies*. Boulder, CO: Lynne Rienner, 1999.

Shaw, Robert. "At Last, the Diabolical Forces of Impunity Are in Retreat." *Daily Nation*, November 17, 2009, http://www.nation.co.ke/oped/Opinion/-/440808/687226/-/4pod8d/-/index.html.

Tettey, Wisdom J. "The Media and Democratization in Africa: Contributions, Constraints and Concerns of the Private Press." *Media, Culture, and Society* Vol. 23, No. 1 (2001): 5–31.

———. "The Politics of Media Accountability in Africa." *The International Communication Gazette*, Vol. 68, No. 3 (2006): 229–248.

Wafula, Ken. "Special Tribunal Only Way Out." *Daily Nation*, November 16, 2009, http://www.nation.co.ke/oped/Opinion/-/440808/686660/-/4pnr5e/-/index.html.

Warah, Rasna. "After the Events of 2008, We Can't Claim Sovereignty." *Daily Nation*, November 15, 2009, http://www.nation.co.ke/oped/Opinion/-/440808/686656/-/4pnr4o/-/index.html.

Part II
Africa in the New Global Economy

5 Toward a Contextualized Appraisal of Securities Regulation in East Africa

June McLaughlin

> "History is thus neither empirical nor imaginative but rather a continual dialectical confrontation of insight with evidence, of intuition and empirical induction, of past and present, of mutually challenging awareness of the self and of the world."[1]

The establishment of a national stock exchange is embedded with ideological dimensions. A stock exchange is a symbol of economic success for a nation—a sign that it has entered the global economic arena. Additionally and more problematically, stock exchanges are artifacts of market-based economies. The free-market economic thinking behind the proponents of stock exchanges is neoclassical theory, which makes unrealistic assumptions about decision making devoid of any cultural context.[2] They have also been described as vestiges of neocolonialism.[3] Therefore, if western economic hegemony is perpetuated by the reproduction of western institutions in former colonies to the detriment of domestic interests, then stock exchanges are the prime examples of such reproduction.

This chapter provides a preliminary examination of the context of western hegemony in the case of East Africa and securities regulation. It examines in an introductory way some of the larger issues that arise when considering securities regulation in East Africa, specifically the historical role of development institutions in the creation of exchanges along with dominant economic policies. Additionally, it addresses some of the common concerns that arise when discussing exchanges in Africa such as exchange integration. The chapter considers each stock exchange in the East African Community individually: the Nairobi Stock Exchange, the Uganda Securities Exchange, the Dar es Salaam Exchange, and the Rwanda Over-the-Counter Exchange. It then explores the various important disciplines that have produced scholarship on stock exchanges. While a comprehensive analysis is beyond the scope of this chapter, each separate discipline provides insight in to how stock exchanges developed in Africa in general and East Africa in particular as well as how they are regulated. Finally, the conclusion attempts to conflate these perspectives in order to provide a better understanding of regulation of stock exchanges by understanding the interdisciplinary context in which they operate.

STOCK EXCHANGES

Determining what a stock exchange is can be complex.[4] This chapter defines a stock exchange as an organization for raising capital. Specifically, companies want to expand their operations and need money to do so. That money can be obtained by selling shares to investors, which can be individuals or other corporations. The money raised is then used by the company issuing shares for product development or physical plant expansion. The efforts to grow by the company can make it more profitable, increasing the value of company shares and allowing it to pay dividends to shareholders.[5]

In most of the world, exchanges are themselves public corporations that trade in the secondary market. In East Africa, exchanges have not demutualised and exchanges function as quasi-governmental organs.[6] What follows is a description of the three established stock exchanges in East Africa: the Nairobi Stock Exchange, the Uganda Securities Exchange, and the Dar es Salaam Stock Exchange in Tanzania, as well as the development of Rwanda's Over-the Counter-Exchange. Also reviewed are the regulations and regulatory bodies that govern these securities markets.

NAIROBI STOCK EXCHANGE

Stock trading in Kenya began in the 1920s under the Nairobi Stock Exchange (NSE). In 1954, the NSE reorganized under the Societies Act as a voluntary association of stockbrokers. During this time, the NSE was recognized by the London Stock Exchange (LSE) as an overseas stock exchange assisting it to gain credibility and values. The self-regulatory framework at that time borrowed from the LSE, with a committee of five people established to manage and govern the NSE. In 1963, and immediately after independence from Britain, the government adopted a Kenyanisation policy. This policy had the primary goal of transferring all economic and social control to citizens of Kenya.

For a short period of time, the NSE did function as a regional market listing companies from Tanzania and Uganda. The then East African Community collapsed in 1975; currently the NSE has fewer listed companies than it had at independence in the 1963. In 1991, the NSE was registered under the Companies Act as a limited company. With the implementation of the Central Depositories Act, the NSE in 2006 developed an automated trading system (ATS). The system matches buy and sell orders of member firms of the NSE, facilitating the ease of trading and displaying the market in real time. Foreign investors have been attracted to the NSE because of the ATS. Additionally, the system provides the capability of producing a complete audit trail of transactions.

Capital Markets Authority Act

The Capital Markets Authority (CMA) Act created the Capital Markets Authority Kenya,[7] now the primary securities regulatory authority.[8] A chief executive of the CMA Kenya is appointed by the president of Kenya upon the recommendation of the minister of finance.[9] Section 11 (1) of the CMA Act lists the objectives of the CMA Kenya as follows: to develop the capital markets; to facilitate a nationwide system of stock market and brokerage services; to create, maintain, and regulate a securities market where trading is orderly, fair, and efficient;[10] to ensure investor protection;[11] to operate an investor compensation fund;[12] and to implement the development of electronic commerce.[13] At its inception, the CMA Kenya was financed by the Government of Kenya as well as from donor support of the United States Agency for International Development Aid (USAID).[14] It currently is self-financing and is funded by fees paid to it from the NSE and licensed members.[15]

In 2004, the World Bank provided US$18 million in credit to help fund reform Kenya's financial and legal sectors.[16] During the project appraisal the World Bank determined that the enforcement of market rules, as well as the supervision of market participants, was weak in Kenya.[17] Part of the stated development outcomes and goals of the project was the development of legal institutions for a market economy.[18] A 2008 World Bank *Report on the Status of the Projects in Execution*[19] stated that the project was making progress, including the development of an electronic central depository system for the NSE in 2005.[20] This CMA Act of 2000 expanded the CMA Kenya's power to make rules that were previously the purview of the Ministry of Finance.[21] Part II, section 12(1)–(3), provides that the authority has the power to formulate rules, guidelines, and regulations as required for the purpose of carrying out its objective to regulate, all with the consultation of the minister.[22]

UGANDA SECURITIES EXCHANGE

The predecessor to the Uganda Securities Exchange, the Kampala Stock Exchange, was organized in 1962.[23] Trading was very informal and there was no statutory framework. The government controlled the exchange with the participation of the Uganda Development Corporation (UDC).[24] The Uganda Securities Exchange (USE) was established in 1997.[25] It conducts trading manually through the traditional call out system.[26] However, there is some indication that it will begin electronic trading very soon.[27] There are currently twelve companies traded on the USE.[28] The securities exchange is regulated by the Capital Markets Authority (CMA) Uganda. CMA Uganda is created by the Capital Markets Authority Act, Chapter 84 of the laws of Uganda.[29]

The CMA Uganda is responsible for promoting, developing and regualting the Uganda capital markets.[30] This act establishes the Uganda Securities Exchange and governs participants in the markets by, for example, issuing licenses for share dealers,[31] and giving the CMA authority to approve stock exchange rule amendments.[32] Both the CMA Uganda and the USE are in close contact with the International Organization of Securities Commissions (IOSCO). The CMA became a member in 2000 and both organizations strive to achieve the regulatory goals and objectives of IOSCO. In order to achieve these goals, the CMA Uganda is authorised under the CMA Act with specific powers, duties, and functions.[33] These include registering and licenseing those involved in the capital markets,[34] providing guiding principles for the securities industry,[35] and protecting against insider trading.[36] The CMA Uganda's Legal and Compliance Department[37] also focuses on investor protection.

CMA Uganda

The CMA Uganda is governed by a board of twelve members—six from the public sector and six from the private sector.[38] It is run day to day by its management team, which consults with the board regularly.[39] The board's Legal and Compliance Committee meets quarterly.[40] The committee oversees development of the capital market legal and regulatory framework. It also approves applications for licenses and public issuance of securities, as well as considering enforcement actions. In 2009, the committee promulgated regulations regarding the Securities Central Depositories Act 2009.[41] The CMA Uganda is autonomous and charged through the Capital Markets Act with the regulation and development of the capital markets industry in Uganda.[42] Market participants are intended to be self-regulatory under the CMA Uganda and the securities market orderly, fair, and efficient.[43] Additionally, the CMA Uganda is responsible for the removal of impediments to long-term investment.[44]

Central Depositories Act

Recent developments for this national system have included the passage of the Securities Central Depositories (SCD) Act of 2009.[45] This act facilitates electronic trading on the exchange when such trading begins.[46] The upgrade to electronic trading from manual trading is progress for the USE. Electronic trading will make cooperation with other exchanges easier for things such as cross-listing and eventual integration. Additionally, funding from the government will be used to acquire a surveillance system for the SCD.[47] For the first six months of the SCD, paper shares will be immobilized or kept on deposit with the exchange.[48] After a year, paper shares will no longer be necessary as the SCD moves to dematerialization.[49] Investors will be required to open an account with a Securities Central Depository

Agent (SCDA) during the first year until the transition to the SCD is complete. The ultimate goal of an SCD is to allow the exchange to transition to automated trading. During the first year of the SCD, the USE will remain manual with an open outcry system.[50]

DAR ES SALAAM STOCK EXCHANGE

The Dar es Salaam Stock Exchange Limited (DSE) was incorporated in 1996 under the Companies Act 2002 (Cap. 212) and opened for trading in 1998. Currently, the DSE has ten listed companies[51] and recently celebrated its ten-year anniversary.[52] One of the first exchanges to automate, the DSE has electronic trading and a central depository system. It is a self-regulatory organization (SRO). There are regulations and rules promulgated by the DSE; these are contained in a book popularly known as *The Blueprint*.[53]

In Tanzania, the Capital Markets and Securities Authority (CMSA) is a government agency that regulates the securities business in Tanzania.[54] The Capital Markets Securities Act established the CMSA in 1994,[55] before the stock exchange. The CMSA was established along with a number of other economic liberalization reforms that took place in the early 1990s in Tanzania[56] The Commonwealth Secretariat[57] as well as the International Finance Corporation (IFC) provided technical assistance in drafting the CMSA Act, which was extensively amended, leading to the speculation that its passage was expedited to comply with reform benchmarks.[58] The purpose of the CMSA is to regulate and monitor the securities industry to ensure that it is fair and efficient. The CMSA is charged with advising the minister on matters relating to the securities industry, creating the necessary environment for the growth of the capital markets and protect the markets against the abuse of insider trading among other duties.[59] The CMSA can approve stock exchanges and their rules.[60] The CMSA, as an administrative agency, is subject to judicial review.[61] Additionally, the power to issue regulations under the CMSA Act is reserved for the minister of finance.[62]

RWANDA STOCK EXCHANGE

In 2008, the Capital Markets Advisory Council (CMAC) Rwanda signed the East Africa Securities Regulatory Authority (EASRA), becoming the fourth member.[63] The Rwanda Stock Exchange was established in 2005.[64] The Rwanda Over- the-Counter Market (ROTCM) was established in January 2008 by the CMAC of Rwanda.[65] Over-the-counter trading involves direct trades between buyers and sellers without the involvement of a securities exchange—companies need not be listed on the exchange in order for their shares to be traded, and the exchange need not publish share prices. As the CMAC explains:

The Rwanda OTC market operates a dual trading process. Firstly members trade securities directly with investors and among themselves. Secondly, open outcry trading sessions are conducted at the trading floor of the OTC market at the CMAC Secretariat every day from 9:00 a.m. to 12:00 p.m. At the open outcry trading floor, members' representatives get together and trade between each other.[66]

The very basic level of the market for and regulation of such trading is illustrated by the fact that the CMAC issued a brochure to educate the public about the exchange, including details of the seven steps required to sell/buy shares.[67] That document, along with a slim handbook, represented the sum total of the rules covering trades on the market. In May 2008, it was reported that that the CMAC was still in search of a consultant to establish a legal and regulatory framework for the market.

COMPARISON

The four functioning exchanges in East Africa are very similar in almost all manner of comparison. This is intentional. The exchanges of Tanzania and Uganda developed their capital markets in the late 1990s. Much of this was accomplished through the funding of the International Monetary Fund (IFM) and World Bank programs. Many of these projects funded by those actors required certain legislation to be in place before monies were disbursed. As previously mentioned, for Tanzania, the Capital Markets Regulator was established with a barebones Capital Markets Act years before a stock exchange was developed. In contrast, Kenya had an older exchange that transitioned after independence and eventually took on the same regulations as Uganda and Tanzania. However, the NSE in Kenya has historically functioned much more independently from the government than other East African exchanges.[68] It was self-sustaining and self-regulating for many years.[69] This is partly due to a wealthy resident European community that permanently resided there. This is in contrast to Uganda, whose business community was dominated by Asians prior to 1972, when they were forced to flee under the government of Idi Amin.[70] Assets were expropriated and businesses were put under UDC and government ministries to manage. While this was going, on Rwanda and Burundi were suffering political and civil unrest so no capital markets development occurred during the same time period.

As all of these countries are members of the East African Common Market, as signatories to the East African Community Treaty, there has always been the intention that a regional exchange would make sense. Therefore Kenya, Uganda, Tanzania, and now Rwanda strive to make their regulations more similar and uniform with one another with the intention of one day combining to form a regional East African Exchange. This is the guiding principle in the adoption of central depositories and automated trading systems. Certainly those things do aid in facilitating trading, but for exchanges that are thinly traded and illiquid with few listed companies automation is not paramount. It will, however, facilitate the eventuality of a regional exchange where shares can trade seamlessly across borders in a common market.

INTEGRATION

Regional integration is consistently recommended for economic reasons throughout Africa to support economies of scale.[71] Individually, small markets have a harder time achieving the liquidity necessary for profitability. There are plans to harmonize securities regulations across the East African Community and several smaller markets combined can achieve the liquidity needed faster. Kenya, Uganda, and Tanzania are currently working toward linking their stock exchanges.[72] When Burundi eventually establishes a capital market, it will be able to simply adopt the harmonized rules rather than drafting its own. Furthermore, the East African Securities Exchange Association (EASEA) has been instrumental in driving an effort to allow companies and investors from any nation to participate on any exchange.[73] Cooperation between the nations that make up the EAC has its own tensions. Historically, Kenya has been economically dominant in the region and the capital flow has been in its favor.[74] Uganda and Tanzania have through time been more interested in preserving national autonomy over continued integration. Nevertheless, integration is on the schedule.

DEVELOPMENT

Development policies permeate much of the discussion of African stock exchanges. Development is actually the industry that grew from the concept of foreign aid,[75] promoted through the policies of the World Bank, created after World War II.[76] The World Bank's purpose is to provide technical and financial assistance to developing countries.[77] It provides financial assistance through loans offered by the International Finance Corporation.[78] Eventually an entire industry grew around development. Government agencies of various nations were formed and became active in developing regions of the world such as the United States Agency for International Development[79] (USAID), the Swedish International Development Cooperation Agency[80] (SIDA), and the United Kingdom's Department for International Development[81] (DFID). Along with the development of the World Bank, after World War II the International Monetary Fund (IMF) was established.[82] The IMF's focus is international monetary cooperation, exchange rate stability, and international trade.[83]

One orthodox belief of development policies is that a stock exchange is necessary for economic advancement.[84] At the end of the 1970s, the World Bank and the IMF began to shift their focus from project lending to program lending.[85] A stabilization program would be agreed upon with the government and the International Finance Institutions (IFI) such as the IMF. Then the IMF would design and help implement it. The programs were focused on particular sectors, and loans meant to be short-term instruments became conditional upon changes made in those sectors by debtor nations.[86] At the same time, the IMF began its push for structural adjustment programs (SAPS) focusing on structural changes in nations such as trade liberalization and the privatization of state-owned companies. Privatization involved the establishment of stock exchanges where those newly privatized companies would issue shares and operate on funds received from investors rather than be wholly government owned. The IMF and World Bank policies overlapped. The World Bank policies focused on the freedom of markets as well.

Divestment of state-owned enterprises was included in the push for structural reforms to governance and the banking sector. This is based on the premise that private ownership of assets is superior to public ownership.[87] The real political consequence of this economic argument, however, is that debtor nation's governmental policies were heavily influenced by the IFIs rather than from the polity.[88] Regulations were selected for noneconomic reasons and selected for political reasons external to the nation involved. Not every nation capitulated to the demands of the international development industry.

Tanzania, for instance, resisted stabilization and structural adjustment. From independence in 1960 until 1985 it faced rising oil prices, growing inflation, and a devaluation of its currency.[89] Eventually, after savings and investment sharply declined, Tanzania entered into both stabilization and structural adjustment in 1985. Since then productivity in the country increased but external debt had to be serviced and reduced many times.[90] Many countries in East Africa never again saw levels of growth comparable to the decades between independence and the late 1980s. This could be attributed to a general deterioration in world markets due to the oil crisis.[91] The failure of states, as claimed by the IFIs, would not have been a valid reason for new programs to be imposed on developing countries if there were other economic explanations. Some positive economic changes did occur—trade liberalization, for example—but even the description of anything positive coming from these activities is debatable.[92] Undoubtedly the existence of stock exchanges in East Africa is due to requirements of the IFIs.

Exchanges, as discussed earlier, were created in order to achieve the economic policies that were promoted during the IFIs, such as the privatization of state-owned companies.[93] This was without regard for the general lack of banking or legal infrastructure to support the exchanges.[94] Indeed, some researchers claim that these programs or structural adjustment were not motivated at all by the economics of the developing nation but entirely by the politics and economic struggles of western corporations and banks.[95] Stock exchanges must be regulated in order to promote investor confidence and simply keep individuals and companies from cheating one another. In the United States, the Securities and Exchange Commission[96]—the U.S. governmental agency tasked with overseeing markets—spends a majority of its time regulating markets in order to build investor and global confidence and frequently failing.[97] Indeed, the SEC holds itself out as the world's preeminent market regulator. Criticism of developing market exchanges for "corruption" can seem humorous in light of the Madoff Ponzi scheme, which went undetected by the SEC.[98]

Having now provided some context for the establishment of exchanges in East Africa, creating a pinpoint on our map, we consider now regulation of those exchanges. Exchanges are institutions that, once created, must be managed by an agency or board that has the power to enforce regulations that prescribe activities on the exchange. Investors will not buy shares without confidence in the safety of that investment to provide a return and trade in an orderly manner on the exchange. Very much like any financial institution exchanges are regulated. When the IFIs asked for stock exchanges as a condition of loans they also suggested regulations, implanting model laws from other jurisdictions. Laws that regulate financial markets are discreet and specific laws. Research exists across disciplines—legal[99] and nonlegal[100]—much as research regarding exchanges as financial institutions cross disciplines. Our next pinpoint in the map is considering those regulations and their implantation in East Africa.

Choice of Regulation

According to prominent economic research, the legal origin of regulation can be predictive of the success of the capital markets.[101] This research, conducted by economists La Porta, Lopez de Silanes, Sheifler, and Vishny, commonly known as LLSV, considers the success of capital markets whose historical roots where either civil law, as in French colonies, or common law, as in British colonies. The research finds that common-law legal origins lead to more successful capital markets, meaning the choice of regulation system for a new exchange might be determinative of whether or not that exchange is profitable. The research finds that regulation originating from common-law jurisdictions provides superior investor protections, explaining why those exchanges are successful. The civil law does not provide those protections; hence securities regulation originating from civil law results in less successful exchanges.[102]

This is such a dominant view that it has influenced policy makers at development agencies.[103] Development agencies encourage developing nations to establish exchanges and dictate the kind of securities regulation that is to be adopted. An alternative view has been expressed. One researcher has stated an alternative view, that legal origin does not alone explain why some capital markets succeed and others struggle.[104] The law is important, but only in the context of history, economics, and politics. It is also possible that because common-law systems are dominant in the world capital markets, similar systems rise with the tide. International securities regulators are dominated by American regulators. It is not legal origin that is expressing itself but the current dominant regulatory scheme that assists its own. It is not the efficiency or excellence of regulation that supports common-law capital markets but rather the dominance of common-law markets that explains why legal origin is significant.

Considering all these matters within context might result in a different understanding of securities exchanges in East Africa.[105] Active securities markets are often vibrant because the polities in the given nation support them regardless of the legal origin of securities laws. Nations fighting communism after World War II were focused on their labor markets and not on building capital markets, which explains why those markets are underdeveloped.[106] Legal origins had little to do with why those markets were not active or vibrant. If legal origin is not as determinative of success as once thought and international development agencies still rely on the concept, those policies are flawed.[107] It is efficient for the IFIs to require legislation is implanted from somewhere else. Certainly most East African nations did not have a securities regulator or securities regulation before their exchanges were established. Also, there are international harmonies to consider. Securities regulation on the books that is recognized and understood allows for speedier membership into international organizations. It is a box that can be ticked in terms of development.

With that said, it is unclear whether laws on the books are of real interest beyond the theoretical. Where the important and relevant information is obtained is from oral data and an understanding of how these exchanges function and are regulated outside of the structures that IFIs impose.[108] This is similar to the securities industry in any nation where practice diverges from official policy. Transparency in the world's major financial systems improved considerably but not completely after the subprime crisis, which led to the subsequent recession. As we begin to understand how connected we are as a global financial community, we can begin to appreciate the variety of cultures that influence each individual nation. This is certainly a goal of comparative studies, but more is necessary.

CONCLUSION

Much of the literature on stock exchanges is from the perspective that markets are purely economic and self-interested institutions. If they are more than that, then how do those additional "things"—such as culture, power, and our understanding of institutions—affect the law that regulates those exchanges? This chapter cannot answer that question but only raise it and then provide some preliminary thoughts that might encourage further research. Sociologists define an institution as "an enduring set of ideas about how to accomplish goals generally recognized as important in society."[109] In terms of stock exchanges as institutions, some sociologists state that markets are dominated by elite or insiders' interests and simply reproduce the advantages of those interests over the long term.[110] Economists consider exchanges and markets as tools to create efficiency. Economic sociologists look for alternative explanations for markets including from a political-cultural perspective.[111] This perspective looks at markets not as profit maximizers but rather as organizations utilized to reduce uncertainty.

These are all alternatives for looking at the existence of exchanges, economic, political, and sociological. How exchanges develop historically informs how we think about them. Once they exist, we need to examine them within their context. As the quote at the beginning of this paper states, history is 'continual' dialectic.[112] There is a continued tension created by the simple existence of stock exchanges in Africa. Exchanges represent the archetype of Anglo-American capitalism and thus a potential tool for neo-colonialism. But they exist, function, and are developing in ways that both do and do not move beyond their beginnings. Developing exchanges still strive to become members of the global financial community that implicitly requires homogeneity. With the world economy currently besieged it is difficult to function without that membership. Things may change once the economy improves.

In conclusion, traditional legal studies awkwardly incorporate, if at all, historical, political, and cultural contexts. Optimistically, this chapter has mapped out a beginning for incorporating some of these. The challenge moving forward is to allow that dialectic and tension to be free and flexible rather than rooted. The challenge is to acknowledge the beginnings of theses exchanges, which may be negative, but also to understand that they have become more than that a decade or so on.

NOTES

1. Joseph Miller, "History and Africa/Africa and History," *The American Historical Review*, Vol. 104 (1999): 1–32.
2. Beinhocker, supra note 2 at 429. Neoclassical economics has dominated economic thinking, therefore development thinking, assuming a world of rational decision makers with the goal of maximizing self-interest.
3. Charles Pouncy, "Stock Markets in Sub-Saharan Africa: Western Legal Institutions as a Component of the Neo-Colonial Project," *University of Pennsylvania Journal of International Economic Law*, Vol. 23 (2002): 85.
4. Ruben Lee, *What Is an Exchange? The Automation, Management, and Regulation of Financial Markets* (Oxford, UK: Oxford University Press, 1998), 1.
5. The dividend paid is usually small such as US$0.25 for every share owned.
6. *Demutualization* describes the transformation of a stock exchange from a mutual association (member-owned) to a company with shareholders.

Samuel Onyuma, "Demutualization of Stock Exchanges in Africa: Prospects and Problems," *OSSREA Bulletin*, Vol. 3 (2006): 36, 37.
7. Capital Markets Authority Act (1990), Cap. 485A Kenyan [hereinafter CMA Act].
8. Ibid., §5(1) (establishing the CMA Kenya). The CMA Kenya replaced the Capital Issues Committee of the Ministry of Finance. See World Bank, Africa Regional Financial Sector Division, *Capital Market Integration in the East African Community*, December 2002, 34, note 28.
9. CMA Act, Part II §8(1).
10. Ibid., §11(1)(c).
11. Ibid., §11(1)(d).
12. Ibid., §11(1)(e).
13. Ibid., §11(1)(f). Electronic commerce refers to technology that links market participants and assists in order executions. Ibid., §11(2)(a–c).
14. Rose Ngugi, "Development of the Nairobi Stock Exchange: A Historical Perspective," *Kenya Institute for Public Policy Research and Analysis Discussion Paper*, Vol. 27 (2003): 27.
15. Ibid.
16. World Bank, "Financial and Legal Sector Technical Assistance Project": http://web.worldbank.org/external/projects/main?pagePK=104231&piPK=73230&theSitePK=40941&menuPK=228424&Projectid=P083250
17. Ibid., 2.
18. Ibid.
19. World Bank, *Status of Projects in Execution—FY08—Africa Region—Country: Kenya*, 10, http://www1.worldbank.org/operations/disclosure/SOPE/FY08/Country/SOPE_AFR_KEnya.pdf
20. Iwa Salami, *The Financial Crisis and a Regional Regulatory Perspective for Emerging Economies in Africa*, Vol. 25, No. 3, (2010).
21. Supra note xx at 34. (Capital Market Integration)
22. CMA Act, Part 11 § section 12(1)–(3).
23. Note, "Securities Marketing and Stock Exchanges in Black Africa," *Columbia Law Review*, Vol. 67, No. 5 (1967): 892, 909.
24. The UDC was formed by the British in 1952 and functioned as a quasi-governmental organization. OBOWONA infra.
25. Uganda Securities Exchange: History, http://www.use.or.ug/
26. See Uganda Securities Exchange, Listing Rules (2003) Part IV, "Methods and Procedures for listing securities on the exchange."
27. Tom Minney, "Uganda Goes Electronic Trading," *Africa News*, September 15,2009. http://www.africanews.com/site/Uganda_goes_electronic_trading/list_messages/26930
28. Uganda Securities Exchange: Listed Securities, http://www.use.or.ug
29. CMA Act c. 84, § 4–22.
30. Ibid., §5 (1–2).
31. Ibid., § 31.
32. Ibid., § 25(1).
33. Ibid., §5(2)(a–k).
34. Ibid., §5(2)(c). Individuals such as investment advisors, registrars, securities brokers, and dealers and their agents.
35. Ibid., §5(2)(d).
36. Ibid., §5(2)(f).
37. http://www.cmauganda.co.ug/ic.php?pID=34&p=Legal%20and%20compliance&menu=1
38. Capital Markets Authority (Uganda) Annual Report 2009, 8 [hereinafter CMA Annual Report]. The Board is appointed by the Minister of Finance, Planning and Economic Development and serves for 3 years.

39. Ibid.
40. CMA Annual Report, 13.
41. Ibid.
42. CMA Annual Report.
43. CMA Act, §5(1)(b).
44. Ibid., §5(1)(a).
45. Securities and Central Depository Act (2009) (Uganda): http://www.cmauganda.co.ug/ic.php?pID=106&p=Laws%20and%20regulations
46. Regulatory Notice No. 01/2009, Capital Markets Authority, Parliament Passes Law to Establish a Central Depository in Uganda (2009), http://www.cmauganda.co.ug/ic.php?pID=36&p=Legal%20notices
47. CMA Annual Report 2008, 2.
48. CMA Uganda,12(1), *Quarterly Review*, 5, (January-March 2010).
49. Ibid.
50. Ibid.
51. DSE Annual Report 2008. Tanzania Breweries Ltd., TOL Gases Ltd., Tanzania Tea Packers Ltd., Swissport Tanzania Ltd., Tanzania Cigarette Co., Tanga Cement Co. Ltd., Tanzania Portland Cement Co., Ltd., Kenya Airways Ltd., East African Breweries Ltd., Jubilee Holdings, Ltd.
52. Dar es Salaam Stock Exchange, "DSE 10th Anniversary," *DSE Journal*, 35 (2008).
53. Ibid., 17. These rules address membership and business conduct, listing, trading, clearing, settlement, and depository as well as foreign investors.
54. Capital Markets & Securities Authority, *About CSMA: Overview*, http://www.cmsa-tz.org/about/overview.htm
55. Capital Markets Securities Act, 1994, No. 5, Part II, (1994) (Tanzania): http://www.parliament.go.tz/polis/PAMS/Docs/5-1994.pdf
56. Hamisi Kibola, "The Regulation of Capital Markets in Tanzania; Is there Room for Improvement?" *DSE Journal*, 35 (2008). Other reforms include divestiture of public enterprises, trade liberalizations, relaxation of exchange controls, and deregulation of interest rates.
57. A voluntary organization of fifty-four nations working toward democracy and development. Nineteen nations in Africa are members of the Commonwealth Secretariat: Botswana, Cameroon, the Gambia, Ghana, Kenya, Lesotho, Malawi, Mauritius, Mozambique, Namibia, Nigeria, Rwanda, Seychelles, Sierra Leone, South Africa, Swaziland, Uganda, United Republic of Tanzania, and Zambia. http://www.thecommonwealth.org/Internal/191086/191247/the_commonwealth/http://www.thecommonwealth.org/Internal/191086/191247/the_commonwealth/
58. Supra note 56 at 14.
59. CMSA Act, §10.
60. *Capital Market Integration in the East African Community*, World Bank 2002, Africa Region, Financial Sector Division, p 36.
61. Ibid., 16.
62. CMSA Act, §147.
63. CMA Uganda, Annual Report 2008, p. vii.
64. http://www.rse.rw/.
65. http://www.cmac.org.rw/downloads/CMAC%20brochure.doc
66. http://www.cmac.org.rw/
67. http://www.cmac.org.rw/profile.php#role
68. Supra note 23 at 906.
69. Ibid.
70. Marios B. Obwona, "Determinants of FDI and Their Impact on Economic Growth in Uganda," *African Development Review*, 13 (2001): 46, 50.
71. Ibid., 69.

72. The United Nations report on commodities exchanges in Africa called on the African Union to play a bigger role in the development of exchanges. This would include organizing workshops and conferences.
73. http://www.dse.co.tz/main/index.php?page=12
74. Supra note 23 at 24.
75. William Easterly, *The White Man's Burden* (New York: Penguin, 2006), 24.
76. www.worldbank.org
77. A total of 187 nations are members of the World Bank. http://web.worldbank.org/WBSITE/EXTERNAL/EXTABOUTUS/0,,pagePK:50004410~piPK:36602~theSitePK:29708,00.html
78. http://www1.ifc.org/wps/wcm/connect/corp_ext_content/ifc_external_corporate_site/about+ifc
79. http://www.usaid.gov/
80. http://www.sida.se/English/
81. http://www.dfid.gov.uk/
82. http://www.imf.org/external/about/overview.htm
83. Ibid.
84. Ha-Joon Chang, *Kicking Away the Ladder: Development Strategy in Historical Perspective* (London: Anthem Press, 2002), 97.
85. Matthew Lockwood, *The State They're In: An Agenda for International Action on Poverty in Africa* (Warwickshire, UK: Practical Action, 2006), 50.
86. Anthony Boardman and Aidan Vining, "Ownership and Performance in Competitive Environments: A Comparison of the Performance of Private, Mixed and State Owned-Enterprises," *Journal of Law and Economics*, 32 (1989): 1–33.
87. Charles Pouncy, "Stock Markets in Sub-Saharan Africa: Western Legal Institutions as a Component of the Neo-Colonial Project," *University of Pennsylvania Journal of International Economic Law*, 23 (2002): 85, 103.
88. Supra note 85 at 11.
89. Colin Stoneman, Deborah Potts, and Tanya Bowyer-Bower, eds., *Eastern and Southern Africa: Development Challenges in a Volatile Region* (London: Pearson Education, 2004), 73.
90. Ibid., 75.
91. Ibid., 82.
92. See, Issa G. Shivji, arguing that claims of corruption, human rights violations, and free and fair elections is the new way for the IFIs to dominate Africa, in "Democracy and Democratisation in Africa: Interrogating Paradigms and Practices," *Pambazuka News*: http://www.pambazuka.org/en/category/features/78361. In contrast see Sarah Bracking, "Structural Adjustment: Why It Wasn't Necessary and Why It Did Work," *Review of African Political Economy*, 80(20):207–226 (1999).
93. Sonny Nwankwo and Darlington C. Richards, "Privatization: The Myth of Free Market Orthodoxy in sub-Saharan Africa," *International Journal Public Sector Management*, Vol. 14, No. 2 (2001): 165, 168.
94. Easterly, supra note 75 at 77.
95. Stoneman, supra note 89 at 59.
96. www.sec.gov
97. See Office of Inspector General, Case No. OIG-509, "Investigation of Failure of the SEC to Uncover Bernard Madoff's Ponzi Scheme": http://www.sec.gov/news/studies/2009/oig-509-exec-summary.pdf
98. Ibid.
99. See Julia Black, "Empirical Legal Studies in Financial Markets: What Have We Learned," Law, Society and Economy Working Papers 4/2010, London

School of Economics and Political Science; Michael Blair and George Walker, *Financial Markets and Exchanges Law* (Oxford, UK: Oxford University Press, 2007); Joanna Gray and Jenny Hamilton, *Implementing Financial Regulation* (Sussex: Wiley, 2006).
100. Voluminous articles from economics and political economy. The most prominent are the articles by financial economists La Porta, Lopez-de-Sillanes, Shleifer, and Vishny, aka LLSV.
101. Rafael La Porta; Florencio Lopez-de-Silanes; Andrei Shleifer; National Bureau of Economic Research, "What Works in Securities Laws?" *Journal of Finance*, Vol. 61 (2006). La Porta; National Bureau of Economic Research; et al., "Law and Finance," *Journal of Political Economy*, Vol. 106 (1998): 1113.
102. "The results support the view that the benefit of common law in this area comes from its emphasis on market discipline and private litigation. The benefits of common law appear to lie in its emphasis on private contracting and standardized disclosure and in its reliance on private dispute resolution using market-friendly standards of liability" Ibid., 28.
103. Mark Roe, "Legal Origins and Modern Stock Markets," *Harvard Law Review*, Vol. 120 (2006): 460, 462.
104. Ibid.
105. See, generally, Ha-Joon Chang, *Kicking Away the Ladder: Development Strategy in Historical Perspective* (London: Anthem, 2005), 135. Chang concludes that development institutions dominated by rich nations of the West impose on developing countries policies and institutions that were not part of the success of the West. The imposition of these "good" policies can impede growth rather than foster it.
106. Ibid., 489.
107. Ibid., 516. Due to the potential for inherent flaws in development agency policies a conscious attempt is made by the author of this paper to rely as little as possible on the publications of those institutions.
108. While researching colonial monetary concepts in West Africa, this author concluded that any accurate assessment of how monetary policy affected indigenous currency exchanges had to be based on "oral data and a deep understanding of regional economy outside the European-style monetary zones." Ames Webb Jr., "Toward the Comparative Study of Money: A Reconsideration of West African Currencies and Neoclassical Monetary Concepts," *The International Journal of Africa Historical Studies*, Vol. 15, No. 3 (1982): 466.
109. http://www.enotes.com/oxsoc-encyclopedia/institution
110. James M. Jasper, Mitchel Abolafia, and Frank Dobbin, "Structure and Strategy on the Exchanges: a Critique and Conversation about Making Markets," *Sociological Forum*, Vol. 20 (2005): 473, 480.
111. Neil Fligstein, *The Architecture of Markets: An Economic Sociology of Twenty-First-Century Capitalist Societies* (Princeton, NJ: Princeton University Press, 2001)
112. See infra.

REFERENCES

Beinhocker, Eric. *The Origin of Wealth: Evolution, Complexity and the Radical Remaking of Economics*. Boston: Random House Business Books, 2006.
Black, Julia. "Empirical Legal Studies in Financial Markets: What Have We Learned?" London: London School of Economics and Political Science and Law Department, 2010.

Bracking, Sarah. "Structural Adjustment: Why it Wasn't Necessary and Why it Did Work." *Review of African Political Economy* Vol. 26, No. 80 (1999): 207–226.
Chang, Ha-Joon. *Kicking Away the Ladder: Development Strategy in Historical Perspective.* London: Anthem Press, 2002.
Easterly, William. *The White Man's Burden.* New York, New York: Penguin, 2006.
Fligstein, Neil. *The Architecture of Markets: An Economic Sociology of Twenty-First Century Capitalist Societies.* Princeton: Princeton Universtiy Press, 2001.
Hamilton, Jenny, and Joanna Gray. *Implementing Financial Regulation.* Sussex, UK: Wiley, 2006.
Jasper, James M., Mitchel Abolafia, and Frank Dobbin. "Structure and Strategy on the Exchanges: A Critique and Conversation about Making Markets." *Sociological Forum*, Vol. 20 (2005):473–486.
Kibola, Hamisi. "The Regulation of Capital Markets in Tanzania: Is There Room for Improvement?" *DSE Journal*, 2008, http://www.dse.co.tz/upload/15.pdf.
Kotz, David H. "Investigation of Failure of the SEC to Uncover Bernard Madoff's Ponzi Scheme." Report of Investigation, United States Securities and Exchange Commission, 2009.
La Porta, Rafael, Florencio Lopez-de-Silanes; Andrei Shleifer; National Bureau of Economic Research. "Law and Finance." *Journal of Political Economy*, Vol. 106 (1998):1113–1115.
———. "What Works in Securities Laws?" *Journal of Finance*, Vol. 61 (2006): n.p.
Lee, Ruben. *What Is an Exchange? The Automation, Management, and Regulation of Financial Markets.* Oxford, UK: Oxford University Press, 1998.
Lockwood, Matthew. *The State They're In: An Agenda for International Action on Poverty in Africa.* Warwickshire, UK: Practical Action, 2006.
Miller, Joseph. "History and Africa/Africa and History." *American Historical Review*, Vol. 104 (1999):1–32.
Minney, Tom. "Uganda Goes Electric Trading." *African Capital Markets News*, September 15, 2009, http://www.africancapitalmarketsnews.com/78/electronic-trading-in-uganda-another-step-to-east-african-market/.
Ngugi, Rose. "Development of the Nairobi Stock Exchange: A Historical Perspective." Kenya Institute for Public Policy Research and Analysis Discussion Paper, 2003.
Obwona, Marios B. "Determinants of FDI and their Impact on Economic Growth in Uganda." *African Development Review*, Vol. 13 (2001):46–81.
Onyuma, Samuel. "Demutualization of Stock Exchanges in Africa: Prospects and Problems." *OSSREA Bulletin*, (2006):14–21.
Pouncy, Charles. "Stock Markets in Sub-Saharan Africa: Western Legal Institutions as a Component of the Neo-Colonial Project." *University of Pennsylvania Journal of International Economic Law*, Vol. 23 (2002):85–117.
Richards, Sonny Nwankwo, and C. Darlington. "Privatization: The Myth of Free Market Orthodoxy in sub-Saharan Africa." *International Journal Public Sector Management*, Vol. 14, No. 2 (2001):165–180;
Roe, Mark. "Legal Origins and Modern Stock Markets." *Harvard Law Review*, Vol. 120 (2006):460–527.
Salami, Iwa. "The Financial Crisis and a Regional Regulatory Perspective for Emerging Economies in Africa." *Journal of International Banking Law and Regulation*, Vol. 25 (2010):128–139.
"Securities Marketing and Stock Exchanges in Black Africa." *Columbia Law Review*, Vol. 67, No. 5 (1967):892–925.
Shivji, Issa G. "Democracy and Democratisation in Africa: Interrogating Paradigms and Practices." *Democracy and Democratisation in Africa*, November 30, 2011, http://pambazuka.org/en/category/features/78361.

Stoneman, Colin, Deborah Potts, and Tanya Bowyer-Bower, eds. *Eastern and Southern Africa: Development Challenges in a Volatile Region*. London: Pearson Education, 2004.

Vining, Anthony, and Aiden Boardman. "Ownership and Performance in Competitive Environments: A Comparison of the Performance of Private, Mixed and State-Owned Enterprises." *Journal of Law and Economics* Vol. 32 (1989): n.p.

Walker, Michael, and George Blair. *Financial Markets and Exchanges Law*. Oxford, UK: Oxford University Press, 2007.

Webb Jr., Ames. "Toward the Comparative Study of Money: A Reconsideration of West African Currencies and Neoclassical Monetary Concepts." *International Journal of Africa Historical Studies*, Vol. 15, No. 3 (1982):455–466,

World Bank. "Capital Market Integration in the East African Community." Financial Section Division, Africa Region, 2002.

World Bank. *Status of Projects in Execution-FY08-Africa Region-Country: Kenya*. World Bank, 2008.

6   The Impact of Changing Global Power Relations on African Governance of Foreign Direct Investment

Roshen Hendrickson

African governments seek foreign direct investment (FDI). Investors from Europe and the United States have traditionally been the main sources of FDI in Africa, but in recent years developing countries such as China, Malaysia, and India have significantly boosted their investment, thereby attracting a great deal of attention, enhancing the opportunities that African countries have in the global economy, and altering the context for the governance of FDI. Unlike the multilateral trade regime centralized in the World Trade Organization (WTO), there is no comprehensive multilateral set of rules governing FDI. Paul Haslam describes the governance of foreign direct investment as a "multi-layered patchwork of agreements."[1] This patchwork includes national investment rules, bilateral investment treaties (BITs), free trade areas of various types, and some multilateral rules such as WTO agreements. These legally binding international investment agreements focus primarily on protecting investors' interests.[2] Governance of FDI also includes efforts to require particular environmental, social, and developmental behavior on the part of investors through national and international rules as well as voluntary agreements.

Research on the link between FDI and economic growth in Africa does not establish a clear finding that increasing FDI leads to economic growth.[3] Historically, most foreign investment in Africa has been in the petroleum and mining sectors and has therefore been concentrated in resource-rich countries. While foreign investors have enriched themselves, the process of resource extraction has often resulted in human rights violations, environmental destruction, and negative economic effects.[4] The potential for FDI to contribute to economic development in Africa depends on the way rules, agreements, and norms impact the likelihood that FDI will create jobs, transfer knowledge and technology, and protect the environment, workers' rights, and human rights. The development of governance depends on the strengthening of domestic and international institutions, the interaction between states and nonstate actors, and the impact of changing ideas about governing corporate behavior.

In this chapter, I explore some ways that changing power relations between major actors in world politics might affect the constraints and opportunities for developing governance of FDI. I argue that the increase in power of developing nations has the potential to provide greater bargaining leverage for African states seeking FDI and improve their chances of maintaining some policy autonomy, while global civil society is placing pressure on all states and multinational corporations to achieve greater transparency and accountability in an effort to increase the economic and social benefits to the societies that host FDI. I start with a brief history of the governance of FDI in relation to the protection of investors' interests as well as societal interests. Then I address several changes at the global level that have altered the global context for FDI in Africa and consequently the implications for its contribution to economic development in Africa. I explore the changing role of the formerly hegemonic United States as it declines in relative power, with some commentary on the role of European powers; then I turn to the increasing influence and initiatives of major developing nations. I conclude with an analysis of the potential impact on African nations.

PROTECTING INVESTORS' INTERESTS

The international governance of FDI has been institutionalized in response to two distinct pressures: the effort of home governments and private investors to protect the interests of their companies and the efforts of host governments and host societies to extract the highest possible contribution from this investment. Historically, foreign investors relied on customary international law, specifically the "Hull rule" that "no government is entitled to expropriate private property, for whatever purpose, without provision for prompt, adequate and effective payment therefore."[5] Starting in the 1950s, developing countries expressed opposition to this rule, in part through a wave of nationalizations but also through collective action at the United Nations. In the 1960s and 1970s, several resolutions were passed in the UN General Assembly regarding states rights to their own resources.[6]

Expropriations rose through the 1960s and into the early 1970s but started to decline in the later 1970s and continued their decline until they practically disappeared in the 1990s, with a small resurgence over the last decade. During the period 1960–1992, the region that had the highest number of expropriations was Africa.[7] Stephen Kobrin's 1984 analysis of the decline of expropriation activity, later confirmed by Michael Minor, points to several reasons for this. First, by 1976, the most sensitive industries, such as mining and petroleum, were nationalized in decolonized African nations. Second, these newly independent countries had begun to gain confidence and take a more practical approach to their relationship with foreign investors so as to derive the greatest possible benefits from FDI. Third, these countries had improved their governmental capabilities, which gave them additional bargaining power. Finally, while international economic conditions by the late 1970s contributed to some benefits from FDI, developing countries were constrained by recessionary conditions that increased their debts and hence their need for more FDI. These underlying conditions gave the World Bank and International Monetary Fund (IMF) greater power to demand changes in governmental policies regarding FDI and its expropriation.[8]

Starting in the 1950s, states started to negotiate directly with each other and use bilateral investment treaties to provide clear commitments on treatment of investors.[9] Because there are not multilateral rules governing FDI, states rely primarily on BITs to both encourage and govern FDI. These agreements address various issues and disputes that might arise between the host governments and investors related to the establishment and operation of corporate activities:

> BITs typically require national treatment[10] and most-favored-nation treatment of foreign investments in the host country, protect contractual rights, guarantee the right to transfer profits in hard currency to the home country and prohibit or restrict the use of performance requirements. Finally, and perhaps most importantly, BITs provide for international arbitration of disputes between the investor and the host country, typically through the International Center for Settlement of Investment Disputes (ICSID) or the UN Commission on International Trade Law (UNCITRAL).[11]

According to Haslam, these treaties serve two major purposes. First, they provide greater security for the foreign investor by reducing the options for government intervention and ensuring means of compensation in the case of expropriation. Second, they set up mechanisms for international dispute settlement. While these measures are often implemented to attract FDI, they may undermine the host government's ability to ensure that foreign investment contributes to government goals.[12]

Many of the first BITs were between European and African countries. Because the United States was focused on ensuring the dominance of the Hull rule, it did not really engage in BITs until the 1980s.[13] Although the United States originally sought multilateral institutionalization at the World Trade Organization (WTO), the inability to make progress in the Doha Round of negotiations resulted in the United States focusing on bilateral agreements.[14] There are various types of BITs with some providing for more policy autonomy than others. Haslam finds that in Latin America there was competition between the European and American standards of international investment agreement, but over time the role of private international investment arbitration contributed to the harmonization of the regime and the dominance of the more liberal American version.[15] Developing countries signed on to BITS because they were competing for capital;

it was not until the 1990s that Least Developed Countries (LDCs) really started embracing BITs with each other.[16]

By 2009 African countries had signed a total of 715 BITs, or 27 percent of all BITs. In 2008, most new BITs were signed with developed countries in Europe; African countries were still the least likely to establish BITs within their regions.[17] According to Alec Johnson, African governments sign BITs in the hopes of attracting much-needed FDI even though there is no clear evidence that BITs have successfully contributed to greater investment in Africa. He argues that in addition to their failure to attract FDI, BITs have failed in Africa because they are concentrated in extractive industries that are especially vulnerable to price fluctuation. They are also problematic because they are structured to include requirements for unrealistic and overly complex institutional reform and reliance on international arbitration that might undermine the development of local rule of law and good governance, but they have inadequate provisions to stimulate the local economies, as through the promotion of infrastructure.[18]

Regional foreign direct investment is encouraged through institutions such as the Free Trade Area of the Southern African Development Community (SADC) and the East African Community (EAC), but there are many overlapping regional agreements with inconsistent investment-related measures.[19] Forty sub-Saharan countries are members of the WTO and consequently bound by the multilateral agreements of the Trade-Related Investment Measures Agreement (TRIMS), the General Agreement on Trade in Services (GATS), the Agreement on Trade-Related Aspects of Intellectual Property Rights (TRIPS), and the Agreement on Subsidies and Countervailing Measures (ASCM), despite fears that some aspects of these measures will undermine economic development. African governments also seek to attract investment through the passage of national laws that protect foreign investment or make expropriation illegal. One example is the Tanzanian National Investment Protection Policy Act, which protects against nationalization and eliminates local equity mandates in several sectors.[20]

PROTECTING HOST SOCIETIES' INTERESTS

The 2010 United Nations Conference on Trade and Development (UNCTAD) overview of world investment finds that while it is true that national investment regimes have become more liberal in their focus on improving conditions for foreign investment, more governments are taking another look at the role of regulation of FDI to achieve public policy objectives such as environmental protection, the alleviation of poverty, and national security. There are various emerging elements of global governance of FDI related directly to the impact of investment on economic development, environmental health, and social issues.

Developmental issues include the use of capital to stimulate industry, create jobs, and build new infrastructure. Although investment agreements are supposed to lure capital to the host country, there is no clear evidence that the signing of BITs ensures an increase in FDI.[21] There is, however, clear evidence that investment treaties undermine the policy autonomy of host countries by restricting the policy tools that governments are allowed to use.[22] But international investment agreements can include restrictions on investors and thus provide some policy flexibility for host governments. According to UNCTAD, one recent trend in treaty negotiation, especially in Latin America, has been to pay more attention to reviving the state's right to regulate by clarifying corporate obligations. There has been an increase in clauses focused on the environmental and social practices of multinational corporations.[23] One third of new investment policy measures in 2010 were regulations and restrictions mostly focused on resource-based industries and financial services, although African governments mostly adopted measures that facilitated private investment.[24] One exception was Zimbabwe, whose 2007 Indigenization and Economic Empowerment Act has indigenization provisions.[25]

Over the last couple decades, corporate social responsibility (CSR) standards for the impact of trans-national corporations (TNCs) on human rights, labor standards, the environment, and other social concerns have been developed and adopted by governments and industries. Although some of these standards are embodied in national laws, most are currently voluntary. There are multiple initiatives, including intergovernmental organization standards such as those of the United Nations, International Labor Organization, and the Organisation for Cooperation and Development (OECD); multiple-stakeholder initiatives developed by interaction between civil society, business, labor, and consumers; industry association codes and individual industry codes. In the first category, the UN Global Compact encourages participating companies to embrace ten principles in the areas of human rights, labor, the environment, and anticorruption; the International Labor Organization (ILO) has influential conventions on multinational behavior and labor rights; and the OECD has its Guidelines on Multinational Enterprises. These are the main but not exclusive sources of CSR standards.[26]

Given the many different CSR initiatives, there are significant gaps in coverage, overlapping initiatives, inconsistent rules, and inadequate methods of measuring, comparing, and ensuring compliance.[27] Multinationals are working with powerful international organizations to promote long-term liberal strategies that institute liberal rules and regulations preconditioned on an expanding liberal economy while increasingly signing on to CSR initiatives that consist largely of voluntary efforts on their part. There are various efforts to provide standardized reporting mechanisms, such as through the Global Reporting Initiative (GRI), which has formulated a sustainability reporting framework to help organizations "measure and report their economic, environmental and social performance."[28] There are also initial efforts to include CSR standards in international investment agreements. For example, CSR has been addressed in some free trade agreements such as the North American Free Trade Agreement (NAFTA), and the Canadian and European parliaments are both seeking the addition of CSR clauses to future free trade agreements.[29]

Some grassroots activists and nongovernmental organizations (NGOs) fear that voluntary initiatives are inadequate and that multilateral regimes ultimately serve corporate interests at the expense of local stakeholders. For example, the members of the G-20 have called on companies to abide by the International Principles for Responsible Investment in Agriculture established by UNCTAD, the Food and Agriculture Organization of the United Nations, the International Fund for Agricultural Development, and the World Bank Group. This initiative is supposed to "enhance the benefits of FDI in agriculture while mitigating its potential downsides, thereby contributing to strengthening food security and local development."[30] Some grassroots groups oppose it, believing that it legitimizes the corporate appropriation of smallholders' agricultural land.[31]

Most African countries have legal protection of the environment, labor conditions, and human rights, but the real issue is their ability to enforce these laws. There is a proliferation of grassroots organizations demanding greater rewards from FDI and more ethical corporate behavior. International efforts to change the impact of multinationals on society range from the Kimberley process, designed to oversee the diamond trade; the Extractive Industry Transparency Initiative, a multilateral voluntary initiative to promote transparency of payments in the natural resources sectors; to a plethora of initiatives to protect the environment or address global climate change.

THE IMPACT OF CHANGING POWER RELATIONS

In this second section I look at changing power relations in the global economy and suggest the potential impact they may have on the governance of FDI. I will address the decline in power of the United States with some comment on Europe and then the rise in economic power and influence of the major developing countries with a focus on China. I do not argue that shifts in power relations between states are the exclusive sources of change but that these shifts in power relations have altered the context in which states, international organizations, businesses and NGOs act.

The United States and Western Power

The United States' share of the global economy has declined since World War II, when it accounted for about half of global economic output to about 20 percent (on a purchasing power parity basis) today. However, this sharp decline took place a few decades ago and, as the largest national economy, the United States still plays a major role in decision making in international economic institutions because of its effective veto power in the IMF and World Bank, its influence in the WTO, and its potential to strengthen or weaken multilateral rule making. The significant shift in recent years is the rapid growth of developing countries that now account for half of the global economy, while the OECD predicts that the OECD share of the global economy will decline to 43 percent by 2030.[32] Despite this trend, developed countries' transnational corporations (TNCs) still account for the majority of FDI inflows into Africa in 2010.

The United States has been a leading promoter of the institutionalization of investment protection, with an agenda to provide "stable preferential access to the U.S. market in exchange for acceptance of norms that limit countries' ability to develop industrial policy."[33] However, Philips argues that the U.S. shift in focus from investment governance at the multilateral level to a focus on bilateral treaties reveals the decline in influence of the United States.[34] According to Haslam's analysis, at the bilateral level in Latin America, U.S. negotiators actually reduced the amount of investment protection in BITs because of congressional legislation that sought to maintain space for government regulation within the United States.[35] The liberal investment regime has also been challenged because several developing countries have either withdrawn or reduced their cooperation with the International Center for the Settlement of Investment Disputes owing to a perception of bias toward corporate interests. South Africa expressed opposition to the liberal regime by refusing to sign a BIT that held to the U.S. model.[36]

Despite its extensive history of investing in Africa, the United States has fallen far behind European nations in some measures of institutionalization. The United States has BITS only with Cameroon, Democratic Republic of Congo, Congo, Egypt, Morocco, Mozambique, Senegal, and Tunisia. It has no FTAs with sub-Saharan Africa, and only one in North Africa, with Morocco. Instead, the United States has established Trade and Investment Framework Agreements (TIFA) with the East Africa Community (EAC) and the countries of Angola, Ghana, Liberia, Mauritius, Mozambique, Nigeria, Rwanda, and South Africa as well as a trade and investment cooperative agreements with the Southern African Customs Union (SACU). These are intended to provide the institutions to encourage greater investment by monitoring economic and investment relations and encouraging greater investment. But Benjamin Leo argues that TIFAs, which are not legally binding, have little impact on investment and should be abandoned so that institutional resources can be devoted to more productive efforts.[37]

The United States led an effort to negotiate a comprehensive Multilateral Agreement on Investment (MAI) at the OECD despite opposition from developing countries and a well-orchestrated campaign by some NGOs, which argued that this would "threaten human rights, labor and environmental standards, and LDC development."[38] Ultimately, France withdrew from the negotiations so the initiative failed and the effort moved back to the WTO. During the Doha Round of WTO negotiations, the EU, Japan, and South Korea led efforts to pursue four investment related issues termed the "Singapore issues," which include trade facilitation, trade and investment, and competition policy as well as transparency in government procurement, but the issue of investment was extremely contentious and finally they agreed only to address trade facilitation.

At the bilateral level, in African countries, the U.S. government has played a significant role in encouraging and protecting private investment and carrying out market reforms through development assistance programs such as the United States Agency for International Development (USAID), the Overseas Private Investment Corporation (OPIC), and the Trade and Development Agency (TDA), among others. The African Growth and Opportunity Act of 2000 provided benefits to American investors by making trade benefits contingent on progress toward a market-based economy and rule of law, requiring national treatment, protecting intellectual property rights, providing a means to solve investment disputes, and requiring that countries abide by obligations to the IMF. As Carol Thompson points out, these measures benefit investors in several ways: the implications of enforcing intellectual property rights will be an increase in royalty payments for technology use and possible limitations on technology transfer; elimination of barriers to investment include reduction of corporate tax rates; privatization requirements provide great opportunities for foreign investors in the sectors of telecommunications and power production. Also, large multinationals can easily borrow money and evade taxes, thus enhancing their ability to compete with local corporations.[39]

The role of the United States in relation to the development of environmental and social governance of FDI is very complex as one has to take into account the interaction between the government and interest groups of all types. U.S. development assistance has increasingly incorporated environmental and social conditions. As early as the 1970s, environmental interest groups succeeded in getting USAID to pay attention to environmental concerns and to institute environmental regulations on development assistance, thus establishing USAID as an environmental leader in the global donor community[40] OPIC has environmental, developmental, and worker and human rights requirements for all its projects and also for its investment funds. In 2007, it signed on to a commitment to support green technology and reduce greenhouse emissions in its projects. It has increased the transparency of its own portfolio by publishing project details on its website and it endorses the Extractive Industries Transparency Initiative (EITI). Despite these efforts, NGOs in the United States continue to express concern that implementation of environmental, labor conditions, and human rights safeguards is inadequate. They claim that OPIC does not have a good record of improving the quality of life of the people who live near its projects.[41]

Flohr et al. argue that the United States is less activist on the formation of environmental and social governance than European governments, and that American companies are much less likely to be "norm entrepreneurs" because rule making in the United States is less collaborative than in Europe and more likely to be challenged by the concerned industries. Because of this, companies are much less likely to engage in international processes that result in the development of norms.[42] On the other hand, Jedrzej Frynas finds, in a study of CSR in the oil and gas sector, that while European companies initiated reforms in response to pressure from stakeholders, American companies' social and environmental policies eventually converged with the European companies' policies because of their pursuit of entrepreneurial strategies such as adapting to climate change or competing for new markets.[43] TNCs are increasingly being held accountable by consumers, the media, and their own stockholders for all the effects of their business practices. Frynas finds that companies are most likely to take part in CSR if they seek international expansion or international credit because both opportunities can be influenced by reputation.[44]

While many of the governance mechanisms to improve the environmental and social impact of foreign investment originated in western nations, government action has been hesitant at best. For example, although Great Britain led on the establishment of the EITI, it has not yet committed to implementing it. In 2011, the United States was the first G8 country to commit to actually implementing the global initiative. In a recent development, the United States 2010 Dodd-Frank financial reform legislation requires American manufacturers to monitor "conflict minerals" from Central Africa in their supply chains. The European Commission has proposed legislation that would require European companies that exploit natural resources to publicly disclose all payments to governments.

From these examples one can glean several potential effects of changing power relations. First, OECD efforts to pass stronger protection of investors' interests have stalled at various levels and are facing more concerted resistance from developing nations. After World War II, the United States took a historic leadership role in setting up multilateral economic institutions including the World Bank, IMF, and the trade regime eventually embodied in the WTO. Now its decline in power is reflected in part in the inability to pass major multilateral agreements such as the Doha Round of the WTO, Multilateral Investment Rules, or even the Singapore issues. In addition, the adoption of the neoliberal approach to development that requires rapid liberalization has been checked by the global financial crisis originating in the United States in 2008 and the faltering economy of the model itself, the United States. Also, it has been challenged by the alternative development models of China and other rapidly growing LDCs.

Second, power has shifted in part to international organizations like the WTO but also to NGOs that have a major influence on global rules, the encouragement of new norms, and the creation of new institutions such as voluntary codes, which in turn influence domestic policies. Domestic activism resulted in the incorporation of environmental and social conditions into development assistance programs, as well as in U.S. pressure on multilateral development banks to pay attention to environmental concerns.[45] Progressive requirements have been incorporated into domestic institutions dealing with African affairs. Although these are not necessarily thoroughly implemented or well monitored, alongside more rigorous expectations for multilaterals and European countries they have contributed to a change in expectations about the role of FDI and the calculation of benefits and costs. Western investors, as the major source of FDI for Africa, increasingly set the standard either because of external pressures or because of entrepreneurial advantage.[46]

Third, because of the pervasive incorporation of liberal market rules and the current American and European budgetary crisis, which places downward pressure on development assistance, the U.S. Congress is reluctant to provide more subsidies for multinational corporations. Under great pressure to deal with budget deficits, by late 2011, the U.S. Congress committed to significant cuts in foreign assistance and some European countries have also been reducing assistance levels. The influence of the United States and Europe in Africa appears to be waning while the influence of China is rising.

The Increased Influence of Major Developing Countries

Developing countries account for half of the world economy and by 2030 may account for close to 60 percent.[47] While developing countries have long held a majority in major international organizations such as the United Nations, in the powerful international economic institutions their influence has been limited until recently. The latest reform of IFI voting increased the share of developing countries, by 3.13 percent in the World Bank (to 47.19 percent), and in 2010 the IMF agreed to increase by about 6% the voting shares of developing countries to 44.7 percent of voting power. Developing countries have tended to oppose limitations on host government policies, so they opposed the MAI negotiations in the OECD and severely limited the investment related issues that could be discussed at the WTO.[48]

Developing countries have historically sought weaker BITs, or at least BITs that have more room for state regulation.[49] This does not indicate less of an interest in institutionalization—China has larger BIT coverage with African countries than the United States[50]—but it does reflect their varied experiences in development pathways. Developing countries such as China, India, and Brazil have maintained a much bigger role for the state in development policy than that prescribed by liberal economic theory. TNCs from these countries, especially China, Malaysia, India, and the countries of the Cooperation Council for the Arab States of the Gulf have significantly increased their proportion of capital flows from 18 percent in the late nineties to 21 percent during 2000–2008.[51] When these major developing countries boost investment in Africa, they serve not merely as alternative sources of capital but also as alternative models of development.

While the increasing role of LDCs has an impact on preserving some space for domestic policy autonomy in international investment agreements, the liberalization and privatization trend continues for now. In an analysis of historical expropriation trends, Minor suggests that this is largely because the state-owned enterprises that resulted from expropriation often failed to deliver satisfactory results but that there is a possibility of reversal if the gains from privatization are not substantial, if the population feels that foreigners have gained overwhelming control of state resources, or if they continue to fault IFI policy for economic problems. Minor also suggests that support for privatization is a result of an acceptance of the potential benefits of foreign capital and that this is eased by measures instituted to limit the amount of control foreigners can have. He concludes that a "demonstration effect" can go either way. The likelihood of expropriation in the future is directly affected by the impact of current foreign direct investments on societies.[52]

Although developing countries involvement in Africa may challenge liberal economic norms, they are increasingly influenced by governance trends that demand accountability on environmental and social concerns. For example, according to Frynas in his study of oil companies, when TNCs from developing countries internationalize their operations, they are likely to respond to pressures to adapt to new environmental and social standards. Brazil's Petrobras and Indian Oil both joined the UN Global Compact, while Kuwait Petroleum adopted higher environmental standards as a strategic tool to win European markets.[53] China, the Philippines, Indonesia, India, Brazil, and Mexico—as well as many smaller economies including African countries like the Sudan, Kenya, and Ethiopia—have all signed on to the UN Global Compact.[54]

China's activities in Africa have received the most attention from scholars as they debate whether China is simply the latest external power to exploit Africa's resources or whether it is providing a significant boost to African economies.[55] By the early 2000s, China was proclaiming the "Beijing consensus" as an alternative to the "Washington consensus." This Chinese alternative model is supposed to allow for a diversity of development pathways rather than the imposition of one method of economic development imposed with rigorous conditions by western institutions. In addition, it is seen to be more socially oriented and more focused on the development of an industrial base by financing the building of infrastructure and enriching of human capital.[56] China has come under sustained criticism for its lack of attention to environmental issues, human rights, and labor standards. Some of this attention is hypocritical given the terrible history of western involvement in Africa, but there are many cases where Chinese companies have committed egregious violations.

In response, China is working on improving the standards followed by its companies and addressing these concerns. In Sudan, China responded to international criticism over Sudan's repression of the people of Darfur with efforts to pressure the government to allow peacekeepers into the country. The Chinese government has already expressed concern about corruption in Angola and Zambia.[57] In 2008, the World Bank and Chinese development bodies agreed to work together on aid programs in Africa in an effort to make sure that development aid is sustainable and assistance transparent.[58] China is also working with the World Bank on developing its corporate social responsibility policies.[59] In South Africa, China engages in publicly monitored joint ventures that are "framed in terms that conform to international legal norms and responsibilities."[60] China has demonstrated acceptance of some environmental standards—for example, by ending the use of ramin wood once its trade became regulated.[61]

There are several ways in which the increasing power of developing countries may condition choices for African states in their efforts to attract foreign investment. Changing power relations in IFIs will enable these institutions to better reflect both developing country experiences, such as government retention of policy options as well as developing countries' interests, for example, to retain some policy autonomy. The evidence of dramatic growth in developing countries provides alternative ideas about development pathways. The growth of these developing countries also provides alternative sources of capital. But as companies from developing countries become more integrated into global economic institutions, they will be more vulnerable to traditional activist pressure tactics such as "naming and shaming" or shareholder activism on companies that list on western stock exchanges.[62] If economic liberalization provides benefits for African countries and greater transparency and accountability is gained from TNCs, this will increase the chances of the internationalization of more progressive governance; but the opposite is possible if liberalization fails to lead to significant growth or schemes to govern FDI falter.

THE IMPACT ON GOVERNANCE OF FOREIGN DIRECT INVESTMENT IN AFRICA

Africa still attracts less than 2 percent of global FDI. Although there were notable inflows of investment after the year 2000, especially with major developing countries seeking African natural resources to fuel their own dramatic growth, the rate fell after 2008 as the global economy slumped. Most TNCs investing in Africa are still from developed countries, so it is the arrival of developing countries seeking raw materials and investment opportunities during the last decade that has stimulated hopes for a more dynamic investment environment.

This interest in Africa has the potential to translate into greater opportunities for African governments to attract investment that contributes to sustainable growth. Since the debt crisis of the 1980s, IFIs have been focused on trying to increase FDI in Africa. Although liberal economists argue that liberal reforms in Africa have resulted in more FDI, the impact of neoliberal trends on sustainable investment in Africa is unclear. African countries are in dire need of investment in infrastructure and manufacturing. In 2010, some 43 percent of investment was in the primary sector, 29 percent in manufacturing, and 28 percent in services.[63] The future impact of FDI on African economies will depend on the nature of investments, African power in multilateral institutions, the ability of African governments to bargain for favorable terms, and the effect of governance on specific projects.

The ability of African countries to fight for their economic interests in international forums has been limited by their marginal role in the global economy and the recent changes to African voice in the international financial institutions have been slight. According to an analysis by the Bretton Woods Project, Africa's share has increased by only 0.19 percent in the International Bank for Reconstruction and Development (IBRD, World Bank), eleven African countries received a diminished share of the vote in the International Development Association (IDA, World Bank), and no low-income countries were among the top ten to acquire greater voting power.[64] Whether the 2010 IMF decision to double African quotas increased shares of developing countries and protected the shares of the poorest members is as yet unclear.

Greater government capacity and transparency may strengthen the hand of African governments as they bargain with TNCs for greater contributions to national development. This is one aspect of the entry of the developing countries into competition for Africa's resources that has received the most attention. For example, in Angola, financing from China allowed Angola to put off resorting to the IMF for a loan that would have been conditioned on higher standards of accountability.[65] In their efforts to compete for access to Angola's oil, all the major oil companies (from Italy, France, the United States, and China) have engaged in development projects; although the effectiveness of these development projects has yet to be determined.[66] Niger reportedly courted the Chinese with promises of uranium rights, only to offer them to the French company Areva when it improved its bid.[67] Despite the challenges to the neoliberal order, African governments still have incentives to sign on to western-dominated governance rules when the majority of FDI is still from developed nations and major developing TNCs are also moving in the direction of incorporation into liberal governance regimes. It is too early to evaluate the impact of these governance trends but there are a plethora of reforms with potential to improve the chances that FDI contributes to sustainable growth. Below, I give several examples.

In South Africa, the Johannesburg Stock Exchange requires companies to use Global Reporting Initiative Guidelines when they file sustainability reports.[68] Central African Republic, Ghana, Liberia, Mali, Niger, and Nigeria are compliant with EITI and several African countries are candidates. Frynas points out, however, that although studies show that transparency has great benefits for economic development, these benefits may be dependent on effective societal governance and thus more difficult to achieve in African resource-rich countries.[69] Both Ghana and Botswana have written model BIT agreements, including CSR provisions that would require contributions to "human capital formation, local capacity-building, employment creation, training and transfer of technology."[70] Although these are not yet implemented, they indicate possible future pathways. African governments will need greater governance capacity to carry out the regulations that they already have on the books and to implement new ones. However, they are under pressure from local and global democratizing forces, including local and international efforts to promote transparency. There is a proliferation of local social movements seeking the protection of workers' rights, environmental protection, and protection of human rights as well as global activist networks demanding greater attention to these concerns that continue to place pressure on international investors.

CONCLUSION

We see the steady incorporation of African countries into new global governance institutions—for example, through the spread of BITs, incorporation into the WTO, and the embrace of new voluntary efforts such as EITI. With the competition for FDI encouraging greater liberalization there has been a reduction in some constraints on foreign investors. More recently, the focus has turned to international pressures on companies to contribute to sustainable development as well as the ability of African governments to ensure that these companies at least follow laws on environmental and social issues. Development assistance from both developed and developing countries, when successful, can contribute to building the capacity of governments. Also, civil society can make demands for transparency, more effective regulation, and greater developmental results from investments.

The progressive nature of governance of FDI will depend on several factors. First, liberal economic reforms can have an impact if they result in the attraction of productive investment. Second, powerful developing countries can have a positive or negative impact on African economies, depending on the extent to which they bring productive investment and provide investment agreements that enable African governments to ensure measurable returns and monitor social and environmental effects. This also depends on whether African governments' agreements with foreign investors are designed to meet societal needs, rather than serve elite interests. Third, the progress of democratization and the impact of social movements depend in part on local economic growth but also on global support.

The United States and European powers have been leaders in the effort to establish greater transparency and accountability on the part of governments and business, but the United States also promoted a neoliberal agenda that limited governments' options in their developmental pathways. The United States economic and leadership crisis as well as the rapid growth of states like China and Brazil have opened up discourse over the role of the state in the economy in a way that may loosen the constraints on African governments that were imposed by neoliberal economic reforms. In addition, greater competition for Africa's resources and opportunities can provide governments the chance to make greater demands on investors. The possibility of both of these structural changes contributing to more sustainable growth in Africa will depend on the capacity of African governments and continued organized pressure from African populations and global civil society.

NOTES

1. Paul Alexander Haslam, "The Evolution of the Foreign Direct Investment Regime in the Americas," *Third World Quarterly*, Vol. 31, No. 7 (2010): 1181.
2. Ibid., 1181–1183.
3. Stephen Kosach and Jennifer Tobin, "Funding Self-Sustaining Development: The Role of Aid, FDI and Government in Economic Success," *International Organization*, Vol. 60 (2006).
4. Oxfam, "Lifting the Resource Curse: How Poor People Can and Should Benefit from the Revenues of the Extractive Industries," Oxfam Briefing Paper (December 2009): www.oxfam.org
5. Cited in Zachary Elkins, Andrew Guzman, and Beth A. Simmons, "Competing for Capital: The Diffusion of Bilateral Investment Treaties, 1960–2000," *International Organizations*, Vol. 60, No. 4 (2006): 813.
6. Ibid., Charles Lipson, *Standing Guard: Protecting Foreign Capital in the Nineteenth and Twentieth Centuries* (Berkeley: University of California, 1985).
7. Michael S. Minor, "The Demise of Expropriation as an Instrument of LDC Policy, 1980–1992," *Journal of International Business Studies*, Vol. 25, No. 1 (1994).
8. Ibid.
9. Elkins et al, "Competing for Capital," 814.
10. National treatment prohibits a country from giving incentives to its own companies that are not available for foreign companies.
11. Elkins et al., "Competing for Capital," 814.
12. Haslam, "Evolution of the Foreign Direct Investment Regime," 1183.
13. Elkins et al., "Competing for Capital."
14. Haslam, "Evolution of the Foreign Direct Investment Regime."
15. Ibid.
16. Elkins et al., "Competing for Capital."
17. UNCTAD, "Recent Developments in International Investment Agreements (June 2009), *IIA MONITOR* No. 3: http://www.unctad.org/templates/Page.asp?intItemID=3766&lang=1

18. Alec R. Johnson, "Rethinking Bilateral Investment Treaties in Sub-Saharan Africa," *Emory Law Journal*, Vol. 59, No. 4 (2010): 919–922.
19. UNCTAD, *World Investment Report 2011* (New York and Geneva: United Nations, 2011), 44.
20. Douglas E. Corkran, "Tanzania Opens Its Doors to U.S. Business," *Business America*, Vol. 112, No. 13 (July 1, 1991).
21. Haslam, "Evolution of the Foreign Direct Investment Regime," 1183.
22. Ibid.
23. UNCTAD, *World Investment Report 2010*, 22.
24. UNCTAD WIR 2011, 94–95.
25. UNCTAD WIR 2011, 98.
26. UNCTAD, WIR 2011, 111–120.
27. Ibid.
28. Global Reporting Initiative, "What Is GRI": http://www.globalreporting.org/AboutGRI/WhatIsGRI/
29. UNCTAD, WIR 2011, 119–120.
30. UNCTAD, WIR 2010, 23.
31. FIAN International, Focus on the Global South, La Via Campesina, REDE SOCIAL, "Why We Oppose the Principles for Responsible Agricultural Investment (RAI)" (October 2010): http://www.tni.org
32. OECD, "Economy: Developing Countries Set to Account for Nearly 60% of World GDP by 2030, According to New Estimates": http://www.oecd.org/document/12/0,3343,en_2649_33959_45467980_1_1_1_1,00.html
33. Haslam, "Evolution of the Foreign Direct Investment Regime," 1192–1193.
34. N. Phillips, "The Politics of Trade and the Limits of U.S. Power in the Americas," in *Political Economy of Hemispheric Integration*, cited in Haslam, 1193.
35. Haslam, "Evolution of the Foreign Direct Investment Regime," 1188–1189.
36. Network for Justice in Global Investment, "Alternative Proposals": http://justinvestment.org
37. Benjamin Leo, "Where Are the BITS? How U.S. Bilateral Investment Treaties with Africa Can Promote Development," Center for Global Development, CGD Essays (July 21, 2010): http://dspace.cigilibrary.org/jspui/handle/123456789/29383
38. Theodore H. Cohn, *Global Political Economy* (New York: Pearson Longman, 2008), 311.
39. Carol Thompson, "U.S. Trade with Africa: African Growth and Opportunity?" *Review of African Political Economy*, Vol. 101 (2004):457–474.
40. Vernon W. Ruttan, *United States Development Assistance Policy: The Domestic Politics of Foreign Economic Aid* (Baltimore, MD: Johns Hopkins University Press, 1996), 373.
41. House Committee on International Relations, *Renewing OPIC and Reviewing its Role in Support of Key U.S. Objectives*, 108th Cong., 1st sess., June 10, 2003.
42. Annegret Flohr, Lothar Rieth, Sandra Schwindenhammer, and Klaus Dieter Wolf, "Variations in Corporate Norm-Entrepreneurship: Why the Home State Matters," in Morten Ougaard and Anna Leander, eds., *Business and Global Governance* (Routledge, 2010), 245.
43. Jedrzej George Frynas, *Beyond Corporate Social Responsibility* (Cambridge, UK: Cambridge University Press, 2009).
44. Ibid.
45. Ruttan, *United States Development Assistance*, 373.
46. Frynas, *Beyond Corporate*.
47. OECD, "Economy: Developing Countries Set to Account."

48. Cohn, *Global Political Economy,* 311–312.
49. Haslam, "Evolution of the Foreign Direct Investment Regime."
50. Leo, "Where are the BITS?"
51. UNCTAD, WIR 2010, 34.
52. Minor, "Demise of Expropriation."
53. Frynas, *Beyond Corporate,* 30–34.
54. Global Compact: http://www.unglobalcompact.org/ParticipantsAndStakeholders/business_associations.html. Its principles are derived from The Universal Declaration of Human Rights; The International Labour Organization's Declaration on Fundamental Principles and Rights at Work; The Rio Declaration on Environment and Development; and The United Nations Convention Against Corruption.
55. For a thorough analysis of these issues, see, for example, Deborah Brautigam, *The Dragon's Gift: The Real Story of China in Africa* (Oxford, UK: Oxford University Press, 2009); Serge Michel and Michel Beuret, *China Safari: On the Trail of Beijing's Expansion in Africa* (New York: Nation Books, 2009); Chris Alden, *China in Africa* (New York: Zed Books, 2007).
56. Barry Sautman and Yan Hairong, "Friends and Interests: China's Distinctive Links with Africa," *African Studies Review* Vol. 50 (December 2007): 81–85.
57. Alden, *China in Africa,* 114.
58. *Financial Times,* "World Bank to Work with China and Africa Aid Projects" May 18, 2007.
59. Brautigam, *The Dragon's Gift,* 303–4.
60. Alden, *China in Africa,* 45.
61. J. Stephen Morrison, "China in Africa: Implications for U.S. Policy," Testimony before the U.S. Senate Committee on Foreign Relations Subcommittee on African Affairs, June 4, 2008.
62. Ndubisi Obiorah, "Who's Afraid of China in Africa? Towards an African Civil Society Perspective on China-Africa Relations" in Firoze Manji and Stephen Marks, eds., *African Perspective on China in Africa* (London: Pambazuka Books, 2007).
63. UNCTAD,WIR 2011, 41.
64. Bretton Woods Project, "At Issue: Analysis of World Bank Voting Reforms: Governance Remains Illegitimate and Outdated": http://www.brettonwoodsproject.org/doc/wbimfgov/wbgovreforms2010.pdf
65. Alden, *China in Africa,* 68.
66. Daphne Eviatar, "Africa's Oil Tycoons," *Nation* (April 12, 2004).
67. Serge Michel, "When China Met Africa," *Foreign Policy* (May/June 2008).
68. UNCTAD, WIR 2011, 118.
69. Frynas, *Beyond Corporate.*
70. UNCTAD, WIR 2011, 120,122.

REFERENCES

Alden, Chris. *China in Africa.* New York: Zed Books, 2007.
Brautigam, Deborah. *The Dragon's Gift: The Real Story of China in Africa.* Oxford, UK: Oxford University Press, 2009.
Bunduku-Latha, Paul. *L'administration Clinton Et L'afrique.* Paris: L'Harmattan, 1999.
Charveriat, Celine, Marita Hutjes, Trini Leung, and Daniela Perez Gavidia. "The Emperor's New Clothes: Why Rich Countries Want a WTO Investment

Agreement." Oxfam International Briefing Paper 46: http://publications.oxfam.org.uk/oxfam/display.asp?K=002P0083

Cohn, Theodore H. *Global Political Economy.* New York: Pearson Longman, 2008.

Corkran, Douglas E. "Tanzania Opens Its Doors to U.S. Business." *Business America,* Vol. 112, No. 13 (July 1, 1991): 11.

Elkins, Zachary, Andrew Guzman, and Beth A. Simmons. "Competing for Capital: the Diffusion of Bilateral Investment Treaties, 1960–2000." *International Organizations,* Vol. 60, No. 4 (2006): 811–846.

Eviatar, Daphne. "Africa's Oil Tycoons." *The Nation,* April 12, 2004.

FIAN International, Focus on the Global South, La Via Campesina, REDE SOCIAL. "Why We Oppose the Principles for Responsible Agricultural Investment (RAI)." October 2010: http://www.tni.org

Flohr, Annegret, Lothar Rieth, Sandra Schwindenhammer, and Klaus Dieter Wolf. "Variations in Corporate Norm-Entrepreneurship: Why the Home State Matters." In Morten Ougaard and Anna Leander, eds. *Business and Global Governance.* New York: Routledge, 2010.

Frynas, Jedrzej George. *Beyond Corporate Social Responsibility.* Cambridge, UK: Cambridge University Press, 2009.

Global Reporting Initiative. "What is GRI": http://www.globalreporting.org/AboutGRI/WhatIsGRI/

Haslam, Paul Alexander. "The Evolution of the Foreign Direct Investment Regime in the Americas." *Third World Quarterly,* Vol. 31, No. 7 (2010): 1181–1203.

Johnson, Alec R. "Rethinking Bilateral Investment Treaties in Sub-Saharan Africa." *Emory Law Journal,* Vol. 59, No. 4 (2010): 919–922.

Kosach, Stephen, and Jennifer Tobin. "Funding Self-Sustaining Development: the Role of Aid, FDI, and Government in Economic Success." *International Organizations,* Vol. 60 (2006): 205–243.

Leo, Benjamin. "Where Are the BITS? How U.S. Bilateral Investment Treaties with Africa Can Promote Development." Center for Global Development CGD Essays. July 21, 2010: http://dspace.cigilibrary.org/jspui/handle/123456789/29383

Lipson, Charles. *Standing Guard: Protecting Foreign Capital in the Nineteenth and Twentieth Centuries.* Berkeley: University of California, 1985.

Michel, Serge. "When China Met Africa." *Foreign Policy,* May/June 2008:38–46.

Michel, Serge, and Michel Beuret. *China Safari: On the Trail of Beijing's Expansion in Africa.* New York: Nation Books, 2009.

Minor, Michael S. "The Demise of Expropriation as an Instrument of LDC Policy, 1980–1992." *Journal of International Business Studies,* Vol. 25, No. 1 (1994): 177–188.

Morrison, Stephen J. "China in Africa: Implications for U.S. Policy." Testimony before the U.S. Senate Committee on Foreign Relations Subcommittee on African Affairs. June 4, 2008.

Network for Justice in Global Investment. "Alternative Proposals": http://justinvestment.org

Obiorah, Ndubisi. "Who's Afraid of China in Africa? Towards an African Civil Society Perspective on China-Africa Relations." In Firoze Manji and Stephen Marks, eds. *African Perspective on China in Africa.* London: Pambazuka Books, 2007.

OECD. "Economy, Developing Countries Set to Account for Nearly 60% of World GDP by 2030, According to New Estimates." June 16, 2010: http://www.oecd.org/document/14/0,3343,en_2649_33959_45467980_1_1_1_1,00.html

Oxfam. "Lifting the Resource Curse: How Poor People Can and Should Benefit from the Revenues of the Extractive Industries." Oxfam Briefing Paper. December 2009: www.oxfam.org

Ruttan, Vernon W. *United States Development Assistance Policy: The Domestic Politics of Foreign Economic Aid*. Baltimore: Johns Hopkins University Press, 1996.
Sautman, Barry, and Yan Hairong. "Friends and Interests: China's Distinctive Links with Africa." *African Studies Review,* Vol. 50, No. 3 (2007): 75–114.
Thompson, Carol. "U.S. Trade with Africa: African Growth and Opportunity?" *Review of African Political Economy,* Vol. 101 (2004): 457–474.
UNCTAD. *World Investment Report 2010*. New York and Geneva: United Nations, 2010.
UNCTAD. *World Investment Report 2011*. New York and Geneva: United Nations, 2011.
UNCTAD. "Recent Developments in International Investment Agreements (2008–June 2009)." *IIA MONITOR* No. 3: http://www.unctad.org/templates/Page.asp?intItemID=3766&lang=1
U.S. Congress. House Committee on International Relations. *Renewing OPIC and Reviewing its Role in Support of Key U.S. Objectives*. 108th Cong., 1st sess., June 10, 2003.

7 Globalization and Regional Impulses from the Global South
A Comparative Study of ECOWAS and ASEAN

Okpeh Ochayi Okpeh Jr.

The end of the Cold War in the last quarter of the twentieth century ushered in a radical transformation process that has continued to significantly affect the world. Indeed, since then, the changes the world has experienced are as complex as they are profound, affecting virtually every aspect of human existence. For example, communications have become more rapid and complex, working patterns are fast-changing, markets for goods and services have immensely transformed, and the movement of money across national boundaries has been spontaneous and less encumbered. *Globalization* is the catch-all word used to describe these changes. In broad terms, the term refers to a process of change in which countries of the world and their economies are increasingly integrated as a consequence of intense transborder economic and other transactions and the revolution in information technology that enabled these interventions.[1]

As a concept, it means the expansion of human activities and interests in the areas of transportation, communication, trade, and financial exchange, as well as nuclear targeting around the world. The immediate consequence of this development is the phenomenal increase in the sociocultural, economic, and political integration of nations of the world, both nationally and supranationally. While it is important to point out that historically globalization is not an entirely new phenomenon,[2] it should, at the outset, be noted that its contemporary manifestation, especially in the post-Cold War period, has been most revolutionary indeed. Similarly, while we acknowledge that it is and should be understood as a multidimensional phenomenon, it is also necessary to bear in mind that its economic aspects remain the core of the globalization process, underscoring the enormous attention it has continued to receive from development scholars.

Globalization discourse has generally elicited various and sometimes contentious reactions from scholars and policy makers who have attempted to study its dynamics and its implications for the development process. Expectedly, the debate is between those who see and understand it in terms of the opportunities it has thrown up in the international economy, enabling nations to grab and actualize economic growth and development, and those who insist that it is the latest phase of imperialism in the life cycle of global finance capital. The contentions of both schools of thought are as fluid as the evidence they have continued to marshal to buttress their passionate claims and counterclaims. For example, defending the phenomenon and its benefits, it is tersely stressed that:

> Globalization does present new opportunities for eliminating global poverty. By providing many types of interactions with wealthier people in other countries, globalization can potentially benefit poor countries directly and indirectly through cultural, social, scientific, and technological exchanges, as well as through conventional trade and finance. A faster diffusion of productive ideas, such as a shorter time between innovation and adoption of new technologies around the world, might help developing countries catch up much more quickly.[3]

A summary of the above argument would suggest, among other things, that globalization

1. Allows the free flow of capital across national boundaries, and that this would help increase the level of domestic investment;
2. Gives nations of the world free access to foreign technology, thereby facilitating technology transfer;
3. Allows nations of the world access to cutting-edge information, thereby improving their capacity to actively participate in the realities of global changes;
4. Allows nations of the world to avail themselves of the advantages of economies of scale, otherwise called large-scale production, as a result of their direct access to the world market through the instrument of trade liberalization;
5. Guarantees and enhances global peace through the harmonization and homogenization of divergent interests between nations of the world;
6. Encourages the migration and diffusion of vital technical skills for national development.

However, if the globalization optimists insist on the above benefits, there are those who think differently: the globalization pessimists. This strand of thought anchors its view on a historical assessment of the structure of the globalization process, and concludes as follows:

> The environment of globalization is an unequal one. The dominant binary couplets: rich/poor, industrial/agricultural, etc, means that one hemisphere is inherently advantaged and the other disadvantaged. It means countries in the northern hemisphere are in a position to avail themselves of the best offered by globalization of production and trade [while] the countries of the southern hemisphere are not in the same

position because they neither have the technology nor the economic competence to be active and equal participants.[4]

Arising from the above, it is argued that globalization

1. Intensifies the centuries-long development crisis confronting many countries in the global south;
2. Deepens inequality between nations and regions and within regions of the world;
3. Worsens the poverty of some developing countries, especially those at the periphery of the international trading system;
4. Intensifies global conflicts, since it has sharpened cultural fault lines between races, social groups, ideologies, and nations;
5. Promotes a production and consumption pattern that has deepened global environmental crisis.

Thus Stiglitz's conclusions on the impact of the globalization process are relevant here and therefore instructive. According to him:

> Globalization today is not working for many of the world's poor. It is not working for the environment. It is not working for the stability of the global economy. The transition from communism to a market economy has been so badly managed that, with the exception of China, Vietnam, and a few Eastern European countries, poverty has soared as incomes have plummeted.[5]

The preceding foray into perspectives on the subject is intended to acquaint the reader with the nature of the globalization discourse and explain why the polemic will rage for a fairly long time to come. What is necessary at this point is to understand the logic of particular arguments and what they are attempting to explain about globalization. This is the case because the phenomenon is many things to different people and because nations of the world are experiencing it in ways that are not at all the same. The task before development analysts is to understand this and interrogate how these nations are responding to both the challenges and opportunities that globalization has created and how this would, in the final analysis, determine their survival in the new world order of the twenty-first century. It is against the backdrop of this very important challenge that this chapter sets out to analyze how countries in the global South are responding to the globalization process. Situated in the context of the global rise of regionalism both as a response to and a consequence of the new world economic order, the chapter isolates and analyzes the Economic Community of West African States (ECOWAS) and the Association of Southeast Asian Nations (ASEAN) as supranational regional groupings and relates the experiences of member nations with the globalization dynamics. It also compares both bodies and assesses their performance, while drawing far-reaching conclusions on their prospects in the new world economic order of the twenty-first century.

THE GLOBAL CONTEXT OF THE "NEW" REGIONALISM

Regional impulses have always been part of the international system. In this sense, their ubiquity has been a distinguishing feature and characteristic of past and particularly present world orders.[6] While the focus of this paper is not strictly on past regional integration schemes, it is important to note that both past and present impetus for cooperation between nations have been informed by the protection and promotion of strategic economic and other interests within the global system. Indeed, it is such considerations and the need to constantly guarantee and actualize their advantages that underlines the particular attention most nations of the world give regional schemes in their foreign policies. Thus, emphasizing this important point, A. I. Asiwaju conceptualizes the phenomenon to mean a novel category of international collaboration forced on adjacent sovereign states. Such states are compelled to interact for reasons not only of common interests in human and natural resources due to a shared international boundary, but also of common concerns about cross-border environmental consequences and/or acts of God.[7] It also presupposes agreements between groups of countries in a region to reduce, and eventually remove, restrictions on economic and political transboundary interactions necessitated by the logic of geographical contiguity.[8]

Theoretically, regionalism has been justified on both economic and political grounds. Anchored on the Smithian theory of international trade, in economic terms it is assumed that unrestricted free trade would allow countries to specialize in the production of those goods and services that they can produce most efficiently. This is in addition to ensuring foreign direct investment and the transfer of technological, marketing, and managerial know-how between interacting and integrating nations. Thus regionalism is an attempt to maximize the gains from the free flow of trade and investment between countries beyond those attainable under international agreements such as the General Agreement on Tariff and Trade (GATT) and the World Trade Organization (WTO).[9] Politically, regionalism promotes interdependence between nations on a wide range of issues. For example, by linking neighboring economies and making them increasingly dependent on each other, incentives are created for political cooperation between neighboring states. As a result, the potential for violent conflicts between them are reduced, while their political influence in the international system is enhanced.[10]

On this basis, we would proceed by declaring that the recrudescence of regionalism in global politics since the mid-1980s is significant in a number of respects. For, although before this time there were regional efforts in Europe and parts of Africa, these were not pursued with the vigor, intensity, and commitment that now characterize such efforts by nations. Indeed, during this period, the attention of nations was concentrated on institution building as a mechanism for warding off state protectionism, which was the norm in international relations. Certain developments on the global scene altered this state of affairs and generated the need for stronger and more viable regional economic and political blocs. Arising from their importance in understanding the nature and character of the world order they help established and given the implications of this on the actions of state and nonstate actors in the international system, it is necessary to isolate and critically examine their basis.

First, there was the collapse of the Soviet Union and the emergence of what has been referred to as a unipolar world order.[11] As part of this process, there was the removal of the Iron Curtain and the unification of Germany, then the last major hurdle to the accelerated integration of Europe as a major political and economic bloc. A distinguishing feature of this unipolarity underscores the preeminent status of the United States in world affairs. According to Krauthammer, after the exit of the Soviet Union, the United States became the only superpower that had the military, diplomatic, political, and economic resources to be a decisive player in any conflict in whatever part of the word it chose to involve itself.[12]

Second, there was the seemingly aggressive behavior of microactors, in a context energized by the progress of multilateralism, and the generalization of adjustment and deregulation policies. Arguing in favor of the latter forces, the International Monetary Fund (IMF) and World Bank (WB) have attributed these trends to structural changes that have enhanced the role of market forces in strengthening economic growth.[13]

Third, there is the rapid expansion of the international financial market, which outpaced growth in trade itself. The internationalization of the financial market was marked by at least four other important features, namely: (a) the optimization of returns on world trade levels and the unrestrained mobility of capital, (b) the increasing importance of financial flows across national boundaries, (c) the movement of private investment funds involving amounts that are larger than those in national central banks, and (d) the stupendous growth in telecommunications and information technology.

Fourth, and as a corollary of the above, there was the partitioning and gradual concentration of world trade and investments between three major economic blocs, namely, North America (made up of the United States and Canada), Europe (dominated largely by Britain, France, and Germany), and Asia Pacific (dominated by China and Japan), and the corresponding intensive competition from emerging nations in Asia (the "Asian Tigers") and Latin America.[14] The emergence of these economic power blocs provoked responses from other parts of the world in the direction of transnational protectionism on a regional basis.

Fifth, there is globalization and the increasing integration of the world's economies. As a result of what was assumed to be the uneven environment of the globalization process, countries that feel endangered by the overwhelming influence of the major economic powers alluded to earlier on, welcomed "'delinking" from the global trading system as a possible viable option.[15]

Sixth, from 1990, following the collapse of the Soviet Union and the subsequent crumbling of the eastern bloc, there was the prospect of the transformation of the European Union (EU) into "fortress Europe." When, on January 1, 1993, the EU became a single market with 360 million consumers, it sent trepidations and shock waves around the world, particularly in North America and the Asia Pacific, for very obvious reasons. Besides signaling the Europeanization of Europe, it was a union that had a gross domestic product (GDP) of more than US$2.7 trillion, an estimated GDP annual growth rate of 4 to 7 percent, an export potential worth more than US$680 billion, and an import capacity of well over US$708 billion.[16]

Seventh, there was the apprehension from many nations around the world associated with the uncertainty surrounding the Uruguay Round of negotiations.[17] The replacement of General Agreements on Tariffs Trade (GATT) with the World Trade Organization (WTO) confirmed these fears and encouraged regional tendencies.

And finally, there are threats to local cultures, whereby regions with sociocultural homogeneity and affiliations tend to more intensely integrate with each other against their neighbors, whom they now see as rivals in the global competition for both influence and resources. Some analysts have emphasized this increasingly dominant position of cultural forces in the New World Order (NWO) and contended that following the exit of the ideologically framed bi- or multipolar world systems, culture, and its spinoffs—including but not exclusive to religion, ethnicity, and technology—has within the context of the "iron law of duality" become a critical factor in the way people relate with each other and forecast the future.[18] The specific argument relating culture and regionalism was forcefully articulated by S. P. Huntington. Advancing this thesis, he persuasively avers that:

> Regions are a basis for cooperation among states only to the extent that geography coincides with culture. Divorced from culture, propinquity does not yield commonality and may foster just the reverse. Military alliances and economic associations require cooperation among members, cooperation depends on trust, and trust most easily springs from common values and culture. The overall effectiveness of regional organizations generally varies inversely with the civilizational diversity of their membership. Single civilization organizations do more things and are more successful than multicivilizational organizations.[19]

It was against the background of all these factors that bilateral economic and other agreements and regional groupings mushroomed and became a preponderant feature of the emergent NWO. Such regional supranational protectionism emerged as responses to the new patterns of trade, economic, and other relations in the international system. Underpinned by the emergence of a NWO, they sought to either protect themselves or re-organize in order to fit into and benefit from the unfolding neoliberal transformation process underscored by the globalization process. It should, however, be noted that the new regionalism under close scrutiny often implies many things to the different nations involved with the phenomenon.[20] In one dimension, it describes the reforming of the so-called first-generation regional organizations, which came into existence in the early 1960s to promote economic integration through import substitution strategies and delinking from the global capitalist market. In another, it entails the establishment of relatively new bodies, like the North American Free Trade Area (NAFTA) and Common Market of the South Americas (MERCOSUR), the Asian-Pacific Economic Conference (APEC), the Caribbean Community (CARICOM), and the Free Trade Agreement of the Association of South East Asian Nations (ASEAN) in Asia. In Europe, the expansion of the EU encouraged the establishment of the European Economic Area (EEA), while in West Africa the challenges faced by the subregional Economic Community of West African States prompted moves by the erstwhile Organization of African Unity (OAU) for the formation of the transcontinental African Economic Community (AEC) in 1991.

Yet in another dimension, these developments connote the initiation of dialogue between mutually relating nations, directed toward the expansion of preexisting institutions and the attainment of interregional agreements. In the final analysis, such a process is directed at enhancing the bargaining power of member states while at the same time tapping the externalities of the NWO. Therefore the global context of new regionalism suggests the following:

1. The NWO is yet to deliver on its promises for a more humane world and economic prosperity;
2. Nations of the world, especially those from the global south, are apprehensive of the deepening worldwide inequality and the accentuation of poverty arising from the restructuring of trading relations under the WTO;
3. Although the world is globalizing, trade within regions has grown faster than trade between regions;
4. New regional impulses are direct consequences of the domination and division of world trade between the most economically powerful nations of the world;
5. This phenomenon suggests the regionalization of international politics, with far-reaching implications for the management of issues relating with economics, peace, and security in regional theaters across the globe;

6. This trend would continue and even intensify in the decades ahead, creating a new platform for contestations between nations in the international system. Global conflicts would as a result be more dominated by economic issues than with military and political concerns of nation-states in the global system, bearing in mind the fact that the latter issues could provide the justifications for violent confrontations.

Thus, as we intend to demonstrate in the remainder of this paper, for the nations of the global south, regionalization holds the key to their survival in a NWO characterized by neoliberal integration and powered by globalization. Their responses to the unequal economic and political environment of the NWO and the multilateral world trading system under the hegemony of the WTO, the WB, and the IMF also play a role. Critics of this order have justified these reactions as appropriate because of the crises they have continued to generate in the international trading system and the implications of this on the prospects for economic growth and development in the global south.[21] Indeed, it is now obvious that their very economic survival in the globalized world would be contingent upon the extent to which they utilize these platforms to negotiate with their more advanced counterparts and the degree to which they sustain their protection on regional basis.

FROM THE PAST TO THE PRESENT: THE BASIS OF REGIONALISM IN AFRICA AND ASIA

In analyzing the driving force for regional impulses in developing countries, Asiwaju identifies at least four critical variables which we find useful in explaining the experiences of West Africa and East Asia.[22] Analyzing the first factor, Asiwaju contends that the tendency towards regional cooperation and integration is underscored by the pervasive presence of what he calls "vivisected or partitioned" ethnic nationalities. According to him, these transborder peoples have continued to maintain a wide range of socioeconomic, cultural, and even political links with each other notwithstanding imposed administrative boundaries and other barriers. Citing the examples of the Shona—across the Monica sector of the Zimbabwe-Mozambique border, the Ketu Yoruba straddling the Niger-Benin border, or the Baatonu of Nikki kingdom of Borgu astride the Nigeria-Benin border—Asiwaju concludes that the significance of ethnic nationality dimension of transfrontier solidarity in Africa is underscored by its ubiquity.[23]

One of the oldest factors facilitating contacts and interactions and therefore integration in Africa, cross-border trade has had the most profound influence in new regional impulses. Reinforcing this claim, Asiwaju points out that although hitherto ignored, trade across boundaries has increasingly captured the attention of development scholars, who are now clamoring for a market-driven integration process.[24] The new emphasis on economic forces such as trade is well placed, perhaps because of its earlier role in promoting cooperation between communities in the premodern times. In Africa, records have shown that ancient empires thrived because of their control of trade and trade routes.[25] In the West African region for example, Ghana, Mali, and Songhai, as well as the Borno kingdom, among many others, emerged as formal entities following informal trade interactions and cooperation between and between communities in the region. The region was knitted together into an economic hub by trade routes and markets, along and within which group solidarities and crosscutting loyalties were constructed.

A third factor is transborder natural resources, the significance of which is underscored by the usage of rivers, lakes, mountains, and forests as boundaries. In Africa, rivers like the Zambezi, Limpopo, Mano, Nile, Niger, Senegal, and Orange; lakes like Chad, Victoria, and Malawi; and mountains like Cameroon, Adamawa, and Kilimanjaro, and so on, demarcate boundaries that have promoted cooperation as well as conflicts between groups with common access to these resources. The Gulf of Guinea Coast offers an interesting example of a transborder resource that has paradoxically encouraged integration and provoked bloody conflicts between the frontier nations of the African continent. Indeed, its offshore hydrocarbon resources facilitated the economic integration of the West African subregion and promoted bilateral and multilateral cooperation between neighboring states, just as contested claims for access to these resources have sometimes degenerated into aggressive litigations and open conflagrations between these states. Available records indicate that the Gulf of Guinea was a factor in the formation of the ECOWAS in 1976.[26] Similarly, its resources are known to have sparked off violent confrontations between Nigeria and Cameroon.[27] Other transborder resources with similar histories include the Aouzur Strip (between Libya and Chad), Agacher Corridor (between Mali and Burkina Faso), and Lake Chad (between Nigeria, Niger, and Sudan).

The fourth factor is historical and cultural links; it suggests the unifying power of the past and preexisting crosscutting and other shared values between contiguous polities in the continent. Thus, far beyond the formal structures of the state in Africa, it is argued that intergroup relations founded on the power of historical and cultural affiliations between ethnic nationalities separated by territorial boundaries encouraged regional integration in Africa.[28] Sociocultural bonds underpinned how economic and political interactions were constructed in and between some countries in the continent before, during, and after colonization. In recent years, the rich history of such interactions has been invoked to generate awareness, galvanize, and justify newer forms of economic relationships between contiguous territories in Africa. It is also the basis of certain bi and multilateral cooperation, pacts, and alliances from which involved African nation-states mutually benefit. Thus, and as Asiwaju aptly asserts,

The point to stress is that contact between the various peoples of Africa has worked not only to generate common experiences over broad and distant areas of the continent, but also to leave behind common threads of which have been woven into the societal fabric in accordance with the varying degrees of receptivity of the diverse local cultures.[29]

It remains to be added that this process of cultural harmonization predicated on cultural variables and the history of the people are resilient forces in the drive for cooperation, integration, and regionalism in modern Africa.

To a certain degree, the drive toward regionalism in East Asia was (and is still) influenced by a combination of the factors examined in the preceding paragraphs. For example, available evidence is clear on how trade provided a credible and positive platform for the interactions of peoples from diverse cultural backgrounds.[30] Similarly, there is evidence that the nations of Southeast Asia had thriving trading relations dating as far back as the second century.[31] Trading and commercial interactions between these nations has continued to modern times in spite of the enormous social and political changes Southeast Asia has undergone over the centuries. The incentive for intraregional trade in Southeast Asia has been given further boost by the challenge posed by the rise of China to global prominence and of course by the dynamics of the globalization process. With regard to cultural and historical linkages, the countries of the region share a few things in common, even though they are largely culturally heterogeneous. For example, to varying degrees, the nations of Southeast Asia have been affected by the Hindu, Buddhist, and Islamic cultures. A source argues that in the remote past, the growth of the Indian civilization had a great influence on the region. As a matter of fact, as early as the first century, Indian traders had begun a prosperous sea trade with Southeast Asia; by the Gupta age, Brahmins and Buddhist monks were already spreading Hinduism and Buddhism in the region.[32]

Therefore, long before formal institutions began to emerge during the last two centuries, the process of integration was already ongoing in both West Africa and Southeast Asia. This was expressed in the complex patterns of socioeconomic networks and other forms of relations that prevailed in the two regions. In this regard, it could be argued that these remote regional impulses predated the present and provide important examples of how societies in these regions organized and conducted economic and other relations before the rise of the West. These relations, however, were consolidated following contacts with the outside world, especially with the West as from the fifteenth century onward. The rise of western imperialism was consistent with the emergence of what became the global economy, in which notions of production and distribution beyond the nation and region increasingly became popularized. Underpinned first by the cutting-edge revolution in navigation technology and later the industrial revolution, western imperialism created a world order that was by and large anchored on the universalization of western values. It is this hegemonic agenda that defines the dichotomy between the global north and the global south, and also frames the dialogue around and reactions to the NWO and the globalization process. In this sense, regionalism in West Africa and Southeast Asia represent both the consequence and antithesis of the emerging world economic order after the Cold War and the globalization process energizing it.

LOOKING IN THE MIRROR: ECOWAS AND ASEAN COMPARED

We have already made the point that the decline of the bipolar world order created an enabling environment for the regionalization of global politics. As a result, the emerging NWO, contrary to general expectations, was fragmented in the sense that the "region" as a geographical unit and regional supranational bodies as entities became agents for economic diplomacy in the global system. As a result, scholarly concerns with how regional bodies are faring in the dynamics of the international system are on the rise.[33] At least three reasons make this particularly important. First, such close examination has enabled us assess the performance of these bodies against the backdrop of their set aims and objectives. Two, it has created the possibilities for us to relate the individual experiences of nations that are directly involved with this development in global politics. Finally, arising from such reflections, we are in the position to draw far-reaching conclusions on the interplay between globalization and the changes in the world economy on the one hand and regionalism and economic development on the other. In the final analysis, the data being generated on these would help validate or refute prevailing notions regarding the nexus between globalization, the emergence of the NWO, and regionalism.

It is against this background that, in the subsequent analysis in this section, we attempt to look in the mirror and see to what extent ECOWAS and ASEAN compare and contrast. Both regional groupings offer useful and interesting examples for the analysis of regional efforts directed at addressing practical challenges confronting members as they try to maximize opportunities in the competitive international system. They also offer good illustrations for the analysis of comparative regionalism in the era of neoliberal globalization. The preferred parameter for the juxtaposition attempted here is formulated based on a synthesis of existing ideas regarding regional integration.[34] For the avoidance of doubts, some of these include (but are not limited to) historical experience, size, and geographical compactness; the structure and composition of the regions; the degree of progress so far recorded; and the specific place of hegemonic powers in the experiences of both regions. The analysis of these variables is done in the context of an appraisal of what ECOWAS and ASEAN have in common and what they do not.

Similarities

ECOWAS and ASEAN have a few features in common that also contrasts them as regional organizations with the EU. These features say a lot about their profile, consummation process, and operational character. Both regional supranational organizations comprise of countries that have the history of being dominated by other nations. There is enough evidence to buttress the point that at different periods in their past, these countries were victims of western imperialism. For example, in the nineteenth century, colonial powers like Britain, France, Germany, and Portugal established dominion over the countries that later became ECOWAS members.[35] In the same vein, Russia, Britain, Germany, France, Portuguese, the United States, and later Japan all had some measure of influence in Southeast Asia in the heyday of imperialist expansion into the region in 1857–1914.[36] Unfortunately this history had serious implications for foreign policies long after the colonial nations' political independence from their overlords, since the newly independent nations still retained some connections with the latter. Indeed, the influence of former colonial powers still compromises global politics involving both sides as well as attempts to objectively resolve ontradictions. In the context of the dichotomy between the global north and the global south, this poses a critical problem related to the inability of regional bodies in the former to effectively operate and positively affect the development of member states. However, this contrasts the EU from ECOWAS and ASEAN in the sense that the EU is largely made up of countries that do not have a colonial history and therefore operate as truly independent nation-states in the regional body.

Second, like the EU, ASEAN and ECOWAS were all products of the Cold War politics between the East and the West. The EU started from the formation of the European Coal Steel Community (ECSC) in 1951. This was the first supranational organization in contemporary world history. It initially began as a six-nation organization, but was later joined in 1958 by other organizations with similar goals and objectives. By 1967, it expanded both its mission and membership, requiring a new identity and a more vigorous focus in the context of the bipolar world order of the era. The result was the European Economic Community (EEC). Reacting to the phenomenal changes occurring at the global scene, particularly, the exit of Soviet Union, the emergence of the NWO, and globalization, the body became into the EU in 1991.[37] ASEAN emerged and operated, by and large, as a response of member states to a common enemy, namely communism, which had allegedly threatened the survival of these states. However, the diminishing influence of communism in Asia also affected its activities. From its initial conception as a military alliance of concerned states, ASEAN has since moved into promoting sociocultural cooperation, encouraging economic collaboration between its members. On its part, ECOWAS has been affected by global changes, compelling it to either adjust or formulate new notions for sustaining and deepening economic cooperation and integration between its members. It should be mentioned that although these mutations are never without serious challenges, the regional body has, mutatis mutandis, continued to trudge onward.

Unlike the EU, ECOWAS and ASEAN are basically multicultural and multicivilizational regional supranational organizations whose consummation processes are consistent with the pluralist model of integration. Under this framework, there is an overarching concern with the sovereignty of members as the basis for economic cooperation and achieving integration. This is besides the fact of diversity in the level of economic development or military power as well as of the divergent civilizational backgrounds of member states. We will illustrate this point by isolating and explaining a couple of issues concerning these organizations. At its inception in 1967, ASEAN was said to be made up of one Sinic, one Buddhist, one Christian, and two Muslim states (Indonesia, Malaysia, Philippines, Singapore, and Thailand), all of which were threatened by communist insurgencies and real ones from Vietnam and China.[38] At this point, all members were also grappling with serious economic and social problems. As essentially loose organizations, members of both regional bodies were at liberty to belong to other associations which they deemed fit. For the next 10 to 15 years, these diversities continued to be part of their existence and in fact seriously affected their overall performance. Similarly, ECOWAS is predominantly dominated by Muslim and Christian states that partly engage global issues as they affect the region on the basis of these divergent cultural backgrounds but more so from the angle of their level of development.[39]

The relationship between cultural heterogeneity and the slow pace of regional economic and political integration has been established by leading scholars of development studies.[40] It is argued that although geographical contiguity offers enormous advantage and incentive for contacts, interactions, and integration between nation-states, realizing the full potential of these could be constrained by the contradictions inherent in cultural plurality. This is the case because, as S. P. Huntington, a major influence in this school of thought, argues:

> Regions are geographical not political space. Regions are a basis for cooperation among states only to the extent that geography coincides with culture. Divorced from culture, propinquity does not yield commonality and may foster just the reverse. Military alliances and economic associations require cooperation among their members, cooperation depends on trust, and trust most easily springs from values and culture. As a result, while age and purpose also play a role, the overall effectiveness of regional organizations generally varies inversely with the civilizational diversity of their membership. By and large, single civilization organizations do more things and are more successful than multicivilizational organizations.[41]

Extrapolating from the above, it is easy to understand why ECOWAS and ASEAN have had problems actualizing their set goals compared with their counterparts, like the EU and CARICOM. ECOWAS and ASEAN have a lot in common at the level of the type of membership they possess and the geographic distances between them. We have already emphasized the place of geography in the process of regional integration. It suffices here to underscore the point that the more geographically contiguous the location of member states, the more likely it is that there would be a sustained and fairly extensive pattern of contacts and interactions between them over time. Where this is matched with the membership size of a regional group, it has the potential of promoting interactions beyond strictly economic matters, leading eventually to the possibility of the emergence of regional identity cutting across diverse interests.[42] The membership of ECOWAS and ASEAN are by and large developing nations of the global south, a vast majority of whose citizens belong to the world's poorest. This point is particularly true with respect to ECOWAS member states, where more than half of the population live on about US$1 per day. Since their inception, both regional organizations have focused on typical developmental issues[43] while trying to increase their membership for greater leverage in a fast-changing and highly competitive world. With regard to membership size and expansion, ASEAN appears to be less successful than ECOWAS. The latter began with fifteen member states at its inception on June 23, 1976, and has since expanded to include virtually all the nations in the West African region.[44] On the other hand, ASEAN began in 1967 with just five members and have been making slow progress in expanding its membership.[45]

Finally, both organizations share in common the advantage of being geographically compact, a favorable condition for accelerated integration. The significance of this factor becomes immediately obvious if we measure the greatest geographic distances between the capital cities of member states in both regional organizations. With a total land area of 5,112,903 square kilometers, most ECOWAS member states are easily linked by land, sea, and air from Senegal to Nigeria (the farthest distance between the states), making this a perfect example of a regional organization that is contiguous in every sense of the word. In its original composition, the maximum distance within ASEAN was is 3,018 kilometers (Hanoi to Jakarta). When it became ASEAN Plus Three, the estimated maximum distance became 5,212 kilometers (from Jakarta through Indonesia to Beijing). This to a very large extent distinguishes both ECOWAS and ASEAN from the EU, the spread of which is presently estimated at 7,796 kilometers.[46] We must point out that geographical compactness can sometimes be a problem for regional economic integration, as demonstrated by the experience of ECOWAS. Though geographically ECOWAS member states belong to a closely knit region, their recent history has been completely bereft of any form of cohesive development. Indeed, affiliations of members with foreign powers have continued to polarize the regional organization into two principal colonial cultures, French and British.

Divergences

The above similarities notwithstanding, ECOWAS and ASEAN manifest a lot of differences in conception, composition, operational character, and, above all, the degree of success in performance since their emergence as supranational organizations in the international system. In the first place, both fundamentally differ in their initial conceptions and philosophies as well as their operational focus. When it emerged, ASEAN was originally conceived as a bulwark against the spread of communism in East Asia. This initial conception limited and eventually attenuated its capacity to rapidly expand, in addition to encumbering its socioeconomic and political relevance to member states for several years. In the 1990s, however, ASEAN broke away from this largely narrow conception and moved on to broader socioeconomic and political issues.Today has the following as its reviewed aims, objectives, and primary focus:

1. To accelerate the economic growth, social progress, and cultural development in the region through joint endeavors in the spirit of equality and partnership in order to strengthen the foundation for a prosperous and peaceful community of Southeast Asian nations;
2. To promote regional peace and stability through abiding respect for justice and the rule of law in the relationship among countries of the region and adherence to the principles of the United Nations Charter;
3. To promote active collaboration and mutual assistance on matters of common interest in the economic, social, cultural, technical, scientific, and administrative fields;
4. To provide assistance to each other in the form of training and research facilities in the educational, professional, technical, and administrative spheres;
5. To collaborate more effectively for the greater utilization of their agriculture and industries, the expansion of their trade, including the study of the problems of international commodity trade, the improvement of their transportation and communications facilities, and the raising of the living standards of their peoples;
6. To promote Southeast Asian studies;
7. To maintain close and beneficial cooperation with existing international and regional organizations with similar aims and purposes, and explore all avenues for even closer cooperation among themselves.[47]

From the above and in this regard, the organization affirmed its new focus on (1) accelerating economic growth, social progress, and cultural development in the region through joint endeavors in the spirit of equality and partnership in order to strengthen the foundation for a prosperous and peaceful community of Southeast Asian nations and (2) promoting regional peace and stability through abiding respect for justice and the rule of law in the relationship among countries in the region and adherence to the principles of the United Nations Charter.[48] It should be pointed out that this seeming paradigm shift is not unconnected with the diminishing global influence of communism as an ideology of development following the collapse of the Soviet Union, the emergence of a NWO, and the restructuring of the Chinese economy, among many other things.[49] From the point of view of geostrategy, this restructuring was appropriate at this point because globalization threw up new challenges that weakened state actors in the international system while underscoring the rising profile of regional supranational bodies.

On the other hand, ECOWAS was from the outset basically concerned with promoting economic cooperation and integration in West Africa. This much is clear from the treaty establishing the organization, which explicitly articulates its specific aims and objectives as follows: "(to) promote cooperation and integration, leading to the establishment of an economic union in West Africa in order to raise the living standards of its people and to maintain and enhance economic stability, foster relations among Member States and contribute to the progress and development of the African Continent."[50] The strategies for achieving these economic objectives in stages include the following:

1. Harmonizing, coordinating national policies, and promoting integration programs, projects, and activities;
2. Promoting the establishment of joint production and joint venture enterprises;
3. Establishing a common market;
4. Establishing an economic union through the adoption of common policies in the economic, financial, social, and cultural sectors and the creation of a single monetary zone;
5. Strengthening relations and promoting the flow of information among populations, organizations, media, businessmen and women, workers, and trade unions.[51]

It is important to point out that the level or depth of economic integration so far attained by both organizations is partly explained by the ideas that underpinned their objectives in the first instance. To this extent, ASEAN's rather slow-paced experience is not unconnected with its initial conception as an alliance against the expansion of communism into East Asia by states who felt their sovereignty was under serious threat. Thus, before the twenty-first century, its major focus was economic *cooperation,* not *integration,* for, as Huntington, citing Palmer and Reckford, emphasizes, "On the economic front, ASEAN was from the beginning designed to achieve economic cooperation rather than economic integration, and as a result regionalism has developed at a modest pace, and even a free trade area is not contemplated until the twenty-first century."[52]

On the flip side, the ultimate goal of ECOWAS is to ultimate goal is to actualize the economic integrate of the West African subregion. A cursory look at the treaty of the organization reveals a deliberate connection of each article with this ultimate goal. There is great liberalization of trade between the ECOWAS states, in addition to the free mobility of people across national boundaries. The move is also on for the establishment of a common currency that would be accepted across national boundaries of all member states. On all these stages of integration, ECOWAS has done rather better than ASEAN if this is measured against the backdrop of the years the two have so far existed and the quantum of progress recorded. The point should be made that both are nowhere near the EU in this regard.

There are arguments in support of the critical role of hegemonic powers in regional economic integration efforts.[53] According to this thesis, the more involved are regional hegemonic powers in an integration process, the greater its chances of success and quality of performance. Others argue that relative symmetry in capabilities (economic, political, and military) among prospective members impact more positively on regional integration efforts.[54] The explanation here is that nations with approximately equal power would better be able to negotiate greater cooperative arrangements, without fear of being dominated by the strongest among them. The experiences of ECOWAS and ASEAN illustrate these divergent perspectives. The leadership role Nigeria has continued to provide ECOWAS has been applauded as one of the critical factors for the emergence, growth, development, and remarkable success of the regional body.[55] ECOWAS has immensely benefited from the resourcefulness of the country right from its inception. But for this, the regional intervention force, the Economic Community of West African States Monitoring Group (ECOMOG) would never have seen the light of the day and West Africa would probably have been severely affected by the civil wars in Liberia and Sierra Leone.[56] Indeed, the survival of ECOWAS is largely contingent on the involvement of Nigeria, the regional hegemonic power. ASEAN has not been very lucky, because it comprises of nations that are approximately "first among equals." Its attempt to involve regional powers like China and Japan in its activities is ongoing and has yet to yield positive results. Consequently economic integration here is lethargically slow and ongoing.[57] On the other hand, we should make the point that the role of hegemonic power in regional integration efforts could stall the process. In the specific example of ECOWAS, the leadership role of Nigeria is viewed with trepidations by some member states, who understand this as a form of "internal colonization." For example, the decisions that led to the establishment of an intervention force in the crises in Liberia and Sierra Leone were met with stiff opposition by some members not because they lacked merit but because of the symbolic meaning of the critical role Nigeria played in their actualization.

CONCLUSION

The preceding represents an attempt to outline in broad strokes, the dynamics of regionalism in the global south in the era of modern day globalization. Analyzing this trend as a basic feature of the post-Cold War global order, I have been able to provide some insights on how countries in the global south are responding to the challenges of the globalization process and the ways in which these reactions are in turn scoping and dimensioning the patterns of the economic and political relationships emerging within and between regions of the world. It was revealed that while regionalism, like globalization, has come a long way, it is equally true that the contemporary manifestations of this phenomenon are both partly reactions to, and products of the emerging NWO and the globalization process. They are reflections of how globalizing nations of the world are redefining alliances in order to protect their economic interests in the context of emerging challenges and opportunities. In explaining this development, we isolated and analyzed the examples of ASEAN and ECOWAS, which although have many things in common, differ in a number of obviously significant ways. The experiences of these regional bodies have been determined by the history of their conception and emergence, the character of the environment in which they operate, and more importantly, how they are affected by the NWO and globalization process. The extent to which they would survive and actualize their set economic and political objectives during the course of the twenty-first century will be largely determined by developments in the international system and particularly the nature and character of the globalization process.

What then would be the future of the NWO as it relates with the neo-liberal globalization process and rising regionalist tendencies? First, the stability of the international system envisaged in the increasing integration of the world as a consequence of globalization appears elusive. Indeed, the more unipolar the world becomes, the more regionalist tendencies proliferate in various parts of the world. It is important to understand these tendencies as both consequences of and reactions to the emerging post-Cold War order, which means many things to different people. Second, regionalism as a phenomenon would remain a major force in the redefinition of world order politics during the twenty-first century. For the developing countries of the global south, especial those that feel particularly apprehensive of the unequal environment of the globalization process, regionalism offers a viable option for negotiating their strategic interests in the NWO. Third, the increasing significance of regionalist tendencies in the post-Cold War global order would ultimately alter the foreign policies of the world's nations. For the global south, the reality of the political economy of the NWO has compelled the need for deepened South–South cooperation in favor of economic survival in an increasingly competitive world. Fourth, global economic recession would put enormous pressure on nation-states, and as some of them try to adjust, there could be political upheavals characterized by social unrests and growing insecurity about the future. In the final analysis, how nations in the global south adjust to these changes will depend a lot on the capacity of their economy, the quality of leadership, and the responsiveness of functioning institutions they possess. These would ultimately impact on the kind of regional supranational organizations they are members of and the extent to which these would help realize their aspirations during the twenty-first century.

NOTES

1. See O. O. Okpeh Jr., "Globalization and the African Question in the 21st Century," in *African Journal of Economy and Society (AJES)*, Vol. 2 (January-December, 2000): 43–60; and R. M. Kanter and T. L. Pittingsky, "Globalization: New Worlds for Social Inquiry," *Berkeley Journal of Sociology*, Vol. 40 (1995–1996): 1–19.
2. The question of whether globalization is a consequence of the contemporary world or has origins that go far back into humanity's past has been raised by and remains contentious between scholars. For details see M. Khor, *Globalization and the South: Some Critical Issues* (Ibadan: Spectrum Books, 2000); E. Toyo, *Background to Globalization* (Ibadan: Academic Staff Union of Universities Educational Publication Series 2, 2000); O. O. Okpeh Jr., "Globalization and the African Question in the 21st Century," in *African Journal of Economy and Society (AJES)*, Vol. 2 (January-December, 2000): 43–60; A. G. Hopkins, ed., *Globalization in World History* (New York: Norton, 2002); P. L. Berger and S. P. Huntington, eds., *Many Globalizations: Cultural Diversities in the Contemporary World* (Oxford, UK: Oxford University Press, 2003); K. S. Jomo, ed., *Globalization Under Hegemony: The Changing World Economy* (Oxford, UK: Oxford University Press, 2006); and C. Kessler, *Globalization: Familiar Issues, but a New-Fangled Discourse—or "Dejavu all over Again"* (Pangi, Malaysia: Institut Kajian Malaysia dan Antarabangsa, 2006).
3. See M. P. Todaro and S. C. Smith, *Economic Development* (Mumbai: Pearson Education, 2003), 511. Similarly consult *Can Africa Claim the 21st Century?* (Washington, DC: World Bank, 2000); and International Monetary Fund, "Globalization: Threat or Opportunity," *Issues Briefs* (2002).
4. See D. Galin, "Inside the New World Order: Drawing the Battle Line," in *Nigerian Fact Labor Sheet*, Vol. 2, No. 1 and 2 (January-April, 1997): 1. For similar strong antiglobalization views, read M. Khor, *Globalization and the South: Some Critical Issues*; E. Toyo, *Background to Globalization*; O. O. Okpeh Jr., "Globalization and the African Question in the 21st Century"; M. Rupert and H. Smith, eds., *Historical Materialism and Globalization* (London: Routledge, 2002); P. L. Berger and S. P. Huntington, eds., *Many Globalizations: Cultural Diversities in the Contemporary World*; K. S. Jomo, ed., *Globalization Under Hegemony: The Changing World Economy* (Oxford, UK: Oxford University Press); P. Bond, *The Looting of Africa: The Economics of Exploitation* (London; Zed Books, 2006); and M.H.K. Timamy, *The Political Economy of Technological Underdevelopment in Africa* (Lagos: Centre for Black and African Arts and Civilization, 2007). See M. P. Todaro and S. C. Smith, *Economic Development* (Mumbai: Pearson Education, 2003), 511.

5. See J. E. Stiglitz, *Globalization and its Discontents* (New York: Norton, 2003), 214. It should be added that Stiglitz was Chief Economist at the World Bank until January 2000. Before that he was chairman of President Clinton's Council of Economic Advisors. Currently he is professor of finance and economics at the Columbia University. His versatility and knowledge of the field earned him the Nobel Prize for Economics in 2001.
6. Read interesting accounts of past and present regional integration efforts in R. Strassoldo, *Frontier Regions: An Analytical Study* (Council of Europe, 1973); V. von Malchus, *The Cooperation of European Frontier Regions: State of the Question and Recent Developments* (Strasbourg, France: Council of Europe, 1975); G. Vedovato, *Transfrontier Cooperation and the Europe of Tomorrow* (Strasbourg, France: Council of Europe, 1995); M. Anderson and E. Borts, eds., *The Frontiers of Europe* (London: Frances Printer, 1998); R. Laverge, ed., *Regional Integration and Cooperation in West Africa* (Trenton, NJ: Africa World Press, 1997); D. Bach, ed., *Regionalism in Africa: Integration and Disintegration* (London: James Currey, 1999); A. I. Asiwaju, *Transfrontier Regionalism; Perspectives on the European Union and Postcolonial Africa with Special Reference to Borgu*, Occasional Publication No. 12 (Ibadan: Institut Francais de Recherche en Afrique [IFRA]), 1999.
7. I. Asiwaju, *Transfrontier Regionalism*, 1.
8. World Trade Organization, *Regionalism and the World Trading System* (Geneva: World Trade Organization, 1995); and C.W.L. Hill, *International Business: Competing in Global Marketplace* (New York: McGraw-Hill, 1998).
9. C. W. L. Hill, *International Business: Competing in Global Marketplace*, 226–227.
10. The establishment of European Community (EC) in 1959 was largely informed by these considerations. Europe had suffered the devastating consequences of two wars during the first half of the twentieth century as a result of the unbridled ambitions of nation-states. The unification of Europe was therefore intended to checkmate the future occurrence of these episodes. Europe also suffered further fragmentations after the WWII, which politically weakened it in the emerging bipolar world order. The founders of EC conceived of a supranational organization that would provide a credible platform for Europe in world politics. For details see D. Swann, *The Economics of Common Market*, 6th ed. (London: Penguin Books, 1990); and C.W.L. Hill, *International Business: Competing in Global Marketplace*, 226.
11. This presupposes a world order dominated by one or very few powerful nations, defending one ideological, economic, and political system (in this case capitalism). Some useful perspectives on this may be found in N. Chomsky, *World Orders: Old and New* (London: Pluto Press, 1997); S. P. Huntington, *The Clash of Civilizations and the Remaking of World Order* (London: Free Press, 2002).
12. See C. Krauthammer, "The Uni-Polar Moment," *Foreign Affairs*, Vol. 70, No. 1 (1991): 23–33. It remains to be added that this power was eloquently illustrated in its role in ousting Slobodan Milosevic of Yugoslavia; the global war against terrorism, especially in countries like Afghanistan, Iraq, and lately Iran; and the championing of the globalization of liberal values of democracy.
13. For a critical assessment of such assumptions see J. E. Stiglitz, *Globalization and Its Discontents*; E. Toyo, *Background to Globalization*; and O. O. Okpeh Jr., "Globalization and the African Question in the 21st Century."
14. By 1992, these economic blocs controlled 46 percent of world trade. For details see O. O. Okpeh Jr., "Globalization and the African Question in the 21st Century," 44.

15. The proposal for delinking from the neoliberal driven global economy of the twenty-first century has remained popular in the developing countries of the world. For more on the rudiments of this proposal, consult B. O. Onimode et al., *Alternative Strategies for Africa: Coalition for Change*, Vol. 1 (IFRAA, 1990); Economic Commission for Africa (ECA), *Beyond Recovery: ECA's Revised Perspectives of Africa's Development, 1990–2008* (Addis Ababa, 1989); and O. O. Okpeh Jr., "Globalization and the African Question in the 21st Century."
16. See H. O'Neil, ed., "Europe," *Journal of Development Studies* (1990): 188–225. Similarly, read N. Colchester and D. Buchan, *Europower: The Essential Guide to Europe's Economic Transformation in 1992* (London: Economist Books, 1990); "One Europe, One Economy," *Economist* (November 30): 53–54; and I. L. Bashir, "The New World Order and Socio-Political Transition in Africa in the 1990s and Beyond," in B. Caron, A. Gboyega and E. Osaghae, eds., *Proceedings on the Symposium on Democratic Transition in Africa* (Ibadan: CREDU, Institute of African Studies, University of Ibadan, 1992).
17. Many countries of the global south realized early enough that the debates at the Uruguay world trade talks were dominated by interests of the countries of the global north. They observed that their agitations for a fairer trade, an end to persistent global poverty and inequality, and a total restructuring of the world trade failed to appeal to their rich counterparts, who insisted on neoliberal reforms. For details of these positions see United Nations Commission on Trade and Development (hereafter UNCTAD), *Capital Flows and Growth in Africa* (Geneva: UNCTAD, 2000); UNCTAD, *Least Developed Countries Report*, (Geneva: UNCTAD, 2000); O. O. Okpeh Jr., "Africa and the International Trade: A Historical Analysis," *African Journal of Economy and Society (AJES)*, Vol. 5, No. 2. (July-December 2005): 117–128.
18. For details of this argument and its place in shaping the NWO, consult A. A. Mazrui, *Cultural Forces in World Politics* (Portsmouth, NH: Heinemann, 1990); S. P. Huntington, *The Clash of Civilizations and the Remaking of World Order*; and O. O. Okpeh Jr., "The New World Order, Diaspora Africans and the Racial Identity Question: A Historical Reflection on Some Emerging Issues," *Lagos Historical Review*, Vol. 6 (2006): 91–117.
19. See P. Huntington, *The Clash of Civilizations and the Remaking of World Order*, 130–131.
20. For these diverse perspectives see D. Bach, ed., *Regionalism in Africa: Integration and Disintegration*; and R. I. Onwuka and A. Sesay, eds., *The Future of Regionalism in Africa* (London and Basingstoke: Macmillan, 1985).
21. See for example, M. Khor, "Present and Future Shape of the WTO and the Multilateral Trading System," Briefing Paper, No. 2 (Pangi, Malaysia: Third Word Network, hereafter TWN, 2001); Oxfam International, *Rigged Rules and Double Standards: Trade Globalization, and the Fight Against Poverty* (New York: Oxfam International, 2002); and Oxfam International, "Africa at the Crossroads: Time to Deliver," Oxfam Briefing Paper No. 19 (New York: Oxfam International, 2002).
22. See A. I. Asiwaju, *Transfrontier Regionalism: Perspectives on the European Union and Postcolonial Africa with Reference to Borgu*, 14–19.
23. Ibid., 15. Also see A. I. Asiwaju, ed., *Partitioned Africans: Ethnic Relations across Africa's International Boundaries, 1884–1984* (London: C. Hurst, 1985).
24. A. I. Asiwaju, *Transfrontier Regionalism; Perspectives on the European Union and Postcolonial Africa with Reference to Borgu*, 16. For more on this strategy of regional integration, consult P. N. Echessah, *Unrecorded Cross-*

Border Trade between Tanzania and Her Neighbors: Implications for Food Security (Nairobi: USAID Regional Economic Development Support Office, 1997); J. Egg and J. Igue, *Market-Driven Integration on the Eastern Sub-region: Nigeria's Impact on its Immediate Neighbors* (Paris: Club du Sahel/OECD, 1993); and R. Lavergne, ed., *Regional Integration and Cooperation in West Africa* (Trenton, NJ: Africa World Press and Ottawa International Research Development Committee, 1997).

25. See R. Gray and D. Birmingham, eds., *Essays on Trade in Central and East Africa before 1900* (Oxford, UK: Oxford University Press, 1970); A. B. Aderibigbe, "West African Integration: An Historical Perspective," *Nigerian Journal of Economic and Social Science*, Vol. 5, No. 1 (March, 1963): 9–18; J. S. Triminghan, "West African States" in R. O. Collins, ed., *Problems of African History* (London: Prentice Hall,1968); A. A. Boahen, "The Caravan Trade in the Nineteenth Century," in R. O. Collins, ed., *Problems of African History*, 297–312; A. I. Asiwaju, "Socio-economic Integration of the West African Sub-region in Historical Context: Focus on the European colonial Period," in A. B. Akinyemi, ed., *Readings and Documents on ECOWAS* (Ibadan, Nigeria: Macmillan, 1984); and D. O. Omagu, *Regional Peace and Security: A Historical Perspective of ECOWAS in Liberia and Sierra Leone* (Calabar, Nigeria: Ushie Printing, 2002).
26. See A. B. Aderibigbe, "West African Integration: An Historical Perspective"; and A. I. Asiwaju, "Socio-economic Integration of the West African Sub-region in Historical Context."
27. For details of this see O. O. Okpeh Jr., "Resource Conflicts in the Gulf of Guinea Coast: Implications for Regional Security," commissioned paper for the Department of History, Vanderbilt University, Nashville, TN, March 22, 2011.
28. See for example S. Adotevi, "Cultural Dimensions of Economic and Political Integration in Africa," in R. Laverge, ed., *Regional Integration and Cooperation in West Africa* (Trenton, NJ: Africa World Press, and Ottawa: International Development Research Centre, 1997); A. B. Aderibigbe, "West African Integration: An Historical Perspective;" and A. I. Asiwaju, "Socio-economic Integration of the West African Sub-region in Historical Context." J. S. Trimingham in an earlier publication shows how the Islam that came into West Africa from North Africa became a strong ideology for social cohesion and also trade between Muslims in West Africa on the one hand and between them and their North African counterparts on the other. For details see J. S. Trimingham, *A History of Islam in West Africa* (Oxford, UK: Oxford University Press, 1962).
29. A. I. Asiwaju, *Boundaries and African Integration: Essays in Comparative History and Policy Analysis* (Abuja, Nigeria: Panaf Publishing, 2003).
30. E. Sakakibara and S.Yamakawa, *Regional Integration in East Asia: Challenges and Opportunities* (World Bank East Asia Project, undated); A. A. Badawi, *Towards an Integrated East Asian Community* (Kuala Lumpur: Second East Asian Forum, 2005); And L. P. Ping et al., eds., *The Emerging Eat Asian Community: Security and Economic Issues* (Pangi, Malaysia: Universiti Kebangsaan, 2006).
31. See Hanes, W. T., T. Falola, and T. Raab, eds. *World History: Continuity and Change* (Austin: Holt, Rinehart and Winston, 1997). Scc in particular chapter 12, 220–350.
32. *World History: Continuity and Change.*
33. For example see A. Hurrell, "Explaining the Resurgence of Regionalism in World Politics," *Review of International Studies,* Vol. 21 (1995); S. P. Huntington, *The Clash of Civilizations*; L. Faecett and A. Hurrell, eds.,

Regionalism and World Politics: Regional Organization and International Order (Oxford, UK: Oxford University Press, 1995); M. Schul, F. Soderbaum, and J. Ojendel, eds., *Regionalization in a Globalizing World: Comparative Perspective on Forms, Actors and Processes* (London: Zed Books,1997); and A. Acharya, "The Role of Regional Organizations: Are Views Changing": http://www.ndu.edu/inss/symposia/pacific2004/acharya.htm

34. By this we mean that we benefited from preexisting theories of and conceptual perspectives on the conditions for successful regional integration, some of which include neorealism, neofunctionalism, neoliberalism, geographical determinism, and intergovernmentalism. Find detailed accounts of these in S. Walt, *The Origins of Alliances* (Ithaca, NY: Cornell University Press, 1987); D. Mitrany, *A Working Peace System* (Pittsburgh: Quadrangle Books, 966); E. Haas, *Beyond the Nation-State: Functionalism and International Organization* (Stanford, CA: Stanford University Press, 1964); E. Haas, *The Obsolescence of Regional Integration Theory* (Berkeley: Institute of International Studies, 1975); J. Nye, *Peace in Parts: Integration and Conflict in Regional Organizations* (Boston: Little Brown, 1971); R. Keohane, *After Hegemony Cooperation and Discord in the World Economy* (Princeton, NJ: Princeton University Press, 1984); M. L. Brown, *Developing Countries and Regional Economic Cooperation* (Westport, CT: Praeger, 1994); and E. Solingen, *Regional Orders at Century's Dawn* (Princeton, NJ: Princeton University Press, 1998).

35. There an impressive account of the colonial episode in Africa in A. Adu Boahen, ed., *Africa Under Colonia Domination, 1880–1935* (Paris: UNESCO, 1985).

36. See Hanes, W. T., T. Falola, and T. Raab, eds., *World History: Continuity and Change,* 579–591.

37. See G. Grin, *The Battle of the Single European Market: Achievements and Economic Thought, 1945–2000* (London: Kegan Paul, 2003).

38. S. P. Huntington, *The Clash of Civilizations,* 132.

39. All ECOWAS member states are multireligious. Christianity and Islam as dominant ideologies are always in contention for the imposition of their identities on some of these states. Since the foreign policies of these states reflect their domestic and external environments, they also affect the nature and character of their involvement with the supranational regional body.

40. See for example I. Wallerstein, *Geopolitica and Geoculture: Essays on the Changing World System* (Cambridge, UK: Cambridge University Press, 1992); A. A. Mazrui, *Cultural Forces in Global Politics* (London: James Currey, 1990); and S. P. Huntington, *The Clash of Civilizations,*130–131.

41. S. P. Huntington, *The Clash of Civilizations,*130–131.

42. We must, however, add that the revolution in information technology and the globalization process has reduced to almost nothing the significance of geographical variables in contacts and interactions between people, groups, and nations. As a result, technology has expanded its reach, shrinking distances and reducing boundaries so that what we call regions are nothing more than what has been aptly described as "elusive entities" that essentially have no boundaries. For an elaboration of these notions see M. F. Schulz and J. Ojendal, eds., *Regionalization in a Globalizing World: A Comparative Perspective on Forms, Actors and Processes* (London: Zed Books, 1997); and T. Falola, *Transnationalization, Denationalization and Deterritorialization: Contemporary Cultures in the Context of Globalization* (Kaduna, Nigeria: Kaduna State University, 2010).

43. Issues such as economic cooperation between member states, economic integration of the regions, infrastructure development, regional peace and

stability, and so on remain the major highlights of both regional groups' main concerns.

44. Apart from Mauritania, which opted out in 2000, and Ivory Coast, which was suspended in 2011 following the election crisis that literally plunged the country into civil war, all the West African nation-states are members of ECOWAS.
45. ASEAN's program of expansion includes persuading Japan, China, and even India to join the organization. Consequently, today we have "ASEAN plus Two" and "ASEAN plus Three" as part of this broad and sustained program. For details see R. B. Palmer and T. J. Reckford, *Building ASEAN: 20 Years of Southeast Asian Cooperation* (New York: Praeger, 1987); P. J. Katzenstein et al., eds., *Asian Regionalism* (Ithaca, NY: Cornell University, East Asian Program, 2000); R. Stubbs, "ASEAN plus Three: Emerging East Asian Regionalism?" *Asian Survey*, Vol. 42 (May/June, 2002); and I. P. Ping et al., eds., *The Emerging East Asian Community: Security and Economic Issues* (Pangi, Malaysia: Penerbit Universiti Kebangsaan, 2006).
46. P. F. Diehl, "Can East Asia Be Like Europe? Exploring Selected Conditions for Regional Integration" in I. P. Ping et al., eds., *The Emerging East Asian Community*, 31–57. Similarly see R. I. Onwuka and A. Sesay, eds., *The Future of Regionalism in Africa*; and D. O. Omagu, *Regional Peace and Security*.
47. http://www.aseansec.org/about_ASEAN.html. Also see R. B. Palmer and T. J. Reckford, *Building ASEAN: 20 Years of Southeast Asian Cooperation*.
48. See R. B. Palmer and T. J. Reckford, *Building ASEAN: 20 Years of Southeast Asian Cooperation*.
49. See M. F. Schulz and J. Ojendal, eds., *Regionalization in a Globalizing World*.
50. See Economic Community of West African States, *Text of Revised Treaty of Economic Community of West African States* (Abuja, Nigeria: ECOWAS, 1976). Also consult Economic Community of West African States, *The Economic Community of West African States Information Brochure* (Abuja, Nigeria: ECOWAS, 1998).
51. Economic Community of West African States, *The Economic Community of West African States Information Brochure*, 2; And D. O. Omagu, *Regional Peace and Security: A Historical Perspective of ECOWAS in Liberia and Sierra Leone*, 45–48.
52. See *The Clash of Civilizations*, 132. Also see R. B. Palmer and T. J. Reckford, *Building ASEAN: 20 Years of Southeast Asian Cooperation*; P. J. Katzenstein et al., *Asian Regionalism*; R. Stubbs, "ASEAN plus Three: Emerging East Asian Regionalism?"; And I. P. Ping et al., eds., *The Emerging East Asian Community*.
53. For example, see R. Keohane, *After Hegemony Cooperation and Discord in the World Economy* (Princeton, NJ: Princeton University Press, 1984); A. Hureell, "Regionalism in Theoretical Perspective," in L. Fawett and A. Hureel, eds., *Regionalism in World Politics* (Oxford, UK: Oxford University Press, 1995), 37–73; E. Sollingen, *Regional Orders at Century's Dawn* (Princeton, NJ: Princeton University Press, 1998); and P. F. Diehl, "Can East Asia Be Like Europe" in I. P. Ping et al., eds., *The Emerging East Asian Community*, 33–57.
54. See P. Schmitter, "A Revised Theory of Regional Integration," *International Organization*, 836–868; and J. Greico, "Systemic Sources of Variation in Regional Institutionalization in Western Europe, East Asia, and the Americas" in E. Mansfield and H. Milner, eds., *The Political Economy of Regionalism*, 164–87.

55. See for example, A. B. Akinyemi, ed., *Readings and Documents on ECOWAS* (Ibadan, Nigeria: Macmillan, 1984); G. O. Olusanya and R. A. Akindele, eds., *Nigeria's External Relations: The First Twenty-Five Years* (Ibadan: University of Ibadan Press, 1986); and D. O. Omagu, *Regional Peace and Security: A Historical Perspective of ECOWAS in Liberia and Sierra Leone*.
56. ECOMOG is the acronym for the ECOWAS Cease-Fire Monitoring Group, which was set up to intervene in the civil wars in Liberia and Sierra Leone. It is argued in some quarters that Nigeria provided more than half of the resources (in cash, personnel, and military equipments) that sustained the activities of this body. For details read M. A. Vogt, ed., *The Liberian Crisis and ECOMOG: A Bold Attempt at Regional Peace Keeping* (Lagos: Gabumo Publishing, 1992); and D. O. Omagu, *Regional Peace and Security: A Historical Perspective of ECOWAS in Liberia and Sierra Leone*.
57. This is not denigrate the successes so far recorded in this regard but to emphasize the point that had regional powers been actively involved from the beginning with ASEAN, it would have since advanced beyond the current level.

REFERENCES

Acharya, A. "The Role of Regional Organizations: Are Views Changing": http://www.ndu.edu/inss/symposia/pacific2004/acharya.htm

Aderibigbe, A. B. "West African Integration: An Historical Perspective." *Nigerian Journal of Economic and Social Science*, Vol. 5, No. 1 (March, 1963): 9–18.

Adotevi, S. "Cultural Dimensions of Economic and Political Integration in Africa." In R. Laverge, ed. *Regional Integration and Cooperation in West Africa*. Trenton, NJ: Africa World Press and Ottawa: International Development Research Centre, 1997.

Akinyemi, A. B., ed. *Readings and Documents on ECOWAS*. Ibadan, Nigeria: Macmillan, 1984.

Anderson, M., and E. Borts, eds. *The Frontiers of Europe*. London: Frances Printer, 1998.

Asiwaju, A. I. "Socio-economic Integration of the West African Sub-region in Historical Context: Focus on the European colonial Period," in Akinyemi, A. B., ed., *Readings and Documents on ECOWAS*. Ibadan, Nigeria: Macmillan, 1984.

———. *Transfrontier Regionalism: Perspectives on the European Union and Postcolonial Africa with Special Reference to Borgu*, Occasional Publication No. 12. Ibadan: Institut Francais de Recherche en Afrique (IFRA), 1999.

———. *Boundaries and African Integration: Essays in Comparative History and Policy Analysis*. Abuja: Panaf Publishing, 2003.

Asiwaju, A. I., ed. *Partitioned Africans: Ethnic Relations across Africa's International Boundaries, 1884–1984*, London: C. Hurst, 1985.

Bach, D., ed. *Regionalism in Africa: Integration and Disintegration*. London: James Currey, 1999.

Badawi, A. A. *Towards an Integrated East Asian Community*. Kuala Lumpur: Second East Asian Forum, 2005.

Bashir, I. L. "The New World Order and Socio-Political Transition in Africa in the 1990s and Beyond." In Caron, B.Gboyega, A. and Osaghae, E., eds. *Proceedings on the Symposium on Democratic Transition in Africa*. Ibadan: CREDU, Institute of African Studies, University of Ibadan, 1992.

Berger, P. L., and Huntington, S. P., eds. *Many Globalizations: Cultural Diversities in the Contemporary World.* Oxford, UK: Oxford University Press, 2003.

Boahen, A. A. "The Caravan Trade in the Nineteenth Century." In R. O. Collins, ed. *Problems of African History.* Upper Saddle River, NJ: Prentice Hall, 1968.

Boahen, A. A., ed. *Africa under Colonia Domination, 1880–1935.* Paris: UNESCO, 1985.

Bond, P. *The Looting of Africa: The Economics of Exploitation.* London, Zed Books, 2006.

Brown, M. L. *Developing Countries and Regional Economic Cooperation.* Westport, CT: Praeger, 1994.

Chomsky, N. *World Orders: Old and New.* London: Pluto Press, 1997.

Colchester, N. and Buchan, D. *Europower: The Essential Guide to Europe's Economic Transformation in 1992.* London: Economist Books, 1990.

Diehl, P. F. "Can East Asia Be Like Europe? Exploring Selected Conditions for Regional Integration." In I. P. Ping et al., eds. *The Emerging East Asian Community.* Pangi, Malaysia: Pernerbit Universiti Kebangsaan Malaysia, 2006.

Echessah, P. N. *Unrecorded Cross-Border Trade between Tanzania and Her Neighbors: Implications for Food Security.* Nairobi: USAID Regional Economic Development Support Office, 1997.

Economic Commission for Africa (ECA). *Beyond Recovery: ECA's Revised Perspectives of Africa's Development, 1990–2008.* Addis Ababa: ECA, 1989.

Economic Community of West African States (ECOWAS). *Text of Revised Treaty of Economic Community of West African States.* Abuja, Nigeria: ECOWAS, 1976.

———. *The Economic Community of West African States Information Brochure.* Abuja, Nigeria: ECOWAS, 1998.

———. *The Economic Community of West African States Information Brochure.* Abuja, Nigeria: ECOWAS, 1998.

Economist. "One Europe, One Economy," *Economist* (November 30): 53–54.

Egg, J., and J. Igue. *Market-Driven Integration on the Eastern Sub-region: Nigeria's Impact on Its Immediate Neighbors.* Paris: Club du Sahel/OECD, 1993.

Faecett, L., and A. Hurrell, eds. *Regionalism and World Politics: Regional Organization and International Order.* Oxford, UK: Oxford University Press, 1995.

Falola, T. *Transnationalization, Denationalization and Deterritorialization: Contemporary Cultures in the Context of Globalization.* Kaduna, Nigeria: Kaduna State University, 2010.

Galin, D. "Inside the New World Order: Drawing the Battle Line." In *Nigerian Fact Labor Sheet,* Vol. 2, Nos. 1 and 2 (January-April, 1997): 1–17.

Gray, R., and D. Birmingham, eds. *Essays on Trade in Central and East Africa before 1900.* Oxford, UK: Oxford University Press, 1970.

Greico, J. "Systemic Sources of Variation in Regional Institutionalization in Western Europe, East Asia, and the Americas." In E. Mansfield and H. Milner, eds. *The Political Economy of Regionalism.* New York: Columbia University Press, 1997.

Grin, G. *The Battle of the Single European Market: Achievements and Economic Thought, 1945–2000.* London: Kegan Paul, 2003.

Haas, E. *Beyond the Nation-State: Functionalism and International Organization* Stanford, CA: Stanford University Press, 1964.

Haas, E. *The Obsolescence of Regional Integration Theory.* Berkeley: Institute of International Studies, 1975.

Hanes, W. T., T. Falola, and T. Raab, eds. *World History: Continuity and Change.* Austin: Holt, Rinehart and Winston, 1997.

Hill, C.W.L. *International Business: Competing in Global Marketplace.* New York: McGraw-Hill, 1998.

Hopkins, A. G., ed. *Globalization in World History.* New York: Norton, 2002.
Huntington, S. P. *The Clash of Civilizations and the Remaking of World Order.* London: Free Press, 2002.
Hureell, A. "Regionalism in Theoretical Perspective." In L. Fawett and A. Hureel, eds. *Regionalism in World Politics.* Oxford, UK: Oxford University Press, 1995a.
———. "Explaining the Resurgence of Regionalism in World Politics." *Review of International Studies,* Vol. 21 (1995b):4.
International Monetary Fund. "Globalization: Threat or Opportunity." *Issues Briefs* (2002).
Jomo, K. S., ed. *Globalization under Hegemony: The Changing World Economy.* Oxford, UK: Oxford University Press, 2006.
Kanter, R. M., and T. L. Pittingsky. "Globalization: New Worlds for Social Inquiry." *Berkeley Journal of Sociology,* Vol. 40, (1995–1996): 1–19.
Katzenstein, P. J., et al., eds. *Asian Regionalism.* New York: East Asian Program, Cornell University, 2000.
Keohane, R. *After Hegemony Cooperation and Discord in the World Economy.* Princeton NJ: Princeton University Press, 1984.
Kessler, C. *Globalization: Familiar Issues, but a New-Fangled Discourse—Or "Deja vu all over Again."* Pangi, Malaysia: Institut Kajian Malaysia dan Antarabangsa, 2006.
Khor, M. *Globalization and the South: Some Critical Issues.* Ibadan: Spectrum Books, 2000. Khor, M. "Present and Future Shape of the WTO and the Multilateral Trading System." Briefing Paper, No. 2. Pangi, Malaysia: Third Word Network, hereafter TWN, 2001.
Krauthammer, C. "The Uni-Polar Moment." *Foreign Affairs,* Vol. 70, No. 1 (1991): 23–33.
Lavergne, R., ed. *Regional Integration and Cooperation in West Africa.* Trenton, NJ: Africa World Press and Ottawa: International Research Development Committee, 1997.
Malchus, V. von. *The Cooperation of European Frontier Regions: State of the Question and Recent Developments.* Strasbourg, France: Council of Europe, 1975.
Mazrui, A. A. *Cultural Forces in Global Politics.* London: James Currey, 1990.
Mitrany, D. *A Working Peace System.* Pittsburgh: Quadrangle Books, 1966.
Nye, J. *Peace in Parts: Integration and Conflict in Regional Organizations.* Boston: Little Brown, 1971.
O'Neil, H. "Europe." *Journal of Development Studies* (1990): 188–225.
Okpeh, O. O. "Globalization and the African Question in the 21st Century." *African Journal of Economy and Society (AJES),* Vol. 2 (January–December, 2000): 43–60.
———. "Africa and the International Trade: A Historical Analysis." *African Journal of Economy and Society (AJES),* Vol. 5, No. 2 (July–December 2005): 117–128.
———. "The New World Order, Diaspora Africans and the Racial Identity Question: A Historical Reflection on Some Emerging Issues." *Lagos Historical Review,* Vol. 6 (2006): 91–117.
———. "Resource Conflicts in the Gulf of Guinea Coast: Implications for Regional Security." Commissioned paper for the department of history. Nashville, TN: Vanderbilt University, March 22, 2011.
Olusanya, G. O., and R. A. Akindele, eds., *Nigeria's External Relations: The First Twenty-Five Years.* Ibadan: University of Ibadan Press, 1986.
Omagu, D. O. *Regional Peace and Security: A Historical Perspective of ECOWAS in Liberia and Sierra Leone.* Calabar: Ushie Printing, 2002.

Onimode, B. O., and H. Sumonu, et al., eds. *Alternative Strategies for Africa: Coalition for Change*, Vol. 1. Interfaith Forum on Religion, Art and Architecture, 1990.

Onwuka, R. I., and A. Sesay, eds. *The Future of Regionalism in Africa*. London and Basingstoke: Macmillan, 1985.

Oxfam International, *Africa at the Crossroads: Time to Deliver*, Oxfam Briefing Paper No. 19. New York: Oxfam International, 2002.

———. *Rigged Rules and Double Standards: Trade Globalization, and the Fight against Poverty*. New York: Oxfam International, 2002.

Palmer, R. B., and T. J. Reckford. *Building ASEAN: 20 Years of Southeast Asian Cooperation*. New York: Praeger, 1987.

Ping, L. P., et al., eds. *The Emerging Eat Asian Community: Security and Economic Issues*. Pangi, Malaysia: Universiti Kebangsaan, 2006.

Rupert, M., and H. Smith, eds. *Historical Materialism and Globalization*. London: Routledge, 2002.

Sakakibara, E., and S. Yamakawa. *Regional Integration in East Asia: Challenges and Opportunities*. World Bank East Asia Project, undated.

Schmitter, P. "A Revised Theory of Regional Integration." *International Organization*, Vol. 24 (1970): 836–868.

Schulz, M. F., and Ojendal, J., eds. *Regionalization in a Globalizing World: A Comparative Perspective on Forms, Actors and Processes*. London: Zed: Books, 1997.

Schulz, M., F. Soderbaum, and J. Ojendel, eds. *Regionalization in a Globalizing World: Comparative Perspective on Forms, Actors and Processes*. London: Zed Books, 1997.

Sollingen, E. *Regional Orders at Century's Dawn*. Princeton, NJ: Princeton University Press, 1998.

Stiglitz, J. E. *Globalization and its Discontents*. New York: Norton, 2003.

Strassoldo, R. *Frontier Regions: An Analytical Study*. Strasbourg, France: Council of Europe, 1973.

Stubbs, R. "ASEAN plus Three: Emerging East Asian Regionalism?" *Asian Survey*, Vol. 42 (May/June, 2002):440–55.

Swann, D. *The Economics of Common Market*, 6th ed. London; Penguin Books, 1990.

Timamy, M.H.K. *The Political Economy of Technological Underdevelopment in Africa*. Lagos: Centre for Black and African Arts and Civilization, 2007.

Todaro, M. P., and Smith, S. C. *Economic Development*. Mumbai, India: Pearson Education, 2003.

Toyo, E. *Background to Globalization*. Educational Publication Series 2. Ibadan: Academic Staff Union of Universities, 2000.

Trimingham, J. S. "West African States." In R. O. Collins, ed. *Problems of African History*. London: Prentice Hall, 1968.

———. *A History of Islam in West Africa*. Oxford: Oxford University Press, 1962.

United Nations Commission on Trade and Development (UNCTAD). *Capital Flows and Growth in Africa*. Geneva: UNCTAD, 2000.

———. *Least Developed Countries Report*. Geneva: UNCTAD, 2000.

Vedovato, G. *Transfrontier Cooperation and the Europe of Tomorrow*. Strasbourg, France: Council of Europe, 1995.

Vogt, M. A., ed. *The Liberian Crisis and ECOMOG: A Bold Attempt at Regional Peace Keeping*. Lagos: Gabumo Publishing, 1992.

Wallerstein, I. *Geopolitica and Geoculture: Essays on the Changing World System*. Cambridge, UK: Cambridge University Press, 1992.

Walt, S. *The Origins of Alliances*. Ithaca, NY: Cornell University Press, 1987.

World Bank. *Can Africa Claim the 21st Century?* Washington, DC: World Bank, 2000.

World Trade Organization. *Regionalism and the World Trading System.* Geneva: World Trade Organization, 1995.

8 The Political Implication of Past and Present Nigerian Financial Crises

Muhammed Tanko

The global financial and economic crisis that began in the United States and the United Kingdom in 2007 brought the credit market to a halt. It compounded the already existing problems of the world's economy when it continued to spread and deepen in several countries. It persisted until mid-2008, when the effect was seen in almost all the world markets, leading to the most severe global recession since the Great Depression of the 1930s. Although the problem began in industrialized countries, the financial crisis quickly spread to emerging markets and other developing economies. This led many investors to pull their capital out of countries that were perceived to have a certain level of risk exposure. The result was that the values of stocks and domestic currencies plunged. Slumping exports and commodity prices have added to developing countries' woes (Ajakaiye and Fakiyesi 2009; Arieff 2010). In 2009, the International Monetary Fund (IMF) estimated that the global economy had contracted by 1.1 percent.

In Nigeria, the initial response of the policy makers was mild. This was associated with a lack of understanding of the magnitude of the crisis. In general, they thought of the crisis as only a "storm in a teacup." Even when the capital market had started bleeding uncontrollably, they insisted that the fundamentals of the financial system looked impressively strong. While the principal government officers continued to exhibit their ignorance of the crisis, it is pertinent to note that in Nigeria, 99 percent of the country's foreign income and 85 percent of local revenues were directly derived from activities related to the export of a single commodity—oil. It is estimated that 58.4 percent of Nigeria's exports went to the United States and up to 25 percent to the Eurozone; 67 percent of its other-than-oil exports went to western Europe and 20 percent to Asia, while the Economic Community of West African States (ECOWAS) accounted for only 11 percent in 2007. The stock of Nigeria's foreign reserves is kept in European capitals—where financial markets had tumbled and banks were severely distressed.

In the literature, the consequences of the financial and economic crises have been established to typically include increased unemployment, decreased consumer and business spending, and declining stock prices. Specifically, the following common outcomes were identified as the result of the crises (Ogunleye 2009):

1. Commodity prices collapse (especially that of oil)
2. Revenue contraction (possible "bust" syndrome)
3. Declining capital inflows in the economy
4. Deaccumulation of foreign reserves and pressure on exchange rate
5. Limited foreign trade finances for banks due to systemic distress in the banks
6. Capital market downturn, divestment by foreign investors with attendant tightness, and secondary effects on the balance sheet of banks through increasing provisioning for bad debts and the attendant negative impact on profitability

On the other hand, the Nigerian lawmakers looked at their banks as being robust enough to withstand the shocks of the economic and financial crisis, especially as the sector witnessed a consolidation that saw the contraction in the number of banks from 89 banks to just 24. Soludo (2009) observed, "Resource flows and capital flows around the world were frozen. Nigeria depended for more than 95 percent of its foreign exchange on oil, whose price had crashed to the extent that from about July 2008 the outflow of foreign exchange had actually far outstripped the inflows." Soludo further observed that, in 2008, Nigeria sold about a billion dollars a month to the bureau-de-change, but since the beginning of 2009 the inflow had been about US$800 million a month.

Appiah-Dolphyne (2009) also addressed the loss of ₦9 trillion clipped off from investors in the nation's capital market. Obi (2009) lamented that the productive sector, which could have given stimulus to financial market's growth, has been on a long recess in Nigeria. Furthermore, the national coordinator of the Independent Shareholders Association of Nigeria (ISAN), Sunny Nwosu (in Ogundipe 2009), explained that while some other nations had recovery plans that were well spelt out, Nigeria remained virtually inactive in taking revival steps to bring the economy out of the woods. This chapter, therefore, interrogates the implications of the past and present global financial meltdown for the world's economy generally for the Nigerian economy more specifically.

OVERVIEW OF THE NIGERIAN ECONOMY PRIOR TO THE CRISIS

Prior to the crisis of 2007, the Nigerian economy was performing with mixed results. While some were of the opinion that the economy was doing fine, others felt that its performance was far below projected growth. Specifically, the estimated GDP growth of 6.2 percent was below the set target of 10 percent. However, in general the economy was growing, as the figure was higher than the 6 percent recorded in 2006. This growth was driven primarily by the non-oil sector, which grew by 9.6 percent (CBN 2008b); it was largely attributable to the agricultural sector, which grew by 7.4 percent—led by crop production, livestock, and fishing. Other drivers of growth in non-oil GDP included wholesale and retail trade, building and construction, and services, which recorded growth rates of 15.3 percent, 13.0 percent, and 9.8 percent, respectively. Industrial output fell by 3.5 percent, attributable mainly to the 5.9 percent drop in crude oil production occasioned by the Niger Delta crisis. By year-end 2007, crude oil production stood at 0.9 million barrels a day. Official confirmation from the Nigerian National Petroleum Company (NNPC) showed that the country lost ₦16.9 billion daily to petroleum pipeline vandalism.

The downstream sector of the petroleum industry remained comatose and the country relied on imported refined petroleum products for domestic and industrial operations. It has been indicated that Nigeria consumed about 14.13 billion liters of refined petroleum products, or 38.7 million liters per day, in 2007, with premium motor fuel accounting for 9.81 billion liters. By end-September 2007, the Manufacturers Association of Nigeria (MAN) reported a drop in the utilization of manufacturing capacity from 44.06 percent in 2006 to 43.5 percent, owing to the difficult operating environment. The industrial sector made a negative contribution of 0.78 percentage points. The agriculture sector, on the other hand, contributed almost half of the GDP growth rate of 6.2 percent.

Meanwhile, earnings from non-oil exports—such as finished leather products, cocoa and its products, sesame seeds, and manufactured products like cosmetics and toiletries—rose during the year to about US$1.38 billion. By the end of 2008, this value rose to US$1.8 billion, the highest in the country's history. In addition, gross official external reserves rose by 20 percent to stand at about US$50.75 billion by end-December 2007, against US$42.3 billion in December 2006. The 2008 GDP growth rate

Table 8.1 Sectoral Contribution to GDP Growth in Nigeria, 2003–2007 (percent)

	2003	2004	2005	2006	2007
Agriculture	2.58	2.65	2.85	2.93	2.65
Crop production	2.42	2.36	2.56	2.64	2.67
Industry	6.12	1.22	0.47	-0.62	-0.78
Crude petroleum	56.02	0.84	0.12	-0.93	-1.08
Building and construction	0.12	0.14	0.18	0.2	0.21
Wholesale and retail	0.69	1.24	1.82	2.16	2.34
Services	0.06	1.32	1.19	1.36	1.49
Communications	0.36	0.36	0.43	0.59	0.74
Total GDP	9.57	6.58	6.51	6.03	6.22
Non-oil GDP	3.44	5.36	6.04	6.65	6.99

Source: CBN, 2008.

of 6.77 percent was higher than that of 2007 (at 6.2 percent). Growth was again driven by the non-oil sector, especially the agricultural sector, which contributed 41.7 percent out of the 83.71 percent total contribution of the non-oil sector to GDP in 2009. This improvement in output, especially in the first half of 2009, was attributed partly to moderate weather, especially the early rains experienced in the southern and northern states of Nigeria. Other factors that helped to boost agricultural production included several government intervention measures, like the National Agricultural Project, the National Special Programme for Food Security, zero tariffs on imported agrochemicals, and export expansion grants as well as tightening of controls on illegal imports of agricultural products. The country maintained a balance of payments surplus in 2009, fueled by the current account surplus.

METHODOLOGY

The aim of this paper is to consider the financial implications of past and present crises that have bedeviled Nigeria. The discussion follows a two-step analysis of the data collected. First, we discuss the various items of development and how they were affected by the financial meltdown. Then we analyze employment as the main variable that determines the level of economic activity. The data under consideration in this section were taken from National Bureau of Statistics (NBS) for the year 1992. Two regression methods were used in the analysis. In the first method, the model for the unit root test is specified as

$$\Delta X_t = \alpha + \sigma t + \beta X_t - 1 + \Sigma \lambda \Delta X_t \ldots 1 + \mu t$$

Where X_t = the variable under consideration; ΔX_t = the difference of the variable under investigation; μt = the random error term; and $\alpha + \sigma t$ indicates when the test is carried out with intercept and trend. The null hypothesis of nonstationarity is rejected if the t—statistics are greater than the critical t value. The t—statistics here are the augmented Dickey-Fuller statistics. They are compared with the Mackinnon critical value and decide for unit-root when t—statistics less t—critical value is less than zero and for stationarity when t—statistics less t—critical value is greater than zero.

For the second method, we used a linear regression model that expresses the composite unemployment rate as dependent variable NAT(Y), whereas the URB(X1) and URB(X2) are the urban and rural unemployment rates respectively. Thus:

$$NAT(Y) = + [URB(X1), RUR(X2)]$$
$$NAT(Y) = \beta 0 + \beta 1 \ URBX1 + RURX2 + \mu$$

Where NAT = the national (composite) unemployment rate; URB =→the urban unemployment rate; RUR =→the rural unemployment rate; μ =→the statistical error term; and β0, β1, and β2 are coefficients to be estimated.

IMPACT ON THE CAPITAL MARKET

There are concerns regarding how rapidly the global financial crisis penetrated the Nigerian capital market, especially given that the country's domestic mortgage market is rudimentary. The decline of indicators of activity on the Nigerian Stock Exchange (NSE) before the escalation of the crisis in July 2008 became a source of concern for many. Emerging facts reveal that the crisis may have been made evident in the capital market through various channels. For instance, foreign portfolio investment withdrawals and withholdings for servicing financial problems of the foreign investors home as well as prospects of reduced foreign direct investment (FDI) are bound to affect investor confidence in the economic health of Nigeria. Evidence of the foreign portfolio withdrawals shows that the total financial inflows to Nigeria between 2007 and 2008 increased by 21 percent, while those between 2008 and 2009 declined by 38.6 percent. The adoption of a public-private partnership (PPP) policy platform to implement huge investment plans such as oil and gas exploration, power plants, railways, and other infrastructural projects, therefore, exposed the country more to FDI uncertainties and vagaries.

The credit crunch experienced by lending institutions, particularly banks, affected businesses that require short- and long-term money, including banks lending to corporate organizations as well as engaging in interbank short-term lending. In an economy like Nigeria's, where mortgages and credit card purchases are not well developed, this credit crunch becomes manifest in deteriorated risk assets of banks that had given out loans to some investors to invest in other financial instruments (particularly secondary market purchase and initial public offerings [IPOs]) in the hope of making quick returns through a quick turnaround of their portfolio. This is what is termed "margin lending." It may also be termed Nigeria's own version of the subprime problem, resulting in an exploding domestic stock market and stock prices and astounding returns to both speculators and providers of margin funds (the banks).

Other factors that have had a serious impact on the capital market are called "intensifiers." These include policy interpretations by the market, which may have been induced by the government's slow initial stand on the economy. This also includes the interpretation of announcements, proclamations, and rumors by the market. Examples include the proposed capitalization plan of the stock market players (stock broking firms), as well as the termination of the margin lending by banks. The all-share index and market capitalization of the 233 listed equities on the NSE has grown over the years from a value of ₦12,137 in 2002 to ₦66,371 in March 2008, with market capitalization at about ₦12.640 trillion, after which values began to fall precipitously to 22,349 points in January 2009, with a market capitalization of ₦4.998 trillion owing to the financial meltdown. By the end of the first week of March 2009, values had declined to 21,893 points with a market capitalization of ₦4.900 trillion. This value had further declined to 21,608 points, with a market capitalization of ₦4.836 trillion, by the end of the second week of March 2009. This reveals that between March 2008 and March 2009, the all-share index had lost a total share of 67 percent, while market capitalization had lost 62 percent of its value.

IMPACT ON FEDERAL MEDIUM- AND LONG-TERM BONDS

The federal government issued fourteen bonds between January and December of 2007, with a total value of ₦504.8 billion. The maturity profiles of the instruments in the portfolio were mainly 3 and 5 years, with only 2 having 10-year maturities. Issuance in 2008 was reduced to only 5, but one had a 20-year maturity in November 2008. The total value of bonds issued in 2008 was around ₦95 billion. However, toward the end of the last quarter of 2008 and from the first quarter of 2009 to date, the yield curve of the bonds appeared to be affected by the global financial crisis. Prices for 3- and 5-year bonds fell while the yield curves rose. The long-term impact of the crisis appeared negligible, which seemed to suggest confidence in the bond market.

IMPACT ON EXTERNAL TRADE AND FINANCIAL FLOWS

The balance-of-payments position remained impressive, with an increase of 8.2 percent in the current account surplus and a reduction by 61.1 percent in the capital and financial account deficit in 2007. The surplus in the current account was driven by a robust account, occasioned by the positive developments in the international oil markets. The average price of Nigeria's reference crude oil, Bonny Light 370 API, for example, rose from US$66.39 per barrel in 2006 to US$74.96. Nigeria's external sector had remained relatively viable in the previous 3 years, with an impressive balance of payments surplus of ₦999.0 billion in 2008 compared with ₦41.6 billion and ₦1073.3 billion in the corresponding period and in 2007, respectively. This development reflected the favorable trade balance occasioned by high crude oil prices and huge capital inflows in the form of diaspora remittances as well as foreign direct and portfolio investments. The current account surplus represented 17.3 percent of GDP, while the deficit in the capital and financial account narrowed from 2.4 percent and 4.6 percent of GDP in the first and second halves of 2007 to 1.1 percent in

2008. The current account surplus for the first half of 2008 was ₦2335.9 billion, compared with ₦1269.5 billion and ₦2371.4 billion in the corresponding second half of 2007, respectively. Although the surplus in the current account narrowed slightly by 0.7 percent from the level in the second half of 2007, the huge net inward transfer overwhelmed the deficits in the services and income accounts, which was reduced by 34.6 percent and 19.1 percent, respectively, when compared with their level in the corresponding period of 2007 (CBN 2008b; 2008c).

The International Monetary Fund (IMF) has estimated a reduction of global economic growth from 5 percent in 2007 to 3.7 percent in 2008. In 2009, the expected growth rate was projected to be only 2.2 percent. It was estimated that industrialized countries, for the first time since World War II, would experience negative growth (—0.3 percent) in 2009. Growth was to slow down considerably, particularly in emerging markets and developing countries—from 7 percent during 2004–2007 to only 4.5 percent in 2008–2009. For developing countries, the ill effects of the financial crisis would be dependent on a number of factors: the level of interdependence with international capital markets, the level of export trade diversification and of FDI, the level of liabilities in foreign currencies, the level of foreign currency reserves and the trade deficit, the level of inflation and the budget deficits, the diversification of local economy and macroeconomic stability, and the performance of local institutions.

A number of factors have affected Nigeria. The major one is the reduction in the demand for crude oil, which alone generates more than 80 percent of Nigeria's foreign earnings. This impact is evident in the volume of sales, which have gone down from 1.69 million barrels a day to 1.49 million on a half-year basis in 2007 and 2008 (owing partly to the financial crisis and youth restiveness in Niger Delta region) and declined in value because of the considerable fall in prices from a peak of US$147 to about US$47, as discussed earlier. Official flows, private flows from both capital and current accounts, and remittances were also affected.

In the medium to long term, however, different negative impacts on the various sectors of the economy are more obvious. This is especially the case considering the sharp drop in the demand for commodities and the resulting decrease in commodity prices. Other determinants are the impacts of the crisis on private capital flows (already threatening to be large) and Official Development Assistance (ODA) levels. To evaluate their impact on the Nigerian economy, four basic areas are highlighted:

1. The direct impacts of the crisis on the Nigerian finance and banking system
2. The direct impacts on private capital flows and ODA levels
3. The direct impacts on commodity demand and prices
4. The direct impacts on macroeconomic indicators, growth and the millennium development goals (MDGs)

Regarding impacts on private capital flows and ODA pledges, FDI as well as private equity flows to sub-Saharan Africa have increased considerably since the burst of the dotcom bubble in 2001. Additional capital inflows can be indicative of the progressive establishment of Africa as an emerging destination for investments and can also contribute to providing urgently required capital for additional investments on the continent. In principle, the current crisis has also provided opportunities for rising financial capital inflows into Africa, as investors might look for strategies to diversify their risks and to explore opportunities for higher returns. In 2007, average returns of FDI coming to Africa were 12 percent higher than average returns on FDI for all developing countries taken together, which were around 10 percent. It is important to note, however, that the bulk of FDI coming to Nigeria still goes to primary resource extraction and communication sectors. Alternative investment opportunities remain limited owing to the high cost of doing business in Nigeria, most especially with regard to the poor state of the infrastructure. Therefore high returns on FDI are also linked to the recent hikes in commodity prices.

IMPACT ON THE NON-OIL SECTOR IN NIGERIA

Data from the NBS indicated that Nigeria's GDP of constant basic prices grew by 6.1 percent in the first half of 2008 from the 5.5 percent recorded in 2007. Aggregate growth was driven by the non-oil sector, which grew by 8.7 percent and contributed 80.7 percent of GDP, as oil sector output declined further by 3.3 percent and contributed the remaining 19.3 percent of GDP. Growth in non-oil GDP was broad-based, as building and construction grew by 13 percent, wholesale and retail trade by 12 percent, services by 10.3 by percent, and agriculture by 6.3 percent. Agriculture remained dominant in terms of sectoral contributions, accounting for 39.8 percent of GDP; industry, services, wholesale and retail trade, and building and construction followed, with contributions of 22.1 percent, 18.1 percent, 17.9 percent, and 2.1 percent respectively.

IMPACT ON THE OIL SECTOR IN NIGERIA

The changing international oil market poses grave concerns for Nigeria's fiscal outlook. The global financial crisis has led to slow growth across the world's economies, resulting in lower demand for commodities, especially oil. This impact has been transmitted through several sources to the Nigerian economy, especially through (1) earnings and revenue, (2) the fall of the Naira's exchange rate, (3) the balance of payments through narrowing of the surplus on the current account balance, (4) the capital account through reduction in capital flows because of reappraisal of planned investments or complete stoppage of previously committed programs of investment, and (5) the contraction of fiscal space for policy. While speculative behavior and investment activities helped buoy up crude oil prices internationally, the reality of the global recession and the adverse impact of the crisis are more evident and direct in terms of the international prices of oil. The recent movements of oil prices are apparent in their unprecedented decline from records highs of about US$147/barrel in July 2008 to about US$50/barrel in January 2009. The figures on the daily basket price hovered between US$38 and US$44 in the third week of February and the first week of March 2009.

The global economic crisis has resulted in about a 71 percent decline in the basket price of crude oil, as shown above. Accordingly, Nigerian policy makers have adjusted the benchmark price, on which the 2009 and 2010 budgets were based. Demand for crude oil in the United States and Europe dropped in 2009, even though it grew slightly in 2010, leading to a rise in the price per barrel. As a country whose earnings and expenditures are tied to the profits from oil, the impact of the financial crisis on Nigeria has been tremendous. As a matter of fact, the financial crisis will most likely further intensify the search by many developed countries for alternative sources of energy. Usually oil shocks are defined in terms of price fluctuations, but these may in turn emanate from changes in either the supply of or demand for oil. In practice, it is unlikely that demand will grow rapidly enough to cause a price shock unless it is motivated by fears of supply shortages. The supply side has been primarily responsible for observed oil price shocks, at least as an initial trigger. Moreover, expectations and speculation about future demand and (especially) supply conditions play a large part in the determination of crude oil prices on the futures and spot markets, particularly when inventories are low.

The federal government of Nigeria finances its annual budget largely through the sale of crude oil. Consequently oil revenue drives economic activities and hence inflation in Nigeria. As of October 2010, the country's foreign reserve was about US$33.9 billion, as against the US$64 billion recorded in 2008. The drop in the price of crude oil had affected federal and state governments' spending and budget performance. Several reasons account for this development. The implication is that Nigeria's economy is based on only one commodity, crude oil, and negative developments in the global oil market will have similar impacts on government funding. Simply put, a persistent drop in crude oil prices means that the government will have less to spend for capital projects in the years ahead.

IMPACT ON THE BANKING SECTOR

In a globalized world, transactions are carried out in different countries in integrated markets. The world has over the past two decades headed toward liberalization and deregulation, with the goal of integrating world markets. Nigerian markets, although not well integrated into the world market, have been facing serious destabilizing effects since the emergence of the global financial crisis in July 2008. The capital market has been shrinking, major international hedge funds have been withdrawn, and the international credit line has phased out available loan funds for domestic industries. The gravity and depth of the crisis in the banking sector can be seen from the following indicators.

Prudential Indicators

These show declining level in the quality of risk assets. The main component considered is nonperforming loans (NPLs) as a percentage of total commercial bank loans. This ratio is likely to increase in the foreseeable future as the loans granted in 2008 become due for payment. Some of these are consequent to the activities of the stockbrokers in the use of margin loans in funding their capital market activities as well as those who received loans to finance share purchases when their prices were still high. These became problems when prices tumbled. Margin lending allows money to be borrowed using existing shares, managed funds, or cash as security. This indicates estimated value based on the amount of margin loan swept by the crash in the capital market. The total margin loan (₦1 trillion) represents 20 percent of total credit granted by the banking system. With the escalation of the financial crisis and by mid 2009, most of the loans entered the nonperforming loans (NPL) profile.

Capitalized Value of Quoted Banks

These have been seriously eroded since the crisis, owing to the decline in the quoted values of these institutions at the stock exchange. This has seriously endangered their tier-one and tier-two capital.

Activity Indicators

The activity indicator is captured by the ratio of security investment to total commercial banks' assets. Available data show a continued decline in the ratio from its peak in 2007. According to the Central Bank of Nigeria (CBN), initially bank lending witnessed growth of about 60.9 percent, which was an indication that Nigerian banks were doing well in the face of financial crisis. However, the situation in the interbank market, which holds meetings weekly, has since indicated otherwise—that is, that banks are experiencing reduced liquidity. For instance, as of December 31, 2008, the Nigerian interbank offer rate (NIBOR) went up in all segments of the lending market, with the 7-day NIBOR up from 14.8 percent to 15.3 percent, the 30-day NIBOR up from 16.7 percent to 17 percent, and 60-day NIBOR up from 16.7 percent to 17.0 percent. The 90-day NIBOR rate also rose from 16.7 percent to 17.2 percent, the 180-day NIBOR from 16.7 percent to 17.4 percent, and the 360-day NIBOR from 16.9 percent to 17.8 percent. The rising interest rate is an indication of fewer funds to lend out. This may have occurred as a result of the exposure of banks to the margin loan and other capital market funding activities discussed above.

Impact on the Labor Force and Unemployment

Statistics on the nation's labor force released by the National Bureau of Statistics (NBS) have indicated that about 9.9 million Nigerians were unemployed as of March 2009. The report further indicated that the total unemployment rate constituted about 19.7 percent of the entire labor force, put at 50.6 million, and has risen sharply from the 14.9 percent recorded in March 2008. That rate is the highest since the year 2000 and was evident at the inception of the financial crisis. For many years, a high unemployment has been a key challenge to the Nigerian government, aggravated by youth restiveness and other vices in all parts of the country, particularly the Niger Delta region. In fact, a World Bank report on employment and growth released in 2009 indicates clearly that Nigeria was facing a growing employment crisis, with youth unemployment on the rise.

The World Bank report (2009) noted that "the share of young people between the ages of 15 and 24 outside the labour force is growing, despite the country's strong growth performance over the years." There are even greater concerns that the number of people without jobs may have increased considerably following the mass sacking, especially in the banking sector, prompted by the Nigeria's Central Bank reforms. For instance, it was reported that as many as 7,500 of the banking staff lost their jobs as of February 2010 and that the figure was still rising. A National Bureau of Statistics (NBS 2009) report showed that the highest number of the unemployed fell within the 22- to 44-year age bracket, indicating that young Nigerians suffered more unemployment challenges than the younger and older folks. Following closely were those between 15 and 25 years, while the elderly, whom the bureau classified into 45- to 64-year group, suffered the least unemployment.

REGRESSION RESULTS

The regression result is presented in Table 8.2. This result was obtained by employing E-views statistical package 3.0 using the OLS method. A regression was run using the data obtained from the NBS to establish a relationship between the composite unemployment variable and the urban and rural unemployment variables.

The result indicates a "good fit" in the statistical sense, given that R^2 = 0.996273 and adjusted R^2, which is better measure of goodness of fit, 0.995776, indicating the over 99 percent variation in the dependent variable

Table 8.2 Regression Results

Dependent Variable: NAT				
Method: Least Squares				
Date: 06/25/10 Time: 19:44				
Sample: 1992 2009				
Included observations: 18				
NAT=C(1)+C(2)*URB+C(3)*RUR				
	Coefficient	Std. Error	t-Statistic	Prob.
C(1)	-0.236672	0.199998	-1.183374	0.2551
C(2)	0.349004	0.032624	10.69782	0.0000
C(3)	0.685332	0.027298	25.10524	0.0000
R-squared	0.996273	Mean dependent var		10.15556
Adjusted R-squared	0.995776	S.D. dependent var		6.151826

is explained by the explanatory variables. It was observed that two coefficients were statistically significant after differencing all the variables. The constant term shows that with zero value for all the explanatory variables, the value of the composite unemployment rate will be −0.236672. The other coefficients indicate that a one percent of urban unemployment will increase the national unemployment by 0.349004 and likewise rural unemployment rate will increase the national unemployment rate by 0.685332. All the signs of the variables conform to a priori of a positive relationship between the dependent and explanatory variables. That is, they indicate a positive relationship between the national unemployment rate and the urban and rural unemployment rates.

The trend of the national urban and rural unemployment rate and the residual showed a very sharp upward movement from 1998 to 2000. It stabilized from 2000 to 2007, but there was another stiff movement in 2008. This is not unconnected with the fact that 2008 was the year the global financial crisis started in the United States and thousands of Nigerians in the United States and the United Kingdom lose their jobs and came back home, thus adding to the increasing unemployment rate. It can be seen that this trend is on the increase because government measures since 2008 to cushion the effect in terms of employment have not yet yielded the desired results.

CONCLUSIONS AND POLICY RECOMMENDATIONS

The impact of the crisis on the Nigerian economy has different ramifications for the capital market, the banking sector, foreign exchange, and the balance of payments as well as the real sector. The Nigerian financial system, particularly the banking sector, mirrored global trends but was largely contained because of its limited integration with the global financial system. While offshore funding of the domestic banking system was growing before the crisis, its scale was manageable and the Central Bank was able to accommodate commercial banks' foreign exchange needs in the depth of the global crisis. Coupled with major internal management problems in some of the banks, the crises impacted the economy through various channels—including the significant decline in oil revenue—leading to revenue attrition for all tiers of government; reduced capital inflows into the economy; significant drawdown of external/foreign reserves; demand pressure in the foreign exchange market; substantial decline in stock market capitalization and share prices; huge bank losses on margin loans and share-backed facilities as well as loans to the downstream oil and gas sector; low valuation with many banks trading below book value; declining asset values; and declining credit growth.

Market capitalization fell by 45.8 percent in 2008, a sharp reversal of growth from 2007, when the market grew by 74.7 percent (Okereke and Onyiuke 2009). The crude oil price (Bonny Light) declined precipitously from US$147 per barrel in July 2008 to US$47 per barrel in January 2009, prompting the government to seek other sources of financing for the 2009 fiscal year, as it could rely on earnings from crude oil exports. Eventually, there was a huge budget cut at all tiers of government and social spending—on education, health, and other basic MDGs—were deeply affected. The Naira, has also depreciated against the U.S. dollar, and this has implications for foreign reserves, which dropped from US$67 billion in June 2008 to US$53 billion in December 2008 and US$33.9 billion in October 2010.

The combined implications of this crisis on the Nigerian economy can be seen clearly from the point of view of rising unemployment levels in the country. The consequences of a growing unemployment phenomenon are so severe that no economy can afford to ignore them. Such implications are glaring in the economy of Nigeria, where many negative developments are traceable to the nonavailability of jobs for the teeming population of its energetic youth, which had led to the restiveness of the youth of the Niger Delta and caused a sharp drop in oil production and its concomitant negative effects on revenues and external reserves. Therefore the need to address this ugly development promptly becomes paramount. While the government must take the lead in providing employment by creating an enabling environment for economic activities, it is necessary to note that the battle against unemployment cannot achieve the desired result without first addressing the fundamental weaknesses of the economy.

This chapter seeks to make the following policy recommendations for moving the Nigerian economy forward and away from future crisis. First and foremost is the urgent need to diversify the economy from its present state of monoculture to a more diversified model that will require attention to the other key sectors. Government should have the political will to rethink policies and amend institutional frameworks as the need arises. Regulatory authorities should strengthen the regulatory and supervisory processes in a coordinated manner to stem corruption and the mismanagement of resources. Maintaining a safe and sound banking sector is essential, given the key role that banks play in facilitating economic growth and financing development projects, particularly key infrastructure, agriculture, and industry. Most emerging market economies have been known to use domestic financial institutions to execute real sector big-ticket projects, and financial institutions in Nigeria should not be an exception if the country hopes to achieve its developmental objectives. There should also be a strong commitment to instill good governance and transparency in all affairs of the nation and to end the past practice of seeking quick fixes and easy solutions. A resilient economy requires hard work, intelligence, consistency, and time. Finally, as the CBN governor, (Sunusi 2010) said, there is no uniform effect, neither is there a single remedy to every crisis. Each brings its own surprises and risks. The key is to take lessons from the past and tailor them appropriately to address future situations of potential crisis.

REFERENCES

Abubakar, M. "The Implication of Global Financial Crisis on International Marketing." Unpublished M.Sc. Assignment on International Marketing, Bayero University, Kano, 2008.

ActionAid. *Where Does It Hurt? The Impact of the Global Financial Crisis*. London, UK: ActionAid International, 2009.

Adamu A. "The Effects of Global Financial Crisis on Nigerian Economy." Paper Presented at the Msc Workshop, Organized by the Department Of Business Administration, Bayero University Kano, 2009.

"African Growth in the Changing Global Economy." Paper Presented by Ambassador of Tanzania and Dean of the African Diplomatic Corps in Japan. GRIPS-ODI-JICA Joint Seminar African Growth in the Changing Global Economy. November 27, 2008.

Ajakaiye O., FakiyesI T., and M. Oyinlola. "Impact of the global financial crisis on the social services sector in Ghana and Nigeria". *CESifo Forum*. Vol. 10, No. 4 (2009):36–42.

Arieff, Alexis, Martin A. Weiss, and Vivian C. Jones. *The Global Economic Crisis: Impact on Sub-Saharan Africa and Global Policy Responses*. Ft. Belvoir: Defense Technical Information Center, 2009.

Avery, C. and P. Zemsky. "Multidimensional Uncertainty and Herd Behavior in Financial Markets." *American Economic Review,* Vol. 88 (1998): 724–748.

Avgouleas, E. "Financial Regulation, Behavior Finance, and the Financial Credit Crisis in Search of a New Regulatory Model," 2008: http://papers.ssrn.com

Bannock, G. et al. *Penguin Dictionary of Economics*. New York: Penguin Books, 1998.

Baker, Dean. *The Housing Bubble and the Financial Crisis*. Washington, DC: Center for Economic and Policy Research,2008.

Briggs, J. E. "Unemployment Statistics and What They Mean." *Monthly Labour Bulletin*, 1973.
Chari, V., and P. Kehoe. "Financial Crises as Herds: Overturning the Critiques." *Journal of Economic Theory*, Vol. 119 (2004): 128–150.
Cipriani, M., and A. Guarino. "Herd Behavior and Contagion in Financial Markets." *The B.E. Journal of Theoretical Economics*, Vol. 8, No. 1 (2008): 1–54.
Crotty, J. "Structural Causes of the Global Financial Crisis: A Critical Assessment of the 'New Financial Architecture.'" Political Economy Research Institute (PERI) University of Massachusetts Amherst. Working paper No. 180. Amherst, MA: PERI, September 2008.
Central Bank of Nigeria. *Statistical Bulletin*, Vol. 17. Abuja, Nigeria: CBN, 2006.
———. "Nigeria: Performance of the Economy, 2000–2008." Abuja, Nigeria: CBN, 2008a.
———. "Annual Report and Statement of Accounts," Year ended December 31, 2007. Abuja, Nigeria: CBN, 2008b.
———. "Remittances Data," Trade and Exchange Office. Abuja, Nigeria: CBN, 2008c.
Federal Ministry of Agricultural Development Abuja. *New Agricultural Policy Thrust*. Abuja, Nigeria: Ministry of Agricultural Development, 2001.
Damachi, N. A. "Evaluation of Past Policy Measures for Solving Unemployment Problems." *CBN Bulletin*, Vol. 25, No. 4 (October/December, 2001).
Dell'Ariccia, G., D. Igan, and L. Laeven. "The Relationship between the Recent Boom and the Current Delinquencies in Subprime Mortgage." CEPR Discussion Paper. London: CEPR, 2008.
Douglason, G. U. and A. Gbosi. "The Dynamics of Productivity and Unemployment Nexus: Implications for Employment Generation in Nigeria NES 2006." Annual Conference, Ibadan, Nigeria, 2006.
Dymski, G. *From Financial Exploitation to Global Banking Instability: Two Overlooked Roots of the Subprime Crisis*. Sacramento: University of California, 2007.
Gbosi, A. N. *Modern Labour Economics and Policy Analysis*. Abakaliki, Nigeria: Pack Publishers, 2006.
Gujarati D. N. *Basic Econometrics*, 4th ed. New York: McGraw-Hill, 2003.
Ishola, R. A. "Reducing Unemployment through the Informal Section: A Case Study of Nigeria." *European Journal of Economics, Finance and Administrative Sciences*, 2008.
Kindleberger, C. P., and R. Aliber. *Manias, Panics, and Crashes: A History of Financial Crises*, 5th ed. New York: Palgrave Macmillan, 2005.
Krugman, P. "The Widening Gyre." *New York Times*, October 27, 2008. http://www.nytimes.com/2008/10/27/opinion/27krugman.html?_r=0.
Laeven, L., and F. Valencia. "Systemic Banking Crises: A New Database." International Monetary Fund Working Paper 08/224, 2008.
Mtango, E. E. E. "African Growth, Financial Crisis and Implications for TICAD IV Follow-Up." GRIPS-ODI-JICA Joint Seminar African Growth in the Changing Global Economy. November 27, 2008.
National Bureau of Statistics, Nigeria. *The Nigerian Statistical Fact Sheets on Economic and Social Development*. Nigeria: Federal Office of Statistics, 2009.
Nigeria Stock Exchange. *Annual Reports*. Abuja, Nigeria: NSE, 2002–2007.
Ogundipe, Odunayo. *Introduction to environmental issues: causes, effects and solutions*. Central Milton Keynes: Author House, 2009.
Ogunleye, G. A. "The global financial crisis : lessons for deposit insurance systems in developing countries." In LaBrosse, John Raymond, Rodrigo Olivares-Caminal, and Dalvinder Singh, eds. *Financial crisis management and bank resolution*. London: Informa Law, 2009.

Okereke-Onyiuke, N. "A Review of Market Performance in 2008 and the Outlook in 2009: The Nigerian Stock Exchange," 2009: www.scribd.com/doc/10585651/Nigerian-Stock-Exchange-Official-2008-Review-and-Outlook-for-2009

Sagagi, M. "A Budget of Despair? Perspective on the International Financial Crisis and the Federal Government 2009 Budget." Paper Presented at the Policy Support and Advisory Forum, 2008.

Soludo, Chukwuma C. *The challenges of ensuring appropriate inflation rate, exchange rate and interest rate regimes in Nigeria: a background presentation.* Nigeria: Central Bank of Nigeria, 2009.

Sunusi, L. S. Keynote Address to the Annual Bankers Conference. Abuja, Nigeria, 2010.

Tairu, B. "Attacking Unemployment Hurdles in the Fragile Economies of the sub-Saharan Africa: The Experience of Nigeria." Paper presented at the Economics for the Future Conference. Cambridge: United Kingdom, 2003.

Te Velde, D. W. "The Global Financial Crisis and Developing Countries." In *Oversea Development Institute Background Notes.* London: Oversea Development Institute, 2008.

9 Transcending an Elitist Approach and Making a Paradigm Shift from Growth without Development to "Populist" Development

Hauwa'u Evelyn Yusuf and Adefarakan Adedayo Yusuf

Every generation produces its own group of men and women who are the initiators of fundamental change in the society. They are forerunners of creative ideas, innovations, and inventions. They champion development and exhibit leadership in order to demonstrate how these new ideas could be implemented. Postindependence Africa has indeed produced its own such elite. However, the historical epoch that gave birth to them, particularly the ravaging capitalist system and the prevailing international economic order, affected not only their conceptualization of issues but also their ability to promote progress in the region. The continent, therefore, when compared with other regions that have similar features, has been drifting.

In the last five decades or so, the drift has been so acute that the pace of development, the quality of development, and the interest in such a development has continued to attract the interest of scholars. At independence, the international community had high hopes for some of the nations in Africa because of their vast populations and great mineral and agricultural potential. The discovery of oil in Nigeria and the growing mining industry in South Africa, to mention just two examples, gave credence to this. Unfortunately this has remained a mirage because many of the postcolonial leaders have demonstrated a dearth of vital leadership and emotional competence. However, such competence is needed to implement the desires and aspirations of a large segment of the population as regards their economic, political, and social policies and programs.

This chapter takes a historical view of development and changes in Africa from independence to date; the individual African nations of Nigeria, Ghana, Egypt, Tanzania, and South Africa are used as case studies. Ghana and Tanzania started off with African socialism but abandoned it for capitalism. Nigeria and Ghana had a history of military elitist control of government for many decades. At one time, Ghana's economy was so backward that many Ghanaians migrated to Nigeria. Currently the situation has been reversed and many Nigerian companies are moving their investments to Ghana, as Ghana seems to be doing relatively well compared with Nigeria. South Africa and Egypt are said to have "productive economies," and both are examined to provide the way for the continent. The chapter also uses Malaysia and Singapore as models for African elites because the elite of these two nations became more visionary, with a mission for selfless service. They have equally been able to raise the scale of populist development above standards. At independence, both were more or less on par with many African nations, particularly Nigeria, Ghana, and Tanzania. However, today they are ranked high among the "Asian Tigers" in terms of gross domestic product (GDP), national per capita income, and diversification of the economy.

The chapter has been organized into three main sections. The first part focuses on the potential of the continent and how, in spite of this, it is lagging behind. The second section examines how the elites have conceptualized and approached development. The last part looks at how emotional intelligence can be used to make a paradigm shift to populist development.

THE CONTINENT'S POTENTIAL

The African continent is blessed with abundant human and natural resources; with the right emotional competence of its leaders, its nations would surely develop. The region has an estimated population of about 880 million.[1] However, this potential has not been properly utilized by the political elite to establish an inclusive development strategy that would redistribute wealth and expand the demand base of the continent.

In the field of agriculture, Africa is endowed with countries like Egypt, Ethiopia, Nigeria, South Africa, and Sudan, which have the largest areas of land under cultivation.[2] The region produces both food and export crops. Staple food crops include corn, millet, rice, sorghum, wheat, cassava, potatoes, and yams. Other important staple food crops include various legumes (peas, peanuts, and beans), fruits, and vegetables. The continent's leading export crops include cocoa, coffee, cotton, kola nuts, palm oil, sugar, and tea.[3] Africa is equally endowed with mineral resources and a large mining industry. It has among the world's largest reserves of chromium, cobalt, gold, manganese, phosphates, platinum, uranium, and vanadium. There are equally substantial quantities of other metals including bauxite (aluminum ore), copper, iron, nickel, and zinc. It is also a major producer of oil and gas. South Africa, for example, is the world's largest producer of gold.[4]

However, in spite of these resources, overwhelming evidence suggests that the continent is seriously behind in many indices of development. Meredith posits that Africa is the world's poorest region, and it is falling further and further behind all other region of the world. The average per capita national income is one-third lower than that in the world's next poorest region, South Asia.[5] Most of these countries have lower per capita income now than they had in 1980, and half of their entire populations live on less than US$1 per person per day.[6] According to a 2004 World Bank report, the economy of Africa has assumed a deteriorating pattern over the years. The general average growth rate in the 1970s was 5 to 6 percent, even rising to 7 to 8 percent in some cases. In the 1980s and beyond, the growth rate has been less than 3 percent on average.[7]

Furthermore, in the early 2000s, the average annual per capita income in Africa was about US$650. Even then, more than thirty countries had annual per capita income less than US$500.[8] Africa's total annual GDP in 2002 was about US$1.75 trillion, compared with US$10.4 trillion for the United States.[9] Africa's share of world trade has declined to half of what it was in the 1980s, amounting to just 1.6 percent. Adebayo posits that in terms of a composite comprehensive index of human development within a global comparative context, African countries were ranked as among the lowest across the world.[10] Only Botswana, Libya, Mauritius, Egypt, Gabon, Ghana, Sudan, and Cameroon were ranked "medium" in the human development category. Africa is the only continent where school enrollment is falling and illiteracy is still commonplace; two in five Africans and half of all African women are illiterate, compared with one in every eight adults in East Asia or Latin America.[11] It is the only region where life expectancy is falling.

The UN Development Programme declared that all the twenty-five countries that ranked lowest in terms of human development were African.[12] By 2003, some 1.7 million children were still receiving no schooling at all. Eight million adult could not read or write. Six million people had no constant access to clean water, a quarter of the adult population was unemployed, and the gap between the rich and poor has led to in high levels of street crime.[13] This gap was accentuated by the fact that as at 2000, the nations of Africa experienced little growth or even declined in agricultural production. Food production has grown more slowly than the population. Most fertile land and resources such as fertilizer are used for the production of cash crops grown for export rather than food crops. There is, therefore, a food shortage that has to be offset by food imports.[14]

Human immunodeficiency virus / acquired immunodeficiency syndrome (HIV/AIDS), which is now ravaging Africa, introduced a new dimension to the continent's struggles. Sub-Saharan Africa is home to 10 percent of the world's population but has more than 70 percent of the world's HIV/AIDS cases. By 2004, some 20 million people had died from AIDS and 30 million were infected by the virus; their number was then rising by estimated 3 million new cases each year.[15] This ugly trend can be attributed to the fact that the political elite lacked the will to mobilize available resources to deal with the epidemic proactively.

THE ELITIST FRAMEWORK FOR DEVELOPMENT

The poor socioeconomic and political state of the African continent stems largely from the conceptualization of development by the elite's lack of confidence in themselves and their inability to develop an inclusive strategy that focuses on the grassroots. Development emanates from a conceptualization of different schools of thought. It is a contested, multidimensional, and multifaceted concept looked at from different perspectives. The growing concern for progress in many areas of development, however, has led to the recurring themes of modernity, development and underdevelopment, self-reliance, and revolution.[16]

Seers refer to it as the creation of conditions for the realization of human personality, reduction of poverty, social inequalities, and the improvement in creating employment opportunities.[17] In the same vein, Torado posits that it is a multidimensional process involving major changes in social structures, popular attitude, national institutions, the acceleration of growth and reduction of inequality, and the eradication of absolute poverty.[18] The United Nations Development Programme (UNDP), however, explores the human angle. To this agency of the United Nations, development is about enlarging people's choices. It identifies four important elements in the concepts of development, particularly human development as productivity, equity, sustainability, and empowerment. It involves the process of moving from a low to a higher and more advanced stage in a various contexts—socially, politically, economically, legally, morally, administratively, and so on.[19]

By far the most dominant of these concepts that has continued to rebound in the conceptualization by the elite is "modernization," which has given birth to the modernization school of thought. The modernization theory, according to Ake, posits an original state of backwardness or underdevelopment that is characterized among other things by low rate of economic growth.[20] This school sees capitalism or the West as the only mode of production for all nations. Nations in their quest for development must, therefore, copy the capitalist model—in other words, it is held that these nations must go through the stages that capitalism passed through. As such, existing traditional institutions and structures standing in the way of capitalism must be removed. The African elite have, in the light of this model, been attempting to copy what happened at the center. Specifically, this view involves an accumulative system within the national boundaries at the expense of the traditional/local economies.[21] These advocates hold that a "modernizing" society will have to be created within the national boundaries in such a way that traditional safeguards that used to stand in the way of unbridled accumulation are removed.[22]

Underdevelopment from the perspective of this school is a transactional phenomenon that can be removed sooner or later by creating certain favorable conditions within the underdeveloped region and ensuring the appropriate interaction between it and the developed regions.[23] Ake argues that the modernization theorists use an evolutionary scheme that regards the ideal characteristic of the West as the end of social evolution.[24] In any case, is it possible to modernize local economy in such a way as to create a full-fledged capitalist economy? Will the "center" allow the local economy to develop its industries, improve its agricultural products, and create a atmosphere conducive for the marketing of goods from Africa? This issue is addressed later in this chapter.

On the other hand, the dependency school is opposed to the modernization conceptualization of development. It developed a radical, explicitly Marxist critique of orthodox development studies.[25] It argues that there is an inverse relationship between the West (capitalist) and the underdeveloped African continent. The underdevelopment of Africa led to the development of capitalism, and the development of capitalism brought about the underdevelopment of Africa.[26] Rodney describes the various stages of this development of underdevelopment as a process that was ongoing for about four decades before political independence and included the transatlantic slave trade era and the period of "legitimate trade," including the period of colonial domination and subjugation.[27] The human and natural resources of the African region were plundered to feed the industries in Europe and the West. With necolonialism, the so-called multinational corporations continued their exploitation through an international economic system that fostered African dependency on the globalized capital system.[28] Rucco and Simon contend that on methodological grounds, the dependency theory is vaguely or tautologically defined and cannot be measured effectively.[29] The theory has been faulted for an inadequate exploration of the role of the state, varieties of dependency, class relations, and culture.[30] Scott observes that both developmentalism and dependency developmentalism are ideologies, as they justify capitalism on their mutual hatred for imperialism.[31]

However, above all this, these various concepts, terms, and phrases associated with development in Africa and indeed the Third World have remained to a very large extent what the the Hausa-speaking people of northern Nigeria called *dogon turanci*—that is, long-winded sentences or phrases. They have not in any way translated to improved and advanced progress in the quality of their lives. Proactively speaking, they have not guaranteed a better life in the future. They open their taps but there is no water available, and the environment is daily being polluted and degraded by heaps of refuse. Educational infrastructure has collapsed, hospitals have become consulting clinics, and the roads are death traps. In spite of this, the elite have continued to favor the externally oriented system of development because they do not understand the international order that the elites in the West have institutionalized and entrenched.

This is, however, not unconnected with different circumstances that gave rise to the elites in West and Africa. A clear understanding of the meaning of the elite will throw more light on the issue being addressed here. The concept of *elite* is used to describe certain fundamental features of organization social life.[32] It is a descriptive term used to designate those who hold high positions in society.[33] The elite is an exclusive, carefully selected group or class, usually small, which possesses certain advantages either of wealth, privilege, education, training, stations, or political power, among others.[34] The elites are those minorities who are set apart from the rest of the society by their preeminence in authority, symbols[35] of common life, and the embodiments of their values. As a minority group, they may be found in separate spheres and with quite different responsibilities, sources of power, and pattern of selection and rewards. They exist in virtually every activity and every corresponding spheres of social life—there are elites of soldiers, of artists, bankers, politics, etc.[36] Some of them have more social weight than others because their activities have greater social significance but all have a disproportionate amount of public decision-making power.[37] The position of elites at the top of the social strata invariably puts them in positions of leadership and often subjects them to pressure to maintain their positions as part of the elite.[38]

In the industrialized societies of the world, the characteristic attributes of the larger society are mirrored in the strategic elite. This refers to those elite who claim or are assigned responsibilities for them that society tries to realize its main goals and projects.[39] In this part of the world (the industrialized world), the function of the elite appears to symbolize the moral unity of a collectivity by emphasizing common purposes and interests, to coordinate and harmonize diversified activities, combat factionalism and resolve group conflict, and to protect the collectivity for external danger. The overriding goals of these elite are the preservation of the ideals and practices of the societies at whose apex they stand.[40] The elite in the West have a vision and a mission. They have a larger picture of their own society and its place in the global economic order. They have continued both their institutionalization and entrenchment of the world capitalist system. Scholars, statesmen, and various stakeholders—such as the World Bank and the International Monetary Fund—do churn out concepts and strategic plans of actions that they thrust in the throats of the African political elite. The African elite are always at the receiving end in the umbilical cord that links them with the western elite, and their citizens are the worse off for it.

The historical epoch of colonialism and neocolonialism and the ever-spreading unequal international economic environment caused the African elite to be closely bound up with the world economy. These elite naturally seek to maintain their own class interests and in practice their strategies to do this are often harmonized with the needs of the international capital.[41] Consequently they have not been able to broaden consumption to talk of the redistribution of wealth and class power. Meanwhile, accumulated wealth did not translate into growth because accumulated value that arose from past growth is siphoned off directly to the West in the form of profit on investment or debt repayment. This has in no small measure contributed to capital flight from the continent. The World Bank in 1993 blamed the local elite for their "irresponsibility" in this regard. It estimated that the capital flight of the developing nations was 32.3 percent of the country's GDP.[42] The model of the African elite in many ways has continuously bypassed the grassroots[43] and has over the last five decades unleashed growth without development as well as calamities of serious magnitude.

At this juncture, it is pertinent to examine the various manifestations of elitist approach to development so that we shall not only appreciate its essence but also the need to move away from it. Greed and self-centeredness, a dangerous trend, is the order of the day, as majority of the African elites find it difficult to rise above it. They use every opportunity that comes their way, including elective posts, appointments, and connections and contracts to enrich themselves at the expense of the citizens. Meredith[44] observes that in postcolonial Nigeria, ministers are rewarded with princely salaries as well as rent-free air-conditioned residences replete with stewards, gardeners, drivers, generators, car allowances, an entertainment budget, free telephones, and free electricity. The situation is not different in other nations. In the Central African Republic and Côte d'Ivoire, about 58 percent of the total budget is allocated to civil service salaries. To compound the situation, the new elite ostentatiously display their acquired wealth in grand houses, luxury cars, and a lavish life-style.[45] The citizens of these nations are so taken aback by this life-style that the elite are given all sorts of names. In Abidjan they are said to lead the "platinum life," while in East Africa they were nicknamed *Wabenzi*, a term describing rich politicians, government officials, and businessmen who drive about in expensive Mercedes-Benz cars.[46]

This greed and self-centeredness has continued to spread by leaps and bounds. In a country like Nigeria, greed accounts for the astronomical growth in overhead costs, which recently pitted the national legislators against the governor of the Central Bank. As a matter of fact, the monthly and annual take-home pay of the legislators is shrouded in secrecy. Various sums running into the millions have been advanced. Meanwhile, even the minimum wage of ⦾18,000, negotiated between workers and the federal government, is too low to provide for the workers and their families and is threatened even before its implementation. State governors are crying out to anyone who cares to listen that they cannot pay that amount to their workers. Greed and self-centeredness have resulted in the misplacement of priorities or "white elephant" projects. The elite find it difficult to rightly place their priorities. Funds are diverted to presidential palaces, conference halls, airports, airlines, hotels, grand highways, and embassies abroad. These have led to all sorts of abandoned projects in the nooks and crannies of a country like Nigeria.

Hosting of the annual summits of the Organization of African Unity (OAU) (now the African Union, or AU), produce nothing but rhetoric from the heads of states and become a conduit pipe for enriching themselves through white-elephant projects. In 1965, Kwame Nkrumah, the former president of Ghana, built a palace that contained sixty luxury suites and a banquet hall capable of serving 2,000 guests. Omar Bongo of Gabon, on his part, constructed several seafront hotels in Libreville with rotating rooms and a private nightclub costing over US$200 million. On the same summit, however, Togo spent US$120 million, half of Togo's national budget, in building a 30-story hotel and conference center in Lome, which included fifty-two presidential suites.[47]

These elites have continued to plunge the African continent into unnecessary and very costly wars and civil unrest. Meredith contends that since 1970, more than thirty wars have been fought in Africa, the majority of them intra-state in origin.[48] Personal aggrandizement and ego are largely responsible for most of these wars. In 1966 alone, fourteen of the fifty-three countries were affected by armed conflict, accounting for more than half of all war-related deaths worldwide and resulting in more than 8 million refugees, returnees, and displaced persons.[49] These wars have seriously undermined Africa's efforts to ensure the long-term stability, prosperity, and peace that are needed for development to take place. In 2000, there were more than ten major conflicts under way in Africa. One–fifth of all Africans lived in countries battered by war. Some 12 million were classified refugees—40 percent of the world's total.[50]

One of the most devastating manifestations of the elitist approach to development is the increasing trend toward a "sit tight" syndrome and an unprecedented high level of corruption. Both the big and small nations of the continent have not escaped this attitude. With the exploration of oil in Equatorial Guinea, its oil revenue rose to US$700 million in 2004. However, this remained the private preserve of dictator Obiang Nguema and members of his family. Meredith contends that the use of oil revenue remains a "state secret."[51] It seems the international and national political economy of oil exploration and refining is a mirage in Third Wolrd countries. This is particularly true in Nigeria, where the quantity of oil taken out for refining, the amount that comes back into the country, and that dispensed by the Nigerian National Petroleum Corporation (NNPC) has remained a mystery. The mystification has lent itself to yet more corruption in high places.

Oil exploration made Nigeria the world's sixth largest oil producer with revenue soaring to US$24 billion a year. Instead of investing this revenue in infrastructural development and raising its citizens' standard of living, the government set off various scrambles for political offices and the wealth that went with them.[52] Access to government spending became the gateway to fortune. This is why the country has continued to sustain a paradox that people find difficult to understand. The Shagari's administration of the 1970s to 1980s was termed "a government of contracts." Meetings of Shagari's cabinet and party councils were described as venues where the resources of the state were put up for auction.[53] An official enquiry in 1980 established that the cost of government contracts was inflated by kickbacks, which were 200 percent higher in Nigeria than in Kenya. Another enquiry found that the costs of construction in the country were three times higher than in East Asia or North Africa. Even with the coming to an end of the oil boom in the 1980s, politicians and contractors have continued "to bribe, steal, smuggle, and speculate, accumulating vast illicit fortunes, displaying them lavishly in stunning disregard for public sensitivities."[54]

The struggle for power among the elite is all about sending a particular clique who has corruptly enriched themselves out and replacing them with another set. When Kenya's Daniel Arap Moi stood down at the end of 2002 after 24 years in power, investigators estimated that he and his cronies had looted as much as US$3 billion. The "Karbinet syndicate"—the Kalenjin politicians—were replaced by the "Kibakis mountain Kenya Mafia" of Kikuyu politicians who moved swiftly to set up their own lucrative deals.[55] The irony of the African situation is the fact that the money obtained from the international community in the form of foreign loans and aid is used to corruptly enrich the political elite. At times it is even diverted to fight unnecessary wars. The situation is so pathetic that Edward Clay, once the British high commissioner to Kenya, said that the names of honest ministers and senior officials would fit on the back of a postage stamp.[56]

In order to sustain corruption at all levels of government, the political elite have adopted a sit-tight approach to power, the promotion of "big men," and a very costly liberal democracy. They are always preoccupied with strategies and methods for staying in power at all costs. Consequent upon this, they operate a patrimonial system that keeps supporters loyal to them in various sectors. Many of these loyalists are without any vision about qualitative governance. Political activity has, therefore, been reduced to palace politics—an area for the ruling elite to maneuver for their own interest.[57]

The system equally fosters big men, a product of the rising profile of corruption which the "dash" or giving of gifts for services rendered created. The elite among these and their cohorts have continued to drain a huge proportion of state resources. They commandeer further riches by acting as gatekeepers for foreign companies. Apart from the ostentatious living mentioned earlier, some of the diverted state revenue is stashed away in foreign bank accounts and foreign investment. The World Bank estimated that 40 percent of Africa's private wealth is held offshore. A report prepared for the African Union in 2002 estimated that corruption cost Africans US$148 billion annually—more than a quarter of the continent's entire GDP.[58]

The high level of corruption and a skewed developmental approach has institutionalized and entrenched poverty and infrastructural breakdown or decay. Ghana, Egypt, and South Africa have posted some appreciable growth indices. Ghana's economy has been growing on an average of over 6 percent a year for the past 5 years with the present focus on improved cultivation of cocoa. It is rated second among the ten nations with the fastest-growing GDP across the world, and, according to the 2011 forecast by the Economist Intelligent Unit,[59] it is set to grow by 14 percent in 2011. Foreign direct investment (FDI) has doubled from US$551.30 million in 2009 to US$1.11 billion in 2010.[60] However, most of the Ghana's poor live in the rural areas without basic services such as health care and clean water.

South Africa, on the other hand, has emerged as a well-managed democratic state with strong institutions and a system of checks and balances firmly entrenched in a modern constitution.[61] It is not only the world's largest gold producer but has also been able to attract bank loans, government bonds, and corporate bonds of about US$62 million, which have helped the country to do well in the international arena.[62] But even with this, the majority of the poor blacks are yet to be integrated fully into the economic system, and this has compounded the problem of poverty giving rise to a high rate of crime. As a matter of fact, the criminal tendencies even threatened the 2010 World Cup that was staged in South Africa. Ultimately, however, the government was able to put its act together to record success.

On the other hand, the picture in Nigeria and Tanzania is one of complete despair. Tanzania is one of the poorest countries in the world. The income per capita over the period of 1994 to 2000 was about US$270, compared with US$470 for sub-Saharan Africa generally. Some 42 percent of the total population and 50 percent of the rural population lived below the poverty line.[63] What is more, infrastructure and the education system are an impediment to economic development. In 2000, only 4.2 percent of the Tanzania road network was paved, compared with 16.5 percent for low-income countries in general. Gross tertiary school enrollment stood at only 0.66 percent by 1997, and gross secondary enrollment was 6.5 percent, while adult literacy was 24.9 percent in 2000.[64] Living conditions have worsened and unemployment is on the rise.

However, it is in the so-called giant of Africa, Nigeria, more palpable than elsewhere on the continent that living conditions have progressively continued to decline and infrastructures have collapsed or are on the verge collapsing. The educational system is broken down, with a breakdown of the system due to incessant strikes by teachers over salaries, welfare, dilapidated structures, and poor equipment. As a result, candidates have continued to record poor results in their school-leaving certificate examinations.[65] The graduates are equally half-baked to the extent that they are finding it difficult to contribute effectively to national development. The insecurity of lives and properties is on the increase, thereby making the business environment not conducive and the power supply unpredictable: "Power supply has been erratic; road conditions are deplorable while governance has been below par."[66]

The elite of the continent find it extremely difficult to discard their colonial mental image, which has made them see the salvation of the region in terms of heavy reliance on western assistance in one form or another—loans and favorable atmosphere in the West to accommodate and sell goods from Africa. They are yet to realize the need to subject their various national interests to the needs of the continent. Meredith[67] posits that most of the nations in the region are effectively bankrupt, weighed down by debt, and barely able to raise sufficient funds on their own account to provide minimum public services. By the late 1990s, most African countries relied on western aid to fund as much as 50 percent of government budget and 70 percent of public investment.[68] Meanwhile, the West is fed up and has adopted a lukewarm attitude toward increased demand for aid.

This has become inevitable because, since independence, Africa has received far more foreign aid than any other region in the world. More than US$500 billion of western aid has been sunk into the continent with little discernible result. During the 1990s, international government aid for Africa fell from an average of US$24.86 billion a year to US$16.4 billion.[69] A testimony to this development was what transpired at the G8 Summit of World's richest nations in Canada in 2002. Thambo Mbeki of South Africa, who led the African delegation and called for the support for the New Partnership for African Development (NEPAD), received only a lukewarm response. Rather, the G8 only made a pledge of US$6 billion, which was seen as peanuts.[70]

In addition to their heavy reliance on the West, African governments have been calling on the various nations of Europe and America to change their trade and agricultural policies to favor the economic development of the continent. But the western governments have continued to demonstrate in very clear terms that they are not ready to alter their policies to satisfy the needs and aspirations of the continent. The various nations are even more determined to protect their own producers. As a matter of fact, while urging African nations to remove all subsidies, they have intensified the application of subsidies to their farmers. It may be recalled with the International Monetary Fund (IMF) Structural Adjustment Programs of the 1980s, African nations were forced to remove subsidies for agricultural and social services like education, health, water, and electricity supply.[71]

In the area of agriculture, for example, the total value of subsidies amounts to US$1 billion dollars a day, about US$370 billion a year—a sum larger than the GDP of all of sub-Saharan Africa.[72] Furthermore, there are tariff barriers to protect their agricultural produce—for example, cotton. The region is the world's third-largest producer of cotton, turning out high-quality cotton at competitive prices. The West African subregion produces large quantities of cotton and provides a living for a million farmers. Cotton production in Francophone West Africa has gone up from 100,000 tons a year at independence in the 1960s to 900,000 tons today. In countries like Benin, Burkina Faso, Chad, Mali, and Togo, cotton represents between 5 and 10 percent of GDP, more than a third of export income, and more than 60 percent of agricultural export income.[73] However, the subsidies given by the West to its own farmers have continued to have a negative impact on African farmers, raising to a very high level the cost of producing cotton in Africa. For example, the cost of production of cotton in West Africa is about 38 cents; in the United States, it is more than twice as high. But the United States provides its 250,000 cotton farmers with an annual subsidy of US$4 billion, more than the value of their entire crops.[74] These subsidies help U.S. farmers to export cotton at one-third of what it costs them to produce it. Over a period of 15 years, they have gained nearly one third of the world's market.[75] A study carried out by Oxfam in 2003 showed that as a result of the U.S. subsidies, the world's price for cotton was 25 percent lower than it would be otherwise.[76]

Consequent upon this, cotton production has been made more costly for the African cotton producers. Oxfam estimates that the cost to Burkina Faso is 1 percent of its GDP or 12 percent of its exports; to Mali 1.7 percent of its GDP or 8 percent of its exports; and to Benin 1.4 percent of GDP or 9 percent of its exports. It concludes that U.S. farm subsidies led to trade losses for the eight West African main cotton exporters to outweigh the benefit they received from the U.S. aid.[77] In the same vein, the European Union (EU) has continued to maintain subsidies. It supports its cotton producers with subsidies amounting to about $1 billion a year.[78] Meanwhile, a World Bank study estimates that it would be three times cheaper for Europeans to import cotton than to grow it in Spain or Greece, where the subsidy paid to farmers is far more than the market price of cotton.[79] Between 1998 and 2002, West African production rose by 14 percent but receipts fell by 31 percent. The World Bank has established that eliminating cotton subsidies altogether would raise West Africa export income by US$250 million a year.[80]

TRANSCENDING THE ELITIST APPROACH

This chapter up to this point is an historical excursion into the various ramifications/manifestations of the elitist approach to development on the African continent. It is obvious that development is a multifactorial issue. However, this chapter recognizes the elite as a critical factor in bringing about change because their actions and omissions are highly influenced and shaped by political decisions that, in turn, influence the environment in which actions operate. The elite in leadership give vision and strategies and create a conducive environment for the implementation of formulated policies. Goleman, in his book *Emotional Intelligence* and *Primal Leadership*, has been able to demonstrate critical issues in this competence. For Goleman, it is all about the capacity of people, particularly those in the leadership, to recognize their leadership and others (subjects, citizens) for motivating ourselves and managing emotion in ourselves and our relationships. It develops in the leadership executive intelligence that comprises the accomplishment of tasks, working with other people, and being able to judge one's own performance. The competence leads to a set of interconnected abilities consisting of the foundation needed for executive talent and proficient decision making. For the political elite and indeed all those in authority to achieve this, they must apply an ethical mind to conceptualization and implementation. They have to survey a wide range of sources, dissect and decide which is important and worth paying attention to, and cast about for new ideas and practices, innovate, take chances, and discover.[81]

Self-awareness, self-regulation, self-motivation, empathy, and social skills are fundamental components of emotional intelligence. Self-awareness brings about an accurate self-assessment of self, the community, and the nation as well as self-confidence in ourselves and our nation or region. Self-regulation on the other hand involves knowing our emotional status and developing in us trustworthiness, conscientiousness, adaptability, and innovativeness. Self-motivation ensures an achievement drive, commitment, initiative, and optimism, appreciating setbacks and objectively analyzing the factors responsible. Empathy and social skills are two other equally important factors. In the case of empathy, the elite must be able to put themselves in the shoes of others (subject, citizens, etc.), modify behavior, and develop relationships, as well as other service orientations.[82] African elite are deficient in these emotional intelligence components.

Ake[83] argues that many African elite lack self-confidence, self-reliance, and self-realization. He contends that it is lack of confidence that makes them to believe that the major business is catching up with industrialized nations. It has made them not to understand that self-reliance is a development that cannot be received; it has to be experienced as participation in the process of bringing out. He opines that it is about responsibility for producing a development project and producing resources to carry it through.[84] It has to be practiced at all levels—from the level of national policies and relation between states it has to spread to regions—federal units, communities, and households.

A high level of emotional intelligence of the elite of Singapore and Malaysia has improved the economies of the two nations tremendously. Malaysia's total economy has been improving at 6 to 7 percent a year from 1970 to 2000. The number of poor persons has fallen to fewer than a million, or 3.9 percent of the population of about 26.6 million. The per capita yearly income was at about US$5,300 in 2007.[85] Capital formation in the economy rose sharply from an average of 17 percent of GDP in the 1960s to 25 percent in 1970s and 29 percent in the 1980s. It peaked at 44 percent in 1995, before the Asian financial crisis, but even then it has stood at an average 22 percent of GDP since 2002.[86] On the other hand, the GDP of Singapore was put at US$25,190 in 2007. Self-confidence of leaders and their ability to take calculated risks made these giant strides possible.

The elite in Malaysia, through confidence about themselves and their country, moved the economy to areas in which they had no strong advantage. They passionately took up the diversification of the economy. The nation was moved away from its traditional reliance on rubber and tin to palm oil and later to light and heavy industries.[87] Such a move requires political determination, stability, attention to growth with equity, experimentation, and an ability to learn through implementation.[88] This confidence produced the political will and determination. Economic policy, therefore, became a product of boldness and vision of government planners and their ability to mobilize support for the experiments.[89]

In the case of agriculture, Malaysia's palm oil production increased significantly, from about 99,000 acres in 1960 to about 335,000 in the 1970s. Similarly, palm oil production increased from 90,000 tons in 1960 to 396,000 tons in 1970s.[90] Confidence begot the taking of calculated risks. The elite took calculated risks and developed risk taking in their institutions. There was rapid diversification away from resource-based industrial exports toward non–resource based industries. There was investment in electronic components, for example, semiconductors and printed circuit boards, as well as industrial products. Investments were channeled into telecom equipment, official equipment, and multimedia products, which recorded the fastest growth in gross exports.[91]

The electronics industry developed Malaysia as a regional products and distribution center for high-end electronic products.[92] Similarly, the political elite that took over at independence under the leadership of Lee Kuan Yew in Singapore were very confident about themselves and their mission. They were men of honesty and integrity and made sure this was institutionalized and entrenched in the society. They were very strong about what they wanted: They must build a kind of economy that would try new methods and schemes never tried anywhere previously. They said Singapore could not live by the begging bowl and turn itself into a nation that depended perpetually on the injection of aid.[93] Steps were therefore taken to make the nation self-reliant.

Singapore, which has no petroleum resources, started oil refining. By 1990, it had a total refining capacity of 1.2 million barrels per day, and it has becomes the third largest refining center after Houston and Rotterdam. Meanwhile, the painful British withdrawal after independence was turned into opportunity. Great Britain had a dockyard in Singapore, and it spend huge amount of money to maintain—a total of about US$450 million a year. The base was converted to the Sembawang Shipyard. The workers that were laid off were retained and retrained to form the nucleus of a new shipping line, the Neptune Orient line, in 1968. In 1972, a container complex was built and Singapore became the container transshipment center of the Southeast Asia. By 1975, it was the world's third busiest port behind Rotterdam and New York.[94]

The same self-confidence, the need to be self-reliant, and empathy were exhibited in the construction of housing estates and the Changi International Airport. The elite in Singapore replaced a once expansive coastal mangrove forest with development areas and by so doing added 17 percent to the nation's total land area. They therefore embarked on aggressive housing estates that produced well-planned and coordinated high-rise buildings. The houses were provided with gas, electricity, and pipe-borne water and then were made available to low-income earners who were encouraged to buy them and pay by installment. Payment was staggered over a period of 20 years.[95] Similarly, in spite of advice from foreign and local experts—who all said a new airport should not be constructed and that the existing one should be expanded—Lee Kuan Yew insisted and got the new airport constructed, now the Changi International Airport. It not only became one of the best in the world but was completed in 6 years instead of the envisaged 10. Above all, instead of the projected cost of US$1.5 billion, only US$1 billion was spent.[96]

The elite in both nations were proactive. They were always in search for a new growth areas and always pushing toward value added and knowledge-based industries. They took time off before formulating policy and made detailed considerations of options before implementation. Furthermore, they involved a large segment of the public and business sector in the specific design of policies and bundled related policy measures into packages that overcame legislative and coordination problem[97]—that is, the "reform cluster" approach. To get grassroots support, a system of visits to parliamentary constituencies and branch offices of ruling political parties were embarked upon to explain policies and get their support.

CONCLUSION

It is clear from the foregoing that the African elite must rethink and relearn development. It has to be conceptualized from an inclusive and not exclusive perspective. It must spring up within the society in a way that is targeted, and it must be an effort of, by, and for the people. Development has to be people-centered, with a focus on the fulfillment of human potential and improvement of the economic, social, and political well-being of the people. It must be advocated at the grassroots and community levels, where people's participation is total. Opportunities must be expanded so as to address people's needs, abilities, and concerns within their economic, social, cultural, and political models. These efforts must merge the interrelated goals of development and empowerment of the people. The African continent will experience development when the elite, both in and out of government, acquire, institutionalize, and entrench emotional intelligence at all levels and in all sectors and develop themselves into individuals and groups of honest, trustworthy, credible, empathetic, and self-confident elements.

NOTES

1. Martin Meredith, *The State of Africa: A History of Fifty Years of Independence* (London: Simon and Schuster, 2005).
2. World Bank, *World Bank Encyclopedia* (Chicago: Scott Fetzer, 2008).
3. Ibid., 126.
4. Ibid., 127.

5. Meredith, *The State of Africa*, 681.
6. Ibid., 682.
7. Ninalowo Adebayo,"The Status Quo: State as antidote to failure A sociological inquiry to Underdevelopment," *The Nation,* December 23, 2010.
8. World Bank, *World Bank Encyclopedia.*
9. Ibid., 125.
10. Adebayo, "The Status Quo," 36.
11. Meredith, *The State of Africa*, 682.
12. Ibid.
13. Ibid.
14. World Bank, *World Bank Encyclopedia*, 126.
15. Meredith, *The State of Africa*, 682.
16. Catherine V. Scott, *Gender and Development. Rethinking Modernization and Dependency Theory* (London: Lynne Rienner, 1995).
17. U. Seers, "Capitalism and Development in Latin America, The Dependency Paradigm Revisited," *Journal of Development Studies,* Vol. 18 (1972).
18. D. Torado, *Development in Historical Perspective, Populism, Nationalism and Industrialization* (London: Dictman, 2003).
19. United Nations Development Programme, *Human Development Report 1997* (UNDP, 1997).
20. Claude Ake, *Democracy and Development in Africa* (Abuja, Nigeria: Spectrum Books, 2003), 10.
21. R. Biel, *The New Imperialism: Crisis and Contradictions in North/South Relations* (London: Zed Books, 2000), 73.
22. Ibid., 72.
23. Ake, *Democracy and Development*, 10.
24. Scott, *Gender and Development*, 3 .
25. Ibid., 1.
26. A. G. Frank, "The Development of Underdevelopment," *New York Monthly Review,* Vol. 18 (1996): 17–31.
27. Walter Rodney, *How Europe Underdeveloped Africa* (London: Boggle L'Ouverture, 1981).
28. Samir Amin, "Accumulation on a World Scale," *New York Monthly Review* (2001).
29. D. Rucco and L. H. Simon, "Radical Theories of Development: Frank, the Modes of Production School and Amin," in Charles K. Wilber, ed., *The Political Economy of Development and Underdevelopment* (New York: Random House, 1973).
30. Scott, *Gender and Development*, 3.
31. Ibid., 2.
32. David L. Sills, ed., *International Encyclopedia of Social Sciences Vol. 5 and 6* (New York: Macmillan and the Free Press, 1995), 26.
33. S. S. Shashi, *International Encyclopedia of Social Sciences* (New Delhi: Anmol Publications, 2007), 1579.
34. Ibid.
35. Sills, *International Encyclopedia of Social Sciences*, 26.
36. Ibid.
37. Shashi *International Encyclopedia of Social Sciences*, 1579.
38. Ibid.
39. Sills, *International Encyclopedia of Social Sciences*, 27.
40. Ibid.
41. Biel, *The New Imperialism*, 197. .
42. Ibid., 200.
43. Ibid., 214.

44. Meredith, *The State of Africa*, 171.
45. Ibid.
46. Ibid.
47. Ibid.
48. Ibid., 172.
49. Ibid.
50. Adebayo, "The Status Quo," 36.
51. Ibid.
52. Meredith, *The State of Africa*, 679.
53. Ibid., 687.
54. Ibid., 22.
55. Ibid., 687.
56. Ibid.
57. Ibid., 175.
58. Ibid., 687.
59. B. Bakare, "Enhance FDI to Boost Power, Others Say the World Bank," *The Nation*, January 18, 2011, 22.
60. *The Nation* January 20, 2011, 29.
61. Meredith, *The State of Africa*, 686.
62. Bakare, "Enhance FDI to Boost Power," 25.
63. Agrawala Shardul et al., *Development Climate change in Tanzania: Focus on Mountain Kilimanjaro* (Paris: Organisation for Economic Co-operation and Development, 2003).
64. World Bank, *World Bank Encyclopedia*.
65. Y. Gowan, "Alarming Decline in Education Standards: Reversing It and Moving Forward," *The Nation*, January 27, 2011, 6.
66. Bakare, "Enhance FDI," 25.
67. Meredith, *The State of Africa*, 683.
68. Ibid.
69. Ibid.
70. Ibid.
71. Ake, *Democracy in Historical Perspective*; and Meredith, *The State of Africa*.
72. Meredith, *The State of Africa*, 684.
73. Ibid.
74. Ibid.
75. Ibid.
76. Ibid.
77. Ibid.
78. Ibid., 685.
79. Ibid.
80. Ibid.
81. H. Gardner, "The Ethical Mind," *Harvard Business Review,* March 2002.
82. D. Goleman, *Emotional Intelligence* (New York: Bantam Books, 1995).
83. Ake, *Democracy in Historical Perspective*, 16.
84. Ibid., 140.
85. Zainab A. Yusuf and Deepak Bhattasali, *Economic Growth and Development in Malaysia: Policy Making and Leadership World Bank* (Washington, DC: The International Bank for Reconstruction and Development, 2008).
86. Ibid., 2.
87. Yusuf and Bhattasali, *Economic Growth and Development in Malaysia*, 4.
88. Ibid., 11.
89. Ibid., 5.
90. Ibid.

91. Ibid., 11.
92. Ibid.
93. D. Sani and A. A. Yusufu, "Yar'adua in the Mold of Lee Kwan Yew," Unpublished article, Kaduna Business School, 2009.
94. Ibid., 9.
95. Ibid., 15.
96. Ibid., 11.
97. Shardul, *Development Change in Tanzania*, 15.

REFERENCES:

Adebayo, Ninalowo. *The Status Quo: State as Antidote to Failure A Sociological Inquiry to Underdevelopment.* Lagos, Nigeria: University of Lagos Press.
Ake, Claude. *Democracy in Historical Perspective, Populism, Nationalism and Industrialization.* London: Dictman, 2003.
Amin, Samir. *Accumulation on a World Scale.* New York: Monthly Review Press, 1974.
Bakare, B. "Enhance FDI to Boost Power, Others Say the World Bank." *The Nation*, January 18, 2011: 22.
Biel, R. *The New Imperialism Crisis and Contradictions in North/South Relations.* London: Zed Books, 2000.
Frank, A. G. "The Development of Underdevelopment." *New York Monthly Review*, Vol. 18 (1996): 121–50.
Gardner, H. "The Ethical Mind." *Harvard Business Review*, March, 2002: 51–56.
Goleman, D. *Emotional Intelligence.* New York: Bantam Books, 1995.
Gowon, Y. "Alarming Decline in Education Standards: Reversing It and Moving Forward." *The Nation*, January, 27 2011: 36.
Liang, J. "Intelligence Strategy: The Integrated 3 C-Ok Framework of Intelligent Human Organization." In *Human System Management.* Lansdale, PA: IOS Press, 2004.
Meredith, Martin. *The State of Africa A History of Fifty Years of Independence.* London: Simon and Schuster, 2005.
Rodney, Walter. *How Europe Underdeveloped Africa.* London: Boggle–L 'Ouverture, 1981.
Rucco, D., and L. H. Simon. "Radical Theories of Development: Frank, the Modes of Production School and Amir." In Charles K. Wilber, ed. *The Political Economy of Development and Underdevelopment.* New York: Random House, 1973.
Sani, D., and A. A. Yusuf. "Yaradua in the mold of Lee Kaun Yeu." Unpublished article, Kaduna Business School, 2009.
Scott, Catherine V. *Gender and Development. Rethinking Modernization and Dependency Theory.* London: Lynne Rienner, 1995.
Seers, U. "Capitalism and Development in Latin America, The Dependency Paradigm Revisited." *Journal of Development Studies* Vol 18 (1972): 21–36.
Shardul, Agrawala et al. *Development Climate Change in Tanzania: Focus on Mountain Kilimanjaro.* Paris: Organisation for Economic Co-operation and Development, 2003.
Shashi, S. S. *International Encyclopedia of Social Sciences.* New Delhi: Animal Publications, 2007.
Sills, David L., ed. *International Encyclopedia of Social Sciences*, Vols. 5 and 6. New York: Macmillan and the Free Press, 1972.

Tornado, D. *Development in Historical Perspective: Populism, Nationalism and Industrialization*. London: Dictman, 2003.
United Nations Development Programme. *Human Development Report 1997*. New York: UNDP, 1997.
World Bank. *World Bank Encyclopedia*. Chicago: Scott Fetzer, 2008.
Yusuf, Zainab A., and Deepak Bhattasali. *Economic Growth and Development in Malaysia: Policy Making and Leadership*. Paris: World Bank/The International Bank for Reconstruction and Development, 2008.

Part III

Forging New International Connections

10 The Political Economy of Rising Asian Interests in Africa
Problems, Prospects, and Challenges

Olusegun M. Osinibi

The vast natural resources available in Africa, the corresponding energy needs, an increased demand for raw materials in Asia, and the need to forge diplomatic coalitions that will counterbalance western dominance has spurred rising Asian interests in Africa. In spite of the limitless opportunities that such an association potentially offers, it remains to be seen whether Africa will benefit in the long run from Asian involvement as well as whether Asia can maximize the potentials its rising interests in Africa offer. This chapter examines these issues, first looking at the historical basis for the present cooperation between Asia and Africa. The second part gives an overview of various political and economic initiatives already taken to strengthen Afro-Asian ties; this is followed by an analysis of the political economy of rising Asian interest in Africa. The final part addresses the reasons why Africa is seemingly retrogressing and offers solutions that could aid Africa to fully maximize the benefits of the rising Asian interest.

HISTORICAL BACKGROUND

Africans and Asians both have a history of migration, interaction, and cultural sharing. They share a history of European colonization, decolonization, and independence as well as neocolonization and dependency (Kochiyama 1998). Despite this, there is a dearth of literature on the ancient historical interactions between Asia and Africa. There are several examples that relations between the two continents have existed for centuries. For one, archaeological excavations at Mogadishu (Somalia) and Kilwa (Tanzania) have led to the discovery of ancient Chinese coins, which lend credence to the prior existence of trade relations (East African Coast, n.d.). In the field of medicine, the spread of humoral medicine from the Mediterranean to South Asia and eastern and southern Africa as well as the long-term evolution of Swahili medicine as an Asian/African hybrid also reveal a long history of interaction between the two continents (Welcome Unit, 2005).

In modern times, however, the need to promote Afro-Asian economic and cultural cooperation and to oppose colonialism or neocolonialism, specifically the United States and the Soviet Union during the Cold War, brought about the convergence of the representatives of African and Asian countries in Bandung, Indonesia, from April 18 to April 24, 1955. Popularly referred to as the Bandung Conference, the purpose of this convergence was to promote the political and diplomatic autonomy of less developed countries in the face of international Cold War politics and to promote the highest aspirations of the peoples of Asia and Africa in terms of economic and cultural cooperation, human rights, and national self-determination as well as the promotion of international peace (Sneyd 2005). In addition to this, there was a call at the conference for the world superpowers to suspend their nuclear tests, reduce armaments, and increase economic aid (Sneyd 2005).

Furthermore, a ten-point "Declaration on the Promotion of World Peace and Cooperation" was unanimously adopted. It incorporated the principles of the United Nations Charter and the five principles espoused by the former Indian Prime Minister Jawaharlal Nehru, which are mutual respect for other nations, territorial integrity and sovereignty, nonaggression, noninterference in internal affairs, equality and mutual benefit, and peaceful coexistence (Encyclopedia Britannica 2011). It is unfortunate that all the resolutions and declarations of the Bandung Conference turned out to be mere rhetoric.

In the course of the decade subsequent to the conference, even though the decolonization process progressed, friction among members increased and the concept of Asian-African solidarity became less and less meaningful. Major divisions among the sponsors of the original conference emerged and, in November 1965, the second Asian-African conference, scheduled to be held in Algiers, was indefinitely postponed, making it less likely that another Asian-African convergence of the magnitude of the Bandung Conference would materialize (Encyclopedia Britannica 2011). It is worthy of note that in 2005, on the fiftieth anniversary of the original conference, leaders from Asian and African countries met in Jakarta and Bandung to launch the New Asian-African Strategic Partnership (NAASP), where they pledged to promote political, economic, and cultural cooperation between the two continents (Tokyo International Conference n.d.).

AFRO-ASIAN POLITICAL AND ECONOMIC INITIATIVES IN THE POST-BANDUNG ERA

Tokyo International Conference on African Development

The Tokyo International Conference on African Development, also known as TICAD, was launched in 1993 to promote high-level policy dialogue between African leaders and development partners; it has since evolved into a major global framework to facilitate the implementation of initiatives for promoting African development under the dual principle of African "ownership" and international "partnership." A central feature of this framework is the cooperation between Asia and Africa. The first Conference, TICAD I, took place in 1993, where commitments were made to reverse the decline in development assistance for Africa occasioned by the end of the Cold War. The Tokyo Declaration on African Development was adopted, committing to the pursuit of political and economic reforms in Africa, increased private sector development, regional cooperation and integration, and the harnessing of Asian experience for the benefit of African development (TICAD n.d.). In 1998, the second Conference, TICAD II, was held with the primary theme being commitment to Africa's developmental challenges, the reduction of poverty, and the integration of Africa into the global economy. This culminated in the adoption of the Tokyo Agenda for Action, which identified shared goals, objectives, and guidelines for actions to be taken by Africa and its partners.

The third Conference, TICAD III, was held in 2003. The highlight of this was an explicit commitment for the TICAD Initiative to support the African Union's New Partnership for Africa's Development (NEPAD)—a blueprint for Africa's peace, socioeconomic growth, and development. TICAD III was held in Tokyo with high-level participation of African leaders, including twenty-three heads of state and ten heads of international organizations. It was heralded as one of the largest international conferences on African development (TICAD n.d.). Under the overall objective of fostering a vibrant Africa, the fourth conference (TICAD IV), held in 2008, addressed the three major objectives of boosting economic growth: ensuring human security, including the achievement of the Millennium Development Goals and the consolidation of peace and democratization, and addressing environmental issues and climate change (TICAD n.d.).

Forum on China-Africa Cooperation (FOCAC)

The Forum on China-Africa Cooperation (FOCAC), an official forum between the People's Republic of China and the states of Africa, was established by means of a ministerial conference held in Beijing, China, in 2000, providing a platform for collective dialogue between China and African countries. The founding of FOCAC represents a major strategic choice that China and Africa made in rising to the challenges of globalization and the need to seek common development through joint efforts. It involves building a new type of strategic partnership featuring political equality, mutual trust, economic cooperation, and cultural exchanges (FOCAC 2010).

Four international conferences have been held so far to promote the objectives of the forum. The first conference heralded the Beijing Declaration of the Forum on China-Africa Cooperation and the Program for China-Africa Cooperation in Economic and Social Development. However, the most notable of the conferences was the fourth Conference of 2009, held in Egypt, where China pledged support for Africa by announcing the establishment of a US$1 billion special loan for small and medium-sized African businesses (Jopson and Anderlini 2009). Other promises made by China for Africa's benefit included the construction of 100 new clean-energy projects in Africa covering solar power, biogas, and small hydropower; the gradual reduction of customs duties on 95 percent of products from African states having diplomatic ties with China; the undertaking of 100 joint demonstration projects on scientific and technological research; the sending of fifty agricultural technology teams to Africa and the training of 2,000 agricultural technology personnel to help strengthen Africa's ability to ensure food security; the provision of medical equipment and antimalarial materials worth ¥500 million to the thirty hospitals and thirty malaria prevention and treatment centers built by China; and the training of 3,000 doctors and nurses for Africa. China also offered to train a total of 20,000 professionals of various fields for Africa over a 3-year period (China.org.cn n.d.).

India-Africa Forum

The India-Africa Forum Summit is the official platform for Indian-African relations. It was first held from April 4 to April 8, 2008 in New Delhi, India, and is an initiative aimed at strengthening ties between India and African countries and furthering cooperation in areas such as environment, health, education, energy, and mining as well as international issues such as the fight against terrorism, climate change, and World Trade Organization negotiations (Payal 2008). Accordingly, India has taken certain steps to strengthen its bond with Africa, including its decision to expand unilateral duty-free and preferential market access for exports from all the fifty least developed countries, thirty-four of which are in Africa, and its offer of lines of credit amounting to US$5.4 billion to these countries; the enhancement of India's budget for technical assistance and training programs, which provide greater opportunities for African students to pursue studies in India; fostering cooperation with the regional economic communities of Africa and with the African Union; and broadly working together for United Nations reforms aimed at making the United Nations more representative and democratic (Payal 2008).

The New Asian-African Strategic Partnership (NAASP)

This partnership was formed during the Asia-Africa Summit held in April 2005 in Jakarta, Indonesia, marking the fiftieth anniversary of the Bandung Conference. At the summit, leaders from Asian and African countries met and declared the New Asian-African Strategic Partnership (NAASP) as a blueprint to bolster Asian-African cooperation in the future. The partnership is seen as a venture to build a bridge between Asia and Africa, with particular focus on the three broad pillars of partnership, namely political solidarity, economic cooperation, and sociocultural collaboration (Ministry of Foreign Affairs 2009). This is particularly necessary because 50 years after the Bandung Conference, the world has witnessed profound changes that have left many countries in Asia and Africa lagging behind in their economic and social development, thus hampering their efforts to benefit from the opportunities offered by globalization (Department of Foreign Affairs 2006). The theme of the summit, "Reinvigorating the Bandung Spirit: Working towards a New Asian-African Strategic Partnership," was described as a pointer to the dawn of a new era of cooperation among the countries of Asia and Africa as they strive toward a more peaceful and prosperous future (Department of Foreign Affairs 2006). Subsequent to this summit, a number of initiatives have been carried out through joint efforts of Asian and African countries, including the International Training on Business Incubator to Develop Small and Medium Enterprises for Asian, African, and Pacific Countries, which took place in Jakarta in November 2006; the NAASP-United Nations Environmental Project Workshop on Environmental Law and Policy held in Jakarta in December 2006; the Asian-African Forum on Genetic Resources, Traditional Knowledge, and Folklore; and the NAASP Workshop on Satellite Communication and Technology and Its Application, held in Bandung in 2007 (Ministry of Foreign Affairs, Indonesia 2009).

THE POLITICAL ECONOMY OF ASIAN INTEREST IN AFRICA

Trade Flows

It can be argued that the rise of Asian interest in Africa is fundamentally driven by motivations such as the quest for resources, business opportunities, diplomatic openings, and strategic alliances (Pham 2007a,b). For example, China's sharply accelerating domestic energy demand, combined with declining domestic petroleum production and insufficient coal output, has spurred the Chinese government to pursue stable overseas sources of hydrocarbon fuels. China is acknowledged as the world's second largest oil consumer behind the United States, but Asian oil and natural gas production is not growing fast enough to meet Chinese demands because a large portion of Middle Eastern oil and gas production is normally allotted to United States and European markets (Brookes and Shin 2006). Hence, China looks to African nations as likely targets for the acquisition of hydrocarbons (Brookes and Shin 2006).

The increase in trade flows between Africa and Asia in recent times is reflective of the growth of south-south trade and is driven by the evolving middle class in Asia's emerging economic giants, particularly China and India, whose appetite for Africa's commodities is growing, and by rising economic growth in sub-Saharan Africa, where the demand for Asian manufactured goods is increasing. Thus this south-south alliance is said to be fostering trade that is qualitatively different from Africa's traditional north-south commerce with the European Union (EU) and the United States, where trade flows have been stimulated largely by preferential arrangements (Broadman 2007). It is worth noting that owing to the poorly developed technology of most African countries, manufactured products account for only 20 percent of Africa's total exports, consistent with the pattern of Africa's exports to Asia (Broadman 2007).

The lopsided state of trade relations between Asia and Africa, especially sub-Saharan Africa, is exemplified by the fact that while commodities account for about 86 percent of Africa's exports to Asia, 80 percent of Africa's imports from Asia are manufactured goods. One must not lose sight of the fact that Africa, with its rich resources, has a natural comparative advantage in producing raw materials, including energy resources, while China and India, with their rich supply of skilled labor, have a comparative advantage in manufactured products (Broadman 2007). There is, however, no gainsaying that with this arrangement, Africa, whose manufactured imports from Asia exceed its manufactured exports to Asia, has an unfavorable balance of trade vis-à-vis Asia. It has been observed that the growing populations in China and India with higher incomes are motivating purchases of commodities and raw materials from Africa and, at the same time, Africa is importing Asian manufactured products for consumption by households and for use as capital goods in the manufacturing sector, in which growth is taking off (Broadman 2007.) Africa exports mainly petroleum and raw materials to China and non-oil minerals to India, but Africa imports more value-added commodities such as textiles and apparel, electric machinery and equipment, and such consumer products as medicine, cosmetics, and batteries from Asia. Apart from the balance of trade, which is already skewed against Africa, the imposition of high Asian tariffs on some African products may be discouraging African exports to Asian countries. Of note are the high Indian tariffs on agricultural products, which negatively affect products in which African countries have growth potential (Broadman 2007).

The economic impact of Asia's trade relations with Africa were aptly stated by Kofi Annan, former secretary-general of the United Nations Organization, when he raised some concerns about Asian and in particular Chinese investment projects in Africa. He pointed out that Asia's trade with and investment in Africa is not necessarily converted into growth and poverty reduction across the continent and that, beyond the circles of the elite, Africans were not benefiting sufficiently from the revenues and partnerships generated by the ongoing extraction of natural resources. He cited the issue of considerable trade imbalances between Africa and Asia, noting that African exports to Asia are dominated by low-value raw materials—such as unrefined oil, minerals, and timber—while processed goods from

Africa, especially in agriculture, face both tariff and nontariff barriers imposed by Asian countries (Annan 2010).

Dumping of Products in Africa

Apart from the fact that the balance of trade between Asia and Africa is heavily weighted in favor of Asia, the dumping of mostly substandard products in Africa by Asian countries, particularly China, has become a cause for concern. Over the past one and half decades, there has been a global increase in demand for products made in China partly due to the fact that Chinese products are reasonably priced compared with competing products from Europe and America. However, although Chinese products are cheap, they are often substandard or counterfeit (Omoneyi 2009). These products range from drugs to household consumables. Most African markets are flooded with fake television and radio sets; satellite dishes and signal receivers; computers, watches, and mobile phones; and an array of domestic appliances including substandard electrical cookers, refrigerators, blenders/mixers, and washing machines. The list also includes detergents, absorbents, spare parts for motor vehicles, agricultural inputs, industrial and domestic chemicals, pharmaceuticals, building materials, textiles, clothes, food and beverages, and alcohol, among others. Some observers even posit that for every original product in the market there is a fake version by the side, and sometimes it takes laboratory analysis to tell the difference between originals and fakes (Omoneyi 2009).

For example, China has always been accused of being the brain behind the influx of fake products into Nigeria and the largest percentage of fake products circulating in Nigeria are exported from China. The director general of the Standards Organization of Nigeria, John Akanya, while leading a Nigerian delegation to visit the vice minister of the General Administration of Quality Supervision, Inspection, and Quarantine of the People's Republic of China in Beijing, recently observed that it is worrisome to see substandard industrial goods being exported to Nigeria from China given the common knowledge that very high quality goods are being exported from China to other parts of the world, including the United States and Europe (Standards Organization of Nigeria, 2003). In addition, the chairman of the Governing Council of Standards Organization of Nigeria, Samuel Ortom, stated that an average Nigerian believes every substandard product in Nigeria is from China, which according to him is not good for the reputation of China as a developed economy and one of the largest trading partners of Nigeria (Standards Organization of Nigeria 2003). The Manufacturers Association of Nigeria has also bitterly condemned China's dumping of "cheap and substandard" products on the Nigerian market, describing the situation as "disastrous" (Ori 2010). According to the association, the expansion of Chinese goods in Nigerian markets makes nonsense of recent government policy that banned importation of some foreign products as part of a campaign to support local industry, as Nigeria's major commercial cities are now overloaded with substandard textiles, machinery, and auto parts (Ori 2010). The fallout of these gross complaints is a proposed agreement on inspection, certification, and surveillance of all industrial goods export, which is aimed at promoting greater cooperation between Nigeria and China as trading partners and substantially improving the quality and safety of industrial goods exports to Nigeria (Standards Organization of Nigeria 2003).

It is worth noting that the influx of cheap Chinese products to the detriment of local African industries is not limited to Nigeria but affects many sub-Saharan countries (Hitchens 2010; Mugabe 2009). International observers also say that the way China does business, particularly its willingness to pay bribes, as documented by Transparency International (2010) and attaching no conditions to aid money, undermines local efforts to increase good governance and international efforts at macroeconomic reform by institutions like the World Bank and the International Monetary Fund (Hanson 2008).

Apart from substandard and counterfeit products, the continent of Africa has also had the misfortune of being made the dumping ground of fake drugs manufactured in Asia. In this regard, India is the most culpable party, notorious for its exportation of fake pharmaceutical products. Drugs made in India are sold around the world, and the country's substandard drug trade represents a grave public health threat that extends far beyond the subcontinent. As such, unless serious steps are taken to improve the quality of the Indian drug supply, the global spread of unsafe pharmaceuticals will persist (Bate 2010). The statement from India, however, is that it is Chinese counterfeit medicines that are being pushed into Africa with fake "Made in India" labels and that India is in favor of close interaction between Indian drug regulators and their African counterparts to jointly fight against the menace (Bhaumik 2011). Even Europe is not spared the menace of fake pharmaceuticals from Asia, as the European Union reported in 2008 that many of the fake pharmaceuticals seized in Europe originated from India (EU Business 2009). Regardless of the particular Asian country responsible for dumping fake pharmaceuticals in Africa, the bottom line is that Africa is the worse for it.

Another worrisome trend is the escalating influx of used Japanese cars into African countries. Quite a number of the used cars are exported as scrap from Japan but are refurbished and used on African roads—causing road accidents or constituting sources of environmental pollution (Awoniyi 2001; Comins 2005). This has led some African governments to ban certain used cars imported from Asia. For example, Zimbabwe recently announced the ban on second-hand vehicles that are more than 5 years old (Zimbabwe Mail 2010). A new directive to ban the importation of outdated second hand cars to Ethiopia is to be ratified shortly (Muluken 2010). It is curious that the Nigerian government on its own part has decided to extend the age limit of used cars imported into Nigeria from 10 to 15 years (All News Nigeria 2010).

Political Relations

In the sphere of politics, Asian superpowers have been shown to support African leaders who serve Asian interests—notwithstanding the tyrannical or despotic tendencies of such African leaders. For example, Sudan's government has long abetted and perpetrated genocide against large non-Muslim populations in its Darfur region. While the United States, the European Union, Japan, and other western democracies have sought to impose United Nations sanctions against the Sudanese regime over the issue, China has opposed UN actions against Sudan. Over the past several years, the Sudanese government has forced hundreds of thousands of people to flee their homes in southern oil fields largely owned by the Chinese oil company, CNPC (Brookes and Shin 2006).

In fact, Sudanese government troops and government-aligned militias have used Chinese-made helicopter gunships, based at airstrips maintained by Chinese oil companies, in raids that devastated hundreds of towns and villages around the oil installations (Harman 2008; Herbst 2008). The position of China on the Sudanese crisis can be accessed from a comment attributed to the Chinese Deputy Foreign Minister Zhou Wenzhong in a recent interview thus: "Business is business. We try to separate politics from business. Secondly, I think the internal situation in the Sudan is an internal affair, and we are not in a position to impose upon them" (Brookes and Shin 2006).

Furthermore, in September 2004, the UN Security Council passed Resolution 1564, which condemned the mass killing of civilians in the Darfur region but stopped short of imposing oil sanctions if Khartoum did not act to stop the killing. China abstained from the vote and threatened to veto any further move to impose sanctions (CNN 2004). African dictatorships are regular buyers of Chinese weapons and military equipment, which they often use to oppress minority populations, squash political opposition, harass neighboring countries, and extinguish any glimmers of democratization. In 2004, despite the U.S. and EU arms embargo against Zimbabwe, China sold Zimbabwe fighter aircraft and military vehicles for US$200 million (Brookes and Shin 2006). In addition, China provided a military-strength radio jamming device, which the Harare government used to block broadcasts of antigovernment reports from independent media outlets during the 2005 parliamentary election campaign (McLaughlin 2005).

The Congressional Research Service reports that China views these sales as a means of "enhancing its status as an international political power, and increasing its ability to obtain access to significant natural resources, especially oil" (Hanson 2008). In the period from 2003 to 2006, China's arms sales to Africa made up 15.4 percent, approximately US$500 million, of all conventional arms transfers to the continent. Notable weapons sales include those to Sudan, Equatorial Guinea, Ethiopia, Eritrea, Burundi, Tanzania, and Zimbabwe. Beijing has also sent Chinese military trainers to help their African counterparts. Arms sales and military relationships help China gain important African allies in the United Nations—including Sudan, Zimbabwe, and Nigeria—for its political goals (Hanson 2008). Conversely, it is important to note that China has contributed greatly to United Nations peace-keeping efforts in conflict zones in Africa. For example, China is involved in the UN Mission in the Democratic Republic of Congo (MONUC); the UN Integrated Office in Sierra Leone (UNIOSIL); the UN Mission in Ethiopia and Eritrea (UNMEE); the UN Mission in Sudan (UNMIS); and the UN Mission in Côte d'Ivoire (UNOCI), As of May 2007, 1,800 Chinese troops were participating in peacekeeping operations in Africa in Liberia, Sudan, and the Democratic republic of Congo (Pham 2007a,b).

THE TRAGEDY OF AFRICA'S CONTINUED RETROGRESSION

It has been observed that at the time of decolonization in the 1950s and 1960s, the level of economic development in most of Asia was at par with that of Africa. For instance, four decades ago, the per capita income of South Korea was comparable with that of the Sudan in Africa. However, since the 1960s, South Korea has achieved an incredible record of growth to become one of the twenty-six richest countries in the world and was able to join the trillion-dollar club of world economies in 2004, while the Sudan is still one of the thirty-three least developed countries in sub-Saharan Africa (Annan 2010; Political Articles 2009). This is in spite of the fact that African countries have relatively larger endowments of natural resources than Asian countries. While Asian countries have engaged in high rates of savings, investment in education, capital accumulation, sound macroeconomic management practices, relatively open trade policies, dynamic agricultural sectors, the maintenance of relatively equitable income distribution, and political credibility, African countries, with the exception of a few, have done the exact opposite (Political Articles 2009).

The main obstacle to African development is the corrupt autocratic leadership and incompetent government that most African countries have been saddled with since independence. In comparison, most governments in Asia are charting the course and actively driving the agenda for the continued growth and development of their nations. The Chinese government, for example, has been instrumental in driving coordinated policy reforms for the country's remarkable transformation from an agrarian to an industrial economy (Annan 2010). In Singapore, the state has created a knowledge economy through targeted investments in high-quality lifelong education. This great institution is testimony to the success of this policy (Annan

2010). Across the region, governments have led a green revolution that has enabled them to feed their citizens. In India, for example, the government invested in irrigation, roads, education, and subsidies for fertilizers, energy, and credit. We cannot underestimate the importance of improving agricultural productivity. Progress simply cannot be delivered unless governments ensure their people are fed (Annan 2010).

Africa is widely considered among the world's most corrupt places, a factor seen as contributing to the stunted development and impoverishment of many African states. Of the ten countries considered most corrupt in the world, six are in sub-Saharan Africa, according to Transparency International, a leading global watchdog on corruption (Furphy 2010). A 2002 African Union study estimated that corruption cost the continent roughly US$150 billion a year. To compare, developed countries gave US$22.5 billion in aid to sub-Saharan Africa in 2008, according to the Organization for Economic Cooperation and Development (Hanson 2009). Transparency International's 2010 Corruption Perceptions Index, released in October 2010, identified Africa as the most corrupt region in the world (Transparency International 2010). Sub-Saharan Africa is also one of the most underdeveloped regions on earth (United Nations 2010). While governments commit large sums to addressing the plethora of problems hindering development on the continent, corruption remains a major obstacle to achieving much needed progress (Furphy 2010). Corruption results in the deviation of funds intended for development and undermines a government's ability to provide basic services. It also undermines the rule of law, breeds inequality and injustice, and discourages foreign investment, thus further impeding development (Furphy 2010).

With regard to the rising interest of Asia in Africa, concern has been expressed about the rise in Chinese investment in Africa in particular, suggesting that China's no-strings-attached approach to aid is undermining anticorruption efforts. Critics suggest that China will continue to make deals with corrupt governments, such as its multi-billion-dollar agreement with the Democratic Republic of Congo, as long as it obtains access to prized natural resources (Hanson 2009). It is also clear that Africans who do not belong to elite circles are not benefiting sufficiently from the revenues and partnerships around the ongoing extraction of natural resources.

The nontransparent nature of many deals has also helped undermine, deliberately or unwittingly, political accountability in Africa and risks fueling corruption and instability (Annan 2010). Asia's investment and loans also raise concerns about debt sustainability, risk sharing, and cost recovery. Asia's growing interest in African land has further led to accusations of land grabbing. It has pushed the Food and Agriculture Organization (FAO), the World Bank, the United Nations Conference on Trade and Development (UNCTAD), and African governments to formulate a new code of conduct for land purchases, which should later lead to an international protocol (Annan 2010).

CONCLUSION

The prospect of strong sociopolitical and economic cooperation between Africa and Asia raises much optimism in view of the boundless human and natural resources available on both continents. At present, the identified goals of the Asia-Africa partnership—such as political solidarity, economic cooperation, and sociocultural collaboration—are far from being realized, as Africa continues to retrogress under the burden of corruption, poverty, bad governance, and an unfavorable balance of trade. The rising interest of Asia in Africa has not conferred tangible benefits on Africa, not simply because Asia is out to serve its own interests but because Africa has not positioned itself to reap the vast benefits that strong Asia-Africa ties can confer.

There must be concerted efforts to entrench true democracy all over Africa. The need for effective institutions that provide checks and balances as well as credible accountability mechanisms, which will ensure that benefits are spread equitably, cannot be overemphasized. These include a free press and strong civic society. African governments need to demonstrate a clear commitment to human rights and the rule of law, because it is only when a government is grounded in the rule of law, fairly and consistently applied to leaders as well as their citizens, can society rest on a solid foundation. Only when the rights of all, including minorities, are respected will there be stability and prosperity (Annan 2010).

There is even a greater need for corruption to be effectively tackled in Africa, as any benefits that may accrue from Asia-Africa cooperation is at present very vulnerable to be siphoned by corrupt government officials and their cronies. Africa's image as the most corrupt region in the world needs to be improved. In this vein, Asia needs to avoid providing support, whether military or financial, to despotic governments in Africa, using the excuse of separating business from politics.

On the economic front, African governments stand to gain a lot if the Asian model for development in the last couple of decades is adopted and pursued vigorously. Such measures would include increased savings, investment in education, capital accumulation, sound macroeconomic management, a relatively open trade policy, a dynamic agricultural sector, and the maintenance of relatively equitable income distribution. Increased foreign direct investment and transfer of technology from Asia to Africa will also go a long way in alleviating the problems of Africa as opposed to food or financial aid. For example, Asian automobile powerhouses like Japan, Korea, and China can set up car-assembly plants in Africa instead of exporting an avalanche of used cars to Africa. This is without prejudice to the fact that Africa on its own part needs to provide a conducive and stable environment for foreign investments. Increased Asian investment in Africa will be immensely beneficial to both continents.

There is a need for concerted efforts on the part of Asian governments, particularly China and India, to curtail the export of fake and substandard products to Africa regardless of the profits accruable, as this breeds a loss of confidence and will not assist in forging a long-term economic partnership. In the area of international trade, the real challenge of Afro-Asian policy makers is to ensure that patterns of Asian-African trade do not replicate north-south linkages. As such, trade between Asia and Africa must be informed by new trade rules in which the fruits of value chain are equitably distributed, the dependency of debtor-creditor relationships is largely absent, the rules of origin encourage investments and technology transfers at the source, and the weaker partners are protected (Patel 2005).

Asia must not only continue to champion Africa's cause in areas like global governance, international trade, or climate change but must also recognize the competitive challenge they themselves pose to Africa. Asia must reexamine policies that inhibit the potential export of African products into Asian markets even though it may be a difficult balance to strike. Asia has been reaping benefits from its relationship with Africa, including greater market access, for years. It now has a responsibility to help Africa along the path of development it has itself trodden so well (Annan 2010). It is then that the immense benefits of Asia's rising interest in Africa will be evident for all to see.

REFERENCES

All New Nigeria. "Jonathan Reverses Obasanjo's Ban on Used Cars," November 30, 2010: http://www.allnewsnigeria.com/nigerianewsbusiness/2571-jonathan-reverses-obasanjos-ban-on-used-cars.html

Annan, Kofi. "Asia and Africa: Past Lessons, Future Ambitions," 2010: http://kofiannanfoundation.org/newsroom/speeches/2010/03/asia-and-africa-past-lessons-future-ambitions

Awoniyi, Femi. "Review Policy on Importation of Used Cars!" 2001: http://www.nigerdeltacongress.com/rarticles/review_policy_on_importation_of_.htm

Bate, Roger. "India's Fake Drugs Are a Real Problem." *Wall Street Journal,* May 19, 2010: http://online.wsj.com/article/SB10001424052748703315404575249901511960396 .html?mod=WSJ_latestheadlines

BBC News."China is fuelling war in Darfur," July 13, 2008: http://news.bbc.co.uk/2/hi/7503428.stm

Bhaumik, Anirban. "India, Africa to Check Fake Drug Menace," 2011: http://www.deccanherald.com/content/58228/india-africa-check-fake-drug.html

Broadman, Harry G. "Connecting Africa and Asia." *Finance and Development,* Quarterly Magazine of the IMF, Vol. 44, No. 22 (June 2007): http://www.imf.org/external/pubs/ft/fandd/2007/06/broadman.htm

Brookes, Peter, and Ji Hye Shin. "China's Influence in Africa: Implications for the United States": http://www.heritage.org/research/reports/2006/02/chinas-influence-in-africa-implications-for-the-united-states

China.org.cn. "Full Text of Wen's Speech at 4th Ministerial Conference of FOCAC": http://www.china.org.cn/world/2009–11/09/content_18849890.htm.

CNN. "Sudan Faces Threats of Sanctions," September 18, 2004: http://www.cnn.com/2004/WORLD/africa/09/18/sudan.unsanction

Comins, Lyse. "Dodgy Vehicle Imports End up on SA Roads," 2005: http://japanese-used-car.com/dodgy-vehicle-imports-end-up-on-sa-roads.htm

Department of Foreign Affairs, RSA. "The First New Asian African Strategic Partnership (NAASP) Senior Officials Meeting (SOM), the first step of the NAASP," 2006: http://www.dfa.gov.za/docs/2006/naasp0817.htm

East African Coast: Select Documents from the First to the Earlier Nineteenth Century: www.mirabilis.ca/archives/cat_history_archaeology.html Freeman-Grenville

Encyclopedia Britannica. "Bandung Conference," 2011: http://www.britannica.com/EBchecked/topic/51624/Bandung-Conference

EU Business. "Fake Drugs Trade on the Rise, Says EU," December 8, 2009: http://www.eubusiness.com/news-eu/pharma-health-drugs.1t3/

Europaafrica.net. "Competing Models of Peace-Keeping: The Role of the E.U. and China in Africa": http://europafrica.net/2010/06/25/new-publication-competing-models-of-peacekeeping-the-role-of-the-eu-and-china-in-africa/

FOCAC. "Commentator of the People's Daily," October 10, 2010: http://www.fmprc.gov.cn/zflt/eng/ltda/

Furphy, Claire. "Corruption in Africa: A Crime against Development," 2010: http://www.consultancyafrica.com/index.php?option=com_content&view=article&id=605:corruption-in-africa-a-crime-against-development&catid=87:african-finance-a-economy&Itemid=294

Hanson, Stephanie. "China, Africa, and Oil," 2008: http://www.alipac.us/ftopict-160799.html

Harman, Danna. "How China's Support of Sudan Shields a Regime Called 'Genocidal,'" 2008: http://www.csmonitor.com/2007/0626/p01s08-woaf.html

Herbst, Moira. "Oil for China, Guns for Darfur." *Bloomberg Newsweek*, 2008: http://www.businessweek.com/globalbiz/content/mar2008/gb20080314_430126.htm

Hitchens, Peter. "How China has Created a New Slave Empire in Africa": http://propagandistmag.com/2010/10/22/china-creates-slave-empire-africa

Jopson, Barney, and Jamil Anderlini. "China Pledges $10 Billion in Low-Cost Loans to Africa." *The Washington Post*, November, 9, 2009: http://www.washingtonpost.com/wp-dyn /content/article /2009/11/08 /AR2009110818002.html

Kochiyama, Yuri. "A History of Linkage." *Model Minority*, 1998: http://www.modelminority.com/joomla/index.php?option=comcontent&view=article&id=202:a-history-of-linkage-&catid=40:history&Itemid=56

McLaughlin, Abraham. "A Rising China Counters U.S. Clout in Africa." *Christian Science Monitor*, 2005: http://www.csmonitor.com/2005/0330/p01s01-woaf.html

Ministry of Foreign Affairs, Republic of Indonesia. "The New Asian-African Strategic Partnership (NAASP)," 2009: http://www.deplu.go.id/Pages/IFPDisplay.aspx?Name=RegionalCooperation&IDP=10&P=Regional&l=en

Mugabe, David. "Made in China–Do We Get Value for Money?" 2009: http://allafrica.com/stories/200906180329.html/

Muluken, Yewondwossen. "Ethiopia to Ban Outdated Second Hand Cars," 2010: http://horncarshippers.com/ethiopia-to-ban-outdated-second-hand-cars

Omoneyi, Patrick. "Made in China: Destination Africa," 2009: http://themarketmagazine.com/index2.php?option=com_content&do_pdf=1&id=695

Ori, Konye Obaji. "Nigeria: Manufacturers Frown at China's Dumping of Cheap Products," 2010: http://www.afrik-news.com/article17137.html

Patel, Chandrakant. "Bandung and Afro-Asian Cooperation: Rhetoric or Transformation in Relations?" 2005: http://www.seatini.org/bulletins/8.5.php#future

Payal, Jain. "India-Africa Relations," May 17, 2008: http://articles.maxabout.com/politics-government/india-africa-relations /article-7017

Pham, J. Peter, "Pandas in the Heart of Darkness: Chinese Peacekeepers in Africa," 2007a: http://worlddefensereview.com/pham102507.shtm

———. "Welcoming an Asian Elephant in Africa," 2007b: http://nationalinterest.org/commentary/conservative-columnist-welcoming-an-asian-elephant-in-africa-1746?page=1

Political Articles.net. "Asia's Development Miracle and Africa's Development Tragedy of the Late 20th Century: Key Lessons," January 26, 2009: http://www.politicalarticles.net/blog/2009/01/26/asias-development-miracle-and-africas-development-tragedy-of-the-late-20th-century-key-lessons/#

Sneyd, Adam. "Bandung Conference," 2005: http://www.globalautonomy.ca/global1/glossary_entry.jsp?id=EV.0026

Standards Organization of Nigeria. "Substandard Goods—China Keen to Regain Nigeria's Confidence," June 13, 2003: http://www.sononline.org/main/readNews.php?id=4

TICAD. "What is TICAD?": http://www.ticad.net/what_is_ticad.html

Transparency International. "Corruption Perceptions Index," Transparency International, 2010: http://www.transparency.org/policy_research/surveys_indices/cpi/2010/results

Tokyo International Conference on African Development, "About TICAD": http://www.ticad.net/about.shtml

United Nations. "The Millennium Development Goals Report, 2010": http://www.un.org/millenniumgoals/pdf/MDG%20Report%202010%20En%20r15%20-low%20res%2020100615%20-.pdf

Welcome Unit for History of Medicine. "Hybrids and Partnerships: Comparing the Histories of Indigenous Medicine in Southern Africa and South Asia," 2005: http://www.wuhmo.ox.ac.uk/events/Hybrids%20Conference /hybrids_info.htm

Zimbabwe Mail. "Zimbabwe Bans Import of Vehicles More than Five Years Old," September 27, 2010: http://www.thezimbabwemail.com/zimbabwe/6194.html

11 The Impact of the BRICS Countries on Africa's Socioeconomic Development in the Post-Cold War Era

*Alexius Amtaika**

The post-Cold War era has seen an evolution of new players in global politics—notably Brazil, Russia, India, China, and South Africa—which came to be known as the BRICS countries. Their influence is evident in the political economy, trade, investment, and decision-making spheres; in international bodies; and in the affairs of other countries beyond their continents. The term *BRICS*, coined by the firm Goldman Sachs in 2001, reflects the changes of the post-Cold War era that compelled developing countries to begin working together as an economic bloc and thus to counter the monopoly of the western European countries in the global economy. Although such collaborations can be traced back to 2001, the first formal summit of the BRICS countries took place only in 2009, in Russia, to rival the influence of the G8 countries.

During the Cold War, the BRICS countries (with the exception of Russia) were classified as developing countries, the influence of which was limited to their continents or regions. Their economic growth and expansion were eclipsed by the politics of the Cold War, which was sparked by differences in ideology between the United States, which advocated capitalism and a free-market economic system, and the Soviet Union, which advocated communism. Schools of thought, such as realism, justified the inevitability of such a conflict in global politics as empirical evidence of the logic of power politics based on superior military means. Because of their obsession with power politics, "realism" became the dominant philosophy among scholars, politicians, and diplomats during the Cold War (1945–1990). Its core assumption was that states, as guardians of the political community, use their internal and external powers not only to maximize their national interests but also to achieve their "ultimate goal of survival." Survival in the lexicon of the realists was a precondition for attaining all other goals. It was assumed that "all states have predatory aims and that if a state lies unguarded or unprotected it invites an attack by its neighbors" (Nicholson 1998: 91), just like a vulnerable animal. The realists regarded the notion of state sovereignty as sacrosanct, seeing it as the rallying point for the need for "national (state) security." Thus, for the realists, the notions of security and power were symbiotic in that power, national interest, and military security formed the central elements of the strategy of states to ensure their survival. Realists referred to this view as realpolitik, involving issues of "high politics." In the vocabulary of the realists, *high politics* traditionally referred to matters of defense, war, security, and foreign policy (see Dunne 1998: 115).

The end of the Cold War not only expanded global issues to include development and environmental matters but also heralded a new era in the history of capitalism. Rapid economic growth and development in developing countries began corroding the dominance of western European countries in the global capitalist economic system. Scholars of international relations, especially realists, failed to predict this, as they were preoccupied with the politics of the Cold War. The BRICS countries, on the other hand, made huge strides in economic growth and development and began reasserting their status and influence only after the end of the Cold War and the disintegration of the Soviet Union. They reinvigorated capitalism and ushered in the "new world order," in which states from developing countries emerged as major players. Such sudden global changes not only usurped the monopoly and dominance of the western European countries but also brought into the global economic system a new form of imperialism and competition for resources in poor countries. Such competition brought about twin problems: first, it threatened the survival of the western European countries, which depend on raw materials from developing countries; second, it raised fears of continued underdevelopment in the developing countries due to the competition of the imperialist West and of the BRICS countries. Thus, while the rise of the BRICS countries is celebrated as a glimmer of hope for developing countries, it also raises concerns about new forms of imperialism, in which rich and powerful "capitalist states control foreign territory by economic [and cultural] domination, while respecting the states' formal political independence" (Heywood 1997: 409).

The power and influence of the BRICS countries in the global capitalist system are evident in their shares of the global economy. The 2010 reports on global states' gross domestic product (GDP) released by three independent global financial institutions—the International Monetary Fund (IMF), the World Bank, and the CIA in its World Factbook—rank China as the second biggest economy in the world after the United States, with a GDP of US$5.9 trillion. The reports also rank Brazil at position seven, with GDP of US$2 trillion; India at position ten, with a GDP of US$1.6 trillion; Russia at position eleven, with a GDP of US$1.4 trillion; and South Africa, the smallest economy among the BRICS countries but Africa's biggest economy, at position twenty-eight, with a GDP of US$363,704 billion. China is not only ranked as the second largest economy in the world but its GDP is also larger that the GDPs of all the other BRICS countries combined. South Africa is by far the smallest economy among the BRICS countries; its GDP is sixteen times smaller than that of China, five times smaller than that of Brazil and India, and four times smaller than that of Russia. The graph below shows the BRICS countries' share of the global economy.

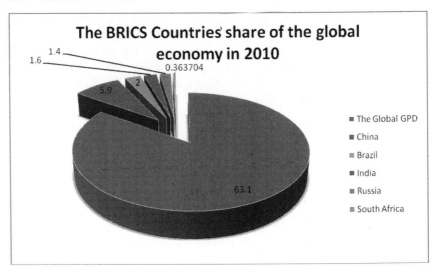

Figure 11.1 The BRICS countries' share of the global economy, 2010.

As can be seen, the GDPs of the BRICS countries constitute 17.6 percent (18 percent) of the total GDP of the global states, amounting to US$63.1 trillion. China's GDP alone constitutes 9.2 percent of the global GDP, Brazil's 3.2 percent, India's 2.5 percent, Russia's 2.2 percent, and South Africa's 0.6 percent. This suggests that China's influence in global affairs is greater than that of South Africa, owing to the size of its economy. Thus the bigger the economy, the greater the power the country wields in global affairs. With this in mind, this chapter focuses on relationships between the four BRICS countries minus South Africa on the one hand and the African countries including South Africa on the other. It positions African countries at the center of competition for resources between the BRICS countries on the one hand and the western European countries on the other and highlights disadvantages of the African countries in both situations.

The chapter also acknowledges the difficulty in using the term *African countries* as an entity and of presenting the analysis of their economic development from a general perspective. The African continent comprises fifty-four countries at different stages of economic growth and development. Generalizations regarding their economic outlooks and stages of development can be dangerous. However, if there is a danger of excessive generalization and the imposition of a false uniformity across space and time, there is an equal and opposite danger in the insistence that everything is unique. Scholars of African politics are particularly prone to feeling that the historical and economic characteristics of the African countries are so distinctive that generalization across the continent is far less valued than prolonged and detailed study of a single country. Many are inclined to argue that any analysis of the economic status of African countries requires a thorough knowledge of the relevant economic activities of the regions where these countries are located, and they insist that almost any attempt to generalize will be either misleading or premature. I have some sympathy for this view and readily recognize that the enterprise undertaken here would be entirely impossible if I could not draw upon the work of such specialists. However, there is nothing more likely to deter potential scholars of African politics and economics than the false claim that nothing can be achieved without an apprenticeship served in an in-depth study of a single country.

Although African countries share a previous past of colonial subjugation, they differ in their outlooks and in terms of their levels of economic of development, resources, needs, and disparities in wealth and poverty. Four categories of African states can be identified in this regard. First, there are African countries that rely on the export of minerals and surplus oil. Second, there are those whose economic growth exceeds their population growth rates. Third, there are those whose rates of economic growth equal those of their populations. Finally, there are those whose rates of economic growth are lower than those of their populations. Most importantly, the majority of African states rely on subsistence agriculture for their survival. These disparities make it difficult to generalize their situations in the global political economy even though they share a colonial past of subjugation. The term *Africa* must therefore be used cautiously, as the continent comprises fifty-four states divided into five regions, namely northern, western, central, eastern, and southern Africa. The only sane way of analyzing these states, then, is in terms of their ranking in GNP per capita. Such analysis is also not always adequate, since its usefulness lies only in distinguishing between states' wealth in terms of gross domestic product. Thus the distribution of their actual income and welfare level, which would ultimately portray severe social disparities within and among states, would remain hidden. In short, as a single category of states, African countries are inadequately depicted owing to their diversity—geographically, economically, socially, and politically. A comparison of African states as a single entity with any single state among the BRICS countries is inappropriate, since Africa is a continent whereas China, Brazil, India, and Russia are individual countries. If we are to get accurate results and pictures, we can only compare similar entities. That being the case, this chapter does not seek to make comparisons between the African states and the BRICS states but rather focuses on the role and the influence of the BRICS countries—in socioeconomic and political matters—on African states in contrast to the roles and influences of the European countries.

This calls for a critical look at the changes of the post-Cold War era and their impact on the African states and their relationships, not only with the BRICS countries but also with European countries, in order to see if such changes ushered in the new world order in the global economic system. The term *new world order* gained prominence in the aftermath of the Cold War in the 1990s, signifying the end of ideological conflicts between western and eastern European countries. The term is not only ambiguous as to what it means, especially in developing countries, but is also a relative term, as it elicits various emotions, such as optimism and pessimism, among scholars. In short, it means different things to different people, as discussed below.

THE VARIANTS OF THE NEW WORLD ORDER

In both academic and political circles, people talk of the new world order, which is roughly traced back to 1989, the fall of the Berlin Wall, and the collapse of the Soviet Union. Conceptually, the term fits in perfectly with the assumptions of the theory of liberalism, which advocates plurality or diversity or a multiplicity of actors in the international system, both politically and economically (see Heywood 1997: 410). Liberalism is a school of thought in international relations holding the view that world politics is shaped by states as well as by a broader range of interests and groups. It views state and nonstate actors—such as international organizations, nongovernmental organizations, multinational and transnational corporations, and religious movements, including militant Islamic movements—as actors in their own right and not just the tools of states (Nicholson 1998: 98–99). Pluralism, therefore, is a strand of liberalism, since it presupposes a specific view of power that is not necessarily concentrated in the hands of one actor but is diffused or shared among a plurality of competing groups. Thus the manner in which the term *new world order* is interpreted and used reflects the plurality of views that seek to explain how the world has been transformed from the old paradigm of realpolitik, characterized by conflict, to the new paradigm, characterized by issues of low politics such as economic development, trade, aid, and environmental matters.

Three competing interpretations of the term *new world order* are evident in the works of three renowned international scholars, namely Francis Fukuyama, Samuel Huntington, and Immanuel Wallerstein. Fukuyama belongs to a broader school of liberalism called neoliberal internationalism, advocating the democratic peace thesis, which holds that liberal states do not go to war with other liberal states. Neoliberal internationalism presupposes that liberal states tend to be wealthy and therefore have less to gain from engaging in conflicts than do poorer, nonliberal states. Thus, for neoliberal internationalism, peace is logical, since liberal states are "friendly" with other liberal states because they share the same system.

It was in this context that Francis Fukuyama popularized the term *new world order* in his controversial essay titled "The End of History?" (1989). In the face of the demise of the Soviet Union, he celebrated the triumph of liberalism over all other ideologies—notably fascism, Nazism, socialism, and communism—which had dominated the international political and economic landscape of the twentieth century. He viewed liberalism, in the form of democracy and capitalism, as a common heritage of humanity that should be embraced by all societies of the global community. Globalization helps to achieve this goal (Fukuyama, 1989: 9). He contended that liberal states were more stable internally and more peaceful in their international relations. This thesis also served to emphasize the superiority of American values, thereby providing legitimacy to those who sought to "export" liberalism (Dunne 1998: 155). Such values could be spread through various instruments of liberal values, including military options, forcible humanitarian intervention, and nonmilitary or political instruments such as the use of international institutions. A good example of the latter is the way in which conditionality, via institutions such as the International Monetary Fund (IMF) and the World Bank, have influenced the policies of developing countries. These countries have been forced not only to liberalize and privatize their economic sectors, but also to comply with the principles of good governance and human rights in exchange for economic benefits such as loans or investment. It becomes apparent that the process of exporting or globalizing liberalism can often be rather aggressive.

Fukuyama presented liberalism and capitalism as the domain of western European countries. However, he did not anticipate the rise of the new actors the in nonwestern world, notably the BRICS, to offset the competition with the western European countries and even overshadow western European countries in exporting capitalism to other parts of the globe. The BRICS countries in general and China in particular monopolize trade and investment in countries that were predominantly seen as the backyards of the western European countries. Consequently the optimism of a liberal world of capitalism and the free market system, which Fukuyama anticipated, has led to the dwindling and the diminishing of western European influence in the developing countries. Nonetheless, this development has opened up new doors and choices for trade in many developing countries, as rich countries, to keep their economies afloat, compete for partnerships and resources in poor countries.

Contrary to Fukuyama's celebratory view of the new world order, Samuel Huntington paints a gloomy picture of the post-Cold War era. He views it not in terms of economic development but rather of new political conflicts. Thus Huntington's views may fall into the context of the realist school of thought. He reasons that the end of the ideological war between the West and eastern European blocs ushered in a new era of conflict between cultures. Contrary to the idea of a universal global community, bound by shared values of democracy and liberal values, Huntington feels that individuals and societies are conscious and concerned about the survival of their own identities, cultures, beliefs, values, and traditions (Huntington 1993: 25). The consequence of this is the resistance that has taken the form of nationalism and fundamentalism—hence "the clash of civilizations." Unlike Fukuyama's view of the new world order, Huntington's essay—entitled "The Clash of Civilizations?"—gives us a pessimistic picture of the global community characterized by the rise of global terrorism perpetrated by Islamic fundamentalists and the rearrangement of global security architectures.

Immanuel Wallerstein shares such pessimism in his "world-systems theory," which analyzes disparities between the poor and the rich in the global economic system. Wallerstein belongs to a neo-Marxist school of thought that falls under the broader umbrella of structuralism. Other notable neo-Marxist scholars who belong to this school of thought include dependency theorists such as Andre Gunder Frank, Samir Amin, and Fernando Cardoso. The neo-Marxists are more interested in analyzing how elements of the international structure and the actions of different actors serve as mechanisms of domination and exploitation in the global economic system. They are interested in structures such as production or economic structures and the different places taken up by states, societies, and classes in those structures. They focus on the hierarchies of states in the international system and reason that the structure of the global economic system determines all else—therefore that politics is driven by the economy. In short, the structuralists or neo-Marxists view "economy as the key to understanding world politics and the contemporary international system" (Viotti and Kauppi 1987: 10). They view the unequal division of power—that is, the relative positions that groups of states and classes have in the structure—as determining who owns control over the means of production in the world economy. In other words, this division decides which nations are the "haves" and which nations are the "have nots" (Nel 1999: 67; Evans and Newnham 1998: 520).

It is in this context that the dependency relations between the developed or industrialized states of the north and the developing countries—or less developed countries (LDCs) of the south (Africa, Latin America, and parts of Asia)—are maintained. Hence their argument that poor states and their societies are underdeveloped not because they have failed to develop capitalist economic systems or are poorly integrated into the world capitalist system but because of too much capitalism (Viotti and Kauppi 1987: 10). In short, the structuralists reason that the structure of the global capitalist system keeps the developing countries dependent on the rich states of the north, and in so doing perpetuating unequal and exploitative relations that benefit particular classes, notably the capitalists.

It was in this context that Wallerstein's world-systems theory came to the fore, refuting the notion of the new world order and asserting the continuity of the old order, dominated by the exploitative capitalist system. Wallerstein's central argument is that the global capitalist system determines political and social relations between states and other international bodies and that economics is central to these relations (Cohn 2003: 132–133). No state exercises global control, and the lack of a central authority has facilitated the development of world capitalism. The behavior of states, markets, and other international actors is determined by the three broad economic arenas that make up the hierarchy of the world system, namely the core, the semiperiphery, and the periphery (Kegley and Wittkopf 1999: 215). The core has the power to exploit the periphery and dictates economic relations. Such a strictly structured system is not anarchic but hierarchical in nature, with a few key economic powers controlling global relations. Although the actors within the world capitalist economy change over time, the system itself remains hierarchical and exploitative. It can be transformed only by revolutionary (antisystemic) forces (Hoogvelt 1998).

In dismissing the notion of the new world order, Wallerstein contends that historically there had only been two types of world orders or systems, namely world empires (e.g., the Roman Empire) and world economies. The modern world system is an example of a world economy that can be traced back to the sixteenth century, when capitalism was institutionalized as a global economic system (Hobden and Wyn Jones 1998: 132). The modern world system has both spatial and temporal features. The spatial features constitute the geographical division of the world system into core, semiperipheral, and peripheral states. Each of these plays a different economic role and they are linked together in an exploitative relationship, in which the richer areas benefit at the expense of the poorer.

The temporal features—namely cycles, trends, contradictions, and crises—are the periods of expansion and contraction in the world economy and account for its continued existence since the sixteenth century. Cycles are the recurrent boom and bust periods of expansion and contraction. Trends are seen in the long-term growth or contraction of the world economy. Contradiction can be understood in terms of the crisis of underconsumption. According to Wallerstein, in the short term, capitalists aim to maximize profits by keeping the wages of the workers low. But since the workers also represent the potential consumers, the lower their wages are kept, the less purchasing power they have, so that the capitalists are unable to sell their goods and maintain profit margins. Crises are situations in which contradictions, trends, and cycles within the system combine in such a way that the system cannot continue to reproduce itself. This leads to the demise of a system and its replacement by another system. Wallerstein states that this has not yet happened, because the modern world system has remained remarkably stable since the sixteenth century. He contends that the boundaries of the world systems have extended to other parts of the world, but that the three-way spatial division between core, semiperiphery, and periphery has remained. Wallerstein's theory allows for the possibility that some countries in the semiperiphery can move up in the hierarchy, but only a few can do this since there is not enough room at the top for everyone.

The most crucial point in Wallerstein's theory is that, while world systems are exploitative and hierarchical in nature, the interstate system, in which states in different zones of the world economy play different roles, has provided stability. It is therefore no coincidence that the system of nation-states arose at the same time in world history as did the world capitalist system, suggesting that the state system and capitalism need each other and that states provide the framework for property rights and reduce the contradictions generated by capitalism through the establishment of a social welfare system.

Judging global affairs from Wallerstein's perspective, one can contend that the collapse of the Soviet Union and the end of the Cold War did not change the economic structures of the global economic system. Rather, the system expanded to include new global players who mastered the art of imperialism. The world systems remain the same: exploitative, unequal, and favoring industrialized countries at the expense of poor countries. This suggests that the rise of the BRICS countries did not bring any changes to the structures of the global economic system but rather added up the number of new actors in world systems. It also suggests that actors may come and go but the system remains the same. In other words, Wallerstein's theory assumes that the system is self-contained and that there is a basic continuity in world politics. Continuity exists in that there have been groups that controlled the means of production and benefited as a result. There have also been groups that have had little or no control and that have suffered as a consequence. Continuity therefore exists in a world where privilege and exploitation coexist.

The perspectives of the new world order presented above—namely the evolving one of Fukuyama, the chaotic one of Huntington, and the hierarchical and exploitative one of Wallerstein—reflect debates on the plight of states in the post-Cold War era among liberals (liberalism), conservatives (realists), and neo-Marxists (structuralists), respectively. The question then is: What is the impact of this system on African states?

THE IMPACT OF THE NEW WORLD ORDER ON AFRICAN STATES

Africa's entry into global economic system and the so-called new world order did not begin with the fall of the Berlin wall in 1989 but rather with the Berlin Conference of European States in 1884. This conference was crucial in the creation of the African states as it also marked the beginning of the post—Cold War era. Since the Berlin Conference of 1884, African states have experienced several world orders that determined their status and position in the international global political and economic system as peripheral states. The first of such world orders began with what came to be called the "Scramble for Africa" or the "partition of Africa," in which the European states divided the continent among themselves as their colonies in search of resources and raw materials for their economic growth and development. This resulted in the establishment of the African states, modeled on the European concept of statehood (Mazrui and Tidy 1986: 373–374). When African countries gained independence in the 1960s, they did not abolish the colonial states but maintained the borders and adopted the concepts of self-determination and sovereignty from Europeans. The

European concept of sovereignty was adopted to distinguish between the colonial and postcolonial states. Thus independence was more psychological, since ties and dependence of the former colonies on the former colonial countries continued unabated. Twin factors were responsible for such dependence: the first was that the former colonial powers could not maintain their economies without "association" with their former colonial territories. The second was that the former colonies could not survive in the world system without the financial support of the former colonial powers. Consequently African countries were not allowed to have democratic economic choices. Their fate was shaped and decided upon by European countries. In short, European countries decided what kind of economy Africans were to build so as to continue their role as suppliers of raw materials for Europe's economic development and growth.

It was during this period that African states were condemned to the category of peripheral states whose roles in the international economic system, according to Wallerstein, was providing raw materials to the core and semi-peripheral states of the western and eastern European countries. This led dependency theorists, an offshoot of the neo-Marxists, such as Andre Gunder Frank, Fernando Cardoso, and Samir Amin, to claim that countries in the developing world were not poor because they were inherently backward or undeveloped. Rather, it was because they were deliberately underdeveloped by the rich countries of the developed world (Kegley and Wittkopf 1995: 38). Thus formal independence increased the number of states in the global political system and integrated the African territories more fully into the global economy. Nevertheless, they remained vulnerable. Their domestic economic structures remained unchanged and fragile. Solutions to the problems posed by their national economies were not necessarily locked in domestic policies but depended on international factors and foreign assistance. This had several implications and problems. First, it entailed a continuation of dependence of postindependence states on former colonial powers for models of governance, economic policies, and aid. Second, postcolonial states inherited the capitalist economic systems but without the capitalists. Finally, it entailed integration of these countries into the global economic systems, governed and regulated by the Bretton Woods systems, namely, the World Bank, the IMF, and the World Trade Organization (WTO).

These factors were compounded by the fact that many of the world's poorest countries rely very heavily on the export of a single raw material or agricultural product while they also import a whole range of consumer and luxury goods. The problem is that the terms of trade of these countries gradually worsen, since the price of raw materials and some agricultural goods tends to decline over time while the price of manufactured goods rises. Consequently poor countries are forced to borrow more and more to stay alive, perpetuating and increasing the inequality in the world economy.

Another way in which the inequality is maintained or even exacerbated is through the international flows of investment capital. One would imagine that the poorer countries would benefit from a relatively free flow of investment capital, especially since labor and infrastructural costs are generally lower in developing countries, with their so-called emerging markets. However, since most of the capital that comes into these emerging markets is short-term (invested in stocks and bonds), it leads to a very unstable and volatile situation. Capital can leave the country just as quickly as it enters it. Examples where this happened include Mexico (1994), South Africa (1996), Thailand, Malaysia, South Korea, and Indonesia (1997–1998) (Nel 1999: 64). This begs the question of what the purpose or meaning of independence may have been. What are the meanings and implications of the terms *independence* and *sovereignty* to Africans? Naturally dependence corrodes sovereignty and independence. Can a state claim to be sovereign while depending on aid from other countries for its economic development and survival? This continuing dependency has given birth to a new era of aid regimes, marking the birth of the second new world order in the evolution of African states.

Mazrui and Tidy (1986: 336) explain that the dependence of African countries on western European states led to the setting up of aid regimes by former colonial powers and other European states under the terms of the 1952 Strasbourg Plan. It urged wealthier countries to set up an aid framework and begin trading with their former colonies. It was followed by the signing of the Lomé Convention of 1975 between Europe and developing countries of Africa, the Caribbean, and the Pacific (ACP), allowing the ACP countries to export 99 percent of their manufactured goods and 95 percent of their processed agricultural products to European markets without restrictions of any kind, with no quota or tariff barriers (Mazrui and Tidy 1986: 339).[1]

In accordance with its original intention, aid was supposed to be temporary, in that once the African countries developed the capacity for self-sustaining growth, aid would no longer be required. However, far from achieving such economic growth, most African countries still rely on aid for survival. They have made very little progress in economic and technological development. Four factors account for this. First, the availability of aid from the developed countries created a dependency syndrome that discourages African people and countries from discovering their own resources to combat poverty and the problems associated with underdevelopment. Second, systems that are based on the interests of donors, such as structural adjustment programs and political conditionality, instead of the needs of the recipients, make development assistance inefficient. Third, aid as an instrument of imperialism appears to have established as a priority the importance of influencing domestic policy in the recipient countries. Fourth, foreign aid is wasted on overpriced goods and services from donor countries and by corruption in recipient countries. As a result of this, too little aid reaches the poor.

From the above account, two issues stand out in the relationship between African states and countries in the developed world. These are trade and aid.

In the 1960s, for instance, the United Nations Charter urged rich countries to contribute 1 percent of their annual GNP to poor countries as part of their moral obligation towars the poor.[2] A decade later, in 1970, rich nations agreed in the UN General Assembly to spend 0.7 percent of their GNP on Official Development Assistance (ODA) (Mansbach 1994: 349–350). Three decades later, in 2000, the nations of the European Union pledged to spend 0.56 percent of their gross national income (GNI) on poverty reduction by 2010 and 0.7 percent by 2015 (Cropley 2010). In spite of setting up of these targets and agendas, rich countries have failed consistently to reach their agreed obligation of 0.7 percent. In 2005, for instance, rich countries promised to double aid by up to US$50 billion in 5 years at the G8 summit in Gleneagles, Scotland (Cropley 2010). They pledged to give African states aid totaling US$25 billion, of which only about US$13 billion was honored (Cropley 2010). At the same summit, rich countries made other pledges, such as (1) giving more support to Africa's peacekeeping forces, (2) increasing investment in education, and (3) helping African countries to combat HIV/AIDS, malaria, and tuberculosis (Cropley 2010). Rich countries also pledged to end their protectionist trade practices and cancel Africa's debt of US$40 billion (Cropley 2010). However, rich countries failed to honor their pledges, mainly because of economic downturn and budget crunches in western European countries. This resulted in economic crises in countries such as Greece, Ireland, and other Eurozone countries. It was compounded by the decrease of economic growth in the Eurozone. These problems have led to cuts in aid donations to poor countries and to changes in the policies of European countries in terms of now giving loans instead of grants to poor countries. These developments have exacerbated the debt crises, not only in African countries but also in other poor countries.

The fact that the majority of African states still depend on aid from rich countries makes any debate about the new world order hit a wall, because aid still remains their lifeline for survival—two decades after the end of the Cold War. The 2009 World Bank report on aid to African countries shed light on the significance of aid to African economies. It points out that in the 2008 overall aid to sub-Saharan Africa was US$38 billion, or 5 percent of output. This ratio jumps to 7.5 percent when South Africa, Africa's biggest economy and a member of the BRICS countries, is excluded (Cropley 2010). The most worrying factor is that, while the need for aid increases, the amount of debt owed by African states also increases. A study conducted by the IMF in 2010 shows that the total public debt for low-income countries rose from 30 percent of GDP in 2008 to 35 percent in 2010 (Cropley 2010). Thus, while the rich countries are willing to give aid to poor countries in the form of loans, they are unwilling, and find it harder, to cancel debts.

Coupled with debt crises is the decline in trade between poor and rich countries. This is mainly due to the expiry of the Lomé Convention in February 2002. As pointed out earlier, the Lomé Convention was signed in 1975. Negotiations for a new trade deal have been ongoing since 2002 and no agreement has been reached, in spite of completing the drafting of the new agreement in 2004. The negotiations for the new deal were launched earlier, before the expiry of the Lomé Convention in 2002, at the Doha Round in the Qatari capital in 2001. The launch was attended by 149 WTO nations with the aim of boosting global economy and helping poor nations to export more (*Mail and Guardian* 2007a). The Doha Round had four objectives:

1. Freeing up trade in goods from food to clothing and cars
2. Freeing services like banking and telecoms
3. Reducing subsidies, customs duties and other trade barriers
4. Using commerce to give developing countries access to rich countries' markets while helping developing countries export their way out of poverty

In spite of these objectives, no agreement was reached, as rich and poor countries as well as exporters and importers squabbled over the need to create new business opportunities while protecting sensitive industries and farm sectors. This, in effect, led to the collapse of the Doha "Development" Trade Round in 2006. Three issues were responsible for the collapse of the Doha Round. They included (1) domestic farm subsidies provided by the United States, (2) import tariffs on agricultural goods levied by the European Union; and (3) market access in developing countries for industrial goods and services (*Mail and Guardian* 2006).

Reports show that the United States nailed the Doha Round into its coffin owing to U.S. insistence that developing countries should open up their markets, just as the United States was being asked to do (Prowse 2009). The United States was infuriated after the poor countries and other developing countries made three demands. First, they demanded that the farm subsidies in European countries be limited and fall by 80 percent while the ceiling on U.S. farm subsidies should drop by 70 percent, to US$14.5 billion. This was not unreasonable, since it was still above the current outlays of about US$7 billion but well below the current ceiling of US$48.2 billion (Lynn 2008). Second, they demanded that the industrial tariffs in developed countries should be capped at 8 percent, while in developing countries their ceiling should be at an average between 11 percent and 12 percent, with a maximum of 25 percent, subject to tariff cuts. Third, they demanded exemption from the "anticoncentration clause," asking that they should be allowed to use waivers to shield entire industrial sectors from lower duties—a key U.S. and EU concern (Lynn 2008).

While the argument of the United States, that rich countries open up their markets and poor countries do the same in return, seems like a fair deal, it negates history, in that the rich countries and the poor countries have never been equal in terms of origin, power, social, and economic needs. Poor countries have always been subjugated by rich countries as former colonies and as peripheral states—hence the root causes of the underdevelopment of poor countries. More importantly, the fact that poor countries lack the capacity and ability to process their raw materials means that global trade will be skewed in favor of rich countries. Opening up poor countries' markets would perpetuate unequal global trade in the guise of equality.

Consequently the procrastination of the negotiations at the WTO has led to losses of international markets by many African counties. In 2005, for instance, several African states—namely Lesotho, South Africa, Swaziland, Nigeria, Ghana, Mauritius, Zambia, Madagascar, Tanzania, Malawi, Namibia, and Kenya, to mention but twelve—lost their international markets for textiles after the expiration of a quota system in industrial nations that had provided a ready market for textiles and apparel from poor African and other developing countries. This, in turn, led to losses of thousands of jobs in these countries, leading to problems of unemployment, which affected millions of individuals and their family members (Mutumi 2006). This was a reversal of the 1974 arrangement between poor and rich countries, when the United States, Canada, and the European Union (the world's biggest markets) set up the Multi-Fibre Arrangement, designed to protect producers in these countries from the more efficient ones emerging in Asia at the time (Mutumi 2006). The arrangement set a limit to the volume of textiles other countries could export to the largest markets. This limit mainly affected the world's major producers, such as China, India, Hong Kong, Taiwan, and South Korea (Mutumi 2006). These restrictions yielded advantages to many smaller textile-exporting countries, which now stepped in to fill the gap. The end of the quota system therefore meant that the WTO rules opened up the market in a sector that had previously, for three decades, been protected and reserved for African textile producers.

SUBJUGATION, POLITICAL CONDITIONALITY, AND STRUCTURAL ADJUSTMENT PROGRAMS

As dependent countries, African countries are subjected to a number of conditions in order to receive aid from the rich countries. Such subjugation fits in perfectly with the Marxist-Leninist theory of imperialism, war, social conflict, and revolution. It assumes that (1) all history is the history of class struggle between a ruling group and an opposing group; (2) capitalism uses war to further its own ends (profit) and gives rise to competing classes, the bourgeoisie and proletariat; and (3) the bourgeoisie is in control because this class controls the capitalist mode of production. *The mode of production* refers to the fact that the means of production are privately owned, labor power is hired as a commodity, and goods and services are produced for sale in a market that has profit as its sole objective (Nel 1999: 63). In the main, Marxism focuses on the contradictions in the capitalist system, namely a structure that emphasizes individual interest at the expense of social equity and the well-being of the community. In short, Marxist-Leninist theory entails the idea that wherever unequal relationships exist, subjugation and exploitation become the order of the day. This applies to the politics of aid between the rich countries of Europe and poor countries in Africa.

The decline in aid and trade between Africa and Europe was accompanied by the imposition of the Political Conditionality and the Structural Adjustment Program by Europe on Africa. Between 1980 and 2000, developed countries made developmental aid accessible, either through IMF grants or direct foreign aid. However, access to funding was restricted to those that fulfilled certain requirements or adopted specific programs and was denied to those that did not. Restrictions came either in the form of structural adjustment programs (SAPs) or political conditionality. Political conditionality and the SAPs served a general purpose. Both were concerned with ensuring that the benefits brought about through international development aid were reaped to the maximum. Political conditionality sought to establish good governance with regard to human rights, corruption, democratization, and other political issues (Baylies 1995: 244). SAPs sought to establish good governance in a different sense; they sought the establishment of sound economic methods and sound financial (both monetary and fiscal) policy (Baylies 1995: 244). The primary distinction between the two was that SAPs were concerned with economic issues only, while political conditionality made political issues a concern. SAPs and political conditionality were first tied to development aid in the early 1990s. Prior to this, aid had been directed at supporting anticommunist movements in the developing world.

The consequences of SAPs have been very different from consequences of political conditionality. SAPs have mostly been criticized as being one-sided economic policies that focused on the market rather than on long-term development. They have been criticized for failing to encourage investment and human capital development, both of which are seen to be essential to long-term growth prospects. One of the key problems with SAPs has been their forcing of developing world budgets away from education and infrastructural development. In reducing the state's role in economics and the market, they have forced the state away from education and the provision of public goods. Both of these consequences have been problematic. A lack of education provision meant that the development of human capital was stunted, while privatization had often been unsuccessful owing to a lack of technically competent capitalists in these states. While neoliberal approaches to development succeeded in the economies of the East-Asian "tigers," the SAPs have not been so successful in Africa. This is mostly due to the state in which African countries were left after decolonization. They were not left with the infrastructure, capital, or human resources needed to implement neoliberal growth plans effectively.

The rise of the BRICS countries as new actors in the global economic system has presented African countries with new alternatives for aid. Encouraged by aid from China and India, African countries have begun challenging and openly rejecting the exploitative tendencies of the European countries. This was particularly evident at the EU-Africa Third Summit in December 2010, when the former Libyan leader Moammar Gadhaffi demanded a better economic deal with the European Union. He pointed out Africa's readiness to do business elsewhere, apparently in reference to BRICS countries. He lamented Africa's failed economic partnership with Europe, in which European emphasis was on governance and human rights, whereas Africa's emphasis was on economics, not politics. Such divergent interests resulted in exploitation and not on symbiotic relations based on mutual interest (Rosemberg 2010). Gadhaffi's statement reopened old wounds between former colonial powers and African nations that date back to the colonial period and continued throughout half a century of Africa's independence. The failures of the summit to seal a "new equal" partnership, as well the failure of the WTO to reach agreement with developing countries, resonates well with the assumption of the neo-Marxists of domination/advantage versus exploitation/disadvantage, which perpetuate dependency relations between the developed or industrialized states of the north and the developing countries of the south (see Viotti and Kauppi 1987: 10).

In response to Gadhaffi's demand, the EU president, Hermann van Rompuy, pointed out that "In Europe's experience, the perspectives for economic growth are closely linked to elements of good governance. Africa is not an exception. Business-friendly policies attract private investment, where corruption is not tolerated, where the rule of law is respected, and transparency valued" (Rosemburg 2010). Van Rompuy's assertion was the continuation of the European attitude toward African states, which dates back to colonial rule, that European systems of governance are ideal models for Africa's systems of governance and African countries have an obligation to follow what the European countries demand of them. To show Europe's supremacy over African states, Jose- Manuel Barroso, president of the European Commission, reminded delegates to the summit that Europe remains the globe's top provider of "aid for trade" and delivered more than €10 billion in 2008. He stated that Europe went to Tripoli with the fascinating long-term perspective of a Euro-African economic area in mind, which would provide opportunities for 2.5 billion citizens by 2050 (Rosemburg 2010).

This was the third time that Africa stood up against European subjugation and said no to imperialism. The first instance took place in 2003, when the First EU-African summit was cancelled owing to Europe's barring of Robert Mugabe, Zimbabwe's president, from attending the summit because of his poor human rights record. In response, African countries refused to attend the summit without Robert Mugabe (*Mail and Guardian* 2007b). The second instance took place in December 2007, at the Second EU-Africa

Summit, in Lisbon, Portugal, when European countries attempted to force African countries to sign a new trade agreement by December 31, 2007, in accordance with the Cotonou Convention of 2000, which wound up the 1975 Lomé accords. To the surprise of the European countries, African countries rejected the straitjacket of the economic partnership agreements. Led by Abdoulaye Wade, president of Senegal, African states denounced the strong-arm tactic of the European Union and refused to sign any deal with it at that summit. They also rejected a complete liberalization of trade in rebellious pride and branded it as a colonial pact (*Mail and Guardian* 2007b). Africans across the continent disapproved of the economic partnership agreement between Europe and Africa. Social movements as well as trade union organizations south of the Sahara mobilized against them. The revolt bore fruit and led to the failure of the summit to reach any agreement, forcing the president of the European Commission, José Manuel Barroso, to back down and accept African countries' call for further discussions (*Mail and Guardian* 2007b). In 2007, African leaders, as in 2003,[3] insisted that Mugabe attend the summit unconditionally and the European Union acceded to this demand (*Mail and Guardian* 2007b).

Such an opposing and rebellious attitude would have not been possible in the 1970s and 1980s, when African countries sorely depended on European countries for aid and trade. The alternative opportunities for foreign direct investments from the BRICS countries have somehow loosened the dependency of African countries on European countries and in so doing empowered African countries to say no to unfair deals. More importantly, the decline in European investment in Africa and the massive increase in Chinese investment, coupled by soft loans it gives to African countries and its principle of noninterference in the internal affairs of African states, makes China a good partner of African countries for economic development. Analysts predict that China will overtake the European Union as one of the continent's principal suppliers and could beat the United States in becoming its most important client by 2015 (*Mail and Guardian* 2007b). This drastically changes the way aid and trade is now regulated and suggests that the time has passed when Europe could impose disastrous SAPs on African states. The rise of the BRICS countries as major global players has not only raised hope for Africa's development but also resuscitated old friendships between African states and the BRICS countries.

FORGING A NEW PARTNERSHIP WITH OLD FRIENDS

The relationship between the African states and the BRICS countries is not only economic but also sociopolitical. Politically, the relationship between African states and individual BRICS countries dates back to the preindependence era and revolved around fighting colonialism and imperialism of the western European countries. The early relationship between Africans and Russians, for instance, evolved in response to the western world's domination of Africans as colonized people. In spite of western European countries' early contacts with Africans in the fourteenth century, it was the Russians who had a better understanding of the plight of Africans as oppressed people dominated by western imperialism. Russia had more sympathy with African nationalism than most European countries had. Russia offered support to African countries in the struggle for freedom and independence. It was in this context that African nationalism got its inspiration from the domestic socialist policies of the Soviet Union and from the ideas of Vladimir Lenin's theory of imperialism. Mazrui and Tidy (1986) contend that Lenin's theory of imperialism inspired many African nationalists not only to speak against colonialism and imperialism but also to revolt against domination by colonial powers. Lenin viewed imperialism as the highest stage of capitalism and reasoned that the first revolution against western capitalism was a revolution against its highest stage. Domestic socialism was, for him, the appropriate economic policy suitably positioned to counter imperialism, which was the cornerstone of international capitalism. Lenin's views resonated well with the aspirations of many Africans, who detested western imperial domination and demanded independence.

The beginning of the Cold War in the aftermath of the Second World War saw the intensification of the relationship between the Soviet Union and African states. The Soviet Union presented itself as a country that had the interests of poor countries at heart. During the 1950s and early 1960s, the Soviet Union, under the leadership of Nikita Khrushchev, actively supported Africa's revolution and instructed Soviet scholars to defend African nationalism and support revolution against imperialism on the continent. One Russian scholar, I. I. Potekhin, perfectly contextualized and linked the idea of Pan-Africanism with the Russian philosophy of socialism and imperialism when he stated that:

> Pan-Africanism as an ideology contains much of what is alien to our (Soviet) ideology. However, Pan-Africanism aims at uniting all the peoples of Africa for the struggle against colonialism and imperialism, and for their national liberation. In addition, from this point of view Pan-Africanism deserves the support of all people of goodwill who are striving for the ideals of progress and democracy (Mazrui and Tidy 1986: 367).

The Soviet Union supported African states when many western countries, including the United States, were reluctant to extend moral support to freedom fighters towing to the socioeconomic and political relations they had with minority regimes in Africa. In 1973, for instance, after many global countries recognized Guinea Bissau's independence from Portugal, the United States vetoed its application for United Nations membership (Mazrui and Tidy 1986: 367). The continued support for Portugal by western countries was based on its membership of the North Atlantic Treaty Organization (NATO), despite the fact that Portugal was under the fascist rule of Salazar and Caitano and was reluctant to liberate its colonies in Africa, notably Angola, Guinea-Bissau, and Mozambique.

Russia's contribution to the independence of Africa can be summarized in three ways. First, Lenin's philosophy of domestic socialism and his theory of anti-imperialism provided a theoretical attack on economic imperialism (Marxism or socialism) in the struggle for the liberation of the continent. It extended considerable financial and material support to the movements engaged in liberation struggles in Africa. Second, the Soviet Union's socialist policies provided practical examples of raising an economically backward country to an industrial one through widespread literacy programs and the massive introduction of social welfare policies. The Soviet Union not only condemned imperialism and colonization in Africa but also provided solutions and alternatives through its socialist policies. Third and most importantly, the Soviet Union was one of the world superpowers and had a permanent seat and veto powers in the Security Council of the United Nations. This gave the Soviet Union moral authority and a platform to speak against colonialism and defend the plight of poor countries in Africa. Comparatively though, the United States spent more money on Africa than the Soviet Union, especially in alleviating poverty and underdevelopment.

Likewise, India's links with Africa date back to the period of the British colonial rulers, when India and some African countries became part of the British Empire. During that period, thousands of Indians were taken from India to Africa as indentured laborers. Many stayed on and today the population of people of Indian ethnic origin living in Africa has surpassed 2 million. As with Russia, India's contribution to Africa's independence and freedom was enormous; the major contribution came from the philosophy of passive resistance of Mahatma Gandhi. Gandhi not only helped in shaping the strategy of anticolonialism in Africa but had himself lived in Africa (South Africa) and experienced racism, segregation, imperialism, and colonialism. His experiences in Africa and India helped him to design and shape his ideas on the principles of absolute nonviolence or passive resistance, which included legitimate political agitation, newspaper and education campaigns, the constitutional application of strikes, and boycotts (Mazrui and Tidy 1986). Gandhi first tried some of his tactics in South Africa, but he could not soften the stance of the segregationist regime in South Africa.

Such limitations forced African leaders to forge links with China, with the objective of borrowing revolutionary tactics from the Chinese leader Mao Tse-Tung. Mao is famous for his views legitimizing the use of force as a means of attaining freedom and independence. His influence is evident in his philosophy of war, which presupposes that "progress is born in chaos" and "originality comes from destruction." *Destruction* is the key word here. He contended that the success of the Chinese Cultural Revolution depended on the destruction of China's old system of production, old ideology, and old customs. In his essay titled *"The Guerilla Warfare,"* Mao formulated three classic phases of his model of guerilla warfare, which freedom fighters—mainly from the southern African countries of Mozambique, Zimbabwe, and South Africa—adopted during the liberation struggle. Mao states that in phase one, the guerrillas must earn the support of the population by distributing propaganda and attacking the organs of government, so that ordinary citizens will provide cover to the guerillas and support them. In phase two, the guerillas must launch escalating attacks on government's military forces and vital institutions so as to paralyze government's ability to wage a full-scale war. In phase three, he gives guerillas options of using conventional warfare and fighting to seize cities or to overthrow the government and then assume control of the country (Mao 1961). His theory provides options of shifting between phases in either directions, depending on the circumstances, and that the phases might not be uniform and evenly placed throughout the countryside (Mao 1961).

The Liberation Front of Mozambique (FRELIMO) perfectly executed Mao's plan for guerilla warfare, defeating the Portuguese colonial government and becoming the only revolutionary movement in Africa to successfully seize power from a colonial government by military means, without any negotiated settlement or elections. Mao's guerilla tactics included intelligence, ambush, deception, strikes, terror, sabotage, and espionage. Such tactics have undermined white minority regimes in South Africa, Zimbabwe, and Mozambique through long, low-intensity confrontations with governments, which increased the cost of maintaining these governments and made governance impossible. China, like Russia, provided military support and trained cadres during the wars of liberation in the southern African region. China, like Russia, was and is a permanent member of the Security Council of the United Nations, had and has veto powers, and used the Security Council as a platform in defense of colonized countries. However, China, unlike Russia, focused on the economic development of African countries. In solidarity with Africa, China built railways and football stadiums and organized projects that were frowned upon by the World Bank.

Although Brazil did not play a major role in the political liberation of Africa, its links with Africa date back to the period of the slave trade. Many slaves from Africa were taken to Brazil by Europeans, making Brazil the country with the second-largest black African population in the world, after Nigeria; 44 percent of Brazil's 200 million people are classified as black (38.4 percent mixed race, or black and white; and 6.8 percent black). Nigeria has a population of about 158 million people.

The above account suggests that links between African countries and the BRICS countries are not new; they are historical. The rise of the BRICS countries as major global players in the aftermath of the Cold War therefore resuscitated and reinvigorated old friendships and cooperation in the global political and economic systems. Levels of engagement between the

BRICS countries and African countries vary from country to country. Russia is probably the smallest trading partner of African states among the BRICS countries. During the independence period there were many exchanges between Russia and African states. Such connections collapsed into low levels of economic engagement during the 1970s and 1980s, the arms trade being an exception. One of the major barriers that impacted on this co-operation and relationship negatively was language. Many Africans speak western European languages, such as English, French, and Portuguese. These languages indirectly link African countries to the economies of western European countries. This suggests that language and economics are interlinked, since business cannot be done without a medium of communication, and communication cannot take place in the absence of language. This explains why African countries have maintained their close relationships with former colonies, in spite of a bitter past of oppression and imperialism.

Some nations, such as the French and the British, have encouraged Africans to study their languages, with awards, trips to their countries, and the establishment of schools that use their models of education. Such ties have cemented the relationships between the former colonial powers and their former colonies. These continue even today, although disagreements and dissatisfaction on political and economic matters often arise. Only Brazil and India have language advantages over Russia and China in their relationships with African states. Brazil has a language connection with Mozambique, Guinea Bissau, Cape Verde, and Angola, while India has colonial and Commonwealth connections as well as the English language connection with all Anglophone African countries. Although China does not have any language connection with Africa, Chinese leaders have been successful in establishing bilateral agreements with African nations through active engagement and offering good deals to African governments.

Against the backdrop of growing trade ties between African states and China-India-Brazil, low levels of contact between Russia and African countries have led to calls being made by African governments to the Russian government to review its policies toward Africa. Trade between Russia and Africa amounted to only US$6 billion in 2009 (Klomegah 2008). This is a small figure compared with billions in trade between African countries and China or India. Low levels of trade with Russia are mainly blamed on the lack of knowledge and expertise among African economies in entering into the challenging Russian markets. Apart from its sheer size and language problems, Russia presents a serious challenge to many African countries in terms of the bureaucratic hurdles that make doing business with that country difficult, as African countries lack the resources to help their companies do business with Russia. Consequently African countries prefer to stick to their regional or traditional markets—such as the European Union, Canada, Japan, and the United States—where they receive trade benefits. A good example of such benefits is the Africa Growth and Opportunity Act

(AGOA), which was set up by the United States with the aim of increasing trade between the United States and African states by approximately 240 percent between 2000 and 2010 (Klomegah 2008).

India and China have been fostering trade ties with African countries by hosting international trade forums for corporate business leaders and entrepreneurs. Yet Russia has never hosted a forum of this nature in spite of the high average annual growth in gross domestic product of 5 percent among African states. Trade forums have been credited with creating measures leading to the simplification of import-export procedures, such as customs, warehousing, and transportation between these partners (Klomegah 2008). Chinese and Indian leaders have made numerous trips to Africa in their quest to boost trade. Russian leaders have made only two visits to Africa—one in 2009, when Russian President Dmitry Medvedev visited four African countries—namely Egypt, Nigeria, Namibia, and Angola (Smolchenko 2009). In 2006, former Russian President Vladimir Putin visited Africa. These visits reflect positive developments in revitalizing the Russian-African relationship and reasserting Moscow's clout in a former Soviet sphere of influence.

Ties between Africa and Brazil have traditionally been insignificant, as Brazil preferred to engage with fellow Portuguese-speaking African countries, mainly Angola and Mozambique. As a former colony of Portugal, Brazil became the first "western" country to recognize the Movimento Popular de Libertação de Angola (MPLA) government in Angola when Angola gained its independence in 1975 (White 2010). In recent years, Brazil has expanded its influence in Africa as it seeks to embrace its new role as a global player. It has started using its cultural connections to boost its trade relationships with African states. One example of this was the announcement of establishment of direct flights from Fortaleza in Brazil to Dakar in Senegal (White 2010). In spite of its historical ties with Lusophone (Portuguese-speaking) countries, South Africa has now become Brazil's major partner in Africa, mainly owing to South Africa's strategic importance on the continent. Trade between Brazil and South Africa increased to nearly US$1.7 billion in 2009. In 2010, the two countries signed trade agreements that included annual political consultations (White 2010). In 1994, Brazil's former President Fernando Henrique Cardoso became the first Brazilian head of state to visit South Africa, and the two countries began collaborating on the issue of HIV drug patents. The relations intensified after Luis Lula da Silva took office in 2003, which resulted in the establishment IBSA, a trilateral alliance of India, Brazil, and South Africa, in which governments and civil society exchange expertise in areas in which they face similar challenges, such as the fight against HIV/AIDS, cash-transfer programs, combating poverty, and fostering social mobility.

Of the four major BRICS countries, only China and India have made huge strides in boosting trade with Africa, particularly in the areas of mining, telecommunications, agriculture, oil, and the exporting of commodities

(O'Neill 2006). Cooperation in these areas has boosted aid and led to heavy investment in Africa. In 1991, trade between Africa and India, for instance, amounted to only US$967 million. By 2008, trade between India and Africa was estimated at US$35 billion. This figure is low compared with China's trade with Africa, which stood at US$100 billion during the same period (Majumdar 2009). Evidence shows that, a decade ago, China trailed India in trade with Africa. However, China's investments have since risen considerably on the back of major energy, construction, and mineral extraction projects.

The deepening of trade between India and Africa is evident in the three summits that these two parties have held between 2005 and 2010, when Indian and African leaders as well as the business fraternity were able to meet. The first conclave took place in 2005, in which the two parties discussed India's plans to invest US$5 billion in Africa in joint projects (Majumdar 2009). The Indian government also donated US$1 billion to connect all fifty-four African countries through a satellite and fiberoptic network and thus to promote "virtual" medical and educational programs (Majumdar 2009). The 2005 conclave was followed by another in 2006, when about 300 business delegates from thirty-five African countries descended on New Delhi to explore new economic partnerships (Majumdar 2009). During the 3 days of the summit, the two parties discussed projects worth US$17 billion, ranging from oil exploration and construction contracts to software and health care services (Majumdar 2009). The outcomes of these summits have been phenomenal in that between 2005 and 2008 trade between Africa and India grew at an annual rate of about 25 percent. In the 2008 fiscal year alone, trade between India and Africa represented US$11.8 billion.

Following the successes of the first two summits, India and African states held a third summit in 2010 in New Delhi. This summit attracted business leaders and politicians from thirty-two African countries and India to explore ways of improving bilateral trade and relations. Speaking during the summit, the Indian Foreign Affairs Minister, Pranab Mukherjee projected that trade between India and Africa would surpass US$100 billion by 2015, as India intensifies its bilateral relations with Africa in the face of competition from rival China for resources (Mahapatra 2006). The minister made two crucial announcements: first the doubling of credit lines for African countries by the Indian government to US$5.4 billion over a period of 5 years (between 2010 and 2015) and second the provision of US$500 million for projects in Africa from the Aid to Africa budget (Mahapatra 2006). Between 2001 and 2010, India has diversified its investments in Africa to include areas such as agriculture, small industry, mining, information and communication technology, oil pipelines, the chemical industry, and power generation and transmission (Mahapatra 2006). One of the areas that Indian companies dominate is the mobile network. The leading company is Bharti India, which operates mobile phones in fifteen African countries. Other than this sector, only a handful of African countries account for the bulk of India's economic engagement and markets. Most Indian investments are concentrated in a few African countries, such as South Africa, Nigeria, Egypt, and Kenya, where India's top economic players—such as the Tata Group, Ranbaxy Laboratories, and Kirloskar Brothers—have mostly focused their investments (Tripathy and Kuncheria 2010).

Among the BRICS countries, China is by far the biggest trade partner and investor in Africa. Compared with other trading partners, China comes third, after the United States and the European Union. Between 2002 and 2003, China's trade with Africa was worth US$18.5 billion. It then rose by 45.1 percent in 2007 and reached US$106.8 billion in 2008 (*Mail and Guardian* 2009b). This rise was attributed to China's need for resources in Africa and Africa's demand for cheap Chinese-made products. This two-way trade favored Africa in that Chinese exports to Africa stood at US$51 billion and its imports stood at US$56 billion (*Mail and Guardian* 2009b). The Chinese imports from Africa mainly come from oil-rich nations, such as Angola, Equatorial Guinea, Nigeria, the Republic of Congo, and Sudan (Zhihong 2010). However, this figure dropped by 30 percent between December 2008 and January 2009.

Like the Indians, the Chinese believe in hosting bilateral summits. Between 2006 and 2010 China and African countries held two of these. The first took place in Beijing in 2006, where the Chinese government not only pledged US$5 billion of assistance but also signed agreements to relieve or cancel the debt of more than thirty African countries (*BBC News* 2009). This summit was followed by another in 2010, which took place in Sharm el-Sheikh in Egypt. At this summit Chinese Prime Minister Wen Jiabao announced a number of measures aimed at assisting Africa's economic development, ranging from the provision of a US$10 billion low-cost loan initiative, tariff reductions, debt relief initiatives, the creation of 100 clean energy projects, and other environmental programs to the cancellation of debts owed by more than thirty poor African countries. China also has become one of the major investors in Africa. Its foreign direct investment in Africa rose from US$700 million in 2001 to US$50 billion in 2009 (Cornish 2010). In the first half of 2009 alone, its investment in the continent, excluding the financial sector, increased to 79 percent or US$875 million as a result of Chinese economic activities in sectors such as the construction of roads, ports, railroads, apartment blocks, mines, and oil pipelines. In 2008, the total Chinese investment in Africa was pegged at US$26 billion (Cornish 2010).

While Chinese investments, aid, and trade with Africa provide alternative options for Africa's development, some scholars argue that such alternatives are only psychological in that the capitalist systems cannot be entirely free of exploitation and that China's active engagement with Africa and its dealings with African countries are no different from what major powers do traditionally in poor countries. This argument is based on the fact that China's global and regional diplomacy pursues multiple objectives, similar to those that all other great powers pursue, which ultimately results in tension between values and interests at both the national and global levels. Critics reason that China could no more be expected to subjugate its commercial and strategic interests than western powers have done in their African or global policies (Besada 2008). This raises questions whether trade or aid or investment could take place between unequal partners without accusations of imperialism and exploitation. Does China's active engagement with African states herald a new form of imperialism, different from the western one?

The responses to these questions are very interesting in that it is not the African countries that are concerned about the expansion of the Chinese influence on the continent but rather the European countries, which view China as a competitor for Africa's resources. European countries are particularly critical of China's role in Africa and view China's role in three different ways: (1) as a rising superpower that has closed the door on individual rights-based market democracies, focusing instead on collective rights-based development; (2) as a resource-seeking state willing to sustain short-term losses for long-term gain; and (3) as a global creditor actively disengaging from the Washington Consensus's structural adjustment disciplines (Cornish 2010). Western European countries accuse China of plundering Africa's natural resources to fuel its booming economy and of overlooking the human rights records of some governments they do business with. China in turn accuses western European countries of envying China's and Africa's relationship and "of viewing Africa as their own backyard" (*BBC News* 2009).

What these accusations and counteraccusations tell us is that bilateral foreign aid and investment carry risks of manipulation and foreign control. Wallerstein reminds us, in his world-system theory, that actors in international economic systems come and go but the system itself always remains the same. This suggests that while the rise of China, India, Brazil, and Russia, and their relationship with Africa should be welcomed, they too possess some characteristics common to all global creditors and actors, which include the exploitation and predatory behavior that form part of the global economic system. Thus, as global players, their objectives remain similar to those of western European states—namely the extraction of resources from peripheral states.

THE WASHINGTON CONSENSUS COMPARED WITH THE BEIJING CONSENSUS

Fukuyama's celebration of the new world order and the triumph of liberalism in the global systems is perhaps more evident in the rise of the BRICS countries in general and China in particular as a global player. When the Soviet Union collapsed in 1989, a vacuum was created in that the United

States remained as the only global superpower. The rise of China as the second biggest global economy, and the manner in and level at which it mastered capitalism and economic liberalism has restored the balance of power in the international global economy. This has raised concerns among the western European countries that they might lose their power and influence over African countries. Of great concern to the western European countries is the manner in which China conducts its deals with the poor states on the continent. For a long time, the rules concerning trade and aid from western European to African countries were determined by international regimes such as the World Bank and the IMF, which were commonly known as the instruments of the Washington Consensus. These regimes were responsible for setting up preconditions for giving out aid and trade. The rise of China as a global creditor brought about an alternative sources—for aid, soft loans, and trade with poor countries—without any conditions attached. African leaders praise Beijing for not preaching to them over the issues of governance and human rights (*Mail and Guardian* 2010). Such an approach has brought about a new dimension to the global economic system known as the Beijing Consensus. This raises the question: What is the difference between the Washington Consensus and the Beijing Consensus?

The main difference between Washington and Beijing lies in the sizes of their economies. The GDP of the United States is almost three times that of China and is estimated at US$14.6 trillion. China's GDP is approximately US$5.9 trillion. The U.S. GDP constitutes 23.1 percent of the entire global GDP of US$63.1 trillion, whereas China's GDP constitutes 9.4 percent of the entire global GDP. The combined GDPs of these two countries are estimated at 32.5 percent of the total global GDP. This suggests that the influence of these two countries in the other parts of the world, economically and politically, is greater than that of any other countries. Their links with Africa are more evident in the areas of resources, trade, and aid. In 2009, for instance, the total U.S. imports from Africa were estimated at 88 percent, and 24 percent of these imports were petroleum products. During the same period, Chinese total imports from Africa were estimated at 86 percent and 30 percent these came mainly from resources such as oil, gas, and minerals (Sharif 2010). This suggests that both the United States and China have greater trade ties with Africa.

What distinguishes the relationship between China and Africa on the one hand and Africa and the United States or western European countries on the other is the friendliness of China in its dealings with African states. The Chinese aid policies to Africa attach no political conditionality, as opposed to western European countries, which attach conditions to their deals. The Tanzanian Finance Minister Mustafa Mkulo attested to this when he stated that "many Chinese projects in Africa come in the form of the soft loan of between 1.5 percent and 2 percent, far undercutting finance offered by the West" (*Manchester News* 2010). He is of the opinion that African countries get money from the Chinese more easily and cheaply, with fewer preconditions, and for projects that western donors consider costly. Western European governments, according to Mkulo, demand benchmarks on issues such as human rights, democracy, and good governance as preconditions for aid and trade (*Manchester News* 2010). Former Ghanaian President John Kufour also hailed the China-Africa partnership and commended China as a country that came to Africa not as a colonial power but as a guest and on Africa's terms (McConnell 2008). He rebuffed those who accuse China of neocolonialism in its relations with Africa. He reasoned that African countries could now choose their partners in trade (*Manchester News* 2010).

One major complaint among African countries about aid from the West is that the bulk of the aid to Africa from American and western European countries is dedicated to humanitarian matters. This contrasts with aid from China, which focuses on improving infrastructure. Such contrasts in priorities were evident in the statements made by former U.S. President George W. Bush and Chinese President Hu Jintao during their separate visits to Africa in 2008. In his February 2008 trip to five African countries—namely Benin, Tanzania, Rwanda, Ghana, and Liberia—the U.S. president highlighted humanitarian success stories in Africa. He emphasized his administration's humanitarian credentials, stressing the existing US$1.2 billion malaria program and the President's Emergency Plan for Aids Relief, which spent US$15 billion between 2004 and 2008, and a further US$30 billion, which Bush asked the U.S. Congress to approve over the next 5 years (McConnell 2008). In Ghana, Bush unveiled a US$350 million 5-year fund to help fight neglected tropical diseases such as hookworm and river blindness (McConnell 2008). In Tanzania, he signed a US$700 million aid package for Tanzania. In Rwanda, he pledged US$100 million to help train African peacekeepers in Rwanda (McConnell 2008).

In contrast, Hu Jintao's visit during the same period (February 2008) emphasized China's commitment to building infrastructure across the continent—swapping roads, railways, and dams for mining concessions and rights to African resources. He signed a US$9 billion deal to upgrade mining and other infrastructure in the Democratic Republic of Congo in exchange for a majority stake in the state copper mining company, Gecamines (McConnell 2008). In Accra, Ghana, Jintao opened a new building for the Ministry of Defense built by Chinese contractors with Chinese money (McConnell 2008). His government also funded and built two new stadiums for the January 2008 Africa Cup of Nations football tournament in Ghana. In Northern Ghana, his government built a US$600 million hydroelectric dam providing much-needed electricity (McConnell 2008). China paid for improvements to the main road connecting the capital city, Accra, and Kumasi, the second biggest city in Ghana (McConnell 2008). In Mali, the Chinese built a presidential palace, hospitals, and a bridge in the capital, Bamako (McConnell 2008). In Malawi, they built a new parliament (Chen 2009). More importantly, the Chinese contractors and workers are not as demanding as their western European counterparts. They do not demand expensive perks such as housing, school fees, and flights home. They live on-site until the job is finished (Chen 2009). In spite of these contrasts, Bush downplayed the United States and China's growing roles in Africa as a zero sum game. When asked by a journalist in Ghana if their agendas in the continent were creating a sense of competition, Bush reasoned that China was not a competitor.

There is no doubt that China's growing influence in Africa, due to its economic boom and the need for resources for its huge populations, are causes for concern for other countries that rely on Africa's resources for economic growth. Such concerns have fueled fierce competition for resources on the continent. The United States is also competing for Africa's sought-after resources. Although the United States remains Africa's largest trading partner, trade projections show that in 10 to 15 years China will surpass the United States. In 2007, Chinese Prime Minister Wen Jiabao predicted that bilateral trade between China and Africa would surpass US$100 billion by 2010. This presents a huge leap forward, considering the fact that the first trade deals between China and Africa were previously only a US$12 million cotton deal signed between China and Egypt in 1956 (Chen 2009). The fact that trade between China and Africa has tripled makes some people argue that China has taken the place of the West in Africa. However, Tanzanian Finance Minister Mustafa Mkulo disputes this and states that "the Chinese are developing a certain part of the continent, whereas the West has its own interest" and that "each of these players has a role to play in the continent" (*Manchester News*, 2010). However, the biggest problem that African countries face in the wake of these competitions is the absence of regulatory frameworks to govern foreign investment in the continent. Such regulations do not exist in most countries on the continent. Consequently Africa's response to trade with the Chinese and other foreign investors has been incoherent and dissenting. This has led foreign investors to bypass local legislation.

CRITICISMS OF CHINA'S ENGAGEMENT WITH AFRICA

China's indiscriminate dealing with African governments has elicited strong concerns, not only from its Asian neighbors but also from western European and African countries. Western European countries accuse China of taking a neocolonialist attitude toward the continent. They accused China of supporting rogue regimes in Sudan and Zimbabwe, which have poor human rights records. More than 800 Chinese state-owned firms operate in Africa. However, the number of private businesses owned by Chinese nationals is unknown (*Mail and Guardian* 2009b). Critics fear that Beijing's demand for African oil exports and other raw materials has resulted in the perpetuation of Africa's reliance on oil exports, which, in turn, inhibit the growth of more labor-intensive industries such as agribusiness and manufacturing (Hornby 2009). Such criticism pours in from the West in spite of European oil companies' destruction of Africa's ecosystems. A good example of this is Shell's continued exploitation of African oil reserves in areas such as the Niger Delta in Nigeria, where ordinary people live in abject poverty and endure water and air pollution (*Mail and Guardian* 2010).

Ordinary Africans are critical of the proliferation of Chinese small-scale entrepreneurs on the continent, especially retail traders, who have had the greatest impact on their lives. Such impacts are twofold. On the one hand Chinese shopowners bring affordable food to the poor; but on the other they represent negative images of greedy businesspeople who make profit from selling worthless junk. Ordinary people accuse Chinese entrepreneurs of selling cheap, inferior consumer goods, which, in turn, has put local entrepreneurs out of work. Such perceptions sparked a public outcry in a number of African states, such as Lesotho, Zambia, Ethiopia, and Namibia. In Lesotho, street vendors attacked Chinese-owned businesses in November 2007, accusing them of colluding with the government to force them out of the city center of the country's capital, Maseru (Besada 2008). In Zambia, Ethiopia, and Namibia public protests focused on poor working conditions and low pay by Chinese firms (AsiaNews.it 2007).

Others accuse the Chinese investors of impeding job creation by bringing their own labor force to Africa instead of creating jobs for the local population (*Mail and Guardian* 2009b). The Chinese media estimates that over 750,000 Chinese expatriates work in Africa, making them one of Africa's largest foreign communities (*Mail and Guardian* 2009b). The nature of their jobs ranges from doctors and fish farmers to barbers and beauticians. The Chinese foreign direct investment soared to US$13.7 billion in 2007, from US$500 million in 2000. This figure presents, and has contributed to, Africa's greatest economic growth since the 1960s. However, this did not help in solving problems of unemployment in sub-Saharan Africa, which remained at about 30 percent in 2009 (Maclean 2008). According to the International Labor Organization, about 55 percent of working people in sub-Saharan Africa do not earn enough to lift themselves and their families above the dollar-a-day poverty line and 86 percent of people in sub-Saharan Africa live on US$2 a day (Maclean 2008). Such high levels of poverty make sub-Saharan Africa one of the highly sensitive territories for foreign investors. Unemployment has been fueled by an unknown proportion of Chinese workers, who flout African law by staying on after their contracts expire in order to seek their fortunes in Africa. Also problematic is the problem of Chinese illegal immigrants, who come on tourist visas with the intention of looking for work opportunities and then stay on when they find them. This is particularly evident in South Africa, where a significant number of Chinese illegal immigrants are smuggled in (Maclean 2008).

In spite of being criticized over its willingness to ignore human rights abuses and environmental and corruption issues in some countries, China insists that it will continue to invest in Africa. Zhong Manying, its head of the West Asian and African Affairs Department of the Commerce Ministry, put it plainly when he stated, "China will certainly continue to invest in existing areas of our co-operation and also further expand into new sectors. Mining, aviation and other transportation, renewable energy and the financial sector will be the 'priority areas' of China's future investment in African countries" (Maclean 2008). China may be criticized for various reasons, but the sustainability of its investments in Africa and its continued presence on the continent depend on its acceptance by African states as partner.

Many African governments talk more favorably of business relations with China than of those with the West. This contradicts the media's perception, which has created an image of China exploiting Africa. Chinese officials have always insisted and emphasized their government's policy of noninterference in the internal affairs of African states. This does not mean that issues of trust and perception do not exist. Labor issues remain key issues of major concern in many African countries, especially in those countries where China has brought its own workers to help build mines and infrastructure. This has been the root cause of resentment among the local people. Beneficiary states have the power to draw and adopt the local legislations regulating foreign investment. They also have the power to decide whether or not to allow unskilled workers from donor countries to build roads, bridges, or mines quickly or whether to spend time training their own workers to do so. Evidence shows that most African leaders prefer the rapid construction of roads and other infrastructure with the help of the Chinese in order to deliver on their election promises.

THE GLIMMER OF HOPE FOR AFRICA

The rise of the BRICS countries as major global players has opened door for the economic success of other developing countries in general and of African countries in particular. In spite of being an "underdeveloped" continent, Africa has abundant resources, ranging from minerals to good agricultural soils. Most importantly, Africa has one of the lowest population densities in the world, at twenty-nine people per square kilometer. It is also home to 14 percent of the globe's population. Its land surface constitutes 22 percent of the world's land mass and its resources remain underutilized. However, Africa is only slowly emerging from shackles of underdevelopment. Such evolution is evident in the areas of urbanization, an emerging middle class, and an expanding labor force. In 1980, just 28 percent of Africans lived in cities. Today, 40 percent of the continent's billion people live in cities, a proportion roughly comparable to China's and larger than India's (James 2010). Actually economists reason that Africa is at the same point where India and China were about 20 or 30 years ago. By 2030, that proportion is projected to rise to 50 percent, and analysts project that

Africa's top eighteen cities will have a combined spending power of $1.3 trillion (James 2010).

Most importantly, Africa's labor force is expanding, in contrast to what is happening in much of the rest of the world, especially the West, where the economy grew to 1.6 percent in 2011 and was expected to contract to 1.1 percent in 2012. Prospects for economic growth seem favorable, since Africa has more than 500 million people of working age. By 2040, this number is predicted to exceed 1.1 billion, more than in China or India (James 2010). China has been critical about the development of the economies in Africa and has become the source of more than US$60 billion in private investment between 1998 and 2008 (James 2010). Africa accounts for more than one quarter of the world's arable land. The fact that it currently generates only about 10 percent of global agricultural output implies that there is huge potential for growth in a sector now expanding only moderately, at a rate of 2 to 5 percent a year (James 2010).

Agriculture is undoubtedly central to the economies of most non-oil exporting African countries. It constitutes approximately 30 percent of Africa's GDP and contributes about 50 percent of the total export value. It accounts for about a third of overall economic growth in agriculture-based countries in sub-Saharan Africa (*Conference Report* 2005). It is the main economic activity and the source of livelihood of 70 percent of Africans living in rural areas.[4] More than half a billion people live in agriculture-based countries; 49 percent of them live on less than US$1 a day (James 2010). Agriculture accounts for the livelihood of 89 percent of the rural population in agriculture-based countries in sub-Saharan Africa (*Conference Report* 2005), making agriculture the engine of overall growth.

Agricultural growth in sub-Saharan African countries has been credited with accelerating economic growth from 2.3 percent per year in the 1980s to 3.3 percent in the 1990s and to 3.8 percent per year between 2000 and 2005 (James 2010). Agricultural growth has been credited for rural poverty reduction in ten out of thirteen countries analyzed by UN researchers between 1990 and 2010 (James 2010). Agricultural growth has been critical not only to household food security but has also contributed enormously to increases in local food production in remote areas with poorly developed infrastructure and markets. This, in turn, has led to an increase in the incomes of the poor.

The current situation in sub-Saharan African countries is comparable to the situation in which Asian countries were four to five decades ago. Africa, like Asia in the 1960s, has been pummeled by food crises in recent decades owing to political unrest, conflict over land ownership, climate change and its consequences, limited infrastructural development, increasing poverty, and the general lack of economic growth. These problems have adversely affected agricultural production. Asian countries faced similar concurrent food crises between 1965 and 1966, and they responded by adopting the agricultural green revolution, which focused on "the Asian countryside stretching from Turkey to the Philippines, and including the pivotal countries of India and Pakistan" (Brown 1968). Asia was at a disadvantage in that it was very densely populated and traditional agriculture could no longer support the area's growing population, as cropland was becoming severely limited. Because of this, food production could not keep up with the rapid growth of population, especially during the 1950s and 1960s. This was compounded by two successive failed monsoon seasons in India, which exacerbated the gravity of the situation (Brown 1968).

The ensuing revolution was based on the single principle of increasing agricultural yields, especially rice, by means of technology (Herren 2008). The use of technology led to an increase in farming production, which, in turn, led to a decrease in famine. This was complemented by government incentives, such as subsidized inputs, access to better credit, government support, and the improvement of infrastructure. The success of the Asian green or farming revolution not only led to the development of high-yielding grain varieties but also resulted in the depletion of soil fertility and water supplies. These, in turn, caused damage to ecosystems, farmer debt, expensive inputs, decreased crop diversity, and higher urbanization (Herren 2008). Consequently food productivity and the whole concept of the Asian farming revolution became unsustainable (Jhamtani 2009). By 2008, the increase in crop yields had dropped to 1 percent in some Asian countries, resulting in higher prices for inputs, which had a detrimental effect on rural communities.

African states did not adopt the green revolution but rather the Comprehensive Africa Agricultural Development Program of the New Partnership for Africa's Development (NEPAD), whose aim was to improve food security, foster growth, and reduce poverty. This differed considerably from Asian irrigated rice- and wheat-based systems. This was so because sub-Saharan African agriculture is 96 percent rain-fed and highly vulnerable to weather shocks (Conference Report 2005). These diverse agriecological conditions produce a wide range of farming systems, based on many food staples and on livestock. Most sub-Saharan agriculture-based countries are small, making it difficult for them to achieve large-scale economies in research and training. Another important drawback is that nearly 40 percent of Africa's people live in landlocked countries. They face transport costs that, on average, are 50 percent higher than in the typical coastal country (Conference Report 2005). This problem is compounded by vast distances and low population densities, which make trade, infrastructure, and the provision of services not only costly but also difficult. This retards the emergence of competitive markets (Conference Report 2005). On a positive note, areas of low population density on the continent with good agricultural potential represent untapped reserves for agricultural expansion.

The above account demonstrates clearly that Africa has great potential to develop rapidly through agriculture if African countries can adopt a policy agenda that is carefully tailored to the countries' specific circumstances.

Such an approach is needed owing to sub-Saharan African countries' diversity across regions and within countries and also in terms of size, agricultural potential, transport links, reliance on natural resources, and state capacity. Harnessing agriculture's potentials will therefore require improving smallholder competitiveness in high- and medium-potential areas, where returns to investment are highest. Harnessing agriculture will also require improving livelihoods, food security, and resilience in remote and risky environments. In short, harnessing agricultural growth requires the balancing of food staples, traditional bulk exports, and higher-value products, including livestock, with different groups of smallholders likely to participate in each sector. However, in most agriculture-based countries in sub-Saharan Africa, the production of staple crops dominates the production of cash crops owing to the problems associated with subsistence farming. The demands for food in sub-Saharan Africa continue to grow and are expected to reach US$100 billion by 2015.[5] It is therefore imperative that governments not only adopt appropriate approaches to address the wide heterogeneity of rain-fed production systems in sub-Saharan Africa but also increase technologies and support services to women farmers, who produce and process most of the food.

The potential and the prospects for economic growth in sub-Saharan Africa are promising because of the discovery of oil deposits in countries such as Ghana, Uganda, and Zambia (Jere 2006), the eastern Democratic Republic of Congo, and Mozambique. This has increased the number of oil-producing countries in Africa to twenty-five and analysts project that by 2015 about 25 percent of the world's oil imports will come from Africa, essentially from the Gulf of Guinea. The discovery of oil and improvements in agricultural growth alone, however, are not enough to propel the continent into economic prosperity. The economic success of African states will also depend on economic integration and the strengthening of regional blocs. These overlapping blocs will need to be reconfigured and restructured to avoid duplication and the complication of aims, goals, and objectives. Good examples of this are the three trading blocs in southern and eastern Africa, namely the Common Market for Eastern and Southern Africa (COMESA), the East African Community (EAC), and the Southern African Development Community (SADC). The COMESA is home to twenty-two countries, the EAC is home to five, and SADC to fifteen. Some are members of more than one bloc. The establishment of a tripartite free-trade agreement (FTA) including the COMESA, EAC, and SADC could bring together twenty-six countries with a total population of 568 million people and a combined GDP of US$875 billion ($1,540 per capita) (Jere 2006).

However, the creation of FTAs among these regions could pose serious challenges, since the COMESA, EAC, and SADC have FTAs within their own regions; 85 percent of trade within the SADC, for example, is duty-free and is supposed to increase to 100 percent by 2012. The SADC free-trade agreement took six years to conclude (Jere 2006). This could pose serious challenges when it includes more than thirty countries from the COMESA, SADC, and EAC. Challenges could arise from strengthening and streamlining customs operations and standardizing safety issues (Jere 2006). Conversely, the fact that a number of countries are already members of more than one trade bloc could facilitate the establishment of the broader FTA.

It is clear from the above account that Africa's economic growth is on the right track, even though people accentuate the negative rather than giving proper and due acknowledgment to the positive. Africa has made progress not only in economic growth but also politically. Many African countries have democratically elected governments as a key to promoting good governance, accountability, and transparency. These are preconditions for economic development. Many African countries are outwardly more democratic today than they were 20 years ago; more than ten times that number are democratic. They have also steadily improved their rankings on the World Bank's "Doing Business" indicators, even though they remain a long way behind other high-growth markets. Governance is about more than how often elections are held or how countries perform on Washington's business indicators. It requires appreciating the inner stuffing of democracy and understanding the relationship between political access and prosperity.

In spite of the improvements outlined above, foreign direct investment (FDI) flows into Africa have been very low, at an average 2.5 percent of GDP, owing to uncertainty in the global markets and economic turmoil in the Eurozone. Economists reason that Africa's share of foreign direct investment is fair considering Africa's market size compared with the rest of the world (Bolin 2004). One such economist is Alan Gelb, the World Bank's chief economist and senior director, who points out that African FDI inflows are only slightly lower than the 3.1 percent of GDP recorded, on average, in Asia (Bolin 2004). Gelb contends that although about 40 percent of FDI in Africa was directed at extractive industries such as mining, oil, and gas, 36 percent goes into services, and in some African countries FDI was higher than the data indicated (Bolin 2004). Another economist, David Bridgman, a program manager at the U.S. Multilateral Investment Guarantee Agency, agrees. Bridgman observes that Africa was getting "about the right share" of worldwide investment based on its share of the global economy (Bolin 2004). He singles out more than a dozen African countries, such as Tanzania, Uganda, Mozambique, and Mauritius, which are in the process of reforming rapidly and have succeeded in attracting significant amounts of investment. "These countries," reasons Bridgman, "need support to broaden and deepen their reform efforts" (Bolin 2004).

A recent WEF study report corroborates these views. It points out that FDI into Africa was the most profitable compared with that into other developing regions, including Asia and Latin America (Le Roux 2007). It point out that legal restrictions on FDI in Africa were no longer much different to those in any other countries and that the returns from investment were generally higher in Africa than in the other parts of the world. However, the study bemoans the existence of the "red tape and hidden barriers to doing trade and investment" in most African countries, as some of the problems that need to be addressed to improve economic growth (Le Roux 2007) and because market size, both internal and external, are important determinants of FDI. Such factors were instrumental for large inflows of FDI into Europe (before the enlargement of the European Union), Brazil, Mexico, and China in the past decade (Le Roux 2007). African countries can improve the flows of FDI by boosting regional trade, as most African countries have small internal markets.

WHAT CAN BE DONE?

There is no doubt that Africa's billion people are the last untapped market in the world. The challenge is to ensure that foreign investors have a good sense of the opportunities that Africa offers. There is also a need for foreign investors to change their attitudes towards Africa, because "they have traditionally been a little wary of Africa" (Le Roux 2007). Yet the stereotype of Africa as a noncompetitive continent is simply not true. The major challenge, however, lies in realizing the promise of the world-class enterprises found in every African country and in practically every industry. To realize this, African countries need not only to adopt good policies and institutions but also to invest heavily in physical infrastructure and human resources. Such investments are crucial in sustaining the current growth trajectory. High growth rates would have to be sustained over decades for Africa to raise the living standards of its people.

In the past decade, economic growth in African countries was fuelled by variable external factors, such as high commodity prices, debt relief, and a favorable international economic environment. This growth fell short of the estimated 7 percent annual growth required to meet the Millennium Development Goal of halving poverty rates in the region by 2015 (Le Roux 2007). In its assessment of the competitiveness of 29 African states among a sample of 128 countries from around the world, the WEF study report found that "the competitiveness of most countries in Africa continues to lag behind not only among the rest of the world but also among other developing regions" (Le Roux 2007). The report made two recommendations: first for North African countries to work on technological advancement and market efficiency and second for sub-Saharan countries to upgrade infrastructure and improve their health systems (Le Roux 2007). These improvements are not only crucial but also basic requirements for migrating into a higher stage of development. Realizing the continent's potential requires a radical reform of the nature of African politics and politicians. Such reforms may include the reduction of freight charges at African ports, the freeing up of more land for cultivation, and the enforcement of honest and transparent courts of law.

African governments also need to put in place private sector reform, by digging deep into foundations that recognize the essential value of free enterprise, not as prey but as a partner (Holman and Mills 2010).

For the time being, aid from developed countries remains crucial for Africa's development and survival, providing short-term solutions in terms of physical capital. However, for long-term solutions, African countries need ideas and knowledge, since ideas and knowledge lead to technical knowhow and innovation. Undoubtedly Africa's underdevelopment is rooted not in the lack of resources but in the lack of human capacity. As a result, African countries are both importers and consumers of ideas and knowledge invented in the industrialized countries, partly because of their own low levels of investment in research institutions and education. Reports on economic development show that African governments spend very little on specialized areas such as science and technology. The continent's share of investment in research and development is only 0.5 percent of the world's total, and it creates 0.8 percent of the world's scientific publications.[6] This is mainly due to the absence of universities devoted to primary research and has been compounded by human capital flight from the continent in search of greener pastures in developed countries, leaving behind a "skills vacuum" that cannot be filled overnight, since emigrant professionals have not passed on their skills to future generations. This, together with poor investment in education, has contributed to slow economic growth in African countries. Furthermore, there are few measures in place to offset the incentives for highly educated people to emigrate. This is a serious problem.

Economically, the continent faces being left further behind as its growth rates fail to match economic growth in other parts of the world. A joint report by the WEF, the World Bank, and the African Bank forecast Africa's growth at 5 percent in 2011 (Cropley 2010). This was in contrast to a 4.9 percent average growth rate that African countries achieved over 8 years (2001–2009) and 5.5 percent that the continent achieved in 2010, in spite of Africa's better macroeconomic environmental outlook. This average growth rate is lower than the International Monetary Fund's statistics, which put China's growth at 10 percent in 2011, India's at 8.4 percent, and Russia's at 6.4 percent (International Monetary Fund 2009). This raises serious questions about the readiness of African states to influence global events and seize opportunities in the changing world order. Africa still has numerous problems, corruption and tribalism probably being the greatest, but major developments are being seen all over the continent in spite of its ills. If the elites of Africa can transcend parochial interests and seriously undertake the modernizing project, the future need not necessarily be a replay of the past.

NOTES

* The author acknowledges funding from the National Research Fund during the preparation stages of this chapter.

1. See also the Lomé Convention: http://ec.europa.eu/development/geographical/cotonou/lomegen/lomeitoiv_en.cfm
2. See www.un.orga/en/development/other/overview.shml
3. While Europe is increasingly in competition with China over African ties, trade, investment, and influence, there have so far been just three EU-Africa summits, the first in Cairo in 2000, the second in Lisbon in 2007 and the last in Libya in 2010.
4. Climate Change and Agriculture in Africa: http://www.ceepa.co.za/Climate_Change/index.html
5. Ibid.
6. The Global Research Report: Africa, http://paepard.blogspot.com

REFERENCES

AsiaNews.it. "Public Protests against Hu Jintao," May 2, 2007: http://www.asianews.it/news-en/Public-protests-against-Hu-Jintao-8403.html

Baylies, Carolyn. "Political Conditionality and Democratization." *Review of African Political Economy*, No. 65 (1995):

BBC News. "China Pledges $10bn Africa Loans," November 8, 2009: http://news.bbc.co.uk/2/hi/8349020.stm

Besada, H. "A Maturing China-Africa Relationship," 2008: http://www.mg.co.za/article/2008-06-18-a-maturing-chinaafrica-relationship

Bolin, L. "Foreign Investment in Africa Not All That Bad," December 27, 2010: http://www.mg.co.za/article/2004-06-04-foreign-investment-in-africa-not-all-that-bad

Brown, L. R. "The Agricultural Revolution in Asia," December 28, 2010: http://www.foreignaffairs.com/articles/23996/lester-r-brown/the-agricultural-revolution-in-asia

Chen, S. "China Seeks Broader Africa Role," January 3, 2011: http://news.bbc.co.uk/2/hi/asia-pacific/7885045.stm

Cohn, Theodore H. *Global Political Economy: Theory and Practice*. New York: Longmans, 2000.

Conference Report. "Mapping sub-Saharan Africa's Future," 2005: www.dni.gov/nic/confreports_Africa_future.html

Cornish, J. J. "Its Paris Je T'aime for Africa": http://www.mg.co.za/article/2010-06-04-its-paris-je-taime-for-africa

Cropley, E. "Donor Aid Squeeze Set to Increase Africa's Debt," 2010: http://www.mg.co.za/article/2010-10-21-donors-aid-squeeze-set-to-increase-africas-debts

Davie, K. "Zuma's Trade Card," 2010: http://www.mg.co.za/article/2010-11-19-zumas-trade-card

Donnelly, L. "Why China Trumps SA," 2008: http://www.mg.co.za/article/2008-08-10-why-china-trumps-sa

Dunne, Timothy. "Realism." In: J. Baylis and S. Smith, eds. *The Globalization of World Politics: An Introduction to International Relations*. Oxford, UK: Oxford University Press, 1998a.

Dunne, Timothy. "Liberalism." In: J. Baylis and S. Smith, eds. *The Globalization of World Politics: An Introduction to International Relations*. Oxford, UK: Oxford University Press, 1998b.

Evans, Graham, and Richard J. Newnham. *The Penguin Dictionary of International Relations*. London: Penguin Books, 1998.

Fukuyama, Francis. "The End of History?" *The National Interest* No.16 (Summer 1989): 3–18.

Herren, H. "Supporting True Agricultural Revolution": http://www.google.co.za/#hl=enandsource=hpandbiw=1276andbih=820andq=Hans+Herrenpercent2C+co-chair+of+the+International+Assessment+of+Agricultural+Science+and+Technology+for+Development.andbtnG=Google+Searchandaq=fandaqi=andaql=andoq=andfp=9935cf356bc91615
Heywood, Andrew. *Politics*. London: Macmillan, 1997.
Hobden, Steve, and Richard Wyn Jones. "World-System Theory." In: J. Baylis and S. Smith, eds. *The Globalization of World Politics: An Introduction to International Relations*. Oxford: UK: Oxford University Press, 1998.
Holman, K., and Greg Mills. "Politics at the Heart of Africa's Reform Process," 2010: http://www.mg.co.za/article/2010-08-06-politics-at-the-heart-of-africas-reform-process
Hoogvelt, Ankie. *Globalization and the Post-Colonial World: The New Political Economy of Development*. London: Macmillan, 1998.
Hornby, L. "China Tries to Wean African Investors off State Loans," 2009: http://www.mg.co.za/article/2009-11-04-china-tries-to-wean-africa-investors-off-state-loans
Huntington, Samuel. "The Clash of Civilizations?" *Foreign Affairs* (Summer 1993): 22–49.
International Monetary Fund. "World Economic Outlook Update," 2009: http://www.imf.org/external/pubs/ft/weo/2009/update/01/index.htm
James, M. "Comment on Midlife Crisis for Africa," August 2, 2010: http://www.mg.co.za/article/2010-07-30-a-midlife-crisis-for-africa
Jere, D. "Zambia Discovers Oil, Gas near Angola Border," 2006: http://www.mg.co.za/article/2006-10-23-zambia-discovers-oil-gas-near-angola-border
Jhamtani, H. "The Green Revolution in Asia: Lessons for Africa," 2009: http://www.twnside.org.sg/title2/resurgence/2009/223/cover6.htm
Kegley, Charles, and Eugene Wittkopf. *World Politics: Trends and Transformation*, 7th ed. London: Macmillan, 1998.
Klomegah, K.K. "Russia Lags behind in Building Africa's Relations," 2008: http://www.mg.co.za/article/2008-07-15-russia-lags-behind-in-building-african-relations
le Roux, M. "WEF: Africa Still Trailing World in Growth," 2007: http://www.mg.co.za/article/2007-06-13-wef-africa-still-trailing-world-in-growth
Lynn, J. "Lamy Urges WTO Members to Bridge Gaps," 2008: http://www.mg.co.za/article/2008-12-07-lamy-urges-wto-members-to-bridge-gaps
Maclean, W. "Africans Marvel Fret at China's Hard Workers," 2008: http://www.mg.co.za/article/2008-08-21-africans-marvel-fret-at-chinas-hard-workers
Mahapatra, J. "Africa-India Sees Promise for Its Booming Business," 2006: http://www.mg.co.za/article/2006-10-16-in-africa-india-sees-promise-for-its-booming-businesses
Mail and Guardian. "WTO Nations Endorse Trade-Talks Freeze," July 27, 2006: http://www.mg.co.za/article/2006-07-27-wto-nations-endorse-tradetalks-freeze
———. "EU Says SA Summit Could Help WTO Talks," October 18, 2007a: http://www.mg.co.za/article/2007-10-18-eu-says-sa-summit-could-help-wto-talks
———. "EU Officials Can't Exclude Mugabe for Being a Dictator," October 25, 2007b: http://www.mg.co.za/article/2007-10-25-eu-official-cant-exclude-mugabe-for-being-a-dictator.
———. "Oil Find Sparks New Hope for Uganda," August 27, 2009a): http://www.mg.co.za/article/2009-08-27-oil-find-sparks-new-hope-for-uganda
———. "China Wants to Set Up Factories in Africa," December 5, 2009b: http://www.mg.co.za/article/2009-12-05-china-wants-to-set-up-factories-in-africa

———. "Oil Discovery off Shore from Mozambique," August 17, 2010: http://www.mg.co.za/article/2010-08-17-oil-discovered-off-shore-from-mozambique
———. "China Plans to Expand Investment in Africa," October 14, 2010: http://www.mg.co.za/article/2010-10-14-china-plans-to-expand-investment-in-africa
Majumdar. B. "India to Triple Trade with Africa," January 21, 2009: http://www.mg.co.za/article/2009-01-21-india-to-triple-trade-with-africa
Manchester News. "UK Seeks China Aid Partnership in Africa," October 5, 2010:http://www.manchesterwired.co.uk/news.php/96308-UK-seeks-China-aid-partnership-in-Africa
Mansbach, Richard W. *The Global Puzzle: Issues and Actors in World Politics*. Boston: Houghton Mifflin, 1994.
Mazrui, Ali A., and Michael Tidy. *Nationalism and New States in Africa*. Nairobi: Heinemann, 1986.
McConnell, T. "Bush: Africa's New China," February 25, 2008: http://www.mg.co.za/article/2008-02-25-bush-africas-new-china
Mutumi, G. "International Textile, Garment and Leather Workers Federation Report." *African Renewal*, Vol. 20, No. 1 (2006): 3–4.
Nel, Phil. "Theories of International Relations." In P. Nel and P. J. McGowan, eds. *Power, Wealth and Global Order: An International Relations Textbook for Africa*. Cape Town: Cape Town University Press, 1999.
Nicholson, Michael. *International Relations: A Concise Introduction*. London: Macmillan, 1998.
Niewoudt, S. "Is Inviting Africans to G8 Meeting Window Dressing?" June 23, 2010: http://www.mg.co.za/article/2010-06-23-is-inviting-africans-to-g8-meeting-windowdressing
O'Neill, B. "What's in It for Africa?" 2006: www.ony.unu.edu/seminars/2006/whatsinitforafrica/oecdreport.pdf
Prowse, S. "Doha and Global Crisis: Briefing Paper 57." Overseas Development Institute: http://www.odi.org.uk/resources/download/4160.pdf
Ramonet, I. "Africa Says No," January 13, 2008: http://www.mg.co.za/article/2008-01-13-africa-says-no
Rosemberg, C. "Africa-EU on Summit Collision Course," November 30, 2010: http://www.mg.co.za/article/2010-11-30-africa-eu-on-summit-collision-course
Sharif, K. "Beijing Consensus: No Strings Attached," 2009: http://www.pambazuka.org/en/category/africa_china/62364
Smolchenko, A. "Russia Ventures Back to Africa," June 21, 2009: http://www.mg.co.za/article/2009-06-21-russia-ventures-back-to-africa
Tripathy, D., and C. J. Kuncheria. "Bharti Africa's Potential Makes Zain Deal Value Fair," February 25, 2010: http://www.mg.co.za/article/2010-02-25-bharti-africas-potential-makes-zain-deal-value-fair
Tse-Tung, Mao. "Selected Works of Mao Tse-tung: Vol. IX," 1961: http://www.marxists.org/reference/archive/mao/works/1937/guerrilla-warfare/
Viotti, Paul R., and Mark V. Kauppi. *International Relations Theory. Realism, Pluralism, Globalism*. New York: Macmillan, 1987.
White, L. "World Cup the Symbol of a New Postcolonial Order," June 21, 2010: http://www.mg.co.za/article/2010-06-21-world-cup-the-symbol-of-a-new-postcolonial-order
Zhihong, W. "Crude Oil Imports Jumps to 33 percent," February 11, 2010: http://www.chinadaily.com.cn/cndy/2010-02/11/content_9460006.htm

12 How Ready is Nigeria for Chinese Investments?

John E. Anegbode and Cletus E. Onakalu

African states have vast expanses of land that are rich in natural resources, with a huge potential for development. After a series of international political conferences on the emancipation of African states from their various colonial masters, these states won their independence. Since then, African countries have been conscientiously exploring a road to development suited to their national conditions while also seeking peace, good governance, a reduction of corruption and poverty, political stability, and economic development. African countries have participated actively in the formation of the Organization of African Unity (OAU), now the African Union (AU). The political situation in African has been stable on the whole, while regional conflicts are gradually being resolved. The New Economic Partnership for African Development (NEPAD) and the African Peer Review Mechanism (APRM) have also drawn an encouraging picture of African rejuvenation and development.[1]

Alongside this internal development, there has also been political development in terms of international relations, including relations with China. Africa has a long history of relations with China, which began slowly in the 1960s after the Bandung Conference (1955) and attempts by Beijing to assert its leadership role in the Third World and sub-Saharan Africa. Nigeria's contact with China started unofficially in 1957, through Egypt. At that time, Chinese relations with Africa were essentially with North Africa. Momoh explains that Chan Hiang-Kang, the commercial officer in the Chinese Embassy in Cairo, established this relationship.[2] Since this period, China has progressed on a platform of communism or refined socialism colored by some influx of capitalist ideas and has retained a stable society. The United States and the rest of developed West have maintained a system of capitalism mixed with socialism which, for the want of better name, may be tagged "welfarism."[3]

Nigeria and China signed the joint communiqué on the Establishment of Diplomatic Relations between the People's Republic of China and the Federal Republic of Nigeria in 1971. Since then, both nations have supported each other and cooperated in international affairs, both on bilateral trade as well as cultural and technological cooperation.[4] According to Meidan,

African attention was drawn to China as a result of the isolation of China by the United Nations in the 1960s: "The flag of third world solidarity was raised and China's international condemnation and isolation for violation of human rights was moderated by the support of African countries in the UN." African support in this multilateral forum allowed Beijing to be voted into the UN Security Council instead of Taiwan. This influenced some of the most important relations between African nations and China because they assisted in the realization of the Beijing's goals, giving birth to a new paradigm in China's African policy and relations.[5] China's activities in sub-Saharan Africa today cover the range of economic activity, including banking, railways, manufacturing, energy, transport, agriculture, and even street trading. China also provides developmental assistance in a manner that is often considered questionable. For instance, Chinese trade activities price foreign and African countries out of the African market.

China, the most populous country in the world with about 1.6 billion people, has made great economic strides over the past two decades, the same period during which Nigeria has witnessed some economic problems. These were caused by insensitivities of the previous regime in implementing policies that would abate the suffering of the people. In discussing China's relations with Africa in general and with Nigeria in particular, this chapter first examines the historical relationship that has existed between Africa and China. Regarding the present day, it highlights the implications of Niger Delta crisis, corruption, and leadership challenges to Chinese investments in Nigeria. Finally, it recommends possible solutions to these problems.

CHINA'S AFRICA POLICY: RATIONALE AND MEANING

China's reemergence on the African continent had been occurring for a long time before it became the focal point of international attention. In the early 1990s, China significantly stepped up its efforts to make its "all-out" policy successful in this particular region. China's African policy during this period was strictly offensive rather than defensive, as African government officials helped to strengthen Chinese companies' positions as vendors of "made in China" goods or as key merchants in raw materials. Around 2002, this venture started to capture international attention. Between 2000 and 2003, China's share in Africa's exports doubled and reached 7 percent. This evolution concurred with the completion of ambitious Chinese mining projects in countries like Zambia and Sudan, the construction of public infrastructure, and the omnipresence of the new Chinese diaspora.[6] However, China appeared not to be Africa's only new trade partner, as the growing economic interest in the region's resources from other countries like the United States, Brazil, and Canada, made China's competing aspirations develop into an issue of concern.

As bilateral trade and economic cooperation have grown, consultation and coordination in international affairs is also on the increase. China's Africa policy has five principles intended to contribute to peace, stability, and common prosperity. Part one encompasses Africa's position and role. Here we have the strategic position in which Africa is situated, including natural endowments like gold, zinc, oil, arable land for farming, etc. Part two entails China's relations with Africa, including frequent visits and exchange of high-level officials as well as technical assistance. Part three speaks to enhancing solidarity and cooperation within the tradition of China-Africa friendship as well as establishing a new type of strategic partnership with Africa. Specifically, the one-China principle (as opposed to the recognition of the second China, or Taiwan) is the political foundation for the establishment and development of China's relations with African countries and regional organizations. Part four emphasizes "enhancing all-round cooperation between China and Africa," which is subdivided into five parts. The political field describes all governmental official visits, exchange between legislative bodies, exchange between political parties, consultation mechanisms, cooperation in international affairs, and exchanges between local governments. The economic field covers trade, investment, financial cooperation, agricultural cooperation, infrastructure development, resource cooperation, tourism, debt reduction and relief, and multinational cooperation. Part three, social development, covers such aspects as education, science, culture, and health, as well as disaster reduction, relief, and humanitarian assistance. Peace and security includes military cooperation, conflicts settlement and peacekeeping operations, judicial and police cooperation, and nontraditional security areas. Finally, part five comprises the Forum on China-African Cooperation, which was launched in the year 2000 to serve as the platform for an effective mechanism for the collective dialogue and multilateral cooperation between China and Africa. China will work with African countries within the framework of the forum to explore new ways to enhance mutual political trust and promote pragmatic developmental cooperation.[7]

Having analyzed the Africa-China relationship and China's Africa policy, it must be questioned whether Africa has benefited from these bilateral and multilateral relations with China. The answer to this question depends on one's perspective. Oluwole buttresses this when he asserts, "these countries [China and India] were racing to Africa for economic survival and Nigeria should not be carried away by their offers."[8] He stresses that China and India have the largest populations in the world and the fastest-growing economies.[9] Although he did not advocate a retraction of their offers, he said that Nigeria must make sure that it is not exploited and financially ruined by these desperate countries. However, a contrary view, presented by Oluwole, asserts that China and other Asian Tigers are important to the development of Nigeria. He notes that Nigeria should work closely with these countries because it would learn from their developmental strategies.[10]

Similarly, Chukwuemeka, political adviser to former President Olusegun Obasanjo, argues Chinese investors should come to invest in the country because the Nigerian government is fiscally prepared for their massive investments. He adds that the potential for positive relations is increased because Nigeria and China are the biggest countries in terms of population on their respective continents.[11]

THE NEW FACE OF CHINESE BUSINESS RELATIONS IN NIGERIA

In the last decade, the trade volume between Nigeria and China has been on the increase. China's exports to Nigeria in 1996 stood at US$178 million, which rose to US$860 million in 2000. Nigeria's total export value to China stood at US$121 million in 1996 and has also increased.[12] According to the Economic and Commercial Office of the Chinese Embassy in Nigeria,[13] the total volume of bilateral trade between China and Nigeria was US$860 million in the year 2000. Nigeria has become the third trading partner of China in Africa after South Africa and Egypt. The trade value already reached US$870 million in the first 9 months of 2001, which represents a 50 percent increase over the same period in 1999 and is greater than the figure for 2000.[14]

Less than 10 years later, as reported by Ochu, China's current investment in Nigeria stands at US$3 billion, while trade as at the end of 2007 amounted to US$4.3 billion.[15] According to the World Bank's weekly report, Sino-African trade generally exploded from US$2 billion in 1999 to US$55.5 billion in 2006 and US$73 billion in 2007. This demonstrates that Chinese trade with Africa is growing faster than its trade with the rest of the world and is making a significant contribution to China's economic success.[16] For instance, China's recent business activities in Nigeria increased to an all-time high of US$2.83 billion in 2005. Shao Huixiana confirms the increase in transactions between China and Nigeria. He adds that the trade between Shanghai and Nigeria alone amounted to US$172 million, 10.3 percent higher as compared with the previous year.[17] It is believed in diplomatic circles that the increasing tempo of China's activities is meant to consolidate its hold on Nigeria as Africa's most important trading partner south of the Sahara.

In addition to trade, Chinese government firms have invested billions of dollars in Nigeria. For example, Chinese firms invested in Petro-China in July 2005 with a US$800 million deal with the Nigerian National Petroleum Corporation (NNPC) to purchase 30,000 barrels of oil per day for a year.[18] Also, in 2006, the China National Offshore Oil Corporation (CNOOC), after failing to acquire American-owned Union Oil Company of California (Unocal), purchased a 45 percent stake in a Nigerian offshore oil and gas field for US$2.27 billion and promised to invest an additional US$2.25 billion in field development.[19] This was reported as the CNOOC's largest foreign investment ever. Profits will be shared with NNPC in a ratio of 70:30 in favor of CNOOC. Oil production commenced in 2008 and has reached a peak of 225,000 barrels a day.[20] The Nigerian government has also awarded contracts to Chinese firms for the Rehabilitation of Nigeria Railways project, the dredging of the Calabar port, and the Abuja Games Village construction of 5,000 housing units in the new Abuja National Stadium Complex.[21] The Chinese Civil Engineering and Construction Company (CCECC) built the Nigerian Communications Commission building in Abuja, and Huawei Technologies, China's largest telecommunication equipment manufacturer, has started doing business in Nigeria, with offices in Lagos and Abuja.

Between 2000 and 2003, the number of Chinese-funded enterprises grew from 499 to 638 and spread across all African countries and regions. China is one of Nigeria's top trading partners and has set up thirty companies (some solely owned, some jointly owned with Nigerians) in Nigeria. This includes Huawei, which signed a deal to provide Nigeria with US$200 million worth of telecommunication equipment to set up nationwide mobile phone services using Code Division Multiple Access (CDMA) technology.[22] Chinese business has also created "Chinatowns" in major cities in Nigeria. These markets are managed by International Cooperation Industry Nigeria Limited. One such market consists of 120 shops, with about 40 shops belonging to Nigerians, while the other 80 shops belong to Chinese traders. The center acts as a market for products like apparel, textile and lace materials, shoes, handbags, Christmas decorations, baby wear, household utensils, and electrical appliances.

THREATS TO CHINESE INVESTMENTS IN NIGERIA

From the above, Chinese-Nigeria trade relations appear to be rewarding to both sides; however, these investments in Nigeria are under threat while the Niger Delta crisis continues, corruption is on the increase, kidnapping occurs on a daily basis, and a leadership crisis persists. So, how safe are China's investments in the face of these issues?

The Niger Delta Crisis

The Niger Delta crisis has generated a lot of controversy among scholars of development, environmentalists, politicians, and government agencies regarding the need to find a lasting solution to the continuous threat to the economy of Nigeria and the world in general posed by this geopolitical zone. Some of the problems of the Niger Delta are traceable to the total negligence of both the government and multinational companies operating in the zone, which have disregarded their social responsibility to the host communities. Onosede asserts that the growth profile of the petroleum industries over the years has been accompanied by a parallel growth in awareness and discontent in host communities. This is fostered by perceptions of manifest inequity in the distribution of petroleum-generated wealth, social amenities, and opportunities. He adds that the juxtaposition of deprivation, social neglect, and environmental degradation in the oil activity areas—with islands of privilege sustained by this wealth–creating industry—has continued to sustain deepening community resentment and constitutes a veritable recipe for instability.[23] This dissatisfaction has given birth to different militia groups and organizations operating in the region—such as the Movement for the Emancipation of the Niger-Delta (MEND) and the Movement for the Survival of Ogoni People (MOSOP)—fighting to actualize their goals and interest.

Since 2006, MEND has declared series of "oil wars" against foreign-owned oil companies working in the region. Chinese interest in Nigeria—an Oil Petroleum Export Countries (OPEC) member state—is based on oil. Therefore MEND attacks are aimed against the oil ventures of China, the United States, France, and oil-producing firms like Royal Dutch Shell, Exxon Mobil, Total, Eni, and Chevron. On June 21, 2009, MEND attacked the Shell Petroleum Development Company (SPDC), Afremo offshore oil fields, and two others in Rivers State. This new war was declared by MEND as a way of protesting military war by the Joint Task Force (JTF) in their region. According to Jomo, it was "Hurricane Piper Alpha" meted out to the Shell offshore Afremo oil fields. He adds that this was the first attack of MEND in an offshore facility since May 13, 2009.[24]

Following an exacerbation of the crisis in the Niger Delta, the federally collected revenue in the first quarter of 2009 stood at ₦1,183.72 trillion, representing a decline of 10.8 and 31.9 percent from the proportionate budget estimate and the level of the preceding quarters. At ₦842.26 billion, oil receipts constituted 71.2 percent of the total revenue, representing an increase of 8.2 percent over the budget estimate but a decline of 39.5 percent from the level of the preceding quarter. Nigeria's crude oil production, including condensates and natural gas, was estimated at 1.68 million barrels per day, or 151.20 million barrels per day for the quarter, while in the second quarter for 2009, it dropped significantly to 1.22 million barrels per day on the average. To cushion the effects of the onslaught against oil and gas exploration and production, the multinationals have commenced the layoff of nonessential staff, with Chevron threatening that 5,000 jobs in the region may be at risk.[25]

Corruption

At the inception of the present political dispensation, Nigerians were hopeful that corruption, which has been rampant both in the public and private spheres, would be drastically reduced. This hope was further raised with the establishment of the Independent Corrupt Practices and other Related Offences Commission (ICPC) in 2000 and the Economic and Financial Crime Commission (EFCC) in 2004. The enthusiasm started to wane with the lackluster performance of the ICPC, but it was rekindled with EFCC, which was able to achieve superlative feats while it lasted. For example, according to Adeniran, Obasanjo's regime promised power up to about 10,000 megawatts, but this was not to be despite the US$16 billion expended on a supplementary national integrated power project between 2004 and 2007. He added that contracts were fraudulently awarded, with full contract sums paid up front to fraudulent firms with illegal, fictitious, and questionable qualifications and standing. Rather, what the regime had to show for itself was power degeneracy to less than 3,000 megawatts.[26]

Another grievous consequence of corruption in Nigeria can be seen in the energy crisis currently ravaging the entire country in terms of electricity production, generation, and distribution. Nigeria trails behind the world in the production of electricity for its people and its comatose industry. Table 12.1 below shows electricity production in some African countries.

Table 12.1 Electrical Energy Production in Some African Countries

S/N	Country	Population (Millions)	Electrical Energy Production (Megawatts)	Planned Improvement (Megawatts)	Electrical Energy Consumption per Million People
1	South Africa	44	40,000	80,000 by 2025	4.2
2	Libya	5.5	4,710	12,000 by 2011	3.33
3	Botswana	1.7	434	700 by 2011	1.0
4	Egypt	81	14,250	29,000 by 2011	0.92
5	Kenya	31	22,000	12,000 by 2015	0.80
6	Ivory Coast	16	8,900	12,000 by 2010	1.0
7	Algeria	33	6,188	8,200 by 2011	0.71
8	Morocco	34	3,592	N/A	0.45
9	Zimbabwe	12.8	2,000	6,000 by 2010	0.44
10	Ghana	20	2,000	2,800 by 2015	0.43
11	Somalia	9	800	N/A	0.40
12	Liberia	3	200	500	0.22
13	Senegal	12	221	N/A	0.20
14	The Gambia	1.7	100	N/A	0.011
15	Uganda	25	270	2,000 by 2025	0.010
16	Nigeria	140	1,800	N/A	0.06

N/A = Not available.
S/N = International Energy Agency, "Africa: Statistics," http://www.iea.org/stats/regionresults.asp?country_code=11.

The table demonstrates that Nigeria, with 140 million people, is generating only 1,800 megawatts of power, without any reasonable plan of improvement. However, Nigeria is competing with countries like Morocco, Somalia, Senegal, and Gambia in power generation.

The problem with the power sector has much to do with a wide gap between supply and demand. The total demand is estimated to be within the range of 8,000 and 10,000 megawatts; of this, only a meager 3,500 megawatts was generated as of September 2010, which represents 30 percent of the total demand. It also means that 70 percent of customers connected to the national grid go without electricity. According to a report on the Nigerian investment climate authored by the World Bank and the African Development Bank, more than 80 percent of firms reported that electricity was the most binding constraint to doing business in Nigeria. Consequently the report notes that electricity-induced indirect losses account for 61 percent of total revenue loss.[27]

The manufacturing sector in particular is groaning under a shortfall of 1,658 megawatts of electricity, despite generating about 575 megawatts privately through existing power plants. The manufacturers, who also put their power demand in the next 5 years at 6,000 megawatts, said that they consumed 8.7 million liters of fuel per week for their operations, amounting to about ₦903 million and ₦3.6 million monthly. According to the chairman of the infrastructure committee of the Manufacturers Association of Nigeria (MAN), Reginald Odiah, while the electricity demand in the sector is 2,500 megawatts, the Power Holding Company of Nigeria is able to supply only 266.86 megawatts to the companies, adding that 575 megawatts is being generated independently through their power plants. He said that the number of manufacturing companies had been reduced from 4,850 in 1980s to 2,000 registered members today, producing at less than 60 percent of capacity.[28] MAN had earlier estimated that over 800 firms—including multinationals, conglomerates, and service providers—had left the shores of Nigeria for other countries, especially other West Africa countries, where there is stable power supply. Owing to the high cost of production, especially the high cost of self-produced electricity, many small-scale industries have collapsed. Relatively strong ones have relocated to other neighboring countries such as Ghana.[29]

Adding to the above, shortly before he left office in 2008, Nuhu Ribadu, then chairman of the Economic and Financial Crime Commission (EFCC), asserted that Nigerian leaders had stolen US$500 billion (₦85 trillion) within the past 40 years.[30] Corroborating Ribadu's claims, the eight recently troubled banks (Finbank, Union Bank, Afribank, Intercontinental Bank, Spring Bank, Bank PHB, Equatorial Trust Bank, and Oceanic Bank) were accused of granting loans indiscriminately to the tune of ₦747 billion, potentially making the Nigerian economy unstable for investment.[31] Corrupt practices were also associated with some international companies, such as the bribery scandals of Halliburton, Wilbross, Siemens, Sagem ID Card, and Pentascope, among others.

More significantly, the importation of substandard goods from China has been a source of concern for both governments, particularly that of Nigeria. The Standards Organization of Nigeria (SON) told the Chinese in October 1996, "Unless steps were taken urgently to rectify the situation, Nigeria would have no option but to lodge a formal protest with the World Trade Organization."[32] However, the fact is that Nigerians themselves request inferior goods for marketing in Nigeria, and the Chinese also, either as accomplices or otherwise, acquiesce to producing such substandard commodities for them.[33] In the face of bribery and corrupt practices in the country, what is the positive hope of the huge investments of the Chinese republic in Nigeria? Will it be protected or be destroyed for selfish reasons? The fact remains that, with the incidence of corruption in Nigeria, most of these investments will not yield expected results.

Leadership Challenges

Leadership can be seen as the process through which one individual or group of people consistently exerts more influence than others in the pursuit of their particular goals. In Nigeria, the political class is far from being productive, but relies on the control of state structures to amass economic reward or wealth. Obi and Seteolu observe that the challenge of leadership is to evolve a political class based on ideology, which should refocus politics and governance to critical development imperatives.[34] Evidence of Nigeria's leadership challenge is seen in the prevailing corruption, over invoicing, electoral malpractice, kidnapping, armed robbery, massive unemployment, and the demand for outright bribes. Nigeria leaders lack transparency and accountability and as such are unresponsive to the citizens' plights, needs, and aspirations.

This verdict is further buttressed by Amina Ibrahim, senior special adviser to the president on Millennium Development Goals (MDGS), in the second and third quarterly meeting of the presidential committee held from September 2–3, 2009, when she asserted that for Nigeria to meet the MDGS, the country would have to overcome the evil of inadequate funding, capacity building, transparency, and accountability in project executions, which is one of the banes to development in Nigeria. She added that to date, what has been appropriated is ₦321 billion for 2006 to 2008, without a meaningful impact in the lives of the people.[35] The case of plea bargaining justice strategy gave room to administering only slaps on the wrist as punishment for convicted corrupt criminals like former Inspector General of Police Tafa Balogun and former Edo State Governor Lucky Igbinedion, among others. It also gave relief to suspected former governors like James Ibori, Peter Odili, and Akume George, whose cases were handled with little punishment.

More recently, the chief executive officers of the eight troubled banks—Okey Nwosu, Erastus Akingbola, Cecilia Ibru, Sebastine Adegwe, Franics Atuche, Ike Oraekwotu, Charles Ojo, and Bartholomew Ebong—were accused of allowing nonperformance loans in their various banks. The leadership problem has also pushed jobless youth into criminality and kidnapping, which they now see as an avenue for quick moneymaking ventures. This can scare away prospective international investors. The development of states in Nigeria as a result of bad leadership and the misplaced priorities of the people have heightened frustration and aggression, thereby making these investments unsafe for the Chinese as well as any other investors.

Conclusions and Recommendations

Having analyzed China-Nigeria relations, we conclude that it is likely that China means well for Nigeria. However, owing to the aforementioned problems and challenges, the country is not yet ready for further economic development. With the Niger Delta crisis, corruption, and leadership problems, Chinese investments are not safe and Nigeria is not yet ready to accommodate China's investment. It is the recommendations of this work that first, the Nigerian government should address these multifaceted problems before inviting international investors to come in. Nigeria should be ready to toe the line of China in fighting corruption by making official corruption a capital offense punishable by death as a deterrent to anyone hoping to profit from bribery and corruption. Finally, Chinese investors in Nigeria should, as a matter of necessity, be aware of their social responsibilities in their various host communities.

NOTES

1. J. E. Anegbode, "An Assessment of the Africa Union (AU) as an Instrument for African Development and Regional Security," *Focus on Contemporary Issues* (Ekpoma, NAWACS, 2004), 11.
2. S. Momoh, "How Tidy Is Nigeria–China Relations," Part 1, *Business Day*, January 11, 2009, 1.
3. S. Imohiosen, "Politics of Deregulation," *The Nigerian Observer*, May 20, 2009, 32.
4. A. Layi and S. Adenkan, "Chinese Incursion into Nigeria: In Whose Interest?" *The Financial Punch*, January 6, 2008, 1.
5. M. Meidan, "China's African Policy: Business Now, Politics Later," *Asian Perspective* Vol. 30, No.4 (2006): 74.
6. J. Holsag, "Friendly Giant? China's Evolving Policy," *Asia Paper*, Vol. 2, No. 5 (2007): 3, http://www.vub.ac.be/biccs.org
7. M. Madukwe, "China's Africa Policy," 2006, 10–16: http://www.fmpic.gov.cn/eng.htm
8. Layi and Adekan, "Chinese Incursion into Nigeria," 3.
9. Ibid., 4.
10. B. Okundaye, "How Tidy Is Nigeria–China Relations," Part 3, *Business Day*, January 13, 2009, 3.
11. E. Chukwuemeka, "Nigeria Welcomes Chinese Investment," 2001, 11, http://www.china.org.cn.english/fr/21711.htm
12. Ibid., 2.
13. Chinese Embassy in Nigeria, "The Office of Economic and Commercial Department," 2001: http://www.fmprc.china.org.cn.htm

14. Ibid.
15. O. Chinwe, "Nigeria: China's Investments in Country Hit $3 billion," 2008: http://www.nowpublic.com
16. World Bank, "Report: The New China–Nigeria Economic Relations," 2008, 4: http://www.businessdayonline.com.
17. Momoh, "How Tidy Is NigeriaàChina Relations" 4.
18. K. Linebaugh and S. Oster, "CNOOC Pays $2.27 Billion for Nigerian Oil Gas Stake," *The Wall Street Journal*, January 10, 2007, 2: http://wsj.com/article/SB113680307278841473.html
19. Ibid., 3.
20. Ibid., 6.
21. Ibid., 2.
22. Okundaye, "How Tidy Is Nigeria-China Relations" 6.
23. G. Onosede, "Community Expectations versus Health, Safety, and Environment (HSE), and Economic Stewardship of Joint Venture Partners: Finding the Right Balance," Keynote Address, International Seminar on Petroleum Industry and the Nigerian Environment, Port—Harcourt, Nigeria, November 18–21, 1996, 32.
24. G. Jomo, "Militants Hit Shell's Offshore Field in Rivers," *The Nation*, June 22, 2009, 2.
25. T. Obateru and E. Amaize, "Niger-Delta: F. G.'s Revenue Losses Rise," *The Vanguard*, June 29, 2009, 5.
26. A. Thompson, "Power Sector Reform: Giving Jonathan's Roadmap the Teeth," *The Financial Punch*, September 27, 2010, 80.
27. "Power: Manufacturers Groan under 1,658MW Shortfall Spend N3.6bn Monthly on Diesel," *The Financial Punch*, September 27, 2010, 80.
28. Ibid., 15.
29. S. Ephraims, "MDGS: Any Hope for Nigeria?" *The Nigeria Observer*, July 2, 2009, 17.
30. T. Amokeodo, "SHAKE-UP in Banks," *The Financial Punch*, September 4, 2009, 2.
31. D. Adeniran, "Nigeria: Good Business, Bad Managers," *The Nation*, June 2, 2009, 16.
32. D. Omoweh, O. Ogaba, and A. Osita, *Nigeria and China: Bilateral Ties in a New World Order*, Lagos, Nigeria: Institute of International Affairs 2005, 18.
33. Ibid., 17.
34. T. O. Agweda, "The Imperative of Leadership in Governance: The Nigerian Experience," in A. S. Akpotor, et al., eds., *Cost of Governance in Nigeria: An Evaluative Analysis* (Ekpoma, Nigeria: Ambrose Alli University Publishing House, 2007), 20.
35. A. Ibrahim, "Nigeria Needs N4 trillion Yearly to Meet MDGS," *The Guardian*, September 4, 2009, 2.

REFERENCES

Adeniran, D. "Nigeria: Good Business, Bad Managers." *The Nation,* June 2, 2009: 16.
Agweda, T. O. "The Imperative of Leadership in Governance: The Nigerian Experience." In A. S. Akpotor et al., eds. *Cost of Governance in Nigerian (An Evaluative Analysis).* Ekpoma: Ambrose Alli University Publishing House, 2007.
Amokeodo, T. "Shake-Up in Banks." *The Financial Punch*, September 4, 2009: 2.
Anegbode, J. E. "An Assessment of the Africa Union (AU) as an Instrument for African Development and Regional Security." *Focus on Contemporary Issues.* Ekpoma: National Association of Women Academics, 2004.

Chinese Embassy in Nigeria. "The Office of Economic and Commercial Department," 2001: http://www.fmprc.china.org.cn.htm
Chinwe, O. "Nigeria: China's Investments in Country Hit $3 billion," 2008: http://www.nowpublic.com
Chukwuemeka, E. "Nigeria Welcomes Chinese Investment," 2001: http://www.china.org.cn.english/fr/21711.htm
Ephraims, S. "MDGS: Any Hope for Nigeria?" *The Nigeria Observer,* July 2, 2009: 17.
Ibrahim, A. "Nigeria Needs N4 trillion Yearly to Meet MDGS." *The Guardian,* September 4, 2009: 2.
Imohiosen, S. "Politics of Deregulation." *The Nigerian Observer,* May 20, 2009: 32.
International Energy Agency. "Africa: Statistics." http://www.iea.org/stats/region-results.asp?country_code=11.
Jomo, G. "Militants Hit Shell's Offshore Field in Rivers." *The Nation,* June 22, 2009: 2
Holsag, J. "Friendly Giant? China's Evolving Policy." *Asia Paper,* Vol. 2, No. 5 (2007): http://www.vub.ac.be/biccs.org
Layi, A., and S. Adenkan. "Chinese Incursion into Nigeria: In Whose Interest?" *The Financial Punch,* January 6, 2008: 1.
Linebaugh, K., and S. Oster. "CNOOC Pays $2.27 Billion for Nigerian Oil Gas Stake." *The Wall Street Journal,* January 10, 2007: http://wsj.com/article/SB113680307278841473.html.
Madukwe, M. "China's Africa Policy." 2006: http://www.fmpic.gov.cn/eng.htm.
Meidan, M. "China's African Policy: Business Now, Politics Later." *Asian Perspective,* Vol. 30, No. 4 (2006): 74.
Momoh, S. "How Tidy Is Nigeria–China Relations," Part (1). *Business Day,* January 11, 2009: 4.
Obateru, T. and E. Amaize, "Niger-Delta: F. G.'s Revenue Losses Rise." *The Vanguard,* June 29, 2009: 5.
Okundaye, B. "How Tidy Is Nigeria–China Relations," Part 3. *Business Day,* January 13, 2009: 3.
Omoweh, D., O. Ogaba, and A. Osita. "Nigeria and China: Bilateral Ties in a New World Order." Lagos: Nigeria Institute of International Affairs, 2005.
Onosede, G. "Community Expectations versus Health, Safety, and Environment (HSE), and Economic Stewardship of Joint Venture Partners: Finding the Right Balance." Keynote Address, International Seminar on Petroleum Industry and the Nigerian Environment. Port Harcourt, Nigeria, November 18–21, 1996.
"Power: Manufacturers Groan under 1,658MW Shortfall Spend N3.6bn Monthly on Diesel." *The Financial Punch,* September 27, 2010: 80.
Thompson, A. "Power Sector Reform: Giving Jonathan's Roadmap the Teeth." *The Financial Punch,* September 27, 2010: 80.
World Bank. "Report: The New China–Nigeria Economic Relations," 2008: http://www.businessdayonline.com

13 The New Scramble for Africa?
Indo-Kenyan Economic Relations, 1980–2010

Felix Kiruthu, Mary Kinyanjui, and Francis Muchoki

The last few years have witnessed a surge in academic, policy, and commercial interest in the global geography of investment, trade, economic growth, and geopolitical power (Mawdesley and McCann 2010). New trends characterized by the emergence of developing countries as new economic powerhouses—like China, Brazil, and India—can no longer be taken for granted as the new industrial tigers flex their muscles in the global competition for resources and markets. The 1980s and 1990s witnessed almost worldwide radical initiatives aimed at safeguarding national economies (Himbara 1994), and these new industrial tigers strategically positioned themselves accordingly. Among the other countries in Asia that witnessed radical spectacular developments during this period were South Korea, Taiwan, Singapore, and Hong Kong. These states attained global recognition and have since been referred to as newly industrialized countries. They were followed closely and later surpassed by other countries, including India and China, whose transformation was driven by exports and large internal markets.

The new industrial powers of Asia have followed the same pattern as western Europe—of sourcing markets and raw materials from the less industrialized parts of the world, especially in Africa and elsewhere in Asia. On the other hand, African countries have also been attracted to the East during this period, owing to a number of factors that we will explore shortly. However, they have done this hand in hand with pursuing traditional relations with western Europe and the United States. The new attention to Africa from Asian countries in recent times has attracted political, economic, and scholarly scrutiny, and questions have been raised not only regarding the motives for this new interest but also as to the possible impact on the African continent. Most western scholars have attempted to explain this phenomenon in terms of unfettered greed for raw materials and fuel for the rapidly expanding industries. Western media, especially newspapers, have been replete with stories of huge consumer markets ready to be exploited by India and China (Paragiya 1994).

However, while the relations between China and Africa have received a lot of attention, few studies have been conducted to examine why India has shown a renewed interest in Africa and why African countries have reciprocated positively. Moreover, India's engagement with Africa has been analyzed in quite a limited way and almost negligibly at a policy level (Vidyarthee 2008). Yet after the first India-Africa Forum Summit in April 2008, the Indian government viewed Africa with a lot of enthusiasm. Commenting on the extant literature from the West on the renewed interest of some of the eastern powers, like the Chinese, Michael Chege points out that:

> Like the dependency theorists, this literature treats Africans as inert pawns in a big power game. In condescending terms, some of its authors make the case for more Western technical advice on building of institutional capability to enable Africans to weather the self-serving schemes of a cunning China. This ignores the diverse forces of agency among African states, investors, and business groups (Chege 2010: 18).

Our study, therefore, examines the resurgence of India's interest in Africa since 1980, focusing on the specific relations between India and Kenya. The reasons, nature, and the dynamics associated with these new economic relations between the two friendly states are interrogated using a political economy approach. The study lays special emphasis on the impact of the Indo-Kenya economic relations using historical lenses in order to trace the evolution of these relations over the years. It is argued here that Indo-African relations after independence have been characterized by issues that are deemed to be of mutual interest to African countries like Kenya and India regardless of whether they are political, social, or economic in nature. These mutual interests are the glue that has enabled such positive relations to thrive in spite of various challenges experienced over the years.

METHODOLOGY

This study involved the collection of archival, oral, and secondary data, especially on the relations between India and East Africa. Archival data were collected from the Kenya National Archives, while secondary data were gathered mainly from various libraries in Nairobi. Rather than focusing only on the postindependence period, a deliberate effort was made to collect archival data from colonial newspapers, Asian community magazines, handing-over reports, annual reports, and trade reports on Asian activities in Kenya since colonialism at the Kenya National Archives. Oral data were gathered between 2009 and 2010 by conducting oral interviews with Indian and local businesspeople on India-Kenya economic relations. Owing to the lack of records, the number of small-scale actors in trade between Kenya and India is not known. It was therefore difficult to construct a sampling frame for the selection of case studies. The researchers approached retail businesses in Mombasa and Nairobi and asked them

The New Scramble for Africa? 281

whether they stocked imported goods from India. If they stocked goods from India, they were asked if they could participate in research project involving the gathering of data on small-scale actors in trade between India and Kenya. The majority declined and only nineteen agreed to the request. Of the nineteen, eleven were from Mombasa and eight were from Nairobi. Upon agreeing to participate in the research project, an interview date was scheduled. The interviews were carried out at the retail outlets (shops) and the interview went on in between the selling. If a customer came to the shop, the interview would be stopped and then resumed after he or she left. As a result a typical interview took between one and two hours. An interview guide was used in the interviews and the responses were recorded by hand. After the interviews, in the evening, the notes would be edited and cleaned and the information keyed into a computer for analysis, employing a multidisciplinary method in order to capture a holistic view of the dynamics of Indo-Kenya relations since 1980.

INDIAN VERSUS ASIAN ISSUES IN KENYA

One of the conceptual issues that demands attention in any study of Indo-Kenyan relations is to distinguish between the role of Kenyan Indians and Indians from the subcontinent living in Kenya. Given that many Kenyan Indians still go back to India to visit relatives and friends, it is usually difficult for the ordinary person to make out who is a Kenyan of Indian origin and who is not. In the same vein, it is difficult to establish Indian enterprises in Kenya that are fully owned by local Indians or even those that are jointly owned with the friends and relatives in the diaspora or at home in India, as often there occurs an overlap in the socioeconomic and other affairs of the Indian diaspora and those of Indians of Kenyan origin. This state of affairs blurs many issues involving Indo-Kenyan relations. Second, it is important to note that during the colonial times, India and Pakistan were under British rule. Therefore, some of the investments associated with South Asians in Kenya do not necessarily belong to Indians but to Pakistani nationals. However, for the purposes of the study, Asians who originated from Pakistan and started their economic activities in Kenya prior to India's independence in 1948 are still considered part and parcel of the Indian population.

ORIGINS OF INDO-KENYAN RELATIONS

Although a rising trend in economic relations between Kenya and India has been noted since the 1980s, a deeper study of this phenomenon indicates that this has not been a sudden development. Immigrants from the Indian subcontinent have, for many years, played an important role in advancing commerce and industry in the East African region since precolonial days (Himbara 1994). The architecture in Kenyan urban centers and elsewhere in East Africa illustrates a great Asian contribution (Seidenberg 1985). Indian masons and building contractors constructed not only the schools and government offices but also the most imposing business and residential dwellings in colonial Kenya. The unique Kipande House at the junction between today's Loita Street and Kenyatta Avenue was erected before the First World War by an Indian, Gurdit Singh Nayar (Seidenberg 1985). The Shia Ismaili Mosque on the junction of today's Moi Avenue and Biashara Street was constructed by Indians in the early 1920s. Asian building contractors also pioneered in the quarrying operations in Nairobi near Quarry Road and Eastleigh, where the pioneer stone mines were to be found. In the process, they apprenticed many Africans in building trades such as masonry and quarrying (Kiruthu 2007). The work of A. M. Jeevanjee, who later bequeathed the famous Jeevanjee Garden in Nairobi, Kenya's capital city, as a leisure park is particularly notable, especially because the garden serves thousands of Kenyan people. Most of the pioneer government buildings in Nairobi, including the Commissioner's House and Nairobi's pioneer Municipal Market, were constructed by Jeevanjee, in addition to the Indian Bazaar on Biashara Street (Patel 1997). Indian architecture has blossomed, especially in the erection of Hindu temples and other holy places such as the mosques in Nairobi's Parklands Estate.

Similarly, many terms of Indian origin and expressions like *duka* ("shop") and *harambee* ("pooling together") are firmly embedded in the Kiswahili language, which is spoken in most countries in the eastern region of Africa. Bharati (1972) observes that to the Africans and whites in East Africa, the Indian was the shopkeeper (*dukawallah*), as during colonialism Indians had established shops where goods such as soap, spices, and food could be found. People of Indian origin therefore have many reasons to feel at home in East Africa, particularly in Kenya. For example, it is not uncommon to find Indian restaurants in the larger urban centers such as Nairobi, Mombasa, and Kisumu, among many others that sell Asian cuisine. Indeed, dishes such as *Kachumpari, biryani, pilao, samosa,* and *chapattis* were introduced by Indians in colonial times (Kiruthu 2007). As such, these are as much Indian food as they are Kenyan dishes.

People in the region have embraced some of these foods, including the heavily spiced, as their own. It is interesting to know that most of these foods are derived from India and have greatly enriched the East African culture by combining African and Asian cuisine. One author has argued that, in a sense, every time an East African sits down to eat, he is connecting to India and Indians (Vidyarthee 2008). There are Indian malls and a number of Indian restaurants offering delicious cuisine from different corners of India. Bollywood films are popular and the latest songs from Indian movies can be heard in Nairobi, Mombasa, and Kampala as well as in other urban centers in East Africa. Indeed, some Indians have also learned the local languages, such as Kikuyu and Dholuo. Kiswahili for instance, which is the official language in Kenya, is spoken by most Indians, and given that it is also the language of commerce, it makes it easy for the Indian community to interact with East African communities. Consequently an Indian is sure to feel at home in East Africa, home to an over 200,000-strong Indian diaspora.

Bore (1994) has observed that historical relations between countries provide an important base for bilateral relations. In this regard, India shares the Indian Ocean with Kenya, and for centuries, traders from the two countries transacted trade. Kenyan Indians have managed to preserve their culture partly because of the close geographical proximity of the two countries. Indian men in Kenya have been able to marry Indian girls from India, who are then brought to reside in Kenya (Bharati 1972: 10). This inevitably has made it easier for the two countries to forge friendly relations in the global era. Therefore, the current interests of India in Kenya and East Africa should not be surprising and perhaps ought to be understood in terms of continuity rather than being seen as a sudden development. Moreover, such cooperation is also boosted by other factors, including a similar outlook in international relations. It is our contention that these factors, among others, have contributed to the positive growth of Indo-Kenyan relations since the 1980s.

The people of India and Africa are known to have had close and friendly relations for centuries (Jones 2007). The *Periplus of the Erythrean Sea*, a guide on Indian Ocean trade, which was authored by a Greek merchant around the first century of the common era, documents some of the trading activities between the peoples of India and those of eastern Africa. Among the goods transported by dhows from East Africa were ivory and rhinoceros horns, while East Africans imported glassware, cotton, wheat, and honey (Ogino, Kiruthu, and Akala 2008; Jones 2007: 16). Rhinoceros horns have been highly valued by the Asian communities mainly for making aphrodisiacs, while ivory was used to make ornaments and other items for the wealthy. In East Africa, these relations were further intensified when Sultan Seyyid Said invited Indian Banyans to Zanzibar to lend money to Zanzibari and Swahili traders in the first half of the nineteenth century. The advent of British colonialism from the second half of the nineteenth century onward further contributed to more interaction between India and Kenya. Given that both states were British colonies, a number of interactions were inevitable even among the colonial subjects. The Indian Baluchi soldiers from India for instance, were used by the British to fight and conquer the communities of Kenya that opposed British colonial authority, especially along the Kenyan Coast. These included the Mazrui Arabs, who were unhappy with British interference in their traditional succession (Ochieng 1985).

When the construction of the Kenya-Uganda Railway line commenced in 1896, the British had no alternative than to hire thousands of Indian indentured workers to provide labor for construction (Patel 1997; Seidenberg

1985). This was mainly because the British already appreciated the importance of Indian skilled labor. As already noted, Indian skilled labor and traders were instrumental in the colonial administration in Kenya. For instance, in 1891, the Bohra family from Karachi, led by Alibhai Mulla Jeevanjee, established a family business in Mombasa (Patel 1997). This businessman was later contracted by the British government to construct government buildings not only in Mombasa but also in Nairobi. The links established by the Indian traders, businessmen, and civil servants who were seconded from the Indian colonial public service played a significant role in the strengthening of relations between the two countries (Bore 1994: ii). In addition, a number of networks between India and East Africa were created in the late nineteenth century by Indian communities residing in Kenya. These included Sir Sultan Mahomed Shah, grandfather of the present Aga Khan and predecessor as imam of the Shia Imami Ismaili Muslims. Consequently, some community associations were established to meet the needs of the Ismaili Community in East Africa, andsome of these have become global agencies in their own right. One of the best examples of these is the Aga Khan Foundation, which runs a number of businesses and other activities in Kenya (Ogino et al. 2008). Allidina Visram on the other hand, was the most prominent businessman in Uganda prior to the First World War and had opened trading stores in different parts of the protectorate (Jones 2007).

During British colonialism in East Africa, Indians also played a key role in introducing a money economy to the African communities. In Kenya, Indians established their shops initially in the colonial *bomas*, such as Machakos, Nyeri, Kisii, Nakuru, and Nyeri; from there, they reached out to Africans in remote villages and plantations, where they exchanged imported wares for African goods and in the process encouraged Africans to embrace a money economy (Ogino et al. 2008). It is important to note that Indians have continued to prosper in commerce and industry in eastern Africa up to the present time. During the struggle for political independence in Kenya, many people of Indian origin living in Kenya also played active roles.

By 1902, Ali Mulla Jeevanjee had established the *East African Standard*, the predecessor of the newspaper that still goes by that name today (Jones 2007; Patel 1997). The newspaper was later acquired by Europeans, who recognized its great value as an instrument of communication. Indians like Jeevanjee took center stage in fighting against British oppression of the other races through land discrimination and political discrimination. By so doing, they not only taught Africans how to fight for their rights but also inspired Africans to fight for their political freedom. The British had wanted to make Kenya a white man's colony. But owing to Indian political contests with the white settlers, the British issued the Devonshire White Paper in 1923, affirming that the African interests in Kenya were supreme (Ochieng 1985).

Some of the pioneer Indians who participated in Kenya's freedom struggle, apart from A. M. Jeevanjee, included trade unionists such as Makhan Singh and traders such as Patel. Makhan Singh worked closely with other African trade unionists in Kenya, like Fred Kubai and Chege Kibachia, and greatly contributed to the improvement of workers' welfare in Kenya by teaching African trade unionists some of the skills, acquired in British India, they needed in organizing the labor movement. Other Indians, such as M. A. Desai, published the *East African Chronicles* in the 1930s and helped Africans in Kenya to channel their grievances against the British colonial government. Other great Kenyan nationalists of Indian origin include people like Pio Gama Pinto, who participated in the Mau Mau nationalist war against the British in the 1950s. This could explain why, in the postindependence scenario, Kenya was one of the first countries in Africa where India established a diplomatic mission (in 1948), which, after Kenya gained independence in 1963, was raised to the status of a high commission. Nationalists like Tom Mboya were greatly inspired by Indian leaders, especially Jawaharal Nehru, to continue in the struggle against colonial rule.

Among the Kenyan freedom fighters was Joseph Murumbi, a Kenyan with some Indian roots and educated in India, who later became Kenya's second vice president. He was to prove one of the most dedicated sons of Africa. He is immortalized in the collection that he donated to the Kenya National Archives. Kenyan students have pursued higher education in India since 1950s, which has contributed positively to the country's development in various ways. Among the prominent Kenyans who acquired their professional training in India also included the late Silvano Melea Otieno (S. M. Otieno), who was educated at Bombay University and emerged among the most famous Kenyan criminal lawyers after independence. As Cohen and Atieno-Adhiambo (1992) opine, an independent India in the 1950s provided the context for Kenyans to socialize and gather in ways unknown in colonial Kenya. Every year, many Kenyans take training in India and many of them benefit from various scholarships sponsored by the Indian government, such as the Indian Commonwealth scholarships. Kenya's defense personnel, for instance, attend defense training programs in India. The two countries have established a cultural exchange program to enhance their cultural ties, and this has had a positive impact on their economic relations.

A number of factors can explain why Kenya is home to many people of Indian descent. The country became independent in 1963 and altered its nationality law. Consequently individuals of African descent and others whose families had lived in Kenya for some time during the colonial era acquired Kenyan citizenship automatically. However, other foreigners in Kenya, including the Europeans and most of the Asians, were given two years to comply with the new conditions for Kenyan citizenship. This required that Indians renounce all other citizenships, including Indian and British citizenship, because the Kenyan constitution at independence, which was in place up to 2010, did not accommodate dual citizenship. The British government did not underscore the urgency on the part of Asian and European communities to apply for local citizenship at independence. Consequently many Asians and Europeans failed to act on these conditions in time.

Indeed, the majority of United Kingdom nationals opted to retain their status as British citizens, possibly because they were afraid that the African government in Kenya would be hostile to foreign nationals (Randall 1999: 816). Out of about 185,000 Asians and 42,000 Europeans, fewer than 20,000 had submitted applications for Kenyan citizenship by the deadline. Thus, those who remained in Kenya after December 1965 continued to work, but their place within postindependence Kenya was threatened owing to the suspicion that Asians used their economic position, especially in commerce and industry, to exploit Africans. The fact that a substantial number of Indians acquired Kenyan citizenship at the time of Kenya's independence obscures the difference between Kenyans of Indian descent and diaspora Indians living in Kenya. This makes the analysis of Indo-Kenyan relations in Kenya quite complex. However, these historical ties have been very instrumental in driving the economic, political, and cultural cooperation between the India and Kenya.

The political leaders in East Africa and India have also contributed to the evolution of good relations between the two regions, especially since the 1960s, when most African states attained political independence. Efforts of Jomo Kenyatta, Kenya's first president, and Mwalimu Nyerere, the founding father of Tanzania, have particularly contributed positively to the enhancement of good relations between India and East Africa for the following reasons. First, the common approach to politics between African leaders and Indian leaders such as Mahatma Gandhi and Jawaharlal Nehru wove strong cohesion in Indo-Africa relations. India played a substantial part in Africa's decolonization and its fight against apartheid. When the Non-Aligned Movement (NAM) was founded in Belgrade in 1961, a leading role was played by both India and African nations. Second, India joined African countries in tackling international issues of mutual concern. This included cooperation in international forums like the United Nations, the Commonwealth, G-77 and G-15, as well as the Indian Ocean Rim Association for Regional Cooperation. Third, India decided not to interfere with political issues involving the internal affairs of the three East African countries. This approach has endeared India not only to the East African countries but also to most other African states which view India as friendly and respectful to African leaders.

With regard to Kenya and India specifically, the two states pursued policies that resonated quite well after Kenya's independence in 1963. India's support for Kenya's freedom struggle and in the Non-Aligned Movement was greatly appreciated by Kenyan leaders. The Non-Aligned Movement advocated for neutrality in the relations between the western and eastern blocs, which were antagonistic during the Cold War. Both India and Kenya also supported the antiapartheid campaign in South Africa. Ultimately this agreement in the foreign policy made it easy for the two countries to work together even in their bilateral relations. In addition, India chose to tread carefully in commerce, education, and philanthropic activities in Africa. Except in Uganda in 1972, when President Idi Amin expelled Asian businessmen, India's role in East Africa is not viewed as imperialistic, as is the role of the West. Indeed, India has been seen as a source of entrepreneurship and commerce for East Africa. Most of the trade that was carried out between India and Kenya, especially before the present millennium, was through small-scale actors, in spite of the fact that global power is usually mediated and transferred through large-scale multinational and multilateral institutions.

PIONEERING INDIAN ECONOMIC INVESTMENTS IN KENYA

A wide range of business ventures and sociocultural projects were introduced by Indian entrepreneurs in East Africa since colonial times. As we have already seen, investors such as the Aga Khan and A. M. Jeevanjee made large investments in Kenya during colonialism (Ogino et al. 2008). Others, including the late Allidina Visram, had invested all over the East African region. These enterprises have included banking, insurance, schools, hospitals, and manufacturing and have continued to thrive more than half a century since they were introduced. It should be noted that in spite of its economic challenges, India was able to produce a number of entrepreneurs even prior to the 1990s, when reforms gained impetus. Indeed, the attractiveness of Kenya's domestic market during this period indicates that contrary to western media reports, India, like China, did not perform as poorly in promoting economic growth (Paragiya 1994: 205).

In the field of banking, the Aga Khan group of companies has operated in the East African region since precolonial times. For example, Diamond Trust Bank, which was started in Kenya in the 1930s, has been instrumental in harnessing the local savings of members of the Asian community, especially prior to independence, when few Africans in Kenya could afford to open a bank account. After independence, the bank teamed up with other banks to help the business community harness savings into loans especially for small-scale businesses. Today it has operations in Tanzania and Uganda and offers a range of retail banking products as well as innovative business products such as asset finance. Other Indian-owned banks in Kenya include the Bank of Baroda, Bank of India, Habib Bank, and Chase Bank. These financial institutions have played a key role in advancing trade not only between Kenya and India but also trade among the Kenyans themselves, especially in the East African region. Ogino and colleagues (2008) have observed that globalization has made it easier for Asians to maintain their relations with their kin overseas. There is no doubt that their ability to maximize on these diasporic networks has given them a head start in trade relations with the rest of the world.

Similarly, Indians have played a major role in the development of the insurance industry in the region (Ng'ang'a 2006; Ogino et al. 2008). This has also assisted business people in both countries to make headway. The Aga Khan Group of companies, for example, has been instrumental in the establishment the Jubilee Insurance Company. This was initially established in the 1930s and 1940s. The company operates on a regional basis in the East African region, covering not only clients in Kenya but also those in Tanzania and Uganda. The company offers general insurance as well as life and medical insurance and is listed on the Nairobi Stock Exchange. Other Indian-owned insurance companies in Kenya include the Pioneer Insurance Company and the Kenindia Insurance Company, which have also operated in Kenya for many decades. The Pioneer Insurance Company was started by Osman Allu, who had great commercial interests not only in Nairobi but also upcountry in Nyeri town in Central Kenya (Ng'ang'a 2006: 629).

Indo–Kenyan relations have also been promoted through development of the media. Indian companies have invested in television and radio stations in the East African region. While some of these stations have been established with the specific aim of serving economic and sociocultural interests of certain Indian communities, others have a broader focus. For example, the Nation Media Group, which is owned by the Aga Khan Group of Companies, is listed on the Nairobi Stock Exchange, and many Kenyans invest in it. Today, the *Nation* newspaper is the most widely read daily in the country. Founded in 1960, the company has its origins in Kenya's *Taifa* and *Nation* newspapers, which were set up to provide an independent view of the Kenyan situation during the years immediately before the country acquired political independence from the British. In 2003, the Aga Khan Group became the largest shareholder. Operations include a growing number of English and Kiswahili national newspapers, a regional weekly, and radio and television stations. In recent years, the group has expanded its operations into Uganda and Tanzania. It operates several newspapers including the Nation Newspapers in Kenya, which include the *Daily Nation*, the *Sunday Nation*, and *Taifa* newspapers. Others include the *Weekly Coast Express* and the regional weekly *The East African*. The broadcasting wing of the company includes the Nation TV and Nation FM radio. The Group operates the Monitor Publications Limited (Uganda), which publishes the daily and Sunday *Monitor* and operates Monitor FM radio and is also represented in Tanzania (Ogino et al. 2008).

Tourism is another business that has seen the entry of Indian investments in Kenya. The presence of a sizeable number of people of Indian origin in Kenya plays a vital role in the Kenya's economy, which adds an important dimension to India-Kenya relationship, and this has been facilitated by the historical relations between the two countries. A number of Indian investors have promoted tourism in the country by building and managing hotels, resorts, and lodges that contribute to economic growth. A good example of these investments, in addition to the major international Kampala Serena Hotel, is the Serena lodges. The pioneer investment of the company in Kenya was in the 1970s. Today these ventures have extended across the border to Uganda and Tanzania, where safari lodges and luxury tented camps are among the popular destinations for tourists from different parts of the world.

Among the leading industrialists of Indian descent in Kenya is Manu Chandaria, who studied in India and in the United States, where he acquired a master's degree in engineering from Oklahoma University (Ng'ang'a 2006). He started working for the Chandaria Group of Industries in 1951 and rose to become a major investor in the steel industry in his own right, the famous Mabati Industries, which conduct business in the entire East and Central African region and beyond (Ng'ang'a 2006; Ogino et al. 2008: 270). Confirming Indians' heavy investment in the textile sector in the country, McWilliams (1996) has observed that Kenya has been significant for direct investment from India over the years. From about 1965, when a relatively small firm invested in a textile mill in Kenya, a lot of textile industrial expansion was experienced to the extent that by the end of the 1960s, the largest single Indian operation overseas was a woolen textile plant in Kenya (McWilliams 1996: 127). Other Indian investors, such as the Birla Group, established a paper mill in 1975, which by 1981 produced half of Kenya's paper and packaging requirements. However, it has been argued that such Indian-owned conglomerates have behaved just like other international companies, whose main motive has been to make profit. Therefore whenever profits in the Kenyan market decline, such companies have been quick to pull their investments out from the country.

Although the Kenyatta regime (1963–1978) has been accused of not having been friendly to Indian investment in Kenya (Himbara 1994), his regime's economic policies, which favored laissez faire, gave a boost to Indian enterprise. It not only shaped Kenya's economic outlook but also facilitated the accumulation of Asian capital by cementing conditions of private property, extending the basis of an industrial labor force, and securing the provision of social infrastructure for private investment (McWilliams 1976). Unfortunately the fact that Asians in Kenya dominate the commercial manufacturing, insurance, and wholesale trade in the country has set them apart as the bourgeoisie that exploits cheap African labor; this has quite often alienated them from other Kenyans (Ogino et al. 2008: 268). This and the lack of intermarriage between most Indians and other Kenyan communities can explain why the Asian community in Kenya was singled out and harassed by looters during the abortive coup d'etat against President Moi's regime in August 1982.

GLOBALIZATION AND THE EMERGENCE OF NEW ECONOMIC RELATIONS

The relationship between India and East Africa since the advent of globalization has not been interrogated in most studies (Vidyarthee 2008). Yet India's rise to the status of a global power has not been seen as political threat in Africa. This calls for attention, especially in the face of the globalization era in the 1980s when most parts of the developing world were adversely affected by neoliberal policies. The interactions between India and Africa are still inspired by the statement of former Indian Prime Minister Jawaharal Nehru that Africa's significance to India stems from the fact that though Kenya is separated by the Indian Ocean from India, it is in a sense India's next door neighbor. The India-Africa neighborhood concept was again echoed in 2002 by External Affairs Minister Jaswant Singh during the inauguration of the Africa Centre at the Indian Council of World Affairs. This neighborhood concept forms the basis of India's policy toward Africa, which began with support for Africa's liberation struggles and then moved on to focus on economic and technological cooperation after the end of the Cold War. The concept serves as a platform for India's regional strategy, in the much talked about admonition to "look east" for alternative development. In this new arrangement, India would shift its position as Africa's partner in the fight against imperialism to become bedfellows with the West in bringing peace and prosperity to Africa (Vidyarthee 2008).

From the time of independence in 1948 until the early 1990s when India began to be recognized as one of the Asian powers, relations between India and East African countries were in the main based on ideological complementarities and were mostly politically oriented (Vidyarthee 2008). It is no secret that India was lumped by the western media together with the underdeveloped countries of the world characterized by poor technology, underdeveloped infrastructure, and poor gross domestic product. India, like other less developed countries at the time, was struggling with her own developmental problems and was a major recipient of aid. Indeed, in the 1950s, when India initiated a development program, the Soviet Union was regarded as a role model in terms of development, and India followed its development pattern, anchored in planned development (Paragiya 199: 194). Given this situation, prior to India's dramatic advancement in the 1990s, the country had little capital to invest abroad. Its trade was also characterized by the familiar pattern of most less developed countries whose trade is overwhelmingly with the western countries of the world along the pattern set during colonialism. In addition, there existed many import controls in India, which mainly benefited the industrialists and the political class. In this way, India shares many similar historical experiences with many African countries, a factor that its leaders have exploited to the country's advantage, especially in commercial relations (Vidyarthee 2008).

Economic reforms in India can be traced back to the 1980s with the shift in the national government's attitude in favor of private sector business and the abating influence of the state in business. However, real reforms came following India's 1991 balance of payments crisis, when India was forced to liberalize her economy. This makes India's industrial expansion quite different in character, especially compared with developments in China during the globalization era. To this extent, India and Kenya experienced economic downturns during the advent of globalization, and it is remarkable that India was able to turn its economy around to a sound position within a relatively short period. This could explain why Kenya and other African countries have found it easier to identify with India, especially in the area of industrial expansion, as India has inspired the others to see that it is possible for poor countries of the world to make industrial progress.

Beginning July 1991, India systematically liberalized its economy. Prior to 1991, a complex array of restrictions, ranging from foreign exchange controls to tariff rates averaging 120 percent and beyond, characterized trade policy (Paragiya 1994: 193). Since then, import quotas have been withdrawn with exception of tariffs on consumer goods and few intermediate goods. Moreover, the rupee was now made convertible on the current account. This advancement is important given that India faces even more formidable challenges than most other countries owing to its large population. For instance, it is no secret that India is the world's most populous democracy, yet it is one of the few developing countries that have functioned as true democracies. This makes India's experience in economic reform quite unique and perhaps worthy to be emulated by African states. By 1993, most transactions were taking place at the market rate (Paragiya 1994). These developments gave India a head start in economic development and greatly contributed to its economic success. By extension, the above factors also earned India great admiration from most countries in the African continent that were experiencing economic turbulence.

Toward the end of the 1980s, the Structural Adjustment Program (SAP) had become an article of faith with the multilateral donor agencies, especially the World Bank and the International Monetary Fund (IMF), with regard to Third World economies. The SAP advocated by these international donors normally had the following conditions, aimed at helping Third World economies to recover: the devaluation of local currencies aimed at promoting exports; a reduction of tariffs so as to facilitate exports through the elimination of price controls; the encouragement of domestic savings; and a reduction of government expenditure on social services and employment as well as privatization of government-owned organizations, commonly known as parastatals (Ikiara 1991).

A number of factors can explain why the international community began to impose SAPs on Kenya and other African countries in the 1980s. Weakened by the economic and financial crisis, which affected it since 1970s, the continent was devalued in the estimation of the great powers

(Bayart, Ellis, and Hibou 1999: 2). The reasons for this include the end of the East-West rivalry of the Cold War and the beginning of peace negotiations between Israel and its Arab neighbors. These two conflicts had hitherto enabled the African elite to gain substantial political capital and enhanced its importance to the European Union. The combination of this loss of diplomatic importance with an economic and financial crisis resulted in a stark erosion of effective sovereignty in almost all the states in the continent, which were now subjected to increasingly rigorous conditions by both multilateral and bilateral donors. Among the main requirements of the SAPs was the import liberalization strategy. This implied that the less developed countries under the SAPs had to open up their doors to trade with other nations, particularly through the removal of tariff barriers. This, in turn, was expected to generate more competitive and productive industrial growth, as inefficient government-subsidized parastatals would be phased out or privatized (Fatton 1992).

India was among the Asian countries that benefited from the liberal policies imposed by western Europe and the United States. In particular, the vast potential of Kenya as a gateway to Africa, particularly central, eastern, and southern Africa, was fully exploited by India. The trade links between India and Kenya that were strengthened in the postindependence era were further boosted during the SAP era, when the western bilateral partners of Kenya insisted on economic and political reforms as the prerequisite for further financial aid. Following the signing of Indo-Kenya Trade Agreement in March 1981, under which both countries agreed to accord each other "most favored nation" status, a significant increase in the volume of trade was experienced. After the introduction of economic liberalization in both countries in early 1990s, the trade volume grew further. The sessions of the India-Kenya Joint Trade Committee, the India-Kenya Joint Business Council, and regular buyer-seller meetings between the business communities have also played a key role in boosting economic ties.

For Kenya, the opening up of the economy since the 1980s adversely affected a number of domestic companies, leading to their collapse and causing massive unemployment. The clothing industry was one of the first casualties, as direct commercial importation of textiles from India and other parts of the world was now allowed. The result of this importation was the closure of companies that used to deal with textile products. Examples of such firms included the Kisumu Cotton Mills (Kicomi), Nanyuki Textiles, and the Kenya Textile Mills (KTM). These firms encountered a myriad of problems thanks to liberalization of the economy. First, they faced serious difficulties importing raw materials and technology, particularly from western countries, owing to their limited purchasing power. Second, locally produced textiles and garments were found to be expensive and of poor quality not only in the export market but also in Africa's domestic markets (Hansen 2000: 88–89). The leather industry was not spared either. Leather manufacturers such as Bulleys in

Thika, the Bata Shoe Company in Limuru, and Twiga Shoes in Nairobi also experienced a downturn due to the severe competition posed by the influx of foreign shoes. These firms responded by retrenching most of their workers. Those retrenched joined the large army of the unemployed, especially in the urban centers (Kiruthu 2007).

A number of scholars have observed that although the domestic capital was weakened during the 1980s, Kenyan Asians continued to thrive, as illustrated by the fact that they acquired a number of western assets as well government corporations that were being privatized. A good example of the latter is the East African Bag and Cordage Company in Juja near Thika town in Kenya, which was renamed the Premier Industries. Kanyinga (1995) explains this in terms of the need of Kenya's former president, Daniel Moi, to create a new base of patronage capital. He argues that Asian capital now replaced Kikuyu capital and that this enabled Asians to make quick profits through blatant infringement of currency regulations, including holding foreign exchange reserves abroad, with collusion of the regime, in return for financial support to the political class (McWilliams 1996). At a time when indigenously owned banks were collapsing following strict government regulations in the 1980s, the *1995–96 Kenya Fact Book* documented that 70 percent of the nonbank financial institutions (NBFIs) in Kenya were Asian-owned by 1987. This contradicts the argument of Himbara (1994) that the African bourgeois in Kenya was based on state support, given that Asian capital benefited tremendously from state support, especially under Moi, who used the Asians to undermine the Kikuyu bourgeoisie, which was threatening his political leadership.

Nevertheless, Indian genius in trade must be recognized in spite of some of the inappropriate strategies employed by some of the businesspeople to have an edge over African competitors. The fact that a number of Kenyan Indians, including the Bohras and the Oshwals, live in communities has the inevitable effect of galvanizing community support in different sectors and thereby gives them a head start as compared with other local investors. Zarwan (1971) observes that although many Asians arrive in Kenya with little capital, they are able to create capital through family partnerships based on personal contacts and trust. This is perhaps a virtue that other communities in East Africa are yet to master on a similar scale.

In regard to trade between India and Kenya, India's principal exports to Kenya have been identified as comprising assorted commodities and manufactures including home appliances, machinery, drugs and pharmaceuticals, synthetic products, transport equipment, dyed fabric, rice, chemicals, and fabrics. On the other hand, Kenyan exports to India mainly comprise primary commodities. These include cashew nuts, leather and leather products, scrap metal, inorganic chemicals, dyeing, tanning and coloring materials, pearls, precious and semiprecious stones, soda ash, fluorspar, diatomite, pulse wattle bark extract, sisal, and African handicrafts. Trade between India and Kenya reached US$450 million in 2004–2005, which was an increase of nearly 55 percent over 2 years (Vines and Oruitemeka 2008). This dramatic increase in trade highlights the increasing scale of trade between the two countries in the new global dispensation. However, it is also quite obvious that Kenya has been exporting unprocessed primary commodities to India, which are usually bought cheaply owing to the lack of added value. On the contrary, India has been exporting processed goods and therefore has been reaping a handsome profit in this trade.

India's economic reforms, which began in the early 1990s, brought about a significant change in its trade, finance, and industrial configurations and patterns, which have given that country a great advantage compared with others that are less developed and that failed to undertake economic reforms. There has been unprecedented economic growth during the beginning of present millennium, placing India among today's powerful industrial tigers, with the potential of developing into a major power within the next quarter century. Currently, India has substantial capital to invest and technologies for enhancing productivity, especially in the field of information technology and pharmaceuticals. Another area where India has an edge over other less developed countries like Kenya is the existence of a large market for exports. In its quest for further development, India has reinvented her terms of engagement with various nations, especially in Africa, and has utilized its historical relations with most African countries to enhance this new engagement (Vidyarthee 2008: 19). This could explain the increasingly diverse portfolio of investment by a number of Indian companies in Africa, especially in the new millennium.

While some of these companies are relatively small family enterprises, others are large. These include Essar and Bharti Airtel, global giants in the telecommunications field. These companies had managed to penetrate eastern and southern African market by 2008 (Mawdesly and McCann 2010). In January 2008, the Essar Group announced that it would invest millions of dollars in two local projects. These operations involved the Econet Subsidiary in Kenya and the Kenya Petroleum Refineries, in which the Kenyan government has a 50 percent stake. Essar has been involved in laying down the multifiber optic cable connecting East Africa with other parts of the world. This development has revolutionized the information technology industry in the region by making it less costly to transact trade as well as in terms of connecting the East African region with the rest of the world.

Bharti Airtel, an unlisted entity until 2001, now ranks among India's top fifteen companies, with net sales of Rs 42,000 crore.[1] The firm is reported to be the fifth largest profitable company in India, with a net profit of Rs 9,163 crore. The company bought out the Kuwait-owned Zain Kenya, a telecommunications firm providing cell phone and other related services to a large group of Kenyan citizens, and renamed it Airtel in 2010. Since then, the population of mobile phone users in Kenya has grown exponentially. Locally, this has also sparked a tough competition for customers between Vodacom and Bharti Airtel in Kenya and has brought down user charges, further attracting more transactions using Internet-based communication in the region (*Weekly Economic Bulletin* 2010). The use of mobile money transfer using the cell phone, such M-pesa and Zap, has completely revolutionized trade transactions in the Kenyan market; the decline of user cell phone charges has played an important role in this development.

Other large Indian-owned firms have also been active in the East African region, especially in Kenya. According to Mawdesley and McCann (2010), the Railway Technical and Economic Services (RITES), the consultancy arm of the Indian Railways, has been engaged in profit-making projects in sub-Saharan Africa for nearly two decades. Although we may not know how much employment such ventures are creating in East Africa, the potential economic benefit from such ventures is not in doubt. For example, RITES secured a US$500 million contract to manage Malawi Railways.

RITES and the Indian Railway Construction Company Limited (IRCON) also signed an agreement with the Sudanese government in March 2004 to refurbish Sudan's aging railway infrastructure. Other projects being undertaken by the company in eastern Africa include erecting a railway connection to enable Mozambique to transport coal to the port of Beira, from which the coal can be exported across the Indian Ocean. In Kenya, RITES has been involved in several projects including the operations of the Rift Valley Railway, which runs Kenya's railway line. The latter, ironically, was erected using Indian labor during the early days of colonialism in Kenya (Patel 1997). Given that the railway services in Kenya have been underutilized for the last two decades, the revitalization of these facilities has the potential to create enormous employment opportunities, while at the same time easing transportation problems.

Another Indian company that has expressed interest in investing in East African region is the Indian Oil Corporation Limited, which declared interest in investing not only in Kenya but also in Tanzania and Mozambique. In particular, the giant oil company offered to support Mozambique by building a compressed natural gas network and gas-based petroleum plant in the country (Vines and Oruitemeka 2008). Tata, another Indian conglomerate that manufactures motor vehicles, has been supplying not only commercial trucks and pickups but also smaller passenger vehicles in different parts of the continent. Although its vehicles are few in the African market as compared with those supplied by the Japanese manufacturers, the company has managed to penetrate the market owing to its affordable prices. The company even supplied the Kenyan government with a brand of police vehicles known as Mahindra during the 1990s. Tata small pickup trucks and larger trucks are now common in different parts of East Africa. The conglomerate has interests across a huge range of sectors from telecommunications, IT consultancy, and steel in South Africa as well as soda ash production in Kenya's Lake Magadi (Mawdesley and McCann 2010). The Aga Khan group of companies has also invested in the power sector, thus providing essential power that is in great demand in order to promote industrial development. In Kenya, the Tsavo Company has invested in an energy project named Tsavo Power. The Aga Khan group has acquired another similar energy project in West Africa under the Malian privatization program known as Energie du Mali.

Indian firms have also invested in the cut-flower industry in Kenya as well as in the horticulture industry. Many flower farms around Lake Naivasha in Kenya, which export cut flowers especially to the European market, are Indian-owned. Although majority of the firms have local shareholders, the investment from India and the Indian diaspora has played a big role in developing this industry in Kenya. Others have invested in the construction industry. Indeed, the majority of the medium-sized construction companies belong to Indian families and corporations. The Aga Khan Development Network, for instance, operates a number of manufacturing firms in Kenya, one of which is All Pack. The company manufactures polypropylene bags and corrugated carton packaging for a range of goods, including horticultural products. Another successful Indian venture in Kenya is the Magadi Soda Company, whose shareholding includes a significant Indian investment. This is one of the most successful companies in the country with a consistent track record of making profits since the colonial era.

Whether the Indian investments in Kenya impact the economy differently from other multinational investments is an important question. However, it should be noted that the situation of Indian investment in Kenya has not been consistently smooth. The Pan Paper Mills, a Kenyan parastatal company, manufactures paper and other related materials. It has gone through difficult times over the years and was acquired by Indian investors during the SAP era. They ran it successfully up to 2009, when it closed down after accumulating a lot of debt. Similarly, some of the Indian investments in Kenya have been accused of involvement in shady deals in collaboration with some of the corrupt state officials. Many such merchants are diaspora Indians who use their Kenya-based friends to engage in fraud. In 1992, for example, Alnoor Kassam, a former chairman of the now defunct Trade Bank Limited, ripped off Kenya's Central Bank by using fake export documents for which he was compensated by the government of Kenya for exports to France and Germany, which eventually proved to have been fictitious (Nyanchoga 1996).

India has played an important role in the development of health care in Africa, particularly in Kenya. Many Kenyan medics have acquired their training and education in Indian institutions over the years since independence in 1963. This has mainly been motivated by the cheaper cost of sending students to India for specialized training in kidney disease, heart conditions, eye problems, and other medical conditions. Moreover, India capitalizes on its ability to produce cheaper pharmaceuticals (Mawdesley and McCann 2010: 7). The "triple-A technology"—which stands for adaptable, affordable, and available technology—enables the pharmaceutical sector to produce products that are better designed and suited to particular

African markets than those of western competitors. For instance, in 1997, the Indian firm Shantha Biotechnics launched a hepatitis vaccine that it sells for US$0.40 per dose, as compared with the cost of US$8 to 10 for the imported vaccine. Thus cooperation between the two countries has enabled Kenya to benefit from cheaper drugs and vaccines (Juma and Yee-Cheong 2005: 1105–1107). However, this has not been without a number of challenges. For example, the government of Kenya has been embroiled in disputes with Indian pharmaceutical firms over the registration of some of their products in the country.

Another aspect of this cooperation in the field of health is spearheaded by Indian-based organizations that operate in Kenya. Among the leading include the Aga Khan Federation, run by Sir Aga Khan, which operates several health centers in different parts of Kenya, and Save by Sight, which is sponsored by the Lions Group. The Aga Khan Health facilities are also linked internationally through networkwide policies and strategies in primary health care, clinical services, nursing development, and human resource management. The national service companies are working with government health services and other institutions to improve and build effective national health systems (Aga Khan 2007: 20–41; Ogino et al. 2008). The Aga Khan University School of Nursing, which began operations in 1980, provides education in nursing in the East African region as well as offering medical care, including laboratory and maternity services. In 2001, Aga Khan University started its Advanced Nursing Studies program in Kenya, Uganda, and Tanzania. The program provides continuing and higher education up to the bachelor's level to working nurses, allowing student nurses to remain at their workplaces as they pursue professional development. In 2004, the university began offering postgraduate programs in Kenya and Tanzania at the Aga Khan University Hospital in Nairobi and Aga Khan Hospital, Dar-es-Salaam.

INDO-KENYAN COOPERATION IN THE JUA KALI SECTOR

Indian machine tool exports have shown better growth performance since late 1990s. These machines were initially exported to industrially advanced regions, especially the European market, before Indian companies realized the great potential lying in Africa. India is still dominated by low and medium technology, although it is relatively advanced as compared to many developing countries such as Kenya. The fact that the cost of her machine tool exports is far lower as compared with American and European products further endears India to many African countries. Indeed, India's position is threatened only by the Chinese companies in terms of pricing and demand (Vidyarthee 2008).

India's positive attitude toward Kenya's small-scale industries has led to the signing of agreements in this area, something difficult to achieve in relation to the more developed countries. Dinsha Patel, minister of state for micro, small, and medium enterprises, reported that the National Small Industries Corporation (NSIC) of India, which operates under the Ministry of Micro, Small, and Medium Enterprises, signed an Agreement on Mutual Cooperation with Kenya Industrial Estates (KIE) Ltd., a government of Kenya state corporation, in May 2009 (Vines and Oruitemeka 2008). The purpose of the agreement was to enhance cooperation in the development of micro, small, and medium enterprises in both the countries. The agreement, among other things, stipulated that NSIC would assist KIE in carrying out industrial potential surveys and feasibility studies to identify thrust areas and opportunities for the development of small enterprises in Kenya on mutually agreed terms. This was born out of the realization of the enormous untapped potential in the informal or *jua kali* sector in Kenya, which could borrow useful technology and innovation skills from India in the spirit of south-south cooperation (Vines and Oruitemeka 2008).

The agreement also stated that the NSIC would also assist KIE in setting up of business incubator centers for demonstration and training on technologies for Kenyan startup entrepreneurs. The Indian corporation was also expected to assist Kenya through the KIE in developing policy and institutional frameworks for small and medium enterprise development and to provide advisory services for capacity building, marketing, credit support, and technology support on mutually agreed terms. It was anticipated that this collaboration would also facilitate technology transfer from India in specific industrial sectors. On the other hand, KIE was expected to facilitate and assist NSIC in holding machinery and equipment expositions in order to market the Indian innovations in the wider East African region. Both NSIC and KIE would facilitate the exchange of business missions to help initiate technology transfer and sustainable business alliances between enterprises in India and Kenya. Furthermore, they would assist each other in holding virtual exhibitions on their respective websites regarding products and services offered by small and medium enterprises (SMEs), in both countries. It was anticipated that the development of sustainable business alliances and technology transfer between medium and small enterprises in India and Kenya would mutually benefit both the countries. Moreover, the advisory services being offered by NSIC on commercial terms were expected to generate revenues in foreign currency, earning both countries substantial revenues.

The sixth session of the Kenya-India Joint Trade Committee Meeting was held in Nairobi on October 12–13, 2010, in accordance with article ten of the trade agreement signed between the Republic of Kenya and the Republic of India on February 24, 1981, in New Delhi. The Indian delegation was led by Anand Sharma, minister for commerce and industry of the government of India, while the Kenyan delegation was led by Chirau Ali Mwakwere, minister for trade, government of Kenya. The Kenyan minister is quoted as specifically having called for further collaboration in the areas of transfer of technology, support for SMEs and business process outsourcing in information communication technology (ICT), increasing training opportunities, registration of pyrethrum products in India, increased lines of credit with favorable terms, issuance of multiple visas to Kenyans traveling to India on business, and increasing international landing points in India to Kenya Airways, as well as developing ICTs in Kenya (*Weekly Economic Bulletin* 2010). It is important to note that since the trade relations with India are imbalanced in favor of India, the Kenyan government has deemed it prudent to strategize in order to ensure that that, besides expansion of imports from Kenya, India also transfers technological skills to Kenyans.

HOW SMALL-SCALE ACTORS COUNTER HEGEMONIC RELATIONSHIPS: STRATEGIES USED IN INDIA BY SMALL-SCALE ACTORS

Global power is mediated and transferred through large-scale multinational and multilateral institutions. The role of small-scale and middle-level traders, financiers, and institutions is hardly considered in the power relationship brokerage dynamics. They are rarely involved in trade negotiations, policy formulation, or memorandum of understanding (MOU) signing or in the making of financial concessions. The mediation of power relations between nations is carried out with teams of experts, senior civil servants, concerned ministers, and the "who's who" in the business world and chambers of commerce.

Small-scale actors in trade between Kenya and India are nevertheless able to overcome hegemonic relationships in trade between India and Kenya by combining market and nonmarket strategies, such as the use of social relationships both in India and Kenya. The positioning of India in close proximity to Kenya makes travel between India and Kenya very easy. Kenya Airways operates direct five-hour flights to India every day. Thus small-scale actors are able to participate in trade between Kenya and India because of the short distance. The travel distance between India and Kenya is relatively short compared to that of Europe, North America, and China. The travel costs are low, and it is also easy to process travel documents with the Indian High Commission. Nearly all the respondents said that acquisition of travel documents to India was relatively easy compared with other developing countries. Easy access to India means that goods are also priced favorably in the Kenyan market compared with similar goods imported from Europe and North America.

The small-scale actors also observed that purchasing goods in India is easy and there is less paperwork. They purchase commodities from small-scale traders in India, and face-to-face contacts are widely used in transactions. Some of the small-scale actors purchased goods from long-term acquaintances that they had to come to know through trade. A few purchased goods from relatives in India. Transactions were kept to the minimum; hence they were less expensive, as they were facilitated by personal contacts and face-to-face relationships.

Cross-Border Trade Challenges for Small-Scale Traders

As more people enter the informal sector, the face and pace of growth have changed dramatically and the existing policy framework has been inadequate to deal with the changing and increased demands. Moreover, the cross-border traders experience difficulties in the day-to-day running of their businesses. The overwhelming majority of these traders hold visitors' visas, suggesting that they wish to travel and trade legally. No country in the region has a specific category of permit for traders. Most have to provide paperwork and have to pay relatively costly visa fees to enter foreign countries. The traders find these increasing restrictions and demands for documents costly (in time and money), difficult to meet, and a hindrance to their businesses.

Duties paid at the border are a significant drain on the profit margin of traders. They also come with costs to the Department of Customs and Excise, which has to administer the collection of relatively small duty fees against complex tariff schedules. Small-scale traders find it difficult to sell their goods in foreign countries owing to the licenses they are supposed to obtain in order to do so. Intraregional trade growth would benefit from official convertibility of most of the region's currencies at fixed exchange rates or the establishment of a common currency. Currency convertibility would lessen the foreign exchange constraint. Fixed (regional) exchange rates would facilitate joint monetary policy aimed at controlling transactions between the region and the outside world. It would also make it possible to coordinate and harmonize the monetary policies required to avoid inconsistent and contradictory actions and signals.

Small-scale export traders find it difficult to sell their goods in foreign countries because of the licenses they are supposed to obtain in order to do so. There are unclear government policies on the development and protection of the informal sector. For example, it is only large firms from the formal sector that are able to obtain import permits for capital equipment components and raw materials or tariff rebates on duties paid on imported inputs and materials used in the production of export products. Another bias relates to government procurement policies that discriminate against informal operators. For example, only large firms can supply large orders and can afford the payment of security bonds. Finally, small-scale export traders cite finance as a critical problem. They are unable to borrow money from formal financial institutions since they cannot provide collateral. Hence they fund their activities from their personal savings or through backstreet moneylenders, friends, and relatives. Only a small fraction is able to raise money from banks or savings and credit societies.

CONCLUSION

From the foregoing, it is quite clear that Indo-Kenyan cooperation was experienced at several levels—cultural, historical, economic, and political—even prior to the 1980s. This provided the right environment and cultural contacts that consolidated the foundation for the current socioeconomic and political relations between the two countries. Consequently both large- and small-scale enterprises from India have made inroads into the Kenyan economy, especially since the 1980s. The large Indian conglomerates that have been very active include Bharti Airtel, Tata Enterprise, and Indian government–owned bodies. There is no doubt that commercial relations between the two countries have been aided by the historical ties between India and Kenya, which can be traced to precolonial times.

However, the economic relations between India and Kenya do not appear to significantly improve Kenya's acquisition of sophisticated technological skills in areas such as pharmacy and information technology. Thus trade transactions appear to echo the trade between the western world and poor countries in Africa, whereby African countries export raw materials while the western countries export manufactured products. It has been argued that indeed China and India have emerged as strong competitors not only between themselves and other western conglomerates within African countries but have also competed against the few African producers of manufactured goods, since cheap Chinese and Indian manufactured products have increasingly flooded local African markets. Kenya, therefore, needs to renegotiate better terms so that Kenyans can benefit more in terms of skills and technology acquired from the more advanced Indian firms. The operations of cell phone companies in Kenya, such as Airtel from India, have contributed to a better business environment owing to their low calling charges, which have inspired more Kenyans to increase trade transactions using such information technology such as mobile banking and money transfer.

East Africa, and Kenya in particular, is favored by these trade relations because of the presence of persons of Indian origin. Whether they provide skills transfer in the region is a matter that is still open to conjecture. This is significant in improving India-U.S. relations, especially in view of the role played by Indian nationals who have studied information technology in the United States. Silicon Valley in the United States has an equivalent in Kerala, India, and the benefits of this advancement could as well be flowing into Kenya. The use of English in both Kenya and India has particularly enhanced the possibilities of passing on skills. This is unlike the case in China-Africa relations, which is complicated by the failure of Chinese technicians to understand and communicate in English.

This study has established that small-scale traders have made tremendous progress in the Indo-Kenyan trade. This has been aided by the historical relations, the short distance between the two countries, the political cooperation between the two states, and even more importantly the strong cultural relations, given the close family networks of Indian families and communities. Such networks seem to have surpassed even the officially supported country-to-country trade networks. This indicates the need for more studies to investigate the role of informal operators, political dynamics, and social capital in this trade.

NOTES

1. A crore is a unit in the South Asian numbering system equal to ten million.

REFERENCES

Bayart, J. F., S. Ellis, and B. Hibou. *The Criminalization of the State in Africa.* Indianapolis: Indiana University Press, 1999.

Bharati, Agehananda. *The Asians in East Africa; Jayhind and Uhuru.* Chicago: Nelson-Hall Co., 1972.

Bore, Benjamin. "Kenya-India Relations 1963–1990." Ph.D. dissertation, Department of Political Science. New Delhi: Jamia Millia Islamia University, 1994.

Calestous, Juma, and Yee-Cheong Lee. "Reinventing Global Heath: the Role of Science, Technology and Innovation." *Lancet,* Vol. 365, No. 9464 (2005): http://belfercenter.hks.harvard.edu/publication/644/reinventing_global_health.html.

Cohen, David, and Atieno-Adhiambo. *Burying SM: The Politics of Knowledge and the Sociology of Power in Africa.* London: James Currey, 1992.

Chege, Michael. "Economic Relations between Kenya and China, 1963–2007." *U.S.-China-Africa Collaboration,* 2010: www.csis.org

Fatton, R. *Predatory Rule: State and Civil Society in Africa.* Boulder, CO: Lynne Rienner, 1992.

Hansen, K. T. "A Salaula State: Secondhand Clothing and Topography of Consumption in Zambia." *Codesria Bulletin,* Vol. 2, Nos. 3–4 (2000): 61–68.

Himbara, David. *Kenyan Capitalists, the State and Development.* Nairobi: EAEP, 1994.

Ikiara, Godfrey. "Policy Changes and Informal Sector: A Review." In P. Coughlin and G. K. Ikiara, eds. *Kenya's Industrialization Dilemma.* Nairobi: EAEP, 1991.

Jones, Stephanie. "Merchant-Kings and Everymen: Narratives of the South Asian Diaspora of East Africa." *The Journal of East African Studies,* Vol. 1, No. 1 (March 2007): 16–33.

Kanyinga, Karuti. "The Changing Development Space in Kenya: Socio-Political Change and Voluntary Development Activities." In P. Gibbon, ed. *Markets, Civil Society and Democracy in Kenya.* Uppsala: Nordiska Afrikainstitutet, 1995.

Khan, Aga. *Development Network: Imprimeries Reunies.* Geneva: Aga Khan Development Network, 2007.

Kiruthu, Felix. "The History of Informal Enterprises in Kenya: A Case Study of the Jua Kali Sector of Nairobi, 1899–1998." Ph.D. dissertation, Department of History, Archaeology and Political Studies. Nairobi: Kenyatta University, 2007.

Kenyan National Archives (KNA). KNA/VQ/1/54. "Establishment of Nairobi Municipal Markets," 1937–1949.

KNA/C/TRDS/AT/IK. "Minutes of the Nairobi Municipal Council Trading Activities." 1941–1946.

KNA/PC/CP/8/1. "Political Record Book Nairobi," 1899–1915.
Mangat, J. S. *A History of Asians in East Africa, 1886–1945.* Oxford, UK: Clarendon Press, 1969.
Mawdesley, Emma, and Gerard McCann. "The Elephant in the Corner? Reviewing India-Africa Relations in the New Millennium." *Geography Compass,* Vol. 4, No. 2 (2010): 81–93.
McWilliams, Scott, and M. Cowen M. *The Kenyan Capitalists.* Helsinki: Institute of Development Studies, 1996.
Ng'ang'a, Wanguhu. *Kenya's Ethnic Communities: Foundation of the Nation.* Nairobi: Gatundu Publishers, 2006.
Nyanchoga, Samuel. "Asians in Colonial Kenya: A General Perspective." *The East African Journal of Historical and Social Sciences Research,* Vol. 1. No.1 (1996): 77–94.
Ochieng, William Robert. *A History of Kenya.* Nairobi: Macmillan Kenya, 1985.
Ogino, Francis, Felix Kiruthu, and Jumba Akala. "A Critical Analysis of the Social and Economic Impact of Asian Diaspora in Kenya." In Toyin Falola and Niyi Afolabi, eds. *Trans-Atlantic Migration: the Paradoxes of Exile.* New York: Routledge, 2008.
Paragiya, Arvind, "India: A New Tiger on the Block?" *Journal of International Affairs,* Vol. 48, No. 1 (Summer 1994): 193–221.
Patel, Zarina. *Challenge to Colonialism: The Struggle of Alibhai Mulla Jeevanjee for Equal Rights in Kenya.* Nairobi: Publishers Distribution Services, 1997.
Randall, Hansen. "The Kenyan Asians, British Politics, and the Commonwealth Immigrants Act, 1968." *Historical Journal,* Vol. 42, No. 3 (1999): 809–834.
Seidenberg, Diana. *Uhuru and the Kenya Indians: The Role of Minority Community in Kenyan Politics.* New Delhi: Vikor Press, 1983.
———. *Mercantile Adventurers: The World of East African Asians 1750–1985.* New Delhi: New Age International Limited Publishers, 1985.
Vidyarthee, Kausha. *India's Trade Engagements with Africa: A Comparison with China.* Oxford, UK: Wolfson College, 2009.
Vines, Alex, and Bereni Oruitemeka. "India's Engagement with the African Indian Ocean Rim States." *South African Journal of International Affairs,* Vol. 14, No. 2 (Winter/Spring 2007): 111–123.
Weekly Economic Bulletin. "Indian Telcos Follow Global Peers, Tap Mobile Apps Biz for Growth." January 5–11, 2010: http://www.indiainbusiness.nic.in/business-news/news-bulletin/jan5–11_10.pdf.
Zarwan, J. I. "Indian Businessmen in Kenya during the 20th Century: A Case Study." Ph.D. Dissertation, Yale University, 1977.

Part IV

The Way Forward for Twenty-First-Century Development

14 French Foreign Policy in Rwanda
Language, Personal Networks, and Changing Contexts

Céline A. Jacquemin

At the end of May 2010, at the France-Africa summit held in Nice, French President Nicholas Sarkozy attempted to redirect French policy toward African states on the basis of mutual interests and shared goals rather than continuing the previous blanket Francophone loyalty. In the past, France committed unconditional support to any French-speaking African state. Since the end of the Cold War, several African countries have started using more English in official documents; some have even altered the list of official languages by removing or replacing French. The policy of favoring the French language often concealed much deeper personal connections between African leaders and French government officials, as was the case with Rwanda. This chapter examines past connections and potential new ground for improved interactions between France and Rwanda and the implications for the continent. Can France really shift its foreign policy in meaningful ways that would prevent it from reproducing earlier mistakes? What are the articulated mutual interests or shared goals Sarkozy outlined at the Africa-France summit? Can these serve as mutually beneficial foundations for foreign relations between Rwanda and France?

At the end of May 2010, the Twenty-Fifth Africa-France summit brought together African presidents, foreign ministers, top officials, and over 200 African business leaders, all invited to discuss the future of Franco-African relations. That year also coincided with the fifty-year anniversary of independence for many African countries. But was this summit truly a break in the old French foreign policy, as announced? Could France overcome its five decades of favoring all African governments who spoke French regardless of their human rights records, economic interests, or military and geopolitical position? This chapter shows that the Francophone policy has remained central in many ways to French foreign policy. While some substantive changes toward specific African countries have occurred, the primacy of language remains central to interests on the African continent even though recent French presidents have realized that these connections are no longer sufficient

Colonial ties ran so deep that, despite a clear need to address the shortsightedness of French Francophone policy, recent French presidents have simply found a way to supplement the original policy to provide the option to engage also with English-speaking countries in Africa. One of the French strategies to gain new allies rests on France's active support of a new permanent seat on the UN Security Council for either South Africa or Nigeria, Africa's powerhouses. France is finding competition not only from the United Kingdom and the United States but also from China and India, both of whom are particularly active on the African continent. So at a time when humanitarian and military interventions have shifted to more regional allies, France found itself less relevant until it started promoting French openness toward the new English-speaking African elites. Furthermore, France continues to support most of its old French-speaking long-time friends. France may never completely leave its Francophone policy behind because of the confidential access it has retained since the independence of its former African colonies.

ORIGIN OF FRANCOPHONE POLICY AND ITS CONTINUED INSTITUTIONAL STRENGTH

The French style of colonial administration forced both linguistic and cultural assimilation. Even prior to the Second World War, France had many ways of fostering cultural diplomacy with book donations in places where French was commonly used and even establishing French libraries where there were none before. This policy had many deep layers, some that were obviously based on language as the basis of imperial ties and that obfuscated some close personal connections.

After decolonization, France intended to retain power through language, military aid, and close personal connections. Fifty years after independence, a majority of African leaders in former French colonies still retained their close personal ties with French officials. These ties often began when these Africans attended schools, universities, or military training establishments in France. Blaise Compaore, the current president of Burkina Faso, studied at the School of Infantry of Montpellier (France) from 1975 to 1977.[1] Paul Biya, president of Cameroon, received his education from several French schools, including the University of Paris for law and political science, the Institut d'Etudes Politiques in Paris, and the Institut des Hautes Etudes d'Outre-Mer.[2] Lt Gen. Idriss Deby, President of Chad, earned his pilot's license from L'Institut Aeronautique Amaury de la Grange in 1976.[3] Laurent Gbagbo, contested president of Cote d'Ivoire, first studied at the University of Lyon and then continued his studies at the University of Paris, Sorbonne, where he earned his master's degree in 1970; he completed a doctorate in 1979 from the University of Paris VII.[4] Gbagbo is in good company, as Ali Bongo Ondimba, president of Gabon, also studied at the University of Paris, Sorbonne, where he earned his doctorate in law. Even Abdoulaiye Wade, president and head of government in Senegal, who has become very vocal about his opposition to France's military policies, studied and even taught law at the Lycée Condorcet in France.[5] These prominent lycées—high schools, highest states schools, renowned universities, and military institutes—are where most French elites also study. The most notable connection, which came to be known in 1994, was the very close friendship that Jean Christophe Mitterand, the son of François Mitterrand, had developed while at university with Juvenal Habyarimana of Rwanda. The implications of this connection are described below under both the impact on the continuity of Francophone policy and for the assessment of the interactions between France and Rwanda specifically.

France acquired eighteen colonies in Africa (Ager 1996). Its presence, with large resettlements of French people, was strongest in Algeria. Large contingents of French people were also present in the Ivory Coast, Senegal, Chad, and Morocco. Decolonization hit France especially hard: in the span of seven years it lost all its colonies except for the smallest, Djibouti. It lost Tunisia and Morocco (1956); Guinea (1958); the Malagasy Republic, Gabon, Congo, Cameroon, Chad, the Central African Republic, Niger, Burkina Faso, Mali, Ivory Coast, Senegal, Togo, and Mauritania (1960); Algeria (1962); and finally also Djibouti (1977). The war with Algeria depleted France's resources, demoralized its people, and inflicted a terrible blow on its grand French ego.

General Charles de Gaulle was elected president of the French Republic in 1958, amid the mounting crisis in Algeria. From this moment on French foreign policy toward the African continent focused on the importance of the African colonies to the French nation. Short of saving France's imperial control over these territories, de Gaulle intended to preserve at least the linguistic hegemony that the French culture enjoyed in northern, western, and central Africa. de Gaulle understood that France's standing in the world depended on its ability to preserve its strong connections to the African continent. He saw French greatness as inextricably linked to its foreign policy (Mahoney 2000: 17–20). France had already lost its imperial foothold in Asia when it was forced out of Indochina in 1954, and now it was seeing its position on the African continent in serious jeopardy. de Gaulle had hoped that by giving independence to thirteen colonies in 1960, it might free enough troops and resources to focus on the war in Algeria. Two years later, France was forced to acknowledge that Algeria had won its independence.

Yet French foreign policy continued to bet on the special status of the French language on the African continent. A decade later, France extended its influence by bringing into its Francophone club, the Organisation Internationale de la Francophonie (OIF), the newly independent former Belgian colonies of Congo Kinshasa (1977), Burundi (1970), and Rwanda (1970) (OIF, 2011). The OIF has continued to grow, bringing in observer states that do not have large French-speaking populations but that understand the power of such an institution and the symbolism added by new members, such as Romania and Bulgaria (OIF 2011). The Francophone club was not only a circle of influence but had become a full-fledged platform for France's foreign policy.

There are several very distinctive elements of France's Francophone policy. First, this policy crossed parties from the late 1950s to the 1990s (Kroslak 2004), and I would argue that this continues still today, even if to a slightly lesser extent. Second, successive French presidents have jealously guarded their exclusivity over making and implementing foreign policy on the African continent. In fact, instead being handled by the Quai D'Orsay, as the French Ministry for Foreign Affairs is known, decisions about Africa were managed by a separate Ministry of Cooperation. Third, during the Mitterrand years, the presidential hold over Africa was tightened by the appointment of Jean Christophe Mitterrand to run the "Cellule Africaine," or the advisory African unit attached to the president for counsel on all African matters. Jean Christophe Mitterrand remained in charge from 1986 to 1992 (Kroslak 2004). During these years, General Juvenal Habyarimana, who had come to power in a coup in 1973, enjoyed special access and support from France. Habyarimana and Jean Christophe Mitterrand had gone to school together in Paris and had forged a powerful friendship (Reyntjens 1995: 30). This is not the only very personal connection. Mitterrand's son enjoyed with African leaders; notoriously he visited Thomas Sankara in Burkina Faso in 1983, which allegedly may have been one of the actions that resulted in Sankara's imprisonment (Brockman 1994). However, Francophone policy did not rest solely on personal contacts; it was facilitated by a very strong institutional framework embodied by several institutions, including the multiple bilateral military agreements signed with former colonies, the zone of the French franc, the establishment of the Ministry of Cooperation, and the OIF. In the case of Rwanda, the CFA—a most versatile acronym that went from describing the Colonies of France in Africa, to the French Community in Africa, to now the African Financial Community—is not as relevant a tool to assess the relationship between France and Rwanda since Rwanda had used the Belgian Congo franc since 1916. It was later replaced by the Rwandan franc issued in 1964.

French imperialism could live beyond independence by furthering the idea of French grandeur with a shared identity between French and African governing elites (Chafer 2002: 13–15). French colonial officials also had much closer relationships to their African counterparts than was the case in the British colonies (Chafer 2002: 14). Connections that were made before independence continued on for generations when sons of African elites studied in the same state schools, universities, or military academies in France. Contacts between French soldiers and Africans also occurred on the African continent, where the French continued to maintain ten major military bases and where the French intervened militarily to prop up their favored regimes as often as necessary. Chafer reports that, since 1960, between 50 to 75 percent of French bilateral economic development aid was consistently given to its former sub-Saharan colonies (2002: 12). This aid helped to foster the relationship between France and its former colonies, a bond that had been solidified by the membership of all of these countries in the OIF.

The OIF celebrated its 40-year anniversary and held its thirteenth summit in Switzerland in October 2010; it met in the Democratic Republic of Congo for the fourteenth summit in 2012. The Francophone policy is nowhere near retirement despite a perceived decrease in the power of the French language, especially in its western counterparts: Belgium and Canada, respectively. Indeed, during the most recent summit, five new observing states were added and the themes clearly intended to address the importance of this organization in world governance as its first topic. Next, the summit dealt with both sustainable development in the face of changing climates and the challenges faced by the French language and education for diversity and innovation (OIF Summit 2011). This is extremely significant, as even if France has recently repeated openly to its African partners that international relations must be based on more than the shared language, France continues to be perceived as attributing very great importance to the furthering and protection of the French language and culture. Indeed, while three major western powers—France, Canada, and Belgium—belong to the organization, France hosted the OIF summit twice, Canada three times, and Belgium has not hosted it yet. The summit also took place four times in French-speaking African countries (Senegal, Mauritius, Benin, and Burkina Faso), and the connection between the organization and France remains very strong. A good sign came when the French government gave the OIF a very large building in Paris's Seventh Arrondissement to enable the organization to house all its offices under one roof (OIF 2011). All of these actions further support the fact that France has no intentions of moving entirely away from its Francophone policy but rather seems motivated to enlarge its sector of influence on the African continent and around the world.

So is France truly interested in overcoming its colonial past? Or will it continue to struggle to establish new genuine paths based on mutual interests within equally beneficial partnerships with its African allies? Rwanda provides a very interesting and important case study because of the way in which it can more directly test the enduring strength of France's Francophone policy, the power of French officials' personal contacts, and France's will to move forward based on reciprocally advantageous agreements. Rwanda, which originally integrated into French foreign policy because of language, provides a singular insight into French foreign policy on the African continent.

It may appear odd to focus on Rwanda, at first a German and then a Belgian colony, to assess the changes in French foreign policy toward the African continent, but it is indeed one of the best cases to illustrate the power of the connection to the French language and culture in the eye of the Paris government, since Rwanda had indeed not been a former French colony.

Rwanda is also the major actor that, following the end of the Cold War, revealed the French failure and betrayal of Rwanda's people in 1994, marking a very clear need for reassessing France's standing in Africa and the foundations of its foreign policy. Rwanda's government in the last decade has been very openly critical of France's role, which led to a three-year termination of diplomatic relations between the two countries, providing a most useful hiatus to help start new relations based on common economic interest instead of personal connections or language.

FRANCE AND RWANDA

Rwanda became a member of the OIF in 1970 (OIF 2011), three years before General Habyarimana took power in a coup. At the time, French was indeed one of its three official languages. Today, only English and Kinyarwanda remain, although Rwanda has retained its member status in the OIF. Rwanda fell under Belgian control following World War I, when Germany lost all its colonies. It was only in the 1960s, following Rwanda's independence, that the interactions between France and Rwanda started to flourish. Belgium had established many important institutional elements that made France's move as Rwanda's special connection much easier, such as the language, trade routes, and the possibility for studying at a French university for those graduating from Belgian Catholic schools. Rwanda became the first of the three countries to sign a civil cooperation agreement with France on December 7, 1962 (Quiles 1998a). However, it was last to sign a Military Cooperation Accord with France in 1975 (Charbonneau 2008: 62). Military agreements enabled France to send military advisors and troops whenever needed. So how had French foreign policy on Africa remained the prerogative of French presidents rather than becoming simply one more area of authority for the Quai d'Orsay—the French Foreign Ministry? Could we see any substantive difference between how Giscard D'Estaing, Mitterrand, and Jacques Chirac handled their relations with Rwanda? Did Sarkozy truly break with past Francophone policies? Or were French policies toward Africa so influenced by the power of the Francophone tradition that no qualitative variation could be found?

D'ESTAING'S, MITTERRAND'S, AND CHIRAC'S CLOSE CONNECTIONS WITH RWANDA

The myth of France's benevolent project in Africa, once called its *mission civilisatrice*, was preserved after decolonization (Charbonneau 2008: 11à45). Under the pretext of security, France was able to maintain a very strong hold over its former African countries and even to develop new dependent associations with Belgium's former colonies. The Francophone policy gave France a much larger sphere of influence and made Rwanda a relevant partner. The invoking of security during the Cold War curtailed debates about the policies or opposition to decisions by the president. This was the case with three presidents from three different political parties who retained similar policies, levels of development aid, and types of military support in Francophone Africa. France saw its role on the African continent as a matter of personal prestige (Chafer in Maclean and Szarka 2008: 37–56). This followed in the vision that de Gaulle had powerfully imposed onto French identity. Thus French presidents worked at developing and sustaining close connections with all heads of state within the Francophone area of the continent, including some of its most ruthless dictators.

Despite changes in political parties and several different presidents, the power of the Francophone tradition remained, because General de Gaulle—when he established the Ministry of Cooperation, designed to manage French African policy in regards to decolonization in 1961—had created an institutional framework that made it possible for French foreign policy to remain the exclusive domain of future French presidents (Kroslak 2004: 63). de Gaulle had given independence to most French colonies with the exception of Algeria, where a war raged on. This had been an attempt at focusing French military efforts in Algeria, and it was a very clever way to earn international approval and continued support from these former colonies while also focusing on the conflict in Algeria.

France's guiding principle during Giscard D'Estaing's presidential term was clearly in line with its earlier favoring of Francophone countries. D'Estaing was the first to attempt to widen the sphere of French influence in Africa beyond the Francophone countries. He also showed some initiative when he withdrew troops from Chad to avoid confrontations with Libya and stopped the sale of weapons to South Africa (Moisi 1982: 353). Yet the rest of his interactions and policies offered no remarkable change of course. The bilateral aid and focus of France's foreign policies in Africa during his presidency remained focused on the Francophone policy.

When Mitterrand came to power in 1981 it was clear that he shared de Gaulle's faith in France's special mission in the world (Moisi 1982: 347), even if he did not see the state as above its people but shared the vision of France's destiny and place in history (Smouts 1983: 157). Like his predecessors, Mitterrand understood matters relating to Africa as the privileged realm of the Elysée Palace under sole presidential authority (Smouts 1983: 155). Mitterrand openly supported some of the demands by the "Group of 77" to address the mounting concerns over balances of payments, prices of raw materials, and the distribution of power within the most oppressive organizations such as the International Monetary Fund (IMF) and the World Bank (Smouts 1983: 164–166). African Francophone countries knew they could count on Mitterrand's support for more fairness; even when France's position in the world may not have necessarily enabled these countries make significant changes, it provided validity and legitimacy to these claims. Many African countries were shocked when, in response to the end of the Cold War, Mitterrand announced that France was intending to pursue new principles for its foreign policy.

In 1990, Mitterrand, in his speech at La Beaule, proposed a new kind of French foreign policy in Africa that would replace the long-standing practice of the French "right" and "left" presidents based on close economic ties, military assistance, and direct intervention with new guiding principles where economic assistance would now rest instead on support for democracy and good governance (Bowen 2005: 102). Tiersky (1995b: 120–121) suggests that despite Mitterrand's wish to alter policies toward African countries, the only change that occurred was forced by France's economic situation. Mitterrand's government had to reduce the amount of aid and subsidies given to Francophone African countries, diminishing France's role as a colonial patron. The most prevalent case was Rwanda, where France decided to decrease support (Tiersky 1995b:121).

Mitterrand did slowly reduce support for France's African partners. In 1999, when the French did not intervene in the Ivory Coast and when they closed two of the seven largest military bases on the continent, reducing troops by 20 percent to only 6,000 men, some African governments feared that this retrenchment might have turned into abandonment (Bowen 2005: 102). It did represent a very serious change and it seemed to have come a decade after most other countries had adapted their policies to a changing post-Cold War world. However, despite a steady decline in material and economic support from France, Francophone ties survived even France's efforts to alter the institutional framework that had fostered the importance of Francophone principles.

The first institutional reform within the French government as to how foreign policy concerning Africa was to be implemented began in 1974 but was only completed in 1998, when the Ministry of Cooperation became a part of the foreign ministry. Chirac resisted this integration, and while low-level bureaucrats had been transferred to the foreign ministry, Chirac insisted that the "minister for cooperation and Francophonie" would retain a position on his cabinet (Kroslak 2004: 63). When one looks closely at the very slow and incremental changes in foreign policy toward Africa, it seems that the changes emerged out of reactions to several major scandals that forced officials to review policies and provided support for slow reforms rather than changes as desired by presidents. Kroslak cites three major events: the scandal of Elf-Aquitaine that involved top-level officials; the accusation that Michel Roussin had committed illegal financing schemes for Chirac's political party; and finally, the enormous hit France took for its extremely controversial role leading up to and during the Rwandan genocide (Kroslak 2004: 64–67). In France's attempt to increase its influence in Central Africa, Rwanda became important in Francophone policy.

RWANDA AS AN IMPORTANT CENTRAL AFRICAN COUNTRY

In the four tomes delivered in 1998 to the French National Assembly, Quiles, president of the Mission of Common Information, reported that France developed only a late influence in Rwanda. He wrote that it took France 10 years after the Rwandan independence to set up a stable and permanent presence (Quiles 1998a: 19). The assistance that Rwanda received was qualified as "honorable" and "not determinant." Yet the Rwandan government received what Andre Guichaoua described as France's strategy of implantation by providing the elite in power a form of military protection (Quiles 1998a: 20). Robert Galley, Minister of Cooperation from 1976 to 1978, explained that Rwanda mattered to France because it was General de Gaulle who, after independence, had reached out to President Kayibanda in the interest of defending all Francophone countries. This had, in turn, enabled the first connections between the two nations (Quiles 1998a: 30–32).

Rwanda represented an important ally for the Francophone cause in Central Africa (Jere-Malanda 2008: 70). France had always provided military training to the army, police, and presidential guards, but once the Rwandan Patriotic Front (RPF) invaded on October 1, 1990, France extended its military support even further with Operation Noroit (Quiles 1998b: 131–198; Kroslack 2008: 4). Rwanda was seen on the front line against the onslaught of the Anglo invasion as seen by the French. The French thought that it was as important to resist the invasion by the RPF not only because it challenged Habyarimana's rule but also, and maybe even more importantly, because it challenged France's interest in retaining its Francophone influence over the region (Charbonneau 2008). It was this dual loyalty to France's friends in Africa and to its own identity as a Francophone power that led France to hold such a pivotal position. Kroslack (2008) analyzed the role France played in the Rwandan genocide and argued that this was "The French betrayal of Rwanda." She investigated very systematically to what extent the French government had specific knowledge of the impending genocide, the degree to which French officials and French military were involved in the events prior and during the genocide, and the level of capabilities that France had to stop the genocide. The original "Investigation on the Rwandan Tragedy," or *Enquete sur la tragedie Rwandaise (1990–1994)*, completed for the French National Assembly by its Mission d'Information Commune (Quiles 1998a, b, c, d) and many recent works, including that of Krolak, which is heavily based on these four volumes of primary sources, reveal that France had actively participated in assisting Habyarimana's regime to fight against the RPF. In 1993, when Kagame's RPF troops were just north of Kigali, France decided not to engage its own soldiers directly in combat and pushed Habyarimana to take part in the negotiations of the Arusha Accord, which heavily favored Kagame, since his troops had the upper hand in the military conflict. However, this is where the French and the West severely miscalculated both Habyarimana and his government's commitment to a forced democratic transition, which gave the Tutsi 50 percent of the officer positions and 40 percent of the enlisted positions in this newly integrated Rwandan Army (Jacquemin 2003). This fueled the furor of the extremists in the government and the military officers, leading them to support, design, and implement the fastest genocide ever carried out.

FRANCE AND THE RWANDAN GENOCIDE

During the genocide, France mounted two military operations. The first, Operation Amaryllis, was intended to evacuate French personnel from the embassy and all other French nationals following what was a clear escalation of violence after the plane transporting the presidents of Rwanda and Burundi was shot down on April 6, 1994. The second, Operation Turquoise, was a much larger military intervention under the guise of providing a "safe zone." It actually set up a safe corridor for all *genocidaires* and Rwandan army personnel to leave Rwanda and flee the advance of Kagame's RPF troops via a safe passage to Goma, Zaire, now the Democratic Republic of the Congo. Yet both operations came under great fire. Video of how the French military was willing and able to evacuate the pet dogs for the embassy personnel but refused to take with them the Tutsi secretary and others who had worked for the French government for over 20 years demonstrated a degree of callousness that would only be amplified later on, with some of the worst implications of the actions of the French troops under Operation Turquoise.

France tried to defend its failure in Rwanda by arguing that it had been the only country to send troops with Operation Turquoise (Quiles 1998a: 294–332). In mid-June 1994, France announced that it would send troops to Rwanda "to stop the massacres and to protect the populations threatened with extermination" (Juppe 1994 in Quiles 1998c). At the time, French political leaders labored to convince the press and public of the humanitarian nature of the operation, and four years later they were still defending the reasons for undertaking it. Even those reportedly opposed to Operation Turquoise in 1994, such as then Prime Minister Edouard Balladur, responded angrily to criticism sparked by a National Assembly inquiry in 1998. Balladur insisted that France had sent its soldiers because it had a "duty to try to save lives." He found it "revolting" that others who had done nothing brought charges against France, "the only country in the world to have acted" (Quiles 1998d). Over time, these excuses have completely lost their weight and the role of France before the genocide, and especially since the beginning of the civil war in 1990, clearly showed that France had been very much involved and intent on preserving Habyarimana's form of Hutu power despite his assassination in April 1994.

The investigative commission of the National Assembly concluded that, besides saving lives, Operation Turquoise was meant to preserve the necessary conditions for a cease-fire and subsequent political negotiations—that is, "territory and legitimacy" for the interim government (Quiles 1998a). However, much evidence seemed to suggest otherwise: France did not save lives except those of *genocidaires*, which endangered or led to the death of many Tutsis who had managed to hide. French soldiers in sync with local authorities were too slow in rescuing a group of Tutsi at Bisesero, an incident that came to symbolize French indifference to the genocide. On June 26, journalist Sam Kiley informed French soldiers that Tutsi were being attacked nightly at Bisesero, a site of resistance. Kiley located on a map the place where the Tutsi were located, which was only a few miles from a French camp. The commanding officer, Captain Marin Gillier, sent a small patrol team in that direction the next day. According to Tutsi survivors, they spoke with these soldiers, who promised to return in 3 days. The Tutsi relate that local authorities accompanied the soldiers and that, by having come out to speak with the French, they exposed themselves to an attack that, soon after, killed many of them.[6]

Gillier requested permission on June 27 and again on June 28 to investigate the situation in Bisesero. He received no response and hesitated to move on his own authority, as he later explained, because his forces—according to the press nearly seventy elite French troops—might be put at risk he was unwilling to take any action (African Success 1994; Quiles 1998b). On June 29, Defense Minister Léotard came to the French post near Bisesero on an inspection visit. Gillier briefed him on the situation, including the possibility that there were Tutsi in need of rescue in the area.[7] On a mission to evacuate a priest, who was beyond Bisesero, French soldiers discovered the horror of the genocide at first hand: hundreds of bodies, many of persons recently slain. Gillier described this as "intolerable" (Quiles 1998b). The human rights violations were even more obvious, since soldiers discovered neither weapons nor other evidence of RPF infiltrators. The commander of Operation Turquoise, General Lafourcade, declared that Rwandan officials had engaged in a deception to keep the French from intervening at Bisesero (Lesnes 1994; McGreal 1994). French top officers operated under the premise that the Hutu were a legitimate power and the target of the RPF insurgencies, as they had been for the previous three years (Bonner 1994). Confronted finally with the reality of the genocide, these French troops provided protection, food, and medical relief to Tutsi survivors. Some 300 of the 800 who straggled out of the bush needed medical attention, about 100 of them urgently so (Quiles 1998b).

The French launched Operation Turquoise as much to prevent an RPF conquest of the entire country as to save civilian lives. In the end, the French soldiers did rescue thousands of persons, but instead of arresting the perpetrators of genocide, they permitted—and in some cases apparently helped—them to escape (Human Rights Watch 1999). On July 6, the French and the RPF decided not to fight each other. The French government asked the Security Council to authorize the creation of a "secure humanitarian zone" to "ensure that the people are safe from any threat from any side" as a condition for French soldiers to remain in Rwanda. The Security Council never authorized or approved the zone but did acknowledge what amounted to a unilateral extension of the French mandate. The French troops withdrew from Gisenyi, leaving the interim government and its troops unprotected. France had come to accept the inevitable accession to power of the RPF. The French government finally denounced the illegitimacy of the interim government representatives. However, the French refused to arrest *genocidaires* even under harsh criticism in the UN. Furthermore, French authorities allowed Rwandan genocide soldiers to transit through, and even sometimes stay in, the secure zone. French soldiers continued to help Rwandan soldiers on their flight (Human Rights Watch 1996; Quiles 1998a). France had invested so much in supporting the Hutu government and its military forces that even once it launched Operation Turquoise, French soldiers on the ground continued to understand their mission as the continuation of the implementation of the Arusha Accord. This meant to oppose and stifle RPF forces instead of halting the government planned genocide of Tutsi (Jacquemin 2003: 51–119).

There have been many investigations of France's role in the Rwandan genocide (Chretien 2007, 2009; Chretien et al. 1999; Kroslak 2007; Mucyo 2008; Quilles, 1998a, b, c, d). All of these investigative reports agree on three major points: France knew of plans for genocide by extremist Hutu in the Habyarimana government, France provided weapons even during the genocide, and French soldiers committed a wide range of human rights violations from their lack of protection of civilians to individual acts of rape and murders against the Tutsi during Operation Turquoise. With the publication of the Mucyo Commission Report in 2008, one might have expected France to shy away from reconnecting with Rwanda, and indeed, for his first three years in power, Sarkozy did not visit or invite Kagame. Therefore the French president's actions in 2010 marked a major shift in policy. Whether this shift can be seen beyond French-Rwandan relations is the subject of the following discussion, which analyzes the Africa-France summit and the subsequent months of French-African interactions.

TWENTY-FIFTH AFRICA-FRANCE SUMMIT MAY-JUNE 2010

One of the main implementations of French foreign policy comes through every few years at the conference of heads of states from France and African countries. I compiled the summary and translated the titles of each summit to provide a sense of how the focus shifted over time and to show how, institutionally, the Francophone policy had clearly remained central until 2010. Three years after the OIF was founded, in 1973, these summits began, but they were not primarily intended to foster French language and culture. Instead, they were intended to harness political power for France, which had suffered such a blow from its losses during decolonization. France always liked to position itself in a nonaligned economic way toward its African partners, despite France's clear allegiance to the North American Treaty Organization. In 2003, the topic of the summit suggested a first effort in putting Africa back at the center, but the summit itself retained its title of *Francafrique*, its France-centric name.

French Foreign Policy in Rwanda 319

Table 14.1 Conference of Heads of States from France and African Countries[a]

Dates	Place	French Theme	Theme Translated into English
XXV Mar. 31–June 1, 2010	Nice, France	Le role de l'Afrique dans la gouvernance mondiale	The role of Africa in global governance
XXIV Feb. 15–16, 2007	Cannes, France	L'Afrique et l'equilibre du monde	Africa and world stability
XXIII Dec. 3–4, 2005	Bamako, MaliMali	La jeunesse africaine: sa vitalite, sa creativite, ses aspirations	Africa youth: its vitality, creativity, and aspirations youth: its vitality, creativity, and aspirations
XXII Feb. 20–21, 2003	Paris, France	L'Afrique et la France, ensemble, dans le nouveau partenariat	Africa and France in a new partnership
XXI Jan. 18–19 2001	Yaounde, Cameroon	L'Afrique face aux defis de la mondilalisation	Africa in the face of globalization
XX Nov. 27–28, 1998	Paris, France	La securite en Afrique	Security in Africa
XIX Dec. 4–6, 1996	Ouagadougou, Burkina Faso	La bonne gouvernance et le developpement	Good governance and development
XVIII Nov. 7–9, 1994	Biarritz, France	Securite et interventions militares	Security and military intervention (Rwanda's new government was excluded)
XVII Oct 5–7 1992	Libreville, Gabon	La rigueur economique	Economic austerity
XVI June 19–21, 1990	La Baule, France	Prime a la democratisation?	Democratization's reward

Continued

Table 14.1   Continued

Dates	Place	French Theme	Theme Translated into English
XV Dec 14–16 1988	Casablanca, Morocco	*Vers la resolution des conflits regionaux?*	Toward the resolutions of regional conflicts
XIV Dec. 10–12, 1987	Antibes, France	*La dette et les matieres premieres*	Debt and raw materials
XIII Nov 13–15, 1986	Lome, Togo	*Un Plan Marshall pour l'Afrique*	A Marshall Plan for Africa
XII Dec. 11–13, 1985	Paris, France	*L' endettement croissant de l' Afrique*	The growing debt of Africa
X Oct 3–4 1983	Vittel, France	*L' integre du Tchad*	The integration of Chad
IX Oct. 8–9, 1982	Kinshasa, Congo	*Le dialogue Nord-Sud face a la crise mondiale*	North-South dialog amid world crisis
VIII Nov. 3–4, 1981	Paris, France	*Solidarite et developpement*	Solidarity and development

VII May 8–9, 1980	Nice, France	Le trilogue à l'honneur	Honoring the trilogue
VI May 21–22 1979	Kigali, Rwanda	Les relations euro-africaines	Euro-African relationships
V May 22–23, 1978	Paris, France	Securité et developpement	Security and development
IV Apr. 20–21, 1977	Dakar, Senegal	La montee des perils en Afrique	Increased perils in Africa
III May 10–11, 1976	Paris, France	Priorite au developpement	Priority to development
II Mar 7–8, 1975	Bangui, Central African Republic	Le nouvel ordre economique mondial	The new economic world order
I Nov. 13, 1973	Paris, France	Un nouveau cadre de dialogue	A new frame for dialogue

[a]Table created and themes translated by Céline A. Jacquemin with information from the News Archive on the Ministère des Affaires Etrangères et Européennes displayed on the France Diplomatie Website. http://www.diplomatie.gouv.fr/fr/pays-zones-geo_833/afrique_1063/sommets-afrique-france_326/xxveme-sommet-afrique-france_20187/sommet-afrique-france-declaration-finale-01.06.10_82713.html

Nicholas Sarkozy brought a much more "pragmatic approach to French policy," as described by Irondelle (2008: 165). And indeed in many areas of policy, Sarkozy brought about clear and substantive changes. His close relationships to Bush and Blair were at times alarming to French citizens. His many unpopular domestic policies were met by countless rounds of strikes, public demonstrations, and an open show of defiance by the French people, workers' unions, and other groups. Many of these policies were indeed often tempered a bit in response. So when Sarkozy stated his intention to also change the way France interacted with African countries by designing a new type of forum in Nice instead of Paris, this announcement was met with a certain level of anxiety. This was going to be Sarkozy's first summit to unite France and African states. His first departure from business as usual came when he made the effort of openly connecting with Rwanda's President Paul Kagame. In early 2010, Sarkozy went to visit Rwanda and met in person with Kagame (Sundaram 2010). No French president had visited Rwanda since the genocide in 1994, but, more significantly, Rwanda had ended all diplomatic relations three years prior because of France's denial of its role in the genocide and because of the growing number of former *genocidaires* that France was protecting within its borders.

Sarkozy's visit to Rwanda marked a clear turning point in the relations between the two countries, which was apparent when Kagame accepted the invitation to attend the Africa-France Summit held in France in May 2010. The French President stopped short of an official apology while in Rwanda. Yet his statement that "What happened here is unacceptable, but what happened here compels the international community, including France, to reflect on the mistakes that stopped it from preventing and halting this abominable crime," quoted in the *New York Times* on February 26, 2010, went much further than any French president had ever done before. He admitted that France had "grossly misjudged" the situation in 1994 and that it, like the rest of the world, had failed to recognize the genocidal intentions of the government at the time. This was easier for Sarkozy to say than it would have been for any of his predecessors. First, he did not hold any key position in the French government in 1994. Second, he did not have any personal connections to any of the genocide's main actors. Finally, Sarkozy expressed support for punishing all *genocidaires*, even those who may have taken refuge in France. So reestablishing direct contact with Rwanda ahead of the summit and ensuring that Kagame would visit France was a very big step for France in changing its earlier policies, and there were some other symbolic and substantive changes that were initiated by Sarkozy for the Twenty-Fifth Africa-France Summit.

This summit presented emblematic changes that clearly marked a departure from the way France had always conducted business previously. The first change addressed the name of the summit itself while in the past, these summits were always named *Francafrique*, making Africa part of France, dating back from colonial times. For this summit, things were different and

Africa was first in a new much more awkward arranging of terms for the French language to say *Afrique-France*. Yet this clearly showed France's intention to put Africa first. Second, France invited 52 of the total of 53 African nations, which existed at the time. The only country France ostracized was the Sudan because of the indictment by the International Criminal Court of President Omar Al Bashir. France was determined about this exclusion and decided to move the summit from Egypt to France in order to make sure France controlled who was invited. This is very important as it would have given France the opportunity to keep out Rwanda's Kagame in light of the renewed controversy and accusations laid against France. Instead, Sarkozy not only delivered the official invitation to Kagame during his own visit to Rwanda in February but also met privately with Rwanda's president while in Nice.[8] Such a landmark visit and change in tone from France's President ushered in the changes that were implemented at the Twenty-Fifth Africa-France Summit in Nice.

Indeed, the tone and composition of this summit were different. For the first time fifty-two African states were invited, whether French-speaking or not. Sarkozy made a great effort to put in evidence his new friendships with two major English-speaking countries: Nigeria and South Africa. The presence of Abdelaziz Bouteflika seemed to show a slight warming of relations between France and Algeria (*L'Expression* 2010a). This summit included 80 French business leaders and 150 African entrepreneurs along with trade union organizations. Of the 52 African states invited, 38 sent heads of state while others sent high-level government representatives. Finally, the European Union, the OIF, the UN Food and Agriculture Organization, the African Union Commission, and the World Bank each also had a seat at the table. The UN General Secretary Ban Ki-Moon attended the summit, making it one of the most important for the African continent in decades. The Elysée Palace had announced that no major international problem could be resolved without a dialogue with Africans; this assumed that African leaders had an important place in international institutions such as the UN or the G20.[9] However, to what extent was this summit to usher in a new set of foundational principles beyond the Francophone policy and to what extent could it really not simply name Africa first in titles but give African countries equal standing in the world? Was it all rhetorical? Or have substantive changes already been implemented? Was France truly giving its Anglophone African friends a new role at the heart of its foreign policy and not only at the heart of the summit?

CONCLUSION: GENUINE PARTNERSHIPS OR FEAR OF ADVANCING INTERNATIONAL COMPETITION IN AFRICA

The skeptics were rewarded by France's typical favoring of only its closest African Francophone partners for the state dinner given on July 13, 2010, on the eve of France's Bastille Day celebration. Leaders from thirteen countries (Benin, Burkina Faso, Cameroon, the Central African Republic, The Republic of Congo, the Ivory Coast, Gabon, Mali, Mauritania, Niger, Senegal, Chad, and Togo) sat down to dinner with Sarkozy. The only one who had declined the invitation was Laurent Gbagbo, who was unhappy with France's lack of support for his continued holding onto power (*L'Expression* 2010c). Some of the human rights organizations pointed to this event and especially to the inclusion of African soldiers in the Military March in Paris on Bastille Day as a continuation of the too familiar Francophone policy favoring dictators and human rights violators. Yet the French government vehemently denied that this provided such evidence. Instead, former Minister Jacques Toubon, in charge of the festivities for the fiftieth anniversary of African independence, offered a different analysis. He suggested that the traditional military march on the Champs Elysées for Bastille Day was to honor those soldiers who had fought on behalf of France (*L'Expression* 2010c). Yet, some on the African continent were also very critical and saw France doing business as usual by favoring countries with which it had imperial ties. The Algerian Abdelhamid Mehri argued that reconciliation with France could not be possible or effective as long as France continued to glorify colonialism (*L'Expression* 2010d).

Taylor and Williams (2004) wrote that Africa remains in the forefront of world politics even if the media only sporadically focuses on tragic events such as war, genocide, and natural disasters. To more openly pursue the inclusion of African countries in all major international decisions, France has been very proactive in advocating for Africa to be given a stronger role in many of the most powerful international organizations. France is the only power on the UN Security Council that is actively promoting the possibility of giving Africa a permanent seat. Yet in many ways this is very cheap diplomacy where France can advocate for something that is unlikely to happen, as all reforms of the Security Council have been blocked since its inception while it legitimizes the demand by African powerhouses like South Africa and Nigeria to be given their rightful place at the world table.

What are some of the motivations behind France's renewed interest in Africa? Competition from the United States and English-speaking economic partners has become fierce. Is France really honest about equal partnership or simply scared by the competition it faces from China and others in areas that were previously its exclusive parts of the African continent? The competition between France and the United States for influence in Africa has become more visible, especially following the emergence of new English-speaking elites who, thanks to their well-trained guerrilla forces, have toppled dictators and are pushing for more "responsive and accountable" governments without necessarily intending fully democratic ones (Schraeder 2000: 418). This is the case with Afwerki in Eritrea, Zenawi in Ethiopia, Museveni in Uganda, and Kagame in Rwanda.

One can also notice a transformation in the attitudes of France and other global powers toward military and humanitarian intervention. There has been a shift from relying on western powers to expecting participation in humanitarian or military missions by regional neighbors on the African continent. The countries listed above, plus Nigeria and South Africa, have been at the forefront of most recent interventions (Schraeder 2000: 416–418). In the case of Rwanda, things became more complicated, as the government once praised for halting the 1994 genocide has now come under increasing fire for its contentious role within the borders of the Democratic Republic of Congo and for minimizing political opposition within its own borders. Sarkozy's visit to Rwanda in 2010 and the invitation of Kagame to the Africa-France summit openly mended diplomatic relations. The substantive changes made to French foreign policy do not intend to erase the Francophone principle but instead are meant to supplement it by including new opportunities for connecting with non-Francophone African countries. One cannot deny that the Francophone tradition still remains the main foundation of the relationship between France and its former colonies. As long as France understands that its own standing in the world is based on its standing in Africa, it will be difficult for many top French officials not to want to play the Francophone card.

Despite the end of the Cold War, a third wave of democratization, and many other changes in the world, the importance of language in the French circles has remained an essential component to understand the continuity between France foreign policy over time and African countries. One cannot deny that the links that were established during colonial times and were nurtured after decolonization have survived despite the end of the Cold War. Even when we have seen a gradual distancing from autocratic leaders like Laurent Gbagbo, France was not as ready or as swift to condemn or attack Gbagbo as it was to attack Lybia's Gadhaffi. The Francophone association has remained more of a close-knit club for French-speaking friends that degenerated into a phony policy of closeness with France. Over time, fierce competition for access to African resources and the emerging markets from the United Kingdom, the United States, and new actors such as China and India have forced French presidents to realize the urgent need to supplement the Francophone policy. This can help explain the tenacity of French connections and the occasional deviations from old habits.

NOTES

1. http://saharanvibe.blogspot.com/2007/07/blaise-compaore-burkina.html
2. http://www.notablebiographies.com/newsmakers2/2006-A-c/BiyaPaul.html#ixzz1EWCqa1zA
3. http://www.answers.com/topic/idriss-d-by#ixzz1EWDWqOLq
4. http://www.encyclopedia.com/doc/1G2-3430900033.html

5. http://news.bbc.co.uk/2/hi/africa/8238860.stm and http://www.africansuccess.org/visuFiche.php?id=68&lang=en
6. Gillier, perhaps seeking to preempt questions about why he did not act on information from the journalists, describes the encounter with misleading vagueness and says he brought these officials for intelligence purposes (Quiles, 1998: 404). African Rights, *Resisting Genocide*, Bisesero, April–June 1994, Witness no. 8, 61–64.
7. Raymond Bonner, "Grisly Discovery in Rwanda Leads French to Widen Role," *New York Times*, July 1, 1994; Corine Lesnes, "M. *Léotard craint de nouvelles difficultés pour le dispositif 'Turquoise,'*" *Le Monde*, July 1, 1994. Asked twice to comment on the accuracy of this account, Mr. Léotard replied that it would be inappropriate to resume debate on this "aid operation whose results have since enjoyed undisputed international recognition." François Léotard to Catherine Choquet, FIDH, September 25, 1996 (Quiles 1998c).
8. BBC's Geoffrey Mutagoma gave Focus on Africa's Peter Ndoro more details with an excerpt of Sarkozy's speech in Rwanda on February 25, 2010, 17:31 GMT, on http://www.bbc.co.uk/worldservice/africa/2010/02/100225_rwanda.shtml
9. My translation from the quote in *L'Expression* of May 31, 2010: *On ne pourra résoudre aucun problème international majeur sans parler aux africains. Cela suppose qu'ils aient une place juste dans les institutions internationales* (ONU, G20).

REFERENCES

African Success. Agence France Presse. "Des Forces du FPR Seraient Parvenus Jusqu'au Lac Kivu." *169 Agence France Presse*. BQA No. 14245. June 30, 1994.
Adelman, Howard. "Humanitarian and Conflict-Oriented Early Warning: Historical Background Sketch." In K. van Walraven, ed. *Early Warning and Conflict Prevention: Limitations and Possibilities*. The Hague: Kluwer Law International, 1998.
African Rights (Organization). *Resisting Genocide: Bisesero, April-June 1994*. London: African Rights, 1998.
Ager, Dennis E. *"Francophonie" in the 1990's: Problems and Opportunities*. Clevedon: Multilingual Matters, 1996: http://www.netlibrary.com/urlapi.asp?action=summary&v=1&bookid=16735
Amuwo, Kunle. "France and the Economic Integration Project in Francophone Africa." *African Journal of Political Science*, Vol. 4, No. 1 (1999):1–20.
Banerjee, Debdas. *Globalisation, Industrial Restructuring, and Labour Standards: Where India Meets the Global*. New Delhi: Sage Publications, 2005.
Barbier, Edward. *Natural Resources and Economic Development*. Cambridge, UK: Cambridge University Press, 2005.
Berman, Bruce, Dickson Eyoh, and Will Kymlicka. *Ethnicity & Democracy in Africa*. Oxford, UK: James Currey, 2004.
Bonner, Raymond. "Grisly Discovery in Rwanda Leads French to Widen Role." *New York Times* (July 1, 1994). http://www.nytimes.com/1994/07/01/world/grisly-discovery-in-rwanda-leads-french-to-widen-role.html.
Bowen, Norman. "Multilateralism, Multipolarity, and Regionalism: The French Foreign Policy Discourse." *Mediterranean Quarterly*, Vol. 16, No. 1 (2005):94–116.

———. "France, Europe, and the Mediterranean in a Sarkozy Presidency." *Mediterranean Quarterly*, Vol. 18, No. 4 (2007):1–16.
BBC (British Broadcasting Corporation). "Sarkozy in Rwanda." *British Broadcasting Corporation*, February 25, 2010. http://bbc.co.uk/worldservice/africa/2010/02/100225_rwanda.shtml
Brockman, Norbert C. *An African Biographical Dictionary*. Denver, CO: ABC-CLIO, 1994.
Brosius, Peter J., Anna Lowenhaupt Tsing, and Charles Zerner. *Communities and Conservation: Histories and Politics of Community-Based Natural Resource Management*. Walnut Creek, CA: Alta Mira Press, 2005.
Chafer, Tony. *The End of Empire in French West Africa: France's Successful Decolonization?* Oxford, UK: Berg, 2002.
Charbonneau, Bruno. *France and the New Imperialism: Security Policy in sub-Saharan Africa*. Aldershot, UK: Ashgate, 2008.
Chrétien, Jean-Pierre. *Burundi, l'histoire retrouvée: 25 ans de métier d'historien en Afrique*. Paris: Karthala, 1993.
———. *The Great Lakes of Africa: Two Thousand Years of History*. New York: Zone Books, 2006.
Chrétien, Jean-Pierre and Richard Banegas. *The Recurring Great Lakes Crisis: Identity, Violence and Power*. London: Hurst, 2008.
Crook, Malcolm, et al. "Book Reviews and Short Notices." *Modern & Contemporary France* Vol. 17, No. 1 (2009):83–121.
Daley, Patricia. "The Role of France in the Rwandan Genocide—By Daniela Kroslak." *Journal of the Royal Anthropological Institute*, Vol. 16, No. 3 (2010): 696–698.
de Freitas Barbosa, Alexandre, Thais Narciso, and Marina Biancalana. "Brazil in Africa: Another Emerging Power in the Continent?" *Politikon: South African Journal of Political Studies* Vol. 36, No. 1 (2009):59–86.
Des Forges, Alison Liebhafsky. *"Leave None To Tell The Story": Genocide in Rwanda*. New York: Human Rights Watch, 1999.
Destexhe, Alain, and Laure Delcros. *Rwanda: essai sur le génocide*. Bruxelles: Ed. Complexe, 1994.
Dramé, Patrick-Papa. *L'impérialisme colonial français en Afrique: enjeux et impacts de la défense de l'AOF, 1918–1940*. Paris: Harmattan, 2007.
Du Preez, Wilhelmus Petrus. *Genocide: The Psychology of Mass Murder*. London: Boyars/Bowerdean, 1994.
Editor's Note. *Journal of Cold War Studies*, Vol. 2, No. 3 (2000):1–3.
Eide, Trine. "The Role of France in the Rwandan Genocide, by Daniela Kroslak." *African Affairs*, Vol. 109, No. 434 (2010):169–171.
Englund, Harri, and Francis B. Nyamnjoh. *Rights and the Politics of Recognition in Africa*. London: Zed Books, 2004.
Exploring Africa. "Unit Two: Studying Africa Through the Social Studies": http://exploringafrica.matrix.msu.edu/teachers/curriculum/m8/map2.php
French Embassy in Australia. "25th France and Africa Summit: Final Declaration." Last modified June 1, 2010: http://www.ambafrance-au.org/france_australie/spip.php?article3815
French Embassy in the United Kingdom."2010 Africa-France Summit": http://www.ambafrance-uk.org/France-Africa-Summit-conclusions.html
Fabricius, Christo, Eddie Koch, Stephen Turner, and Hector Magome. *Rights Resources and Rural Development: Community-based Natural Resource Management in Southern Africa*. London: Earthscan, 2004: http://www.UCM.eblib.com/EBLWeb/patron?target=patron&extendedid=P_429918_0&
"France/Africa: Remaking an Old Relationship." *Africa Confidential*, Vol. 50, No. 18 (2009):4–5.

Fontaine, Andre. "What Is French Policy?" *Foreign Affairs,* Vol. 45, No. 1 (1966): 58–76.
Fretwell, J. 1991. "Western Europe." *International Affairs,* Vol. 67, No. 4 (1991): 805.
Friguglietti, James. "Three Guides to Research in Paris." *French Historical Studies,* Vol. 14, No. 2 (1985):269–273.
Heidenrich, John G. *How to Prevent Genocide: a Guide for Policymakers, Scholars, and the Concerned Citizen.* Westport, CT: Praeger, 2001.
Holslag, Jonathan. "The New Scramble for Africa." *New Presence: The Prague Journal of Central European Affairs,* Vol. 9, No. 2 (2007):23–24.
Human Rights Watch. "The Rwandan Patriotic Front 1999": http://www.hrw.org/hrw/reports/1999/rwanda/Geno15-8-02.htm
Irondelle, Bastien. "European Foreign Policy: The End of French Europe?" *Journal of European Integration,* Vol. 30, No. 1 (2008):153–168.
Jacquemin, Celine Andree. "Human Rights Crises and International Response: Framing Rwanda and Kosovo." Ph.D. dissertation. Irvine, CA: University of California, 2003.
———. "Allied against All Odds to Fight Genocide: How Far Has the U.S. Come?" *Revista Espaco Academico,* November 2008: http://www.espacoacademico.com.br/090/90esp_jacquemin_ing.htm\
Jere-Malanda, Regina. "Rwanda Genocide Haunts France Again." *New African,* Vol. 471 (2008): 70.
Jones, Adam. *Genocide: A Comprehensive Introduction.* London: Routledge, 2006.
Jong, Lammert de. *Extended Statehood in the Caribbean: Paradoxes of Quasi Colonialism, Local Autonomy and Extended Statehood in the USA, French, Dutch and British Caribbean.* Amsterdam: Rozenberg, 2006.
Juppe, Alain. *Conseil Affaires Generales—Interview du Ministre des Affaires Etrangeres Alain Juppe aux Radios Francaises.* In United Nations. *The United Nations and Rwanda, 1993–1996.* New York: United Nations, Department of Public Information, 1996.
Kroslak, Daniela. "France Policy towards Africa: Continuity or Change?" In Ian Taylor and Paul Williams, eds. *Africa in International Politics: External Involvement on the Continent.* London: Routledge, 2004.
———. *The Role of France in the Rwandan Genocide: The French Betrayal of Rwanda.* London: Hurst, 2007.
Lesnes, Corine. "M. Léotard craint de nouvelles difficultés pour le dispositif 'Turquoise'." *Le Monde,* July 1, 1994. http://www.lemonde.fr/cgi-bin/ACHATS/acheter.cgi?offre=ARCHIVES&type_item=ART_ARCH_30J&objet_id=330914&xtmc=m_leotard_craint_de_nouvelles_difficultes_pour_le_dispositif_turquoise&xtcr=1.
L'Expression. « *Sommet France-Afrique: 38 dirigeants africains pour parler business et stabilite.*" *L' Expression,* May 31, 2010a: http://www.lexpressiondz.com/internationale/78707-38-dirigeants-africains-pour-parler-business-et-stabilit%C3%A9.html.
———. "*Un coup d'épée dans l'eau.*" *L' Expression,* June 3, 2010b: http://www.lexpressiondz.com/chroniques/analyses_du_professeur_chitour/135423-un-coup-d-epee-dans-l-eau.html.
———. "*L'invitation a l'Afrique contestee.*" *L' Expression,* July 12, 2010c: http://www.lexpressiondz.com/chroniques/analyses_du_professeur_chitour/85440-L%E2%80%99ing%C3%A9rence-continuelle-de-l%E2%80%99Occident.html
———. "*Mehri pose les conditions d'une reconcillation.*" *L'Expression,* July 19, 2010d: http://www.lexpressiondz.com/actualite/137619-mehri-pose-les-defis-de-l-avenir.html.

Lumumba-Kasongo, Tukumbi. *Liberal Democracy and Its Critics in Africa*. Dakar: CODESRIA Books, 2005.
Lüthy, Herbert. "de Gaulle: Pose and Policy." *Foreign Affairs* Vol. 43, No. 4 (1965): 561–573.
Maack, Mary Niles."Books and Libraries as Instruments of Cultural Diplomacy in Francophone Africa during the Cold War." *Libraries and Amp: Culture,* Vol. 36, No. 1 (2001): 58–86.
Maclean, Mairi and Joseph Szarka. *France on the World Stage: Nation State Strategies in the Global Era.* Basingstoke, UK: Palgrave Macmillan, 2008.
Mahoney, Daniel J. *De Gaulle Statesmanship, Grandeur, and Modern Democracy.* New Brunswick, NJ: Transaction Publishers, 2000.
McGreal, Maurice. *A Noble Chance: One Pilot's Life.* Wellington, New Zealand: M. McGreal, 1994.
McKinley, James C. "Firing Squads Execute 22 Convicted of Genocide in Rwanda." *Times News Services,* April 25, 1998:
Melvern, Linda. *A People Betrayed: the Role of the West in Rwanda's Genocide.* London: Zed Books, 2000.
Moïsi, Dominique. "Mitterrand's Foreign Policy: The Limits of Continuity." *Foreign Affairs* Vol. 60, No. 2 (1982): 347–357.
Moravcsik, Andrew. "De Gaulle Between Grain and Grandeur: The Political Economy of French EC Policy, 1958–1970 (Part 2)." *Journal of Cold War Studies* Vol. 2, No. 3 (2000): 4–68.
Mucyo, Jean de Dieu. 2008. *Commission nationale independante charge de rassembler les elements de prevue montrant l'implication de l'Etat francais dans la preparation et l'execution du genocide perpetre au Rwanda en 1994.* Ministère de la Justice du Rwanda.
Naidu, Sanusha, Lucy Corkin, and Hayley Herman. 2009. China's (Re)-Emerging Relations with Africa: Forging a New Consensus?. Politikon: South African Journal of Political Studies. 36, 1 (2009): 87–115: http://www.informaworld.com/10.1080/02589340903155419.
Nasong'o, Shadrack Wanjala, and Godwin Rapando Murunga. "Lack of Consensus on Constitutive Fundamentals: Roots of the Sudanese Civil War and Prospects for Settlement." African & Asian Studies, 4, ½ (2005): 51–82.
Nasong'o, Shadrack Wanjala. *Contending Political Paradigms in Africa: Rationality and the Politics of Democratization in Kenya and Zambia.* New York: Routledge, 2005.
Newbury, Catharine. *The Cohesion of Oppression: Clientship and Ethnicity in Rwanda, 1860–1960.* New York: Columbia University Press, 1988.
Nhema, Alfred G. *The quest for peace in Africa: transformations, democracy and public policy.* Addis Ababa, Ethiopia: OSSREA, 2004.
Nyankanzi, Edward L. *Genocide: Rwanda and Burundi.* Rochester, VT: Schenkman Books, 1998.
OIF (Organisation Internationale de la Francophonie). "*Le monde de la Francophonie*": http://www.francophonie.org/-Etats-et-gouvernements-.html
OIF Summit (Organisation Internationale de la Francophonie). "*Sommet de la Francophonie.*" *Le Sommet de l'Organisation Internationale de la Francophonie 2008–2011 & Rwanda*: http://www.francophonie.org/Le-Sommet.html
Pedaliu, Effie G. H. ""A Sea of Confusion": The Mediterranean and Détente, 1969–1974." Diplomatic History, 33, 4 (2009): 735–750. Power, Samantha. *A Problem from Hell: America and the Age of Genocide.* New York: Basic Books, 2002.
Quilès, Paul, Pierre Brana, and Bernard Cazeneuve. *Enquête sur la tragédie rwandaise (1990–1994): rapport d'information. Tome II, Annexes.* Paris: Assemblée nationale, 1998a.

———. *Enquête sur la tragédie rwandaise (1990–1994): rapport d'information. Tome I, Rapport.* Paris: Assemblée nationale, 1998b.
———. *Enquête sur la tragédie rwandaise (1990–1994): rapport d'information. Tome III, Auditions. Part I.* Paris: Assemblée nationale, 1998c.
———. *Enquête sur la tragédie rwandaise (1990–1994): rapport d'information. Tome III, Auditions. Part II.* Paris: Assemblée nationale, 1998d.
Reyntjens, Filip. *L'Afrique des Grands Lacs en Crise: Rwanda, Burundi, 1988–1994, Les Afriques.* Paris:Karthala, 1994.
Reyntjens, Filip. *Burundi: breaking the cycle of violence.* London: Minority Rights Group, 1995.
Risse-Kappen, Thomas. *Bringing Transnational Relations Back In: Non-State Actors, Domestic Structures, and International Institutions.* Cambridge, UK: Cambridge University Press, 1995.
Ross, George, Stanley Hoffmann, and Sylvia Malzacher. *The Mitterrand Experiment: Continuity and Change in Modern France.* New York: Oxford University Press, 1987.
Rwanda Embassy. "Country Information 1999": http://www.rwandemb.org/info/geninfo.htm
Salhi, Kamal. *Francophone Post-Colonial Cultures: Critical Essays.* Lanham, MD: Lexington Books, 2003.
Schraeder, Peter J. "Cold War to Cold Peace: Explaining U.S.-French Competition in Francophone Africa." *Political Science Quarterly,* 115, 3 (2000): 395.
Smouts, Marie-Claude. 1983. "The External Policy of François Mitterrand." International Affairs (Royal Institute of International Affairs 1944), 59, 2(1983): 155–167.
Sundaram, Anjan. "Sarkozy Tries to Mend Rift With Rwanda." *New York Times,* February 26, 2010: http://blume.stmarytx.edu:2063/hottopics/lnacademic/
Taylor, Charles, and Amy Gutmann. *Multiculturalism: Examining the Politics of Recognition.* Princeton, NJ: Princeton University Press, 1994. http://site.ebrary.com/lib/librarytitles/Doc?id=10035810
Taylor, Ian, and Paul Williams. *Africa in International Politics: External Involvement on the Continent.* London: Routledge, 2004: http://www.netlibrary.com/urlapi.asp?action=summary&v=1&bookid=105231
Tiersky, Ronald. "Mitterrand's Legacies." *Foreign Affairs,* 74, 1 (1995b): 112–121.
Tiersky, Ronald. *The Mitterand Legacy and the Future of French Security Policy.* Washington, DC: Institute for National Strategic Studies, National Defense University, 1995a.
Tiersky, Ronald. *François Mitterrand: The Last French president.* New York: St. Martin's Press, 2000.
Tiersky Ronald. "France Returns to Center Stage." Current History, 107, 707 (2008): 99–104.
Toye, J F.J., and Richard Toye. *The UN and Global Political Economy: Trade, Finance, and Development.* Bloomington: Indiana University Press, 2004.
Varat, Benjamin. "Point of Departure: A Reassessment of Charles de Gaulle and the Paris Summit of May 1960." *Diplomacy & Statecraft,* 19, 1 (2008): 96–124.
Watson, Catharine, and Virginia Hamilton. *Exile from Rwanda: Background to an Invasion.* Washington, DC: U.S. Committee for Refugees, 1991.
Wibbels, Erik. *Federalism and the Market: Intergovernmental Conflict and Economic Reform in the Developing World.* Cambridge, UK: Cambridge University Press, 2005.
Xiang, Junbo. "Year of the Pig—The New Scramble for Africa." *Africa Confidential,* 48, 11 (2007): 6–7. Accessed February 6, 2011.

15 The Question of Development in Africa

Ebunoluwa O. Oduwole

This chapter looks at various indices for addressing a nation as developed and concludes that Africa is far behind developing let alone developed. Besides economic factors, the chapter highlights that human development, the environment, and safety are major indices of a developed country. While not denying the potentials and abilities for rapid development, this chapter argues that the social, political, and more importantly, moral climate of Africa is a clog in the wheel of achieving development, and that Africa does not currently have the political consolidation and improvement in governance necessary to achieve this end. Drawing examples from Nigeria, the chapter highlights particular problems affecting the development of the nation. Addressing corruption, which is a not only a bane in the society but a stumbling block of any developmental project, is one of the major concerns of this chapter. The chapter finally advocates that Africa should develop in its own interest by emphasizing internal development through a commitment to political will, both by rulers and the ruled.

WHAT IS DEVELOPMENT?

Development, according to *Longman's Dictionary of Contemporary English*, is the gradual growth of something so that it becomes bigger or more advanced.[1] This definition defines a developed country or nation as a rich industrial nation with a lot of business activity. By contrast, a developing nation is a poor society that is trying to increase its industry and improve trade. When a country is found to be developing, it is assumed that it is making progress. Countries with low levels of material and technological well-being are usually described as developing. They are also countries in which most people have a low economic standard of living. The concept of underdevelopment is that a country that is not developed is underdeveloped. However, a developing country is one that is making some progress at development. Consequently development is about progress. However, while the former is negative development, the latter is positive.

The term Third World refers to the concept of political nonalignment with either the capitalist or communist bloc. It was a concept that gained ground during the Cold War to define countries that were not in line with either capitalism or communism. This became a broad definition provided to categorize the world's nations into three groups based on social, political, and economic divisions. In other words, the term Third World arose as a political idea rather than as a term that describes a developed nation. Coincidentally, the Third World is also considered underdeveloped because of its low level of technological development, low gross national product (GNP), lack of industrialization, and low per capita income; this is the most common view of what constitutes underdevelopment. It is assumed that in all that a developing nation does, it must catch up with the industrialized West.

There are various views and types of development. We have development in the areas of the economic, social, political, spiritual, educational, and scientific arenas, among others. In short, development cuts across all areas of life. There are many development theorists, hence we shall engage in a brief conceptual clarification of some of their ideas on development in order to relate them to the African situation.

On the one hand, development can be technology-based. In this regard growth theorists such as Pearson[2] state that development is partly a process whereby a country can achieve reasonable self-sustaining growth, which facilitates and enhances industrial and technical progress in the interest of the people. By this definition, a nation's progress is measured by its technological advancement. It also assumes that technological development leads automatically to the progress of the people. However, the advancement of technology or industrialization does not automatically lead to societal self-advancement, especially if the drivers of such advancement are capitalists and profit oriented to the core.

On the other hand, development can also be linked with artifacts. Rostow, for example, says that development is determined by the rate at which a country accumulates social, cultural, industrial, technical, and other artifacts.[3] The implication is that countries that do not have these artifacts are not developed. Rostow's view, though more detailed, can be considered an extension of Pearson's. However, in like manner, it also does not consider how the accumulation of the various artifacts leads to the development of the people. It is also commonly assumed that development is about a nation's economy. According to Lewis, development revolves around the world market, or profit, instead of people.[4] Therefore economic indices such as per capita income, GNP, and so on determine the level of development. Thus a country with high per capita income is considered to be more developed and vice versa.

The above views of development are rather material. They do not take into consideration other aspects of development such as the humanistic, moral, and spiritual dimensions. It is assumed that development leads to progress when scientific and technological progress is achieved. From such an analysis, this aspect of development measures a nation's progress by its technological and industrialized advancement. The measure of a country's development then is in such things as the building of highways; forms of transportation, communication, and telecommunication; sources of energy; computer literacy; and so on. The more we conform to these western ideals, terms, and standards of living, the more the society is assumed to be developed. This is a narrow view of development and it is not all-encompassing.

When development programs are preoccupied with economic development, there is great danger of losing the concept of development that fosters real humanity, humanness, fellow feeling, and concern for others. Because of this, there will be a tendency to forget the other aspects of development in our national development plans. There will be no national policy that emphasizes human values. In other words, the neglect of human resources and the morally good can thwart efforts to bring about development even in the economic or political sense.

A broader view involves not only technology, economy, or artifacts but a kind of growth between society and individuals. Rodney argues that development in a human society is a many-sided process. At the level of the individual, it implies increased skill and capacity, greater freedom, creativity, self-discipline, responsibility, and material well-being. Although he states that some of these factors of development are virtually moral categories and are difficult to evaluate depending, as they do, on the age in which one lives, one's class origins, and one's personal code of what is right and what is wrong. However, he considers that the achievement of personal development is very much tied in with the state of the whole society.[5] Be that as it may, society can help to make or mar one's progress and level of development. As such, we need a concept of development that is all-encompassing, all-involving, and takes care of all areas of life.

Some other scholars place their emphasis on human development. Oladipo, in his analysis, claims that development is nothing but human development and that it can be described as a process whose primary goals are human well-being, both in its material and moral dimensions.[6] He argues that the development process is not an abstraction, the integrity of which can be measured simply in quantitative terms, such as the rate of growth in GDP per capita. It is not even the process of social change, whose primary goal is to "catch up" with the more developed societies—a process pervasively but mistakenly called the process of modernization. Rather, it is a process of social transformation, which involves the replacement of those factors that inhibit the capacity of the individual for self-direction and the promotion of social cooperation with those who promote these ideals. It is, in short, the essence of the people's quality of life.

According to Oladipo, development is a social concept standing for the process whereby human beings strive to improve the conditions of their lives. To this end he identifies two broad dimensions of development as the tangible or technical aspect and the intangible or moral aspect. The tangible aspect is concerned with material progress; it involves the control and exploitation of the physical environment through the application of the results of science and technology. The primary goal of this process is human well-being, which involves among other things the eradication of certain human-demeaning social phenomena such as poverty, illiteracy, and low life expectancy and the creation and maintenance of what can be called livelihood opportunities.[7] The intangible or moral aspect of development has to do with improvement of the qualities of human relations between people. It involves the promotion of positive social values—such as freedom, justice, tolerance, compassion, and cooperation—as well as the reduction of social inequity, which globally is a major source of conflicts.

Oladipo analyzed further that the tangible aspect appears most visible but the intangible aspect is crucial. This is because it is that which enhances the capacity of the individual to actually shape his or her own life without being insensitive to the common good.[8] In other words, any development goals and initiatives that do not take into consideration the capacity to shape the individual and the concerns of the common good is not an all-encompassing form of development. Similarly, Sen argues that development is a process of expanding the real freedom that people enjoy. It focuses on human freedom rather than other views of development such as growth of GNP or with rise in personal incomes, industrialization, technological advance, or social modernization. Although he does not deny the importance and relevance of growth of the GNP or of individual income to expanding the freedoms enjoyed by the members of the society, he avers that freedom depends also on other determinants, such as social and economic arrangements (for example, facilities for education and health care) as well as political and civil rights (for example, the liberty to participate in public discussion and scrutiny).[9] Sen opines further that "Human Development, as an approach, is concerned with what I take to be the basic development idea: namely, advancing the richness of human life, rather than the richness of the economy in which human beings live, which is only a part of it."[10] Similarly the Human Development Report (HDR) asserts that: "People are the real wealth of a nation." It maintains that:the objective of development should be to create an enabling environment for people to enjoy long, healthy and creative lives may appear self-evident today. But that has not always been the case. A central objective of the HDR for the past twenty years has been to emphasize that development is primarily and fundamentally about people.[11]

The basic purpose of development is thus to expand people's choices—though in principle these choices can be infinite and can change over time. However, people often value achievements that do not show up at all, or not immediately, in income or growth figures. Greater access to knowledge, better nutrition and health services, more secure livelihoods, security against crime and physical violence, satisfying leisure hours, political and cultural freedoms, and a sense of participation in community activities are also cherished. The objective of development is thus to create an enabling environment for people to enjoy long, healthy, and creative lives.

The human development approach originated as a result of growing criticism of the leading development approach of the 1980s, which presumed a close link between national economic growth and the expansion of individual human choices. Many scholars such as Sen and Mahbub ul Haq, who played key roles in formulating the human development paradigm, came to recognize the need for an alternative development model. This was because of a number of reasons, which included the following four factors. First, there was growing evidence that the then prevailing "trickle down" theory—that market forces would spread economic benefits and end poverty—could not be supported. Second, the human costs of the structural adjustment program became more apparent. Third, social ills (crime, weakening of social fabric, HIV/AIDS, pollution, etc.) were still spreading even in cases of strong and consistent economic growth. Fourth, a wave of democratization in the early 1990s raised hopes for people-centered models.[12]

The basic objective of development, according to Mahbub ul Haq, "is to create an enabling environment in which people can enjoy long, healthy and creative lives."[13] This vision has retained a powerful resonance over the years. By dismantling the idea of development that emphasizes the economic, it is considered here all that people are the real wealth of nations. It is said that the simple truth is sometimes forgotten. Mesmerized by the rise and fall of national incomes (as measured by GDP), we tend to equate human welfare with material wealth. However, the importance of GDP growth and economic stability should not be understated in that both are fundamental to sustained human progress, as is clear in the many countries that suffer from their absence. Thus the ultimate yardstick for measuring progress is people's quality of life.

The Human Development Project is very rich and all-encompassing. It cuts across other themes and issues that are considered central to it. They include social progress in terms of greater access to knowledge, better nutrition and health services, and the importance of economic growth as a means to reducing inequality and improving levels of human development.[14] It also addresses efficiency in terms of resource use and availability, whereby human development favors growth and productivity as long as such growth directly benefits the poor, women, and other marginalized groups. Equity in terms of economic growth and other human development parameters is also one of its concerns. Participation and freedom—particularly empowerment, democratic governance, gender equality, civil and political rights, and cultural liberty (especially for marginalized groups defined by urban-rural, sex, age, religion, ethnicity, physical/mental parameters, etc.)—are further considerations. In addition, sustainability for future generations in ecological, economic, and social terms; human security in daily life against such chronic threats as hunger; and abrupt disruptions including joblessness, famine, and conflict are major concerns of this project.

But how can a nation achieve all these without a well-organized political structure and good leadership? Who is responsible for the organization of the society and how will it be achieved? In a corrupt society where selfish motives and moves characterize the leaders, how then do we achieve these human development goals or any other developmental goals for that matter? Everything boils down to leadership and leadership qualities. There is no doubt that these are the key missing factors in African development.

Leadership and corruption are among the key problems affecting development in Africa. Idakworji emphasizes the inability of most organizations in Nigeria to achieve their desired objectives, stating that this often stems from corruption among leaders on the political and administrative levels.[15] Corruption today, he says, "Stands like a ruin in the societal and political landscape of most African countries. Leadership entails being a builder of special values, a definer of societal mission, a setter of societal goals and a facilitator for goal attainment."[16] No meaningful development can take place when the country and its citizens are corrupt. Idakworji, in his detailed analysis of the nature and effects of corruption in Nigeria, succinctly asserts that, "Corruption not only undermines authority but it displays selfish moves that are counterproductive to development."[17]

Corruption in Nigeria ranges from the handling of elections in an unprecedented way by the Independent National Electoral Commission (INEC) to the weak nature of the national assemblies and legislatures who are the key organs of government, INEC being the major force that institutes these key organs. The various inadequacies of these key organs have had gross negative and degrading effects on the economy as well as on education, health, road networks, water and energy resources, and virtually all the aspects of society. Yagboyaju highlights the ripple effects of weak governance caused by corruption as lack of security, armed robbery, abduction, kidnapping, unemployment, and collapse of manufacturing and technological sectors of the economy, to mention a few. Consequently this represents a total denial of development.[18] Thus the argument of this paper tilts toward good leadership and moral development in order to achieve development in Africa. Africans and their leaders currently place emphasis on foreign aid and assistance. If there are no committed, patriotic leaders to plan in a particular progressive direction, even when the aid comes it may not be utilized to achieve desirable goals of growth and development of individuals and the society at large.

THE MORAL FACTOR IN DEVELOPMENT

It will be grossly inadequate to say that the moral factor is the problem responsible for underdevelopment in contemporary Africa. The factors that militate against development are many. There are economic, ideological, and political factors such as political instability and intrigue, lack of continuity, and lack of clear and coherent ideological policies; economic factors such as level of industrialization, problem of balance of payments, and international economic problems; demographical factors such as the "brain drain," which is affecting our universities, whereby the current highly skilled migrant program and visa lotteries all drain away experts and people at the top of their chosen professions and careers; socioreligious and cultural obstacles such as tribal wars, cultural inferiority, irrational adherence to custom and tradition, and disunity among states, and so forth. Here we single out the moral factor in development. Although it is certainly an aspect of development, it must be contended that it is an all-encompassing aspect of development.

Morality is unique in a number of ways. It is morality that can help government to make policies capable of bringing development to the society. It is also on moral grounds that we can criticize bad governments and bad policies. It is morality that can prevent government from enacting arbitrary and socially iniquitous or inhumane laws that can deprive citizens of their fundamental human rights. It is also morality that can define duties and responsibilities of the government and citizens. But for morality we would have engaged in irrational social acts. Immanuel Kant says that an effort to be immoral is an effort to be irrational.[19]

Morality promotes love, truth, harmony, and social peace, which will breed security and stability in our states. When individuals are stable, their cumulative stability will lead to general stability in our countries. A community of moral individuals will enhance the quality of the lives of individuals and consequently the quality of the wider society. An adequate engagement with this moral factor would necessitate dealing with the total person and seeking to make the best of him or her as a physical, psychological, social, spiritual, and rational being. So, with the development of the moral aspect one will not only be useful to oneself but also to the community and the human race at large.

THE WAY FORWARD IN THE DEVELOPMENT OF AFRICA

There is no gainsaying that political and economic stability can enhance positive development in Africa. However, if the necessary ideals or processes are not put in place to fight corruption, development cannot be achieved. To this end, the mind-set factor—which can be described as a set of ideas that shape one's behavior and outlook and place the interest of society far above that of the self—is crucial.[20] It includes the shunning of corruption as well as acts of patriotism and support of the national identity. Most leaders in Africa have self-centered mind-sets and a lack of discipline. They also lack self-mastery of the situations of their countries, be it on the political, economic, or social level. Even when they do grasp these situations, their self-centered mind-sets will not allow them to lead constructively.

It is an understatement to say that we have not had development modules in Africa over the years. Apart from any individual country's attempts at development in terms of trade and industrialization, leading to economic growth and reflecting in economic indices such as increasing GNP, there are also attempts at securing foreign aid, particularly the raising of funds from the International Monetary Fund and the World Bank to enhance developmental projects. There has also been an attempt by Africa as a continent to come together to discuss and solve developmental problems. The Organization of African Unity (OAU), Economic Commission of West Africa (ECOWAS), and African Union, with its peer-review mechanism, are attempts in this direction. Suffice to say that most of these initiatives both at the internal and external levels have begotten the monsters of colonialism, neocolonialism, imperialism, and most importantly corruption.

As Oladipo rightly mentions, there are no indications as of yet that the African Union and New Partnership for Africa's Development (NEPAD) have made African development a reality.[21] Thus there is an urgent need to secure the conditions for political stability in most African states. In this sense there is a need to develop on the part of the leaders but also on the part of the people. Commitment is needed on both sides—that is, a will to organize the society in order to achieve human development. The factor of the group mind with corporate social responsibility is essential to development.[22] At this level, the masses also need to fight corruption.

Within the limits of this paper, the way forward to Africa's development can be highlighted in the following ways: First, there is a need to terminate imperialism by rejecting dependence on foreign aid and fostering development from within. This will make our development internal. Baah, in his analyses of the history of development, highlights initiatives considered to have been made from within and not from without as the most effective and beneficial to human development in Africa. According to him, country-owned initiatives designed and implemented by African countries rather than those designed for Africa by outsiders have yielded more developmental goals.[23] He argues that Africa should not continue to deceive itself. Rather, Africa should take its destiny into its own hands and develop its own policies based on the needs of its people. Africa's future lies in its own ability to take bold developmental initiatives. Africa's future does not lie in spurious and neocolonial partnerships.[24] McBride in this regard makes an urgent call for Africa to develop in its own interest, which is crucial here.[25] This is a type of development that considers not just growth but also the emancipation of the people. This again is where the human development indices are relevant and meaningful.

Second, our leaders should also be morally sound by showing good examples. As shown earlier, this is lacking in contemporary Africa and it is one reason for its failure. Our leaders most of the time get to power because they are wealthy economically, not morally, and they use their wealth to buy others over. To achieve social stability, our planners and policy makers should evolve urgent educational policies that emphasize the moral rather than the economic aspect of development.

Third, the issue of national identity and patriotism, which is a subject for further research, is also crucial. There is no doubt that the destruction of our economic and political structures due to colonialism and modernization has destroyed our culture. There is a loss of cultural, national, political, and collective identity. However modernization need not necessarily mean obliteration of all elements of traditional culture. Modern African identity does not have to reject aspects of traditional culture that are useful, but it can take note of the good aspects and do a critical and reconstructive self-evaluation. In this sense whatever evolves will not be out of cultural traditionalism but will be an authentic identity based on a conscious and deliberate effort; it will reflect both the new and old ideals of life. There are a number of factors hindering the development of contemporary Africa, the principal one of which involves the moral dimension. A number of concrete steps have been highlighted here and it is my fervent hope that we start from there in order to achieve the desired goals of true development in contemporary Africa and to contribute to the well-being of the entire world.

NOTES

1. *Longman's Dictionary of Contemporary English* (1995), 374.
2. L. B. Pearson, *The Crisis of Development*. (London: Pall Mall Press, 1970), 5.
3. Walt Whitman Rostow, *The Process of Economic Growth* (Oxford, UK: Clarendon Press, 1960), 25.
4. W. Arthur Lewis, *The Theory of Economic Growth* (London: George Allen and Unwin, 1963), 14.
5. Walter Rodney, *How Europe Underdeveloped Africa*. (Abuja, Nigeria: Panaf Publishers, 1972), 12.
6. Olusegun Oladipo, *Philosophy and Social Reconstruction in Africa* (Ibadan, Nigeria: Hope Publications, 2009), 96–97.
7. Ibid., 94.
8. Ibid., 95.
9. Sen Amartya, *Development as Freedom* (New York: Knopf, 2000), 4.
10. Ibid., 4.
11. "The State of Human Development": http://www.hdr.undp.org/en/media/HDR06-complete.pdf. 263
12. "The Real Wealth of Nations: Pathways to Human Development," *Human Development Report 2010: 20th Anniversary Edition:* http://hdr.undp.org/en/reports/global/hdr2010/chapters/, 1

13. "Asian Countries Lead Development Progress Over 40 Years." *Human Development Report 2010: 20th Anniversary Edition:* http://www.hdr.undp.org/en/media/PR6-HDRIO-RegRBAP-Erev5-sin.pdf
14. "The State of Human Development," *Human Development Report 1990:* http://www.hrd.undp.org/en/media/hdr_1998_en_chapl.pdf, 15–37
15. S. P. Idakworji, "Leadership, Corruption and Development," *Canadian Social Science,* Vol. 6, No. 6, (2010): 173–179.
16. Ibid., 175.
17. Ibid., 177.
18. Dhikru Adewale Yagboyaju, "Nigeria's Fourth Republic and the Challenge of a Faltering Democratization." *African Studies Quarterly,* Vol. 12, No. 3 (2011): 93–106.
19. Immanuel Kant, "Fundamental Principles of Metaphysic of Morals." In William Frankena and John T. Granrose, eds., *Introductory Readings in Ethics* (Upper Saddle River, NJ: Prentice Hall, 1974), 113.
20. Emmanuel Onyechere Osigwe Anyiam-Osigwe, *Advancing the Cause for a Holistic Approach to Human Existence Development* (Lagos, Nigeria: Proceedings of the Second Session of the Emmanuel Onyechere Osigwe Anyiam-Osigwe Memorial Lecture Series, 2000): 5–26.
21. Oladipo (2009), 94.
22. Emmanuel Onyechere Osigwe Anyiam-Osigwe, *The Cosmopolitan Expression of the Group Mind Principle* (Lagos: Osigwe Anyiam-Osigwe Foundation, 2003), 13.
23. Anthony Baah, "History of African Development Initiatives": http://www.sarpn.org/document/d0000407/P373_Baah.pdf
24. Ibid., 8.
25. Robert H. McBride, "How Can Africa Develop in Its own Interest?" *A Journal of Opinion,* Vol. 8, No. 4 (1978): 30–34.

REFERENCES

Baah, Anthony. "History of African Development Initiatives": http://www.sarpn.org/document/d0000407/P373_Baah.pdfHuman Development Indicators: http://www.hdr.undp.org/en/media/hdr04_backmatter_1.pdf

Human Development Report: 20th Anniversary Edition, *Asian Countries Lead Development Progress Over 40 Years.* 2010: http://www.hdr.undp.org/en/media/PR6-HDRIO-RegRBAP-Erev5-sin.pdf

———.*The Real Wealth of Nations: Pathways to Human Development.* 2010: http://www.hdr.undp.org/en/reports/global/hdr2010/chapters

Idakworji, S. P., "Leadership, Corruption and Development." *Canadian Social Science,* Vol. 6, No. 6 (2010): 173–179.

Lewis, W. Arthur. *The Theory of Economic Growth.* London: George Allen and Unwin, 1963.

McBride, Robert H. "How Can Africa Develop in Its Own Interest?" *A Journal of Opinion,* Vol. 8, No. 4 (1978): 30–34.

Oladipo, Olusegun. *Philosophy and Social Reconstruction in Africa.* Ibadan: Hope Publications, 2009.

Opafola, S. Olayinka. *The Idea of Development: A Philosophical Analysis.* Abuja, Nigeria: Samtech Communications, 1994.

Pearson, L. B., *The Crisis of Development.* London: Pall Mall Press, 1970.

Reaffirming Human Development: http://www.hdr.undp.org/en/media/HDR-2010-EN-Chapter1-reprintpdrf

Rodney, Walter. *How Europe Underdeveloped Africa*. Abuja, Nigeria: Panaf Publishers, 1972.

Rostow, Walt Whitman. *The Process of Economic Growth*. Oxford, UK: Clarendon Press, 1960.

Sen, Amartya. *Development as Freedom,* New York: Knopf, 2000.

The State of Human Development: http://www.hdr.undp.org/en/media/HDR06-complete.pdf

———. http://www.hrd.undp.org/en/media/hdr_1998_en_chapl.pdf

Yagboyaju, Dhikru Adewale. "Nigeria's Fourth Republic and the Challenge of a Faltering Democratization." *African Studies Quarterly*, Vol. 12, No. 3 (2011): 93–106.

16 A Critique of the Notion of Africa as the "Third World"
Towards a New Perspective

Mike O. Odey

This chapter interrogates two basic ideological premises in relation to Africa in a historical perspective—namely Africa as the "Third World" and Africa as the "developing world." The chapter further questions which of these is more appropriate in regard to Africa in twenty-first-century world affairs. Essentially, the analysis is a critique of the concept of the Third World and attempts to create a new image for Africa. The two concepts of the Third World and developing nations have several things in common—traceable to the same historical circumstances—but they are not necessarily synonymous. For the purposes of this chapter, the concepts are taken as analytical tools as applicable to African countries at different stages of world history. The chapter argues that to conceive of African nations as the Third World in the strict sense of backwardness in the present millennium is to live in the past. Furthermore, to say that Africa has not changed for the better or developed beyond what the continent was under colonial domination amounts to taking too much for granted and may even be tantamount to racial prejudice. The analysis is linked to other issues of global concern, such as interdependence and connectivity, which appear to be more relevant in the present scheme of things, rather than the unchanging ideological posture typical of the past.

It is reasonable to argue that the concept of the Third World is obsolete and should be jettisoned because it belongs more to the post-Cold War era as a preoccupation of the twentieth century in international relations rather than to the present millennium. To some others, the most important perspective from which to see Africa in world politics would be from the current stance of its development efforts, which is a continuous process from the 1950s that belongs to the twenty-first century, rather than from an ideological stance. Thus the point of departure in the present argument is to demonstrate how Africa in twenty-first-century world affairs is emerging from the backwoods of history, overstepping the limits and ideology of the Third World, and moving gradually into an era of development.

The main question is: How has Africa developed since the end of the Cold War? What is the basis for the preference for the concept of development instead of the Third World? The conclusion of the chapter underscores the interdependence of the global world, in which the development of one part largely depends on the others. The implication is that it is unnecessary to categorize the world into ideological spheres as a result of constant shifts in conceptualizations. This bolsters the preference for the concept of development over that of the Third World without prejudice when Africa is considered in the context of world politics since the 1940s. The chapter is divided into four parts, beginning with the background on world classifications and an analysis of key issues. It goes on to demonstrate the necessity for shifting from the concept of the Third World as a basis for arguing that African countries are gradually developing, albeit slowly, despite all odds. The conclusion reiterates the more fundamental issue of our interdependence in a world that is increasingly globalized.

BACKGROUND TO CLASSIFICATIONS OF GLOBAL IDEOLOGICAL DIFFERENCE: A FRAMEWORK FOR ANALYSIS

Most perspectives on Third World and development derive from the ideological leanings of western scholarship. Generally, their meanings and what constitutes development lack precision and are surrounded with much debate. The concept of development is often used in such a broad way that it involves a multiplicity of criteria, especially economic terms such as *modernization, industrialization, westernization*, and growth of some sort involving change and progress, but it fails to show what each of these implies. For the purposes of this chapter, development is taken to mean a multidimensional phenomenon ranging from high income per capita or GDP, as emphasized in the past, and now shifting to the more current criteria of the UN Human Development Index, within which several elements are subsumed, including noneconomic categories such as life expectancy and level of literacy. Human development is the most significant aspect of development, embracing all other elements in one simple and composite index, and it is much deeper and richer than any other criteria in the conceptualization of development. For any country or region to be regarded as developed, three variables must be clearly present, namely life expectancy, educational knowledge and attainment, and as high an income as necessary for a decent standard of living.[1] Added to this, the significance of sustainable development by way of a sustainable environment has become a central element in what constitutes development since the 1997 Kyoto Protocol.

In much of the contemporary western academic literature, this process of change includes social, economic, and political systems, which began in western Europe and North America in the seventeenth century and later spread to the rest of Europe, South America, Asia, and, last, Africa. Thus the West has provided the basis for what usually constitutes the model of a developed society, with the rest of the world seen in terms of traditional or backward societies.[2] Supposedly this signifies a type of continuum, or stages of development, and what colonial powers have always made the Third World countries to believe even when they are beginning to do well in their development efforts. However, the caveat to begin with here is to make room for creativity and shifts in the Africanization of paradigms of development. The essence of this is to underscore the decolonization of the basic concepts from a stereotypical point of view with the realization that for every opinion, there are always alternative views. Furthermore, it is imperative to understand African institutions and cultures within their own context so that the indices for measuring growth rates side by side with poverty could be captured as such simultaneously instead of doing so in isolation.

Thus, as Mahatma Gandhi rightly argued, development should be seen not necessarily from the point of industrialization or mass production by machines. Rather, development involves other forms of progress in human society that are free from destruction and geared toward sustainability and the improvement of human life or society in general with a sense of responsibility attached to whatever is considered as development ad infinitum. Furthermore, there is no direct route or simple formula for development. It is therefore erroneous to think that development must necessarily follow western lines or be judged against western models. For instance, in the past it used to be conceived that an increase in GDP, in productive activities, or industrialization were the only strategies that could bring about development. However, a more popular view is that increases in production, consumerism, and materialistic tendencies have corresponding problems in the development process and would require more understanding to be relevant in the current thinking on sustainability. Furthermore, development, as desirable by all humans in all societies, is expected to be progressive, intending to ensure good living standards and to benefit human beings rather than creating widespread poverty and strangulating the vast majority of the people. Sustainable development underscores fairness, equity, and broad benefits including liberal distribution of available wealth to the majority of people in all societies, broad participation of people in matters that concern them, and so forth. In all these, cultural elements must also be taken into account in the conceptualization of development. That is, every society develops along the lines of its most suitable cultural milieu.

Linked to this is the current classification of the world into countries using several categories of growth per capita, including the employment rate of persons and work per hour, as well as purchasing power parity. Other classifications include the human poverty index, human development index, and percentage of countries living in poverty. More recently, countries have been classified on their digital opportunity index—that is, the number of Internet users and the prevalence of broadband access, as well as number of mobile phone users.[3] In the past, even the conventional meaning of the concept of development did not include some of the current details, which is why it is necessary to constantly keep in perspective the question, "What is development now?"

One other important classification of the world is the categorization of the global north and global south. Although there are objections to this, the idea is helpful in the present analysis. "The North" supposedly refers to the rich industrialized countries in the Northern Hemisphere, and including Australia and New Zealand south of the Equator. The rest are half-industrialized nations such as Brazil and India and the emerging economies of South East Asia, Latin America, and sub-Saharan Africa, which are generally considered to be poor. In between both are several overlaps, leaving one in doubt about where to situate some of them, whether along geographical or ideological lines. In the past, the world was classified into different groups on the bases of historical, economic, political, sociolinguistic, cultural, and ideological criteria. Thus, the bases for world classifications will keep shifting as always from academic euphemism to Cold War terminology and later to the complexities of geopolitical maneuvering. Until the end of the Cold War, the three blocs of nations that appeared most permanent included the First, the Second, and the Third Worlds.

The emergence of the concept of the Third World is closely related to the dynamics of Cold War and characterized by the desire among postcolonial states for autonomous development rather than aligning with the two superpowers, which constituted as it were, the First and Second Worlds, strictly from ideological point of view. The First World was ruled by the capitalist ideology and was led by the United States. The other members of the First World were the highly industrial and very rich western countries, including Japan. The Second World comprised about thirty countries and was led by the Soviet Union under the socialist ideology. In between the two ideological blocs were the Third World countries, which regarded themselves as nonaligned nations and tried to keep their distance from the western and eastern ideological conflicts as exhibited during the Cold War. They were known as nascent nations, emerging from the postcolonial domination and characterized by extensive poverty; they were also seen as aid/grants receivers from donor agencies. Although there are constant shifts in the use and meaning of the term *Third World*, its conceptualization can best be grasped within the context of the politics of the Cold War and the emergence of the nonaligned nations. Both concepts have more than half a century of historical precedent and suggest that neither of them belonged to the First or the Second Worlds. In particular, the Third World nations of the 1960s included postindependent African, Latin American, and Southeast Asian countries.

Like the shift in the use and meaning of the concept, several Third World countries—including Brazil, India and several others in Southeast Asia—are also moving gradually out of abject poverty. However, as *The Economist* argues, "over 60 or so small poor countries still retain Third-World characteristics in its crude form of aid dependency, corruption and violence."[4] When Africa is singled out of the Third World group identity, however, it is seen mostly as a dark continent, with the poorest of the poor and hopeless as far as development is concerned. The Third World has had other nomenclatures over time, all of which are characterized by common features. According to Meier and Rauch, what we now refer to as Third World were those regions of the world considered to be "rude and barbarous" back in the eighteenth century, as "backward" in the nineteenth century, and in the twentieth century as "poor or underdeveloped" countries and "less developed states." Lately, they have come under the rubric of "developing" or "emerging countries" and under a larger umbrella of the "global south."[5]

According to Bauer and Yamey, for over half a century of their existence, the most distinguishing feature of the Third World nations has been their demand for and continued dependence on foreign aid in cash and kind, including technological and managerial assistance, for their development after long years of colonial domination.[6] In recent times, foreign aid is received in many other ways, including development aid from the United Nations and the World Bank as well as international nongovernmental organizations' support during general elections, natural disasters, and in the fight against epidemics. By 2007–2008, approximately US$121.3 billion was received from the 22 richest industrial countries and the European Union, most of it for African countries. Tanzania alone received US$1.8 billion, Sudan and Cameroon received US$1.6 billion, and Ethiopia US$165 million in foreign aid.[7] It has been constantly argued that without foreign aid, the Third World would not exist. But rather than being helpful, foreign aid to Third World countries has in the long run proven to be detrimental to development. In particular, some of the aid has been diverted away for private use instead of serving to promote national economic growth and development, for which it was meant. More importantly, foreign aid has always been an instrument of confrontation, as the superpowers began more aggressively to impose their economic interests on the Third World countries—to complicate their problems of development and exacerbate internal conflicts throughout the period of the Cold War and thereafter.

Undoubtedly foreign aid to Third World countries has constituted a significant element in the relationship between the First and Second Worlds and their allies, whom the Third World originally wanted to keep at a distance during the Cold War period, but they could not do so because of their development needs. This was what Ian Clark referred to as a complex "process of globalization and fragmentation . . . organically linked to the Cold War, to ensure that capital flows to the underdeveloped regions, economic aid and programme of economic development would themselves become integral part of what was happening within the Western system itself."[8] Thus, as Wilber and others further argued, the Third World countries are always caught up in Cold War struggles over which they have no control and in which they are cast as mere pawns:

> and they are absolutely dependent on outside capital, technology, and markets for their products. . . . and other ties for which they cannot

divorce themselves; moreover many of them are entirely dependent for their continued development on external energy sources and thus are the victims of skyrocketing prices that they can ill afford to pay that has wreaked havoc with their national economies.[9]

Aid to Africa is not helping the development of the continent as it should for a number of reasons. First, it usually falls into the hands of corrupt government officials. It is also given with interest, to provide investment opportunities, rather than as free donations to Africa, so the conditionality attached to such aid rather exacerbates poverty levels in the long run. Thus aid to Africa comes for the most part at the expense of poor people and does not in a real sense promote development process.

The concept of Third World also connotes poverty and a lack or slow pace of development for the vast majority of people of not less than 80 percent of the world. Thus, they are generally characterized by backwardness, retardation, stigma, negativism, and misery by the First and Second Worlds because they cannot control more than 20 percent of their natural resources, unlike the global north. For instance, most countries in the global north have stable democratic institutions; they are technologically and scientifically advanced; and they have an equitable distribution of wealth as well as reasonable living standards and manageable population growth. In contemporary parlance, however, it should be observed that most African nations are increasingly becoming aware more than ever before that for them to successfully develop their economies, they must move beyond the backwoods of history in several respects. They must find alternatives to receiving foreign aid, no matter how the forces of neocolonialism act against them are or refuse to back off even after the Cold War. However, the end of the Cold War in the early 1990s did provide an escape route for the Third World nations, given the nature of the differences between the superpowers and the reconfigurations between the emerging basic units of interactions between the south-south and the wider context of international history.

All these have no doubt converged to seriously challenge the relevance of the concept of the Third World in the old sense, despite the fact that some of the bases for categorizing them as Third World nations remain unchanged. Apart from that, even the levels of interactions within and between the same regional groupings have substantially increased in the way that the concepts of global north and south or globalization have demonstrated enough evidence against the continued usage of the concept of the Third World. Indeed, African nations have also shifted from the domain that characterized the concept of Third World. Furthermore, the operations and the phenomena of the Third World have shifted to an arena that may be more specifically defined as sub-Saharan Africa, having less or nothing to do with the generality of Asia and Latin America but rather in search of autonomy and cooperation at bilateral levels for purposes of development.

Historically, the concept of the Third World was practically in use even before the idea was first conceived by Alfred Sauvy in a publication in 1952—initially in reference to the French commoners who were diametrically opposed to the First and Second Estates in France as political economic classifications. According to him, the French commoners are comparable to the Third World nations, with nothing but the wish to be something, while to him the First Estate represented the western capitalist bloc and their allies and the Second Estate represented the Soviet Union and their allies. The nonaligned nations continued to assume autonomy as a third bloc and the posture of noninterference in the power relations of the other two blocs. In several instances, the Third World nations demonstrated that they could stand alone and together, expressing one opinion in world affairs, because to them the doctrines of capitalism and communism were based on wrong principles. This was the posture of the Third World nations until the emergence of the UN Human Development Index (UN HDI), with its emphasis on the basic human needs in 1974. The UN HDI and the new groundbreaking doctrine of the basic human needs has a history of its own, which was to challenge the old concept of development when the concept made its first appearance in an annual speech by the president of the World Bank, Robert McNamara, to its board of governors in 1972.[10] This is how remarkable the shifts in the ideological perspectives and the political economy of nations on the globe have been, and it will continue to be so.

THE NECESSITY FOR DISCARDING THE CONCEPT OF THE "THIRD WORLD" IN TWENTY-FIRST-CENTURY AFRICAN INTERNATIONAL RELATIONS

Implicit in the foregoing argument is the fact that the use of the concept of the Third World partly in reference to Africa was only appropriate during the Cold War era and now appears to be generally obsolete. This is because the post-Cold War era, with its multipolar and multicultural worlds, does not have the overwhelming dominant cleavage of the Cold War era. New alignments are emerging all over the world, not in the manner of the old regime of the East-West ideological divide with the Third World in between, but rather with more dynamism, complexity, and multidirectional relations. There are too many common interests, and the search for cooperation between nations will continue to set the agenda of where to place alignment at a particular time. In this section I want to press further, using a number of arguments, to show that the use of the term *Third World* in reference to African countries fits more into the twentieth century rather than the dynamics of the twenty-first century.

The first misconception is that the concept of the Third World is an apology of historical truth. For practical purposes, there is no such thing as neutrality in international relations. Geographically, the world may be

A Critique of the Notion of Africa as the "Third World" 349

classified into several parts as continents, but not in the ideological sense at all. During the Cold War, two ideologies ruled the world: socialist (Marxist-Leninist) versus capitalist. Until the end of the Cold War, no country was ever able to escape the dilemma of either the capitalist network and imperialist exploitation or the socialist manipulations. According to Jalee, "There is no third choice. The so-called Third World is no more than the backyard of imperialism, which does not mean that it does not belong to the system; quite the contrary."[11]

The understanding of the concepts of the Third World and development depends on western ideological perspective and for anyone to really understand issues about Africa's needs more than one school of thought. Thus it would be misleading to use the criteria of one region with its income levels and distribution of GNP or GDP to classify the developed and less developed nations and by extension for classifying rich and poor nations. Indeed, it is not all true to say that one-third of the world living in the global north is rich and the remaining two-thirds in the global south is poor. Geographically there are some in advanced areas of the Northern Hemisphere that are actually poorer than some in the south, and vice versa. For instance, among the former 145 countries of the Third World, some countries in East Asia, the Middle East, and Southeast Asia are currently richer than several in the Northern Hemisphere. Indeed, nobody can gainsay the fact that the economies of some countries in the global south today are growing even faster than those in the global north.

Next, the pace and patterns of development within the former Third World are not the same and do not allow their categorization in the same demeaning group of the 1960s. Within Africa there are over 700 million people, it is not just one country but fifty-six, and the growth rate of each is different from the rest for different reasons. This can be explained by the type of geographical space they occupy, their peculiar historical circumstances, and differences in their social and cultural environments as demonstrated by their divergent growth rates. Each African country is growing and developing at its own pace under different national government policies. Furthermore, the nature and character of economic policies in different nations have radically shifted in such a way that it is not possible to distinguish between the First-, Second-, and Third-World countries as in the 1960s. What appears to be more popular is changes in the membership and differentials in the levels of development in the Third World countries when it was first conceived.

The concept of the Third World has strong racial undertones and attitudes that engender racial conflicts and hatred between the psychology of "superiority" and "inferiority" relations and should therefore be discarded because, like religious fundamentalism and terrorism in international relations, prejudice and pessimism do not help anyone. Furthermore, there is more optimism about African growth rates now than in the past, and anyone writing and talking about the current state of affairs in Africa must have the same prospect in mind. This is perhaps why the designations of "developed" and "developing" do not really exist in the operational system of the UN except as a statistical convenience and which do not necessarily express a judgment about the stage reached by a particular country or area in the development process.[12]

For purposes of preference, African countries should be seen in the context of development rather than the Third World because the former is a more universal phenomenon with several routes and formulas leading to it and without any stigma attached. And it is erroneous to assume that African nations are not developing because they are not engaging in massive industrial and manufacturing systems or because they are still lagging behind the Asian Tigers with which they were previously classified as part of the Third World. As development is a process between two extremes that makes the coexistence of two dichotomies of the global north and south justifiable, there is therefore no rationale for sticking to the concept of the Third World as a stigma for lack of development. Furthermore, African efforts toward development during the post-Cold War era should be respected and acknowledged as such. Apart from all these, African countries are not as backward as they were in the 1960s and during the Cold War.

Talking more specifically about aid and corruption as indices for the classification of the Third World, it is simply true that avarice and greed are human weaknesses found in all societies, not only in Africa. Africa is not merely receiving aid, as it is the West that depends more on aid giving as a way of exerting influence in Africa and the rest of the Third World, especially during the era of the Cold War. For all aid given and received, there is prestige and profit attached. Jalee puts it as pillage of the Third World and summarizes it as follows: "Aid to the Third World is not gratuitous generosity, and it will be childish to deny the political or commercial motivations of what is variously called aid, technical assistance or cooperation a glance at the map will show that nations without strategic importance gets less than others."[13] This was how donor nations took political factors into consideration before and why aid was an integral part of the Cold War. Of course, there are several arguments regarding foreign aid to Africa, as since the end of the Cold War it appears no longer necessary for western powers to use it to counter the influence of the Soviet Union in Africa.[14] But even now, for all aid given and the more any country doubles its aid to another in the Third World, the more it exerts influence in that part of the world. So who is gaining or losing more?

To some analysts, there are two other plausible arguments to overturn these sweeping assumptions about aid, namely that private capital flow to less developed countries is in the form of investment for most donors, rather than as aid, and that Africa has to depend unavoidably on western nations. Furthermore, a more balanced view regarding foreign economic aid from the West to Africa is that it is not even sufficient for the development of Africa if one is to take it as compensation or reparation for the evil

A Critique of the Notion of Africa as the "Third World" 351

inflicted on Africa by the western world during the transatlantic slave trade and subsequent colonial rule. It was partly in this connection that Walter Rodney demonstrated how Europe underdeveloped Africa. And, finally, one must factor in Samuel Huntington's caveat as expressed in his predictions regarding the fall of civilizations and the breakdown of barriers between peoples in the present century as one of uttermost relevance in the present argument:

> During the Cold War, the world was divided into the First, Second and the Third Worlds. These divisions are no longer relevant. It is far more meaningful now to group countries not in terms of their political or economic systems or in terms of their level of economic development but rather in terms of their culture and civilization.[15]

With the end of the Cold War and the confrontation between the two ideological blocs of the capitalist West versus the communist East during the period, the use of the concept of the Third World becomes increasingly jejune in contemporary world politics. The end of the Cold War has also provided what Krasner regards as "a unique window of opportunity for the Third World,"[16] or what is known in popular parlance as New International Economic Order and the prospect of a brighter future for African development with a new agenda in which several interests regarding the continent converge. However, some scholars are skeptical of the liberation and optimism that the end of the Cold War has brought. They argue that without the Cold War, there would be no mutual rivalry between the West and the East and therefore the superpowers will no longer be interested in the Third World, causing these nations to be "neglected" and "marginalized." Be that as it may, to insist on the use of the concept of the Third World in contemporary international relations amounts to bringing back the idea of the First and the Second Worlds all over again to the center stage in an increasingly globalized world. The world is moving and nobody can stop it.

Indeed, even in our globalized world, fragmentations and compartmentalization cannot be ruled out, but definitely not in the old categorization of the First and Second Worlds. The post-Cold War era is characterized by new forms of negotiations, interdependence, and confrontation, and attempts toward world integration became more apparent than forces of disintegration, as witnessed during the Cold War.[17] However, there is really no uniqueness or purity of racial, religious, or color, as Huntington rightly observes.[18] Another form of international interdependence lies in the global environmental crises, which know neither offenders nor culprits. Thus to discard the use of the concept of the Third World is also to accept the alternative interpretation to the rigid bipolarization of the world and allow for flexibility and interdependence, multilateral relations, and globalization in a complex world that has also brought new economic opportunities for development among the Third World. This is how the Third World is making new appearances to redress the unbalanced world.

RECONSTRUCTING AND HISTORICIZING AFRICAN DEVELOPMENT AS A PROCESS

To appreciate the extent of the African development process and the imperative of using the concept of development rather than Third World, it is significant to recourse to historical antecedent. One of the most radical views about the past African development is that of Walter Rodney in *How Europe Underdeveloped Africa*.[19] Although not many analysts subscribe to his view in absolute terms, there is credibility in the argument considering the time frame of Rodney's analysis. In simple terms, Rodney demonstrated that African ancient kingdoms and empires developed along their own lines long before the advent of colonial rule, and that it was European colonialism that destroyed African civilization and retarded its development. Similarly, in *The Wretched of the Earth*, Frantz Fanon declared outright that to Africa colonialism was bad and that the black continent was not in any way the white man's burden.[20] While it is difficult to say that colonial rule in Africa did nothing good, it appears that the whole gamut of the African developmental process began before colonial rule in Africa but was truncated during the European domination of the continent and began again to pick up after independence by different sovereign African states.

In the past, the African continent had some of the most civilized centers in the world prior to the advent of colonial domination in the nineteenth century. Some of the centers of civilizations included ancient Egypt, ancient Ghana, Mali, the Luba and Lunda, Mwenemutapa, Great Zimbabwe, Swahili city states on the East African Coast, the Oyo Alafinate, the Saifawa dynasty of Kanem-Bornu, and several other kingdoms and empires all over Africa. However, all these drifted into the backwoods of history over time. The reasons for this are numerous; to cite the basic one in passing is to refer to the worst hazards of the African historical past, especially the colonial domination and exploitation of the continent. However, more fundamentally and currently, the lack of growth capacity of the continent is traceable to recurring violence and wars, the persistent traditional rural economy, poor management of resources, corruption of political leadership, and long periods of military dictatorship with unintended consequences of famine, disease, and hunger and the massive deprivation of the majority of the people. But African nations have not been naive about their history, especially the current problem of a slow rate of economic growth and development. Thus several policies have been formulated at national and continental levels to achieve growth, ranging from ideological to practical issues of daily life. The most internationally acclaimed policy framework for African economic growth includes the Lagos Plan of Action of 1982, which encouraged African countries to

A Critique of the Notion of Africa as the "Third World"   353

ban the importation of foreign goods and begin to develop internally as well as to strive toward self-sufficiency. The most recent effort toward the development of the continent is what is known as New Partnership for African Development (NEPAD), which was articulated in 2001 by African heads of state and government endeavoring to make progress slowly.

Since the end of the Second World War, Africa's greatest problem has been how to develop, especially after independence from their respective colonial powers. However, the quest for development is not limited to Africa alone, because the pursuit for development has always "resonated in all parts of the contemporary world."[21] Different nations and regions of the world, including Africa, began to engage in development processes, with each trying to formulate its own theory, public policy, and route it deemed fit for development. Thus, like the classical economists, the postwar growth economists too had to work out the details of economic theory and policy analysis that are most appropriate for their age and environment. And so it was that, with time, the new growth theorists again overstepped the narrowness of the colonial economic anthropologists, but they were still incapable of providing all the growth elements for all the nations of the world owing to the different ideological perspectives and political economies of various nation-states.[22]

There is no doubt that sub-Saharan Africa remains the world's poorest region in the twenty-first century, even within its traditional classification within the Third World. In most cases, there has been little or no progress; and in others, where there appears to be some elements of development, their sustainability may not be secure. However, that does not make the whole of African continent perpetually the wretched of the earth or deny it the possibility of growth and development. And every sincere scholar should be weary of such an argument about a complete absence of African development.

To undermine the deepening crises and the level of poverty in most African nations or to overemphasize the state of affairs in some crisis-prone areas of Africa is to miss the point at two extremes. As we have demonstrated from the beginning of this argument, African countries, especially in the 1970s, generally experienced a period that UN experts referred to as "the lost decade of African development." That was when Africa's dependence on the capitalist nations with huge and powerful financial capital bases became worse and besieged the continent with abject poverty. However, this downturn was not unique to Africa, because the early 1970s marked the end of supergrowth in the world economy, with "falling rates of growth, instability in monetary and exchange rate, widespread inflation and unemployment, anxieties about a return to protectionism, and concerns about access to raw materials."[23] Indeed, the 1980s and 1990s were even worse and more staggering, drifting gradually into what appears to be one of the worst economic meltdowns in world history. But this is not to say that African countries are worse off in the current spate of the global economic crises, nor are they spared from the pangs.

Long before now, Africa had been written off as a basket case of corruption, war, and poverty. Of the 47 countries classified as least developed in the 1990s, 32 were sub-Saharan African nations with very weak productive/growth capacity, huge external debits, and unprecedented social and economic hardships as well as breakdowns in political and institutional frameworks. This is in addition to the nature of their predominantly traditional agrarian economies with low living standards and life expectancies, burgeoning population growth amid slow economic growth, involuntary unemployment, and a disproportionate experience of poverty and illiteracy. There is no gainsaying that all these are familiar in Africa. The plethora of African woes remains a constant and seems to be on the increase in geometric progression.

Be that as it may, this is just one side of the argument and it is practically impossible to completely negate the slow progress that several African countries are making over time. For instance, much of what the developed world is today, especially America and Western Europe, was derived from the African continent through the transatlantic slave trade and later by way of international commodity trade and colonial exploitation. Through the Southern Atlantic System, the African continent was deprived of her labor force, even long after the abolition in form of forced labor outside the agricultural sector. Eventually, when land became more commercialized in the expansion of export production, it was still to the advantage of different colonial governments and agencies as soon as the effective occupation was achieved. Through this means, according to Rodney, the African continent, which was well developed before colonial rule, became exploited through the colonial domination of Africa leading to the underdevelopment of the continent on the long run. All these are familiar African historical experiences that cannot be overemphasized.

The two related trades in slaves and commodities went on for hundreds of years, with the most unfavorable terms of exchange to Africa as dictated by the capitalist system. No one can deny that Africa contributed to world development through these avenues. Even now, the terms of WTO are most unfavorable to sub-Saharan Africa, which would have been otherwise an important precondition for the development of the continent. For instance, during the post-Cold War era, no matter how self-sufficient the global north appears to be, its dependence on the global south for raw materials could not be ruled out. And now that interdependence and integration have become the most important elements in the emerging global economy, the true meaning of development rests on interconnectivity among nations in the north and south. Advanced or highly developed economies of the world can continue to be relevant only by collaborating with the less developed countries of Africa through world trade and capital flow, international labor migrations, supply of raw materials, and as sources of markets for exports. Undoubtedly the economic growth of the West still depends on Africa, and as the connections between the north and south continue to grow, Africa will likely dictate the rate of growth in the very near future.

Furthermore, any spell of economic downturn in the Third World becomes a bad omen for the West. And so it will be that "the wretched shall inherit the earth by about 2025."[24]

One specific area of African development lies in the growing importance of African export markets with China; this trade increased by over 10 percent in the last 5 years and marked a definite shift away from the old trade regime with the West, with all its trade imbalances. Furthermore, the surge in international labor migrations since the twentieth century, facilitated by improvements in communication and transport systems, has assumed new dimensions to such an extent that the rich countries of the global north continue to depend on the unskilled and semiskilled labor force of the global south. In particular, "At present, there are about 20 million migrant workers in the world; about 12 million of them are from developing countries."[25] In the words of Brandt, "it would be highly misleading to present the Third World as an unchanging picture of widespread poverty."[26] In this, African development lags behind the rest of the Third World, although it is moving on at its pace too. As the president of the World Bank, Bob Zoellick, argued, "2009 was the end of what was known as the Third World—that is, the end of a distinct, separate section of humanity that is poor, aid-dependent and does not matter very much."[27] Indeed, aid to the poorer nations will go on for a long time to come and may never be enough as long as the world is divided between the haves and the have nots, but the Third World stands as moderating influences in world affairs now more than ever before. In a number of ways, Africa is beating the odds. For instance, South Africa has just successfully hosted the World Cup and was the poorest nation to do so since 1930. In the most recent world economic meltdown that began toward the end of 2008, African countries demonstrated more resilience than in the past and did not experience the same adverse pangs of debt burdens as the rich countries of the world, just as they have less worry about cutting off gas emissions under the UN Convention on climate change.

According to the report of the International Fund for Agricultural Developmenton on the rate of growth in Central and West Africa, several variables can be used to assess African progress, which differs by country and subregion.[28] One of the most significant indices for explaining this is the current capacity and level of productivity in Africa, because agriculture is the main activity and lifeline of the people. According to the Food and Agricultural Organization, production systems are diverse and heterogeneous, with about thirteen farming systems within a general pattern of either cereal/root crop mixed system, root crop system, and tree crop system. Using per capita income to judge the performance of growth for the 1980s and 1990s, the reports show that there was poor growth and stagnation and deterioration of economic and social indicators in most African countries. However, "economic growth as a whole shows positive signs with a long term average of annual growth rate of about one percent." More importantly, when Africa's agricultural growth rate is, the picture appears to be clearer. Between 2004 and 2006, African annual growth per capita GDP moved up to 5.16 percent. Some of the growth rates are well ahead of global average levels. In 2007, the fastest-growing economies were recorded by the World Bank as follows: Mauritania at 19.8 percent, Angola at 17.6 percent, Sudan at 9.6 percent, Mozambique at 7.9 percent, and Malawi at 7.8 percent.[29]

A more contemporary profile of new opportunities and development in African countries shows that, at a general level of performance, the continent is moving at a modest speed with varying degrees from country to country. According to the Economic Intelligence Unit of the UN, two African countries top the GDP growth rate in a selection of twelve in the group, namely Angola at 12.1 percent and Equatorial Guinea at 11.1 percent. Ethiopia followed with a GDP growth rate of 8.0 percent, Nigeria with 7.8 percent, Egypt with 7.3 percent, Tanzania with 7.2 percent, Uganda with 6.4 percent, and South Africa with 5.1 percent.[30] According to the IMF World Economic Outlook, the cumulative average of Africa's growth, which was 4 percent in 2007, rose to 6 percent in 2009, despite economic instabilities. Apart from the prospects of higher economic growth, the international community appears to engage African countries in business in the amid recurring global recessions, with evidence that the global north is currently experiencing diminishing returns in economic growth far more than the south.[31] Furthermore, investment flows into Africa from China and other emerging economies since 2005 have been unprecedented. Apart from that, some African countries have increased their own investment drives within the continent. For example, South Africa outstripped Chinese investment in Africa between 2006 and 2008 and, under a strategic partnership agreement, China is the most important destination of South Africa's export trade.

In September 2010, when UN Secretary General Ban ki Moon went to Cameroon to assess the UN's MDG performance, he rated that country to have scored very high in development strides, especially in primary education, as well as showing a remarkable decline in infant mortality and improvement in inequality. This seemed to have been a reflection of other African countries and was what informed the UN summit of world leaders in New York in September 2010. There it was said that after the establishment of the MDGs, "the end of extreme poverty in Africa is at hand—within one generation." The review went on to state,

> There is no doubt that socio-economic condition in many African state have improved; there is more money in the system and better economic management. School enrolment is up, easily preventable disease is down. Africa's billion people may generate the same GDP as Brazil and Russia, but the extreme inequality and failing social provision is worse in Africa.[32]

Most African states have become democratized, but this democratization is not in any way perfect, because of political corruption and the failure of political leadership in most countries as well as inequity, inequality in wealth distribution, and social insecurity. Indeed, the tenets of democracy—like the rule of law, good governance, and the provision of social amenities—may be found wanting in most African states. Nevertheless, things are better than they were 50 or more years ago as far as governance in Africa is concerned, as none of the African nations is directly under colonial domination.

It is not possible to assess the level of development in sub-Saharan Africa without examining the Human Development Index (HDI), which measures the degree to which basic human needs are met, including health, education, and a complex matrix of human welfare. According to Brandt, although life expectancy in sub-Saharan Africa is still very low, with an average of about 45 years, people in Africa live much longer today than in previous decades.[33] This is the result of successes since the 1970s in bringing some deadly diseases like smallpox, malaria, and cholera under control. The emergence of HIV/AIDS is a more serious challenge, but it is also receiving attention as much as the general poor health conditions and primary health services, food and nutrition, employment, and wealth distribution. Until now, sub-Saharan Africa has remained a low-developed region, with an HDI Index of about 0.5. South Africa, Gabon, and Equatorial Guinea score the highest and are even moving to the next level of medium development.

The predictions for the fastest growing economies in 2010 by the IMF are even brighter for Africa, including Botswana, the Democratic Republic of Congo (DRC), Angola, Liberia, Malawi, and recently Equatorial Guinea and Nigeria, as shown in Table 16.1.

Table 16.1 Growth Rates of the Fastest Growing Economies in 2010

	Country	Growth Rate
1	Qatar	16.4 percent
2	Botswana	14.4 percent
3	Azerbaijan	12.3 percent
4	Republic of Congo	11.9 percent
5	Angola	9.3 percent
6	East Timor	7.87 percent
7	Liberia	7.53 percent
8	China	7.51 percent
9	Afghanistan	7.01 percent
10	Uzbekistan	7.00 percent
11	Turkmenistan	6.96 percent
12	Iraq	6.69 percent

Economy Watch and Economic Statistics Database.

With an average growth rate of about 7 percent as against the current prevailing range of 2.5 to 3.2 percent, the IMF classified Nigeria in 2010 as one of the fastest-growing economies with improved life expectancy, though still with severe problems amid staggering growth, especially involuntary unemployment, social insecurity, and institutional breakdown. The vast majority of Nigerians still live below the poverty line and generally get low scores on the Human Development Index. But be that as it may, there are also reasons for optimism regarding economic growth. Furthermore, it has been predicted that with more political stability and good governance in other African countries, Ghana will emerge as a leading world economy with an expected growth rate of 16.78 percent, to be followed by Angola and Liberia and then by Mauritania, Liberia, and Niger. The same prediction goes for the rest of Africa, indicating that 2010 to 2020 will be African decade of economic growth and recovery.

Except in Somalia, Sudan, and the DRC, there has been a significant decline in violence in the last few years, with remarkable achievements in peace-building processes and conflict resolution throughout the continent. Peace and security concerns have been given more attention to avert humanitarian or refugee disasters as well. There is also steady progress in educational development in several African countries. School enrollments of both genders at the primary, postprimary, and tertiary levels have been on the increase over time. Adult literacy is also impressive in Africa, since the 1970s, with an increase from 20 to 26 percent. The only problem is how to make tertiary education more relevant to the needs of the continent to employ university graduates.

Another area in which African countries are gradually showing signs of development is the bridging of gaps in gender inequality. In the past, African women were the most vulnerable group, with an unbroken record of the feminization of poverty, inequality, and degradation, but things are gradually changing in their favor. However, twenty-first-century African women have clearly demonstrated that they are indeed dynamic agents of political and economic transformation by which the dream of African development could become a reality. This is buttressed by the fact that traditional perceptions about women are being challenged in Africa more than ever before as more women become more educated. Amazingly and despite all odds, women in several endeavors in Africa are slowly but surely developing a new outlook as agents of motivation, beauty, excellence, resilience, zeal, and accountability, helping to debunk the negative and conventional views held about them in the past. Furthermore, because of the loss of faith in men to bring about the dream of African development to reality, women in Africa are clearly demonstrating that if given the chance, they are capable of bringing the black continent out of the backwoods of the African experience.

Like most of the western images and impressions about African development, ideas about African women in the past were generally biased and negative and women were regarded as housekeepers. However, the truth is that African women are more than mere numbers in the rank of female gender; they are ladies indeed, refined in definite ways, dignified, and great achievers, with so much to offer society. This is generally true of the current revolutionary sweep across Africa about women and several gender groups are emerging and collaborating to eradicate gender inequality and bring about more dynamism in the activities of women in the economy to move the continent forward. In several countries in Africa, women have risen to the challenge of contesting for elective political positions such as female vice-presidents like Phumzile Mlambo Ngcuka in South Africa, Joice Mujuru in Zimbabwe, and Luisa Diogo, the prime minister of Mozambique. President Ellen Johnson Sirleaf of Liberia did so well in her first term as president that she is going for another round. Rwanda has the highest ratio of women in parliament in the world at about 49 percent and occupies the third position of women entrepreneurs in Africa. Generally in sub-Saharan Africa, women occupy an average of 16.8 percent of parliamentary seats, which is nearly the world average of 17.1 percent.[34]

CONCLUSION

The views expressed here represent those of realists and optimists rather than pessimists on African development. I am not an idealist, however, but a humanist, and my natural bent is to be as pragmatic as I can. Throughout the analysis, my line of argument was to reiterate that the international system is very complex without any permanent categorization. It is therefore more reasonable to bear in mind our interdependence on each other rather than how we conceive of each other should be more important to us than issues of classification. The bourgeoning global migrations underscore this. More importantly, the global community should concern itself more with how the trade and financial policies and regulations, which are masterminded by the West, should be adjusted to enhance the future development of countries of the Third World. As part of Africa's dream of rapid economic growth, there is need for cooperation at global level, especially in the World Trade Organization. Aid is good, but competitive trade between nations on the basis of what Africa has is preferable so that local businesses can compete favorably in world trade to break the tradition of depending on aid in cash, technology, and skills.

On the other hand, we need to be more progressive and liberal minded in our current thinking about Africa of the twenty-first century. The economies of all the countries in Africa do not have the same capacity: some are still really poorer than others. All of them have not exhibited the capacity of the emerging economies of the Asian Tigers or Brazil. But many African countries are undoubtedly showing strong signs of economic growth and resilience. The essence is to see African development as a process on the basis of specific regions and countries. Furthermore, what is currently required is to stimulate domestic investments in the continent for sustainable growth, pursue inflation free monetary regimes, and, most importantly, invest in human capital for other regions of the globe to recognize African development more practically. Therefore, from the foregoing, the potential for African development in the near future are enormous and should be harnessed for further world development from the vast natural resources, the avalanche of arable land, and the prospect of being the largest voting bloc in the UN if the fifty-four member countries are given the chance they deserve to speak as one bloc. The stigma of the old Third World will be jettisoned when all these goals are achieved and Africa will wear a new look of development. And that is where we have to go from here.

NOTES

1. United Nations Development Programme, *Human Development Report* (New York: Oxford University Press, 1997).
2. E. A. Brett, *Colonialism and Underdevelopment in East Africa: The Politics of Economic Change, 1919–1939* (New York: Nok, 1977.)
3. W. Brandt, *North-South: A Programme for Survival* (London: Pan Books, 1980).
4. *Economist*, "Rethinking the Third World: Seeing the World Differently," June 12, 2010.
5. Meier, M. G., and James E. Rauch, *Leading Issues in Economic Development*, (New York: Oxford University Press, 2000).
6. M. G. Meier, *Leading Issues in Economic Development*, 4th ed. (Oxford, UK: Oxford University Press, 1984).
7. *Development Magazine*, No. 47 (2009): 14.
8. I. Clark, *Globalization and Fragmentation: International Relations in the Twentieth Century* (Oxford, UK: Oxford University Press, 1997).
9. Charles K. Wilber and Kenneth P. Jameson, eds., *The Political Economy of Development and Underdevelopment*, 5th ed. (New York: McGraw-Hill, 1992).
10. Gilbert, R., *The History of Development from Western Origin to Global Faith* (London: Zed Books, 1977).
11. P. Jalee, *The Pillage of the Third World*, transl. Mary Klopper (New York: Monthly Review Press, 1970).
12. W. C. Kegley, Jr., and R. E. Wittkopf, *World Politics: Trend and Transformation*, 7th ed. (New York: Worth Publishers, 1999).
13. Jalee, *The Pillage of the Third World*.
14. Ulf Himmelstrand, Kabiru Kinyanjui, and E. K. Mburugu, eds., *African Perspectives on Development* (Kampala, Uganda: Fountain Press, 1994).
15. S. P. Huntington, "The Clash of Civilizations? The Debate," *Foreign Affairs* Vol. 72 (1993): 22–49.
16. D. K. Stephen, *Structural Conflict: The World against Global Liberalism* (Berkeley and Los Angeles: University of California Press, 1985).
17. Clark, *Globalization and Fragmentation*.
18. M. P. Todaro, *Economic Development*, 6th ed. (London: Longman, 1998).
19. Walter Rodney, *How Europe Underdeveloped Africa* (London: Bogle L'Ouverture, 1976).

20. Frantz Fanon, *The Wretched of the Earth* (Harmondsworth, UK: Penguin, 1967).
21. Brandt, *North-South: A Programme for Survival*.
22. Meier and Rauch, *Leading Issues in Economic Development*.
23. Clark, *Globalization and Fragmentation*.
24. S. P. Huntington, *The Clash of Civilizations and the Remaking of World Order* (New York: Simon and Schuster, 2003).
25. Codesria, "Rethinking African Development: Beyond Impasse, Towards Alternatives," 11th General Assembly, Maputo, Mozambique, December 6–10, 2005.
26. Brandt, *North-South*.
27. Ibid.
28. International Fund for Agricultural Development, *Assessment of Rural Poverty: East and Central Africa* (Rome: IFAD, 2001).
29. United Nations, *Economic Intelligence Unit Report*, 2008.
30. Ibid.
31. *The Africa Report* No. 25 (November 2010).
32. Ibid.
33. Brandt, *North-South*.
34. M. Ndulo, ed., *Democratic Reform in Africa: Its Impact on Governance and Poverty Alleviation* (Oxford, UK: James Currey, 2006).

REFERENCES

The Africa Report No. 25 (November 2010):
Brandt, W. *North-South: A Programme for Survival*. London: Pan Books, 1980.
Brett, E. A. *Colonialism and Underdevelopment in East Africa: The Politics of Economic Change, 1919–1939*. New York: Nok, 1977.
Clark, I. *Globalization and Fragmentation: International Relations in the Twentieth Century*. Oxford, UK: Oxford University Press, 1997.
Codesria. "Rethinking African Development: Beyond Impasse, Towards Alternatives." 11th General Assembly. Maputo, Mozambique. December 6–10, 2005.
Development Magazine, Issue No. 47 (2009): 14.
Economist. "Rethinking the Third World: Seeing the World Differently." June 12, 2010.
Fanon, Frantz. *The Wretched of the Earth*. Harmondsworth: Penguin, 1967.
Gilbert, R. *The History of Development from Western Origin to Global Faith*. London: Zed Books, 1977.
Himmelstrand, Ulf, Kabiru Kinyanjui, and E. K. Mburugu, eds. *African Perspectives on Development*. Kampala, Uganda: Fountain Press, 1994.
Huntington, S. P. "The Clash of Civilizations? The Debate." *Foreign Affairs*, Vol. 72 (1993): 22–49.
———. *The Clash of Civilizations and the Remaking of World Order*. New York: Simon and Schuster, 2003.
International Fund for Agricultural Development. *Assessment of Rural Poverty: East and Central Africa*. Rome: IFAD, 2001.
Jalee, P. *The Pillage of the Third World*. Transl. Mary Klopper. New York: Monthly Review Press, 1970.
Kegley, W. C. Jr., and R. E. Wittkopf. *World Politics: Trend and Transformation*, 7th ed. New York: Worth Publishers, 1999.
Meier, M. G. *Leading Issues in Economic Development*, 4th ed. Oxford: Oxford University Press, 1984.

Meier, M. G., and James E. Rauch. *Leading Issues in Economic Development.* New York: Oxford University Press, 2000.
Ndulo, M., ed. *Democratic Reform in Africa: Its Impact on Governance and Poverty Alleviation.* Oxford, UK: James Currey, 2006.
Rodney, Walter. *How Europe Underdeveloped Africa.* London: Bogle L'Ouverture, 1976.
Stephen, D. K. *Structural Conflict: The World against Global Liberalism.* Berkeley and Los Angeles: University of California Press, 1985.
Todaro, M. P. *Economic Development,* 6th ed. London: Longman, 1998.
United Nations. *Economic Intelligence Unit Report.* 2008.
United Nations Development Programme. *Human Development Report.* New York: Oxford University Press, 1997.
Wilber, Charles K., and Kenneth P. Jameson, eds. *The Political Economy of Development & Underdevelopment,* 5th ed. New York: McGraw-Hill, 1992.

17 American Pharmaceutical Influence on Uganda's HIV/AIDS Relief System

Ben Weiss and Jessica Achberger

The purpose of this chapter is to explore American pharmaceutical influence on the distribution of antiretroviral drugs in Uganda. These drugs comprise the front-line medical defense against the fatal destruction of the human immune system caused by AIDS. As such, the adequate allocation of said drugs impacts the lives of millions of people. Uganda itself is of particular importance because its HIV/AIDS treatment programs are among the few AIDS-related large-scale success stories in Africa. Because of foreign aid from American programs like the President's Emergency Plan for AIDS Relief (PEPFAR), created in 2003, Uganda has experienced one of the most statistically significant decreases in AIDS rate in the world.

Unfortunately several recent funding developments have led to billion-dollar shortfalls in budgeting for these relief programs. Ugandan clinics are already indicating potential shutdowns. In this chapter, we will discuss current avenues for the distribution of antiretroviral drugs in Uganda and draw conclusions about why shortfalls are forecasted to have such a deleterious effect on a very successful system. That said, we will argue that Uganda is entirely too dependent on American pharmaceutical aid. The basis for this argument lies in fast-changing financial and political realities that affect the Ugandan HIV/AIDS relief infrastructure. Essentially no matter how beneficial American aid is in the short term, pharmaceutical and logistical dependence on the United States will always threaten Uganda's ability to have a sustainable HIV/AIDS treatment program.

THE ECONOMY OF HIV/AIDS

HIV/AIDS is a perfectly treatable and preventable disease. In fact, in the United States and many European nations, it is a manageable chronic illness. Western governments frequently subsidize the costs of treatment for their citizens, and people living with the disease are physically affected by it about as much as someone living with diabetes. However, much like diabetes in parts of Africa, HIV/AIDS is a huge threat to the lives and livelihoods of individuals. A lot of this derives from financial inhibitors that prevent access to the drugs that could make HIV/AIDS manageable in Africa. Even the lowest figures proposed by the *Internet Journal of International Medicine* establish that current treatment regimes can cost about US$110 a month.[1] Although affordable from the standpoint of a citizen in a western nation, this price far exceeds the income of the average citizen of an African nation. In addition, whereas most workers in developed nations enjoy the benefits of health insurance or government assistance, African workers in several nations on the continent routinely do without.

The mining conglomerates in Africa have claimed that providing their employees with antiretroviral treatment is completely infeasible. Even access to reduced prices due to business affiliations has not resulted in costs much lower than US$1,000 a year per individual, generally around the yearly income of a miner. Thus, absent litigation demanding that the mining industry provide treatment, government-funded European-style health care policies would double corporate expenses in Africa. Thus mining companies have little to no incentive to provide HIV/AIDS relief. This is an important problem to note because the mining industry represents a huge venue for the spread of HIV, since the establishment of mining towns almost always leads to the presence of rampant prostitution.

Without sufficient sovereign or corporate relief efforts, the burden of paying for treatment falls on the people of African nations, making the drugs completely unaffordable and death a day-to-day reality. Ezekiel Kalipeni simplifies the problem, pointing out that HIV/AIDS relief undertaken by the international community, rather than being a medical social service or a humanitarian effort, becomes an industry:

> The social, economic, and political forces driving HIV/AIDS are so profound and seemingly ineluctable that many argue AIDS will not see a decline in Africa until the advent of an effective vaccine. Unfortunately, one is not forthcoming in the near future. Pharmaceuticals have funneled disproportionately few resources into vaccine research relative to drug development because drugs have the better profit potential.[2]

In short, aiming the market at profit potential instead of relief potential massively undercuts anyone's ability to provide actual relief to the victims of HIV/AIDS around the world. In fact, this exacerbates the problem of fighting the rise of drug-resistant strains of HIV. When families and individuals are able to scrape enough money together for treatment, that treatment is often affordable for only a few months at a time. The treated end up relapsing, and the drugs used lose some net effectiveness. This creates a huge problem if said relapsed individual spreads the disease to anyone else. Foreign programs like PEPFAR are designed to remediate this effect.

PEPFAR: EMERGENCY RELIEF FROM AN ECONOMICALLY UNFEASIBLE OPTION

Almost 8 years after President George W. Bush's 2003 State of the Union Address announcing the creation of PEPFAR, the HIV/AIDS relief program is producing phenomenal results in prevention and treatment. Program data

Table 17.1 PEPFAR Mother-to-Child Transmission Prevention Program Coverage[5]

Country	Fiscal Year 2004	Fiscal Year 2008
Botswana	58%	68%
Ivory Coast	3%	23%
Ethiopia	0.2%	6%
Guyana	32%	87%
Haiti	8%	53%
Kenya	19%	69%
Mozambique	4%	56%
Namibia	12%	76%
Nigeria	0.4%	12%
Rwanda	11%	59%
South Africa	46%	85%
Tanzania	2%	53%
Uganda	8%	55%
Vietnam	0.1%	17%
Zambia	11%	59%
Totals	6%	32%

Economy Watch and Economic Statistics Database.

Table 17.2 Number of Individuals put on Antiretroviral Drugs by PEPFAR Globally[b]

Year	Target	Reached
2008	2,000,000	2,007,800
2007	1,300,000	1,358,000
2006	900,000	822,000
2005	500,000	401,000
2004	200,000	155,000
2003	Start	0

have shown that, through 2009, more than 2.5 million people were directly supported by its relief infrastructure and were placed on antiretrovirals. In combination with the Global Fund to Fight HIV/AIDS, Tuberculosis, and Malaria, the United States through PEPFAR has committed over US$32 billion to fighting AIDS globally.[3]

Money and effort are spread across more than thirty nations, and the program has not lost any of its initial efficacy. In fact, each month the care and prevention programs expand their operating capacities, aided by the informational support of the partner countries. Each country in which PEPFAR operates has a research division organized for the sole purpose of finding and documenting which segments of the population are most at risk and how the disease spreads demographically. These informational foundations help PEPFAR decide where to allocate both its prevention infrastructure and the necessary treatment facilities.[4] As shown in the tables below, U.S. support has been wildly successful in making sure that targeted segments of the population most in need of antiretroviral treatment have an improved rate of access to necessary pharmaceuticals that they could not otherwise afford.

In alignment with these results, Eric Goosby, the U.S. Global AIDS coordinator, explains,

> We're learning how to do this better than we did in the first couple or three years of PEPFAR. Each month brings in new insights that we are better and better positioned to realize, to see, to document and then to reintegrate that learned advantage or system change into our larger systems of care in each country.[7]

He claims with pride that the United States represents about 60 percent of the international funding for the fight against HIV/AIDS. However, he uses this claim as a springboard to encourage other nations in the world who are able to help to increase their contributions. "We are ready to be the voice to put that challenge out,"[8] he declares.

PEPFAR IN UGANDA—A STORY OF SUCCESS

In particular, Uganda has experienced stellar success in dealing with its HIV/AIDS epidemic, and much of this has been due to foreign HIV/AIDS relief funding and logistical support. Before PEPFAR set up operations in Uganda, anywhere from a fifth to a fourth of the population was infected with HIV. As shown in Table 17.3,[9] access to antiretroviral therapy has greatly increased in in Uganda. The jumps after 2003, right after PEPFAR was created, deserve special attention.

Furthermore, Table 17.4[10] indicates that the majority of the funds that have aided Uganda's HIV/AIDS relief system have come from external actors like PEPFAR.

Table 17.3 Provision of Antiretroviral Treatment from 2000 to 2007 in Uganda

Year	People Covered
June 2007	105,000
April 2007	100,000
December 2006	95,000
June 2006	85,000
December 2005	70,000
June 2005	65,000
December 2004	40,500
June 2004	17,000
December 2003	10,000
December 2002	8,500
December 2001	2,000
December 2000	0

Table 17.4 HIV/AIDS Expenditures in 2006

AIDS Spending Categories	Target Area Government	Target Area Nongovernment	Total	Percentage
Prevention	–	67,883,659,823	67,883,659,823	19%
Care and treatment	6,464,856,763	146,324,634,498	152,789,491,261	42%
Orphans and vulnerable children	–	24,611,793,105	24,611,793,105	7%
Program management and administration	15,630,428,058	64,898,546,671	80,528,974,729	22%
Incentives for human resources	–	1,692,999,066	1,692,999,066	0%
Social protection and social services	–	1,759,592,990	1,759,592,990	0%
Enabling environment and communal development	–	929,011,872	929,011,872	0%
Nonoperations research	–	33,004,475,915	33,004,475,915	9%
Totals	22,095,284,821	341,104,713,939	363,199,998,761	100%
Percentage	6.1%	93.9%		

Regardless of whether the support was externally or internally funded and organized, Uganda has utilized these resources with wild success. In the past 2 years, UNAIDS data charts show that Uganda's HIV/AIDS prevalence rate has fluctuated between 5 and 8 percent, a dramatic decrease from the highest figure of 25 percent in the late 1990s and early 2000s. However, HIV/AIDS remains a significant challenge for the nation.

By the end of 2009, over 200,000 Ugandans were receiving HIV/AIDS antiretroviral treatment. Of these people, PEPFAR programs directly supported 175,000 individuals and their medical treatment regiments. As of 2010, U.S. HIV/AIDS funding to Uganda totaled about US$280 million a year. Ultimately, a total of US$1.4 billion has been spent on fighting HIV/AIDS in Uganda since 2004. This seems remarkable in the context of the floundering markets and frugal budgets that have characterized the last decade. Beating out the U.S. global percentage of HIV/AIDS relief contribution, America makes up an impressive 70 percent of HIV/AIDS-related relief funding in Uganda.[11] Eric Goosby explains PEPFAR's importance to this fight:

> Of course, the key metric is not the amount spent on a particular intervention, but the lives saved. That is why under President Obama's Global Health Initiative (GHI), we are working to save as many lives as possible by addressing the range of health needs people in countries like Uganda face, such as maternal and child health, health systems, neglected tropical diseases, and—of course—HIV/AIDS. By linking our activities, we will have a significant impact on the longevity and quality of life of millions of people now suffering from preventable and treatable diseases. PEPFAR is the cornerstone of this effort, which reflects lessons learned from the success of PEPFAR in Uganda and other countries.[12]

PEPFAR is undeniably of critical value to the Ugandan HIV/AIDS relief system in its ability to provide support. Ironically, PEPFAR'S greatest value to the government and people of Uganda is also its greatest detriment to the country.

LOOMING THREATS TO UGANDA'S HIV/AIDS RELIEF SYSTEM

Unfortunately the unprecedented success Uganda has had in fighting HIV/AIDS coupled with the overwhelming percentage of American foreign aid used in this fight has created unintended consequences. Uganda is dependent upon American foreign aid to avoid drastic slowing in its anti-HIV/AIDS progress or, worse yet, regression to higher transmission rates. Imagine the effect if America were to cut its support in half—a scenario quite possible in today's budget-cutting environment. First and foremost, the antiretroviral supply would be severely inhibited. This alone could destroy Uganda's ability to make progress against HIV/AIDS. However, there are several other ways in which a shortfall in support could damage the nation.

In mid-2010, American leaders began discussing substantial cuts to PEPFAR, cuts that are still on the table for U.S. policymakers. Several very vocal economists and public health officials in the United States, with little expertise specifically in the crisis that HIV presents for sub-Saharan Africa, have been pushing for a reduction in contributions for HIV/AIDS relief infrastructure. These economists argue that donor money ought to be funneled toward building health systems rather than dealing with a specific disease. However, these vocal proponents of funds reduction fail to realize that (1) the link between HIV victims' life expectancy and their economic contribution to GDP in countries like Uganda is strong and (2) a substantial number of health systems have been built solely because they are necessary to accommodate the HIV/AIDS infrastructure. These health systems have garnered unprecedented community involvement in the fight against HIV/AIDS in sub-Saharan Africa as compared with generic health policy or any other specific disease.[13]

Clearly the challenges are significant. On the campaign trail in 2008, President Obama promised a billion-dollar increase in PEPFAR's HIV/AIDS relief funding every single year. However, there has yet to be any meaningful increase.[14] In 2009, despite this significant commitment by the United States, the allocation of the Global Fund to Fight AIDS, Tuberculosis and Malaria was only US$4.2 million (from a grant awarded in 2007). This was far below both the amount allocated and the wildly unrealistic promises of President Obama. The lack of increased funding was attributed to continuing governance issues in Uganda. However, it is much more likely that governance issues this was just a convenient excuse and that foreign relief fell prey to the budget-cutting axe. Although there has been progress in addressing both funding levels and the cited Ugandan governance issues, funding lags recent years have led to the closing of many clinics in Uganda, which in turn has severely increased the pressures on other service sites, the majority of which are supported by PEPFAR. Additionally, the impending withdrawal of medicines donated by the UNITAID health fund has led to a great deal of uncertainty among the ranks of PEPFAR administrative officials regarding supplies for HIV treatment providers.[15]

The effects are extremely personal. Clinics have already started to identify Ugandan citizens who will be cut off from treatment. One clinic alone, Mildmay Uganda, has indicated that at least 4,447 children living with HIV will languish without treatment after the clinic goes through a likely shutdown because of PEPFAR shortfalls.[16] Even more concerning is what these shutdowns could do to the disease itself. Mary Lugembe, an HIV-positive mother of two, was on antiretrovirals prescribed in Uganda by a PEPFAR-supported clinic. Unexpectedly, in November 2009, her health degenerated drastically. Lugembe was adamant that she followed the appropriate treatment regimen as directed by her doctors. However, she also admitted that she was having unprotected sex with her husband. Lugembe was later told that despite being on antiretrovirals, having unprotected sex with another HIV-positive individual exposed her to a more lethal strain of the virus. As Lugembe discovered the hard way, the viral strain of HIV is hard to predict and control because it keeps changing as it multiplies in body cells. This predicament is exacerbated if an individual becomes infected with multiple strains, and that is why Lugembe's antiretroviral treatment failed.[17] Fortunately, Lugembe's story did not end in tragedy. The Joint Clinical Research Centre in Entebbe is one of a limited group of Ugandan clinics that has the medical resources to handle drug-resistant strains. Lugembe was able to receive treatment there. However, like most other clinics in the country, the Joint Clinical Research Centre is PEPFAR-supported. Given the present realities of PEPFAR funding, the future of even this research center is uncertain.[18]

For many, these fears have already become a reality. Health staff at the Hope Clinic in Kampala, a large HIV/AIDS pharmaceutical provider, argue that current trends will make for changes in clinics that have had the capacity to give free treatment to every patient who arrives on site. As of the moment, patients who are already enrolled in antiretroviral treatment through their clinical services will continue to get their drugs for the foreseeable future. However, this clinic cannot operate in the capacity it used to owing to already occurring cuts. Now almost all new patients go on a waiting list. A treatment slot is open only to someone on the waiting list when a current patient dies. Mugyenyi, a spokesperson for the clinic, said that they turn away up to twenty patients every day. "As people who saw the devastation of the past, we fear we may have a setback," he told CNN, "the achievements we have made over the years with PEPFAR—we might begin to see a reversal of the benefits we have seen."[19]

A much larger problem looms when all of the patients who have had access to antiretroviral drugs are no longer able to procure them. When the 4,447 children lose their antiretroviral supplies, a greatly increased risk that HIV/AIDS will evolve into more drug-resistant strains will be born. This will clog care centers that are already unable to treat drug resistant HIV/AIDS until the doctors there realize they cannot treat it, causing the patients to overwhelm the resources of the centers that can treat drug resistance.

In addition to PEPFAR woes, another setback has come on the global scale. The Global Fund to Fight HIV/AIDS, Tuberculosis, and Malaria took a huge credibility hit when it was discovered that the donor contributions were being horribly mismanaged. On January 23, 2011, nearly 200 American and 50 international media outlets ran the story headed "Fraud Plagues Global Fund." The report said that millions upon millions of Global Fund dollars were being embezzled and misappropriated by on-the-ground operations all across Africa. Already, analysts are predicting that the huge hit to legitimacy in the global AIDS fight will translate to widespread donor reductions and thus more budget cuts.[20]

Potentially the worst threat to Ugandan HIV/AIDS relief efforts comes from the international legal arena, and it could be exponentially disastrous for the funds of programs like PEPFAR. The European Union is pushing India into a free trade agreement specific to HIV medications. India produces the same antiretrovirals as European manufacturers at a fraction of the cost. Programs like PEPFAR in Uganda buy these drugs because they can supply a larger portion of the population.[21] Michelle Childs, director of policy and advocacy for Médecins Sans Frontières' campaign for access to essential medicines, explained the free trade deal:

> The European Union is pushing for data exclusivity, which means Indian generics manufacturers would no longer be able to use existing studies to make identical drugs, a practice recommended by WHO [UN World health Organization]—they would have to conduct their own clinical trials, which would be unethical and redundant since we already have evidence that the drug works, but also, the data exclusivity could last anywhere between five and 10 years, delaying poor countries' access to these drugs for long periods.[22]

Beyond the time delay, Indian manufacturers would have to pay for hundreds of millions of dollars worth of testing. This cost would be passed along to the customer, causing antiretroviral prices to skyrocket. Programs like PEPFAR would not only be forced to limit the amount of drugs they could purchase but also to pull patients on antiretrovirals off them, creating more opportunities for drug-resistant strains of HIV/AIDS to proliferate. The EU-India trade deal would generate an enormous amount of profit, but it would also result in death for many Africans. Those who require the newer, second-line drugs (because front-line drugs like Tenofivir are no longer effective) will be subject to years of waiting for the Indian brands—that is, if they prove to be affordable in the first place. Most of the drugs taken in Africa are Indian generics. Anything that changes the nature of the Indian generics system will alter the health and livelihood of millions of HIV-positive people in Africa, and not for the better.[23]

Thus there are a great many factors that threaten the sustainability of the HIV/AIDS relief system in Uganda. The system is almost entirely operated by PEPFAR and external donors, which means it is subject to the pulls of international economic and political battles. Any one of the above scenarios will cause Ugandan HIV/AIDS treatment to grind to a halt. The more daunting yet more likely problem is the occurrence of some combination of these scenarios. Thus it is important to take swift action to minimize the possible impact of these threats.

PEPFAR IN NIGERIA: NOT JUST A UGANDAN PROBLEM

While Uganda has been represented as a success story in fighting HIV/AIDS, Nigeria, a somewhat underrepresented example, also shares similar progress in its battle. As of the end of 2010, PEPFAR had provided more than US$2 billion in foreign aid specifically designed to fight HIV/AIDS in Nigeria. US$500 million dollars of this was sent in the fiscal year 2010 alone, revealing a trend toward more of a commitment to AIDS prevention and treatment in the country, soon to be undermined by what appears to be oncoming budget cuts to PEPFAR. The new United Nations global report on AIDS recently listed Nigeria as one of the 33 countries in the world and one of 22 countries in sub-Saharan Africa where the prevalence rate of HIV has declined by more than 25 percent between in only 8 years. Moreover, this report states that Nigeria is only one of five African countries with large-scale epidemics where the spread of the virus has met international standards to be described as being stabilized, Uganda being one of the others.[24]

In 2004, identifying areas of need, UNAIDS and the World Health Organization estimated that PEPFAR had placed nearly 26 percent of the 750,000 people in need of antiretroviral treatment on the drugs.[25]

Furthermore, in the years since these data were published, the number of people treated in Nigeria by PEPFAR programs increased substantially. Table 17.6 reveals that, in less than a year from the December 2007 statistics, nearly 25,000 more Nigerians were placed on antiretroviral treatments, leaving Nigeria the third-best-supported of PEPFAR's fifteen focus countries. This also means that financial support is rapidly increasing.[26]

However, what is most instilling of hope is not the statistics themselves but what they mean. If one single relief program of one single nation can make such a contribution to Nigeria, covering such a relatively large population of infected individuals, it is a given that the right amount of international support can strangle AIDS globally. These statistics show us that severely limiting or even entirely eradicating HIV/AIDS is a real possibility and not just some utopian thought. We will certainly approach that point soon in Nigeria as long as the support continues to keep the disease in retreat. Alas, as in the case of Uganda, therein lies the pin that can destroy the whole bubble.

Almost every single one of the factors that poses a threat to PEPFAR's operations in Uganda also represents serious risks in Nigeria. In some cases, the threat is even worse. As a country often seen as a haven for economic

Table 17.5 PEPFAR's HIV/AIDS Treatment in Nigeria, 2007

Country	People Receiving Treatment in December 2007	People Needing Treatment in 2007	Treatment Coverage
Nigeria	198,000	750,000	26%

Table 17.6 PEPFAR Provided Treatment In Its Fifteen Focus Nations

Country	American-Provided Treatment July 2004	American-Provided Treatment September 2004	American-Provided Treatment September 2005	American-Provided Treatment September 2006	American-Provided Treatment September 2007	American-Provided Treatment September 2008
Botswana	–	32,900	37,300	67,500	90,500	111,700
Ivory Coast	400	4,500	11,100	27,600	46,000	50,500
Ethiopia	–	9,500	16,200	40,000	81,800	119,600
Guyana	–	500	800	1,600	2,100	2,300
Haiti	–	2,800	4,300	8,000	12,900	17,700
Kenya	2,700	17,100	44,700	97,800	166,400	229,700
Mozambiqu	–	5,200	16,200	34,200	78,200	118,000
Namibia	2,500	4,000	14,300	26,300	43,700	56,100
Nigeria	500	13,500	28,500	67,100	126,400	211,500
Rwanda	100	4,300	15,900	30,000	44,400	59,900
South Africa	3,700	12,200	93,000	210,300	329,000	549,700
Tanzania	100	1,500	14,700	44,300	96,700	144,100
Uganda	7,300	33,000	67,500	89,200	106,000	145,000
Vietnam	–	0	700	6,600	11,700	24,500
Zambia	1,500	13,600	36,000	71,500	122,700	167,500
Totals	18,800	155,000	401,000	822,000	1,358,500	2,007,800

corruption, the cuts to Nigerian aid could be sharper than in Uganda as a result of the aforementioned Global Fund scandal. Furthermore, the problems with PEPFAR drug distribution and expense can also be found in Nigeria, including the threat represented by the loss of production rights by Indian generic manufacturers. It is possible that the strong social forces mandating commitment in marriage may protect members of the Muslim communities in northern Nigeria, but this does little to prevent the spread of HIV/AIDS among those abiding by less stringent religious codes in the metropolitan cities to the south. Many of the ways in which Nigeria and Uganda are at risk of an HIV/AIDS resurgence are similar. Although unfortunate for these countries, the fact that similar situations exist in two different nations, far removed from each other, with completely different social, political, and economic realities, is strongly illustrative of a larger flaw with the way America conducts is policy not only on HIV/AIDS relief in one nation but also across the world. Indeed, these problems may lie in how the United States dispenses foreign aid in general.

INDICATORS OF A MUCH LARGER PROBLEM

In and of itself, the nature of Uganda's—and Nigeria's—position in the battle against HIV/AIDS is precarious at best. However, this situation is only a symptom of the larger disease that plagues Ugandan economic policy. In 2009 alone, the growth rate of the country's gross domestic product took a dive down by about 1.9 percent.[27] In itself, this does not reveal much. However, when put in direct correlation with recent American budget cuts to foreign aid programs in Uganda, we can see not only how dependant Uganda is on the United States for HIV/AIDS relief but also how much the whole Ugandan economic structure relies on foreign support. The frightening conclusion behind this analysis is that much more than health infrastructure is on the line in Uganda. In fact, a major withdrawal of aid there could lead to a full economic meltdown in all sectors. The World Bank estimates that U.S. dollars put into Ugandan economic growth in 2009 were upwards of US$ 16 billion.[28] The unfortunate truth is that a huge chunk of the national budget in Uganda is made up of American dollars.

Even more of a folly is how this funding is allocated. Although PEPFAR claims to provide the countries in which it operates with the supplies necessary to maintain a sustainable HIV/AIDS relief system, it does anything but make the system sustainable per se. The actual ability of the whole health infrastructure to work is reliant on supplies from PEPFAR, including pharmaceuticals, testing kits, and education programs. The local governments and people are often less involved than PEPFAR would like to have the world believe. The problem with this is the same as has been stated above. When and if the funding gets cut, the staff will leave, medicine shipments will end, and logistics support will cease. PEPFAR is not doing enough to make sure that the countries it provides for are able to take up the reins if need be. Based on the figures for Uganda, it is apparent that this phenomenon is a problem across the board for foreign money invested in any of the economic sectors, let alone the health industry.

As shown by the way PEPFAR is organized in Nigeria, the risk is a similar there. In fact, it is not a stretch to say that most of the nations in which PEPFAR operates are ill equipped to handle their own epidemics without overwhelming support from America. The United States is not training these nations in the most historically effective ways to control HIV/AIDS. It is attempting to do the job for them, and there is no security in the completion of that mandate by a particular actor when the world has been engaged in this fight for more than 30 years.

REFORMING HOW WE THINK ABOUT FOREIGN AID: THE FIRST STEP TOWARD FINDING VIABLE LONG-TERM SOLUTIONS

Reduction in HIV/AIDS transmission is integral to a country's stability, especially in the economic sector. Individuals from their mid-teens to about 50 years of age are disproportionably targeted by HIV/AIDS merely because this age group is most likely to be sexually active. Unfortunately these individuals comprise the backbone of the economy as well as the majority of rising political leaders and citizens who are more apt to be politically aware and politically active. PEPFAR needs to look toward more sustainable practices in the fight against HIV/AIDS. Until there is a vaccine that has any claim to long-term efficacy, the treatment infrastructure will never be sustainable because it depends on a constant stream of supplies from external factors, such as antiretroviral market prices, trade patterns, and international politicking. Uganda must begin to think and act beyond the scope of international relief.

Many solutions, while helpful, will remediate only a small part of the problem. As shown in the preceding discussion, the greatest reason international affairs have such a capacity for catastrophic influence on Uganda's HIV/AIDS relief system has to do with the psyche of external dependence, which creates national lassitude. Uganda itself is doing very little to take the lead in its fight against HIV/AIDS. Instead of planning or creating infrastructure, arranging the national budget to contribute to the HIV/AIDS battle, or establishing independent research initiatives, Uganda's government remains in a catatonic state. Foreign aid is, in this case, not the proverbial drug that cures but the drug that sustains an illness, so to speak. Unfortunately this creates a classic conundrum: if the international community and organizations like PEPFAR pull out of Uganda or cut their supplies, the country will be left with very little to work with on its own. Clinics will invariably close. On the other hand, continuous dependence upon fickle foreign aid may, in the long run, make valiant programs such as PEPFAR all for naught.

To meet the need for pharmaceutical independence, Uganda's national government must take the reins and establish itself as the central actor in leading the national response to HIV/AIDS in particular. While the commitment of the United States and PEPFAR has been extraordinary and is greatly appreciated, the United States cannot be the sole resource for reaching the shared global goal of access to AIDS treatment everywhere, including Uganda. Because of the current nature of treatment aid, Uganda's health policy has become stagnant and the government complacent.

For a start, PEPFAR staff around the country ought to work with their Ugandan counterparts to study in great detail the treatment expenditures of the country so that Uganda may develop a plan that results in more people accessing treatment. This should not just be limited to securing supplies but also should take into account the location of clinics, building of roads, and the physical act of distributing antiretrovirals, so that the process can be streamlined. Instead of just procuring external drugs, Uganda should make long-term investments in making HIV/AIDS treatment as widespread and efficient as possible. Although PEPFAR funds could disappear tomorrow, a road that makes a 5-day trek across the Ugandan countryside to the nearest clinic into a 3-hour journey by car will still be years away. One of the biggest and most meaningful investment suggestions might be the development of a Ugandan system of antiretroviral manufacture. South Africa has recently developed such a system, and as a result its HIV/AIDS relief infrastructure is much more self-contained and less susceptible to external shortcomings.

At the end of the day, PEPFAR needs to pursue a new approach to governmental engagement in its HIV/AIDS treatment protocols, an approach that would replace paternalism with real social responsibility. The government of Uganda and the people of Uganda need to be involved in the research, planning, and execution of any decision made about their HIV/AIDS relief system. PEPFAR needs to seek meaningful collaboration and contribution to the HIV response from Uganda, ultimately engaging it in the process of addressing the critical needs of the country. Uganda needs to achieve better health outcomes for the Ugandan population because ultimately, in the event that PEPFAR fails, it is Uganda's future at stake, not America's.

NOTES

1. ISPUB, "A Study on Prescription Pattern and Cost Analysis Of Antiretroviral Drugs," *Internet Journal of International Medicine*, No. 6 (April 2010): http://www.ispub.com/journal/the_internet_journal_of_internal_medicine/volume_8_number_2_18/article/a-study-on-prescription-pattern-and-cost-analysis-of-antiretroviral-drugs.html

2. Ezekiel Kalipeni, *HIV and AIDS in Africa: Beyond Epidemiology* (Malden, MA: Blackwell, 2004): 256.
3. Stephen Kaufman, "PEPFAR Showing Greater Effectiveness, Efficiency Against HIV/AIDS United States Mission Geneva." *United States Mission Geneva*, November 2, 2010: http://geneva.usmission.gov/2010/11/15/pepfar/
4. Ibid.
5. US PEPFAR, "Celebrating Life: Latest PEPFAR Results," 2008: http://www.pepfar.gov/documents/organization/115411.pdf
6. Ibid.
7. Kaufman, "PEPFAR Showing Greater Effectiveness."
8. Ibid.
9. Ministry of Health Records, 2005, 2006, 2007.
10. "The UNGASS National Funding-AIDS Spending Categories by Financing Source for the Financial Years 05/06 and 06/07," HealthNet Consult, 2007.
11. Eric Goosby, "Global Health Progress Media Center PEPFAR Programs in Uganda: An Update," *Global Health Progress*, July 14, 2010: http://globalhealthprogress.org/mediacenter/index.php/pepfar-programs-in-uganda-an-update/
12. Ibid.
13. "Pepfar Funding Threatened: What Does This Mean for HIV Treatment and Prevention Programmes?" *Writing Rights*, February 10, 2010: http://writingrights.org/2010/02/11/pepfar-funding-threatened-what-does-this-mean-for-hiv-treatment-and-prevention-programmes/
14. Tom Odula, "African AIDS Activists Slam U.S. Funding Shortfall," *Chicago Defender*, May 21, 2009: http://www.chicagodefender.com/article-4606-african-aids-activists-slam-us-funding-shortfall.html
15. Goosby, "Global Health Progress Media Center."
16. Issac Khisa and Eunice Rukundo, "Uganda: 4,500 Lives at Risk as Aids Clinic Shuts," October 12, 2010: http://allafrica.com/stories/201010120093.html
17. Haggai Matsiko, "Uganda: HIV's Deadliest Strain," November 2, 2010: http://allafrica.com/stories/201011030093.html
18. Ibid.
19. David McKenzie and Brent Swails, "Funding Threat to Uganda's Winning AIDS Program," June 18, 2010: http://articles.cnn.com/2010–06–18/world/uganda.aids_1_pepfar-plan-for-aids-relief-ugandan?_s=PM:WORLD
20. Bernard Rivers, "Africa: Corruption by Global Fund Grant Implementers," January 27, 2011: http://allafrica.com/stories/201101280926.html
21. IRIN, "EU-India Deal Could Threaten Access to Essential HIV Drugs," November 9, 2010: http://allafrica.com/stories/201011090721.html
22. Ibid.
23. Ibid.
24. U.S. Department of State, "Programs and Events: United States Diplomatic Mission to Nigeria." *United States Diplomatic Mission to Nigeria*, December 1, 2010: http://nigeria.usembassy.gov/prog_12012010.html
25. U.S. PEPFAR, "The U.S. President's Emergency Plan for AIDS Relief (PEPFAR)," *AIDS & HIV Information from the AIDS Charity AVERT*, April 19, 2011: http://www.avert.org/pepfar.htm
26. Ibid.
27. The World Bank, "Economic Policy and External Debt | Data," Spring 2011: http://data.worldbank.org/topic/economic-policy-and-external-debt
28. Ibid.

REFERENCES

FHI 360. "GHAIN: Global HIV/AIDS Initiative in Nigeria." UN Global AIDS Report: Nigeria, 2010: http://www.fhi.org/NR/rdonlyres/ejo6cnei63tdlvxwgky7auvml4jslzkc4ivmxudzvlhwsltwxffofruknca5n4vmmqqjlppvfgh74j/GHAINStrategiesenhv1.pdf

Goosby, Eric. "Global Health Progress Media Center PEPFAR Programs in Uganda: An Update." *Global Health Progress,* July 14, 2010: http://globalhealthprogress.org/mediacenter/index.php/pepfar-programs-in-uganda-an-update/

IRIN. "EU-India Deal Could Threaten Access to Essential HIV Drugs." November 9, 2010: http://allafrica.com/stories/201011090721.html

ISPUB. "A Study On Prescription Pattern And Cost Analysis of Antiretroviral Drugs." *Internet Journal of International Medicine,* April 6, 2010: http://www.ispub.com/journal/the_internet_journal_of_internal_medicine/volume_8_number_2_18/article/a-study-on-prescription-pattern-and-cost-analysis-of-antiretroviral-drugs.html

Kalipeni, Ezekiel. *HIV and AIDS in Africa: Beyond Epidemiology.* Malden, MA: Blackwell, 2004.

Kaufman, Stephen. "PEPFAR Showing Greater Effectiveness, Efficiency against HIV/AIDS: United States Mission Geneva." *United States Mission Geneva.* November 2, 2010: http://geneva.usmission.gov/2010/11/15/pepfar/

Khisa, Isaac, and Eunice Rukundo. "Uganda: 4,500 Lives at Risk as Aids Clinic Shuts." October 12, 2010: http://allafrica.com/stories/201010120093.html

Matsiko, Haggai. "Uganda: HIV's Deadliest Strain." November 2, 2010: http://allafrica.com/stories/201011030093.html

McKenzie, David, and Brent Swails. "Funding Threat to Uganda's Winning AIDS Program." June 18, 2010: http://articles.cnn.com/2010-06-18/world/uganda.aids_1_pepfar-plan-for-aids-relief-ugandan?_s=PM:WORLD

New Vision. "Uganda: Teens with HIV Prefer Religion to ARVs." October 13, 2010: http://allafrica.com/stories/201010140054.html

Odula, Tom. "African AIDS Activists Slam U.S. Funding Shortfall." *Chicago Defender.* May 21, 2009: http://www.chicagodefender.com/article-4606-african-aids-activists-slam-us-funding-shortfall.html

Rivers, Bernard. "Africa: Corruption by Global Fund Grant Implementers." January 27, 2011: http://allafrica.com/stories/201101280926.html

"The UNGASS National Funding—AIDS Spending Categories by Financing Source for the Financial years 05/06 and 06/07." HealthNet Consult. 2007.

U.S. Department of State. "Programs and Events: United States Diplomatic Mission to Nigeria." *United States Diplomatic Mission to Nigeria.* December 1, 2010: http://nigeria.usembassy.gov/prog_12012010.html

U.S. PEPFAR. "Celebrating Life: Latest PEPFAR Results." *US PEPFAR.* 2008: http://www.pepfar.gov/documents/organization/115411.pdf

U.S. PEPFAR. "The U.S. President's Emergency Plan for AIDS Relief (PEPFAR)." *AIDS & HIV Information from the AIDS Charity AVERT.* 2010: http://www.avert.org/pepfar.htm

World Bank. "Economic Policy and External Debt." Spring 2011: http://data.worldbank.org/topic/economic-policy-and-external-debt

Writing Rights. "Pepfar Funding Threatened: What Does This Mean for HIV Treatment and Prevention Programmes?" February 10, 2010: http://writingrights.org/2010/02/11/pepfar-funding-threatened-what-does-this-mean-for-hiv-treatment-and-prevention-programmes/

18 An African's View of the Aftermath of Copenhagen's Climate Change Conference

Olivier J. Tchouaffe

"There are no boundaries in the sky."

This chapter builds upon the Copenhagen Conference of 2009 to foreground Africa at the center of the global environmental crisis. It does this through the relationship prism between power and the environment and how crises are framed in terms of sovereignty and self-interest rather than environmental justice and global public welfare. It analyzes how these discursive frameworks and approaches to global climate change inform the infighting among the superpowers and emerging powers, including the United States, China, India, and the European Economic Community (EEC), and where Africa appears as a residual player irrelevant to contemporary energy problems. Africa is equally disengaged from active participation in emergency activities against climate change. This work argues that these forms of insularity are shortsighted because, when it comes to the environment, there is indeed no place to hide; therefore environmental justice cannot be privatized in the hands of the few. This chapter advocates carbon pricing, the transfer of green technologies, and better communication between science, the media, and individual activism as a way out of this crisis.

Consequently it poses the central question of what constitutes an ethic of public welfare on a global scale, particularly when the continent of Africa remains the most likely to suffer most in a comprehensive environmental collapse, even though its pollution output is very low compared with Europe, America, and Asia. Specifically, this chapter seeks to answer how to think ethically about a phenomenon that will reverberate throughout the rest of the globe, how to reconceptualize our relationship to the environment, and whether or not an anthropocentric conceptualization of the environment is still valid. Indeed, climate change does not recognize borders. As such, handling climate change appropriately is important for the global climate equilibrium and the quality of life on this planet. In kind, climate change is a global challenge that requires substantial questions, definite answers, and incentives.

In itself, this work aims to deconstruct the globalization discourses around climate change and the African continent and examine how cooperation between north and south is crucial in terms of the utilization of resources and the management of diverse ecosystems and species, resources, and land in general. This chapter claims that the logic of climate change relates directly to food security; the prospect of malnutrition and starvation; the collapse of the social order; access to the distribution of food; the role of the state in the farming business; global trade and agriculture; investment; and trade rules, which show unequal power between the north and the south, all of which must be reworked to overcome the challenges of global warming. This chapter emphasizes that this global environmental debate is taking place against the backdrop of a powerful "Promethean discourses" that Dryzek defines as follows:

> For several centuries, at least in the industrializing and industrialized West, the dominant Promethean order has been taken for granted. The industrial revolution produced technological changes that made materials close to home (such as coal and later oil) into useful resources. At the same time, European colonial expansion opened up whole new continents and oceans for exploitation. Against this background, capitalist economic growth became taken as the normal condition of a healthy society.[1]

It is important to couch that critique as central to the global environmental debate. Furthermore, the "Promethean ethos" does not incorporate the proven idea that our planet is finite, fragile, and interconnected in challenging the neoliberal ethos of the "invisible hand of the market," which dominates the environmental discourse.

In this, "the invisible hand" creates the best socio economic outcomes for all because businesses and corporations work to produce goods that benefit all. This Promethean horizon comes packaged with a trickle-down redistributive philosophy of economic progress that must be put into context when it comes to the environment, particularly since 82 percent of climate scientists recognize that human activities are significant contributors in altering climate. Evidence of nonstop climatic catastrophes—recently in New Zealand, Pakistan, Japan, and Haiti—and hunger riots in Mozambique, Zambia, Burkina Faso, and Cameroon (owing to high food inflation, particularly, wheat) led people to the street to protest the high prices of food commodities. In places where people spend up to 80 percent of their income to feed themselves, these riots powerfully challenge the market-oriented drive of the environment that led to the threat of revolutions in Africa.[2] In the same vein, two years of drought, which threatened four million Somalis with hunger, directly shows how the politicization of food aid subjects the African people.[3]

It is necessary to understand that capitalism cannot simply be reduced to a market and a religion of progress that fail to take lives and ecosystems into account. Additionally, scientific authorities are operating in the age of social media, freedom of information requests, and openness of data, which are often used to discourage scientists and inhibit research. It is clear that sound environmental policies have to be based on sound scientific information for a well-balanced and robust policy debate; however, social media adds another layer of complexity to these processes. Social media carry this environmental debate beyond the management and influence of scientific authorities. They introduce a real conundrum about the legitimacy of experts versus ordinary citizens in 24- hour global media sound bites.

NATIVE CONTEXT

This work occurs within a reflection on the role of intellectuals facing a string of rapid events, all occurring abruptly—including the Arab Spring in the Middle East and earthquakes and tsunamis in Haiti, Pakistan, New Zealand, and Japan—creating a series of problems related to intellectual exercise, immediacy, and memory. Precisely, the clash between new media and the rapid global flow of events creates the proper context of interpretation and conditions in which an innovative and pioneering new institutional order can take root. This work will reflect on the relationship between the demands of explication and clarification compared with the complexities of decrypting contexts and the genealogy of events within an accelerating global flow of information.

Indeed, the rising number of natural catastrophes affects interactions between human beings and the land. It becomes clear that every day, as we try to conquer nature, we seem to be creating only more problems. In his 2011 State of the Union Address, Barack Obama claimed that nuclear power was clean energy. After Fukushima, the question seems to be who wants to live near a nuclear reactor.[4] With Fukushima, the earth seems to do what it wants; it seems to have an autonomy of its own and does things that are unpredictable. Within that context, we need humility. Thus a model based on unreasonable development and more spending seems unsustainable.

The appropriation of lands demonstrates that nature is no longer inert, something just there to be possessed. Earth's unpredictability makes speculation about risks very difficult. It begins with a genealogy of events and the fact that there are cities built on waste, such as Tokyo, and houses built on shorelines or fault lines, as in California. We must rethink how we build cities today. Furthermore, catastrophes demonstrate the failure of the state, as seen in Haiti. Even well-prepared countries, such as Japan, struggle with natural disasters like earthquakes and tsunamis. Hence one must not underestimate the difficulties of discussing climate change. For example, discussions about nuclear energy are embedded in notions of classified defense, which creates opacity of information owing to the conflict between national security and alternative energy development. The goal here is to find a functioning paradigm to understand and work through all these events. It means using resources of knowledge to historicize the notion of climate change and thus to design a new global social contract.

The Copenhagen Climate Change Conference of 2009 offered an opportunity to explore why the world is divided on this issue and to address discursive practices around climate science. It begins with unpacking the representation of science, its intercultural esthetics, and its practical values involving its relationship with politics. These processes help flesh out the role that Africa plays in the debate on climate change. This work claims that it requires a radical process of interdisciplinary rethinking. In kind, climate change invokes the influence of culture as a resource for the economy and policy. Culture provides a basis for developmental projects, investment, and consumption practices as well as a rhetorical basis for social change.

The crux of the problem with climate change is that deals mandating emission cuts mean paying more money for green power. It brings in an economic rationality that undermines the threat of global climate change because many countries fear that it might slow down economic growth, particularly in Africa, where many countries still rely on fossil fuels. Hence clean energy does not come cheap, and global warming creates a wedge in the capitalist system because it replaces profits with conservation. As such, climate justice becomes problematic when confronted with notions of a neoliberal market, infinite desire, and profit.[5]

The response to this economic rationality lies in the knowledge that climate change also destroys cultures through neoliberalism and notions of unlimited desire that can be fulfill through market forces and excessive individualism, rather than shared values such as justice and solidarity. The debate around climate change, however, focuses on rhetoric of limited resources on the planet and questions excessive modes of consumption to foreground environmental justice. It comes packaged with questions of norms and quotas and a system of rationing such as global cap and trade and carbon taxes. The inevitable questions are: Shall we create an estimate of nature in order to save it? Within that context, how do we determine justice? Why follow the rules if others do not?

At the core of climate change are the responsibilities of the media and how communication between the scientist and the public can improve. It is about how universities produce research and therefore institutional incentives and systems of rewards and punishments. Copenhagen's failure also attests to the polemic about climatology and how scientists communicate with a vast number of people locked into the fast tempo of the news cycle, in which the Internet gives the public coownership of the news. The discourses surrounding global warming lead to the discussion of the role of global civil societies with nongovernmental organizations (NGOs)—such as Oxfam International, Greenpeace, or Climate Action Networks International—in order to establish the distinction between governmental self-interest and the global civil society.

COPENHAGEN

More than 1,500 journalists covered the Copenhagen Climate Conference, held from December 7–18, 2009. It opened with a call for a global initiative to face the pressing problem of out-of-control greenhouse gas emissions. The conference called for a 50 percent reduction in emissions by 2050 in order to prevent global temperatures from rising 2 to 4 percent. Copenhagen's collective failure to deliver the greenhouse targets showed the tensions between climate science, nationalism, finances, and values on the one hand and climate science and its relationship with media and the quality of its communication on the other.

Thus this failure to provide a binding legal treaty to decarbonize the planet addresses the difficulties to reconcile the rhetoric surrounding global governance and national self-interest. It complicates the consensus around building a universal democratic policy. The lack of a single policy, consequently, highlights the conflict between global political representatives and the consciousness required for new forms of collective actions versus the interferences of powerful governments such as the United States, China, and India, intent on preserving their individual sovereignty. Additionally, Copenhagen raises concerns about supranational institutions such as the United Nations and their strategy to produce a single policy. In kind, the United Nations has 192 members that serve democratically within the charters of the institution. Nobody believes, however, that the UN carries the same weight as a single African nation. Thus the global governance for climate change can become a way to defeat citizens from the Third World.

In the following pages, this work will highlight the role of China and the United States in Copenhagen and how their attitudes complicate the negotiation over climate change and their implications for developing countries in Africa.

CHINA AND THE RIGHT TO POLLUTE

What came out of Copenhagen is that global warming is a matter of perception. It highlighted the problem of global governance and the influence of specific countries such as China, a nation that has a different understanding of global warming than Europe or the United States. As such, Copenhagen appears to be ineffective because China was accused of blocking all the possibilities of creative conclusions for global warming.[6] China announced prior to the Copenhagen Conference its intention to reduce its carbon emissions by 40 to 45 percent by 2020 compared with its 2005 levels. China refuses to open up its borders for independent control of its programs for the reduction of gas emissions. The country believes in its right to develop its industries quickly and without interference. As a result, temperatures will increase by 2 degrees in the coming years, even though

Africans are not responsible for this increase.[7] The fact that China refuses to allow international regulation of its emissions means a death sentence for poor countries in Africa.

This is where global warming turns into climate justice. Even though there are 192 nations, as identified by membership in the UN, China and the United States alone produce more than 40 percent of the world's emission. To broaden that to the G20, these countries account for 80 percent of the world total global emissions as well as 85 percent of the global GDP.[8] China notes that developed countries have produced 80 percent of gas emissions in the past 200 years.[9] Thus the Chinese believe that it is farfetched to use the environment to control the growth of emerging countries. On this point, Chinese scholar and climatologist Wang Feng writes that it is immoral to press China to reduce it gas emissions while the country undertakes its effort to build a strong middle class. Relying on Adam Smith's *The Wealth of Nations*, Feng claims that "it is not from the benevolence of the butcher, the brewer or the baker that we expect our dinner, but from their regard to their own self-interest. We address ourselves, not to their humanity, but to their self-love, and never talk to them of our own necessities, but of their advantages." Thus, as Feng adds, "from the perspective of China's national development strategy, the priority remains economic growth, if only for the sake of improving the standard for its 1.3 billion people."[10]

Copenhagen can wait, particularly with the knowledge that every person living in the United States emits 20 tons of pollution per year while a Chinese person emits only 6 tons. Therefore, should the Chinese be unfairly made to shoulder a heavy burden? If China is to remain competitive, it must retain the right to pollute, and China resents the idea of putting limits on its own economic growth. It demonstrates that global consciousness over climate change is still hugely marginal. Hence, capitalism is more important than the environment. One can see this with the crisis of the banking system in 2008. The dominant countries did not have a problem coming to terms with a bailout of all the leading banks. The same urgency cannot be said about climate change.

Above all, Copenhagen showed that the time of western countries making decisions for the rest of the planet is over because of the weight that countries such as China, Brazil, India, and South Africa are beginning to accumulate on the world stage. However, the fact that these same countries are aiming for similar western lifestyles poses problems. The United States, which represents 5 percent of the world population, already consumes 25 percent of the world resources. Needless to say, this lifestyle is unsustainable.

AMERICA AND THE GLOBAL CRISIS

American attitudes towards global warming are dysfunctional. On the local level, Americans support some radical changes to cope with climate change. At the government level, however, the country lacks the ability to enact and implement climate change laws. Hence, Obama's State of the Union Address was disappointing. If it were about "action," Obama took none. His address in Copenhagen was essentially calibrated to the local American media. As such, Obama's speech disappointed because it did not provide a new target for reducing emissions. Rather, it seemed designed to spin and address a conservative U.S. Congress rather than the rest of the world. Indeed, the U.S. Congress has the last word on treaties and had previously refused to endorse the Clinton administration's signature of the Kyoto Accord. Obama in Copenhagen was not genuinely interested in a legally binding agreement but rather in discrediting China. According to Wikileaks revelations, the United States even put pressure on countries such as Bolivia and Ecuador to make the accords of Copenhagen not binding. Hence, the United States threatened countries that did not toe the line with deep cuts in aid money if they did not go along with the watered-down and ineffective policy supported by the United States.

Obama, therefore, is responding to domestic concerns and trying to appease Republicans' skepticism regarding global warming. This is where local governance confronts global governance head on, because underneath the discourse of climate change is the question of the American way of life.[11] First, Obama's pragmatism is motivated by Americans' desire for energy independence. Second, the field of climate change is extremely recent. It comes packaged with probability that is not fully understood by politicians or the public. It seems, however, that we need another Katrina to move the government into action; whereas, in the case of climate change, Obama could have used the Clean Air Act and the Environmental Protection Agency to directly regulate emissions without congressional approval. American attitudes toward global warming expose the lack of a mechanism to resolve global problems and local governmental concerns. Moreover, people are ready to look the other way when confronted with scientific facts that would cause anxiety.[12] The cultivation of indifference toward global warming explains the American government's half-hearted attempts to develop compelling strategies to combat it. However, some people are subjected to global warming more than others, particularly people living in the tropics.[13]

NATIONALISM, CLIMATE JUSTICE, AND AFRICA: WE CANNOT BARGAIN WITH NATURE

Climate change requires new policies to counter global warming. It requires rich and developing countries to trust each other. Naturally the difficulties of rich countries in committing to pledges to reduce gas emissions complicate the process. This makes it difficult for African countries to trust the process. Already many countries in Africa, such as Senegal and Djibouti, are arid or semiarid. This aridity comes in addition to concerns about the expansion of the immense Sahara desert. Deforestation advances at an alarming rate of 13 million hectares per forest-year, an area representing four times the size of Belgium. The regions most affected are in the tropics, including Brazil, Indonesia/Malaysia, and central Africa, which lose about 7 percent of their forest area annually.

Land grabbing adds another layer to these processes. According to the Food and Agricultural Organization (FAO), African farmers lost another 30 million hectares to countries such as China and the Gulf States to provide food production for their people. Another 20 million hectares are now undergoing trade negotiation, and the buyers include South Korea, with a 700,000-hectare acquisition in Sudan, and 500,000 hectares for Saudi-Arabia in Tanzania. The Democratic Republic of Congo is in a business deal with South Africa involving 8 million hectares, while eighty companies from India are looking to acquire 350,000 hectares in Africa.[14] Thus the pressure on the forest results from the exponential increase in demand for agricultural oil, such as palm oil, and also sugar cane, meats, woods, paper, and minerals. This reality is fast approaching of replacing those ordinary agroecological farmers with corporate global agribusiness. It will install hyperconsumption and pollution as the norm. In the process, the lack of support for the agroecological farmer results in a form of manual farming dependent on rainfall and highly susceptible to insects and poor crops.

The main problem with this deforestation is the participative management of land resources and the percentage of land set aside for reforestation, agriculture, and animal farming. This approach, however, is dominated by the World Bank, IMF, and NGOs with large-scale models of food production that many agricultural corporations think is the panacea for world food sustenance. These processes complicate ordinary Africans' access to the land because their aim is to favor big industrial groups rather than small enterprises. In kind, scholars such as Michael Duffy from Iowa University have shown that a farm with more than 600 to 900 acres is terribly inefficient in the long run. The same logic applies for a farm with more than 1,200 hogs. This farm practice depletes the soil, biodiversity diminishes, and devastation caused by pests increases. Thus, large-scale agribusinesses are unsustainable for reliable food production.[15]

Moreover, deforestation has a direct link to the access of health and education. The lack of water or the abundance of contaminated water can lead to the outbreak of epidemics. It also affects the schooling system because sick children are ostracized. These trends set Africa on the path to suffer disproportionally from the effects of climate change. As natural disasters caused by climate change become more frequent, economic and environmental stresses will give way to failing states because of uncontrolled logging, excessive soil erosion, a loss of biodiversity and medicinal plants, and wholesale food insecurity. Given the large scale of these looming environmental disasters, there will be a tremendous difference between who get to live and who get to die. Indeed, the earth's overheating upsets supplies of food, creates food insecurity, and in turn can even lead to violence.

Dealing with this state of affairs requires a transfer of technology because a lack of rain destroys lives and causes migrations, which pressures remaining land. This is where sovereignty inscribes itself on bodies in the way Achille Mbembe describes as necropolitics.[16] As such, surviving in a degraded environmental system will turn into a question of life and death. It brings into focus the notion of "idealized bodies," and how framing the black body in environmental crisis does not explore the racial aspect of the environmental discourse that is visually present but repressed. It puts into critical perspective the racist aspects of the global environmental debate that reduce Africa to play a residual role, to even become irrelevant, when in fact environmental crises know no borders. In this regard Paul Farmer writes that "rights violation are not random in distribution or effects but symptoms of deeper pathologies of power and are linked intimately to the social conditions that so often determine who will suffer abuse and who will be shielded from harm."[17]

Taking the indigenous part of the equation away is not to understand its role in terms of biodiversity management, rain, food supplies, and ways of life. Whether or not world resources can be genuinely shared gets to the heart of the question. Necropolitics points to the dangers of privatizing energy into few individuals, elected or not, who are making decisions that will lead to the destruction of millions of people. Additionally, necropolitics asks the question of the right to rescue. Who is going to save Africans when a crisis hits? A globalization that relies solely on extraction of natural resources might indicate that these resources matter more than people. Climate change calls for another way to look at the management of resources that puts humans first. It begins by reworking notions such as the "curse of resources" which has led to violent civil wars in places such as Sierra Leone and the Democratic Republic of Congo.

The real issue here is that African countries can hardly trust the process when industrialized countries will not make their commitments binding. The deal, however, is that most of the world's biodiversity resides in Africa and collaboration between north and south is crucial in terms of resource utilization and diverse ecosystems, the management of species and genetic resources, and land management. These problems are both environmental and industrial. In other words, environmental problems are democratic issues. As such, without democracy, the technological dream of mastering the world is just an illusion.

SCIENCE AND MODELS OF COMMUNICATION

Dealing with climate change requires strength of conviction. It also comes packaged with the fear of biopower's scientific dictatorship, mass sterilization, and land-grabbing—ecological imperialism that the likes of activists such as Vandana Shiva decry.[18] It calls for an evaluation of the ways in which scientists communicate and the underlying assumptions about this communication in terms of ownership and agency. Who owns research? This is a question that ties into notions of science and authority. Consequently the science of climate change is highly controversial, to the point that some have called it simply "catastrophism." For instance, the Inter-Academy Council has criticized the idea that the Himalayan glaciers will melt by 2035, and how the Intergovernmental Panel on Climate Change (IPCC) invited critics but did not consider their arguments. There was also weak evidence that climate change would halve the output of rainfed agriculture by 2020.[19] The National Center for Public Policy Research (NCPPR) has called on Michael Mann, a leading expert on climate change, to return the US$1.9 million he received from the NCPPR. This center claims that Mann was leading agenda-guided research:

> Emails and documents mysteriously released from the previously prestigious Climate Research Unit at the University of East Anglia in the United Kingdom revealed discussions [by a closed circle of climate scientists] of manipulation and destruction of research data, as well as efforts to interfere with the peer review process to stifle opposing views. The motivation underlying these efforts appears to be a coordinated strategy to support the belief that mankind's activities are causing global warming.[20]

Moreover, The Pew Research Center recently found a decrease in the number of Americans saying there is strong scientific evidence that the earth has gotten warmer over the past few decades, from 71 percent to 57 percent.[21]

The controversies around climate science indicate that, without trust, science is no longer science but politics. In kind, the failure in Copenhagen was not just a diplomatic failure. It was also a scientific failure. Now the question whether we can really debate about global warming without being involved in politics? And also what role do the media play in this notion of politics? The Internet plays a crucial role in discussions of climate change; it renders gatekeeping unnecessary. Hence, information is now a commodity. The Internet creates a gap between the slow, precise, and careful work of science and the fast-paced media. Additionally, climate science is not predictive but probabilistic, creating a conundrum. This probability is based on the past, not the future, and this is where a subtle distinction has to be made, because scientists are not the ones making the political decisions. Indeed, climate science cannot substitute for democracy, and maybe that is what caused the uproar against the IPCC, because they were viewed as substituting themselves for the democratic process.

Furthermore, the discrepancy between scientific language and everyday ordinary language requires a monumental work of translation. Additionally, there is the peer-review process for the journals, so that scientists' publications add to the confusion. Hence, as widely reported, Phil Jones headed the University of East Anglia's Climatic Research Unit, which was viewed as the holy wellspring of the raw data on which climate science depends—until recently that is, when leaked emails among researchers showed so-called signs of the manipulation of data and evidence. Jones responded in the journal *Nature* that skeptics are attempting to denigrate academics and the educational system in order to skew evidence relating to climate change: "I do not think we should be taking much notice of what's on blogs because they seem to be hijacking the peer-review process," says Jones.

Most of the criticism is that scientists work for ideology or funding. This explains why the IPCC's claims that the glaciers of the Himalayas will melt by 2035 has been labeled by some as the result of groupthink. The main problem is that the scientific method always includes some uncertainty. However, it is part of a long-standing attack by industry and other special interest groups on the credibility of science, especially when it reveals things that threaten profits. There is a sordid history of this, such as attacks by the tobacco industry on scientists claiming that smoking causes cancer.

The attack on climate science as scientism is, however, a whole new level of attack. It comes with accusations of producing false results in order to get government grants. The result is the risk of severe damage to the credibility of science. This equates to severe risk to our modern society and the science that created it. Others scientists, such as Vincent Courtillot, argue that the sun has a lot more to do with global warming than humans. Coutillot argues that global warming is now a form of ideology, a religion with its infidels and heretics. He claims that global warming has a lot to do with a Judeo-Christian culture of sin or culpability and the nature of sacrifice. He is right in part because even the *Washington Post* referred to Phil Jones as the "Archbishop in the Church of Global Warming," which explains in part why the Chinese and others Asians who do not share an apocalyptic Judeo-Christian mentality do not seem to care as much about global warming.[22]

Courtillot understands the role that power and ideology play in the climate change puzzle. It raises the question of nationalism, foundational narration, identity, and uniformity and the role that university plays in that project. Thus it poses the question of mainstreaming and marginalization. It asks how society manages identities and to what extent notions of identities relate to notions of self-preservation, national exclusivity, cultural pride, or arrogance—in brief, community of interest or emotional community. Within that context, the recognition is that universities are part of these processes and that there are positive and negative social conditions at their core. Therefore one must recognize that the foundational narrative of the university began in Bologna in the eleventh century and that this Judeo-Christian, Greco-Latin, and Arab goal was to fight and dominate the barbarians. They were aware that the making of the university was within the confrontational understanding of unity between the Judeo-Christian, Greco-Latin, and Arab world versus the multitudes of the barbarians, whose philosophy was described as *Sophia barbarorum*.

Their lifestyle was deemed uncivilized as well. There was something sacred at the heart of the establishment of universities, and education and culture were, from the outset, a political tool for hegemony, because they recognized the Christian God as the sole repository of philosophy and values.[23] Hence modern universities were set up to create an identity for the Holy Roman Empire under the protection of the Emperor Frederick Barbarossa.[24] There was a concept of what Foucault calls heterotopias, meaning that the university has a clear sense of space, of center-periphery, of inside and outside, and it is the in-betweeness, the space in the middle, that this paper deals with—precisely how contemporary multiculturalism in academia address the question of the stranger: how is the question of otherness is addressed in pedagogy? In kind, it poses the question of the stranger, the one outside of the norms in a process that does not take foreigners into account because it is important to note that more often the "universal" aspect of democratic egalitarian ideals is taken for granted. It helps explain Courtillot's notion of climate change as a kind of Judeo-Christian guilt.

GLOBAL CRISIS AND PREVENTION

A real politics of prevention is actually one of shared responsibility. Prevention of crisis in global warming shows that all nations have to work together and succeed together or fail simultaneously. These processes of crisis prevention have ramifications for sovereignty and law in terms of environmental global rights or transfer of technologies. It raises issues of effective control, supervision, and sanctions, which come in direct confrontation with problems of sovereignty. A clear signal, however, is that global competence can influence national laws. Already there are some agreements on issues such as genocide or torture that derived from international conventions. The same can be applied to environmental laws. The biggest question, however, is whether we can have an economy without carbon and more importantly, recognizing that, world resources are limited. Thus, the world needs a radical reconversion into clean energy.

The role of the United Nations is universal, but it poses the question of democracy, particularly, the UN convention to require unanimity. As such, the twenty-seven nations that signed the Copenhagen Accord did so outside of official UN discussions. To develop strong integrated regulatory systems to manage climate change requires an organization that can provide consensus. It is not surprising that when consensus could be achieved at Copenhagen, there was a rhetorical shift from the universal to the national and China was singled out as the main obstacle to that consensus.

It is also crucial to consider market incentive to deal with carbon emissions in light of the conversations on a global cap-and-trade system and a tax system on every unit of gas pollution.[25] It is important to note that the EU and Japan are already applying cap-and-trade systems. There is a carbon credit in place making carbons one of the hottest commodities on the market. Major financial houses such Goldman Sachs, Merrill Lynch, and Citibank already have carbon desks in London. The UN, however, is still a grinding bureaucratic process, and in this case Copenhagen did not fail because the grinding process is ongoing. It is probably better for the great polluters to form a club and let the peer pressure do the work. This is still not out of the question because nothing is precluding a deal between the United States and China. The most important idea to discuss begins with the recognition that the climate crisis is changing the legal relationships between citizens of the world because its impact is so important that the conversation must move from control to cooperation. The difference here is to become a community of destiny in the face of problems such as climate change, because the sky has no boundaries. Within this context, a nation cannot exercise an absolute form of sovereignty because the problems are all common to the globe. Hence, money saved from carbon taxes will serve to build a new economy based on renewable energy such as wind, solar, and geothermal power plants.

Al Gore's *An Inconvenient Truth* and his Nobel Peace Prize did much for the global warming debate. Within that context, citizens are media consumers and they are not getting the messages they need to perform as responsible citizens. There is no social problem that cannot be handled by the individuals. Groups such as Greenpeace and the Sierra Club are playing a prominent role in keeping this issue in the forefront. Rachel Aitkens from the Sierra Club, who attended the Copenhagen Conference, claims:

> We need to make our priority in this country to be a leader in climate-change issues and to make a difference and have a legally binding agreement. The biggest hurdle to overcome is to get people start discussing climate change with the seriousness that it deserves. The more you talk, the more pressure you will put on our representatives and the more likely they will do something about it.[26]

CONCLUSION

Climate change is about the legitimacy processes of different kinds of political, economic, and scientific rationalities and power. The international policing of the environment is about power and who has the ability to talk about climate change. Additionally, climate change raises questions about the way science works and communicates. In this fashion, this chapter is concerned with the place of Africa in world politics in terms global governance versus national interests, the role of scientists, their communication practices, and ideology in arguing that, in the larger scheme, it is about Africa's place in modernity.

To answer these questions, this work argues that the problem of climate change inserts itself within a project of modernity, which often plays within the illusion of an apolitical project. It shows that debate of climate change engages both a civic responsibility and an ethical question. Indeed, climate change is also a political problem that plays across multilayered spaces of communication such as the scientific, political, economic, and then in the media, which requires a comparative analysis of political economy and forms of self-interest. It results in the knowledge that there is no longer science and the exact representation of nature on one side and politics on the other. Therefore, it matters when it comes to the boundary between the scientist and the consumer, countries, and self-interests.

Moreover, we live in the same ecosystem and ecology disrupts distance, in the sense that pollution is also the pollution of distances, community of effects and instantaneity. In this shrinking world, such designations as *Lebensraum*, meaning "living space," and *Konzentrationlager*, meaning spaces where people are confined to die, are no longer acceptable. Hence one must be honest about universal allocation. We got the earth for free and even the technology was passed down from generation to generation. Being rich has meaning only when it gives a place to the vulnerable at the bargaining table.

Thus Copenhagen was an opportunity to differentiate cultural specificities and value systems generated by globalization versus the nation-state. These problems are therefore environmental, industrial, and cultural, and the solutions must be adjusted in the realities of globalization. It begins with the recognition that the all-or-nothing approach of Copenhagen does not work. A piecemeal approach works better because it allows people to adapt to global warming slowly. Adaptation means agreeing on what is agreeable and defers the tougher issues for later. It might begin with agreeing on conserving the forest and rewarding people who are working to preserve forestry, then moving to industrial pollution and so forth. It also means investing to make clean energy cheap, particularly giving away intellectual property, thereby turning green energy technologies into allies to beat the tough challenge of global warming by making clean energy cheap and available to all.

NOTES

1. John S. Dryzek. *The Politics of the Earth: Environmental Discourses* (Oxford, UK: Oxford University Press, 1997): 46.
2. See Agence France Presse, "Nestle Chief Warns of Food Riots," October 7, 2011.
3. It is also important to note that this kind of famine comes packaged with collateral epidemics such as cholera, measles, and typhoid fever.

4. Barack Obama, "State of the Union Address," *New York Times*, February 1, 2011, p. B1.
5. An example is Vandana Shiva's earth-based democracy and her articulation of *vasudhaiva kutumbakam* as an organizing principle of earth democracy versus multinational corporations such as Monsanto. Shiva calls for the participatory management of land resources and the power of people to access the land resources where they live.
6. One of the points of contention was China's opposition to the creation of an international organization to monitor gas emissions. China sees that as an intrusion into its sovereignty.
7. It is also important to note that islands in Micronesia such as Tuvalu are supposed to disappear from the face of the earth if the temperature rises by 2 degrees.
8. Ted Nordhaus and Michael Shellenberger, "Changing the Energy Conversation," *Wall Street Journal*, November 29, 2010, pp. R1 and R6.
9. "China's Thing about Numbers," *The Economist*, December 30, 2009.
10. Wang Feng, "Behind China's Target," *New China* Vol. 18 (January 5, 2010): 12–13.
11. On June 29, 2009, a Climate Change Bill cleared the House of Representatives. It aims to eliminate the use of all fossil fuels, including coal. Critics such as Bjorn Lomborg have claimed that it will cost US$350 billion, which is half of the American trade deficit. Lomborg argues that only US$40 billion can cure problems of underdevelopment in the world.
12. Ibid.
13. Texas congressman Republican Joe Barton claimed that the only thing to do to fight global warming was to "get a shade" and that "global warming is good for us." See House Energy and Climate Committee, "Press Release: Mankind Always Adapts to Climate Change, Barton Says," March 25, 2009: http://republicans.energycommerce.house.gov/news/PRArticle.aspx?NewsID=6912
14. John Vidal, "Rich Nations Snaffle 30 million Hectares of Third World Farmland" July 5, 2009: http://www.postnewsline.com/2009/07/rich-nations-snaffle-30-million-hectares-of-third-world-farmland-.html
15. From the Report to the Kerr Center for Sustainable Agriculture: http://www.kerrcenter.com/
16. Achille Mbembe, "Politiques de la vie et violence spéculaire dans la fiction d'Amos Tutuola," Cahiers d'études Africaines (2003): 11–40.
17. Paul Farmer, *Pathologies of Power: Health, Human Rights, and the New War on the Poor* (Berkeley: University of California Press, 2003): xiii.
18. *Democracy Now*, July 8, 2010.: http://www.democracynow.org/2010/7/8/gwynne_dyer_on_climate_wars_the.
19. Jeffrey Ball, "Climate Panel Faces Heat," *Wall Street Journal*, August 31, 2010, pp.1 and 12.
20. See Noel Sheppard, "ClimateGate's Michael Mann Received Stimulus Funds, Media Mum," January 14, 2010: http://newsbusters.org Michael Mann's Hockey Stick Theory has been highly controversial. Scholars such as Stephen McIntyre and Ross McKitrick, for example, have challenged his data. Moreover, scholars, such as Phil Jones of the University of East-Anglia, have been criticized for "fudging" data.
21. See John Young, "Everybody's an Expert," *Austin American Statesman*, January 16, 2010, p. A.17.
22. Wesley Pruden, "The Red-Hot Scam Unravels," *The Washington Times*, February 16, 2010, p. 1.
23. In an interview with Peter Robinson in the *National Review* on August 21, 2009, Henri Jaffa blames the rise of cynicism and immorality on the

American university getting away from that tradition. He blames American universities with his contemporary fondness for postmodernism and immorality with the production of serial killers such as Ted Bundy, whose cynicism and nihilism he learned in academia, and that turned him into a monster. Jaffa argues this is because now you can oppose society mainstream values and possibly get away with it.

24. See Universita di Bologna's website: http://www.unibo.it/Portale/default.htm.
25. It is important to note that the European Union and Japan are already using a cap and trade system.
26. In the *Daily Texan*, January 21, 2010, p. 2.

REFERENCES

Agence France Presse. "Nestle Chief Warns of Food Riots." October 7, 2011: http://www.google.com/hostednews/afp/article/ALeqM5iVGNj_X2Q2b2kBpo6nKSId5dTUiw?docId=CNG.e8fbdb7962bb43fdf2294f71e6099162.c1.
Agnew, John A. *Hegemony: The New Shape of Global Power*. Philadelphia: Temple University Press, 2005.
Anderson, Alison. *Media, Culture, and the Environment*. London: University College, London Press, 1997.
Ball, Jeffrey. "Climate Panel Faces Heat." *Wall Street Journal*. August 31, 2010, pp. 1 and 12.
Bookchin, Murray. "Social Ecology versus Deep Ecology: A Challenge for the Ecology Movement." In Nina Witoszek and Andrew Brennan, eds. *Philosophical Dialogues: Arne Naess and the Progress of Ecophilosophy*. Lanham, MD: Rowman and Littlefield, 1999.
Buell, Lawrence. "Toxic Discourse." *Critical Inquiry*, Vol. 24, No. 3 (1998): 639–655.
Bullard, Robert D. "Introduction." In Robert D. Bullard, ed. *Confronting Environmental Racism: Voices from the Grassroots*. Boston: South End Press, 1993.
"China's Thing about Numbers." *The Economist*. December 30, 2009: http://www.economist.com/node/15179774.
Deluca, Kevin. *Image Politics: The Rhetoric of Environmental Activism*. Mahwah, NJ: Erlbaum, 2006.
Dryzek, John S. *The Politics of the Earth: Environmental Discourses*. Oxford, UK: Oxford University Press, 1997.
Farmer, Paul. *Pathologies of Power: Health, Human Rights, and the New War on the Poor*. Berkeley, CA: University of California Press, 2003.
Feng, Wang. "Behind China's Target." *New China* Vol. 18 (January 5, 2010): 12–13.
Glodfelly, Cheryll. "Introduction: Literary Studies in age of Environmental Crisis." In Cheryll Glotfelty and Harold Fromm, eds. *The Ecocriticism Reader: Landmarks in Literary Ecology*. Athens: University of Georgia Press, 1996.
Harvey, David. *A Brief History of Neoliberalism*. Oxford, UK: Oxford University Press, 2003.
House Energy and Climate Committee. "Press Release: Mankind Always Adapts to Climate Change, Barton Says." March 25, 2009: http://republicans.energycommerce.house.gov/news/PRArticle.aspx?NewsID=6912
Luke, Timothy. *Ecocritique*. Minneapolis, MN: University of Minnesota Press, 1997.
Mbembe, Achille. "Politiques de la vie et violence spéculaire dans la fiction d'Amos Tutuola." *Cahiers d'études Africaines* (2003).

Nordhaus, Ted and Michael Shellenberger. "Changing the Energy Conversation." *Wall Street Journal.* November 29, 2010, pp. R1 and R6.
Obama, Barack. "State of the Union Address." *New York Times.* February 1, 2011, p. B1.
Pruden, Wesley. "The Red-Hot Scam Unravels." *Washington Times.* February 16, 2010, p. 1.
Robinson, Peter. "Harry Jaffa and the Apostolic Succession." *National Review.* August 21, 2009: http://www.nationalreview.com/corner/185673/harry-jaffa-and-apostolic-succession/peter-robinson.
Sheppard, Noel. "Climate Gate's Michael Mann Received Stimulus Funds, Media Mum." January 14, 2010: http://newsbusters.org
Vidal, John. "Rich Nations Snaffle 30 million Hectares of Third World Farmland." July 5, 2009: http://www.postnewsline.com/2009/07/rich-nations-snaffle-30-million-hectares-of-third-world-farmland-.html
Young, John. "Everybody's an Expert." *Austin American Statesman.* January 16, 2010, p. A.17.

19 Globalization and Developing Economies
Eco-Tourism and Sustainable Development in Cross River State, Nigeria

Donald Omagu

Tourism, a well-established component of the most recent pattern of globalization, creates contact and communication between peoples from different cultures. Eco-tourism, though a relatively new phenomenon (the term was coined by Hector Ceballos-Lascurain in 1983), is a new form of nature travel[1]; it is currently the fastest-growing sector of the world's largest service industry, tourism. In 1989, eco-tourism, marketed together with adventure travel, had captured almost 10 percent of the tourist market and was growing at a rate of 30 percent a year. In 1990, nature tourism estimates ranged between US$2 and US$12 billion of the US$55 billion of tourism generated in developing countries.[2] Today, the eco-tourism market is estimated to be in excess of US$300 billion. Much of this revenue is generated in developing countries, which perceive eco-tourism as a profitable, environmentally friendly, and sustainable alternative to mass tourism.[3] This growth, which has been phenomenal for the past decade, is due in part to the increasing number of environmentally conscious consumers, who have taken to eco-tourism because it combines an exotic travel experience with the self-satisfying notion of being socially and environmentally responsible.[4]

Eco-tourism presents an environmentally friendly and potentially complementary intervention option to other income-generating and wealth creating activities—such as farming, fishing, and the harvesting of wildlife carried out on a sustainable basis. The complementary role of tourism can be particularly valuable when considered against the background that the "hot spots" of biological diversity in the state are generally the poorest areas, where economic necessity is most likely to drive local people to pursue environmentally damaging options. For the foreign visitor to the state, tourism provides an educational glimpse of a world that is not his or her own, often a world of striking natural beauty and rich cultural heritage that serves to satisfy an educational and spiritual desire and appeal. This can be used to promote cross-cultural exchanges that can form a healthy bridge between industrialized and developing countries.[5] However, in spite of these laudable opportunities, eco-tourism development is threatened by many challenges.

This chapter focuses on the changing global tourism environment, with particular emphasis on the key trends and developments that are likely to occur in the twenty-first century. It argues that without appropriate planning and management, the cost of Cross River State eco-tourism development may accrue to the extent that its benefits are burned out. To avoid this, the chapter identifies some key factors that need to be addressed in order to ensure success for developing eco-tourism in Cross River State.

ECO-TOURISM IN CROSS RIVER STATE: AN OVERVIEW

As one of the twenty-five vibrant biodiversity hot spots in the world, Cross River State, located in the southernmost region of Nigeria, enjoys a rich diversity of attractions and a statewide distribution of sites that offers activities for virtually every traveler including natural, historical, and archeological resources as well as business appeal and conventional tourism. It is considered the wellspring of the country's hospitality industry.[6] Cross River State has succeeded in establishing itself as a reference point for tourism in Africa. The state is endowed with diverse natural and manmade tourist attractions, some of which include Cross River National Park, Kwa Falls, Agbokim Waterfalls, and the Obudu Mountain Ranch Resort. Other attractions include the Tinapa Business Resort, the Calabar Free Trade Zone, the Monoliths, and the Old Residency Museum. Festivals and events are a great complement to the state's ecotourism attraction and include new yam festivals (held annually in ten local government areas of the state), wrestling festivals (in seven local government areas of the state), the Obudu Mountain Race (held once a year), Boat Regatta (in four local government areas), the Ekpe Festival (a masquerade dance that is common among the Efiks and Quo people of the state), and the Christmas Festival (held once a year).

Cross River National Park ("The Pride of Nigeria"),[7] the oldest and largest surviving rainforest in Nigeria, incorporates a large chunk of southeast Nigeria's remaining moist tropical forest between Cross River and the Cameroon border. The park, which is one of the richest natural enclaves in the country, has two separate and noncontiguous sectors: Oban Hills and the Okwangwo sector. It is conceived to protect and conserve the last vestige of the rain forest ecosystem and to promote eco-tourism in Nigeria. Indeed, the state has been identified as the only area in Nigeria that can still lay claim to any meaningful part of the rainforest ecosystem remaining in that country and also as comprising the remaining 10 percent of West Africa's tropical rainforest, about 7,290 square kilometers.[8]

As a preserved rainforest nature reserve, the park is home to many localized species of plants and animals, including chimpanzees, baboons, leopards, and red foxes. The park also hosts a number of endangered species, including the drill monkeys, the lowland gorillas, buffalo, forest elephants, and the newly discovered Cross River gorilla. The park also harbors a rich collection of flora and fauna and is blessed with a total land area of 720 square kilometers of rugged mountain scenery and rolling hills. The Cross River National Park and the Oban Hills region lie beside Korup National Park in Cameroon. This combined area is an important focus for the World Wildlife Federation (WWF) in Nigeria, where work is being done to combat illegal hunting, logging, and land clearing while also implementing conservation action plans.[9] National parks are special natural ecosystems with unique attributes. They play unquantifiable roles vital to national/regional well-being as well as acting as a catalyst for the development of eco-tourism. They also enhance ecological processes and life-support systems such as soil regeneration, protection of nutrient cycles, cleansing, and purifying hydrological cycles.[10] Activities to enjoy in the park include game viewing, bird watching, gorilla tracking, mountaineering/hiking, sport fishing, boating, and visiting the Botanical Garden and Herbarium in Butatong.[11]

The state is home to the Kwa Falls, located in a narrow, steep gorge on the headwaters of the Kwa River, where they cascade down resistant basement rocks and drain through the Oban Hills and mountains. The attractive features of the falls include their sparkling white waters, pleasantly surrounded by green vegetation. A deep plunge pool forms at the bottom of the waterfall, which, before deforestation, was hidden under the thick canopy of the tropical rainforest.[12] There is also the Agbokim Waterfalls, located in Etung local government area, a very short distance away from the Nigeria-Cameroon border. The waterfall lies less than 30 kilometers east of Ikom town in Cross River State and is actually situated on the estuary of the Cross River, where it descends in terraces through the tropical rainforest. The falls are surrounded by green tropical trees, valleys, and steep hills, which are all enveloped by a rainbow-like aura of colors. The Agbokim waterfall, which consists of seven streams, rolls down steep walls at different points, offers a unique natural scene. Both Agbokim and Kwa could be harnessed to generate hydroelectric power.[13]

The Obudu Mountain Ranch Resort, located on the Oshie Ridge Plateau of the Sankwala Mountains, offers another tourist attraction. The ranch, which became functional in 1949, has been repositioned for excellent tourism services under the management of African Sun. Since the ranch's inception, livestock have been bred to provide fresh meat as well as milk, butter, and cheese daily. Other available produce includes eggs, pork, and local honey, all available in commercial quantities.[14] The Obudu Mountain, which is the highest in the state and the hilly lands of the Obudu and Obanliku areas, has an altitude of 1,716 meters above sea level.[15] The mountain also has a unique climatic condition in a predominantly tropical zone. The temperature in the mountain ranges between 26 to 32 degrees centigrade during the warmer months of November and January and the lowest temperature range of 4 to 10 degrees between June and September.[16] Leading up to the Obudu Mountain summit is an 11-kilometer windy route with twenty-two perilous bends.[17] The 11 kilometers of winding road make driving to the ranch at the summit quite exhilarating. This means of transportation was complemented in 2005 with a state-of-the-art cable car, acclaimed as the longest in the world, covering a distance of 4 kilometers up through the clouds, offering dramatic views of green rolling hills.[18]

The Obudu Mountain Resort is also home to the world-acclaimed Obudu International Mountain Race, an annual 11.25-kilometer mountain running competition held in November. First held in 2005, it has a total prize of about US$250,000, including other conciliatory prizes. The men's and women's competition winners receive US$50,000 each. Undeniably this reward attracts competitors from across Nigeria and the world. The Obudu International Mountain Race is an International Association of Athletics Federations (IAAF) recognized event, a World Mountain Running Association (WMRA) associate member event, and is organized by the Local Government Area of Cross River State assisted by the Athletics Federation of Nigeria.[19]

In addition to tourist attractions, Cross River State is acknowledged as one of the most valuable stores of biodiversity on earth, which has not only contributed to sustainable development but has also given the state an identity of global significance. Owing to the enormous potential and opportunity represented by this area, the state government floated a ₦4 billion tourism development bond in 2004 to finance its tourism policy. This loan, which was repaid by the state government from its statutory federal allocation over 4 years, was for the increase of the rentable rooms at the Ranch Resort from 80 to 250 by December 2005, the establishment and commencement of a tourism bureau, the extension of road works at the Ranch Resort, the extension of the runway at Bebi airstrip to admit larger aircraft, and the development of the cable car. Other funds were to be used for the development of a water park on the ranch and the commencement of work to upgrade each site of the tourism circuit to ensure quality services for tourists from creeks to the mountains, including the marina, the falls, the monoliths, and the Drill Ranch.[20]

ECO-TOURISM AND SUSTAINABLE DEVELOPMENT IN CROSS RIVER STATE

The unique attraction of Cross River State has made it a tourist haven in Africa. Tourism, as a worldwide phenomenon, touches the highest and deepest aspirations of all people through the delivery of economic benefits to Nigerians by providing employment, stimulating local markets, and improving transportation and the communication infrastructure.[21] These are vitally important for a developing economy like Cross River, as discussed subsequently.

Transfer of Incomes

The influx of international and domestic tourists who engage in leisure and ecotourism activities in Cross River State has progressively increased since 2004. Recent research shows that the overall income from these tourists is estimated to be over ₦15 million,[22] approximately US$1 million. Communities have generally profited significantly from tourism by providing a complex and varied supply chains of goods and services, such as supporting a versatile labor market with a variety of jobs for tour guides, translators, cooks, cleaners, drivers, hotel managers, and other service sector workers. It must, however, be emphasized that many of these tourism jobs are flexible or seasonal and can be taken on in parallel with existing occupations such as farming.[23]

The benefit of tourism as an excellent vehicle for transferring income from developed to developing countries is often overlooked. Eco-tourism is especially effective in this transfer because tourism as a relatively barrier-free trade commodity offers the opportunity of transferring income from the modernized world that does not involve traditional forms of foreign investment—for example, export-processing zones, in which profits are largely repatriated.[24] Many developing countries, facing debt burdens and worsening trade terms, have turned to tourism promotion in the hope that it brings foreign exchange and investment. Simultaneously, leading international agencies such as the World Bank and United Nations and business organizations like the World Travel & Tourism Council (WTTC) have been substantially involved in making tourism a truly global industry.[25]

A Tool for Job Creation

As an engine for economic development, eco-tourism—with its potential to create jobs and other associated enterprise opportunities—provides one of the largest sources of income in the world. The fact that eco-tourism-related businesses are located in rural and countryside areas provides an additional potential for poverty reduction in locales where there are fewer opportunities for white-collar jobs, industries, and other larger private businesses. Indeed, in 1991, the Drill Ranch establishment in Boki proved to be the largest private employer in the area, providing alternative incomes to mostly young men who might otherwise practice slash-and-burn agriculture, hunting, or logging. In addition, this project offers thousands of people, mostly local citizens who share the drill's habitat, an opportunity to see natural-sized drill family groups and chimpanzees and learn about the animals and the challenges these species face in the wild.[26]

Through eco-tourism, an outlet for new markets for local products is created. Locals are able to sell their goods directly to the consumer without having to use an intermediary. Common craft works sold include beaded bags, beaded wall hangings, and shoes. Others include Ekpe masquerades made with raffia, cane chairs, brass trays, raffia clocks, and motif work. However, while this is great for local businesses, the local citizens themselves are put at a disadvantage. The new market for local goods raises their global price, making it harder for locals to afford traditional goods. In this way, the source of income to the locality is widened and more people are directly and indirectly engaged. Apart from motivating local entrepreneurship, rural-urban drift will be reduced, with increased improvement in the livelihoods of the countryside.[27]

Eco-tourism therefore remains the single most crucial source of employment in the rural areas after agriculture. Farmers can expand quality, variety, and quantities of products for the tourism supply chain. Transportation businesses can expand to deliver customers to the tourism "product." Infrastructure can be developed (and jobs created) that will provide essential services for local communities.[28] The World Bank has recognized this tourism potential by funding the Tourism Employment and Opportunities (TEMPO) project in Cross River State. Tourism has been found to be valuable as it sensitizes the local economy and ensures the redistribution of wealth.

Attributes of Social Cohesion

Perhaps one of the greatest attributes of eco-tourism is its potential to enhance the sociocultural values of indigenous people. Tourism has a critical role to play in facilitating and shaping intercultural dialogue. At a basic level, it provides for direct encounters between peoples from different cultures. Culture-oriented tourists are a new, emerging category of travelers. They treat a vacation as a learning experience—an opportunity to discover an area's unexploited resources.[29] In the words of Kofi Annan, "I see dialogue as a chance for people of different cultures and traditions to get to know each other better, whether they live on opposite sides of the world or on the same street."[30] Tourism can facilitate cultural harmony and understanding among people. More in-depth knowledge of other people's cultures will promote communication, understanding, and integration. So, with this understanding, it is essentially through a process of interaction with others in a cultural context that one develops an understanding of oneself. This understanding of the self is then used as a basis for further interaction and evolves as new experiences, beliefs, and memories are added. Poets, artists, administrators, academics, and travel writers have often used very elaborate systems of subcategories to translate and make meaningful the social life of peoples visited or otherwise encountered.[31]

Tourists can provide an audience for local communities to uphold their heritage and ways of life. Close interaction between tourists and locals creates conditions to dispel myths and stereotypes on both sides. In visiting developing countries, tourists experience the variety, beauty, and liveliness of local cultures while at the same time being exposed to the issues of poverty and environmental degradation. Significantly, tourists and the tourism industry in an era of globalization have moved from generating passive observers of destinations to creating tourists actively involved in improving the social, environmental, and economic well-being of their hosts by raising awareness of human rights abuses and actively engaging in environmental improvement schemes for the host community.

International tourism in Cross River State, for instance, has stimulated the restoration and preservation of historical sites and monuments. The most popular historical sites in the state include the National Museum Old Residency Calabar, which, apart from housing other historical artifacts, has a collection of ritual terracotta and other materials, excavated locally by Professor Ekpo Eyo, dated to 400 to 1500 of the common era. It also contains collections and exhibitions on the history of the slave trade. Built in 1884 on top of Consular Hill, the building is a prefabricated structure of Scandinavian red pinewood that was shipped in knockdown parts from Britain. This building, initially known as the Government House, was the seat of the British colonial administration for the Southern Protectorate of Nigeria. As an imposing two-story structure, it remains one of the best examples of early colonial architecture. The building was declared a National Museum in August 1959 and was converted into a museum of Old Calabar history in August, 1986.[32]

Cross River tourist destinations offer a variety of cuisines of high quality, ranking among the best of African dishes. Some of the popular delicacies of the state include *edikang ikong*, *afang*, *ekpang nkukwo*, *Ogbono* soup, *afia anang* soup, *efere*, *beniseed* soup, *eruru* soup, melon cakes, snails, bush meat, and plantain. Occasionally the area acquires new traditions from strangers; their dress, eating habits, and style of interaction all bring some new uniqueness to the area of their visit.[33] In communities where western and traditional cultures coexist, the eco-tourism industry has the potential to provide real leadership on issues of cultural integrity and greater harmony and integration among cultures.[34]

Interactions and observations of this kind have lifted the level of thinking among visitors, resulting in a positive mind-set toward others and themselves. People have accepted some new favorable cultural traits regarding the diversification of menu or costumes without cutting down their social values constituting their identity. Familiarity with different languages has not only made the communication easier and better but also added a new and useful skill to their life. Tourism has facilitated the development of the sense of place among the people. They are conscious about the heritage that has been preserved from many years. The locales have slowly but surely come to be aware of the secret that is of interest for the people around the world. Consequently more care and protection is devoted to their collective cultural heritage. Such a joint effort not only improves the attraction of the destination but also unites the people.[35]

Infrastructural Development

Tourism development often brings a range of benefits to host communities like improved infrastructure, access services, and new investment opportunities, all of which serve to enhance the lifestyles of communities. It is in recognition of eco-tourism growth potential that the government embarked on several initiatives and programs aimed at improving the economic and social well-being of citizens. Its core passion is the provision of infrastructure in rural communities as a catalyst for economic growth and wealth creation. To drive this agenda, the state government established the Rural Development Agency and State Electrification Agency. Through these agencies, over 500 kilometers of rural roads are today spread across sixteen local government areas of the state. These roads have helped create access to markets for agricultural produce and improved the value of agricultural goods and services while generally improving communication and fostering positive intercommunity relations. This unprecedented focus on rural development also includes the provision of electricity to rural communities. This multifaceted approach to rural development is yielding significant economic value to the people of the state and is a critical index in the growth of the state's economy and the wealth-creation agenda of the government.

The state government has also provided infrastructure and services through its Urban Renewal Program in designated urban cities like Calabar, Ikom, Ogoja, Ugep, Akamkpa, and Obudu. These initiatives are aimed at stimulating the economies of these urban centers and provide requisite amenities that will enhance the overall well-being of the citizens on a sustainable basis.[36] For the sake of tourism, a well-organized public transportation system structured to match prospects of the sector has been introduced. To this end, the use of motorcycles (also known as *okada* and popularly referred to as *alalok* in Efik) as a means of public transportation was banned in Calabar city. Instead, a modern fleet of taxis and buses was introduced.

Tourism is an industry with abundant potential for growth. It creates employment and generates income, including foreign exchange and increased tax revenue. Apart from the financial gains, there is also cultural diffusion. The environment is conserved and beautified while funds are expended on infrastructural development, thereby enabling both visitors and locals to derive benefits from industry. It is hoped that by 2020, Cross River State tourism will be a significant economic sector contributing to the State's GDP through job creation and increased revenues. This process will be driven by a uniquely differentiated internationally competitive product complemented by a comprehensive, fully functional physical infrastructure. Ultimately it will be supported by the people of Cross River State.[37]

MAJOR CHALLENGES AND ISSUES IN ECO-TOURISM DEVELOPMENT

It is unwise to assume that eco-tourism is without challenges. Indeed, developing economies like Cross River State face tough choices by allowing an unregulated influx of tourists in protected areas. With weak laws, eco-tourism could turn this nascent industry into wishful thinking. Some of the key challenges that require urgent attention as we strive to put a sustainable tourism initiative in place for Cross River State are outlined below.

Environmental Impacts

Eco-tourism operations occasionally fail to live up to environmental standards. Although eco-tourism is intended for small groups, even a modest increase in population, however temporary, puts extra pressure on the local environment and necessitates the development of additional infrastructure and amenities. The concentration of visitors in natural areas may result in an unacceptable level of environmental degradation. A *Washington Post* article by Elizabeth Becker, "Don't Go There," discusses how tourism is harming the environment. In this article, Becker notes:

> Global tourism today is not only a major industry it's nothing short of a planet-threatening plague. It's polluting land and sea, destroying wildlife and natural habitat and depleting energy and natural resources. From Asia to Africa, look-alike resorts and spas are replacing and undermining local culture, and the international quest for vacation houses is forcing local residents out of their homes. It's giving rise to official corruption, wealth inequalities and heedless competition. It's even contributing to human rights violations, especially through the scourges of sex tourism.[38]

Eco-tourism activities are themselves issues in environmental impact because they disturb fauna and flora. Eco-tourists believe that because they are only taking pictures and leaving footprints—that they are keeping eco-tourism sites pristine—but even a harmless-sounding activity such as a nature hike can be ecologically destructive. Where the eco-tourism activity involves wildlife viewing, it can scare away animals, disrupt their feeding and nesting sites, or acclimate them to the presence of people. The relative success of gorilla tourism in East Africa[39] has led to the suggestion, at the 2006 Cross River gorilla action planning workshop, that gorilla tourism following the mountain gorilla model be developed for at least one of the Cross River gorilla localities. Indeed, the potential for tourism to generate meaningful revenue throughout the Cross River gorillas' range is in doubt because of the low numbers of gorillas and high degree of threat at each of the localities. This raises questions as to the potential negative impact of tourism. Cross River gorillas present particular challenges for habituation. In addition to their wariness of humans because of a recent history of intense hunting and the dense vegetation in their habitat, the small population is fragmented and individual groups range over large areas in rugged, inaccessible terrain.[40]

The requisite habituation process itself can cause elevated levels of stress for gorillas and alter both their social behavior and ranging patterns.[41] These changes could have significant negative effects on small Cross River gorilla groups, particularly like those at Afi Mountain that may already be living in a somewhat marginal habitat. Increased exposure to humans also heightens the risk that diseases will be transmitted to the gorillas. Several human pathogens, particularly respiratory illnesses, transmitted to wild gorilla populations have resulted in fatalities.[42] The introduction of such pathogens to one of the Cross River gorilla localities could easily result in the extinction of that locality. In addition, the gorillas' forest habitats continue to be eroded and fragmented by farming, burning by pastoralists, and the extension and expansion of roads. The potential for damage to the Cross River gorilla population from tourism appears to outweigh the likelihood of benefits.[43] This is similar to what is happening in Kenya, where wildlife observer disruption drives cheetahs off their reserves, thus increasing the risk of inbreeding and further endangering the species.

Deforestation, an issue high on the global environmental agenda for many years, remains a serious problem for the eco-tourism industry today because of the people's basic economic need to provide for themselves and their families. Indeed, the state has, in the past few decades, witnessed a burgeoning human population pressure, which has prompted farmers to encroach on forest land in order to farm, thus causing deforestation.[44] One of the principal causes of deforestation is the expansion of the agricultural frontier through the extensive shifting of cultivation systems. These land-use systems are becoming increasingly unsustainable as populations increase and the amount of agricultural land available declines, a situation that is often associated with low crop productivity and reduced soil fertility.[45]

In addition to transitory cultivation, other activities such as hunting, fishing, and grazing have been also on the increase and have equally contributed to damage of the ecosystem. Furthermore, the use of chemicals by some fishermen has threatened marine life. Snares set by farmers and hunters to trap smaller animals cause injuries to the larger species. To make matters worse, the increased perennial cattle ranching by Fulani herdsmen along the Bushi-Ranch axis involves hundreds of thousands of cattle grazing on expansive areas in and near forests, to the detriment of the land. Cattle ranching in this manner destroys thousands of square miles of rainforest each year owing to the stripping of the soil. Lamentably, cattle ranchers expand their grazing areas yearly, leading to more destruction.[46]

Indeed, with the global demand for timber used in manufacturing furniture, construction, and a variety of other products, forests are destroyed or degraded owing to the harvesting of wood. Logging, both legal and illegal, is on the rise. Multinational companies, for whom the improvement of forest practices is not a priority, often export the unprocessed timber out of Cross River State. For instance, the Western Metal Products Company (WEMPCO), a Hong Kong-based multinational, started prospecting for wood in the state in 1992, in contravention of extant forest laws and regulations.[47] On July 7, 2004, the company was ordered to close down its logging operations and evacuate the area. Although the closing of WEMPCO operations in Cross River State remains a big step, other international oil and logging companies continue to operate in the area, with little oversight.[48] Other activities that have threatened the forest include rubber tapping and the collection of fungi, nuts, bamboo, and berries. Other nonwood forest products include medicinal compounds, dyes, and fabrics.

Local People

Tourism's impact on indigenous peoples' way of life and on their control of and access to their resources and environment has become more pronounced with the globalization of the world economy. One of Eva Garen's biggest complaints concerning eco-tourism, which is also applicable to Cross River State, is that the resident population is often excluded from the development process and relegated to minimum-wage support jobs or the informal street vendor economy. These rural workers were often previously involved in industries such as logging, poaching, or agriculture, which are incompatible with eco-tourism.[49] However, instead of being compensated for switching to professions in the tourism industry, locals receive jobs that are often low-paying (although better-paying than farming) and limited in their potential for upward mobility. Meanwhile, managerial positions go to foreigners or the urban-educated elite.

Without doubt, most eco-tourism enterprises are owned by foreign investors and corporations that provide few benefits to local communities. An overwhelming majority of the profits are put into the pockets of investors instead of being reinvested in the local economy or in environmental protection. The limited numbers of local people who are employed in the economy enter at its lowest level and are unable to live in tourist areas because of their meager wages and a two-market system.[50] In addition, Garen observes that while one of the standards of eco-tourism is to generate domestic employment and economic opportunities for locals, profits, if not carefully monitored, can leak out of these regions into the hands of elites and wealthier nations. In addition, if developmental projects are monopolized by rich businessmen looking for short-term economic gain, both the local environment and peoples could pay the price.[51] David Western's thoughts regarding the Amboseli Basin in Kenya in the late 1960s, as detailed in his book *In the Dust of Kilimanjaro*, represent the early ideas emerging in the 1960s about what is now known as ecotourism. In his view,

> Time had come for a new approach, an approach resting on fairness and local involvement rather than on alienation and enforcement. Why should local communities not become the principal beneficiaries and ultimate custodian of wildlife, as they have always been, without sacrificing the larger interest of the society?[52]

Globalization and tourism have become a deadly mix for indigenous peoples.[53] While eco-tourism is widely acclaimed as a money spinner, the stakes for indigenous people are growing in leaps and bounds, especially with the eviction of people from their land for eco-tourism space. For example, in the Obaliku Local Government Area of Cross River State, over 1,000 families of the Becheve, Gbakoko, Bagga, and Bellenge communities have been evicted from their ancestral lands to make room for the development of the ranch resort and safari lodges. Another non-Nigerian example of the undesirable impact of tourism is that of the extent of land lost from the Masai culture. In Kenya, the Masai have not gained any economic benefits. Despite the loss of their land, employment favors better-educated workers. Furthermore, the investors in this area are not local and have not put profits back into the local economy. In some cases, game reserves can be created without informing or consulting local people, who come to find out about the situation only when an eviction notice is delivered.[54] The lack of economic opportunities for local people displaced from traditional lands and unfair compensation terms forces them to degrade the environment as a means of sustenance.

Threat to Indigenous Cultures

One of the primary concerns about cultural globalization through tourism is that local cultural differences may become homogenized in the process of catering to the desires of outside consumers. This leads to problem of which "culture" a cultural tourism project decides to market to tourists and concerns over what kinds of things this cleaning up hides.[55] For example, problems might arise when local communities are stereotyped or when tourists, in their search for authenticity, intrude upon locals' private lives.[56] In historical neighborhoods, buildings are refurbished or "preserved" to create a cleaner image of history. Because cultural tourism attempts to highlight and preserve local culture while simultaneously packaging it for tourists, cultural tourism is an important issue through which to study the commodification of culture.[57]

Indeed, the conversion of indigenous culture in response to the perceived or actual demands of the tourist market is one of the major negative cultural impacts associated with international tourism. As already observed, tourism may provide a monetary incentive to revive art forms, crafts, and other cultural attributes of a given local community. However, a problem arises when the inherent quality and meaning of cultural artifacts and performances become less important than the economic motive of earning an income from their reproduction. When this happens, the culture of a given community may be modified to suit the tastes of tourists and its original meaning and significance lost: it becomes a "pseudoculture."[58] Philip and Hezlett recognize the fact that one of the strategic routes used by leisure firms in gaining competitive edge has been through an increased concentration in customer satisfaction.[59] Customer satisfaction is increasingly becoming a corporate goal as more and more companies strive for quality in their products or services. Ceremonies are altered to provide more appeal to tourists, and performances are staged at regular intervals suitable to the tourist market.

Thus authenticity gives way to attractions of a more contrived nature. Prices are set at the highest possible levels allowed by the market. Large amounts of cheaply produced souvenirs are made available for sale. The integrity of the original culture is entirely lost owing to tourism. Without having full control of tourism planning, "the cultures of the host society are as much risk from tourism as the physical environment."[60] Many indigenous cultures affected by tourism are not accustomed to the fast-paced, material-oriented lifestyles of developers and the tourists that soon follow.[61] Tourism's impact on indigenous peoples' ways of life and on their control of and access to their resources and environment has become more pronounced with globalization of the world economy. It is in the same vein, Garen observes that while one of the standards of eco-tourism is to generate domestic employment and economic opportunities for locals, such aims, if not carefully monitored, can cause profits to leak out of these regions into the hands of elites and wealthier nations. In addition, if development projects are monopolized by rich businessmen looking for short-term economic gain, both the local environment and peoples may have to pay the price.[62]

Many indigenous people see globalization as a threat to the traditional family structure, creating a disconnect from cultural traditions. The fear of many indigenous groups is that this global pressure on their culture is only going to lead to the erosion of their traditional values, so that the diversity of culture in the world will be slowly whittled away to the point where there will be only one large homogeneous culture worldwide. The consumerist nature of globalization is often contrary to traditional indigenous values. Globalization does not take into consideration cultural and socioeconomic circumstances. Instead, it looks to further the interests of the larger, more influential countries and corporations that constitute the impetus behind its spread.[63]

As a result of globalization, many indigenous groups are being more widely exploited through the tourism industry. The increasing ease of access to these cultures by western tourists allows for a greater interaction between the two, a process that is not necessarily equal. Western tourists often view indigenous groups as quaint relics of the past that they can observe and report back on to their friends at home. Even though there is interest in the culture of these indigenous groups, there is rarely a sense of equality. The tourists often see themselves as superior and worthy of being served.

Mismanagement

If policies and programs come to naught, the environment might degrade, thereby removing the key travel motive for the eco-tourist.[64] Limited finances, inadequate local expertise, and corruption can all lead to lax enforcement of conservation efforts.[65] As a result, park systems and eco-tourism industries do not reach market potential.[66] Remarkably, developing nations often do not have the resources to train the personnel required to efficiently regulate and protect a national park or wildlife preserve. In Cross River State, for example, protected areas are becoming ever more isolated, with few resources or qualified staff in place to encourage sustainable management. Indeed, Afi Mountain Wildlife Sanctuary is today beset by a number of conservation problems, including encroachment from the communities that surround it as well as more than 600 illegal farms within the sanctuary itself. This problem is also common at Costa Rica's Tortuguero National Park. There, the Western Hemisphere's most important nesting ground for the endangered green turtle is left to the protection of just ten full-time employees. Poachers are a problem in this area and the park has to recruit volunteers to help guard the beach during the nesting season. Another obstacle facing conservation efforts in Costa Rica is the fact that 44 percent of the 3.2 million acres marked for protection remain in the hands of their previous residents and owners. Logging in these areas is often hard to detect or prevent, leading some to argue that Costa Rica's natural resources are protected only on paper.[67]

While governments are typically entrusted with the administration and enforcement of environmental protection, they often lack the commitment or ability to manage eco-tourism sites effectively. The regulations for environmental protection may be vaguely defined, costly to implement, hard to enforce, and uncertain in their effectiveness.[68] Consequently, in Nigeria alone, over 90 percent of tropical lowland rainforests in Cross River State have been lost to deforestation.[69] Forests have frequently come under threat from dry-season fires that spread up the mountain slopes from surrounding farmland. Logging of the surrounding Afi River Forest Reserve and farming threaten to sever the habitat corridor linking Afi and Mbe to the east, isolating Afi and its gorillas. The Mbe Mountains are community-owned land and lack formal protection.[70] Government regulatory agencies, as political bodies, are likely to spend on politically beneficial but environmentally unproductive projects. Because of its prestige and conspicuousness, an attractive visitor's center at an ecotourism site may take precedence over more pressing environmental concerns like acquiring habitat, protecting endemic species, and removing invasive ones.[71]

Security Concerns

Tourism, a phenomenon that is today a universal practice, is threatened by security concerns, caused by years of economic crisis and ethnic-religious conflicts and resentment of the existing sociopolitical system. Undeniably, frustration with the system has bred a society in which armed robbery, human and drug trafficking, ritual killings, prostitution, kidnappings, and fraud scams like 419, which target foreigners worldwide, are increasingly becoming legitimate avenues of escaping from the clutches of poverty. Such safety concerns are vital to this highly important yet fragile global industry because eco-tourists do not travel to areas at risk of war or civil strife or where there are severe health problems. According to Abdullahi:

> Security involves food security and health-care delivery. You do not get anything, far less self-reliance, from people who are hungry or sick. If people are too concerned with their securities, there would be no time to be patriotic or to think of production of goods and services. The young and able-bodied would be too busy seeking other means of survival, begging or stealing . . . Where self-survival is at stake, talk of self-reliance is useless.[72]

Tourism is quite sensitive to political, religious, and economic upheaval as such security issues can easily scare away tourists, damage tourism and park management structures, and degrade the natural resource base. Indeed, people were apprehensive about visiting Nigeria following the 2009 terrorist attempt by Umar Farouk Abdulmutallab and the negative publicity about Nigeria's appalling security situation, which resulted from the indiscriminate bombings by Boko Haram. The security outlook appears positive in Cross River State in spite its location in the volatile Niger Delta, but sudden political instability or escalating crime rates could trigger an unexpected decline in tourism.

Sex Tourism and the Spread of AIDS

Tourism seems to be having the effect of promoting prostitution for tourists, including minors, at their destinations. The phenomenon has been explored by French novelist Michael Houellebecq in his novel, *Platform*[73] and in the nonfiction book by Jeannette Belliveau titled *Romance on the Road*.[74] These works support the idea that sex tourism by both men and women reflects serious problems in the tourists' home countries, including a "dating war" or profound disharmony between the sexes. Particularly important is the 45-minute U.S. documentary *Rent-a-Rasta*, about women who flock to Jamaica in search of the "big bamboo" and the young Rastafarians who cater to them.[75]

The growing sex tourism industry catering to sex-seeking tourists and the growing threat of AIDS has added yet another dimension of concern. It is difficult to obtain statistics on tourism and HIV/AIDS, as governments in developing countries, reliant on the tourism industry to increase their economies, are unwilling to acknowledge the link between HIV and tourism for fear of scaring away tourists. Adult sex tourism becomes a breeding ground for AIDS when tourists in a "holiday mood" have unsafe sex with other tourists or African nationals. A number of studies demonstrate that tourists on holiday feel "free" and are more prone to adopt risky behaviors. Tourists have a higher buying power, which allows them to negotiate the more risky behaviors, like sexual intercourse without a condom, which can promote the spread of sexually transmitted diseases such as HIV/AIDS.[76] Tourists' behavior is also a threat to tourism, as the spreading of AIDS may transform some otherwise attractive destinations into "no-go areas"; moreover, increasingly intense campaigns against sex tourism may also alter tourism flows and motivations.

The proliferation of AIDS, especially in preferred tourist destinations, is an area that demands attention, providing the challenge and opportunity to raise the multiple and interrelated questions of justice, development, gender equity, and health through concrete grassroots programs designed to combat the negative impact of tourism and its pernicious effects on vulnerable populations. Given the spread of HIV/AIDS and its damaging impact on families and communities, there is an urgent need for more evidence-based research into this dimension of modern tourism and to advocate for better policies from governments and the tourism industry.[77]

MEETING THE CHALLENGES OF ECO-TOURISM

Although it has been acknowledged that, compared with other economic sectors, tourism is an important avenue for sociocultural development, the sector is marred by many challenges. Indeed, the future of tourism in Cross River State is dependent on the opportunities and challenges being exploited and addressed to meet the diverse needs, aspirations, and sometimes frustrations of indigenous communities. Admittedly, given the potentials of the state's tourism sector, there is a pressing need to overhaul and develop the industry.

Foreign Exchange and Revenue Leakage

It is already a well-established fact that, in some developing countries, more than two-thirds of the revenue from international tourism never reaches the local economy because of the high foreign exchange leakages. Although an international hotel chain that opens up in a developing country may create jobs in the local community, it will repatriate the profits. In a similar way, host communities might decide that, to keep tourists happy, they have to offer them food and drink with which they are familiar and which have to be imported.[78] Even the voices of the tourism industry in Asia are urging a cautious approach toward globalization. Imtiaz Muqbil, for instance, opines that "The independence of thousands of small and medium size enterprises, including hotels and tour operators, is at risk." This is because most local enterprises will hardly be able to compete with foreign companies. Moreover, Muqbil suggests that as an outcome of globalization, Asian countries may face "the prospects of huge growth in leakage of foreign exchange earnings." This means that the claims that globalization and liberalization of tourism will bring wealth, progress, social achievements, and improved environmental standards to developing countries need to be seriously questioned.[79] Developing countries must try to capture more tourism spending and limit leakage if they are to maximize their revenues from tourism.

Better Management

For this nascent sector to thrive, awareness about eco-tourism must be raised to ensure that the value of eco-tourism is understood by stakeholders. As communities become increasingly aware of the potential that eco-tourism has to improve their livelihoods, there will be a greater level of involvement in its overall conception, design, and management.[80] Indeed, an approach of involving local communities in the management of forests in the buffer zones has been tested with some success in the old and new Ekuri villages in the northwestern part of the Oban division. The Ekuri Community Forestry Project was set up with the help of park officials and foreign donors to improve management of the forest and access to markets. The villagers there had rights to about 250 square kilometers[81] of forest land and were living by subsistence agriculture and the sale of high-value forest products, including the meat of endangered species such as chimpanzees and drill monkeys. With training and financial support, the villagers established ways to harvest the forest in a sustainable way, and they now have a vested interest in its preservation. This contrasts to the negative effects usually seen when external logging or plantation companies enter an area.[82] Moreover, policies governing how forest concessions are awarded, taxed, and enforced encourage highly destructive logging practices. Low fees paid by most loggers also mean that governments fail to capture even a fraction of the full value of their forests. This is potential revenue that could be channeled back into sustainable forest management.

To curtail such encroachment in the buffer zone surrounding the park, government has encouraged programs to establish the backyard farming of bush-meat species, with villagers raising rabbits, poultry, duikers, porcupines, cane rats, giant rats, pythons, crocodiles, and snails for their livelihood. In areas where such government involvement has taken place, the hunting and poaching of animals as bush meat has declined dramatically. Other ways include creating corridors or eco-ducts, highway diversions, and improved policing to protect endangered species.[83] This approach holds promise for the area surrounding the park. Its success will depend on committed government officials at the state and federal levels and the facilitating role played by international development agencies. Undeniably the support of international partners like the World Wildlife Fund (WWF) was vital in establishing tourist destinations at Akamkpa and Boki, where communities have made a significant contribution to both tourism and community development. Optimal local participation is central to ensuring eco-tourism's development.

While it is evident that the government has seen the economic development value of eco-tourism, it has not been as effective in supporting the preservation ideals inherent in the concept, as illustrated by the inadequate funding and management of the national park system. Basically, the government needs to start making preservation as high a priority as economic development. Just as it spends significant money to promote eco-tourism, it needs to spend greater money to support the infrastructure that supports the practice (i.e., the national parks). Additionally, the government will need to take the lead in orchestrating cooperation between a wide range of actors including itself, NGOs (especially environmental groups), tour operators, and local communities. Moreover, all of these stakeholders will need to recognize the limitations of eco-tourism. However, with the sincere and earnest commitment and stewardship of all of these groups, eco-tourism as a means of economic development and environmental sustainability in Cross River State, both now and in the future,[84] should and will be enhanced.

Thus far, the UN General Assembly has adopted a resolution on "sustainable tourism" as part of its Program for the Further Implementation of Agenda 21, an action program adopted at the Rio Earth Summit that acknowledges the need to further consider the importance of tourism in the context of Agenda 21. Among other things, it states, "For sustainable patterns of consumption and production in the tourism sector, it is essential to strengthen national policy development and enhance capacity in the areas of physical planning, impact assessment, and the use of economic and regulatory instruments, as well as in the areas of information, education and marketing." Furthermore, the resolution calls for participation of all concerned parties in policy development and the implementation of sustainable tourism programs.[85] This area leaves much to be desired. Since the local communities have the biggest stake in the outcome of eco-tourism programs, their voices should be heard in establishing sustainable eco-tourism.

Governments need to emphasize the implementation of sound principles and the best practices of eco-tourism rather than fixating on increasing tourism numbers. If it is to benefit local communities and prevent them from being exploited, laws must be enacted to protect the environment from overdevelopment and safeguard the land and livelihoods of communities affected by tourism. With regard to local economic development, the government needs to increase the involvement of local communities within various eco-tourism enterprises. This requires the presence of strong and effective institutions at both the national and local levels.[86]

Peace and Security

Peace and security are preconditions for a thriving tourism sector. It therefore behooves developing countries with ambitions to build a successful tourist industry to maintain an enabling sociopolitical climate[87] and provide a safe environment for potential visitors.[88] Travelers are risk-averse and will not want to spend their vacations feeling anxious about their personal safety or that of their belongings or having to be wary of being ripped off. It is necessary, therefore, to devise multidimensional policies and interventions that will offer a permanent solution to poverty in all its numerous manifestations, including low and unreliable income, poor health, low levels of education and literacy, insecurity and uncertain access to justice, disempowerment, and isolation from the mainstream of socioeconomic development. Combating insecurity in Nigeria must, therefore, as a matter of necessity, begin with a committed and comprehensive war on poverty. While government has a particular responsibility for spearheading action and creating a positive framework, the private sector, nongovernmental, and community-based organizations all have a vital role to play in meeting the challenge of poverty reduction.[89]

CONCLUSION

Eco-tourism, though a new concept, has enjoyed tremendous progress and has become an important engine of sustainable development and cultural diffusion. The extent to which eco-tourism contributes to the socioeconomic development of Cross River State is still a subject of debate. Arguably the sector stimulates economic development through job creation, the transfer of income, and socially, it enhances the exchange of educational, recreational, and cultural values in the state. Indeed, eco-tourism is a great hope for the helpless societies and communities whose resources are deteriorating and untapped. However, there is general agreement among tourist analysts and scholars that if tourism development is not properly planned and managed, the destructive consequences of development will outweigh the benefits for those areas that are particularly at risk of suffering from poor planning in this regard. This chapter concludes that eco-tourism, as evidenced by its potential to generate revenue and improvements in infrastructure, more than any other industry has the potential to lead Cross River State to attain sustainable development.

NOTES

1. Cabeallos-Lascurain, "Tourism, Ecotourism, and Protected Areas: The State of Nature-Based Tourism around the World and Guidelines for Its Development," World Conservation Union (September 1996): 20.
2. Paul H. Whelan and Brad O'Hara, "Ecotourism: A Guide for Marketers," *European Business Review* Vol. 97, No. 5 (1991): 231–236.
3. T. Whelan, ed., *Nature Tourism: Managing for the Environment* (Washington, DC: Island Press, 1991).
4. Eva J. Garen, "Appraising Ecotourism in Conserving Biodiversity," in Tim W. Clark, Andrew R. Williard, and Christina M. Cromley, eds. *Foundations of Natural Resources Policy and Management* (New Haven, CT: Yale University Press, 2000): 222.
5. Draft Report of Cross River State Economic Empowerment and Development (CR-SEED) Strategy (2004): 155.
6. "Harnessing the Power of Tourism for Economic Development," http://africatravelassociation.org/media/documents/CDCNewsletterJune2010v6-7.pdf
7. "Cross River National Park, Cross River State," http://hospitalitynigeria.com/cross_park.php
8. Daniel Ukene, "Marketing Eco-tourism in Cross River State," paper presented at the 2nd Cross River State Tourism Summit, October 23–25, 2003.
9. "Cross River National Park," http://www.keyafrica.com/en/Africa_L2/Nature/Nature-and-Wildlife_C823/Cross-River-National-Park_O1602013
11. "Cross River National Park, Cross River State," http://hospitalitynigeria.com/cross_park.php
10. Cabeallos-Lascurain, *Tourism, Ecotourism, and Protected Areas: The State of Nature-Based Tourism Around the World and Guidelines for Its Development,* World Conservation Union (September 1996) 20
12. "About Cross River State," http://kekerete.tripod.com/CRSG/about.html
13. Ibid.
14. Cross River State, *The New Paradigm* (Calabar, Cross River State: Jodez Press Ltd.): 3.
15. Ibid.
16. Ibid.
17. Paul Ugor, "The Developing Underdevelopment: Democracy, New Political Elites and the Emergence of Mountain Tourism in Nigeria," http://birmingham.academia.edu/PaulUgor/Papers/583308/_The_Developing_Underdevelopment_Democracy_New_Political_Elites_and_the_Emergence_of_Mountain_Tourism_In_Nigeria
18. Ibid.
19. Thomas Olukayode, "Obudu Mountain May Get Grand Prix Status," http://234next.com/csp/cms/sites/Next/Sport/5469527-147/Obudu_Mountain_may_get_Grand_Prix.csp
20. Cross River State Budget (2005).
21. J. Mackinnon, K. Mackinnon, C. Graham, and J. Torshell, *Managing Protected areas in the Tropics* (IUCN, 1992); and S. Ross, and G. Wall,

"Evaluating Ecotourism: the Case of North Sulawesi, Indonesia," *Tourism Management: Research, Policies, and Practice* Vol. 20, No. 6 (1999): 673–682.
22. Report of Cross River State Economic Empowerment and Development Strategy (2004): 155.
23. Martha Honey and Raymond Gilpin, "Tourism in the Developing World Promoting Peace and Reducing Poverty," United States Institute of Peace, Special Report 233 (Washington, DC, October 2009): 2.
24. D. B. Weaver, *Ecotourism in the Less Developed World* (London: Cab International, 1998), 23.
25. "What is Ecotourism," http://www.untamedpath.com/Ecotourism/globalisation.html.
26. "Drill Ranch," http://www.pandrillus.org/projects/drill-ranch/
27. Emmanuel Asuquo Obot, "Eco-tourism—A Tool for Job Creation, Poverty Alleviation and Social Harmony in Nigeria."
28. "Harnessing the Power of Tourism for Economic Development," http://africatravelassociation.org/media/documents/CDCNewsletterJune2010v6-7.pdf
29. Gaetana Trupiano, "Cultural Tourism and Economic Development in the Urban Context of Alexandria," paper presented at the Fourth International Congress on "Science and Technology for the Safeguard of Cultural Heritage in the Mediterranean Basin," Cairo, Egypt, December 6–8, 2009.
30. "United Nations Year of Dialogue Amongst Civilizations in 2001," http://www.un.org/Dialogue/background.html
31. P. Blanchard, S. Blanchoin, N. Bancel, and G. Boëtsch, eds., *L'Autre et Nous: Scènes et Types* (Paris: Syros, 1995).
32. "National Museum Old Residency," Calabar, Cross River State, http://destinationcrossriver.com.ng/index.php?option=com_content&view=article&id=117&Itemid=120
33. R. R. Kunwar, *Anthropology of Tourism: A Case Study of Sauraha* (New Delhi, India: Adroit Publishers, 2002), 104–105.
34. D. Morgan, "Ecotourism Fad or Future for Tourism?" Botanic Gardens Conservation International (BCGI): The Global Network, July 1999, http://www.bgci.org/education/article/371/
35. Pradeep Acharya, "Socio-economic Impacts of Tourism in Lumbini, Nepal: A Case Study," http://www.nepjol.info/index.php/DSAJ/article/viewFile/290/281
36. Report of Cross River State Economic Empowerment and Development Strategy, 155.
37. "Tourism in Cross River State," http://www.crossriverstate.gov.ng/index.php?option=com_content&view=article&id=716&Itemid=37
38. Elizabeth, Becker, "Don't Go There," Washington Post, August 31, 2008:
39. T. M. Butynski and J. Kalina, "Gorilla Tourism: A Critical Look," in Guilland and R. Mace, ed., *Conservation of Biological Resources* (London: Blackwell, 1998).
40. Ephrem Balole-Bwami et al., "Berggorilla & Regenwald Direkthilfe," *Gorilla Journal*, Vol. 22 (June 2001):
41. Butynski and Kalina, "Gorilla Tourism."
42. Ibid.
43. Richard Alexander Bergel, "Conservation Biology of the Cross-River Gorilla," PhD Dissertation, CUNY, 2006, 256.
44. Anthony Anderson, *Alternatives to Deforestation: Steps towards Sustainable Use of the Amazon Rain Forest* (New York: Columbia University Press, 1990).

45. Alexandra Fischer and Liette Vasseur, "The Crisis in Shifting Cultivation Practices and the Promise of Agro-Forestry: A Review of the Panamanian Experience," *Biodiversity and Conservation* Vol. 9, No. 6 (200): 739–756.
46. Ephrem Balole-Bwami et al., "Berggorilla & Regenwald Direkthilfe."
47. "Rain Forest Destruction in Nigeria," http://www.culturalsurvival.org/explore/rainforest-destruction-nigeria.
48. Tracy Kirkland and Kielly Dunn, "Nigeria: Victory for Cross River State!" August 3, 2004, http://www.greengrants.org/2004/08/03/nigeria-victory-for-cross-river-state/
49. Garen, "Appraising Ecotourism in Conserving Biodiversity," 230.
50. "Ecotourism : Environmental Hazards and Local People," http://www.lintangbuanatours.com/index.php/ecotourism-environmental-hazards-and-local-people.html
51. Garen, "Appraising Ecotourism in Conserving Biodiversity."
52. David Western, *In the Dust of Kilimanjaro* (Washington, DC, and Covelo, CA: Island Press/Shearwater Books, 1997).
53. "Globalization and Tourism: Deadly Mix for Indigenous Peoples," http://www.twnside.org.sg/title/chavez-cn.htm; and O. Kamauro, *Ecotourism: Suicide or Development?* Voices from Africa #6: Sustainable Development (UN Non-Governmental Liaison Service, United Nations News Service, 1996).
54. Kamauro, *Ecotourism.*
55. Kevin Meethan. *Tourism in Global Society: Place, Culture, Consumption* (New York: Palgrave Macmillian, 2001); and Melanie K. Smith, *Issues in Cultural Tourism Studies* (London: Routledge, 2003).
56. Peter M. Burns, "Social Identities, Globalization, and the Cultural Politics of Tourism" in William F. Theobald, ed., *Global Tourism* (Amsterdam: Elsevier, 2005), 391–405.
57. Jennifer S. Macasek, "From Huotong to Hostels: Cultural Tourism and the Process of Commodification in Beijing," bachelor of philosophy thesis submitted to the Faculty of Arts and Sciences, University of Pittsburgh, 2010.
58. N. Tahana, and M. Oppermann, "Maori Cultural Performances and Tourism," in *Tourism Recreation Research,* Vol. 23, No. 1 (1998), 23–30.
59. G. Philip and S. A. Hazlett, "The Measurement of Service Quality: A New P.C.P. Attributes Model," *International Journal of Quality and Reliability Management* Vol. 14, No. 3 (1996): 260–288.
60. S. Wearing, "Exploring Socio-cultural Impacts on Local Communities," in David Weaver, ed., *The Encyclopedia of Ecotourism* (Cambridge, MA: CABI, 2001): 395.
61. David Crouch and Scott McCabe, "Culture, Consumption, and Ecotourism Policies," in Ross Dowling and David Fennell, eds., *Ecotourism Policy and Planning* (Cambridge, MA: CABI, 2003), 77–98.
62. Garen, "Appraising Ecotourism in Conserving Biodiversity."
63. "Globalization and its Effect on Cultural Diversity," http://sites.wiki.ubc.ca/etec510/Globalization_and_its_Effect_on_Cultural_Diversity.
64. F. J. Paul Eagles, "The Travel Motivations of Canadian Eco-tourists," *Journal of Travel Research,* Vol. 11, No. 2 (1992): 3–7.
65. Weaver, *Ecotourism in the Less Developed World,* 62.
66. Paul J. H. Eagles, "International Ecotourism Management: Using Australia and Africa as Case Studies," Department of Recreation and Leisure Studies (Waterloo, Canada: University of Waterloo):.
67. Julie Delude, "Trouble in Paradise: Critics Say Lack of Protection Endangers Costa Rica's Famed Nature Preserves," *The San Francisco Chronicle,* December 28, 2000:

68. W. J. Baumol and W. E. Oates, *Economics, Environmental Policy, and Quality of Life* (Englewood Cliffs, NJ: Prentice Hall, 1977.)
69. W. Lawrence, "Reflections on the tropical Deforestation Crisis," *Biological Conservation*, Vol. 3 (1999): 91.
70. "Nigeria" http://www.wcs.org/where-we-work/africa/nigeria.aspx
71. A. Tuohino and A. Hynonen, *Ecotourism—Imagery and Reality: Reflections on Concepts and Practices in Finnish Rural Tourism* (Nordia, Finland: Geographical Publications, 2001): 21–34.
72. M. D. Abdullahi, "Resources Management for Self-Reliance in Nigeria," speech at the 2nd National Conference on Resource Management for Self Reliance in Nigeria, organized by the College of Administration and Management Studies, Hassan Usman Katsina Polytechnic, Katsina, June 28–30, 2005.
73. *Platform* (French: *Plateforme*) is a novel by French writer Michael Houellebecq (translated from the French by Frank Wynne). It has received both great praise and great criticism, most notably for the novel's apparent condoning of sex tourism and anti-Muslim feelings. The author was charged for inciting racial and religious hatred after describing the Islam as "stupid," but saw charges dismissed.
74. This novel written by Jeannette Belliveau discusses the hidden phenomenon that affects hundreds of thousands of traveling women and foreign men: instant vacation love affairs that banish loneliness, provide cultural insights, offer one-on-one, hand-to-hand foreign aid to the world's poor, create international children, and sometimes even change the course of history.
75. *The Ottawa Citizen*, "Sex Tourism: When Women Do It, It's Called 'Romance Traveling,'" http://www.canada.com/ottawacitizen/news/arts/story.html?id=6f1d0124-af59-431a-b9eb-f75a5aa47882
76. "Tourism and HIV AIDS," http://www.ecotonline.org/programs-/tourism-and-hivaids
77. Ibid.
78. Honey and Gilpin, "Tourism in the Developing World: Promoting Peace and Reducing Poverty," 8.
79. "Tourism, Globalization and Sustainable Development," http://www.untamedpath.com/Ecotourism/globalisation.html
80. "The Evolution of Ecotourism in East Africa: From an Idea to an Industry," Summary of the Proceedings of the East African Regional Conference on Ecotourism Organized by The African Conservation Center, Nairobi, Kenya, *IIED Wildlife and Development Series* No. 15 (June 2003): 14.
81. John Terborgh, *Making Parks Work: Strategies for Preserving Tropical Nature* (Washington, DC: Island Press. 2002.)
82. Ernst Lutz, Julian Oliver Caldecott, *Decentralization and Biodiversity Conservation* (World Bank Publications, 1996), 87.
83. Laura K. Marsh *Primates in Fragments: Ecology and Conservation* (New York: Kluwer Academic/Plenum Publishers, 2003).
84. Sujata Narayan, "Below the Surface: The Impacts of Ecotourism in Costa Rica," http://www.umich.edu/~csfound/545/1998/narayans/chap07.htm
85. "Tourism, Globalization and Sustainable Development," http://www.untamedpath.com/Ecotourism/globalisation.html
86. Honey and Gilpin, "Tourism in the Developing World," 8.
87. Ibid.
88. Ibid.
89. Roselyn N. Okech and Mercy Mwagona, "Tourism Contribution in Local economies: Focus on Poverty Reduction in Kenya," http://www.iipt.org/africa2007/PDFs/Roselyne.pdf

REFERENCES

Abdullahi, M. D. "Resource Management for Self-Reliance in Nigeria." Speech at the 2nd National Conference on Resource Management for Self-Reliance in Nigeria. Organized by the College of Administration and Management Studies, Hassan Usman Katsina Polytechnic, Katsina, June 28–30, 2005.

"About Cross River State": http://kekerete.tripod.com/CRSG/about.html

Acharya, Pradeep. "Socio-economic Impacts of Tourism in Lumbini, Nepal: A Case Study": http://www.nepjol.info/index.php/DSAJ/article/viewFile/290/281.

Anderson, Anthony B. *Alternatives to Deforestation: Steps towards Sustainable Use of the Amazon Rain Forest.* New York: Columbia University Press, 1990.

Balole-Bwami, Ephrem, et al. "Berggorilla & Regenwald Direkthilfe." *Gorilla Journal*, Vol. 22 (June 2001):

Baumol, W. J., and W. E. Oates. *Economics, Environmental Policy, and Quality of Life.* Englewood Cliffs, NJ: Prentice Hall, 1979.

Becker, Elizabeth. "Don't Go There." Washington Post. August 31, 2008:

Belliveau, Jeannette. *Romance on the Road: Traveling Women Who Love Foreign Men.* Baltimore: Beau Monde Press, 2006.

"Benefits of Ecotourism": http://www.untamedpath.com/Ecotourism/benefits.html

Bergel, Richard A. "Conservation Biology of the Cross-River Gorilla." Ph.D. dissertation, Ne York: City University of New York, 2006.

Blanchard, P., S. Blanchoin, N. Bancel, and G. Boëtsch, eds. *L'Autre et Nous. Scènes et Types.* Syros, Paris, 1995.

Burns, Peter M. "Social Identities, Globalization, and the Cultural Politics of Tourism." In William F. Theobald, ed. *Global Tourism.* Amsterdam: Elsevier, 2005.

Butynski, T. M., and J. Kalina. "Gorilla Tourism: A Critical Look." In E. J. Milner-Guilland and R. Mace, ed. *Conservation of Biological Resources.* London: Blackwell 1998.

Cabeallos-Lascurain, Hector. "Tourism, Ecotourism, and Protected Areas: The State of Nature-Based Tourism around the World and Guidelines for Its Development." World Conservation Union (September 1996).

Cross River National Park. "Cross River State": http://hospitalitynigeria.com/cross_park.php

———. http://www.keyafrica.com/en/Africa_L2/Nature/Nature-and-Wildlife_C823/Cross-River-National-Park_O1602013

Cross River State. *The New Paradigm.* Calabar, Cross River State: Jodez Press.

Crouch, David, and Scott McCabe. "Culture, Consumption, and Ecotourism Policies." In Ross Dowling and David Fennell, eds. *Ecotourism Policy and Planning.* Cambridge, MA: CABI Publishing, 2003.

Delude, Julie. "Trouble in Paradise: Critics say Lack of Protection Endangers Costa Rica's Famed Nature Preserves." *The San Francisco Chronicle.* December 28, 2000:

Dowling, Ross, and David Fennell. "The Context of Ecotourism Policy and Planning." In Ross Dowling and David Fennell, eds. *Ecotourism Policy and Planning.* Cambridge, MA: CABI Publishing, 2003.

Draft Report of Cross River State Economic Empowerment and Development Strategy (CR-SEED). 2004.

TheDrill Rehabilitation and Breeding Centre. "Drill Ranch." Cross River State, Nigeria: http://www.pandrillus.org/projects/drill-ranch/.

Eagles, Paul F. J. "International Ecotourism Management: Using Australia and Africa as Case Studies." Department of Recreation and Leisure Studies, University of Waterloo, Waterloo, Canada, 1998.

———. "The Travel Motivations of Canadian Eco-tourists." *Journal of Travel Research,* Vol. 11, No. 2 (1992): 3–7.

"Ecotourism: Environmental Hazards and Local People": http://www.lintang-buanatours.com/index.php/ecotourism-environmental-hazards-and-local-people.html

"The Evolution of Ecotourism in East Africa: From an Idea of an Industry." Summary of the Proceedings of the East African Regional Conference on Ecotourism Organized by The African Conservation Center, Nairobi, Kenya, *IIED Wildlife and Development Series* No. 15, June, 2003.

Fischer, Alexandra, and Liette Vasseur. "The Crisis in Shifting Cultivation Practices and the Promise of Agro-Forestry: A Review of the Panamanian Experience." *Biodiversity and Conservation* Vol. 9, No. 6 (2000):

Garen, Eva J. "Appraising Ecotourism in Conserving Biodiversity." In Tim W. Clark, Andrew R. Williard, and Christina M. Cromley, eds. *Foundations of Natural Resources Policy and Management.* New Haven, CT: Yale University Press, 2000.

"Globalization and its Effect on Cultural Diversity": http://sites.wiki.ubc.ca/etec510/Globalization_and_its_Effect_on_Cultural_Diversity

"Globalization and Tourism: Deadly Mix for Indigenous Peoples": http://www.twnside.org.sg/title/chavez-cn.htm

"Harnessing the Power of Tourism for Economic Development": http://africatravelassociation.org/media/documents/CDCNewsletterJune2010v6-7.pdf

Honey, Martha. *Eco-tourism and Sustainable Development: Who owns Paradise?* Washington, DC: Island Press, 2008.

Honey, Martha, and Raymond Gilpin. "Tourism in the Developing World: Promoting Peace and Reducing Poverty." United States Institute of Peace, Special Report 233. October 2009.

"Imoke Identifies Challenges to Forestry Programs": http://www.crossriverstate.gov.ng/index.php?option=com_content&view=article&id=900:imoke-identifies-challenges-to-forestry-programme&catid=209:quick-news

Kamauro, O. *Ecotourism: Suicide or Development?* Voices from Africa #6: Sustainable Development. UN Non-Governmental Liaison Service, United Nations News Service, 1996.

Kirkland, Tracy, and Kielly Dunn. "Nigeria: Victory for Cross River State!" August 3, 2004: http://www.greengrants.org/2004/08/03/nigeria-victory-for-cross-river-state/

Kunwar, R. R. *Anthropology of Tourism: A Case Study of Sauraha.* New Delhi, India: Adroit Publishers, 2002.

Lascurain-Cabeallos, Hector. *Tourism, Ecotourism, and Protected Areas: The State of Nature-Based Tourism around the World and Guidelines for Its Development.* World Conservation Union (September 1996).

Lawrence, W. "Reflections on the Tropical Deforestation Crisis." *Biological Conservation,* Vol. 91, No. 3 (December 1999):

Lutz, Ernst, and Oliver Julian Caldecott. *Decentralization and Biodiversity Conservation.* Geneva: World Bank Publications, 1996.

Macasek, Jennifer S. "From Huotong to Hostels: Cultural Tourism and the Process of Commodification in Beijing." Bachelor of philosophy thesis submitted to the Faculty of Arts and Sciences, University of Pittsburgh, 2010.

Mackinnon, J., K. Mackinnon, C. Graham, and J. Torshell. "Managing Protected Areas in the Tropics." Gland, Switzerland: International Union for the Conservation of Nature, 1992.

Marsh, Laura K. *Primates in Fragments: Ecology and Conservation.* New York: Kluwer/Plenum, 2003.

Meethan, Kevin. *Tourism in Global Society: Place, Culture, Consumption.* New York: Palgrave Macmillan, 2001.

Morgan David, "Ecotourism Fad or Future for Tourism?" Botanic Gardens Conservation International (BCGI): The Global Network.1999: http://www.bgci.org/education/article/371/

"National Museum Old Residency," Calabar: http://destinationcrossriver.com.ng/index.php?option=com_content&view=article&id=117& Itemid=120

"Nigeria": http://www.wcs.org/where-we-work/africa/nigeria.aspx

Obot, Asuquo Emmanuel. "Eco-tourism—A Tool for Job Creation, Poverty Alleviation and Social Harmony in Nigeria." Paper presented at the 2nd Cross River State Tourism Summit held at the State Library Complex, Calabar, 2003.

Okech, Roselyn N., and Mercy Mwagona. "Tourism Contribution in Local Economies: Focus on Poverty Reduction in Kenya": http://www.iipt.org/africa2007/PDFs/Roselyne.pdf

Olukayode, Thomas. "Obudu Mountain May Get Grand Prix Status": http://234next.com/csp/cms/sites/Next/Sport/5469527147/Obudu_Mountain_may_get_Gran d_Prix.csp

The Ottawa Citizen. "Sex Tourism: When Women Do It, It's Called 'Romance Traveling'": http://www.canada.com/ottawacitizen/news/arts/story.html?id=6f1d0124-af59-431a-b9eb-f75a5aa47882

Philip, G., and S. A. Hazlett. "The Measurement of Service uality: A New P.C.P. Attributes Model." *International Journal of Quality and Reliability Management,* Vol. 14, No. 3 (1996).

"Rainforest Destruction, Nigeria": http://www.culturalsurvival.org/explore/rainforest-destruction-nigeria

Ross, S., and G. Wall. "Evaluating Ecotourism: the Case of North Sulawesi, Indonesia." In *Tourism Management: Research, Policies, and Practice,* Vol. 20, No. 6 (1999).

Smith, Melanie K. *Issues in Cultural Tourism Studies.* London: Routledge, 2003.

Sujata, Narayan. "Below the Surface: The Impacts of Ecotourism in Costa Rica": http://www.umich.edu/~csfound/545/1998/narayans/chap07.htm

Tahana, N., and M. Oppermann. "Maori Cultural Performances and Tourism." In *Tourism Recreation Research,* Vol. 23, No. 1 (1998):

Terborgh, John. *Making Parks Work: Strategies for Preserving Tropical Nature.* New York: Island Press, 2002.

"Tourism and HIV/AIDS": http://www.ecotonline.org/programs-/tourism-and-hivaids

"Tourism, Globalization and Sustainable Development": http://www.untamedpath.com/Ecotourism/globalisation.html.

"Tourism in Cross River State": http://www.crossriverstate.gov.ng/index.php?option=com_content&view=article&id=716&Itemid=37

Trupiano, Gaetana. "Cultural Tourism and Economic Development in the Urban Context of Alexandria." Paper Presented at the Fourth International Congress on "Science and Technology for the Safeguard of Cultural Heritage in the Mediterranean Basin" Cairo, Egypt, December 6–8, 2009.

Tuohino, A., and A. Hynonen. *Ecotourism—Imagery and Reality. Reflections on Concepts and Practices in Finnish Rural Tourism.* Nordia, Finland: Geographical Publications, 2001.

Ugor, Paul. "The Developing Underdevelopment: Democracy, New Political Elites and the Emergence of Mountain Tourism in Nigeria": http://birmingham.academia.edu/PaulUgor/Papers/583308/_The_Developing_Underdevelopment_Democracy_New_Political_Elites_and_the_Emergence_of_Mountain_Tourism_In_Nigeria

Ukene, Daniel. "Marketing Eco-tourism in Cross River State." Paper Presented at the 2nd Cross River State Tourism Summit, October 23–25, 2003.

United Nations. "United Nations Year of Dialogue Amongst Civilizations in 2001": http://www.un.org/Dialogue/background.html

Wearing, S. "Exploring Socio-cultural Impacts on Local Communities." In David Weaver, ed. *The Encyclopedia of Ecotourism*. Cambridge, MA: CABI, 2001.

Weaver, D. B. *Ecotourism in the Less Developed World*. London: Cab International, 1998.

Western, David. *In the Dust of. Kilimanjaro*. Washington, D.C. and. Covelo, CA: Island Press/Shearwater Books, 1997.

"What Is Ecotourism": http://www.untamedpath.com/Ecotourism/globalisation.html

Whelan, Paul Herbing, and Brad O'Hara. "Ecotourism: A Guide for Marketers." *European Business Review*, Vol. 97, No. 5 (1991):

Whelan, T., ed. *Nature Tourism: Managing for the Environment*. Washington, DC: Island Press, 1991.

Contributors

Jessica Achberger received her PhD in History from the University of Texas at Austin. Her dissertation focused on the foreign policy and economic development of Zambia, particularly in terms of its relationship with China. An historian of both Africa and Asia, she is interested particularly in linkages between the two continents. She is currently a Fellow at the Southern African Institute of Policy and Research in Lusaka, Zambia.

Alexius Amtaika teaches politics in the Department of Political Studies and Governance at the University of the Free State in South Africa. His research interests include human rights and governance in southern Africa. His new book, entitled *Local Government in South Africa since 1994: Leadership, Democracy, Development and Service Delivery*, is currently in press for 2012 with Carolina Academic Press.

John E. Anegbode received his doctorate in strategic studies in 2009 from the Centre for Strategic and Development Studies (CSDS), Ambrose Alli University, Ekpoma Edo State, Nigeria. He obtained his master's degree in international relations and strategic studies (MISS) in 1999 from the CSDS, Ambrose Alli University, Ekpoma Edo State Nigeria, and a B.Sc. (Hons) in political science with a second-class upper division in 1994 from Edo State University Ekpoma, Edo State, Nigeria. He is currently a senior lecturer in the Department of Political Science, Ambrose Alli University, Ekpoma, Edo State, Nigeria.

Jacob Butler completed a B.A. degree in secondary education in 2003 at Indiana University-Bloomington. As part of his student teaching experience, he spent 8 weeks teaching at a secondary school in Bungoma, Kenya. On returning to the United States, he enrolled in the African studies program at the University of Illinois at Urbana-Champaign, where he received his M.A. degree. At Illinois, he completed research on a myriad of topics including political accountability in Kenya, Nigerian oil politics, education in postgenocide Rwanda, South African xenophobic violence, and the lives of street children in Kenya. Butler is currently a volunteer teacher with WorldTeach at Buko Secondary School near Musoma, Tanzania. On returning to the United States he hopes to begin work toward his Ph.D.

Toyin Falola is the Frances Higginbotham Nalle Centennial Professor in History at the University of Texas at Austin. A fellow of the Nigerian Academy of Letters, he is the author or editor of more than 100 books.

Roshen Hendrickson is an assistant professor of political science at the College of Staten Island, part of the City University of New York. Her research is on U.S. relations with Africa and the economic and political conditions structuring African countries' options in the global economy.

Céline A. Jacquemin received a Ph.D. from the University of California, Irvine, in 2003. She is an associate professor in political science at St Mary's University, where she is currently serving as the associate dean for the School of Humanities and Social Sciences. Her early research examined how international actors understand and frame cases of massive human rights violations and how this impacts the possibilities for intervention. Her expertise covers parts of Europe and the Great Lakes of Africa, where she more closely studies Rwanda. Her recent work examines the links between African countries and former European imperial powers such as France to assess the impact on development and democratization. For St Mary's University Center for Legal and Social Justice, she also serves as a pro bono expert witness for political asylum cases often linked to female genital mutilation.

Mary Kinyanjui is a senior research fellow at the Institute for Development Studies, University of Nairobi, Kenya. Her research focuses on small businesses, informality, and social institutions as well as the trade issues of international development. She has published widely in reputable journals, such as the *International Journal of Entrepreneurship and Small Business* and the *Journal of East African Development and Research*. She has been a visiting scholar at the International Development Centre (IDC), Open University, UK; the United Nations Research Institute for Social Development (UNRISD), Geneva, Switzerland; and Nordic Africa Institute, Uppsala, Sweden. She has a forthcoming book, titled *Vyama, Institutions of Hope: Market Coordination and Society Organisation Strategies*, to be issued by Nsemia Publishers.

Felix Kiruthu teaches history and is the coordinator of public policy and administration programs at Kenyatta University in Nairobi, Kenya, where he has taught at the Department of History, Archaeology, and

Political Studies since 1997. Besides his research interests in political economy and gender studies, he has also researched the urban history of Africa with a special focus on the African informal enterprises. He is the author of *Voices of Freedom* (2001) and has also authored several book chapters and articles in refereed journals. His other research interests include biographies of prominent individuals and pedagogical methods in the study of history and political studies, as well as studies of peace and conflict.

Emmanuel M. Mbah is Assistant Professor of History at the City University of New York, College of Staten Island. His research focuses on colonial and postcolonial African conflict, identity, ethnicity as well as the place of Africa in transatlantic and global interconnections. He is the author of *Land/Boundary Conflict in Africa: The Case of Former British Colonial Bamenda, Present-Day North-West Province of the Republic of Cameroon, 1916–1996* (The Edwin Mellen Press, 2008); "Disruptive Colonial Boundaries and Attempts to Resolve Land/Boundary Disputes in the Grasslands of Bamenda, Cameroon," (*African Journal on Conflict Resolution*, Vol. 9, # 3, November 2009); and editor (with Steven J. Salm) of *Globalization and the African Experience* (Carolina Academic Press, 2012). He has also published numerous chapters in anthologies and edited volumes.

June McLaughlin is a doctoral candidate at Queen Mary University of London.

Francis Muchoki is a senior lecturer in the Department of History at the Catholic University of Eastern Africa, Kenya. He has taught at several other universities in eastern Africa, including Egerton University, and has also served as chairman of the History Department; dean of the Faculty of Arts and Social Sciences; and twice as the deputy vice-chancellor at the Catholic University. Muchoki's main area of interest is the colonial and postindependence economic and political history of Kenya. He is currently completing his Ph.D. at Kenyatta University, focusing on the politics of central Kenya. He has also published articles and books, some jointly with others, in his area of specialization, including *Governance in Africa: Historical and Contemporary Perspectives* and "The Social-Economic Implication of Settlement Schemes in Kenya," an article published in the *East African Journal of Humanities and Sciences*.

Mike O. Odey is associate professor of history specializing in economic history. He is the current head of the Department of History, Benue State University, Makurdi, Nigeria. He has a professional graduate diploma in education (1987), B.A. in history (Hons) (1980), M.A. in history (1994), and Ph.D. in history (2002), all from the University of Jos, Nigeria. His teaching and areas of research interest include Sfrican development studies, poverty analysis/reduction policies, and food security systems, as well as inter-group relations. He has published several articles in both local and international journals and authored several books, including *The Development of Cash Crop Economy in Nigeria's Lower Benue Province,1910–1960* (London: Aboki Publishers, 2009). He is the coeditor of *Historical Research and Methodology in Africa* (Makurdi, Aboki Publishers, 2007).

Dr. (Mrs.) Ebunoluwa O. Oduwole, former head and senior lecturer in the Department of Philosophy, Olabisi Onabanjo University, Ago-Iwoye, Ogun State, Nigeria, has been teaching philosophy for over 20 years. She has attended various conferences both locally and internationally and is a member of the Nigerian Philosophical Association, International Society for African Philosophy and Studies, and Pan-African Gender and Peace Research Group.

Okpeh Ochayi Okpeh, Jr., Ph.D., is a professor of African history in the Department of History, Benue State University. He has contributed numerous scholarly articles in many journals, chapters to several books, and is the current editor of the *Journal of Globalization and International Studies*. Okpeh has also authored many books, including *NEPAD and the African Crisis: The Myths, Realities and Possibilities* (Makurdi: Aboki Publishers, 2005); and *Dimensions and Implications of Military Transition Programmes, 1976–1999* (Makurdi: Book Makers, 2005).

Donald Omagu currently teaches global and African history at Wagner College, New York. He received his Ph.D. from the University of Calabar, Calabar, Nigeria. Dr. Omagu's several peer-reviewed articles have appeared as chapters in edited volumes, in journals, and as monographs. He is a member of several professional organizations, including the Historical Society of Nigeria, American Historical Association (AHA), African Studies Association (ASA), New York Historical Society, and Nigeria Institute of International Affairs (NIIA), Lagos, Nigeria. His research interests include Nigeria and West Africa.

Cletus E. Onakalu received his M.S. degree in international relations and strategic studies in 2010 from the Department of Political Science, Ambrose Alli University, Ekpoma, Edo State, Nigeria. He received his B.A. degree (Hons) in political science with a second-class upper division in 2004 from Ambrose Alli University Ekpoma, Edo State, Nigeria.

Olusegun M. Osinibi is a law lecturer in the Department of Private Law, Faculty of Law, Olabisi Onabanjo University, Ago-Iwoye, Ogun State, Nigeria. His research interests include international economic law, human rights law, and criminal law. He is also seeking avenues for making the law a tool for social engineering. He is an active member of the Nigerian Bar Association and the International Development Ethics Association. He has attended various international conferences in Africa and the United States and is presently a M.Phil./Ph.D. candidate in the Faculty of Law, University of Ibadan, Nigeria.

Jesse Salah Ovadia is a Ph.D. candidate in political science at York University, specializing in African politics, development theory, and political economy. His research is on the politics of oil and development in the Gulf of Guinea, focusing on the effects of national content policies in the oil and gas industry. Ovadia conducted field research in Angola and Nigeria in 2010 and is now writing his dissertation, which is a comparison of the two cases.

Martin S. Shanguhyia is an assistant professor of African history. His research interests include colonial and postcolonial eastern Africa and agrarian/environmental studies.

Muhammed Tanko is in the Department of Accounting at Kaduna State University, Nigeria.

Olivier J. Tchouaffe is a visiting assistant professor at Southwestern University in Georgetown, Texas, where he teaches classes on communication and film studies. He is currently working on a book on Cameroonian cinema and grassroots democratic activism. Besides many book chapters, his other works have also appeared in the *Journal of Applied Semiotics*, POV Online, *Journal of Contemporary Thought*, *Journal of African Cinemas*, *PostAmble Journal*, and in *The International Encyclopedia of Communication*. His most recent publications include "Colonial Visual Archives and the Anti-Documentary Perspective" in the *Journal of Information Ethics* and "Notes on Cultural Flows and Globalization: When China Meets Africa," forthcoming in Blackwell's *International Companion to Media Studies: Production*.

Ben Weiss, working under the supervision of Jessica Achberger and Toyin Falola, is a senior at the University of Texas at Austin, studying government and central African conflict through the liberal arts honors program. He is also pursuing two side majors in philosophy and African and African American studies. His interests in Africa center on HIV/AIDS, genocide, and postgenocide recovery in central and southern Africa. He has made several research and study trips to Africa.

Hauwa'u Evelyn Yusuf, Ph.D., is dean of Students' Services and faculty in the Department of Sociology, Kaduna State University, Nigeria.

Adefarakan Adedayo Yusufu is a 1979 graduate of history at Ahmadu Bello University, Zaria and has had over three decades of teaching experience. He was at different times a lecturer in the College of Advance Studies, Zaria, and Hassan Usman Katsina Polytechnic, Katsina, and a facilitator with the Kaduna Business School, Kaduna, where he was director of programs. He is currently a lecturer with the Department of General Studies and is preoccupied with research in conflict resolution and management. He has a handful of both local and international papers and books to his credit.

Index

A
Abacha, Sani, 61
Abakpwa, 81
Abuja Games Village, 271
Accountability
  and democracy, 94–95
  and the media, 99–101
  definition of, 93–94
  horizontal, 94
  in Kenya, 96–99
  vertical, 94
Accra, 254
Afi Mountain, 405, 409
Africa Growth and Opportunity Act (AGOA), 248
Africa, nationalism, 245
Africa, oil reserves, 256
African Development Bank, 263, 274
African Economic Community (AEC), 153
African Elite, 195, 197, 198
African Peer Review Mechanism, 267
African Union (AU), 36, 37, 124n72, 215, 216, 267, 323, 338
Aga Khan
  Group, 287, 288, 295, 296, 297
  Hospital, 297
  University Hospital, 297
  University School of Nursing, 297
Agacher Corridor, 155
Agbokim Waterfalls, 397, 398
Agribusiness, 256
Aguleri-Unuleri conflict, 76
Airtel, 294, 301
Akum, 81, 86,
Algeria, 309, 313
All Pack, 296
Allu, Osman, 288
Amin, Idi, 116, 287

Anglo-leasing scandal, 97
Angola, 246, 248, 249, 251
Annan, Kofi, 98, 218
Antiretroviral (ARV), 363–372, 375–376
Aouzur Strip, 155
Ardo Sabga, 83
Ardo Umam, 83
Arusha Accord, 315, 318
Asian Tigers, 242, 269
Asian-Pacific Economic Conference (APEC), 153
Association of Southeast Asian Nations (ASEAN), 149–150, 153, 157–163, 170n45
Atlas Mountain, 78
Automated trading system (ATS), 112
Awing, 81–82, 86

B
Bachama, 78
Bafanji, 87
Baforchu, 85
Bafoussam, 82
Bafut, 81
Bali, 81
Balikumbat, 86, 87
Bali-Nyonga, 80–81, 83, 85, 87
Bali-Nyonga, Station, 80
Balladur, Edouard, 316
Baluchi, 283
Bamako, 254
Bambili, 86, 87
Bambui, 86
Bamenda, 81–82, 86
Bandung Conference (1955), 214, 216, 267
Bangang, 87
Bank of Baroda, 287
Bank of India, 287

430 Index

Baoule, 78
Bashir, Omar Al, 323
Bata Shoe Company, 293
Batibo, 81
Beijing Consensus, 253
Beijing, 215, 251, 255
Beinart, William, 24
Belgium, 311, 312
Benin, 82, 254
Benue Valley, 78
Beria, 295
Berlin Conference of 1884, 2, 236
Berlin Wall, 232, 236
Bharti Airtel, see Airtel
Bharti India, 250
Biashara Street, Nairobi, 282
Bilateral Investment Treaties (BITs), 128, 130–132, 134, 137, 141
Birla Group, 289
Bisesero, Rwanda, 317
Biya, Paul, 308
Bohra, 283, 293
Bollywood, 282
Bombay University, 285
Bouteflika, Abdelaziz, 323
Brazil, 228, 229, 230, 231, 247, 248, 249, 252, 262, 268, 384
Breton Woods System, 237
BRICS, 2, 228, 229, 230, 231, 233, 236, 239, 243, 244, 247, 248, 249, 251, 252, 257
Bui, 85
Bulgaria, 310
Bulleys, 292–293
Burkina-Faso, 380
Burundi, 116, 117
Bush, George W., 254, 255

C

Caitano, 246
Calabar Port, 271
Cameroon, 380
Canada, 241, 248, 268, 311
Cancun, 33
Cape Verde, 248
Capital Markets
  Advisory Council (CMAC) Rwanda, 115–116
  and Securities Authority (CMSA) Tanzania, 115, 116
  Authority (CMA) Act (Kenya), 113
  Authority Kenya, 113
  Authority Uganda, 113–114
  Securities Act (Tanzania), 115, 116

Capitalism, 228, 229, 232, 253
Carbon pricing, 379, 391
Cardoso, Fernando, 234, 237, 249
Caribbean Community (CARICOM), 153, 160
Caribbean, 238
Carter, Jimmy, 103
Central Bank of Nigeria (CBN), 185, 188
Central Intelligence Agency (CIA), 229
Chad, 309, 313
Chan, Hiang-Kang, 267
Chandaria, Manu, 289
Chase Bank, 287
Chevron, 272
China National Off-shore Oil Corporation (CNOOC), 270–271
China, 218, 228–230, 231, 253, 257, 262, 263, 268, 279, 357
  and aid to Africa, 243, 244, 254
  and climate change, 383–385, 390, 391, 393n6
  and energy demand, 217
  and FOCAC, 215–216, 269
  and liberation wars, 246–247
  and relations with Africa, 221–223, 248, 251–258, 267, 268–269, 279–280, 301
  and relations with Nigeria, 267–268, 270–271, 275, 276
  and trade with Africa, 219–220, 233, 241, 249–250, 251, 253, 255, 355
  foreign direct investment, 244, 256
  investment in Africa, 128, 140, 251, 355
  rise of, 133, 136–139, 142, 156, 162, 252–253, 255, 279, 301, 308, 324
  threat to India, 297, 301
Chinese Civil Engineering and Construction Company (CCECC), 271
Chinese Cultural Revolution, 246
Chirac, Jacques, 312–313
Chomba, 85
Climate change, 31, 32, 33, 34, 36, 215, 225, 379, 380, 381, 382, 388
Climate justice, 384
Coal, 295
Code Division Multiple Access (CDMA) technology, 271
Cold War, 2, 19, 158, 214, 215, 229, 231, 236, 245, 247, 287, 290, 292, 342, 345, 347, 349, 351

Index 431

Colonialism, 2, 213
Commission of Inquiry in Post-Election Violence (Kenya), see Waki Commission
Common Market for Eastern and Southern Africa (COMESA), 260, 261
Common Market of the South Americas (MERCOSUR), 153
Commonwealth, 286
Communism, 228, 232
Compaore, Blaise, 308
Consultative Group on International Agricultural Research (CGIAR), 35
Copenhagen Conference of 2009, 33, 36, 379, 382, 385, 390, 391
Corporate Social Responsibility (CSR), 132, 133, 136, 141
Corruption, 97, 199, 200, 223, 224, 267, 268, 271, 271, 273, 275, 276, 296, 336, 337–338
Costa Rica, 409
Council of Freely Elected Heads of Government, 103
Cripps, Sir Stafford, 25
Cross River
   gorilla, 397–398, 404–405
   National Park, 397
   State, economic development, 399–401, 403
   State, Rural Development Agency 403
   State, State Electrification Agency, 403
   State, tourism, 397–399, 401–402, 404–407, 410, 411
Cross-border trade, 300
Customs, see Duties
Cut-flower industry, 296

D
D'Estaing, Giscard, 312–313
Dakar, 249
Dar es Salaam Stock Exchange (DSE), 115
Daukoru, Edmund, 57, 61–62
de Gaulle, Charles, 309, 313
Deby, Idriss, 308
Decolonization, 213, 242, 344
Deforestation, 386, 405, 409
Democracy, 93–96, 99, 100, 102, 224, 232, 245
Democratic Republic of Congo, 223, 254, 260, 325, 358, 387

Democratization, 242
Department of Petroleum Resources (DPR), 55–58, 61, 66, 68–69
Dependence, 363, 368, 375
Desai, M. A., 285
Desertification, 21, 31
Development assistance, 135, 137, 141
Development, and morality, 337, 339
Development, definition of, 331–334
Development, human, 333–335, 339
Devonshire White Paper, 284
Dholuo, 283
Dhow, 283
Diamond Trust Bank, 287
Diogo, Luisa, 359
Djibouti, 385
Doha Round, 240
Drill Ranch, 399, 400
Drought, 21, 23, 28, 30, 32, 35
Dukawallah, 282
Dust Bowl, 24
Duties, 300

E
East Africa Securities Regulatory Authority (EASRA), 115
East African
   Bag and Cordage Company, 293
   Chronicles, 285
   Common Market, 116
   Community (EAC), 112, 116, 260, 261
   Exchange, 116–117
   Securities Exchange Association (EASEA), 117
   Standard, 284
Eastleigh, Nairobi, 282
Econet Subsidiary, 294
Economic
   and Financial Crime Commission (EFCC), 272–273, 271, 272, 273, 274
   Community of West African States (ECOWAS), 149–150, 153, 155, 157–163, 169n39, 176, 338
   Community of West African States Monitoring Group (ECOMOG), 163, 171n56
   liberalism, 253
Eco-tourism, 396, 400–401
Eco-tourism, challenges of, 404–410, 411–414
Egypt, 216, 249, 251, 251, 255, 267
El Nino, 32

Electoral Commission of Kenya (ECK), 96, 97
Electricity, 273
Emotional Intelligence, 203
Eni, 272
Equatorial Guinea, 251
Essar, 294
Ethiopia, 220, 222, 256
EU-Africa Summit, 243
Europe, 128–134, 136–138, 141, 142, 238, 242, 244, 262
Europe-African Economic area, 243
European
  Coal Steel Community (ECSC), 158
  Commission, 243, 244
  Community (EC), 166n10
  Economic Area (EEA), 153
  Economic Community (EEC), 158, 379, 391
  Union, 152, 153, 158–159, 160, 163, 218, 220, 221, 292, 323
Extractive Industries Transparency Initiative (EITI), 133, 135, 136, 141
Exxon Mobil, 272

F
Fascism, 232, 246
First World War, 74, 345
Food security, 380
Foreign direct investment (FDI), 180, 181, 182–183, 261, 262
Forum on China-Africa Cooperation (FOCAC), 223, 269
France, 248, 296
  and the Rwandan Genocide, 316–318
  colonial administration, 308, 309, 310, 312
  decolonization, 309, 313, 318
  development aid, 310–311, 314
  foreign policy, 307–323
France-Africa Summit, 307, 318–321, 322–323
Free-market economic system, 228
Free-Trade Agreement (FTA), 260, 261
Fukushima, 381
Fulani, 82–84
Fungie, 86

G
Gadhaffi, Moammar, 243, 325
Gambia, 274
Gandhi, Mahatma, 246, 286, 344

Gbagbo, Laurent, 308, 324, 325
Gelb, Alan, 261
General Agreement on Tariff and Trade (GATT), 150, 152
Germany, 74, 80, 81, 85, 296
Ghana, 75, 241, 254, 255, 260, 352
Gillier, Marin, 317, 326n6
Githongo, John, 97
Global
  Fund, 366, 369–370, 374, 376–378
  Health Initiative, 368
  North, 345, 346
  Reporting Initiative, 132, 141
  South, 345, 346
Global warming, 32, 33, 34
Globalization, 19, 20, 32, 147–148, 215, 217, 233, 407–408
Gold Coast, see Ghana
Goldman Sachs, 228
Good governance, 233, 242, 261
Gore, Al, 391
Great Britain, colonial rule, 246
Great Depression, 19, 23, 26
Great-Zimbabwe, 352
Greece, 239
Gross Domestic Product (GDP), 343, 344, 349, 356
Guinea Bissau, 245, 246, 248
Gulf of Guinea, 47–48, 58, 61, 155, 260
Guzang, 81

H
Habib Bank, 287
Habyarimana, Juvenal, 309, 310, 312, 315, 316, 318
Haiti, 380, 381
Harambee, 282
Hausa, 78, 81
Heywood, Andrew, 229, 232
HIV/AIDS, 194, 239, 249, 347, 350, 357, 363–378, 411
Hong Kong, 241
Huawei Technologies, 271
Hull rule, 129, 130
Human
  capital development, 242
  Development Project, 335–336
  rights, 233, 242
Huntington, Samuel, 232, 233, 236

I
Imperialism, 229, 236, 245
Impunity, 96, 98, 99, 101, 104,

Index 433

Independent Corrupt Practices and other Related Offences Commission (ICPC) Nigeria, 272–273
Independent National Electoral Commission (INEC), 336
India Railways, Railway Technical and Economic Services (RITES), 295
India, 217, 218, 223, 224, 228, 229, 230, 231, 241, 248, 249, 252, 259, 263, 279, 379, 383, 383
 and relations with Africa, 216, 243, 246, 249–251, 269
 economic reforms, 291, 294
 government scholarships, 285
 pharmaceuticals, 220, 296–297, 371
India-Africa Forum, 216
India-Kenya Joint Business Council, 292
India-Kenya Joint Trade Committee, 292
Indian Council of World Affairs, Africa Centre, 290
Indian Ocean Rim Association for Regional Cooperation, 286
Indian Oil Corporation Limited, 295
Indian Railway Construction Company Limited (IRCON), 295
Indigenization Decree, 51–52
Indo-Kenya Trade Agreement (1981), 292
Indonesia, 214, 216
Industrialization, 343, 344
Informal sector, 298, 299–300
Information Communication Technologies (ICTs), 299
Inter-Academy Council, 388
Intergovernmental Authority on Development (IGAD), 35, 36
Intergovernmental Panel on Climate Change (IPCC), 388, 389
International
 Bar Association, 101
 Cooperation Industry Nigeria Limited, 271
 Criminal Court (ICC), 98, 103–104
 Finance Corporation (IFC), 115, 117
 Fund for Agricultural Development, 355
 Labor Organization (ILO), 256
 Monetary Fund (IMF), 30, 86, 95, 102, 116, 117–118, 130, 134–137, 140, 151, 154, 176, 182, 220, 229, 233, 237, 239, 242, 263, 291, 313, 338, 356, 358

Organization of Securities Commissions (IOSCO), 114
Principles for Responsible Investment, 133
Internet, 388
Ireland, 239
Islamic fundamentalism, 234
Israel, 292
Ivoirité, 77
Ivory Coast, 77, 78, 82, 140n44, 309, 314

J
Jakarta, 216, 217
Jakiri, 86
Japan, 221, 224, 248, 345, 380, 381, 391
Jeevanjee Garden, Nairobi, 282,
Jeevanjee, Alibhai Mulla, 282, 284, 285, 287
Jhamtani, 259
Jiabao, Wen, 251, 255
Jintao, Hu, 254
Joint Clinical Research Center (JCRC), 370
Jonathan, Goodluck, 62
Jubilee Insurance Company, 288
Jukun, 78, 89 n.16

K
Kagame, Paul, 315, 316, 318, 322, 323
Kampala Serena Hotel, see Serena Lodges
Kampala Stock Exchange, 113
Kanem-Bornu, 352
Kano, 22
Katrina, Hurricane, 385
Kenindia Insurance Company, 288
Kenya
 Africa National Union (KANU), 96
 Airways, 299
 Broadcasting Corporation, 96
 Industrial Estates (KIE), 298
 Petroleum Refineries, 294
 Textile Mills (KTM), 292
 78, 84, 241, 251
 Central Bank, 296
 Elections (1992), 93, 96
 Elections (1997), 96
 Elections (2007), 97–98, 103, 104
Kenya-India Joint Trade Committee, Meeting (2010), 298
Kenyanisation, 112
Kenyatta, Jomo, 286

Kenyatta, Jomo, administration of, 289
Kerala, India, 301
Khan, Aga, 284, 287, 297
Khrushchev, Nikita, 245
Kibachia, Chege, 285
Kibaki, Mwai, 97, 98, 103
Kidnapping, 271, 275, 276
Kikuyu grass, 84
Kikuyu, 27, 283, 293
Kiley, Sam, 317
Kimbi, 85
Ki-Moon, Ban, 323, 356
Kipande House, 282
Kirloskar Brothers, 251
Kisii, 284
Kisumu Cotton Mills (Kicomi), 292
Kiswahili, 282
Kola nut, 80, 81, 84
Kom, 83
Kombe market, 81
Kubai, Fred, 285
Kuffor, John, 254
Kumasi, 254
Kupolokun, F. M., 57–59
Kwa Falls, 397, 398
Kyoto Protocol, 33, 37, 343, 348

L

Lagos Plan of Action, 352
Lake Chad, 155
Lake Magadi, 295
Lake Naivasha, 296
Latin America, 234, 261
Le Roux, 261, 262
Leadership, 336, 337–338
Lesotho, 241, 256
Liberalism, 236
Liberation Front of Mozambique (FRELIMO), 247
Liberia, 163, 171n56, 254
Libya, 313
Lions Group, 297
Lisbon, 244
Lome Convention of 1975, 238, 239, 240, 244
London Stock Exchange (LSE), 112
Luba, 352
Lunda, 352
Lusophone, 249

M

Mabati Industries, 289
Machakos, 284
Madagascar, 241

Magadi Soda Company, 296
Mahindra, 295
Malaria, 239
Malawi, 241, 254
Malaysia, 193, 204, 205, 238
Mali, 296, 352
Mambilla Plateau, 78
Mamfe, 81
Mango, 80, 84
Mankon, 81
Manufacturers Association of Nigeria (MAN), 178, 274
Mao, Tse-Tung, 246, 247
Marginal Fields Program, 60–62, 69
Marxist-Leninist Theory of Imperialism, 241, 242, 245–246
Masai, 407
Maseru, 256
Mau Mau, 27, 285
Mauritania, 78, 140n44
Mauritius, 241, 261
Mazrui Arabs, 283
Mbatu, 81, 86, 90n26
Mbe Mountains, 409
Mbengwi, 87
Mboya, Tom, 285
Medvedev, Dmitry, 249
Mehri, Abdelhamid, 324
Mexico, 238, 262
Mezam, 85
Millennium Development Goal, 2, 182, 188, 215, 262, 275, 356
Mining, 364
Ministry of Cooperation (France), 310, 313, 314
Mitigation, 33
Mitterand, Francois, 309, 310, 312–314
Mitterand, Jean Christophe, 309, 310
Mjuru, Joice, 359
Mkulo, Mustafa, 253, 254, 255
Modernization, 195, 343
Mogadishu, 213
Moi, Daniel arap, 96–97, 98, 100, 101, 103, 289, 293
Mombasa, 284
Momo, 85
Monitor (Kenya), 288
Moreno-Ocampo Six, 104
Moreno-Ocampo, Luis, 104
Morocco, 78, 274, 309
Mortimore, Michael, 28
Moscow, 249
Movement for the Emancipation of the Niger-Delta (MEND), 272

Movement for the Survival of Ogoni People (MOSOP), 272
Movimento Popular de Libertacao de Angola (MPLA), 249
Mozambique, 246, 247, 248, 249, 260, 261, 295, 380
M-pes, 295
Mucyo Commission Report, 318
Mugabe, Robert, 77, 243, 244
Mukherjee, Pranab, 250
Multi-Fibre Arrangement, 241
Multilateral Agreement on Investment (MAI), 134, 137
Murumbi, Joseph, 285
Museveni, Yoweri, 36
Mwakwere, Chirau Ali, 298
Mwene-Mutapa, 352

N
Nairobi Stock Exchange (NSE), 112, 113, 116, 288
Nairobi, 284
Nakuru, 284
Namibia, 241, 249, 256
Nanyuki Textiles, 292
Nation (Kenya), 288
Nation Media Group, 288
National Center for Public Policy Research, 388
National Museum Old Residency Calabar, 402
National Petroleum Investment and Management Services (NAPIMS), 56–57
National Small Industries Corporation (NSIC) India, 298
Nationalism, 233
Nayar, Gurdit Singh, 282
Nazism, 232
Ndu, 86
Nehru, Jawaharal, 214, 285, 286, 290
Neo-colonialism, 213
Neo-Marxists, 234, 236, 237, 243
New Asian-African Strategic Partnership (NAASP), 214
New Delhi, 216, 250
New Partnership for Africa's Development (NEPAD), 215, 267, 338, 353
New World Order (NWO), 152–154, 157, 158, 162, 164, 231, 232
New-Zealand, 345, 380, 381
Ngcuka, Phumzile Mlambo, 359
Ngyen-Mbo, 85

Niger Delta crisis, 186, 188, 256, 268, 271–272, 276, 409
Niger Delta, 50, 65, 71
Nigeria National Petroleum Corporation, 270–271
Nigeria Railways, 271
Nigeria, 219–221, 241, 247, 249, 251, 256, 267, 269, 270, 271, 272, 273, 274, 275, 276, 308, 323, 324, 325, 365, 372–375, 377–378
and ECOWAS, 163
banking sector, 184–186, 188
capital market, 180
electricity, 273–274
land conflict, 76, 78, 82
leadership challenge, 275–276
non-oil exports, 178–179, 183
oil-exports, 176, 177–178, 181, 182, 183–184, 188
unemployment, 186–187
Nigerian Content Development and Monitoring Board (NCDMB), 56–58, 63–70
Nigerian National Petroleum Company (NNPC), 178
Nigerian National Petroleum Company (NNPC), 51, 53–61, 63–64
Nigerian Stock Exchange (NSE), 180–181
Nkrumah, Kwame, 198
Nkwen, 86
Non-Alignment Movement (NAM), 286–287
Non-Governmental Organizations (NGOs), 133-136
Norms, 128, 134, 136, 138–139
North American Free Trade Area (NAFTA), 153
North Atlantic Treaty Organization (NATO), 246, 318
Nso, 83
Nsongwa, 81, 86, 90n26
Nyerere, Mwalimu, 286
Nyeri, 284, 288

O
Obama, Barack, 368–369, 381, 385, 393
Obasanjo, Olusegun, 56–58, 269, 273
Obudu
International Mountain Race, 399
Mountain Ranch Resort, 397, 398–399
Mountain, 398–399

436 Index

Odinga, Raila, 98, 103
Official development Assistance (ODA), 182–183, 239
Oil palm, 84
Oil Petroleum Export Countries (OPEC), 272
Ondimba, Ali Bongo, 308
Operation Turquoise, 315, 316–318
Organisation Internationale de la Francophonie (OIF), 309–311, 312, 318, 323
Organization for Economic Cooperation and Development, 132, 134, 136, 137
Organization of African Unity (OAU), 103, 153, 267, 228
Oshwals, 293
Otieno, Silvano Melea, 285
Otuocha, 76
Overseas Private Investment Agency (OPIC), 135
Over-the-counter trading, 115–116
Oyo-Alafinate, 352

P
Pacific, 238
Pakistan, 259, 380, 381
Pan Paper Mills, 296
Pan-Africanism, 245
Patel, Dinsha, 298
Perplus of Erythean Sea, 283
Petro-China, 270
Petroleum Act of 1969, 50–51, 55, 60
Petroleum and Natural Gas Senior Staff Association of Nigeria (PENGASSAN), 64
Pew Research Center, 388
Pharmaceutical, 363–364, 366, 370, 374, 376
Philippines, 259
Philosophy of passive resistance, 246
Ping, Jean, 36
Pinto, Pio Gama, 285
Pioneer Insurance Company, 288
Pluralism, 232
Pollution, 379
Populist Development, 193
Portugal, 244, 245, 246, 249
Portugal, colonial government, 247, 248
Poverty, 215, 347
Power Holding Company of Nigeria, 274
Premier Industries, *see* East African Bag and Cordage Company

President's Emergency Plan for Aids Relief (PEPFAR), 254, 363–366, 368–378
Proletariat, 241
Prometheus ethos, 380
Putin, Vladimir, 249

Q
Qatar, 240

R
Ranbaxy Laboratories, 251
Realism, 228, 229, 236
Realpolitik, 229, 232
Refugees, 199
Republic of Congo, 251
Ribadu, Nuhu, 274
Rice, 80, 84
Richards, Paul, 26
Rift Valley Railway, 295
Rift Valley, 78
Rio Earth Summit, 413
Roman Empire, 235
Romania, 310
Rosemberg, 243
Royal Dutch, 272
Rule of Law, 223, 224
Russia, 228, 229, 230, 231, 245, 247, 248, 249, 252, 263
Rwanda Over- the-Counter Market (ROTCM), 115
Rwanda Stock Exchange, 115
Rwanda, 116, 254, 307, 309, 311–312, 314–316, 322, 325
Rwandan Genocide, 314, 316–318
Rwandan Patriotic Front (RPF), 315, 316, 317–318

S
Sahel, 21, 28, 33
Sankara, Thomas, 310
Santa-Njong, 81–82, 86
Sarkozy, Nicholas, 307, 318, 322, 323, 324, 325
Scotland, 239
Second World War, 245, 345
Securities and Exchange Commission (SEC) United States, 119
Securities Central Depositories (SCD) Act of 2009 (Uganda), 114–115
Securities Central Depositories Act 2009 (Uganda), 114
Sefawa Dynasty, 352
Senegal, 244, 249, 274, 309, 385

Serena Lodges, 289
Sex tourism, 410–411
Shah, Sir Sultan Mahomed, 284
Shambaa, 26
Shantha Biotechnics, 297
Sharma, Anand, 298
Shell Petroleum Development Company (SPDC), 65, 256, 272
Shell-BP, 48, 50, 52
Shia Imam Ishmaili Muslims, 284
Shia Ishmail Mosque, 282
Sierra Leone, 163, 1717n56, 387
Silicon Valley, 301
Singapore, 193, 204, 205, 222
Singh, Jaswant, 290
Singh, Makhan, 285
Sirleaf, Ellen Johnson, 359
Small and Medium Enterprises (SMEs), 298–299
Social media, 380, 381
Socialism, 232
Somalia, 98, 274
South Africa, 228, 229, 230, 231, 238, 239, 241, 246, 247, 249, 251, 256, 287, 308, 313, 323, 324, 325, 356, 365, 373, 376, 384
South Korea, 238, 241
Southeast Asia, 156
Southern African Development Community (SADC), 260, 261
South-South Cooperation, 298
Soviet Union, 214, 228, 232, 236, 245, 246, 252, 290
Soviet Union, collapse of, 151, 152, 158, 162
Standards Organization of Nigeria (SON), 275
Stock exchange, definition of, 112
Stock exchange, regulation, 119–120
Strasbourg Plan (1952), 238
Structural adjustment policies, 29, 30
Structural Adjustment Program (SAP), 118, 242, 291–292, 286
Structuralism, 234, 236
Subsidies, 202, 203
Sudan, 222, 251, 255, 268, 295, 323
Sunday Nation (Kenya), 288
Swahili, 352
Swaziland, 241
Swedish International Development Cooperation Agency (SIDA), 117

T
Taifa (Kenya), 288
Taiwan, 241, 267
Tanzania, 118, 241, 253, 254, 261, 288, 289, 295, 297
Taraba, 78
Tariffs, *see* Duties
Tata Group, 251, 295, 301
Tea, 75, 80, 84, 86
Thailand, 238
Theory of Liberalism, 232
Tingno-Waduku, 78
Tiv, 78
Tiv-Jukun conflict, 78
Tokyo International Conference on African Development (TICAD), 214, 215
Tokyo, 214, 215
Total, 272
Toubon, Jacques, 324
Tourism
  and infrastructure development, 403
  cultural, 401–402
  definition of, 396
Trade and Development Agency (TDA), 135
Trade, unfavorable balance of, 217
Trans-Atlantic slave trade, 1, 75
Transparency International, 220, 223
Transparency, 129, 133, 135, 139, 140–142
Traore, Moussa, 31
Tripathy, 251
Tripoli, 243
Tsavo Company, 295
Tuabi, 87
Tuberculosis, 239
Turkey, 259
Twiga Shoes, 293

U
Uganda Development Corporation (UDC), 113, 116
Uganda Securities Exchange (USE), 113–114
Uganda, 260, 261, 287, 288, 289, 297, 363–378
Uluguru, 26
Underdevelopment, 195, 196
Union Oil Company of California (Unocal), 270
United Kingdom's Department for International Development (DFID), 117
United National Global Compact, 132, 138

United Nations, 28, 98, 103, 129, 131, 132, 137, 216, 267, 286, 400, 413
    Charter, 162, 214
    Conference on Trade and Development (UNCTAD), 131–133, 223
    Development Program (UNDP), 194, 195
    Food and Agricultural Organization, 215, 323, 386
    General Assembly, 239, 245
    Human Development Index (HDI), 343, 348
    Program on HIV/AIDS (UNAIDS), 368, 372
    Security Council, 246, 247, 308, 317, 324
United States Agency for International Development (USAID), 113, 117, 135
United States Multilateral Investment Guarantee Agency, 261
United States, 129, 130, 133–137, 140, 151, 214, 228, 229, 240, 241, 245, 246, 248, 249, 251, 253, 255, 324, 325, 363–378, 379, 382, 384, 385, 391
Utomi, Pat, 47–48, 57

V
Visram, Allidina, 287
Vodacom, 294

W
Wade, Abdoulaiye, 308–309
Waki Commission, 98
Washington Consensus, 252, 253
West Asian and African Affairs Department of the Commerce Ministry, 257
Western Metal Products Company (WEMPCO), 406
World Bank, 27, 29, 30, 35, 77, 86, 95, 102, 113, 116, 117–118, 130, 133, 134, 136, 137, 139, 140, 151, 154, 193, 197, 200, 220, 229, 233, 237, 239, 247, 253, 261, 263, 274, 291, 313, 323, 338, 354, 374, 377–378, 400, 401
World Health Organization, 371
World Systems Theory, 234, 252
World Trade Organization (WTO), 128, 130, 131, 134–137, 141, 150, 152, 154, 216, 237, 240, 243, 354, 359
World Travel and Tourism Council (WTTC), 400
World Wildlife Federation (WWF), 398, 412
Wukari, 78, 89n16
Wum, 83

Z
Zain Kenya, 294
Zambia, 241, 256, 260, 268, 380
Zanzibar, 283
Zap, 295
Zimbabwe, 77, 220, 243, 247, 255

An environmentally friendly book printed and bound in England by www.printondemand-worldwide.com

This book is made entirely of sustainable materials; FSC paper for the cover and PEFC paper for the text pages.

#0036 - 020715 - C0 - 229/152/24 [26] - CB - 9780415818889